Lecture Notes in Computer Science   12766

More information about this subseries at http://www.springer.com/series/7409

Sakae Yamamoto · Hirohiko Mori (Eds.)

Human Interface and the Management of Information

Information-Rich and Intelligent Environments

Thematic Area, HIMI 2021
Held as Part of the 23rd HCI International Conference, HCII 2021
Virtual Event, July 24–29, 2021
Proceedings, Part II

Springer

Editors
Sakae Yamamoto
Tokyo University of Science
Tokyo, Saitama, Japan

Hirohiko Mori
Tokyo City University
Tokyo, Japan

ISSN 0302-9743   ISSN 1611-3349 (electronic)
Lecture Notes in Computer Science
ISBN 978-3-030-78360-0   ISBN 978-3-030-78361-7 (eBook)
https://doi.org/10.1007/978-3-030-78361-7

LNCS Sublibrary: SL3 – Information Systems and Applications, incl. Internet/Web, and HCI

This Springer imprint is published by the registered company Springer Nature Switzerland AG
The registered company address is: Gewerbestrasse 11, 6330 Cham, Switzerland

Foreword

Human-Computer Interaction (HCI) is acquiring an ever-increasing scientific and industrial importance, and having more impact on people's everyday life, as an ever-growing number of human activities are progressively moving from the physical to the digital world. This process, which has been ongoing for some time now, has been dramatically accelerated by the COVID-19 pandemic. The HCI International (HCII) conference series, held yearly, aims to respond to the compelling need to advance the exchange of knowledge and research and development efforts on the human aspects of design and use of computing systems.

The 23rd International Conference on Human-Computer Interaction, HCI International 2021 (HCII 2021), was planned to be held at the Washington Hilton Hotel, Washington DC, USA, during July 24–29, 2021. Due to the COVID-19 pandemic and with everyone's health and safety in mind, HCII 2021 was organized and run as a virtual conference. It incorporated the 21 thematic areas and affiliated conferences listed on the following page.

A total of 5222 individuals from academia, research institutes, industry, and governmental agencies from 81 countries submitted contributions, and 1276 papers and 241 posters were included in the proceedings to appear just before the start of the conference. The contributions thoroughly cover the entire field of HCI, addressing major advances in knowledge and effective use of computers in a variety of application areas. These papers provide academics, researchers, engineers, scientists, practitioners, and students with state-of-the-art information on the most recent advances in HCI. The volumes constituting the set of proceedings to appear before the start of the conference are listed in the following pages.

The HCI International (HCII) conference also offers the option of 'Late Breaking Work' which applies both for papers and posters, and the corresponding volume(s) of the proceedings will appear after the conference. Full papers will be included in the 'HCII 2021 - Late Breaking Papers' volumes of the proceedings to be published in the Springer LNCS series, while 'Poster Extended Abstracts' will be included as short research papers in the 'HCII 2021 - Late Breaking Posters' volumes to be published in the Springer CCIS series.

The present volume contains papers submitted and presented in the context of the Human Interface and the Management of Information (HIMI 2021) thematic area of HCII 2021. I would like to thank the Co-chairs, Sakae Yamamoto and Hirohiko Mori, for their invaluable contribution to its organization and the preparation of the proceedings, as well as the members of the Program Board for their contributions and support. This year, the HIMI thematic area has focused on topics related to information presentation, visualization and decision-making support, information in VR and multimodal user interfaces, information-rich learning environments, and information in intelligent systems, as well as work, collaboration and design support.

I would also like to thank the Program Board Chairs and the members of the Program Boards of all thematic areas and affiliated conferences for their contribution towards the highest scientific quality and overall success of the HCI International 2021 conference.

This conference would not have been possible without the continuous and unwavering support and advice of Gavriel Salvendy, founder, General Chair Emeritus, and Scientific Advisor. For his outstanding efforts, I would like to express my appreciation to Abbas Moallem, Communications Chair and Editor of HCI International News.

July 2021   Constantine Stephanidis

HCI International 2021 Thematic Areas
and Affiliated Conferences

Thematic Areas

- HCI: Human-Computer Interaction
- HIMI: Human Interface and the Management of Information

Affiliated Conferences

- EPCE: 18th International Conference on Engineering Psychology and Cognitive Ergonomics
- UAHCI: 15th International Conference on Universal Access in Human-Computer Interaction
- VAMR: 13th International Conference on Virtual, Augmented and Mixed Reality
- CCD: 13th International Conference on Cross-Cultural Design
- SCSM: 13th International Conference on Social Computing and Social Media
- AC: 15th International Conference on Augmented Cognition
- DHM: 12th International Conference on Digital Human Modeling and Applications in Health, Safety, Ergonomics and Risk Management
- DUXU: 10th International Conference on Design, User Experience, and Usability
- DAPI: 9th International Conference on Distributed, Ambient and Pervasive Interactions
- HCIBGO: 8th International Conference on HCI in Business, Government and Organizations
- LCT: 8th International Conference on Learning and Collaboration Technologies
- ITAP: 7th International Conference on Human Aspects of IT for the Aged Population
- HCI-CPT: 3rd International Conference on HCI for Cybersecurity, Privacy and Trust
- HCI-Games: 3rd International Conference on HCI in Games
- MobiTAS: 3rd International Conference on HCI in Mobility, Transport and Automotive Systems
- AIS: 3rd International Conference on Adaptive Instructional Systems
- C&C: 9th International Conference on Culture and Computing
- MOBILE: 2nd International Conference on Design, Operation and Evaluation of Mobile Communications
- AI-HCI: 2nd International Conference on Artificial Intelligence in HCI

List of Conference Proceedings Volumes Appearing Before the Conference

1. LNCS 12762, Human-Computer Interaction: Theory, Methods and Tools (Part I), edited by Masaaki Kurosu
2. LNCS 12763, Human-Computer Interaction: Interaction Techniques and Novel Applications (Part II), edited by Masaaki Kurosu
3. LNCS 12764, Human-Computer Interaction: Design and User Experience Case Studies (Part III), edited by Masaaki Kurosu
4. LNCS 12765, Human Interface and the Management of Information: Information Presentation and Visualization (Part I), edited by Sakae Yamamoto and Hirohiko Mori
5. LNCS 12766, Human Interface and the Management of Information: Information-rich and Intelligent Environments (Part II), edited by Sakae Yamamoto and Hirohiko Mori
6. LNAI 12767, Engineering Psychology and Cognitive Ergonomics, edited by Don Harris and Wen-Chin Li
7. LNCS 12768, Universal Access in Human-Computer Interaction: Design Methods and User Experience (Part I), edited by Margherita Antona and Constantine Stephanidis
8. LNCS 12769, Universal Access in Human-Computer Interaction: Access to Media, Learning and Assistive Environments (Part II), edited by Margherita Antona and Constantine Stephanidis
9. LNCS 12770, Virtual, Augmented and Mixed Reality, edited by Jessie Y. C. Chen and Gino Fragomeni
10. LNCS 12771, Cross-Cultural Design: Experience and Product Design Across Cultures (Part I), edited by P. L. Patrick Rau
11. LNCS 12772, Cross-Cultural Design: Applications in Arts, Learning, Well-being, and Social Development (Part II), edited by P. L. Patrick Rau
12. LNCS 12773, Cross-Cultural Design: Applications in Cultural Heritage, Tourism, Autonomous Vehicles, and Intelligent Agents (Part III), edited by P. L. Patrick Rau
13. LNCS 12774, Social Computing and Social Media: Experience Design and Social Network Analysis (Part I), edited by Gabriele Meiselwitz
14. LNCS 12775, Social Computing and Social Media: Applications in Marketing, Learning, and Health (Part II), edited by Gabriele Meiselwitz
15. LNAI 12776, Augmented Cognition, edited by Dylan D. Schmorrow and Cali M. Fidopiastis
16. LNCS 12777, Digital Human Modeling and Applications in Health, Safety, Ergonomics and Risk Management: Human Body, Motion and Behavior (Part I), edited by Vincent G. Duffy
17. LNCS 12778, Digital Human Modeling and Applications in Health, Safety, Ergonomics and Risk Management: AI, Product and Service (Part II), edited by Vincent G. Duffy

18. LNCS 12779, Design, User Experience, and Usability: UX Research and Design (Part I), edited by Marcelo Soares, Elizabeth Rosenzweig, and Aaron Marcus

19. LNCS 12780, Design, User Experience, and Usability: Design for Diversity, Well-being, and Social Development (Part II), edited by Marcelo M. Soares, Elizabeth Rosenzweig, and Aaron Marcus

20. LNCS 12781, Design, User Experience, and Usability: Design for Contemporary Technological Environments (Part III), edited by Marcelo M. Soares, Elizabeth Rosenzweig, and Aaron Marcus

21. LNCS 12782, Distributed, Ambient and Pervasive Interactions, edited by Norbert Streitz and Shin'ichi Konomi

22. LNCS 12783, HCI in Business, Government and Organizations, edited by Fiona Fui-Hoon Nah and Keng Siau

23. LNCS 12784, Learning and Collaboration Technologies: New Challenges and Learning Experiences (Part I), edited by Panayiotis Zaphiris and Andri Ioannou

24. LNCS 12785, Learning and Collaboration Technologies: Games and Virtual Environments for Learning (Part II), edited by Panayiotis Zaphiris and Andri Ioannou

25. LNCS 12786, Human Aspects of IT for the Aged Population: Technology Design and Acceptance (Part I), edited by Qin Gao and Jia Zhou

26. LNCS 12787, Human Aspects of IT for the Aged Population: Supporting Everyday Life Activities (Part II), edited by Qin Gao and Jia Zhou

27. LNCS 12788, HCI for Cybersecurity, Privacy and Trust, edited by Abbas Moallem

28. LNCS 12789, HCI in Games: Experience Design and Game Mechanics (Part I), edited by Xiaowen Fang

29. LNCS 12790, HCI in Games: Serious and Immersive Games (Part II), edited by Xiaowen Fang

30. LNCS 12791, HCI in Mobility, Transport and Automotive Systems, edited by Heidi Krömker

31. LNCS 12792, Adaptive Instructional Systems: Design and Evaluation (Part I), edited by Robert A. Sottilare and Jessica Schwarz

32. LNCS 12793, Adaptive Instructional Systems: Adaptation Strategies and Methods (Part II), edited by Robert A. Sottilare and Jessica Schwarz

33. LNCS 12794, Culture and Computing: Interactive Cultural Heritage and Arts (Part I), edited by Matthias Rauterberg

34. LNCS 12795, Culture and Computing: Design Thinking and Cultural Computing (Part II), edited by Matthias Rauterberg

35. LNCS 12796, Design, Operation and Evaluation of Mobile Communications, edited by Gavriel Salvendy and June Wei

36. LNAI 12797, Artificial Intelligence in HCI, edited by Helmut Degen and Stavroula Ntoa

37. CCIS 1419, HCI International 2021 Posters - Part I, edited by Constantine Stephanidis, Margherita Antona, and Stavroula Ntoa

38. CCIS 1420, HCI International 2021 Posters - Part II, edited by Constantine Stephanidis, Margherita Antona, and Stavroula Ntoa
39. CCIS 1421, HCI International 2021 Posters - Part III, edited by Constantine Stephanidis, Margherita Antona, and Stavroula Ntoa

http://2021.hci.international/proceedings

Human Interface and the Management of Information Thematic Area (HIMI 2021)

Program Board Chairs: **Sakae Yamamoto**, *Tokyo University of Science, Japan*, and **Hirohiko Mori**, *Tokyo City University, Japan*

- Yumi Asahi, Japan
- Shin'ichi Fukuzumi, Japan
- Michitaka Hirose, Japan
- Yasushi Ikei, Japan
- Yen-Yu Kang, Taiwan
- Keiko Kasamatsu, Japan
- Daiji Kobayashi, Japan
- Kentaro Kotani, Japan
- Hiroyuki Miki, Japan
- Miwa Nakanishi, Japan
- Ryosuke Saga, Japan
- Katsunori Shimohara, Japan
- Takahito Tomoto, Japan
- Kim-Phuong L. Vu, USA
- Tomio Watanabe, Japan
- Takehiko Yamaguchi, Japan

The full list with the Program Board Chairs and the members of the Program Boards of all thematic areas and affiliated conferences is available online at:

http://www.hci.international/board-members-2021.php

HCI International 2022

The 24th International Conference on Human-Computer Interaction, HCI International 2022, will be held jointly with the affiliated conferences at the Gothia Towers Hotel and Swedish Exhibition & Congress Centre, Gothenburg, Sweden, June 26 – July 1, 2022. It will cover a broad spectrum of themes related to Human-Computer Interaction, including theoretical issues, methods, tools, processes, and case studies in HCI design, as well as novel interaction techniques, interfaces, and applications. The proceedings will be published by Springer. More information will be available on the conference website: http://2022.hci.international/:

General Chair
Prof. Constantine Stephanidis
University of Crete and ICS-FORTH
Heraklion, Crete, Greece
Email: general_chair@hcii2022.org

http://2022.hci.international/

Contents – Part II

Learning in Information-Rich Environments

Characterization of Auxiliary Problems for Automated Generation
in Error-Based Simulation 3
  Nonoka Aikawa, Kento Koike, Takahito Tomoto, Tomoya Horiguchi,
  and Tsukasa Hirashima

Development of Collaborative Chemistry Experiment Environment
Using VR 14
  Hisashi Fujiwara, Toru Kano, and Takako Akakura

Enhancing Preparedness for Emergency Alternative Modes of Instruction:
Construction and Evaluation of a Remote Teaching Curriculum 27
  Gabriella M. Hancock, Christopher R. Warren, and Amy Wax

Design of Learning by Logical Empathic Understanding in Technology
Enhanced Learning 38
  Tsukasa Hirashima

From On-Campus to Online Undergraduate Research Experience
in Psychology: Transition During the COVID-19 Pandemic 50
  Ya-Hsin Hung and Robert W. Proctor

Learner Model for Adaptive Scaffolding in Intelligent Tutoring Systems
for Organizing Programming Knowledge 63
  Kento Koike, Yuki Fujishima, Takahito Tomoto, Tomoya Horiguchi,
  and Tsukasa Hirashima

Exploring Human-Computer Interaction in Mathematics:
From Voevodsky's Univalent Foundations of Mathematics
to Mochizuki's IUT-Theoretic Proof of the ABC Conjecture 75
  Yoshihiro Maruyama

Generalization Training Support System Promoting Focusing
Target Changes. 92
  Kosuke Minai and Tomoko Kojiri

Proposal of Learning Support System for Improving Skills in Inferring
Background Knowledge in Conversation 104
  Tomohiro Mogi, Kento Koike, Takahito Tomoto, Tomoya Horiguchi,
  and Tsukasa Hirashima

Development of a Learning Support System for Electromagnetics
Using Haptic Devices   115
   Konoki Tei, Toru Kano, and Takako Akakura

Features Analysis of a Patent Act Based on Legal Condition–Effect
Structure: Conversion of Law Texts into Logical Formulas for a Learning
Support System.   128
   Akihisa Tomita, Masashi Komatsh, Toru Kano, and Takako Akakura

Using User-Guided Development to Teach Complex Scientific Tasks
Through a Graphical User Interface.   141
   Alexis R. Tudor, Richard M. Plotkin, Aarran W. Shaw,
   Ava E. Covington, and Sergiu Dascalu

Preparing Undergraduate Students for Summer Research Experiences
and Graduate School Applications in a Pandemic Environment:
Development and Implementation of Online Modules   156
   Kim-Phuong L. Vu, Chi-Ah Chun, Keisha Chin Goosby,
   Young-Hee Cho, Jesse Dillon, and Panadda Marayong

Advancing Inclusive Mentoring Through an Online Mentor Training
Program and Coordinated Discussion Group.   177
   Kelly A. Young, Malcolm A. Finney, Panadda Marayong,
   and Kim-Phuong L. Vu

Supporting Work, Collaboration and Design

Information Technology Creative Discussion Method
for Collective Wellbeing   197
   Hideyuki Ando, Dominique Chen, Junji Watanabe,
   and Kyosuke Sakakura

Development of a Survey Instrument to Explore Telehealth Adoption
in the Healthcare Domain.   208
   Avijit Chowdhury, Abdul Hafeez-Baig, and Raj Gururajan

Structural Changes in Discussions Using Design Thinking and Their Effect
on Creativity   226
   Mayumi Kawase, Kazumi Matsumoto, Hiroshi Kamabe, Hidekazu Fukai,
   and Kazunori Terada

Evaluation of the Current State of Nippon Professional Baseball
in Digitalization   242
   Masaru Kondo and Yumi Asahi

Digitizing the FlexIA Toolkit - Transforming a Paper-Based Method into a
Flexible Web App.   253
    Christian Kruse, Daniela Becks, and Sebastian Venhuis

Analyzing Early Stage of Forming a Consensus from Viewpoint
of Majority/Minority Decision in Online-Barnga   269
    Yoshimiki Maekawa, Tomohiro Yamaguchi, and Keiki Takadama

Classification of Automotive Industry Salesmen   286
    Yoshio Matsuyama and Yumi Asahi

Impact of Task Cycle Pattern on Project Success in Software
Crowdsourcing   300
    Razieh Saremi, Marzieh Lotfalian Saremi, Sanam Jena,
    Robert Anzalone, and Ahmed Bahabry

Can Community Point System Promote the Interaction
Between Residents?.   312
    Yurika Shiozu, Mizuki Tanaka, Ryo Shioya, and Katsunori Shimohara

Research on the Smart Traditional Chinese Medicine Service System Based
on Service Design.   326
    Junnan Ye, Xu Liu, Jingyang Wang, Menglan Wang, and Siyao Zhu

A Scenario-Based, Self-taught and Collaborative System
for Human-Centered and Innovative Solutions   340
    Der-Jang Yu, Wen-Chi Lin, Meng-Yu Wun, Tian Yeu Tiffany Lee,
    and Tao-Tao Yu

Intelligent Information Environments

Proposal of Credit Risk Model Using Machine Learning
in Motorcycle Sales.   353
    Ryota Fujinuma and Yumi Asahi

Research on Supporting an Operator's Control for OriHime
as a Telepresence Robot.   364
    Kosei Furukawa, Madoka Takahara, and Hidetsugu Suto

Factor Analysis of Continuous Use of Car Services in Japan
by Machine Learning.   373
    Kenta Hara and Yumi Asahi

Creative Design of Gaussian Sensor System with Encoding and Decoding . . .   385
    Yu-Hsiung Huang, Wei-Chun Chen, and Su-Chu Hsu

Smart Speaker Interaction Through ARM-COMS for Health Monitoring
Platform.   396
    Teruaki Ito, Takashi Oyama, and Tomio Watanabe

Proposal of Wisdom Science   406
    Tetsuya Maeshiro

Information Management System for Small Automatic Navigation
Robot Ships   419
    Kozono Rinto, Yutaro Tsurumi, Yasunori Nihei, and Ryosuke Saga

Development of a Presentation Support System Using Group Pupil
Response Interfaces   429
    Yoshihiro Sejima, Yoichiro Sato, and Tomio Watanabe

Extraction and Extended Analysis of Good Jobs from Safety Reports Using
Text Mining - Focusing on the Voluntary Information Contributory
to Enhancement of the Safety (VOICES) Data   439
    Tsubasa Takagi, Ayumu Osawa, and Miwa Nakanishi

Development and Evaluation of a Gaze Information Collection
System in e-Testing for Examinee Authentication   455
    Toru Tokunaga, Toru Kano, and Takako Akakura

An Improved Optimized Route Selection Method for a Maritime
Navigation Vessel   468
    Yutaro Tsurumi, Ryosuke Saga, Sharath Srinivasamurthy,
    and Yasunori Nihei

Novel Motion Display for Virtual Walking.   482
    Minori Unno, Ken Yamaoka, Vibol Yem, Tomohiro Amemiya,
    Michiteru Kitazaki, and Yasushi Ikei

Author Index   493

Contents – Part I

Information Presentation

The Use of New Presentation Technologies in Electronic Sales
Environments and Their Influence on Product Perception............... 3
  María-Jesús Agost, Margarita Vergara, and Vicente Bayarri

Research on Conveying User Experiences Through Digital Advertisement ... 16
  Stephanie Dwiputri Suciadi and Miwa Nakanishi

Preventing Decision Fatigue with Aesthetically Engaging
Information Buttons.. 28
  *Andrew Flangas, Alexis R. Tudor, Frederick C. Harris Jr.,
  and Sergiu Dascalu*

A Modeling Research on How to Solve Ventilator Alarms from Behavioral
and Cognitive Perspectives.................................... 40
  Jun Hamaguchi and Sakae Yamamoto

Evaluating Digital Nudging Effectiveness Using Alternative
Questionnaires Design....................................... 49
  Andreas Mallas, Michalis Xenos, and Maria Karavasili

Cultivation System of Search-Query-Setting Skill by Visualizing
Search Results 61
  Chonfua Mano and Tomoko Kojiri

A Support Interface for Remembering Events in Novels by Visualizing
Time-Series Information of Characters and Their Existing Places 76
  Yoko Nishihara, Jiaxiu Ma, and Ryosuke Yamanishi

Experimental Evaluation of Auditory Human Interface for Radiation
Awareness Based on Different Acoustic Features 88
  *Dingming Xue, Daisuke Shinma, Yuki Harazono, Hirotake Ishii,
  and Hiroshi Shimoda*

Comprehending Research Article in Minutes: A User Study of Reading
Computer Generated Summary for Young Researchers 101
  *Shintaro Yamamoto, Ryota Suzuki, Hitokatsu Kataoka,
  and Shigeo Morishima*

Possibility of Reading Notes as Media to Enrich Communications Between
Reader and Book   113
    Satoko Yoshida, Madoka Takahara, Ivan Tanev,
    and Katsunori Shimohara

Notification Timing Control While Reading Text Information.   125
    Juan Zhou, Hao Wu, and Hideyuki Takada

Visualization and Decision-Making Support

Designing Data Visualization Dashboards to Support the Prediction
of Congenital Anomalies   143
    Tatiana Aparecida de Almeida, Ferrucio de Franco Rosa,
    and Rodrigo Bonacin

Improving User Experience Through Recommendation Message Design:
A Systematic Literature Review of Extant Literature on Recommender
Systems and Message Design   163
    Antoine Falconnet, Wietske Van Osch, Joerg Beringer,
    Pierre-Majorique Léger, and Constantinos K. Coursaris

Research on Innovative Application Mode of Human-Computer Interaction
Design in Data Journalism   182
    Rui Fang, Qiang Lu, and Feng Liu

Evaluating the Impact of Algorithm Confidence Ratings on Human
Decision Making in Visual Search   192
    Aaron P. Jones, Michael C. Trumbo, Laura E. Matzen, Mallory C. Stites,
    Breannan C. Howell, Kristin M. Divis, and Zoe N. Gastelum

NEARME: Dynamic Exploration of Geographical Areas.   206
    Noemi Mauro, Liliana Ardissono, Federico Torrielli, Gianmarco Izzi,
    Claudio Mattutino, Maurizio Lucenteforte, and Marino Segnan

Decision Support for Prolonged, and Tactical Combat Casualty Care.   218
    Christopher Nemeth, Adam Amos-Binks, Natalie Keeney,
    Yuliya Pinevich, Gregory Rule, Dawn Laufersweiler, Isaac Flint,
    and Vitaly Hereasevich

Lessons Learned from Applying Requirements and Design Techniques
in the Development of a Machine Learning System for Predicting Lawsuits
Against Power Companies   227
    Luis Rivero, Carlos Portela, José Boaro, Pedro Santos, Venicius Rego,
    Geraldo Braz Junior, Anselmo Paiva, Erika Alves, Milton Oliveira,
    Renato Moraes, and Marina Mendes

Information in VR and Multimodal User Interfaces

Asymmetric Gravitational Oscillation on Fingertips Increased the Perceived
Heaviness of a Pinched Object   247
   Tomohiro Amemiya

Thematic Units Comparisons Between Analog and Digital Brainstorming . . .   257
   Shannon Briggs, Matthew Peveler, Jaimie Drozdal, Hui Su,
   and Jonas Braasch

On-Demand Lectures that Enable Students to Feel the Sense of a Classroom
with Students Who Learn Together   268
   Ryoya Fujii, Hayato Hirose, Saizo Aoyagi, and Michiya Yamamoto

Research on Perceptual Cues of Interactive Narrative in Virtual Reality   283
   Entang He, Jing Lin, Zhejun Liu, and Yize Zhang

Avatar Twin Using Shadow Avatar in Avatar-Mediated Communication   297
   Yutaka Ishii, Satoshi Kurokawa, and Tomio Watanabe

Effects of Interpupillary Distance and Visual Avatar's Shape
on the Perception of the Avatar's Shape and the Sense of Ownership   306
   Tokio Oka, Takumi Goto, Nobuhito Kimura, Sho Sakurai,
   Takuya Nojima, and Koichi Hirota

Impact of Long-Term Use of an Avatar to IVBO in the Social VR   322
   Akimi Oyanagi, Takuji Narumi, Kazuma Aoyama, Kenichiro Ito,
   Tomohiro Amemiya, and Michitaka Hirose

Multi-modal Data Exploration in a Mixed Reality Environment Using
Coordinated Multiple Views   337
   Disha Sardana, Sampanna Yashwant Kahu, Denis Gračanin,
   and Krešimir Matković

Perception of Illusory Body Tilt Induced by Electrical
Tendon Stimulation   357
   Nozomi Takahashi, Tomohiro Amemiya, Takuji Narumi,
   Hideaki Kuzuoka, Michitaka Hirose, and Kazuma Aoyama

Wearable Haptic Array of Flexible Electrostatic Transducers   369
   Ian Trase, Hong Z. Tan, Zi Chen, and John X. J. Zhang

Investigation of Sign Language Motion Classification by Feature Extraction
Using Keypoints Position of OpenPose   386
   Tsukasa Wakao, Yuusuke Kawakita, Hiromitsu Nishimura,
   and Hiroshi Tanaka

Author Index   401

Learning in Information-Rich Environments

Characterization of Auxiliary Problems for Automated Generation in Error-Based Simulation

Nonoka Aikawa[1]([✉]), Kento Koike[1], Takahito Tomoto[2], Tomoya Horiguchi[3], and Tsukasa Hirashima[4]

[1] Graduate School of Engineering, Tokyo Polytechnic University, Atsugi, Japan
[2] Faculty of Engineering, Tokyo Polytechnic University, Atsugi, Japan
[3] Graduate School of Maritime Sciences, Kobe University, Kobe, Japan
[4] Graduate School of Advanced Science and Engineering, Hiroshima University, Higashi-Hiroshima, Japan

Abstract. Error-based Simulation (EBS) is a learning support framework that visualizes learner's errors. Learning with EBS encourages trial and error, unlike learning by instruction, because learners are required to actively challenge problems. However, when problems are complex and difficult, learners may get stuck. In such cases, it is effective to present auxiliary problems that can support learning of the original problem. Learning with auxiliary problems requires learners to actively challenge problems compared with more passive learning by instruction. However, the creation of many auxiliary problems places a burden on teachers, especially because there are no rules to creating these problems. Therefore, we considered that a system that automatically generates auxiliary problems according to rules would provide the required auxiliary problems. Such a system would lift the burden on teachers who would otherwise need to create the auxiliary problems. In this paper, we discuss characterization and generation rules for the purpose of automated generation of auxiliary problems in EBS. We propose three types of operations that generate auxiliary problems: replace, balanced delete, and simple delete. Using these operations to generate auxiliary problems in a trial, we generated fourteen auxiliary problems.

Keywords: Auxiliary problem · Error-based simulation · Automated generation

1 Introduction

Error-based Simulation (EBS) is a framework that supports learning by visualizing learners' errors [3]. EBS presents learners with simulations that visualize their answers and encourages trial and error. The framework aims to help learners compare their answers with correct answers and to help them become aware of their errors from the difference.

© Springer Nature Switzerland AG 2021
S. Yamamoto and H. Mori (Eds.): HCII 2021, LNCS 12766, pp. 3–13, 2021.
https://doi.org/10.1007/978-3-030-78361-7_1

Learning with EBS encourages trial and error compared with learning by instruction because learners are required to actively challenge problems. The learning effect of EBS has been demonstrated in studies to date [4].

However, EBS has not been shown to support learners who find themselves at an impasse. In the present study, "impasse" is defined as the state where a problem cannot be solved despite the learner's repeated attempts at solving the problem. Problems that are complex and difficult often result in learners getting stuck.

We consider that the presentation of an auxiliary problem is effective in helping learners solve impasses. Auxiliary problems are problems that help in understanding the original problem. Learning with auxiliary problems requires learners to challenge problems actively compared with learning passively by receiving teaching on mistakes. Therefore, learning with auxiliary problems in combination with EBS can better encourage trial and error than with EBS alone.

We have recently created auxiliary problems in EBS for physics [1]. However, the creation of many auxiliary problems places a burden on teachers, especially because there are no rules to creating such problems. Therefore, we considered that a system that could automatically generate auxiliary problems according to rules could create many auxiliary problems, such that teachers would not be burdened with creating these auxiliary problems.

In this paper, we discuss characterization and generation rules for the purpose of automated generation of auxiliary problems in EBS. By creating an auxiliary problem experimentally using the framework of automated generation, we generated fourteen problems. This is seven more than the number of auxiliary problems created in our earlier study [1].

2   Support by Error-Based Simulation

2.1   Physics Error-Based Simulation System

A physics EBS system simulates the "assumed correct" phenomenon based on learner answers, which supports learners in finding their errors [3]. Learners can obtain learning effects by observing simulations and noticing the errors themselves. A physics EBS system first presents a diagram of a certain phenomenon. Then, the learner is tasked with drawing arrows that indicate the forces acting on the objects in the diagram. From the learner input, the EBS system simulates strange behavior if the drawing is incorrect or natural behavior if the drawing is correct (Fig. 1).

2.2   Problems in EBS

The physics EBS system presents a diagram of a phenomenon. A learner solves the phenomenon by inputting arrows that show the forces acting on an object in the diagram. The arrows can express the direction, the point of action, and the size of the forces. While the learner inputs arrows, they consider the force

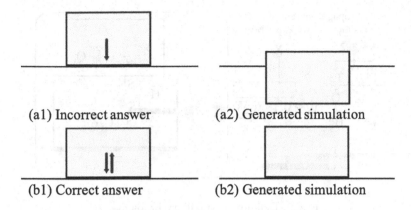

(a1) Incorrect answer   (a2) Generated simulation

(b1) Correct answer   (b2) Generated simulation

Fig. 1. Example of behavior of EBS.

balance and the concept of acting force. However, complicated phenomena are difficult to solve because it is difficult to determine which arrow affects which movement, even if the learner is looking at the simulation.

2.3 Support Using Auxiliary Problems

EBS is learning support that encourages active trial and error in learners. Horiguchi et al. conducted research on support for EBS to identify and suggest the cause of error in EBS [6]. However, in situations where providing support with EBS is difficult, learning is a passive activity, such as in the case where learners receive an auxiliary explanation. Therefore, we considered that providing support in the form of auxiliary problems rather than auxiliary explanations would require learners to challenge problems more actively.

3 Automated Generation of Auxiliary Problems

3.1 Characterization Using Causal Reasoning

The auxiliary problem in a system that provides support in the provision of auxiliary problems was defined by referring to the causal reasoning theory on force and motion of Mizoguchi et al. [8] and applying it to EBS. Causal reasoning estimates the causal relationship of force from motion. Mizoguchi et al. organized and theorized the causality of forces acting on physical phenomena in elementary physics. Based on their work, we ordered the arrows representing the forces acting on the object in the EBS problem based on the force generation propagation relationship in the present study.

The right side of Fig. 2 shows the problem and the force acting on the object, and the left side shows the propagative relation of the force acting on the object. Force propagation sequences are independent of each other owing to the forces generated. In addition, the composed force is treated as a force separate from

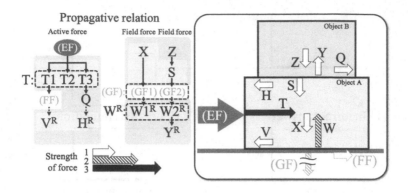

Fig. 2. Defining an auxiliary problem.

the propagation sequence. For example, in the case of the problem in Fig. 2, three points are the sources of the force: force X acting on object A, gravity Z acting on object B, and force (EF) pushing object A from the side. Force W^R is the force of two parts, namely, force $W1^R$ propagating from gravity X acting on object A and force $W2^R$ propagating from gravity Z acting on object B.

In addition, each propagation sequence has a force that acts and propagates, and a force that reacts to it. If the action force and the reaction force are equal, the object stands still in the direction of the force. However, if the action force and the reaction force are not equal, the object accelerates in the direction of the larger force. In the figure, the action force has no subscript, and the reaction force is expressed by adding the subscript "R". For example, in Fig. 2, force X, which is gravity, acts on object A. Force X pushes the ground as a force (GF1), and normal force $W1^R$ is returned from the ground. In addition, force Z, which is gravity, acts on object B. Because object B is on object A, force Z propagates as force S, which pushes down on object A. Force S pushes the ground as a force (GF2), and normal force $W2^R$ is returned from the ground. Then, force $W2^R$ propagates to object B and returns to object B as its normal force Y^R so that object B pushes down on object A. At this time, in object A, forces X and S and forces $W1^R$ and $W2^R$ are balanced, and in object B, force Z and force Y^R are balanced.

3.2 Automated Generation Rule of Auxiliary Problems

Auxiliary problems are generated by simplifying the order of arrows; that is, we consider the force propagation relationship, based on the characterization in Subsect. 3.1. In this paper, we define three types of operations: replace, balanced delete, and simple delete.

"Replace" is an operation that generates an auxiliary problem by replacing a certain force with an external force. The operation is to delete a specific object from two or several existing objects and to save the force propagating from the deleted object. When considering the force in the remaining object, the situation

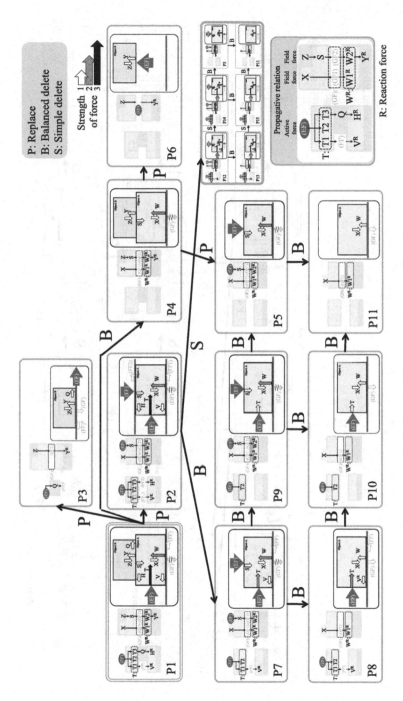

Fig. 3. Characterization of auxiliary problems of P1 to P11.

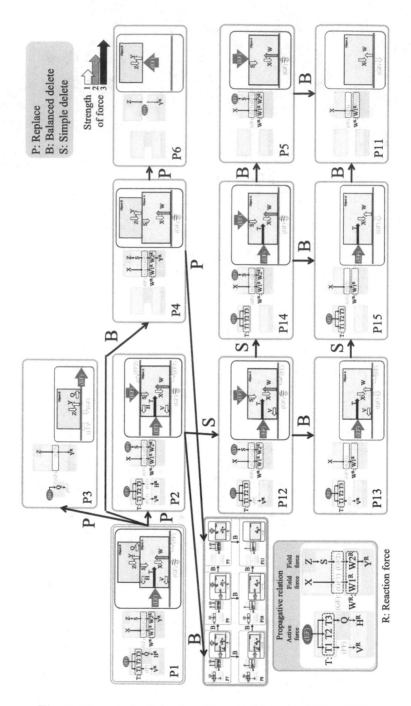

Fig. 4. Characterization of auxiliary problems on P12 to P15.

Table 1. Rules for characterization of auxiliary problems.

Problem ID	Base ID	Type	Operation	Side effect
P1 (Original)				
P2	P1	Replace	Replacing force Z with force (EF) by deleting force Z, Y^R, and Q	Delete object B
P3	P1	Replace	Replacing force T with force (EF) by deleting force T, H^R, V^R, X, W^R, and S	Delete object A
P4	P1	Balanced delete	Deleting force (EF), T, Q, V^R, and H^R	
P5	P4	Replace	Replacing force Z with force (EF) by deleting force Z and Y^R	Delete object B
	P9	Balanced delete	Deleting force (EF) and T2	
	P14	Balanced delete	Deleting force (EF) and T	
P6	P4	Replace	Replacing force W^R with force (EF) by deleting force X, W^R, and S	Delete object A
P7	P2	Balanced delete	Deleting force H^R	Delete the friction at the top of object A
P8	P7	Balanced delete	Deleting force (EF) and S	
P9	P7	Balanced delete	Deleting force V^R	Delete the friction at the bottom of object A
P10	P8	Balanced delete	Deleting force V^R	Delete the friction at the bottom of object A
	P9	Balanced delete	Deleting force (EF) and S	
P11	P5	Balanced delete	Deleting force (EF) and S	
	P10	Balanced delete	Deleting force (EF) and T2	
	P15	Balanced delete	Deleting force (EF) and T	
P12	P2	Simple delete	Deleting force H^R	Delete the friction at the top of object A
P13	P12	Balanced delete	Deleting force (EF), S, and $W2^R$	
P14	P12	Simple delete	Deleting force V^R	Delete the friction at the bottom of abject A
P15	P14	Simple delete	Deleting force V^R	Delete the friction at the bottom of object A
	P13	Balanced delete	Deleting force (EF), S, and $W2^R$	

does not change between the original problem and the auxiliary problem. For example, P5 in Fig. 3 is an auxiliary problem that replaces P4. This is a simplified problem that focuses on the arrow of force S in problem P4. Force S is preserved by deleting object B; that is, the force acting on object A is preserved, and force Z is replaced with an external force. Also, when focusing on the force on object A in this operation, the force relationship $X + S = W^R$ is the same for both P5 and P4.

"Balanced delete" is an operation that generates an auxiliary problem by deleting only a part of the force propagation sequence. Here, the force to be deleted is a series of propagation sequences from the action force to the reaction force or a set consisting of the action force and the reaction force. For example, P8 in Fig. 4 is an auxiliary problem that deletes P7. The force propagation sequence of force (EF), S and $W2^R$ has been deleted.

"Simple delete" is also an operation that generates an auxiliary problem by deleting only a part of the force propagation sequence. However, unlike balanced delete, only the reaction force is deleted from the set consisting of the action force and the reaction force. For example, P12 in Fig. 3 is an auxiliary problem where the simple delete operation was used on P2. Action force T3 is saved and reaction force H^R is deleted, which accelerates object A.

Table 1 summarizes the generation rule of auxiliary problems. "Base ID" is a base problem for generating an auxiliary problem. "Type" is a method for simplifying auxiliary problems. "Operation" is a concrete operation for generating an auxiliary problem. "Side effect" is a changed problem situation as a result of performing "Operation". Auxiliary problems are defined in Table 1 and shown in Figs. 3 and 4. In this way, we generated fourteen auxiliary problems, which was seven more than created in the study by Aikawa et al. [1]. The newly generated auxiliary problems include P6, P7, P9, P12, P13, P14, and P15.

3.3   How to Use Automated Generation of Auxiliary Problems

If the automated generation of auxiliary problems can be realized, it can be expected that impasses that learners face will be solved. Although auxiliary problems are effective in solving impasses, the creation of auxiliary problems is a difficult task for teachers. Therefore, we implement automated generation of auxiliary problems in the EBS system. Accordingly, it can be expected that the learner and the system alone will be able to solve the impasses.

4   Discussion

4.1   Auxiliary Problems

Various studies have been conducted on learning by auxiliary problems.

Hirashima et al. defined a process by which learners solve problems and classified auxiliary problems based on this process [5]. When solving a problem, the learner converts the problem sentence into a computable formula or quantitative relationship to perform the calculation. This process is called the "problem-solving process of mechanics problems". There are three phases in the problem-solving process of mechanics problems (Fig. 4). In the first phase, "detection of surface structure", the relationship between situations from the problem sentence is extracted, expressed structurally, and converted into a surface structure. In the second phase, "specification of phenomenon", the surface structure is converted into a quantity. In the third phase, "detection of solution

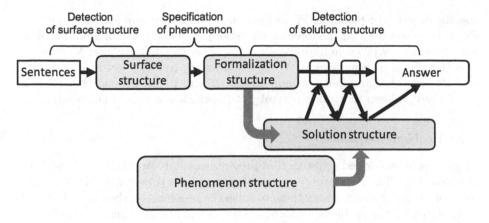

Fig. 5. Three phases in the problem-solving process of mechanics problems.

structure", the solution is assembled to match the problem by applying the formalization structure to the equation in order. Through this series of phases, the learner solves the problem.

The learner also uses three structures to solve the problem. The first is the surface structure, which is the structure of the situation and parameters of the problem and is generated in the detection of surface structure and converted in the specification of the phenomenon. The second is the phenomenon structure, which is the structure of the quantity relationship in the situation of the problem. The third is the solution structure, which is the structure for finding a solution using formalization structure and phenomenon structure.

Hirashima et al. classified the auxiliary problems into three categories according to which of the abovementioned structures was simplified [5]. The first is an auxiliary problem that simplifies the surface structure to something close to a formalization structure. The second is an auxiliary problem that simplifies the solution structure and is called a "partialized problem". The third is an auxiliary problem that simplifies the phenomenon structure and is called a "specialized problem".

We grouped the auxiliary problems from our study according to these categories. As introduced in Subsect. 3.2, our research considered three operations: replace, balanced delete and simple delete. In physics EBS, the situation of a phenomenon is presented to the learner, and the learner solves the phenomenon by drawing arrows that show the force acting on it. The learner inputs the relationship of forces in the phenomenon. Therefore, the problem within physics EBS is the problem of creating a phenomenon structure. In other words, all the auxiliary problems in this paper simplify the phenomenon structure.

However, the auxiliary problem generated by "replace" does not change the situation between the original problem and the auxiliary problem within a specific object. In other words, the phenomenon structure has not changed, and the solution structure is simplified when focusing only on the force acting on the specific object. For example, P5 in Fig. 3 is an auxiliary problem that replaces P4. If it focuses only on the force acting on object A, both the original problem and the auxiliary problem have the same the phenomenon structure: X (gravity) + S (force pushed from top) = W^R (normal force). In other words, because P5 and P4 have the same phenomenon structure, and it can be said that P5 is a partialized problem that takes only object A, which is a part of the solution.

4.2   Problem Sequence

Hayashi et al. developed a system that presents auxiliary problems of elementary mechanics [2]. Their system gives auxiliary problems to learners who failed to solve problems and encourages them to solve the problems on their own. Hayashi et al. simplified the problems by using specialization and partialization, and gave auxiliary problems to learners who were stuck. When an auxiliary problem was solved, a function that was incorporated into the system prompted the learner to think about the difference between the original problem and the auxiliary problem. This difference was considered to be the point of difficulty that learners faced. On the other hand, the purpose of our research is to adaptively give the learner an auxiliary problem and to help them become aware of the problem itself. In particular, the auxiliary problem generated by "replace" is not used in the study by Hayashi et al. and is a problem created so that the learner can easily become aware of a specific force. This auxiliary problem can rouse awareness in learners who are stuck, without rousing awareness of force.

Horiguchi et al. proposed a graph of microworld (GMW) [7], which is a framework for promoting understanding of complex phenomena by presenting complex phenomena in stages from a simulation of a limited phenomenon. Based on the description of the microworld, Horiguchi et al. made possible a transition between microworlds where the difference is small and has educational meaning. They also created the ability to generate a description of the changes in the two microworld models. This enables learner-adaptive microworld migration. Their aims to facilitate adaptive learning and have clear problem goals are the same as ours. On the other hand, as a difference from our study, the graph of microworld need to manually describe by the teacher, in our research, it became possible to generate auxiliary problems by a created framework for automatically generate.

5   Conclusion

In this paper, we defined the characterization of automated generation of auxiliary problems. We proposed three types of operations for simplifying auxiliary problems: "Replace", "Balanced delete", and "Simple delete". These operations were used to generate each auxiliary problem. In future work, we plan to develop a system that automatically generates auxiliary problems and conduct evaluation experiments.

References

1. Aikawa, N., Koike, K., Tomoto, T.: Proposal and preliminary evaluation of a system that presents auxiliary problems to break learners' impasse based on tendency of the error in Error-based Simulation. IEICE Trans. Inf. Syst. (Japanese edition) **103**(9), 644–647 (2020). (in Japanese)
2. Hayashi, N., Shinohara, T., Yamamoto, S., Hayashi, Y., Horiguchi, T., Hirashima, T.: Scaffolding for self-overcoming of impasse by using problem simplification. In: The 22nd International Conference on Computers in Education (2014)
3. Hirashima, T., Horiguchi, T., Kashihara, A., Toyoda, J.: Error-based simulation for error-visualization and its management. Int. J. Artif. Intell. Educ. **9**(1–2), 17–31 (1998)
4. Hirashima, T., Imai, I., Horiguchi, T., Tomoto, T.: Error-based simulation to promote awareness of error in elementary mechanics and its evaluation. In: Proceedings of International Conference on Artificial Intelligence in Education, pp. 409–416 (2009)
5. Hirashima, T., Niitsu, T., Hirose, K., Kashihara, A., Toyoda, J.: An indexing framework for adaptive arrangement of mechanics problems for ITS. IEICE Trans. Inf. Syst. **77**(1), 19–26 (1994)
6. Horiguchi, T., Hirashima, T.: A method of creating counterexamples by using error-based simulation. In: Proceedings of ICCE2000, pp. 619–627 (2000)
7. Horiguchi, T., Hirashima, T.: Graph of microworlds: a framework for assisting progressive knowledge acquisition in simulation-based learning environments. In: AIED2005, pp. 670–677 (2005)
8. Mizoguchi, R., Hirashima, T., Horiguchi, T.: Causality-compliant theory of force and motion. Trans. Jpn. Soc. Artif. Intell. **31**(4), A-F44_1 (2016). (in Japanese)

Development of Collaborative Chemistry Experiment Environment Using VR

Hisashi Fujiwara[1]($^{(\boxtimes)}$), Toru Kano[2], and Takako Akakura[2]

[1] Faculty of Engineering, Department of Information and Computer Technology, Tokyo University of Science, 6-3-1 Nijuku, Katsushika-ku, Tokyo 125-8585, Japan
4617069@ed.tus.ac.jp
[2] Faculty of Engineering, Tokyo University of Science, 6-3-1 Nijuku, Katsushika-ku, Tokyo 125-8585, Japan
{kano,akakura}@rs.tus.ac.jp

Abstract. In recent years, the importance of distance learning has been reaffirmed, but there are some subjects where learning is ineffective owing to the difficulty of interaction. For chemistry experiments, some researchers have tried to conduct remote experiments using head-mounted display (HMD)-based virtual reality (VR). However, in these attempts, there is a concern that collaborative learning, which is important in science education, is lacking. In this study, we proposed a new environment for remote chemistry experiments using network services and HMD-based VR. Specifically, we conducted VR experiments of flame color reaction and metal ion separation and identification, which are often taught in high school chemistry, and then evaluated the effectiveness of the proposed environment using exams and questionnaires. The results confirmed effective learning in the chemistry experiment using HMD-based VR, suggesting that collaborative learning was possible in VR spaces.

Keywords: VR · CSCL · Chemical experiment · E-learning · E-education · Synchronous learning

1 Introduction

1.1 Background

Devices such as personal computers and smartphones, which have become ubiquitous in modern society, can communicate remotely and are expected to become even more widespread in the future. Against this backdrop, Japan's Ministry of Education, Culture, Sports, Science and Technology is aiming to promote distance education [1]. Accordingly, they are improving the information and communication technology (ICT) environment in schools from 2018 to 2022 [2]. However, for subjects that require face-to-face lessons, such as physical education, technology, and chemistry experiments, it is expected that effective learning might be difficult in distance lessons.

Among such subjects, this study focuses on chemistry experiments, in which dangerous equipment and materials are handled. The primary approach in distance

S. Yamamoto and H. Mori (Eds.): HCII 2021, LNCS 12766, pp. 14–26, 2021.
https://doi.org/10.1007/978-3-030-78361-7_2

learning is video demonstration experiments by instructors. However, students cannot interact with such demonstrations, and therefore there is a concern that the students will miss learning opportunities.

In recent years, to address such problems, there have been attempts to conduct science experiments remotely by using head-mounted display (HMD)-based virtual reality (VR) and augmented reality (AR) [3–5]. These attempts were aimed at individuals, but in the science section of the Ministry of Education, Culture, Sports, Science and Technology's curriculum guideline [6], school education is required to include work with others to solve problems. Therefore, collaborative learning is important. In this respect, the previous remote learning attempts were inadequate, and we are also concerned that the advantages of in-person collaborative classes, such as exposure to a variety of opinions and ideas, the development of communication and social skills, and the deepening of one's own understanding through discussion and debate with friends, will not be achieved.

1.2 Purpose of This Paper

From the current situation of distance learning as described above, it is considered necessary to have a distance learning environment in which students can interact and collaborate. Therefore, in this study, we develop a collaborative learning system for chemistry experiments using VR with network services and evaluate its effectiveness.

2 HMD-Based VR and Collaborative Learning

2.1 Trends in HMD-Based VR

In a 2019 survey [7] conducted on 206 people aged between 15 and 69, 91% recognized the term VR, and 21% had actually experienced VR. Of those who had experienced it, 85% responded that they were satisfied with the sensation of reality and presence.

In 2020, an affordable stand-alone HMD-based VR device that does not require a high-spec computer was released [8], which is expected to make VR more widespread in the future and enable its use in the educational field.

2.2 Example of Using HMD-Based VR for Education

Nakamura et al. [3] focused on the gyro sensor of smartphones and tried to develop e-learning materials to teach physics to students experientially. By using the gyro sensor of a smartphone and operating the camera in the virtual space according to the direction a student is facing, the student can freely observe and move in the virtual space to obtain a high sense of immersion. This synchronous e-learning teaching material has the following advantages:

- It is possible to reproduce an environment that is not possible in reality, such as an object with zero mass or a space with zero friction.
- Experiments are easy to repeat
- Experiments such as those dealing with explosives or fragile objects are possible without risk.

Nakamura et al. dealt with physics experiments, but the above advantages might be possible in chemistry experiments as well. However, Nakamura et al. expressed concern that the learning opportunities of the stuis possible to reproduce an environment that dents may not be sufficient because the learning is based on demonstration experiments.

Okamoto et al. [4] conducted a solution experiment of inorganic chemistry using an HMD-based AR device and suggested the possibility of acquiring knowledge about inorganic chemistry. In their research, HMD-based AR equipment was used, but it is expected that the same learning effect can be obtained with HMD-based VR because VR can provide an immersive experience equal to or better than that of AR.

Hayashi et al. [5] used a hand-tracking controller within a VR chemistry experiment environment. They confirmed that chemical experiments involving body movements can be performed in virtual space.

In this study, we focus on collaborative learning, which was not considered the abovementioned studies.

2.3 Collaborative Learning

The Ministry of Education, Culture, Sports, Science and Technology states in its guidance on qualities and abilities to be cultivated in a topic, "What the new curriculum guideline aims for [9]" is "the ability to think, judge, and express oneself in order to share information with others, to understand the similarities and differences in diverse ways of thinking through dialogue and discussion, to sympathize with the ideas of others and to integrate diverse ideas, and to solve problems in cooperation (collaborative problem solving)" and "an attitude of respect for diversity and the ability to work together by making the best use of each other's strengths." In addition, "Thinking ability, judgment ability, expressive ability, etc., experience the scene of independent and collaborative problem finding/solving in which the above-mentioned thinking/judgment/expression is demonstrated in learning. The individual knowledge and skills that you have acquired will also be established by utilizing them in such learning experiences, and you will acquire them while being systematically associated with existing knowledge and skills, and eventually your life. It is expected to lead to a deep understanding of things and mastery of methods that can be utilized throughout."

In this way, collaborative learning is positioned as extremely important for learning in the coming era. In this study, we focused on "collaborative problem solving" and whether the knowledge and skills acquired by it can be systematized and acquired even in VR space.

CSCL. Computer-supported collaborative learning (CSCL) is a research activity that uses a computer to support collaborative learning in which multiple students learn while communicating with each other remotely. Nakahara [10] explains CSCL as follows:

> In conventional learning theory, learning is considered to be the accumulation of an individual student's knowledge, and the transfer of knowledge from the teacher's mind to the student's mind is learning and education. However, CSCL takes a situational cognitive approach that seeks to focus knowledge not only in the mind but also in relation to others and tools. This shift from traditional learning theory to a situational cognitive approach has brought about the following changes in beliefs about teaching and learning:
> - Change in students from "people who are satisfied with sharing the same knowledge" to "people who can cooperate with each other"
> - Change in teachers from "sources of knowledge" to "guides to advanced intellectual resources within the community"
> - Change in learning activities from "means for accumulation of knowledge" to "exercises of knowledge using tools and/or participation in the community"
> - Change in the learning objective from "the cultivation of competent individuals" to "the cultivation of individuals who can demonstrate their intellect when they cooperate while being dispersed in various groups."

In this way, with the progress of ICT and the importance of collaborative learning, the importance of CSCL is increasing and the form of learning is also changing. In this study, we tried to realize collaborative learning, which is important in science, in the form of CSCL.

3   System Overview

In this study, an HMD-based VR device was used by participants in order to conduct chemical experiments in VR space. The advantages of HMD-based VR are that it is highly immersive, it is possible to interact with objects as in an actual experiment, and the presence of others is greater than with an AR device when multiple people participate in a synchronized manner. The HMD-based VR device can transfer the movement of the body in real space to the virtual space by using infrared sensors. There are two types of movement methods: one is to actually walk in an area set in real space, and the other is to move back, forth, left, and right by operating the trackpad of a controller. One can also use the controller to lift objects and drop reagents from pipettes.

The Unity platform [11] was used to build the system, and Photon's PUN 2 package [12] was used as a network service for synchronization. PUN 2 is a multiplayer platform that enables highly reliable and rapid communication.

The experimental scene of this system is shown in Fig. 1. We prepared each subject's avatar and laboratory equipment with PUN 2's original network game object, and implemented it so that multiple people can conduct experiments remotely by sending and receiving object information via the Photon server.

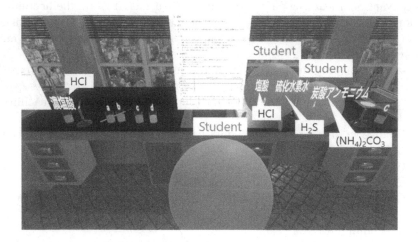

Fig. 1. Experimental scene with multiple people

3.1   Learning Content

This study deals with the flame reaction and metal ionization tendency of inorganic chemical compounds. For the flame reaction, students learn the change in the flame color of a gas burner depending on the sample introduced to it, and for the ionization tendency of the metal, students learn the identify of metal ions by introducing separation reagents into the system. These experiments were selected because they are frequently performed in junior high and high schools, and it is difficult and hazardous for a student to deal with gas burners and dangerous reagents without supervision. Because this system can conduct experiments in a non-hazardous situation, we thought that it would be effective even when students study outside of class hours.

Flame Reaction Experiment. When an alkali metal or alkaline earth metal is heated with a gas burner flame, the flame turns a color that is peculiar to the metal. Using this feature, we conducted experiments aimed at identifying the type of metal. In this experiment, first samples of salt (NaCl), potassium chloride (NaCl), strontium chloride ($SrCl_2$), and copper sulfate ($CuSO_4$) are dissolved in water. We randomly label and arranged them so that students do not know what solution is in any specific beaker. Students first clean the tip of a platinum wire with concentrated hydrochloric acid. Next, the tip of the platinum wire is dipped in a sample solution (Fig. 2), the tip is inserted into the flame of a gas burner (Fig. 3), and the student observes the flame color. This procedure is repeated for each solution. By looking at the color of the flame, the students determine whether the metal contained in the sample is Na, K, Sr, or Cu.

Fig. 2. Dipping the platinum wire into a solution

Fig. 3. Observing the flame reaction color

Metal Ion Separation Detection Experiment. Generally, cations can be divided into six groups by using appropriate separation reagents. In this experiment, students learn that cations of groups I to V can be precipitated, separated, and detected as each separation reagent is added. First, samples of silver nitrate ($AgNO_3$), sodium nitrate ($NaNO_3$), copper nitrate (II) [$Cu(NO_3)_2 \cdot 3H_2O$], and calcium nitrate [$Ca(NO_3)_2 \cdot 4H_2O$] are dissolved in water. We randomly label and arrange the solutions so that students do not know which sample is in any specific beaker. Students add hydrochloric acid (HCl) and hydrogen sulfide solution (H_2S_{aq}) to each beaker (Fig. 4). Then, a gas burner is used to expel hydrogen sulfide from the sample and then ammonium carbonate solution [$(NH_4)_2CO_3$] is added drop by drop, resulting in a white precipitate of silver chloride (Fig. 5), a black precipitate of copper sulfide, or a white precipitate of calcium carbonate. Students observe the results and consider which metal ion, Na+, Ag+, Cu2+, or Ca2+, is in each sample.

4   Evaluation Experiment

The evaluation experiment was performed according to the procedure shown in Fig. 6. Participants were randomly divided into an asynchronous system group, in which an individual uses the system, and a synchronous system group, in which multiple people perform synchronous communication to perform experiments together. First, we conducted a preliminary test (pre-test) on the instructional

Fig. 4. Dropping hydrochloric acid into a solution

Fig. 5. Change in color after the metal cation precipitates

content related to the flame reaction, the ionization tendency of the metal, and the equipment used in the experiment, and then we provided a basic explanation of the HMD-type VR device, such as how to use the controller. Next, in both groups, the experimental instructions existing in the VR space were first browsed, and then the subjects were observed as they carried out the chemical experiments. The synchronized system group used the voice call feature of the LINE app [13] to communicate by voice conversation. The content of the chemical experiments, as shown in Sect. 3.1, was the same for both groups. After that, participants answered a post-test with the same content as the pre-test and finally answered a questionnaire.

4.1 Evaluation Index

The purpose of the evaluation experiment is to determine whether effective collaborative learning can be achieved by multiple people sharing a VR environment with an HMD-type VR device. The evaluation indexes are the scores of a pre-test, post-test, and questionnaire. The questionnaire was composed of several sets of questions rated on a five-point scale (with 5 being positive) and a free-form comment section. The questions common to both groups included VR-related questions, system-related questions, and the comment section. An additional set of questions, also rated on a five-point scale, addressed the individual versus collaborative natures of the two different groups: one set investigated the environment in the asynchronous system (individual) group, and the synchronous system group was asked the other set of questions based on the collaborative learning environment design principles proposed by Mochizuki et al. [14]. Specifically, this environment consists of six design principles based on the division of labor in CSCL, which indicates collaborative learning supported by computers.

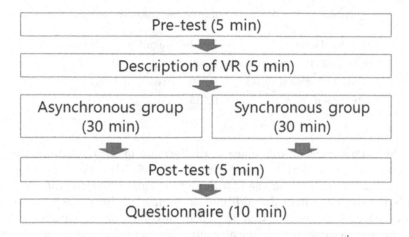

Fig. 6. Experimental flow

4.2 Results and Discussion

Results of Pre- and Post-tests. Eighteen university students participated in the evaluation experiment; nine were in the synchronous system group, and the other nine were in the asynchronous system group. In the synchronous group, the nine people were further divided into three subgroups. The test results are shown in Table 1.

Table 1. Pre- and post-tests results

Test	Synchronous group		Asynchronous group	
	Mean	SD	Mean	SD
Pre-test	3.667	1.054	3.889	0.875
Post-test	4.444	0.831	4.889	0.875

In both groups, the post-test scores were higher than those of the pre-test. Two-way analysis of variance (ANOVA) with replication was performed on the results of Table 1. We set the synchronous system group and asynchronous system group in the specimen elements, set the pre-test and post-test scores in the column elements, with the significance level set to 0.05. The results are shown in Table 2.

Table 2. ANOVA between pre- and post-test results

Variable factor	P-value	Significant difference?
Specimen (between groups)	0.309	No
Column (between tests)	0.010	Yes
Interaction	0.733	No

There was a significant difference in the increase in scores between the pre- and post-tests, which is the column item ($p < 0.05$). However, no significant difference was found between the synchronous group and asynchronous group, which is the specimen item. In addition, no significant difference was found in the interaction. It is possible that the effect of collaborative learning was not fully exhibited because the technical content of the experiment was not very complicated. Therefore, it is necessary to employ experiments dealing with more complicated subjects and verify whether problems can be solved in collaboration.

Questionnaire Results

– About VR
The results of the questionnaire about the VR space are shown in Table 3.

Table 3. "About VR" questionnaire results

Q	Question content	Synchronous group		Asynchronous group	
		Mean	SD	Mean	SD
Q1	I was able to concentrate (become immersed) in the VR space	4.667	0.471	4.556	0.956
Q2	The chemistry experiment in VR space was done in the same way as an actual chemistry experiment	3.222	0.629	3.889	0.737

In Q1, both groups reported high levels of immersiveness, so it is probable that this system created an environment where it was easy to concentrate on the chemical experiments. However, responses to Q2 by the synchronization system group were moderate. One participant reported that "the physical behavior was strange." Therefore, it is necessary to aim for behavior that is closer to reality.

– About the System
The results of the questionnaire about the system are shown in Table 4.

Table 4. "About the system" questionnaire results

Q	Question content	Synchronous group		Asynchronous group	
		Mean	SD	Mean	SD
Q1	There was no discomfort in the flame and its color expressed in the VR space	4.444	0.685	4.333	1.247
Q2	The flame expressed in the VR space and its color change were easy to observe	4.667	0.471	5.000	0.000
Q3	There was no discomfort in the appearance of the liquid expressed in the VR space	3.778	1.227	3.333	1.414
Q4	I was able to observe the precipitation reaction expressed	3.444	1.499	3.667	1.247

From Q1 and Q2, the flame reaction exercise was highly rated overall, and we were able to obtain the opinion that "the color and reaction of the flame are easy to understand" in one of the comments. It was suggested that the flame reaction experiment using the HMD-type VR device was easy to understand and might be effective for learning.

Regarding the metal ion separation detection experiments in Q3 and Q4, the standard deviation was large and the rating was moderate. In addition, comments mentioned low realism of "the appearance of the liquid" and "the appearance of the precipitate." When conducting a metal ion detection experiment in VR space, it is considered necessary to improve the realism of liquid representation.

– Group-specific Survey
In the group-specific questionnaire, "synchronization" was investigated in the synchronous system group, and "environment" was investigated in the asynchronous system group.
The results of the "environment" questionnaire are shown in Table 5.

Table 5. "About environmental" questionnaire result

Q	Question content	Mean	SD
Q1	Work progressed without problems	3.778	1.133
Q2	I was able to work smoothly	3.667	1.054
Q3	I felt like I was performing the experiment with multiple people	4.222	0.916

From Q1 and Q2 in Table 5, it is considered that the content of the chemical experiments dealt with in this experiment were such that individuals could proceed smoothly even while working alone. Therefore, it is considered that there was no significant difference between the groups in Table 2. However, Q3 showed that they were interested in experiments with multiple people, suggesting that they are highly motivated for collaborative learning in chemistry experiments.

In the synchronous group, we investigated the collaborative learning environment design principle advocated by Mochizuki et al. The results of the questionnaire are shown in Table 6. However, for Q7, some students thought that there were no inconsistencies or mistakes in the work, and the experiment was completed without any problems, so the number of valid responses to the questionnaire was six.

Table 6. "About synchronization" questionnaire result

Q	Question content	Mean	SD
Q1	I was able to share the work and carry out the experiment	3.889	0.994
Q2	I was able to carry out the experiment smoothly by sharing the work	3.222	0.916
Q3	I was able to grasp my work situation	3.667	0.943
Q4	I was able to grasp the work status of others	3.667	1.054
Q5	I was able to understand that others understood my work situation	3.111	0.875
Q6	I was able to share the work situation of myself and others and coordinate with them	3.444	0.956
Q7	When dividing labor, there is a contradiction in the work situation of the other party or your own work situation and I noticed a mistake	4.000	1.000

The three items Q2, Q5, and Q6 were rated relatively low, and an associated comment was "I couldn't distinguish avatars." It is possible that the experiment did not proceed smoothly because the similar appearance of student avatars led to communication problems. We also received the comment that "I want to be able to share information not only on the phone but also on VR." By taking fuller advantage of VR, it will be possible to realize smoother progress by presenting information on the progress of the experiment within the VR environment.

Because we were able to obtain a high overall evaluation for all items regarding the collaborative learning design principle, it is considered that collaborative learning was realized in this system. It will be important in the future to build an environment that facilitates collaborative learning by presenting information that visualizes the appearance of avatars and the progress of experiments.

5 Conclusion

5.1 Summary

In this study, we focused on chemical experiments, which are considered difficult to carry out in distance learning. Experiments are considered to be very important for teaching chemistry, but in distance learning, it is not possible to operate laboratory equipment, so students can only watch presentations by teachers or forego remote learning (i.e., go to school to perform experiments hands-on). In recent years, attempts have been made to carry out chemical experiments remotely by using HMD-type VR devices. However, these attempts were aimed at individuals and did not carry out collaborative learning, which is important in science. Therefore, in this study, we proposed an environment in which students can interact with each other and learn collaboratively on a network system using HMD-based VR, and evaluated its effectiveness. We developed a system in which students can carry out flame reaction experiments and metal ion separation and detection experiments remotely and collaboratively, and conducted the experiments by dividing participants into a synchronous group (remote collaborative learning) and an asynchronous group (remote individual learning). Based on the collaborative learning environment design principle [14] proposed by Mochizuki et al., the results indicating whether collaborative learning was realized suggested that collaborative learning of chemistry experiments using HMD-based VR was established. In addition, it was suggested that it is effective in improving the effectiveness of learning, regardless of whether it is collaborative.

5.2 Future Issues

In the collaborative learning environment design principle [14], as implemented in this study, it was not possible for students to distinguish the avatars of other students, so there was a discrepancy in the sharing of progress and communication when experiments were performed with a division of labor. It is necessary to improve the appearance of avatars, and then verify whether this change makes collaborative learning progress more smoothly and achieve a higher learning effect. It was also suggested that the realism of the chemistry needs to be improved. Improving the realism of the appearance and physical behavior of liquids may enhance the immersive feeling and allow more focus on the experiment. In this study, it was confirmed that collaborative learning using an HMD-based VR device was realized, but the content of the experiments could also be carried out by individuals. For this reason, it is considered that there was no significant difference in the learning effect between the pre- and post-tests between the synchronous system group and the asynchronous system group. This suggests that the verification of learning effects in collaborative learning remains insufficient. Therefore, it is necessary to design experiments with more complicated content and verify the learning effect of collaboration.

References

1. Enkaku kyouiku no suishinn nitsuite (About promotion of distance education). https://www.mext.go.jp/b_menu/shingi/chukyo/chukyo3/siryo/__icsFiles/afieldfile/2018/11/21/1411291-9_1.pdf. Accessed 22 Sep 2020 (in Japanese)
2. Gakkou niokeru ICT-kankyou-seibi nitsuite (About ICT environment improvement in school). https://www.mext.go.jp/a_menu/shotou/zyouhou/detail/1402835.htm. Accessed 22 Sep 2020 (in Japanese)
3. Nakamura, S., Akakura, T.: E-learning material synchronized VR environments with smartphone VR headset. IEICE **117**(469), 235–238 (2018). (in Japanese)
4. Okamoto, M., Ishimura, T., Matsubara, Y.: Inorganic chemistry learning support system using head mounted display and augmented reality approach. JSiSE **35**(4), 312–321 (2018). (in Japanese)
5. Hayashi, J., Okamoto, M., Matsubara, Y., Iwane, T.: Virtual chemistry experiments environment using HMD and hand tracking controller. In: JSiSE 2016 Student Research Presentation, Japan, pp. 187–188 (2016). (in Japanese)
6. Science edition, Science and Mathematics edition: Explanation of high school Curriculum guideline (announced in 2018). https://www.mext.go.jp/a_menu/shotou/new-cs/1407074.htm. Accessed 21 July 2020 (in Japanese)
7. VR ni kansuru ishikichousa. VR taiken de kounyuuiyoku wa takamarunoka? (Awareness survey on VR. Will VR experience increase purchase motivation?). https://honote.macromill.com/report/20190207/. Accessed 15 Dec 2020 (in Japanese)
8. Quest 2. https://www.oculus.com/quest-2/. Accessed 29 Dec 2020
9. Atarashii Gakusyuuushidouyouryou ga mezasu sugata (What the new Curriculum guideline aims for). https://www.mext.go.jp/b_menu/shingi/chukyo/chukyo3/siryo/attach/1364316.htm. Accessed 14 Dec 2020 (in Japanese)
10. Dejitaru kyouzai no keifu/manabi wo sasaeru tekunoroji dai4kai misemasu, CSCL no subete: 1 nichi de wakaru kyoutyougakusyuu (Technology that supports the genealogy and learning of digital teaching materials 4th fascinating, all about CSCL: collaborative learning that can be understood in one day). https://fukutake.iii.u-tokyo.ac.jp/archives/beat/seminar/012.html. Accessed 14 Dec 2020 (in Japanese)
11. Unity. https://unity.com/ja. Accessed 2 Sep 2020
12. PUN 2. https://www.photonengine.com/. Accessed 17 July 2020
13. LINE. https://line.me/ja/. Accessed 4 Jan 2020
14. Mochiduki, T., Kato, H.: Reconsidering the theory of emergent division of labor for designing collaborative learning environment. JSiSE **34**(2), 84–97 (2017). (in Japanese)

Enhancing Preparedness for Emergency Alternative Modes of Instruction: Construction and Evaluation of a Remote Teaching Curriculum

Gabriella M. Hancock[✉], Christopher R. Warren, and Amy Wax

Department of Psychology, California State University, Long Beach, 1250 Bellflower Boulevard, Long Beach, CA 90840, USA
Gabriella.Hancock@csulb.edu

Abstract. The COVID-19 pandemic and its associated safety recommendations of social distancing provoked an unprecedented shift from primarily in-person to online educational instruction. This paper details a curriculum of eight professional workshops designed to help faculty develop the knowledge and skills to meet their instructional learning goals and students' accessibility needs in these unique and challenging circumstances. Results identified a number of digital tools and strategies that faculty and students found useful for both synchronous and asynchronous learning contexts. A detailed description of each module as well as faculty-provided recommendations are included herein for the benefit of instructors designing future online courses for alternative modes of instruction.

Keywords: Online learning · Higher education · Remote teaching tools · Learning modes · COVID-19

1 Introduction

The COVID-19 Pandemic has catalyzed an unprecedented and (what will likely be) an enduring transformation in instructional practice across the curriculum. Roughly 90% of the world's students, equating to over 1.6 billion pupils, experienced an abrupt disruption in their education as the result of COVID-19, and see Table 1 [1, 2]. Sweeping school closures were enacted within close proximity of one another as a behavioral measure of controlling the spread of this infectious disease [3], and research suggests that these actions were largely successful in partially mitigating the rise of cases [4]. Despite these beneficial short-term health effects of school closures, educators and the wider public, however, remain extremely concerned about the long-term effects of these closures on students' health, well-being, educational progress, income, and life expectancy [3, 5].

While numerous authorities are structuring plans for a safe return to the traditional in-person classroom [6, 7], instructors worldwide are working at a frantic pace to establish the knowledge, skills, and infrastructure necessary to keep educational activities progressing during the pandemic via distance learning tools and practices, also known

© Springer Nature Switzerland AG 2021
S. Yamamoto and H. Mori (Eds.): HCII 2021, LNCS 12766, pp. 27–37, 2021.
https://doi.org/10.1007/978-3-030-78361-7_3

as alternative modes of instruction (AMI) [8–10]. Moreover, educators are doing so with particular emphasis on building an infrastructure that will continue to serve the best interests of online learners once the emergency conditions have been lifted.

While online and blended learning have increased in popularity in recent decades and have been shown to be virtually as effective as face-to-face instruction [11], these mediums remained relatively less implemented for various reasons including the unavailability or resistance to distance education technologies. However, the global health crisis of 2020 necessitated an emergency shift to alternative modes of instruction, thrusting hundreds of millions of unprepared educators and students into purely remote learning contexts [12]. Beginning with an emergency transition but continuing indefinitely, this "new normal" has been accompanied by stress, a lack of motivation to learn [13], changes in the quantity and quality of inter-student interactions, less active social support systems, less engagement in their community [14], as well as unequal access to digital infrastructure exacerbating educational inequalities [15, 16]. Pivoting to face these challenges, faculty have had to radically alter their attitudes and practices regarding pedagogical instruction, assessment, interaction, and even philosophy. Accordingly, in this work is described the curriculum designed and content generated to prepare faculty to respond to this global educational crisis (and see Fig. 1). Data concerning its efficacy are herein reported, reactions by faculty are summarized, and recommendations to improve future online learning are provided.

Table 1. Impact of COVID-19 on education at the height of school closures in April of 2020 [2].

Total number of affected learners	1,484,712,787
Percentage of total enrolled learners	84.8%
Country-wide school closures	172

The curriculum was designed to help generate online teaching materials, develop relevant technical skills, and expand and improve the digital infrastructure supporting remote classes across all three modes of delivery (synchronous, asynchronous, and blended). Content was presented over the course of a remote, 8-week professional development workshop series in the summer of 2020 (in preparation for fall teaching). Each session was co-hosted by the authors, as well as strategically chosen guest speakers to leverage their expertise with different remote learning practices or technical skills to enhance teaching or promote accessibility for students. Topics included communication for online classes, recording and posting lectures, videoconferencing software (i.e., Zoom), and methods for increasing student participation in virtual environments. The unique differences between online and face-to-face assessments were also covered, along with preparing and administering online exams, virtual drop boxes for written assignments, and how to gauge the effectiveness of online instruction via informal feedback. Moreover, integrated into each of these discussions was a conscientious focus on providing concrete strategies for maximizing accessibility and equity for all students to help bridge the digital divide. The curriculum, moreover, is in keeping with classic literature concerning successful distance learning practices [17–19], and particularly those methods identified as most effective in response to emergency conditions such as the COVID-19 Pandemic [20, 21].

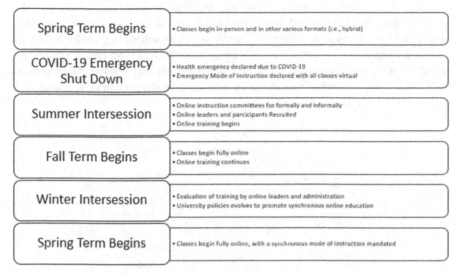

Fig. 1. Timeline of activities in response to the COVID-19 Pandemic and curriculum generation.

The setting for the current pedagogical initiative was a public, state-funded institution of higher learning, offering baccalaureate degrees in a number of disciplines across many colleges, along with master's degrees and some doctoral-level education in conjunction with other local institutions. The specified faculty teach in the Psychology Department, with many of the faculty currently teaching graduate and undergraduate courses. The typical teaching load of faculty in this department, within this college and university consists of 4 courses, or 12 weighted teaching units per semester. The courses in the department normally range from in-person to hybrid and 100% online courses. The average course size ranges from approximately 12 students per course for graduate, to 45 students for undergraduate courses. Faculty all hold a master's degree or higher, and regularly participate in trainings and other developmental opportunities.

2 Curriculum Modules

In order to deliver the desired material in the training to faculty, the Department Chair and the College Dean approved the eight proposed modules and secured funding for participants. Potential participants were then notified of the training that would take place and the opportunity for an award for attending the majority of the modules. Across the sessions offered, 53 faculty members (60.4% women) attended an average of 6.9 of the 8 modules offered across the 8-week period. Given the department the training was held in has approximately 60 tenure/tenure-track and lecturer faculty each semester, this attendance represents the majority of teaching faculty. Each of the eight modules lasted approximately 1.5 h with about 1 h of content including demonstrations of technology by local faculty as guest lectures to leverage their individual expertise (and see Fig. 2). Each session also included approximately 30 min for questions and answers, and a simultaneous chat dialogue utilized to answer questions or concerns or offer additional examples or resources during sessions. An additional module was designed as a "check-in" after the eight modules were concluded. Reminders leading up to each session were provided to faculty and recordings were offered for individuals with scheduling conflicts. In addition to the recorded live sessions, the participants were provided an online site through the local learning management system (i.e., BeachBoard) that housed the recordings, example materials, and other resources, as well as providing another mechanism of communicating with the workshop leaders.

Fig. 2. Training modules for the transition to emergency online education.

2.1 Communication with Students

This first module covered ways of properly communicating the course objectives, methods of delivery (e.g., synchronous versus asynchronous), ways to reach the professor, and critical course components through the syllabi, introductory videos or vignettes, netiquette guides, or other materials. For example, many options for live introductions, pre-recorded introductions, or creative options such as animations (i.e., PowToons). An example of a screenshot from an animated PowToon introductory video can be seen in Fig. 3.

Participants left with examples of policies and procedures most in need of emphasis in online environments to promote student success such as where to obtain technical support or how to address accessibility concerns, and creative ways to meet these ends. A major goal of this module is to set students up for success through course design, manuals, release conditions and other technological methods of keeping students on

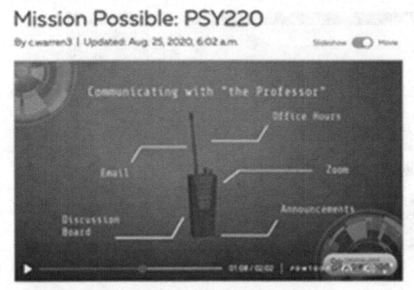

Fig. 3. PowToon introductory video illustrating methods of communicating with the professor throughout the AMI course.

track. The workshop was accompanied by a 30-min question-and-answer period with the hosts and co-hosts.

2.2 Recording Lectures

This workshop covered best practices for structuring video lectures, how to create and edit videos using software like Camtasia, how to record Zoom meetings, how to upload videos to YouTube and subsequently post those links to learning management systems. The workshop also covered how to caption a video in YouTube and provided a brief introduction to recording videos using other software including Kaltura, Audacity, and PowerPoint. This workshop was accompanied by a 30-min question-and-answer period with the hosts and co-host.

2.3 Videoconferencing Software

This session included the basic mechanisms for conducting videoconferencing for course purposes, including the most popular technology currently: Zoom (and see Fig. 4). Discussions were co-led with a guest around best-practices for communicating how and when the class will meet via video-conferencing software, technology options for conducting synchronous sessions, and enhancing participation, while maintaining a safe and secure classroom environment that is accessible to all students. For example, many options exist with personal meeting identification numbers, reoccurring links versus novel links and passwords or registrations for meetings. Equity issues such as technology concerns and mandates for video use by students was discussed, and another guest

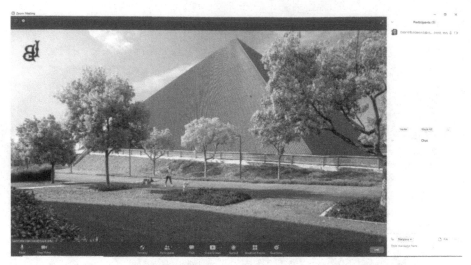

Fig. 4. Zoom videoconferencing interface complete with active video, participants, and chat function visible.

offered a demonstration of whiteboards within virtual environments. The final 30 min was reserved for a question-and-answer session with faculty along with the leaders and co-hosts.

2.4 Increasing Participation

This module focused on how to poll your audience using Poll Everywhere, how to poll your audience using the native polling application in the most widely used video-conferencing software (i.e., Zoom), how to simplify scheduling with Doodle, how to create interesting graphics using Piktochart, how to use the grouping mechanism and record group-level video chats in the local learning management system. The session also covered best practices to increase participation through discussion boards, and the importance of breaks and stretching during class, ideas for holding virtual student socials, assessing student mental health online, and the importance of email blasts for online classes to engage students. This workshop was accompanied by a 30-min question-and-answer period with the hosts and co-host.

2.5 Assessments for Online Classes

This workshop was designed to expand on the idea of assessments beyond traditional quizzes and tests, connecting learning objectives to learning experiences in additional ways. The topics included how to translate existing assignments to virtual delivery formats along with the types of assessments typically utilized in online learning environments (e.g., online participation), while considering accessibility and equity. For example, communicating expectations and technology requirements was emphasized along with the importance of de-linking grades or performance with the bandwidth of their internet connection. Privacy and disability concerns were also covered with attendees, and methods of captioning, recording, and other considerations for audio and video accessibility. Participants were encouraged to work through the learning objectives for their course, ensuring linkages were clear with planned assignments. The final 30 min was reserved for questions and answers with attending faculty along with the leaders and co-host.

2.6 Online Exams

This session covered the capabilities and options for administering different types of exams on the local learning management system (i.e., BeachBoard) by way of the Quizzes function. Faculty were exposed to the mechanics of the interface regarding how to post, administer, and assess exam questions at different levels of Bloom's Taxonomy (e.g., multiple choice, true-or-false, matching, short answer, mini-essay). A demonstration was given on quiz generators, and what to consider to enhance accessibility and equity such as extended time and flexible deadlines. Specific strategies to counteract cheating on electronically administered exams was also covered, as well as the hurdles that some cheating prevention mechanisms can inadvertently impose. The final 30 min was reserved for questions and answers with faculty and hosts.

2.7 Written Assignments and Dropbox

This workshop addressed how to assign, restrict, and evaluate various written assignments via the Dropbox function of the local learning management system, BeachBoard. Demonstrations on how to build and complete grading rubrics were offered to help enhance efficiency and consistency in grading. How to enact and review the technology to properly screen for plagiarism (i.e., Turnitin). The final 30 min of this workshop was dedicated to a question-and-answer session wherein faculty could ask specific questions of the leaders and co-hosts with regard to enacting these practices through their online teaching.

2.8 Soliciting Informal Feedback

This workshop covered how to make an instructor feedback survey or other surveys using popular software, including Qualtrics and Google Forms. Participants were shown how best to construct and distribute a survey, how to download survey data, and the general benefits of using feedback mechanisms, including a start/stop/continue style of feedback form (including when and how to administer it and how/why to give students feedback on their feedback). This workshop was accompanied by a 30-min question-and-answer period with the hosts and co-host.

After the conclusion of the last module, two follow-up sessions were offered through the close of the semester. One of these sessions focused exclusively on concerns related to the evolving definitions of online instruction during the emergency mode. Another was designed as a question-and-answer session to address any concerns moving into the next semester.

3 Results

Following up with departmental faculty in the Fall 2020 semester, it became clear what practices were working well for both instructors and students. Zoom emerged as the most widely implemented and successful video conferencing teaching tool, especially for synchronous instruction. Professors extolled the value of breakout rooms and the chat feature in particular for fostering participation, engagement, and discussion. While Zoom was seen as the most useful tool to assist with the emergency transition to online classes in the early weeks/months of the pandemic, it also retained its perceived importance among faculty members over time, including throughout the Fall 2020 semester and beyond. Overall, Zoom was seen as a critical tool and was virtually ubiquitously used by faculty in order to connect with students.

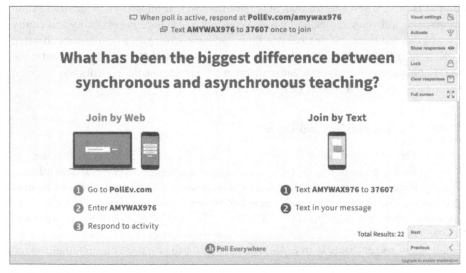

Fig. 5. Poll Everywhere software demonstrating question presentation and the multiple means by which students can participate (i.e., web and text).

In addition to Zoom, other software that faculty noted as having positively impacted their virtual teaching practices included Camtasia, YouTube, Doodle, and Poll Everywhere. For instructors who taught asynchronously, Camtasia and YouTube were of particular importance. Camtasia was the most popular video-recording/-editing application that faculty members used to create recordings of their lectures/lessons, while YouTube was the most popular platform to post these pre-recorded lectures to, because of excellent speed and bandwidth. Doodle was a popular app that faculty used to determine virtual meeting times, while Poll Everywhere was an application that was commonly used to ask/answer questions during synchronous class meetings, to supplement the native Zoom polling function (and see Fig. 5).

Faculty expressed pleasant surprise at the fact that the majority of students (75–95%) were consistently attending synchronous class sessions despite the common availability of recordings. Student engagement, however, was more variable than attendance. A trend emerged wherein graduate students seemed to be more engaged when compared to their undergraduate counterparts; this observation may be due to the seminar-style orientation of most graduate courses, and parallel in nature to traditional instruction. Strategies for enhancing engagement included the presentation of video clips to generate discussion and facilitating the students' ability to guide discussion activities. Faculty reported that such student engagement levels were one of the key differences between synchronous and asynchronous courses this semester.

Another noted trend was students' use of Discord, which is a messaging application. Perhaps due to the students' increased ability to connect with one another en masse, due to the Zoom chat feature, undergraduate and graduate students seemed more prone to create Discord channels devoted to their classes in order to communicate with one another outside of the virtual classroom. This trend highlights one of the silver linings of the pandemic; students have been able to connect with one another and share course-relevant information and tips more easily than they would have been able to in person.

Both students and faculty have reported that time management, workload, and work-life balance have been some of the most significant challenges to their success this year. This educational program was developed to help mitigate these risks to productivity and learning through revision of pedagogical perspectives (prioritizing compassionate teaching, accessibility, and equity), enhancing knowledge of online education practices, developing technical skills for the operation of instructional hardware and software, and the extension of the digital infrastructure of the university. Faculty have provided important initial findings as to what has and has not worked in their teaching efforts, and student perceptions of teaching effectiveness are being collected to compare across semesters.

Finally, it should be noted that, in December 2020, this workshop series qualified our instructors for full certification to teach online in the local SoCal Community College system (namely, at Cerritos Community College) for the Fall 2020 semester. In other words, extramural institutions have recognized this training program and decreed that it meets their expectations for qualification without any further necessary training sessions.

4 Conclusions

In summary, the training initiative that was undertaken was successful in terms of participation and attendance. The old adage if something is built, it will be used was certainly the case with this opportunity to adapt to the emergency mode of instruction necessitated by the pandemic. Faculty reported higher than expected levels of involvement from students and adapted several new techniques and implemented new technological software. The faculty reported concerns with workload through the transition, but demonstrated concern for equity and accessibility in their course offerings. However, the impacts on faculty motivation and subsequent ability to succeed during the emergency mode may have been much more attenuated, while workload concerns may have been higher if reimbursement for the time spent on the trainings were not sought or secured.

Future trainings should take several recommendations to note while attempting to transition faculty to different modes of instruction. First, the added workload and importance of a holistic approach to the training demands remuneration for participants. Without properly rewarding faculty for their time, the attendance and other gains may not have been realized. For future iterations, considerations of the most contemporary educational technology are also warranted. The technologies discussed here will likely evolve and be replaced by more interactive, engaging, or accessible versions that should be integrated where necessary, while also keeping in mind the lessons learned from the previous study, that less is sometimes more. Technology for technology's sake should be avoided given the workload concerns associated with learning numerous new systems simultaneously, as well as the potential exacerbation of inequities felt by our most vulnerable learners [16].

Prior to the COVID-19 Pandemic, there existed already a robust and growing trend for the implementation of online and distance learning [22]. The global health crisis merely necessitated an unprecedented acceleration to this ongoing trend. Major issues arise, however, given that the emergency instructional transition was implemented extremely quickly without systematic redress of the concerns that have long plagued educators regarding online education, namely inaccessibility and inequality [15, 16]. In both short-term and long-term efforts to develop effective distance learning curricula, educators must do so with this awareness that technology offers both solutions and further challenges. Instructors' efforts to cope with these emergency conditions have been fairly successful and this work showcases a variety of useful tools and strategies to improve online learning practices and outcomes. It is important for all educators to heed these recommendations, as well as student feedback [23], as distance learning will no doubt only continue in popular practice and expand in utility in the post-COVID global educational system.

References

1. Edmunds, W.J.: Finding a path to reopen schools during the COVID-19 pandemic. Lancet Child Adolesc. Health **4**(11), 796–797 (2020)
2. UNESCO: Education: from disruption to recovery (2020). https://en.unesco.org/covid19/edu cationresponse. Accessed 11 January 2021
3. Donohue, J.M., Miller, E.: COVID-19 and school closures. J. Am. Med. Assoc. **324**(9), 845–847 (2020). https://doi.org/10.1001/jama.2020.13092
4. Auger, K.A., et al.: Association between statewide school closure and COVID-19 incidence and mortality in the US. J. Am. Med. Assoc. **324**(9), 859–870 (2020)
5. Meara, E.R., Richards, S., Cutler, D.M.: The gap gets bigger: changes in mortality and life expectancy, by education, 1981–2000. Health Aff. **27**(2), 350–360 (2008)
6. Lordan, R., FitzGerald, G.A., Grosser, T.: Reopening schools during COVID-19. Science **369**(6508), 1146 (2020)
7. Sheikh, A., Sheikh, A., Sheikh, Z., Dhami, S.: Reopening schools after the COVID-19 lockdown. J. Glob. Health **10**(1), 010376 (2020). https://doi.org/10.7189/jogh.10.010376
8. Dhawan, S.: Online learning: a panacea in the time of COVID-19 crisis. J. Educ. Technol. Syst. **49**(1), 5–22 (2020)
9. Huang, R., Tlili, A., Chang, T.W., Zhang, X., Nascimbeni, F., Burgos, D.: Disrupted classes, undisrupted learning during COVID-19 outbreak in China: application of open educational practices and resources. Smart Learn. Environ. **7**(1), 1–15 (2020)

10. Mishra, L., Gupta, T., Shree, A.: Online teaching-learning in higher education during lockdown period of COVID-19 pandemic. Int. J. Educ. Res. Open **1**, 100012 (2020)
11. Means, B., Toyama, Y., Murphy, R., Bakia, M., Jones, K.: Evaluation of evidence-based practices in online learning: a meta-analysis and review of online learning studies. Structure **115**(3) (2010)
12. Ghazi-Saidi, L., Criffield, A., Kracl, C.L., McKelvey, M., Obasi, S.N., Vu, P.: Moving from face-to-face to remote instruction in a higher education institution during a pandemic: multiple case studies. Int. J. Technol. Educ. Sci. (IJTES) **4**(4), 370–383 (2020)
13. Di Pietro, G., Biagi, F., Costa, P., Karpinski, Z., Mazza, J.: The likely impact of COVID-19 on education: Reflections based on the existing literature and recent international datasets. Publications Office of the European Union (2020)
14. Marinoni, G., van't Land, H., Jensen, T.: The impact of COVID-19 on higher education around the world. IAU Global Survey Report (2020). https://www.iau-aiu.net/IMG/pdf/iau_covid19_and_he_survey_report_final_may_2020.pdf
15. Engzell, P., Frey, A., Verhagen, M.: Learning inequality during the COVID-19 pandemic. Mimeo, University of Oxford (2020)
16. Doyle, O.: COVID-19: 'exacerbating educational inequalities?' (2020). http://publicpolicy.ie/papers/covid-19-exacerbating-educational-inequalities/
17. Baran, E., Correia, A.-P., Thompson, A.D.: Tracing successful online teaching: voices of exemplary online teachers. Teach. Coll. Rec. **115**, 1–41 (2013)
18. Keengwe, J., Kidd, T.T.: Towards best practices in online learning and teaching in higher education. MERLOT J. Online Learn. Teach. **6**(2), 533–541 (2010)
19. Bailey, C.J., Card, K.A.: Effective pedagogical practices for online teaching: perception of experienced instructors. Internet High. Educ. **12**(3–4), 152–155 (2009)
20. Quezada, R.L., Talbot, C., Quezada-Parker, K.B.: From bricks and mortar to remote teaching: a teacher education programme's response to COVID-19. J. Educ. Teach. **46**(4), 472–483 (2020). https://doi.org/10.1080/02607476.2020.1801330
21. O'Keefe, L., Rafferty, J., Gunder, A., Vignare, K.: Delivering high-quality instruction online in response to COVID-19: faculty playbook. Every Learner Everywhere (2020). https://files.eric.ed.gov/fulltext/ED605351.pdf
22. Palvia, S., et al.: Online education: worldwide status, challenges, trends, and implications. J. Glob. Inf. Technol. Manag. **21**(4), 233–241 (2018). https://doi.org/10.1080/1097198X.2018.1542262
23. Adnan, M., Anwar, K.: Online learning amid the COVID-19 pandemic: students' perspectives. J. Pedagog. Sociol. Psychol. **2**(1), 45–51 (2020)

Design of Learning by Logical Empathic Understanding in Technology Enhanced Learning

Tsukasa Hirashima[✉]

Hiroshima University, Hiroshima, Japan
tsukasa@lel.hiroshima-u.ac.jp

Abstract. Logical Empathic Understanding is to assume the other's conclusions or arguments as correct ones even if they are not the same ones with self-ones, and then try to explain them logically. It is "logical thinking about other's thinking". Empathic Understanding (EU for short) has been originally proposed in the practice of counseling and it has been widely accepted as a basic principle of counseling. EU includes emotional aspects and logical aspect. This paper focuses on the logical aspects of EU and call the specified EU "Logical Empathic Understanding" (LEU for short). Because it requires reflective thinking or metacognitive thinking, it is also promising in teaching and learning. In technology enhanced learning, LEU by teachers or learning support systems have been already investigated as learner modeling or cognitive counseling but there are little studies that deal with LEU by learners. In this paper, a framework of Knowledge Empathic Understanding as a subcategory of LEU is defined. Then, design of learning tasks for LEU with explicit knowledge are proposed based on Open Information Structure Approach. As concrete tasks, problem-posing word problem for a wrong answer in arithmetic, finding missing premises in triangle logic, and re-composition of concept maps are explained.

Keywords: Logical empathic understanding · Open information structure approach · Technology enhanced learning · Explicit knowledge · Critical thinking · Metacognitive thinking

1 Introduction

Empathic Understanding (EU for short) means that accurately understanding the other's thoughts, feelings, and meanings from the other's perspective [1, 2]. EU has been originally proposed as a form of understanding of clients in the practice of counseling and it has been widely accepted as a basic principle of counselling. In EU, a counsellor is requested to empathically understand a patient. EU includes emotional aspects and logical aspect. In the context of education, several investigations mentioned the important role of logical aspects of EU in individual and adaptive learning support [3, 4]. Michita formalized logical aspects of EU as an activity that assumes the other's conclusions or arguments as correct ones even if they are not the same ones with self-ones, and interpret

© Springer Nature Switzerland AG 2021
S. Yamamoto and H. Mori (Eds.): HCII 2021, LNCS 12766, pp. 38–49, 2021.
https://doi.org/10.1007/978-3-030-78361-7_4

them logically [5]. This assumption is often called "principle of charity" [6]. Because such type of EU requires the subjects to think about their own thoughts, and to find "missing premise" that needs to enable logical interpret interpretation, it is a promising activity to promote critical thinking or metacognitive thinking. Because EU formalized by Michita is logical one, we call this type of EU "Logical EU (LEU for short)". In this paper, as an implementation of LEU in technology enhanced learning, a framework of Explicit Knowledge Empathic Understanding is proposed.

In LEU, a teacher or supporter should not say only to wrong for learner's wrong answer. They are requested to regard learner's wrong answer as logically derived one by learner's knowledge. If the knowledge origin of the wrong answer is found, it is possible to correct the wrong from the origin. LEU has been regarded as a promising method for teachers or learning supporters for individual learners. Bug model [7, 8] that is a kind of learner model in technology-enhanced learning is able to reproduce learner's wrong answers by using wrong knowledge (that is, bug) assumed that the learner has. This means that the bug model is an example of LEU in technology-enhance learning. Matz model [9], process driven inference model [10], and perturbation modeling [11] are also similar learner modeling methods.

In [7], the possibility of LEU by learners was also suggested although the bug model is basically proposed as LEU by teachers or learning supporters because it is a function of diagnosis of learner's wrong answers. BUGGY was introduced in [7] as an instructional game for training student teacher (and others). BUGGY is a computerized game based on the diagnostic interaction of a tutor and a student. In the game, BUGGY generates a wrong answer and a player find the bugged procedure that computationally derives the wrong answer. BUGGY was used for student teachers and seventh & eighth grade elementary school students. The results are reported that many student teachers felt that "BUGGY could be used to sharpen a teacher's awareness of different difficulties with addition and subtraction." The paper also reported that seventh & eighth grade students "began to see that he (it) had fundamental misconceptions as opposed to being just stupid.... it paves the way for students to see their own faulty....as a source of data from which they can understand their own errors." These reports mentioned that learning effect of subjects of EU, that is, the student teachers and seventh & eighth grade students.

In this paper, Explicit Knowledge Empathic Understanding (EKEU, for short) as a subcategory of LEU is defined, and a framework of learning from LEU (as EKEU) is proposed. Firstly, specification EKEU in EU is explained. Then, a framework of EKEU by learners and concrete examples are described. In the examples, design of learning tasks for EKEU proposed based on Open Information Structure Approach. As concrete tasks, re-composition of concept maps or arithmetic word problems from provided components are explained.

2 Explicit Knowledge Empathic Understanding

2.1 Overview

Logical Empathic Understanding (LEU) is a kind of empathic understanding where it tries to find the missing/wrong knowledge (or premises) and logically explain the argument of others by complimenting the missing one or by using the wrong one. Logic is often categorized into two categories: formal logic that is able to be written by symbols explicitly and informal logic that is not able to be written by symbols explicitly. Explicitly written symbols used to logical reasoning is often called explicit knowledge. Knowledge used in informal logic are often called implicit knowledge. Therefore, explicit knowledge empathic understanding only deals with formal logic with explicit knowledge. When other's arguments or conclusions are different from self-ones, in explicit knowledge empathic understanding, it is required to find and compliment the missing/wrong explicit knowledge or premises that can logically explain the arguments or conclusions. We call "Explicit Knowledge Empathic Understanding" EKEU in this paper.

There are two types of EKEU: one is EKEU conducted by supporters of learning and the other is EKEU conducted by learners themselves. EKEU by supporters is a sophisticated diagnosis of learner's arguments or conclusions. EKEU by learners is a promising task to promote critical thinking. Since the knowledge dealt with in knowledge engineering is this explicit knowledge, EKEU is a proposal based on knowledge engineering.

In the next subsection, general categorization of EU is explained. Then, EKEU by supporters and learners are explained.

2.2 Categorization of Empathic Understanding

Figure 1 shows a categorization of Empathy and Empathic Understanding. In psychological viewpoint, empathy is widely accepted as an interactive process of affective empathy as an emotional event and cognitive empathy as a cognitive event. On the other hand, Rogers mentioned that "The state of empathy, or being empathic, is to perceive the internal frame of reference of another with accuracy, and with the emotional components and meanings which pertain thereto, as if one were the other person, but without ever losing the "as if" condition" [1]. Cuff mentioned that EU proposed by Rogers was "cognitive-only empathy", and recommended to use difference terms with "empathy" and "empathic understanding" as different [12]. EU includes both affect estimation and logic estimation. In this paper, logic estimation in EU is called Logical EU (LEU for short). LEU conducted by a teacher or learning supporter is useful to individual learning support. LEU conducted by a learner is useful to promote critical thinking. In the next subsection, model of LEU is introduced. Then, based on the model, Explicit Knowledge Empathic Understanding as a computational method of LEU are explained.

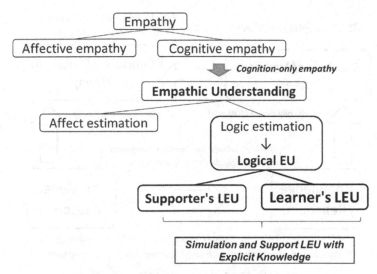

Fig. 1. Categorization of empathic understanding

2.3 A Model of Logical EU

A basic model of LEU is shown in Fig. 2. The process is composed of the following two phases: (1) detection of difference between other's or own conclusion or argument, (2) find knowledge/reasoning that logically explain the other's conclusion/argument by changing own knowledge/reasoning. In the process, there are three assumptions, (i) other's conclusion or argument was derived logically, (ii) own conclusion or argument was derived logically, and (iii) other's knowledge and reasoning process are in the neighborhood of own ones [13].

Detection of difference between other's and own conclusion or argument is the first phase of LEU. In this phase, when it is judged that the difference is important, resolution of the difference is motivated. LEU is a method of the resolution. In order to conduct LEU, the subject of LEU should assume that the other derives the conclusion or argument logically from the other's knowledge/reasoning. Moreover, the subject should also assume (or confirm) that the subject derives the own conclusion or argument logically from the own knowledge/reasoning. One more important assumption of LEU is that the other's knowledge/reasoning is similar with the own ones, so it is possible to derive the other's by modifying the own ones. The modification of knowledge/reasoning is often called perturbation [10, 11]. In this paper, we use this term.

The process of LEU satisfies several important requirements of critical thinking. Critical thinking requests the subject to think about the own thinking. Then, the thinking should be logical one. In LEU, the subject thinks about other's thinking by referring to own thinking. Then, the thinking is necessary to be logical. One of the most important activities in critical thinking is to find "missing premise" to complete the conclusion/argument logically [14]. In LEU, it is naturally requested to derive knowledge/reasoning that logically derives the other's conclusion/argument. Besides, it is

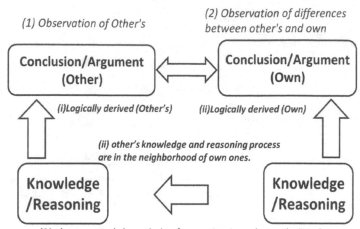

Fig. 2. Model of LEU

possible to confirm that the activity success or not. For these reasons, LEU is promising to promote critical thinking.

3 Explicit Knowledge Empathic Understanding

Although the model of LEU explained in Sect. 2.3 would be enough as a guideline for teachers or learning supporters, it is not enough to develop learning support function in technology enhanced learning and to design LEU as a learning task. The former is LEU by support system, and the latter is LEU by learners. In order to realize such LEU, the process should be computational one. If the knowledge/reasoning is described as explicit knowledge used in knowledge base systems, the conclusions or arguments are logically and computationally derived by using the explicit knowledge.

As an example of EKEU, an interpretation of a wrong answer for multi-digit subtraction is introduced in Buggy. In Buggy, at first, a procedural knowledge network that can conduct multi-digit subtraction correctly is implemented. The network is regarded as the explicit knowledge of a teacher. When a learner derives an answer "43" for "45–8", the network derives the correct answer "37" and judges the learner's answer is wrong. This judgement is not EU. In order to realize EKEU, it is necessary to regenerate the wrong answer by using the explicit knowledge. For the wrong answer, if the learner has knowledge "subtract a small number from a large number" instead of "borrowing" in the network, the wrong answer "43" can be derived. The wrong answer is logically one in the network including knowledge "subtract a small number from a large number". This process is a diagnosis of learner's wrong answer by bug model, and from viewpoint of LEU, it is LEU by supporter.

In the investigation of BUGGY, as introduced in Introduction, LEU by learner was also promoted. However, in the investigation, learners were shown the wrong answers and they discussed the answers outside of the system. So, the system cannot be directly involved in the process. Our research is trying to realize to support the process.

3.1 EKEU as a Learner Task

In this subsection, we consider how to design learning tasks as EKEU that learners perform. In learning, a learner is requested to understand learning materials or contents of lecture. The need for this understanding is clear, but how it is understood is implicit. Implicit goals and methods are the cause of the difficulty of the task of understanding. EKEU is a computational EU as explicit knowledge computation. So, EKEU as a learner task is a promising approach to make explicit the goal and method of the understanding.

In this paper, EKEU by learners is formalized as "re-composition of "thinking or the results of the thinking" of teacher's or other learner's". In this formalization, we assume that thinking is able to be described as mental representation and operation of the representation (representation assumption). Then, we also assume that the mental representation and the operation is able to be externalized with symbols and operations of them (externalization assumption). Based on the two assumptions, firstly, teachers or other learners externalize their thinking or the results of the thinking as symbolic representation, and then, by de-composing the representation, a set of components are prepared. EKEU by learners is designed as re-composition task of the components. In the process of the re-composition, we assume that learners refer to their own thinking (self-reference activity). Through the process, we also assume that they compare their thinking with the other's thinking trying to re-compose (comparison activity). The part that cannot be de-composed is detected as un-EU part. Un-EU also EKEU in the sense of not being able to re-compose. These activities are "thinking about thinking".

EKEU by learners is realized by Open Information Structure Approach. OIS approach is a design approach of learner tasks in technology-enhanced learning. In OIS approach, (1) teachers externalize their thinking and the results of the thinking by describing them as symbolic representation, (2) by de-composing the representation, the components of the representation are generated, and then, (3) learning tasks are designed as re-composition of the thinking or results by operating the components. In the next subsection, EKEU as re-composition is explained.

3.2 EKEU as Re-composition

In usual learning, learners need to understand the content of lectures or textbooks as logical ones with their knowledge. This does not mean to passively accept them as they are. They should actively make logical explanation about the contents. So, we can say it is active acceptance. LEU is usually discussed on the premise that someone who was already familiar with the content would conduct the LEU. However, the purpose of LEU conducted by learners is to sophisticate or complement learners' knowledge that is not completed. So, the difficulty of LEU is high. This is the reason that learners often passively accept the content of lectures or textbooks as they are without LEU. One of the solutions of the difficulty of LEU for learners, EU as re-composition based on open information structure approach [15].

Figure 3 shows the framework of EU as re-composition based on Open Information Structure approach. Information Structure-Oriented approach was originally proposed by Carbonell [16]. The information structure means that externalized mental representation of domain expert, that is, explicit knowledge representation. Carbonell proposed that learning support system should be designed based on the information structure to sophisticatedly and adaptively individual learner. So, the information structure is used by system developer or system itself in information structure-oriented approach. Open Information Structure approach (OIS approach) means to open the information structure for learners. In OIS approach, learner tasks to operates the information structure are designed. Basic design of the tasks is re-composition [17].

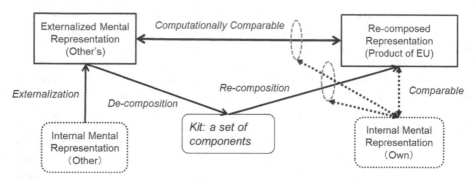

Fig. 3. Framework of EKEU as re-composition

In the framework of LEU as re-composition based on OIS approach, externalized mental representation is necessary. This is the ideal information structure that learner need to acquire. The representation is then decomposed and generated a set of components. As a learner task, learners are requested to re-compose the representation by using the components. The product is re-composed representation that corresponds to other's representation. In the process of re-composition, learners need to refer to own internal representation. Because the re-composed representation is other's one, learners are able to compare it with the own presentation. Moreover, the product of LEU is explicit one, it is possible to judge whether the re-composition, that is, EU, is success or not. Because it is possible to judge the success of LEU, we can call the LEU as "success use [18] of LEU". If a teacher requests a learner to conduct LEU without the method to evaluate the product, it is called "intentional use of LEU".

In the next section, several examples of EKEU as re-composition are introduced.

4   Examples of EKEU by Learner as Re-composition

In this section, four examples of EKEU as re-composition designed based on OIS approach are introduced.

4.1 Empathic Problem-Posing in Mathematic Word Problems

Figure 4 shows the interface of MONSAKUN [19–21]: Interactive Environment of learning by problem-posing in mathematic word problem. A learner poses a problem by fill in three blanks in the left side by selecting three cards from the card set in the right side (There are 6 cards. Numbers are given for this explanation). The posed problem should be satisfied the conditions written in the upper side. The car set is called "card condition" and the condition of posed problem is called "problem condition". A problem-posing assignment is specified by the pair of the card condition and problem condition. In the problem-posing assignment shown in Fig. 4, a problem composed of {1, 3, 5} satisfied the problem condition. Problem-posing of MONSAKUN is designed based on OIS approach. A word problem is represented based on the Three Quantity Proposition Model (TQP model for short) [20]. A concrete representation of a problem is de-composed into the sentence cards. A sentence card represents a quantity proposition. The problem-posing is a re-composition of a problem. MONSAKUN has been practically used in several elementary schools and the learning effects also have been confirmed.

Empathic problem-posing is to create a problem in which the learner's wrong answer is logically derived as correct one. In the assignment shown in Fig. 4, the wrong problem composed of {2, 3, 4} is very popular. Assignment of problem-posing for this problem-posing is to find an assignment in which the problem composed of {2, 3, 4} is correct posed problem by changing the problem condition and/or card condition. In this case, by changing the story from "difference" to "total" in the problem condition, the problem composed of {2, 3, 4} becomes correct one. When a learner poses a problem composed of {1, 6, 5}, by changing "white" in card-5 into "black", the problem becomes a correct one. Because the problem is generated by changing the card condition, this is also an empathic problem-posing.

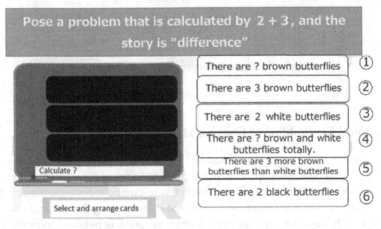

Fig. 4. MONSAKUN: problem-posing of mathematic word problem

4.2 Complement "Missing Premise" in Triangle Logic

Figure 5 shows an exercise of triangle composition. By using the cards in the left side in the interface, fill in the three blanks in the triangle in the right side. Each card represents a proposition. The triangle is a unit frame of logic compose of Claim, Warrant and Evidence that are assigned to each three apexes. A logic structure is explicitly described as the triangle logic. Then, the triangle logic is de-composed into the cards represent propositions. The exercise is re-composition of the logic structure. So, this exercise is also designed based n OIS approach. In the case shown in Fig. 5, Claim: Socrates is mortal, a correct triangle logic is composed of Evidence: Socrates is human, and Warrant: Human is mortal.

In this case, necessary propositions are provided. If one or two of the necessary propositions are missing, they need to be complemented. In the complementation, "complementation of "missing premise"" is indispensable activity. Therefore, a triangle logic assignment with missing necessary propositions is an example of EKEU by learner as re-composition.

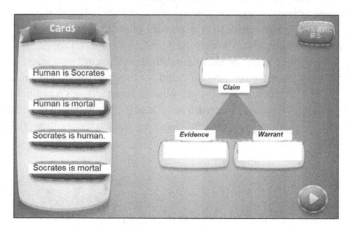

Fig. 5. Exercise of triangle logic re-composition

4.3 Reciprocal Kit-Building of Concept Map

Kit-Build concept map is a kind of framework of re-composition of concept map [17, 22]. In the kit-build concept map, a learner is provided a set of components of a concept map, that is, nodes and links. Then, the learner is re-compose a concept map. The re-composed concept map is automatically analyzed by comparing the original map. Then, by overlapping the re-composed maps by learner group, it is possible to make a group map. The kit-build concept map has been used in practical situation and the learning effect is confirmed. In kit-build concept map, the map is the information structure and the re-composition of the concept map is the re-composition task.

Kit-building itself is a kind of EKEU because learner is required to build other's concept map as externalization of other's understanding. Reciprocal kit-building has more clear the nature as EKEU. Figure 6 shows the process. In reciprocal kit-building, a learner is required to re-compose peer's concept map. Then, by visualization of the difference between the original map and the re-composed map, discussion in the pair is promoted. Through the experimental evaluation, we have already confirmed that (1) reciprocal kit-building promoted valuable talks in the pairs in comparison with the pairs used usual concept map [23] and (2) the quality and quantity of products of the pairs with reciprocal kit-building was better than the pairs with usual concept map [24].

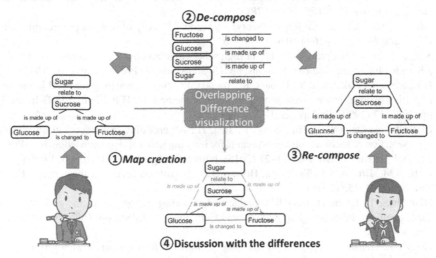

Fig. 6. Process of reciprocal kit-building

5 Conclusion Remarks

Empathic understanding promotes subjects to think about their thinking logically. Thinking about own thinking logically is very important from viewpoint in education as critical thinking or metacognitive thinking. In this paper, learning by empathic understanding as re-composition of information structure is defined. Design of learning tasks for Empathic Understanding with explicit knowledge are proposed based on Open Information Structure Approach. Some tasks of EKEU have been already implemented and evaluated. However, analysis from the viewpoint of LEU has not conducted yet. In future work, in addition to design and developed EKEU in various learning domain, it is necessary to evaluate the effect as LEU.

References

1. Rogers, C.R., Truax, C.B.: The therapeutic conditions antecedent to change: a theoretical view. In: The Therapeutic Relationship and Its Impact: A Study of Psychotherapy with Schizophrenics, pp. 97–108(1967)

2. Rogers, C.R.: Empathic: an unappreciated way of being. Couns. Psychol. **5**(2), 2–10 (1975)
3. Ichikawa, S: Cognitive counselling to improve students' metacognition and cognitive skills. In: Shwalb, D.W., Nakazawa, J., Shwalb, B.J. (eds.) Applied Developmental Psychology: Theory, Practice and Research from Japan, pp. 67–87 (2005). Information Age
4. Uesaka, Y., Seo, M., Ichikawa, S.: Students' cognitive and non-cognitive beliefs about learning as a factor in learning skills acquisition: suggestions from cognitive counselling. In: Proceedings of the 2008 Annual International Conference of ATLAANZ, pp. 89–100 (2009)
5. Michita, Y.: Importance of soft heart in critical thinking. In: Bulletin of Faculty of Education University of the Ryukyus, vol. 60, pp. 161–170 (2002). (In Japanese)
6. Baillargeon, N.: Intellectual Self-Defense. Seven Stories Press, New York (2007)
7. Brown, J.S., Burton, R.R.: Diagnostic models for procedural bugs in basic mathematical skills. Cogn. Sci. **2**(2), 155–192 (1978)
8. Brown, J.S., VanLehn, K.: Repair theory: a generative theory of bugs in procedural skills. Cogn. Sci. **4**(4), 379–426 (1980)
9. Matz, M.: Towards a process model for high school algebra errors. In: Sleeman, D., Brown, J.S. (eds.) Intelligent Tutoring Systems, pp. 25–50. Academic Press, Cambridge (1982)
10. Hirashima, T., Nakamura, Y., Uehara, K., Toyoda, J.: Student modeling for ICAI in view of cognitive science: process driven model inference method. In: IEICE, vol. J73-D-II, no. 3, pp. 408–417 (1990). (in Japanese)
11. Matsuda, N., Ogawa, H., Hirashima, T., Taki, H.: A generating technique and knowledge representation of multiple-answer problems for learning with solving knowledge. Res. Pract. Technol. Enhanc. Learn. **10**(1), 1–21 (2015). https://doi.org/10.1007/s41039-015-0005-1
12. Cuff, B.M., Brown, S.J., Taylor, L., Howat, D.J.: Empathy: a review of the concept. Emot. Rev. **8**(2), 144–153 (2016)
13. Hiarshima, T.: Learning through empathic understanding: tasking empathic understanding for learners. In: Proceedings of 45th Annual Conference of JSISE, pp. 169–170 (2020). (in Japanese)
14. Gough, J., Tindale, C.: 'Hidden' or 'missing' premises. Informal Logic **7**(2), 99–106 (1985)
15. Hirahsima, T., Hayashi, Y.: Design of meta-problem with open information structure approach. In: Workshop in ICCE2018 (2018)
16. Carbonell, J.R.: AI in CAI: an artificial intelligence approach to computer-assisted instruction. IEEE Trans. Man-Mach. Syst. **11**(4), 190–202 (1970)
17. Hirashima, T.: Reconstructional concept map: automatic assessment and reciprocal reconstruction. Int. J. Innov. Creat. Change **5**, 669–682 (2019)
18. Scheffler, I.: The language of education (1963)
19. Hirashima, T., Kurayama, M.: Learning by problem-posing for reverse-thinking problems. In: International Conference on Artificial Intelligence in Education, pp. 123–130 (2011). https://doi.org/10.1007/978-3-642-21869-9_18
20. Hirashima, T., Yamamoto, S., Hayashi, Y.: Triplet structure model of arithmetical word problems for learning by problem-posing. In: Yamamoto, S. (ed.) HCI 2014. LNCS, vol. 8522, pp. 42–50. Springer, Cham (2014). https://doi.org/10.1007/978-3-319-07863-2_5
21. Supianto, A.A., Hayashi, Y., Hirashima, T.: An investigation of learner's actions in posing arithmetic word problem on an interactive learning environment. IEICE Trans. Inf. Syst. **100**(11), 2725–2728 (2017)
22. Hirashima, T., Yamasaki, K., Fukuda, H., Funaoi, H.: Framework of kit-build concept map for automatic diagnosis and its preliminary use. Res. Pract. Technol. Enhanc. Learn. **10**(1), 1–21 (2015). https://doi.org/10.1186/s41039-015-0018-9

23. Wunnasri, W., Pailai, J., Hayashi, Y., Hirashima, T.: Reciprocal kit-build concept map: an approach for encouraging pair discussion to share each other's understanding. IEICE Trans. Inf. Syst. **101**(9), 2356–2367 (2018)
24. Sadita, L., Furtado, P.G.F., Hirashima, T., Hayashi, Y.: Analysis of the similarity of individual knowledge and the comprehension of partner's representation during collaborative concept mapping with reciprocal kit build approach. IEICE Trans. Inf. Syst. **103**(7), 1722–1731 (2020)

From On-Campus to Online Undergraduate Research Experience in Psychology: Transition During the COVID-19 Pandemic

Ya-Hsin Hung$^{(\boxtimes)}$ and Robert W. Proctor

Purdue University, West Lafayette, USA
{hung17,rproctor}@purdue.edu

Abstract. The outbreak of COVID-19 at the beginning of 2020 resulted in a global impact on higher education. This instant change in the research, teaching, and training environment from on-campus to online influenced the "Research Experience in Psychology" courses offered by Purdue's Department of Psychological Sciences. We report results of a survey of faculty members that contained closed- and open-ended questions relating to the changes and challenges faced by them with the transition that occurred in the spring 2020 semester. The survey also included questions regarding alteration of the activities for the course during the fall 2020 semester, when the university campus was re-opened with protective safety procedures and a curriculum consisting of in-person, hybrid, and fully online learning. The survey results showed not only negative aspects of the changes on the undergraduate research experience, but also positive outcomes associated with engagement in different activities and extensive use of online communication. Lessons learned from such knowledge and implications for renovating and developing undergraduate research experience programs in the future are discussed.

Keywords: COVID-19 · Online learning · Research experience

1 Introduction

1.1 Global Pandemic

The year 2020 started with an outbreak of COVID-19 in Wuhan, China, first reported on December 31, 2019 [1]. In the U.S., a case of the virus was diagnosed on January 29, 2020; Donald Trump, then President, declared a Public Health Emergency on February 3 and a National Emergency on March 13 [2]. One consequence of the latter declaration was for most colleges and universities in the U.S. to send students home, close the campus, and switch to online classes. Purdue University in West Lafayette, Indiana, cancelled all in-person classes beginning March 23, the first day after the spring vacation week [3]. Remote instruction was implemented for the remainder of the semester, for which classes ended on May 9.

© Springer Nature Switzerland AG 2021
S. Yamamoto and H. Mori (Eds.): HCII 2021, LNCS 12766, pp. 50–62, 2021.
https://doi.org/10.1007/978-3-030-78361-7_5

The transition from on-campus to online classes was abrupt, and instructors had little time for preparation prior to having to make the change. This characterization is true for most universities and colleges across the U.S. and worldwide, which made it a challenging time for instructors and students in all courses [4, 5]. The challenge was particularly great for those courses in any discipline that involve research experiences [6].

Most colleges and universities were planning to have on-campus classes in the fall 2020 semester, but many decided to forego those classes because the COVID-19 pandemic did not decline over the summer [7]. Purdue was one of the schools that did open the campus in the fall, implementing a variety of safety measures and offering a mixture of on-campus classes, online classes, and hybrid classes. The campus remained open the entire semester, but uncertainty existed throughout the semester as to whether that would be possible. Consequently, the fall semester was an atypical one in which the faculty had to do many things online that they would not normally conduct in that manner and be prepared to switch from on-campus activities to off-campus ones at any time.

1.2 Purdue University's Research Experience in Psychology Course

In this paper, we focus on the course "PSY 390 Research Experience in Psychology" that is offered by Purdue's Department of Psychological Sciences for junior- and senior-level majors in Behavioral and Brain Sciences and in Psychological Sciences. Students sign up with a faculty member and work with that person or postdoctoral researchers and graduate students working in the faculty member's laboratory. Students enrolled in this course are to work 3 h per week for each credit received, with most students being signed up for 3 credits, or 9 h. The students participate as research assistants, with the details of the work performed and instruction decided by the faculty member overseeing the lab in which the student is working. The content, activities, and number of students enrolled are at the faculty member's discretion. Because the research experience centers on working as part of a team, for the most part in a laboratory setting, this course was disrupted more than typical lecture-based classes by the move to online.

We conducted a survey of the department faculty members at the end of the fall 2020 semester to investigate their experiences and actions with respect to the Research Experience in Psychology course during the disrupted spring semester. The survey also contained questions about modifications made to the course in the fall semester. In addition to responses to closed-ended questions, we asked two open-ended questions to allow a wider range of answers and to obtain more personal evaluations of the pandemic's impact on the undergraduate research experience course.

2   Faculty Survey of the Research Experience Course

The goal of the survey was to gain an understanding of the effect of the pandemic on the research activities associated with the Research Experience in Psychology course. The survey included questions oriented toward both the spring and fall 2020 semesters. The survey included questions oriented toward both the spring and fall 2020 semesters. The Purdue Institutional Review Board classified the survey as exempt, and the survey was conducted in accord with the APA Ethical Guidelines for Human Research.

2.1 Method

Participants. An invitation to participate in the survey was sent by email via the faculty mailing list to all faculty members of the Department of Psychological Sciences at Purdue University on December 16, 2020. A reminder was sent on December 18. A total of 21 persons filled out the survey from a maximum of 30 faculty who had supervised students in the Research Experience in Psychology course in the spring semester. All respondents were tenured/tenure-track faculty.

Survey and Procedure. The survey was run online via the Qualtrics platform. Each respondent read a consent form to which they agreed by clicking on a button to proceed. The respondent then indicated in which of six research areas (corresponding to the department's training areas) she or he worked: Clinical Psychological Sciences; Cognitive Psychology; Industrial-Organizational Psychology; Mathematical and Computational Psychology; Neuroscience & Behavior; Social Psychology; an "Other" option was also included. Then, the message "Please provide responses regarding your course PSY 390 Research Experience in Psychology and 390 undergraduate students in the *spring 2020 semester*" was shown, and several questions about that semester were asked. Following those questions, the respondents were instructed, "Please provide responses regarding your course PSY 390 Research Experience in Psychology and 390 undergraduate students in the *fall 2020 semester*", and answered several questions about the fall semester. Any respondent who indicated that COVID-19 influenced their assigned research activities was asked a final, open-ended question for the fall semester, "Please sum up your transition strategies by highlighting the specific arrangements or strategies you employed for your 390 program." The survey ended with the general open-ended question, "Do you have any additional comments regarding the influence of the pandemic on undergraduate research activities?"

2.2 Closed-Ended Responses: Results and Discussion

Of the 21 faculty members, 17 specified only one research area in which they work, whereas 4 indicated two research areas: Cognitive Psychology ($n = 7$), Clinical Psychological Sciences ($n = 6$), Neuroscience & Behavior ($n = 4$), Social Psychology ($n = 3$), Industrial-Organizational Psychology ($n = 2$), Mathematical and Computational Psychology ($n = 2$), and Other (specified as Human Factors; $n = 1$). Of the four who checked two categories, three designatcd Cognitive Psychology plus another area (two specified Mathematical and Computational Psychology and one Human Factors), and the fourth specified Clinical Psychological Sciences and Neuroscience & Behavior.

Spring Semester. Figure 1 shows the frequencies of respondents who reported enrolling various numbers of undergraduate students in the PSY 390 course in the spring semester. Four respondents specified 7 or more, which we treated as 7 for purposes of analysis. A total of at least 88 students were enrolled, with mode $= 3$, median $= 4$, and mean $= 4.19$ ($SD = 2.09$). No obvious patterns were evident between research areas and the number of undergraduates mentored.

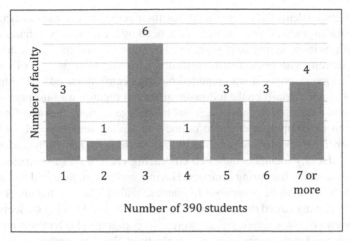

Fig. 1. Number of faculty members who enrolled various numbers of PSY 390 students in the spring semester.

In the survey, respondents were asked to indicate whether the research they conducted prior to the COVID-19 shutdown was in one or more of four study categories: Lab, Observational, Correlational, or Survey. A fifth option, "Other", was also allowed, with an open-text box for specifying the study type. The types of studies the respondents reported conducting are summarized in Table 1. The total was 40 studies conducted, with the largest number being lab studies and the next largest being survey and correlational studies. Eight respondents designated a single study type, of which 6 were lab studies, with the remaining two being Other (one specifying online study and the other not elaborating the answer). Eight respondents indicated 2 study types, 4 specified 3 types, and 1 indicated 4 types. Of those reporting two, 6 designated lab and survey studies. Of the respondents who reported more than two types, two indicated all types excluding lab studies, with one adding a fourth category of "Other" (data analysis). Three faculty members reported three study types, including lab and survey with correlational (2 respondents) or observational (1 respondent). The only additional "Other" response was data processing.

Table 1. Counts for each type of study conducted in the spring and fall semesters.

Type of study	Spring	Fall
Lab study	15	12
Observational study	3	4
Correlational study	8	7
Survey study	10	7
Other	4	9

Eighteen respondents (85%) answered that their research activities associated with the PSY 390 undergraduate students were influenced by the university's shutdown of on-campus activities in the spring 2020 semester. The survey asked about their adjustments or accommodations with respect to the students' activities after the school's shutdown (see Table 2). One respondent who reported having been influenced by Purdue's shutdown did not provide details on the follow-up questions regarding adjustment strategies, leaving 17 valid responses for those questions to analyze. Among the predefined adjustments, moving on-campus meetings to online and having students conduct literature reviews or other review studies were the two most frequent approaches adopted; All but one of the faculty members indicated embracing each of these strategies after the university shutdown in the spring semester. Having students engage in data coding and analysis had the next highest response frequency, with 12 faculty members choosing this approach. Having halted data collection for lab studies and having students conduct literature reviews or other review studies were also common. This halt was required for any on-campus studies that were in progress at the time. Smaller numbers of respondents decided to move or transfer lab studies from offline to online, and a few conducted a survey study to substitute the lab study. Of the 2 respondents who specified "Other", a common theme was having the students engage in extra professional and personal development activities.

Table 2. The adjustments or accommodations faculties utilized after the school's shutdown in the spring semester.

Approach/Strategy	Count	%
Moved offline meetings to online or tele-conference (e.g., zoom, WebEx, Microsoft Team)	16	94%
Halted data collection for lab studies	10	59%
Conducted survey studies online to substitute for the lab study data	2	12%
Transferred onsite lab studies to an online platform or remote setting	5	29%
Had students engage in data coding and analysis	12	71%
Had students conduct literature reviews or other review studies	10	59%
Other	2	12%

By reading the number of strategies been adopted during the spring semester, only 1 respondent reported using just a single strategy to accommodate the PSY 390 research activities. Specifically, 8 of 17 respondents indicated that they used 3 strategies, 4 respondents indicated 4 strategies, and 2 respondents indicated 5 or 6 strategies. There were differences in pairings of strategies, with frequently selected strategies (i.e., strategies with counts of more than 10 in Table 2) were often used together. The most popular 3-strategy combination was online meeting + data analysis + review studies (7 respondents), followed by online meeting + halt lab study + review studies (5 respondents) and online meeting + halt lab study + data analysis (5 respondents). All these involved use of online meetings, which in most cases replaced on-campus meetings.

Fall Semester. For the fall semester, the respondents also indicated the number of students they enrolled in PSY 390 (see Fig. 2). The mode $= 5$, which is larger than that of 3 in the spring semester, but with almost as many faculty having 1 student or 7 or more students. The median $= 4$ and mean $= 3.90$ ($SD = 2.28$), similar to the spring semester. The slightly lower mean and larger standard deviation are due mainly to one faculty member having no students. Compared to the previous semester, of the 21 faculty members surveyed, nine (42.8%) reported having the same number of students, nine reported having less, and only three (14.3%) reported having more students in the fall semester than in the spring. Across the three categories the difference was definitely not significant, $\chi^2(2, N = 21) = 3.43$. $p = .18$, but comparing just the less and more categories, the values was $\chi^2(1, N = 12) = 3.00$, $p = .08$. Particularly, faculty members in the cognitive area tended to have fewer students registered for PSY 390, with six of the seven cognitive faculty reporting a decrease in student numbers. Situations were varied in the Social area as the three respondents' answers were distributed across same, less, and more. The other research areas (Clinical, Industrial-Organizational, and Neuroscience & Behavior) all reported more faculty members had an increase of PSY 390 students, with only one member of those areas reporting a decrease.

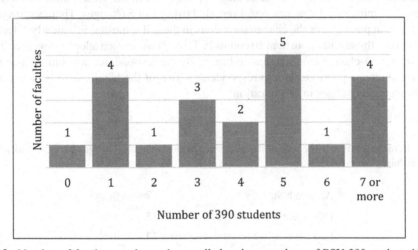

Fig. 2. Number of faculty members who enrolled various numbers of PSY 390 students in the spring semester.

The total number of types of studies conducted in the fall semester was 39 (see Table 1, right numerical column), which was only one less than the 40 reported for the spring semester. However, all of the predefined study types decreased, except observational studies (which increased from 3 to 4). Lab studies and survey studies each decreased by 3 in the fall semester. The reason why the total reported study types decreased by only one is that the number of "Other" studies increased from four to nine. For the fall, the Other category included online adaptations [Qualtrics, virtual treatment trial, online experiments (3 respondents)], as well as coding written response data (2 respondents), and all studies are closed. Note that the increase of "Other" responses basically reflected some of the adaptations and accommodations reported in the following question.

Seventeen (81%) respondents answered that the COVID-19 virus and its related restrictions influenced the research activities that they assigned to their PSY 390 students in the 2020 fall semester. Similar to the spring semester, this time the respondents were asked to provide their perceptions of how they characterized their 390 programs for the fall semester compared to the typical semester prior to the pandemic. However, one respondent did not provide details on the follow-up questions. Of the 16 respondents who provided follow-up information in terms the adjustments they used (see Table 3), a majority (all but one) reported holding more online meetings. Also, more than half specified that they had fewer active research projects or had students analyze previously collected data. Some faculty members reported conducting more studies online and more literature review studies during the fall semester. In general, the strategies to accommodate the restriction to on-campus lab experiences were in line with the trends from the spring semester.

With regard to the number of changes adopted during the fall semester, only 1 respondent indicated using a single strategy. A total of 9 of the 16 respondents marked 3 changes, 2 indicated 2 changes, and 4 reported using 4 or 5 changes. There were again differences in pairings for the change selections in the fall semester. Frequently selected changes (i.e., those with more than 10 counts in Table 3) were often adopted together. The most popular 3-change combination embraced by the respondents was online meeting + fewer studies +previous data (6 respondents). Two of the faculty members selected all 5 predefined changes in this question.

Table 3. In comparison to the typical semester prior to the pandemic, changes the faculty member utilized during the fall semester.

Approach/Strategy	Count	%
Held more online meetings	15	94%
Had fewer active research projects	13	81%
Analyzed previously collected data	11	69%
Conducted more studies online	6	37%
Conducted more review studies	5	31%

2.3   Open-Ended Responses: Results and Discussion

The last two questions on the survey were open-ended. Following typical procedures for coding open-ended answers [8], the authors conducted an initial reading of the answers in which they decided on codes that characterize themes included in one or more response. They then went through each of the answers individually assigning codes and resolved any disagreements through discussion of the answers in question. The coders also referred to participants' responses to the closed-ended questions from the spring and fall semesters to help interpret the written answers in the coding process. The codes fall into three categories, shown in Fig. 3, which lists the code frequencies separately for each of the two questions and in total. Codes related to research activities outnumbered those related to instructors and students in the answers to the transition strategies question ($Ms = 3.4, 1.4$, and 0.5, respectively), but not in those to the pandemic influences question ($Ms = 1.3, 2.0$, and 1.5, respectively).

	Codes	Transition Strategies	Pandemic Influences	Total
Reserch activities related	Online meetings	8	2	10
	Data coding and analysis	4	3	7
	Literature review	3	1	4
	Online experiments	3	1	4
	Conduct on-campus research	3	1	4
	COVID-19 SOPs/Safety trainings	2	1	3
	Independent studies	1	0	1
Instructor related	Slowed research progress	2	3	5
	Change of student number	1	4	5
	Additional learning experiences	2	2	4
	More 390 students show interest	1	1	2
	Fewer meetings	1	0	1
Student related	Wellness concerns	1	2	3
	Less rewarding experience	0	3	3
	Few personal interactions	1	0	1
	Student disengagement	0	1	1

Fig. 3. The frequency of codes assigned to the open-ended questions.

Transition Strategies. The first open-ended question asked respondents to sum up their transition strategies (if any) with respect to the fall 2020 semester, by highlighting the specific arrangements or strategies they employed for the PSY 390 program. Thirteen participants provided answers. Below we summarize the results accompanied with representative quotations, with the participants coded as P1, P2, and so on.

Although the use of online meetings (e.g., Zoom, Webex) was covered in the earlier closed-ended questions, many respondents highlighted this aspect again as part of specific arrangements for their research activities. P7 utilized online meetings to accommodate the international students who worked in the lab, stating, "*390 students and graduate student were all in different locations, including out of the US. All work and meetings were online.*" P13 accommodated a student's desire not to come to campus: "*One 390 student did not want to come to campus - so I held individual weekly meetings with this student to keep him engaged. Other students met in small groups weekly with me and grad students on Zoom.*" where the online meeting was a special arrangement for students who were not available for online on-campus meeting.

This last quote also highlights how the online meetings were integrated into research team activities. For instance, P18 answered, *"Students were divided into two types of teams: lab task teams and research project teams. Students met each week with their team supervisor(s) and peers for at least 15 min per team, which added to about 45−60 min of synchronous meetings."* P11 mentioned a similar approach in the lab as *"Ran more but shorter online meetings with subgroups of students."*

Mention was also made of broader participation of the students in the various aspects of the research being conducted. Added emphasis was placed on data coding and analysis, and the reports indicated that the undergraduate students were assigned more literature reviews. For instance, P6 said, *"The 390 s were assigned secondary data sets to design an analysis for, and conducted literature review for those projects."* P12 described the situation as *"Transitioned many students to secondary data coding, management, and analysis."*

Additionally, the use of online experiments was a noticeable trend. For example, P3 indicated, *"All meetings switched to on-line, which worked pretty well... Most of my experiments were on-line already, so that just continued."* P18 remarked, *"Student lab task activities included running some online projects (both new ones related to COVID and old ones that were already in progress), coding tasks, data cleaning."*

Another highlight was the slowing of on-campus laboratory research, with some respondents indicating that they continued to conduct such research in the fall semester but at a reduced rate, and others indicating cessation of on-campus research. For instance, P13 mentioned, *"We ran in-person studies, but far fewer projects and a slower rate given our efforts to space scheduling of sessions and research assistants to help with distancing and cleaning protocols."* Also, P1 specified, *"I directly supervised the 390 students running lab experiments because the graduate students were not on campus,"* which reduced the number of lab studies that were performed.

Finally, to limit the spread of COVID-19 in the fall semester, Purdue University established the Protect Purdue Plan – a comprehensive strategy to keep the campus and community safe from the virus [9]. A recommended strategy was the use of online meetings to reduce physical contact between individuals, as already emphasized. Another regulation for the fall semester was that research spaces were required to have an approved COVID-19 Standard Operating Procedure (SOP), the intent of which is to confirm adherence to Protect Purdue COVID-19 safety measures in response to the pandemic. All researchers, including undergraduates working in the lab, were required to read, sign, and follow the SOP. The fact that students working in the lab had to learn the procedures was mentioned by several respondents in the verbal answers. For example, P1 noted, *"The 390 students who ran lab experiments became familiar with the Purdue COVID-19 Research Space Standard Operating Procedure, including sanitizing the lab facilities after each participant."*

Influence of the Pandemic on Undergraduate Research Activities. The final question asked respondents to write down any additional comments regarding the influence of the pandemic on undergraduate research activities. Twelve persons provided answers to this question. In their answers, the surveyed faculty members elaborated their general thoughts and overall impressions on the consequences after university shutdown due to the pandemic.

Although not mentioned by all respondents, an obvious influence of the pandemic was its direct impact on the research progress due to the reduced research activities necessitated by the shutdown in the spring and the restrictions in the fall. P14 stressed that the pandemic *"slowed things down by at least one year, maybe more."* P19 indicated frustration with this slowdown resulting in being unable to enroll many new students: *"Given the reduced research activity in my lab, as well as COVID-19 SOP limitations, I have not accepted or sought any new students in PSY 390. Consequently, I have fewer students (just 1) than I typically have in a semester."*

The reductions and changes in research activities caused by pandemic significantly affected students' participation in the course as well. Some labs enrolled fewer students, as specified in the prior quote, whereas others registered more students. P3 stated reasons for turning down some PSY 390 applicants *"I turned down some requests for a PSY 390 (or something similar) because it was not clear how they would contribute to an on-line experiment."* P12 also described the consequences of such changes *"There seemed to be more 390 applicants, especially in Fall 2020, given that some labs had to suspend some research activities while the number of students interested in research experience remained the same."* However, one faculty member, P18, indicated intentionally accommodating for this increased number of applicants: *"I tried to make as much space as possible for students given so many labs were shut down. I do not think we turned anyone away."*

Many of the concerns expressed were related to the teaching and educational aspects, including a negative impact on students' learning experiences. For example, P2 declared, *"It has certainly made it a less rewarding experience, as it is for all of us I assume."* This negative impact continued into the fall semester due to the restrictions on research and physical restrictions such as social distancing after the reopening of the university. P13 also expressed concerns over the lost chances for the students to develop research projects due to the situation: *"I feel bad for the students - it was definitely atypical. If the pandemic had not happened, we certainly would have had more 390 students to collect data for additional projects."*

Although negative impacts on the learning experience were mentioned by some faculty members, several statements emphasized positive aspects, particularly an increased focus on student well-being and mental health. This focus is significant because, during the spring shutdown, a study of undergraduate students at a similar large, state university showed that 71% of undergraduate students reported having increased stress and anxiety due to the COVID-19 pandemic [10]. P18 discussed the need to be concerned about student well-being, indicating that *"...much of our time together involved self-care and general check-in, also about mental health and well-being. Students described these conversations and regular check-ins as critical to their experiences this semester."* P9 addressed a similar topic from the connections and interactions among members of the research group *"Undergraduate researchers seemed to value the continued sense of connection with the lab. Though meetings were all virtual, it still seemed all the more important for students to be connected to our research group."* So, even the online interactions and experiences could serve to help maintain student well-being.

The overall influence from the pandemic and its transitions seems to be negative, but some faculty members viewed the situation more positively. For example, P21 stated, *"Overall it was a smooth transition for us. The 390 s attended weekly online meetings, and we conducted data analysis workshops for them. The students were great."* P6 expressed unexpected benefits that his/her lab eventually gained from the difficult transition from offline to online learning: *"It was hard! We struggled with how to keep the lab running. It was hard to know how many 390 s to even recruit. Silver lining was it forced me to try new activities in the lab (like running analyses in SPSS and designing research analysis projects) which I think I will continue to incorporate even in non COVID semesters."* This latter point needs to be highlighted, as it indicates the potential long-term benefits to instruction in the research experience course as a consequence of the challenges that were faced during 2020.

3   Conclusion

3.1   Lessons Learned

Online Collaborations. The majority of surveyed faculty members indicated that they used online meetings (e.g., Zoom, Webex) to substitute for the on-campus meetings of their lab group. These meetings served not only educational purposes, but provided opportunities for social interactions among the faculty members and students. As almost all students were off campus in the spring semester, and a sizable number in the fall semester, time differences were a concern in scheduling meetings. This concern was particularly pronounced for international students, for whom the discrepancy in time zones from West Lafayette, Indiana, might be great. For example, students in Asia were on approximately an opposite day-night cycle from those in the Eastern U.S. time zone. For this and other reasons, identifying an acceptable meeting time for the team members to work can be difficult. Meeting scheduling services (e.g., Doodle, When2Meet) can be useful for finding times when everyone can meet, but in some cases more than one meeting for the same purpose may need to be held.

Student Engagement. Students' levels of engagement and class involvement can be negatively impacted by the COVID-19 disruption, as found by Perets et al. [11]. Our survey results suggest that the lack of real-world interactions and hands-on practices resulted in a decrease of learners' engagement. Among issues that emerged together with low student engagement, one critical consideration is how to check each student's progress when the research experience course is taught online. Different from the normal PSY 390 experience course, for which the undergraduate students have assigned working times and tasks in the lab, which can be easily monitored, the online students need to function more independently. Setting specific, weekly goals for each student and the research team as a whole seems essential.

Mental Wellness. Human interactions across the students and the instruction team were another concern. People could experience depression or secondary trauma during the pandemic [12], and the situation could get worse after a long period of lockdown without typical interactions with other students. How to motivate students, and assure their well-being, given the limited social interactions is a challenge compared to research experience in the lab. From survey responses, multiple faculty members mentioned holding weekly online meetings or discussion sessions to check-up on student's mental and physical well-being. Perhaps most important, the survey illustrated that being creative and flexible in one's approach to the pandemic situation allowed unique learning experiences and opportunities to interact with the students. And those experiences can be worthwhile to be implemented even in post-pandemic era.

3.2 Final Remarks

Research experience is a crucial part of undergraduate education in psychology, and most higher education institutions offer such opportunities to students. The present paper provides a case study of how faculty members at a single university in the U.S. perceived and dealt with the transition from training students in the lab to training them online entirely in the spring 2020 semester and to a large extent in the fall 2020 semester. We identified strategies adopted by the faculty members to fulfill the research experience online of the students in the spring and to address the range of on- and off-campus options in the fall.

While the hands-on research experience necessarily suffered from the limited time in on-campus labs in both semesters, the experience was also broadened by including the undergraduate students in aspects of research to which they normally would not be exposed, introducing new projects and activities, and engaging in tutorials on topics. Having to address the changes in research and undergraduate involvement imposed by the pandemic provided an opportunity for faculty members to become familiar with, and think innovatively about, ways in which online meetings and activities can be incorporated into the learning process. The knowledge gained should be valuable to instructors for assimilating technology into their post-COVID 19 instructional routines and responding to disruptions to on-campus education that may occur in the future [13].

Although Purdue University plans to return to normal on-campus operations in the fall, 2021, semester, it is likely that more courses will continue to be hybrid, with some parts taught online and some offline. More generally, education will probably continue to be increasingly online, in part or whole. The COVID-19 pandemic has forced instructors to be creative about moving to online and hybrid research experience classes. Because lab-based courses such as the PSY 390 research experience class involve students' hands-on practices more than lecture-based courses do, challenges for such transitions are unique. Hopefully, the lessons learned from our survey will be of use to instructors in renovating and developing the research experience courses of the future.

Acknowledgments. We thank all faculty members who responded to our request and participated in our survey. We also thank graduate student lab members Jeongyun Choi, Tianfang Han, and Qi Zhong for assistance with the undergraduate students.

References

1. Fan, J., Liu, X., Pan, W., Douglas, M.W., Bao, S.: Epidemiology of coronavirus disease in Gansu Province, China, 2020. EID J. **26**(6), 1257–1265 (2020)
2. AJMC Staff: A timeline of COVID-19 developments in 2020. AJMC, 1 January (2021)
3. Bangert, D.: Coronavirus: Purdue ends in-person classes through semester, asks students to move out. Lafayette Journal & Courier, 2020, March 16 (updated March 17)
4. Johnson, N., Veletsianos, G., Seaman, J.: U.S. faculty and administrators' experiences and approaches in the early weeks of the COVID-19 pandemic. Online Learn. **24**(2), 6–21 (2020)
5. Besser, A., Flett, G.L., Zeigler-Hill, V.: Adaptability to a sudden transition to online learning during the COVID-19 pandemic: understanding the challenges for students. Scholarship Teach. Learn. Psychol. (2020). https://doi.org/10.1037/stl0000198
6. Lashley, M., McCleery, R.: Intensive laboratory experiences to safely retain experiential learning in the transition to online learning. Ecol. Evol. **10**(22), 12613–12619 (2020)
7. Inside Higher Ed: Reversals in colleges' fall 2020 reopening plans (2020). https://www.insidehighered.com/coronavirus-colleges-reverse-reopening-plans
8. Gibbs, G.R.: Analysing Qualitative Data, 2nd edn. Sage, London (2018)
9. Protect Purdue Implementation Team: Protect Purdue plan (2020). https://protect.purdue.edu/plan/
10. Son, C., Hegde, S., Smith, A., Wang, X., Sasangohar, F.: Effects of COVID-19 on college students' mental health in the United States: interview survey study. J. Med. Internet Res. **22**(9), (2020)
11. Perets, E.A., et al: Impact of the emergency transition to remote teaching on student engagement in a non-STEM undergraduate chemistry course in the time of COVID-19. J. Chem. Educ. **97**(9), 2439–2447 (2020)
12. Zhong, B., Huang, Y., Liu, Q.: Mental health toll from the coronavirus: social media usage reveals Wuhan residents' depression and secondary trauma in the COVID-19 outbreak. Comput. Hum. Behav. **114**, (2021)
13. van der Spoel, I., Noroozi, O., Schuurink, E., van Ginkel, S.: Teachers' online teaching expectations and experiences during the Covid19-pandemic in the Netherlands. Euro. J. Teach. Educ. **43**(4), 623–638 (2020)

Learner Model for Adaptive Scaffolding in Intelligent Tutoring Systems for Organizing Programming Knowledge

Kento Koike[1]([⊠]), Yuki Fujishima[2], Takahito Tomoto[2], Tomoya Horiguchi[3], and Tsukasa Hirashima[4]

[1] Graduate School of Engineering, Tokyo Polytechnic University, Atsugi, Kanagawa, Japan
k.koike@t-kougei.ac.jp

[2] Faculty of Engineering, Tokyo Polytechnic University, Atsugi, Kanagawa, Japan

[3] Graduate School of Maritime Sciences, Kobe University, Kobe, Hyogo, Japan

[4] Graduate School of Advanced Science and Engineering, Hiroshima University, Higashi-hiroshima, Hiroshima, Japan
https://www.koike.app/

Abstract. Learner models are constructed from learner understanding states regarding learning materials, obtained by observing learner behaviors. A learner model collects information for adaptive tutoring and uses this information to determine system actions such as hints, problem presentations, and explanations appropriate to learner understanding. A learner model thus plays an essential role in intelligent tutoring systems (ITSs). Our previously developed ITSs have adopted a simple learner model that considers once-solved problems as learner-acquired solutions for problem solving. However, such models cannot grasp learner proficiency for solutions, which is an important aspect of constructing learner models because learners often make problem-solving mistakes despite having already learned the solution. In such situations, it is effective for an ITS to apply scaffolding based on learner proficiency regarding the solution. However, excess scaffolding decreases comprehension, a phenomenon known as the "assistance dilemma." A learner model that adaptively scaffolds based on analysis of learner proficiency in solutions can effectively mitigate the assistance dilemma. In this study, we develop and evaluate an ITS with a learner model that considers learner proficiency in solutions. Experimental results indicate that the developed learner model can reduce total feedback without changing learner comprehension.

Keywords: Programming education · Learner model · Adaptive scaffolding · Knowledge organization · Intelligent tutoring system

1 Introduction

Improving problem-solving skills is essential for programming education because general programming exercises do not have unique answers. Our previous

© Springer Nature Switzerland AG 2021
S. Yamamoto and H. Mori (Eds.): HCII 2021, LNCS 12766, pp. 63–74, 2021.
https://doi.org/10.1007/978-3-030-78361-7_6

research has thus developed some intelligent tutoring systems (ITSs) and their underlying technologies [4–8]. These products aim to improve programming problem-solving skills through our original approach for organizing knowledge, called the "Building method that Realizes Organizing Components" (BROCs) approach.

An ITS is a computer-based learning support system designed to provide immediate customized instruction and feedback to learners without human instructor intervention [9,10]. Such support is realized by understanding learner problem-solving processes. To do so, however, the ITS requires a learner model, constructed from the learner's understanding state by observing learner behavior. The learner model collects information for adaptive tutoring and uses this information to determine system actions such as hints, problem presentations, and explanations that are appropriate to the understanding state. The learner model thus plays an essential role in an ITS.

Our previously developed ITSs have adopted a simple learner model that considers once-solved problems as learner-acquired solutions for problem-solving. However, such a model cannot grasp learner proficiency for solutions, which is an important aspect of constructing learner models because learners often make problem-solving mistakes despite having already learned the solution [1]. In such situations, it is effective for an ITS to apply scaffolding based on learner proficiency regarding the solution. However, excess scaffolding decreases comprehension, a phenomenon known as the "assistance dilemma" [3]. A learner model that adaptively scaffolds based on analysis of learner proficiency in solutions can effectively mitigate the assistance dilemma. In this study, we developed and evaluated an ITS with a learner model that considers learner proficiency in solutions.

We conducted evaluations in a counterbalancing method comparing ITSs under two conditions: an experimental condition (EC) in which learners receive limited feedback from our learner model, and a control condition (CC) where learners can always receive unlimited feedback. The results indicated no differences in comprehension between EC and CC, and that fewer learners received the total feedback amount under EC as compared to CC. The proposed learner model can thus reduce the total feedback amount without changing learner comprehension.

2 ITS for Organizing Programming Knowledge

2.1 BROCs Approach

We proposed BROCs as a pedagogy for our developed ITSs for programming education [4–7]. This study similarly uses BROCs as the pedagogy for an ITS developed with the proposed learner model.

BROCs allows stepwise extension of components to support knowledge organization in programming. For instance, Fig. 1 shows presenting tasks in two steps: writing short functions (e.g., swap) by combining primitive components (e.g., assignment, if statements), and writing longer functions (e.g., sort) by

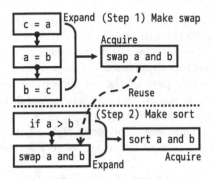

Fig. 1. BROCs approach.

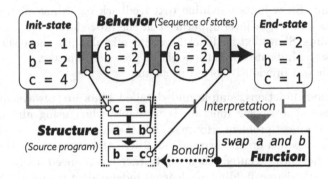

Fig. 2. Programming problem-solving process.

combining already written components. By repeating these steps, learners can structuralize and accumulate components in a stepwise fashion. That is, functionally meaningful sequences of code are defined as components, which learners recognize and learn.

Programming knowledge of components is required for learners to understand them. Component knowledge is defined as a combination of three elements in the programming problem-solving process (Fig. 2): function (what the component achieves), behavior (data state transitions), and structure (source code) [4,7,8]. In this way, code series are linked to functions to help students understand them.

In fact, another study [2] showed that first writing small functions then combining them to build larger functions is an effective learning approach. Therefore, the BROCs approach enhances reusability of programming knowledge and helps learners improve their problem-solving skills.

2.2 Original ITS

We have been developing ITSs to enhance and scaffold learning in the BROCs approach [4–7]. The ITS proposed in this paper is another version of such ITSs, because we aim to investigate the effects of changing the feedback function in previous ITSs according to the proposed learner model.

Figure 3 shows the user interface (UI) for one of our previous ITSs. This system is a Windows desktop application developed using the C# programming language. The upper middle part of the UI shows the target component that learners should acquire, a problem, and problem constraints. The left side of the UI shows a component list for selecting components to add to the workspace to construct the target component. The lower right of the UI is the workspace, where learners can edit component elements, namely textboxes, order, and hierarchy level.

This system also has the following feedback functions for scaffolding learner activities in BROCs:

- Simple hints: Show hints providing text feedback regarding mistakes related to textboxes, order, or level uppermost in the procedure.
- Detailed hints: Show text feedback for fixing mistakes like those shown above.
- Check answer: Indicate correctness of the presented answer.
- Review: Show a previously solved problem.

Among these functions, simple and detailed hints are always available at learner request. The review function is available when using already learned components in a new problem. However, whether use of the feedback function is appropriate depends on the learner's skill. On the other hand, the feedback function is sometimes executed when the learner has no need for it.

To realize adaptive scaffolding in a learner-independent manner, it is desirable for the ITS to automatically generate feedback adapted to the learners' state. To generate adaptive feedback using these functions, therefore, we propose a learner model that utilizes learner proficiency for solutions, and we developed an ITS with the resulting learner model.

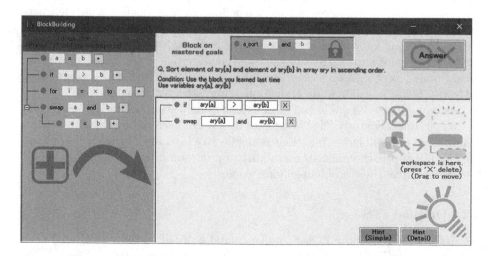

Fig. 3. User interface of our previous system.

3 Learner Model for Adaptive Scaffolding

3.1 Modelization

One effective scaffolding method is to adaptively provide feedback when the learner makes a mistake. However, if the learner makes many mistakes due to random behavior, providing feedback each time can lead to excess scaffolding. On the other hand, insufficient scaffolding often leads to learner impasses. To resolve this assistance dilemma we must maintain appropriate difficulty of problem-solving [3], so it is important to distinguish the causes of learner mistakes.

To construct the learner model, therefore, we define and distinguish learner mistakes due to two states: the insufficient proficiency in solution (IPS) state and insufficient resource of learner (IRL) state [1]. IPS is a state where the learner makes mistakes in solutions that involve already-solved problems using scaffolding. IRL is a non-IPS state, such as when the learner makes mistakes that involve already-solved solutions to other problems with no scaffolding. Our learner model uses these two states to represent the learner state.

By casting both problem-solving states with components in the BROCs approach, learner-acquired components using scaffolding are defined as the IPS component (Fig. 4). When a learner makes mistakes regarding IPS components in problem-solving, we can suppose an IPS state. In contrast, when the learner makes a non-IPS-component mistake in problem-solving, we can suppose an IRL state.

Scaffolding for a learner in an IPS state requires reviewing previous problems related to an IPS component, as shown at the bottom of Fig. 4. For instance, when the model detects the first IPS state of a learner solving problem C_3, the model presents C_2, a problem that was presented when acquiring the learner's IPS component, because learner proficiency in the solution to an IPS component is supposedly insufficient. In the problem under review, the learner model collects components again as IPS or non-IPS, separately and according to the

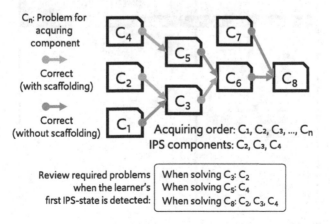

Fig. 4. Our learner model in problem-solving with components.

detection of any received scaffolding by the learner. In Fig. 4, therefore, there is no need to review C_2 when the learner model detects the IPS state in problem C_8, but the learner has already reviewed C_2 and provided a correct answer with no scaffolding. Such a situation can occur when the learner model detects an IPS state in problems C_3 or C_6. Therefore, the constructed learner model can categorize learner mistakes into the above two types and present adaptive scaffolding.

3.2   Implementation

We developed ITS with a learner model that considered IPS and IRL states (described in Sect. 3.1). Figure 5 shows an example of the user interface of our ITS.

In Fig. 5, the upper part of the UI shows the target component for learner acquisition and a problem and constraints for acquiring it (the top of Fig. 6 shows details). To construct the target component, the lower-left part of the UI shows a component list for selecting components to add to the workspace at the lower right. In the workspace, learners can edit the textbox, order, and hierarchy level of components.

Figure 6 shows examples using the learner model in the same system problem. Examples 1 and 2 show how learners separately acquired components as IPS or non-IPS. Example 3 shows the required review of IPS components when the learner makes a mistake. In Example 1, the system judged the learner's answer as correct, following correction based on received feedback. Therefore, this component is acquired as an IPS component. In Example 2, in contrast,

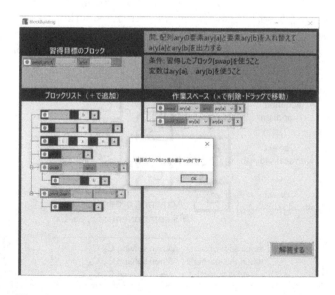

Fig. 5. Example of the user interface and text feedback.

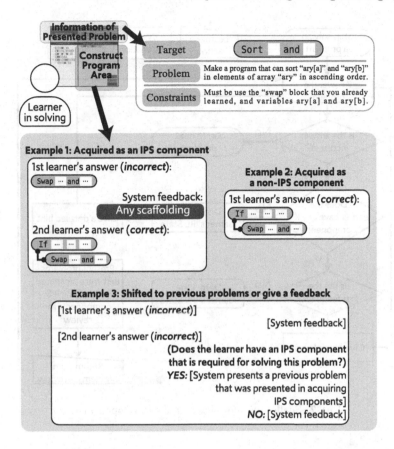

Fig. 6. Examples using our learner model in the developed ITS.

the system judged the learner's answer as correct, but the learner received no feedback. This component is thus acquired as a non-IPS component. In this way, the system estimates whether the learner acquired the IPS components. In Example 3, the system decides whether to present a previous problem for review or to give feedback, according to whether the learner has any IPS components.

Figure 7 shows diagnostic algorithms for detecting and scaffolding the two learner states in the developed system. The system first judges whether the learner's answer is correct. If so, the system presents the next problem, and if not it judges whether the learner has any IPS components. If the learner has no IPS components, the system estimates the learner IRL state and gives a detailed hint. Otherwise, the system judges whether the learner has received feedback yet. If the learner has not received feedback, the system gives a simple hint. Otherwise, the system estimates the learner IPS state and requires the review of problems presented in acquiring IPS components. After problem review, the learner returns to the original problem and attempts it again.

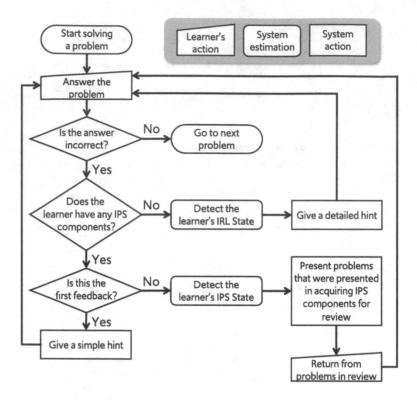

Fig. 7. Scaffolding flowchart in the developed ITS.

As described above, our ITS can generate adaptive scaffolding according to diagnoses from our learner model.

4   Evaluation

4.1   Method

To evaluate the learning gains of our proposed ITS, we compare scaffoldings that depend on learner requests or system learner models. We therefore conduct an evaluation that compares learner model ITSs between two conditions in a counterbalancing method: an experimental condition (EC) in which learners receive limited feedback from our learner model, and a control condition (CC) where learners can always receive unlimited feedback. The evaluation hypotheses are as follows: the learning gains of both systems are equal (H1), and the number of received feedbacks in EC is less than CC (H2).

We prepared both systems for our proposed ITS for EC and a system based on the original ITS for CC. Table 1 shows the functional availability of both systems along with that of the original ITS for reference, the details of which are described in Sect. 2.2.

Table 1. Functional availability comparison between conditions and a reference.

System	Simple hint	Detailed hint	Check answer	Review
EC: Our proposed ITS	Limited	Limited	Free	Limited
CC: ITS based on original's	Free	Free	Free	Free
(Reference: original ITS)	Free	Free	Free	Forced

Participants were twelve undergraduate students who have studied programming for at least three years in programming courses. All participants had already learned basic concepts such as "for" and "if" statements, sorting algorithms, and functions. We divided participants into two groups: a group EG that first learned in EC and then in CC (7 participants), and a group CG that learned in the opposite order (5 participants).

Our evaluation was conducted over two days, divided into each condition for each participant. As the procedure on day 1, we first conducted 25-min pre-tests (12 problems) that can be developed stepwise to measure fundamental programming and design skills. After that, learners used the system under each condition for 30 min. We then conducted 25-min post-tests posing the same problems as pre-tests and a questionnaire. As the procedure on day 2, we first conducted 25-min pre-tests. After that, learners used the system under opposite conditions to day 1 for 30 min. Finally, we conducted 25-min post-tests and the questionnaire.

In each test, learners were instructed to perform structuring such as functionalization or componentization in each problem to the extent possible, and to reuse earlier answers in other problems. These evaluations utilized a procedural scoring that evaluated whether the procedure is correct, and a structuralized scoring that evaluated whether learners functionalized and reused the other problems, regardless of procedure correctness.

4.2   Results: Learning Gains

Table 2 presents results of test scores as the learning gains of both systems. To analyze the differences, we conducted a 2 (groups: EG or CG) $\times$ 2 (test timing: pre- or post-test scores) ANOVA four times for each situation (two days $\times$ two types of scoring). In addition, statistical values are stated in each results: F-value, p-value, significant difference ($**$: $p < .01, *$: $p < .05, \dagger$: $p < .10$), and effect size of partial η^2 (indicated as η_p^2).

In the use of systems on day 1, an ANOVA for procedural scores showed significant difference in the test timing $[F(1, 10) = 5.28, p = .04^*, \eta_p^2 = .35]$. We did not find significant differences in the groups $[F(1, 10) = 0.03, p = .87, \eta_p^2 = .00]$ and the interaction effects $[F(1, 10) = 0.34, p = .57, \eta_p^2 = .03]$. Also, an ANOVA for structuralized scores showed significant difference in the test timing $[F(1, 10) = 20.25, p < .01^{**}, \eta_p^2 = .67]$. We did not find significant differences in the groups $[F(1, 10) = 0.15, p = .71, \eta_p^2 = .02]$ and the interaction effects $[F(1, 10) = 0.27, p = .61, \eta_p^2 = .03]$.

Table 2. A summary of test scores.

$N = 12$ (EG = 7, CG = 5)			Procedural score		Structuralized score	
Day	Group	Condition	Pre	Post	Pre	Post
Day 1	EG	EC	2.86 (2.10)	3.57 (2.38)	1.00 (1.60)	3.86 (2.59)
	CG	CC	2.40 (1.36)	3.60 (1.20)	0.20 (0.40)	3.80 (2.64)
Day 2	EG	CC	3.29 (2.60)	4.14 (3.27)	3.29 (2.49)	6.57 (2.72)
	CG	EC	3.40 (0.49)	5.00 (2.28)	2.60 (1.62)	5.80 (2.32)

Note: Each value described as "Mean (SD)".

In the use of systems on day 2, similar to day 1, each ANOVA in two types of scoring showed significant differences in the test timing; but we did not find any significant differences in the groups and interaction effects (detail in procedural scores: the groups $[F(1, 10) = 0.10, p = .76, \eta_p^2 = .01]$, the test timing $[F(1, 10) = 4.88, p = .05^\dagger, \eta_p^2 = .33]$, and the interaction effects $[F(1, 10) = 0.45, p = .52, \eta_p^2 = .04]$; detail in structuralized scores: the groups $[F(1, 10) = 0.29, p = .60, \eta_p^2 = .03]$, the test timing $[F(1, 10) = 20.37, p < .01^{**}, \eta_p^2 = .67]$, and the interaction effects $[F(1, 10) = 0.00, p = 1, \eta_p^2 = .00]$).

In summary, these four ANOVAs showed statistical differences only in the test timing; but we did not find any statistical differences in the groups and the interaction effects.

4.3   Results: Number of Received Feedbacks

Table 3 presents results of number of received feedbacks in both systems. To analyze the differences, we conducted a 2 (groups: EG or CG) × 3 (feedback types: simple hint, detailed hint or review) ANOVA two times for each day. In addition, statistical values are stated in each results: F-value, p-value, significant differences ($^{**} : p < .01, ^* : p < .05, ^\dagger : p < .10$), and effect size of partial η^2 (indicated as η_p^2).

In the use of systems on day 1, an ANOVA showed significant differences in the groups $[F(1, 10) = 34.34, p < .01^{**}, \eta_p^2 = .77]$, the feedback types $[F(2, 20) = 25.83, p < .01^{**}, \eta_p^2 = .72]$, and interaction effects $[F(2, 20) = 6.36, p < .01^{**}, \eta_p^2 = .39]$. A Tukey post-hoc test revealed significant pairwise difference between EG and CG in the count of detailed hint ($p < .01^{**}$).

Table 3. A summary of number of received feedbacks.

$N = 12$ (EG = 7, CG = 5)			Number of received feedback		
Day	Group	Condition	Simple hint	Detailed hint	Review
Day 1	EG	EC	6.71 (2.31)	19.57 (5.73)	3.00 (1.07)
	CG	CC	16.80 (13.76)	51.40 (19.44)	1.20 (1.47)
Day 2	EG	CC	13.14 (3.98)	23.43 (12.01)	1.14 (1.46)
	CG	EC	5.80 (2.23)	9.20 (6.34)	2.20 (1.47)

Note: Each value described as "Mean (SD)".

In the use of systems on day 2, similar to day 1, an ANOVA showed significant differences in the groups $[F(1, 10) = 7.35, p = .02^*, \eta_p^2 = .42]$, the feedback types $[F(2, 20) = 15.37, p < .01^{**}, \eta_p^2 = .61]$, and interaction effects $[F(2, 20) = 4.19, p = .03^*, \eta_p^2 = .30]$. A Tukey post-hoc test revealed significant pairwise difference between EG and CG in the count of detailed hint $(p = .01^*)$.

On both days, thus EC resulted in significantly fewer received detailed hints as compared to CC.

4.4 Consideration

The results in Sect. 4.2 suggested that the use of both systems contributes to the understanding of algorithms and enhances the reusability of programming knowledge. Such effectiveness of BROCs approach was also confirmed in our previous study [4, 6]. Therefore, these results support the hypothesis H1.

The results in Sect. 4.3 suggested that our proposed learner model can reduce learners' received feedback amount. Especially, the learner model reduced the learners' number of received detailed hints that show text feedback for fixing mistakes as described in Sect. 2.2. That is, the learner model has reduced the number of times learners' see the answer. Therefore, these results support the hypothesis H2.

These results support our hypotheses H1 and H2, so in conclusion, there were no differences in comprehension between EC and CC, and that EC resulted in less received feedbacks as compared to CC. The proposed learner model can thus reduce the total feedback amount without changing learner comprehension.

5 Conclusion

We developed an ITS with a learner model that can mitigate the assistance dilemma by adaptively scaffolding based on analysis of learner proficiency in solutions. To construct the learner model, we defined and distinguished learner mistakes due to IPS state and IRL state [1].

We conducted evaluations in a counterbalancing method comparing ITSs under EC and CC conditions. The results indicated no differences in comprehension between EC and CC, and that fewer learners received the total feedback amount under EC as compared to CC. The proposed learner model can thus reduce the total feedback amount without changing learner comprehension.

Our proposed learner model represents learner proficiency in solution as 0 (IPS state) or 1 (IRL-state); in a normal situation, however, learners' proficiency in solution is not discrete values. Therefore, it is future work that representation of learner proficiency in solution extends to continuous values.

Acknowledgement. This work was supported by JSPS KAKENHI Grant Numbers JP18K11586, JP19H04227, and JP17H01839.

References

1. Hirashima, T., Kashihara, A., Toyoda, J.: Providing problem explanation for ITS. In: Frasson, C., Gauthier, G., McCalla, G.I. (eds.) ITS 1992. LNCS, vol. 608, pp. 76–83. Springer, Heidelberg (1992). https://doi.org/10.1007/3-540-55606-0_11
2. Hu, M., Winikoff, M., Cranefield, S.: A process for novice programming using goals and plans. In: Proceedings of the Fifteenth Australasian Computing Education Conference, pp. 3–12 (2013)
3. Koedinger, K.R., Aleven, V.: Exploring the assistance dilemma in experiments with cognitive tutors. Educ. Psychol. Rev. **19**(3), 239–264 (2007). https://doi.org/10.1007/s10648-007-9049-0
4. Koike, K., Mogi, T., Tomoto, T., Horiguchi, T., Hirashima, T.: Compogram: development and evaluation of ITS for organizing programming-knowledge by visualizing behavior. In: Stephanidis, C., et al. (eds.) HCII 2020. LNCS, vol. 12427, pp. 151–162. Springer, Cham (2020). https://doi.org/10.1007/978-3-030-60152-2_12
5. Koike, K., Tomoto, T., Hirashima, T.: Proposal of a stepwise support for structural understanding in programming. In: ICCE 2017–25th International Conference on Computers in Education, Workshop Proceedings, pp. 471–481, December 2017
6. Koike, K., Tomoto, T., Horiguchi, T., Hirashima, T.: Proposal of the expandable modular statements method for structural understanding of programming, and development and evaluation of a learning support system. Trans. Jpn. Soc. Inf. Syst. Educ. **36**(3), 190–202 (2019). https://doi.org/10.14926/jsise.36.190. (in Japanese)
7. Koike, K., Tomoto, T., Horiguchi, T., Hirashima, T.: Supporting knowledge organization for reuse in programming: proposal of a system based on function–behavior–structure models. In: ICCE 2019–27th International Conference on Computers in Education, Workshop Proceedings, vol. 2, pp. 388–398, December 2019
8. Koike, K., Tomoto, T., Horiguchi, T., Hirashima, T.: Intelligent learning support for reusability oriented knowledge organization in programming learning. Trans. Jpn. Soc. Artif. Intell. **35**(5), C-J82-1-17 (2020). https://doi.org/10.1527/tjsai.35-5_C-J82. (in Japanese)
9. Nwana, H.S.: Intelligent tutoring systems: an overview. Artif. Intell. Rev. **4**(4), 251–277 (1990)
10. Wenger, E.: Artificial Intelligence and Tutoring Systems: Computational and Cognitive Approaches to the Communication of Knowledge. Morgan Kaufmann Publishers Inc., San Francisco (1987)

Exploring Human-Computer Interaction in Mathematics: From Voevodsky's Univalent Foundations of Mathematics to Mochizuki's IUT-Theoretic Proof of the ABC Conjecture

Yoshihiro Maruyama[✉]

Research School of Computer Science,
College of Engineering and Computer Science,
The Australian National University,
Canberra, Australia
yoshihiro.maruyama@anu.edu.au

Abstract. Human-Computer Interaction research features the human-in-the-loop view of computer science and engineering, or system science in general. Here we argue that the same view applies to mathematics as well as computer science, especially in the context of Voevodsky's univalent foundations programme, which involves the human-in-the-loop view of mathematics. At the same time we explicate and articulate the difference between Hilbert's programme and Voevodsky's programme on foundations of mathematics. We elucidate, inter alia, the foundational significance of Voevodsky's programme, which arguably aims at structural realist foundations of mathematics rather than reductive idealist foundations as problematised in Hilbert's programme. Voevodsky's univalent foundations programme pursues the conceptually transparent and logically certified treatment of mathematics qua Big Data, the whole web of knowledge of which goes far beyond a single mathematician's comprehension bound by the finitary nature of the human mind, just as ordinary Big Data does; the fundamental reason we need statistical machine learning for Ordinary Big Data analytics is essentially the same as the reason we need univalent foundations for Mathematical Big Data analytics. Voevodsky's programme is concerned with the computational methodology of ensuring and maintaining the certainty and objectivity of mathematical knowledge, which would arguably help deal with puzzling issues in the mathematical community, such as the recent case of Mochizuki's Inter-Universal Teichimüller Theoretic proof of the abc conjecture, the formal computer verification of which could resolve the perplexing complications and firmly support its mathematical truth.

Keywords: Voevodsky's Univalent Foundations · Homotopy Type Theory · Voevodsky's Programme as opposed to Hilbert's Programme · Mathematical big data · The Human-in-the-Loop view of mathematics ·

© Springer Nature Switzerland AG 2021
S. Yamamoto and H. Mori (Eds.): HCII 2021, LNCS 12766, pp. 75–91, 2021.
https://doi.org/10.1007/978-3-030-78361-7_7

Interactive theorem proving/proof assistant · Formal verification of
mathematics · Mochizuki's Inter-Universal Teichimüller Theoretic Proof
of the ABC Conjecture · The nature of mathematical knowledge · The
objectivity and certainty of mathematical truth

1   Introduction

Human-Computer Interaction can, in principle, be problematized in any system in
which humans and computers interact with each other. Humans involved may be
the general public, and yet at the same time, they may rather be experts such as scientists. In the present paper we focus upon Human-Computer Interaction in Mathematics, in particular Vladimir Voevodsky's Univalent Foundations of Mathematics and Homotopy Type Theory [54], which give novel foundations of mathematics, building upon interactive theorem prover and proof assistant systems (especially, Coq [17]; there are different origins of homotopy type theory, such as Hoff-
man and Streicher's work [23] and Awodey and Warren's work [14], other than
Voevodsky's). Human-Computer Interaction in Mathematics, generally speaking,
has not been paid much attention to in Human-Computer Interaction research so
far. In the present paper we take first steps towards foundational studies on Human-
Computer Interaction in Mathematics, pursuing the human-in-the-loop view of
(the epistemology and ontology) of mathematics (or mathematical activity).

What is striking in recent years is the changing perceptions of interactive theorem provers and proof assistants in the Pure Mathematics community. On the
one hand, interactive theorem provers and proof assistants have long been concerns of symbolic logicians and computer scientists; yet on the other, pure mathematicians mostly kept a certain distance from them. Indeed, computer-generated
proofs, such as the one for the four colour theorem, have been highly controver-
sial in the Pure Mathematics community; some eminent mathematicians, such as
William Thurston, who was generally known for extraordinary mathematical intuition and awarded the Fields Medal for his celebrated work in low-dimensional
topology (which indeed requires special geometric intuition in a certain sense),
have even argued that computer-generated proofs do not get the status of mathematical proofs because they do not give us any insight into (or understanding of)
mathematical mechanisms underlying phenomena concerned (see, e.g., [53]).

The former situation in formalised (or certified) mathematics is comparable
to the current situation in statistical machine learning, especially the black box
nature of deep learning. Recent trends such as Explainable Artificial Intelligence
and Interpretable Machine Learning are rooted in essentially the same kind of concern with the lack of explanation, interpretation, and understanding in computationally complex systems, which may go beyond human apprehension (see, e.g.,
[12, 42, 44, 47]). Powerful computational systems can solve certain problems very
well, and yet they do not necessarily give a fundamental understanding of underlying mechanisms, the elucidation of which, presumably, gives the principal raison
d'etre of (pure) science (rather than engineering, which puts more emphasis on
practical power, such as statistical predictive performance as pursued in ordinary
artificial intelligence research).

The significant change in mathematicians' perceptions has mainly been triggered by the work of Voevodsky and his collaborators, the Fields Medalist who suddenly changed his topic from algebraic geometry (and motivic cohomology theory) to the foundations, verification, and automation of mathematics which, unlike traditional foundations of them, are more mathematician-friendly and keep the same kind of conceptual transparency as pure mathematics has. Voevodsky's work may be seen as improving Human-Computer Interaction in Mathematics, enabling a more natural formalisation of mathematical proofs as, for example, embodied in his univalence axiom, which basically states that "identity is equivalent with equivalence", or to put it simply, "isomorphic objects are identical" (see, e.g., [13]). The mathematician often identifies a mathematical object with another object equivalent with it; this practice, however, has been regarded as an informal trick to make proofs more transparent, more conceptual, and thus more intelligible to the human mathematician. And formal frameworks for interactive theorem proving and proof assistants did not support such tricks as used in actual mathematical practice, and were quite alien to the pure mathematician. Yet they can nevertheless be expressed and exploited in formal foundations of mathematics. Voevodsky's univalence axiom has allowed us to justify the very practice of the mathematician in a formally consistent manner, thus making formal proofs closer to mathematicians' informal, conceptual proofs and thereby improving Human-Computer Interaction in interactive theorem proving and proof assistant systems. Voevodsky's univalent foundations and homotopy type theory have already been implemented in Coq [54], one of the most popular frameworks for interactive theorem proving and proof assistant. Coq is not just a formal verification framework; it arguably has the potential to incarnate mathematical understanding. It is notable, amongst other things, that the Coq framework even allowed us to give a more surveyable and more conceptually transparent proof of the four color theorem [24], thus contributing to mathematical understanding as well as formal verification. Making understanding compatible with formal computational capabilities is the common challenge that is shared by both machine learning and formal verification research. It should be remarked that Wittgenstein puts strong emphasis on the surveyability of proofs, arguing that non-surveyable proofs are not true mathematical proofs, which is concerned with the nature of mathematical understanding; merely formally correct proofs may not count as genuine proofs yielding mathematical understanding and thereby driving mathematical activity (see, e.g., [43] and references therein).

The rest of the paper is organised as follows. In the following we analyse Voevodsky's perspective on foundations of mathematics and verifications of mathematical knowledge (Sect. 2) and discuss the case of Shinichi Mochizuki's interuniversal Teichimüller theoretic proof of the abc conjecture, the formal computer verification of which could settle the surrounding complications and firmly support its mathematical truth (Sect. 3). A virtue of mathematics is its transparency about truth; it gets lost, however, once social controversies arise as to the correctness of proofs, which is unfortunate to mathematics and mathematicians, and yet even in which case, formal verification would help resolve the controversies and bring the mathematics back to what it ought to be. We finally conclude with several remarks upon the nature of Voevodsky's univalent foundations programme and its relationships with Hilbert's programme and recent trends in computer science, artificial intelligence, and philosophy of mathematics (Sect. 4).

2   Voevodsky's Univalent Foundations and Homotopy Type Theory

In the present section we explore Voevodsky's view of foundations of mathematics, especially the certainty and objectivity of mathematics. Voevodsky's interest in foundations of mathematics and computer verifications of mathematical truths did not stem from abstract epistemological considerations as former generations of foundational mathematicians such as Hilbert and Weyl made, but it was rather deeply rooted in his own practical experience on the certainty of mathematical knowledge. In the idealist conception of mathematics, mathematical knowledge is immutable and universally valid, which is, of course, not wrong per se, being a crucial characteristic of mathematical knowledge as different from other kinds of knowledge.

Yet at the same time, mathematics in practice is human activity, and there are various human factors in mathematics, just as Human-Computer Interaction, as a research field, is concerned with human factors in computer science and engineering. Put another way, humans are in the loop of mathematics as well as computer science. The human-in-the-loop view of mathematics allows us to better understand Voevodsky's motivation for his univalent foundations of mathematics and homotopy type theory, or the significance of formal verifications of mathematical truths in general. Human factors in mathematics, as we shall see, led Voevodsky to univalent foundations research. In the following we trace Voevodsky's intellectual history concerning foundations of mathematics and formal verifications of mathematical truths, and analyse what exactly are human factors in the loop of mathematics or mathematical research activity. Grothendieck is a precursor of Voevodsky, having proposed a speculative theory of motives in algebraic geometry and arithmetic geometry in order to capture the fundamental essence of different cohomologies. The theory of (mixed) motives is not completed even now, and yet Voevodsky made major progress along similar lines, and at the same time systematised motivic cohomology theory in a rigorous manner, which is different from the Grothendieck-style theory of motives per se, and yet closely related with each other. Regarding motivic cohomology, Voevodsky [55] argues as follows:

> The field of motivic cohomology was considered at that time to be highly speculative and lacking firm foundation. The groundbreaking 1986 paper "Algebraic Cycles and Higher K-theory" by Spencer Bloch was soon after publication found by Andrei Suslin to contain a mistake in the proof of Lemma 1.1. The proof could not be fixed, and almost all of the claims of the paper were left unsubstantiated. A new proof, which replaced one paragraph from the original paper by thirty pages of complex arguments,

was not made public until 1993, and it took many more years for it to be accepted as correct.

It is presumably the early experience in which Voevodsky came to have some doubts about the idealist conception of mathematics or rather mathematical activity as being infallible. Any human activity is actually fallible, and mathematics qua human activity is no exception, although it is supposed to be infallible in the idealist conception. The same however applies to computer verified proofs, the correctness of which rests upon the correctness of implementations; it is sometimes not obvious how mathematical theories should be formalised in formal proof systems such as Coq. Even so, computer verifications of mathematical proofs yield additional certainties in mathematics, which do matter especially when one is seriously worried with the status of mathematical proofs that may even be intractable to experts in relevant fields, such as Shinichi Mochizuki's interuniversal Teichimüller theoretic proof of the abc conjecture. Voevodsky [55] proceeds as follows (right after the above passage):

> Interestingly, this new proof was based on an older result of Mark Spivakovsky, who, at about the same time, announced a proof of the resolution of singularities conjecture. Spivakovsky's proof of resolution of singularities was believed to be correct for several years before being found to contain a mistake. The conjecture remains open.

The above case is in pure mathematics, in which researchers are not so familiar with (and could be not so much interested in) the formal logical correctness of proofs. In general, logicians, especially proof theorists, tend to be more strict about the formal correctness of proofs (although ultimately it depends upon the nature of each individual logician or mathematician). It is however not unusual even in foundations of mathematics, and even in proof theory among other things, that proofs published in a respected journal and accepted by the relevant research community turn out to be wrong at the end of the day. The consistency of the naïve comprehension principle in Łukasiewicz logic, for example, was once proved with a complex proof theoretic argument (see [57]), but decades later turned out to include a non-trivial mistake (to be precise, there was a significant gap in the proof, the correction of which is seemingly not possible in any straightforward way; see, e.g., [52]). The same actually happened to Voevodsky himself. Voevodsky [55] explains his experience as follows:

> In 1999–2000, again at the IAS, I was giving a series of lectures, and Pierre Deligne (Professor in the School of Mathematics) was taking notes and checking every step of my arguments. Only then did I discover that the proof of a key lemma in my paper contained a mistake and that the lemma, as stated, could not be salvaged. Fortunately, I was able to prove a weaker and more complicated lemma, which turned out to be sufficient for all applications. A corrected sequence of arguments was published in 2006.

Present-day mathematics, especially those fields that require incredibly deep and diverse background knowledge, such as algebraic geometry and arithmetic geometry, consists of a colossal amount of complex arguments, all of which an ordinary single mathematician, or even a mathematician of the most sophisticated sort, may not be able to check in detail within the limited amount of his/her lifetime. When that is the case, one just has to assume that prior knowledge accumulated by past mathematicians is indeed correct, and build his/her own mathematical theory on the basis of the prior work. Yet doing mathematics in such a way risks the certainty of mathematics, ultimately due to the fallible nature of any human knowledge whatsoever (cf. Cartesian scepticism). As to this, Voevodsky [55] argues as follows, from a more realistic point of view:

> This story got me scared. Starting from 1993, multiple groups of mathematicians studied my paper at seminars and used it in their work and none of them noticed the mistake. And it clearly was not an accident. A technical argument by a trusted author, which is hard to check and looks similar to arguments known to be correct, is hardly ever checked in detail.

Voevodsky was definitely a trusted author, and everyone basically trusts his work when there are no particular reasons to question it. Grothendieck's so-called EGA and SGA lay foundations for algebraic geometry and arithmetic geometry, and yet they consist of thousands of pages in total (see, e.g., [25, 26]). The same applies to more recent works on higher categorical foundations of geometry by Jacob Lurie, the total amount of which adds up to thousands of pages as well (see, e.g., [30] and his subsequent massive amount of works such as [31, 32]). The amount of mathematical publications piling up every year is just overwhelming even when only a single field of pure mathematics is taken into account. No single mathematician could actually check the logical, step-by-step details of all the proofs therein; it is just too much for a single mathematician's relatively short lifetime, so that it can happen that a mathematician just assumes the truth of theorems shown by others and attempts to make progress on the basis of them, which however risks the certainty of mathematics. Voevodsky [55] continues in the following way:

> In October 1998, Carlos Simpson submitted to the arXiv preprint server a paper called "Homotopy Types of Strict 3-groupoids." It claimed to provide an argument that implied that the main result of the "∞-groupoids" paper, which Kapranov and I had published in 1989, cannot be true. Mathematical research currently relies on a complex system of mutual trust based on reputations. By the time Simpson's paper appeared, both Kapranov and I had strong reputations. Simpson's paper created doubts in our result, which led to it being unused by other researchers, but no one came forward and challenged us on it.

Mathematics in actual practice is not the Platonist universe of absolute mathematical truths. Mathematics is not practiced by someone living in the Platonist universe and enjoying an eternal lifetime with no worries about his/her life.

Mathematics is just a fallible human activity of the same kind as any other human activities, as Lakatos, Reichenbach, and other philosophers of science have emphasised the fallible nature of mathematics (or rather mathematical activities; see, e.g., [28,50]). Human factors such as trust and reputations make a difference in mathematical activities just as in any other kind of human activities. Some mathematicians and philosophers would still argue for the universal nature of mathematics, but Voevodsky presumably took this human aspect of mathematics (or mathematical activities) at face value, or he had to do so due to his experience on the fallibility or fragility of mathematics as per above. Voevodsky's aforementioned experience had finally impacted and changed his conception of research at a fundamental level as Voevodsky [55] asserts as follows:

> But to do the work at the level of rigor and precision I felt was necessary would take an enormous amount of effort and would produce a text that would be very hard to read. And who would ensure that I did not forget something and did not make a mistake, if even the mistakes in much more simple arguments take years to uncover? I think it was at this moment that I largely stopped doing what is called "curiosity-driven research" and started to think seriously about the future. When I first started to explore the possibility, computer proof verification was almost a forbidden subject among mathematicians.

This is where the formal verification of mathematics comes into play. There may have been no significant rôle that formal verification could play in more tractable mathematics in earlier centuries. Yet in the highly complex body of knowledge in contemporary mathematics, the methods of formal verification can make a difference just as machine learning is able to make a difference in Big Data Analytics. Contemporary mathematics is some sort of (mathematical) Big Data that a single mathematician cannot really oversee. Mathematics today is definitely a collective enterprise and endeavour across time and place, the entirety of which only exists in history rather than any single mathematician's mind. We need Natural Language Processing to analyse the details of all text that exists in the world (wide web). Just likewise, we need the formal computer verification methods to check and analyse the logical details and interconnections of all theorems that exist in the world, even if they are "forbidden subjects among mathematicians" (perhaps in past generations). Voevodsky [55] proceeds in the following way:

> The primary challenge that needed to be addressed was that the foundations of mathematics were unprepared for the requirements of the task. Formulating mathematical reasoning in a language precise enough for a computer to follow meant using a foundational system of mathematics not as a standard of consistency to establish a few fundamental theorems, but as a tool that can be employed in everyday mathematical work.

Hilbert's foundations of mathematics were conceived for verifying meta-theoretical properties of mathematics such as the consistency of mathematics. Yet Voevodsky's foundations of mathematics are conceived for supporting everyday mathematical practice. Hilbert's could be called idealist foundations of mathematics, and Voevodsky's realist foundations of mathematics. Hilbert's programme basically failed due to Gödel's theorems, and yet Voecodsky's programme can still succeed (although there are different kinds of escapes from Gödel's theorems; e.g., the first incompleteness can be escaped with infinitary logic, logic with a certain type of ω-rule, and the like; the second incompleteness is intensional whilst the first incompleteness is extensional, in the sense that the second incompleteness essentially hinges upon the formalisation details of the so-called provability predicate, some implementations of which allow us to escape from the second incompleteness; or one can also formalise everything within a sequent calculus system without the cut rule in order to escape the second incompleteness, which actually does not cause any unsolvable difficulties, since applications of the cut rule are almost always eliminable in concrete proofs). Voevodsky [55] mentions the deficiencies of traditional foundations of mathematics as follows:

> Historically, the first problems with ZFC could be seen in the decline of the great enterprise of early Bourbaki, which occurred because the main organizational ideas of mathematics of the second half of the twentieth century were based on category theory, and category theory could not be well presented in terms of ZFC. The successes of category theory inspired the idea that categories are "sets in the next dimension" and that the foundation of mathematics should be based on category theory or on its higher-dimensional analogues.

Category theory is even useful for traditional foundations of mathematics such as Hilbert's programme. One can actually give partial realisations of Hilbert's programme whilst not violating Gödel's theorems (see, e.g., Coquand [21,22] and his related works with collaborators), which is actually done via categorical duality theory (see, e.g., [34–37,40,41,46]) by eliminating ideal objects through the duality correspondence between point-set and point-free space (in which points are ideal objects, just as the existence of prime ideals as points in algebraic geometry, in general, hinges upon an indeterministic principle such as the axiom of choice or its weaker version; see, e.g., Coquand [21,22] and his related works with collaborators). Voevodsky [55] finally explicates the following three requirements for the realist foundations of mathematics (which univalent foundations and homotopy type theory are supposed to satisfy):

> [A]ny foundation for mathematics adequate both for human reasoning and for computer verification should have the following three components. The first component is a formal deduction system: a language and rules of manipulating sentences in this language that are purely formal, such that a record of such manipulations can be verified by a computer program. The second component is a structure that provides a meaning to the sentences of this language in terms of mental objects intuitively comprehensible to humans. The third component is a structure that enables humans to encode mathematical ideas in terms of the objects directly associated with the language.

The first requirement is concerned with syntax, the second with semantics, and the third with direct structural encodability of mathematical ideas, which is essential for the realist foundations of mathematics, and which involve some aspects of Human-Computer Interaction in Interactive Theorem Proving Systems, since the structural directness of encodings of ideas ultimately boils down to human-sensitive conditions (such as those about user interface design for mathematicians at the most superficial level). The second requirement is concerned with some human factors as well. Natural semantics for mathematicians, such as the homotopy theoretical interpretations of type theory (especially, the notion of homotopy levels to organise mathematical entities ranging from truth values and propositions, to sets and posets, to groupoids and categories, and to higher analogues of them), or what is natural in the first place, is essentially of human nature. We could thus conclude that Voevodsky was actually concerned with Human-Computer Interaction within the specific context of Mathematics in order to ensure and maintain the certainty and objectivity of mathematical practice (rather than philosophically conceived ideal mathematics as in traditional foundations of mathematics).

3 Shinichi Mochizuki's Interuniversal Teichimüller Theoretic Proof of the ABC Conjecture

Shinichi Mochizuki released a series of preprints on his webpage (see [49]), which give a proof of (a certain form of) the abc conjecture, and Masaki Kashiwara and Akio Tamagawa publicly announced in 2020 that Mochizuki's papers will be published in *Publications of the Research Institute for Mathematical Sciences* (see [16]). They are currently expected to be published during 2021. The publication process has taken nearly ten years, which is unusual even in the mathematical community (in which it is not so unusual that the review process takes more than one year especially when results presented are more substantial or more novel than those of ordinary papers).

Mochizuki is a trusted mathematician of high distinction in the international mathematical community, recognised for his path-breaking work even before the proof of the abc conjecture, including his celebrated achievements that settled the Grothendieck conjecture on anabelian geometry in a remarkable, stronger form than Grothendieck expected. Even so, several mathematicians, such as Peter Scholze, have expressed certain doubts about the correctness of the proof of the abc conjecture (see, e.g., [16]). The proof has long been debated since its first appearance in 2012, and its mathematical status is still agreed upon in the international mathematical community even in 2021. There are apparently no concrete substantial evidences for the incorrectness of the proof, and yet the disagreement still persists for some reason, which seems to be quite an unfortunate situation to all stakeholders and to academe as a whole.

How could we resolve this? There would be various factors in the complications surrounding the proof of the abc conjecture. Mathematics is a human activity, and involved in different human factors as we have discussed above.

Yet at the same time, verifying a proof is a purely mathematical problem. Why is it not possible in the present case? It would be just because the proof is too complex for even the most capable kind of mathematicians to understand in a substantial manner within a reasonable amount of time; a superficial, popular science account, or any pseudo-mathematical simplified account, cannot constitute the rigorous verification or refutation of the proof. The colossal amount of preliminary knowledge required for a genuine understanding of the abc proof allows only a handful of mathematicians to grasp what is actually going on in the proof.

Voevodsky, as a matter of fact, had a similar concern with "how to convince others that my arguments are correct", which is basically the same sort of challenge as the abc proof has been facing. And he had his own solution to the problem, which was his univalent foundations and homotopy type theory, or the formal verification of proofs on the basis of them. Indeed, Voevodsky [55] asserts as follows:

> And I now do my mathematics with a proof assistant. I have a lot of wishes in terms of getting this proof assistant to work better, but at least I don't have to go home and worry about having made a mistake in my work. I know that if I did something, I did it, and I don't have to come back to it nor do I have to worry about my arguments being too complicated or about how to convince others that my arguments are correct. I can just trust the computer.

Mathematics today consists of a highly complex body of knowledge. No single mathematician can actually oversee the mathematical landscape as a whole. It is analogous to a gigantic computer system built by countless engineers collaborating across time and place. No one has the whole picture of massive technical details in his/her single, tiny mind.

The same would even apply to contemporary science in general; the problem of the abc proof, or more precisely, the problem as has been uncovered by the abc proof, could be an instance of the universal problem in the contemporary system of knowledge in contemporary science. Contemporary science is ultimately a collective human endeavour. Collective intelligence in the enterprise of science has been essential since the nineteenth century, just as Helmholtz [27] contends as follows (translation by Weingart [56]):

> No one could oversee the whole of science and keep the threads in one hand and find orientation. The natural result is that each individual researcher is forced to an ever smaller area as his workplace and can only maintain incomplete knowledge of neighbouring areas.

The fragmentation of science has threatened the cohesive unity of science since the nineteenth century specialisation of science (or even since the renaissance modernisation, which has allowed the disenchantment of the world in Max Weber's terms, thus promoting fragmentation as a negative effect of specialisation, which is not necessarily negative per se; specialisation has rather essentially driven the advancement of science, making knowledge production more effective and optimised for each local domain, which however has a negative effect on the global unity of knowledge as well.).

There was the same tendency of fragmentation in mathematics as well. Bourbaki's endeavour on their Éléments de mathématique pursued the unity of mathematics as an antithesis to the fragmentation of mathematics, endorsing the organism view of mathematics as a coherent whole. Bourbaki [15] indeed argues as follows:

> [I]t is legitimate to ask whether this exuberant proliferation makes for the development of a strongly constructed organism, acquiring ever greater cohesion and unity with its new growths [...] In other words, do we have today a mathematic or do we have several mathematics? Although this question is perhaps of greater urgency now than ever before, it is by no means a new one; it has been asked almost from the very beginning of mathematical science. Indeed, quite apart from applied mathematics, there has always existed a dualism between the origins of geometry and of arithmetic [...]

Bourbaki clearly aimed at the unity of mathematics, and succeeded to some extent, especially in the standardisation of mathematical language. As to the last point above, the dualism between arithmetic (or algebra) and geometry is united by duality, as has indeed been done in arithmetic geometry (or algebraic geometry). More generally, categorical dualities exist across different fields of mathematics (and the sciences), and thus evidence the unity of mathematics (and the unity of science).

Even so, it is not a single great scientist who discovers and systematises the whole web of scientific knowledge. It may have been possible up to a certain point in the history of science, but it is practically impossible in science today. Scientific knowledge today, including mathematical knowledge, is some sort of Big Data, which only the computer can analyse as a whole; human agents with limited cognitive capacities only have access to fragments of it. Yet the computer cannot work with informal data, which must be formalised for computational analyses and verifications, which, in turn, is what Voevodsky's programme is about (when regarded as the verification of mathematics programme; there are, of course, other elements of the programme also). In the long run, machine learning systems would become capable of learning even from informal, unorganised data, which would further facilitate Voevodsky's programme.

The sociology of mathematics is complex as the sociology of any other human activity is. Yet the correctness/incorrectness of a proof, however intricate it is, has nothing to do with the sociology of mathematics. The complexity of a proof is arguably no excuse for leaving the truth of a proof to any non-mathematical activity. No authoritarian mathematician, whether he/she trusts the proof or not, has the scientific right to make a final judgement about the validity/invalidity of a proof; the correctness/incorrectness of a proof is no human property. When a proof is disputed, Voevodsky's recommendation is to leave it to formal computer verification rather than human verification, which is more fallible due to the cognitive limits of the human being; or rather the idea ultimately goes back to Leibniz's concept of *characteristica universalis*, which allows us to reduce all truths to some sort of calculus, thus being a sort of general algebra as the so-called alphabets of human thought (aka. algebra of thought):

> [A] kind of general algebra in which all truths of reason would be reduced to a kind of calculus. At the same time, this would be a kind of universal language or writing, though infinitely different from all such languages which have thus far been proposed, for the characters and the words themselves would give directions to reason, and the errors – excepting those of fact – would be only mistakes in calculation. [...] When we lack sufficient data to arrive at certainty in our truths, it would also serve to estimate degrees of probability and to see what is needed to provide this certainty.

Any logical disputes about truths can be resolved via calculation in *characteristica universalis*. The passage above comes from Leibniz's 1714 letter to Nicolas Remond (see [29]), which was written when Leibniz's death was quite near. In the following passage, Leibniz compares *characteristica universalis* with arithmetic and algebra (see [29]):

> [A]lthough learned men have long since thought of some kind of language or universal characteristic by which all concepts and things can be put into beautiful order [...] yet no one has attempted a language or characteristic which includes at once both the arts of discovery and judgement, that is, one whose signs and characters serve the same purpose that arithmetical signs serve for numbers, and algebraic signs for quantities taken abstractly. Yet it does seem that since God has bestowed these two sciences on mankind, he has sought to notify us that a far greater secret lies hidden in our understanding, of which these are but the shadows.

Leibniz is called a "one-man embodiment of the unity of science" (see, e.g., [56]), and *characteristica universalis* was supposed to be a language to support the unity of science. In work by Mochizuki and Voevosky, as well as Grothendieck and Lurie, category theory serves as a foundational language; ideally, category theory could serve as a unifying language for mathematics (and the sciences as recent remarkable advances in applied category theory show; see, e.g., [1–11, 19, 20, 38, 40, 41, 43, 48]).

Computer verification is no harm to mathematics. Unlike the case of the four colour theorem, it is not that the mathematical proof activity is eroded per se by the computer; rather it is that the mathematical proof activity is genuinely supported by the computer. That is to say, there is no erosion of mathematical understanding or explainability in the formal verification of proofs. If the human mathematical community cannot tell the truth of a proof, it can nevertheless let the computer tell, which is essentially Voevodsky's insight stemming from his own experience on the truth of mathematical proofs as we have discussed above. Just as LaTeX is part of mathematical activity today, formal verification via

Coq and others could become part of mathematical activity in the future; in philosophers' terms (see [18]), formal verification tools are part of the extended mind, in particular the extended mathematical mind.

Voevodsky's programme reimagined how foundations of mathematics could be. Mochizuki's Interuniversal Teichimüller Theory sheds new light on foundations mathematics from a different angle. Mochizuki [49], especially the last paper IV, emphasises the algorithmic nature of mathematical (especially, geometric) objects (or their constructions). The last piece of the series of papers giving a proof of the abc conjecture is concerned with algorithmic foundations of mathematics, which does not mean anything like computational or recursion-theoretic foundations of mathematics. They are conceptually akin to categorical computer science rather than any traditional foundations of mathematics or any traditional branch of mathematical logic. There have been both pros and cons for Mochizuki's as well as Voevodsky's understandings of foundations of mathematics. Their knowledge about technicalities in mathematical logic might not necessarily be perfect, but that does not mean their remarks on foundations of mathematics do not include novel ideas to be explored in the mathematical logic community. As Voevodsky's idea about foundations of mathematics has eventually enabled significant advances in foundations of mathematics, Mochizuki's, too, could lead to a new kind of foundations of mathematics.

4   Concluding Remarks: The Human-in-the-Loop View of the Mathematical Landscape

Human-Computer Interaction research has featured the human-in-the-loop view of computer science and engineering, or system science in general. We have argued, in this paper, that the same view applies to mathematics as well as computer science, especially that Voevodsky's concerns in his univalent foundations of mathematics programme, which arguably aims at realist foundations of mathematics rather than traditional idealist ones such as in Hilbert's programme, were close to those in Human-Computer Interaction research as we have discussed above, pursuing the (not necessarily computationally but conceptually) effective and certified treatment of Mathematics qua Big Data. Voevodsky's programme thus aligns, in this specific sense, with recent trends in Machine Learning and Human-Computer Interaction. Voevodsky's programme, moreover, is of significance in terms of clarifying the nature of mathematical understanding and explanation, which also aligns with the recent trend of Explainable Artificial Intelligence (XAI) and Interpretable Machine Learning (IML). Mathematics or mathematical knowledge accumulated through the history of human civilisation gives a specific form of (Mathematical) Big Data, and Voevodsky's programme problematises the computational methodology of ensuring and maintaining the certainty and objectivity of knowledge therein (especially in the long run), which would arguably help address puzzling controversies in the mathematical community, especially those concerning the correctness of mathematical proofs which are intractable to most human mathematicians; the computer verification of them, or artificial mathematicians' verification, could resolve complications involved and thereby firmly establish their mathematical truth even if human mathematicians cannot verify the Big Data of mathematical proofs concerned. It may not be easy at all to verify Mochizuki's interuniversal Teichimüller theoretic proof of the abc conjecture in such a manner, but if it could have been accomplished, it would certainly be a significant, path-breaking achievement in both pure mathematics and its formal verification.

Let us finally summarise the difference between Hilbert's programme and Voevodsky's programme. Hilbert's programme was concerned with reductionist foundations of mathematics in the sense that it aimed at reducing the certainty of the whole mathematics to the certainty of Hilbertian finitist mathematics (which is what is called the Hilbert finitism, regarded by Tait [51] as being formally equivalent with Primitive Recursive Arithmetic), i.e., proving that infinitary ideal mathematics is a conservative extension of finitary real mathematics (as Hilbert calls it), which is equivalent to the consistency of (infinitary ideal) mathematics as in the popular science account of Hilbert's programme. According to Hilbert, ideal elements may be used in mathematics, and yet must be eliminated; Hilbert's view, thus, is also called Hilbert's instrumentalism with the possible implication that infiniary mathematics is not real and merely instrumental. It should be remarked that the elimination of ideal objects is a particular method to prove the conservativity of infinitary mathematics over finitary mathematics. In the context of categorical duality theory as we explained above, ideal elements correspond to set-theoretical points, and doing geometry without points allows us to reduce the consistency strength of mathematics, in particular geometry and topology; the duality-theoretical Hilbert's programme is implemented, for example, in scheme theory in algebraic geometry as well as a variety of issues in general topology. Voevodsky's programme, by contrast, is concerned with algebraic topology, in particular homotopy theory, from the outset, and the notion of h-levels, from a homotopy-theoretical perspective, allows us to classify mathematics from logic, to sets, to categories (or groupoids as being more fundamental than categories), and to higher categories (higher groupoids). It should be noted that category theory, as both Voevosky and Lawvere have shown, is a generalisation of set theory, rather than an alternative to it. Voevodsky's programme is not obsessed with the consistency of mathematics or the conservativity of infinitary mathematics over finitary mathematics. It is rather concerned with structuralist foundations of mathematics as the univalence axiom is a structuralist principle. Yet categorical structuralist foundations are not really monolithic. Lawvere's categorical structuralist foundations are foundationalist in the sense as has been criticised in philosophy of mathematics. Voevodsky's categorical structuralist foundations are clearly not. Fondationalist foundations are the foundations that give the idealised absolute foundations of mathematics. Voevodsky's univalent foundations are rather realist foundations as we have discussed above. In particular, there is no foundationalist presupposition that there is an absolute (ontological or epistemological) basis of mathematics as a whole. Voevodsky's programme focuses upon the formal verification of each proof in mathematical practice rather than the consistency proof of the whole mathematics (if it exists at all; no such whole might not exist without the idealisation of mathematical activity). There is a recent trend in philosophy of mathematics, called the philosophy of mathematical practice (see, e.g., [33]; it focuses upon issues of significance to the practising mathematician whereas the orthodox philosophy of mathematics, roughly since the late twentieth century, has made a radical departure from mathematical practice). Voevodsky's univalent foundations have an affinity with that sort of foundational issues in mathematical practice rather than those in traditional philosophy of mathematics. We have only discussed, in the present paper, limited facets of Voevodsky's univalent programme and their significance in foundations of mathematics; a full-fledged elucidation of them is yet to be explored and completed elsewhere.

References

1. Abramsky, S.: Domain theory in logical form. In: Proceedings of the 2nd Annual IEEE Symposium on Logic in Computer Science, pp. 47–53 (1987)
2. Abramsky, S., Coecke, B.: A categorical semantics of quantum protocols. In: Proceedings of the 19th Annual IEEE Symposium on Logic in Computer Science, pp. 415–425 (2004)
3. Abramsky, S.: Temperley-Lieb Algebra: from Knot Theory to logic and computation via quantum mechanics. In: Mathematics of Quantum Computing and Quantum Technology, pp. 415–458. Taylor & Francis (2008)
4. Abramsky, S., Brandenburger, A.: The sheaf-theoretic structure of non-locality and contextuality. New J. Phys. **13**, 113036 (2011)
5. Abramsky, S., Hardy, L.: Logical Bell inequalities. Phys. Rev. A **85**, 062114 (2012)
6. Abramsky, S.: Relational databases and Bell's Theorem. In: Tannen, V., Wong, L., Libkin, L., Fan, W., Tan, W.-C., Fourman, M. (eds.) In Search of Elegance in the Theory and Practice of Computation. LNCS, vol. 8000, pp. 13–35. Springer, Heidelberg (2013). https://doi.org/10.1007/978-3-642-41660-6_2
7. Abramsky, S., et al.: Robust constraint satisfaction and local hidden variables in quantum mechanics. In: Proceedings of the Twenty-Third International Joint Conference on Artificial Intelligence, pp. 440–446 (2013)
8. Abramsky, S., Sadrzadeh, M.: Semantic unification. In: Casadio, C., Coecke, B., Moortgat, M., Scott, P. (eds.) Categories and Types in Logic, Language, and Physics. LNCS, vol. 8222, pp. 1–13. Springer, Heidelberg (2014). https://doi.org/10.1007/978-3-642-54789-8_1
9. Abramsky, S.: Intensionality definability and computation. Outstanding Contrib. Logic **5**, 121–142 (2014)
10. Abramsky, S.: Arrow's theorem by Arrow theory. In: Logic Without Borders: Essays on Set Theory, Model Theory, Philosophical Logic and Philosophy of Mathematics, pp. 15–30, de Gruyter (2015)
11. Abramsky, S., Winschel, V.: Coalgebraic analysis of subgame-perfect equilibria in infinite games without discounting. Math. Struct. Comput. Sci. **27**, 751–761 (2017)
12. Arrieta, A.B., et al.: Explainable Artificial Intelligence (XAI): concepts, taxonomies, opportunities and challenges toward responsible AI. Inf. Fusion **58**, 82–115 (2020)
13. Awodey, S.: Structuralism, Invariance, and Univalence. Philosophia Math. **22**, 1–11 (2014)
14. Awodey, S., Warren, M.A.: Homotopy theoretic models of identity types. Math. Proc. Camb. Phil. Soc. **146**, 45–55 (2009)

15. Bourbaki, N.: The architecture of mathematics. Am. Math. Mon. **4**, 221–232 (1950)
16. Castelvecchi, D.: Mathematical proof that rocked number theory will be published. Nature **580**, 177 (2020). https://www.nature.com/articles/d41586-020-00998-2
17. Chlipala, A.: Certified Programming with Dependent Types: A Pragmatic Introduction to the Coq Proof Assistant. MIT Press (2013)
18. Clark, A., Chalmers, D.: The extended mind. Analysis **58**, 7–19 (1998)
19. Coecke, B.: Automated quantum reasoning: non-logic - semi-logic - hyper-logic. In: Proceedings of AAAI Spring Symposium: Quantum Interaction, pp. 31–38 (2007)
20. Coecke, B., Sadrzadeh, M., Clark, S.: Mathematical foundations for a compositional distributional model of meaning. Linguist. Anal. **36**, 345–384 (2010)
21. Coquand, T.: A logical approach to abstract algebra. In: Cooper, S.B., Löwe, B., Torenvliet, L. (eds.) CiE 2005. LNCS, vol. 3526, pp. 86–95. Springer, Heidelberg (2005). https://doi.org/10.1007/11494645_12
22. Coquand, T.: Space of valuations. Ann. Pure Appl. Logic **157**, 97–109 (2009)
23. Hofmann, M., Streicher, T.: The groupoid interpretation of type theory, Twenty-five years of constructive type theory. Oxford Logic Guides, vol. 36, pp. 83–111, Oxford University Press (1998)
24. Gonthier, G.: Formal proof – the four-color theorem. Not. AMS **55**, 1382–1393 (2008)
25. Grothendieck, A., Dieudonne, J.: Éléments de géométrie algébrique. IHES (1960–1967)
26. Grothendieck, S A.: éminaire de Géométrie Algébrique du Bois Marie. IHES (1960–1967)
27. von Hemholtz, H.: Vorträge und Reden, vol. 1, 4th edn. Vieweg und Sohn (1896)
28. Lakatos, I.: Proofs and Refutations. Cambridge University Press, Cambridge (1976)
29. Loemker, J.: Leibniz: Philosophical Papers and Letters. D. Reidel, Synthese Historical Library (1969)
30. Lurie, J.: Higher Topos Theory. Princeton University Press (2009)
31. Lurie, J.: Higher Algebra (2017). https://www.math.ias.edu/lurie/. Accessed 12 Feb 2021
32. Lurie, J.: Spectral Algebraic Geometry (2018). https://www.math.ias.edu/lurie/. Accessed 12 Feb 2021
33. Mancosu, P.: The Philosophy of Mathematical Practice. Oxford University Press (2008)
34. Maruyama, Y.: Fundamental results for Pointfree convex geometry. Ann. Pure Appl. Logic **161**, 1486–1501 (2010)
35. Maruyama, Y.: Natural duality, modality, and coalgebra. J. Pure Appl. Algebra **216**, 565–580 (2012)
36. Maruyama, Y.: From operational Chu duality to Coalgebraic quantum symmetry. In: Heckel, R., Milius, S. (eds.) CALCO 2013. LNCS, vol. 8089, pp. 220–235. Springer, Heidelberg (2013). https://doi.org/10.1007/978-3-642-40206-7_17
37. Maruyama, Y.: Categorical Duality theory: with applications to domains, convexity, and the distribution monad. Leibniz Int. Proc. Inf. **23**, 500–520 (2013)
38. Maruyama, Y.: Prior's Tonk, notions of logic, and levels of inconsistency: vindicating the Pluralistic Unity of Science in the light of categorical logical positivism. Synthese **193**, 3483–3495 (2016)
39. Maruyama, Y.: Categorical harmony and paradoxes in proof-theoretic semantics. In: Piecha, T., Schroeder-Heister, P. (eds.) Advances in Proof-Theoretic Semantics. TL, vol. 43, pp. 95–114. Springer, Cham (2016). https://doi.org/10.1007/978-3-319-22686-6_6

40. Maruyama, Y.: Meaning and duality: from categorical logic to quantum physics. D.Phil. thesis, University of Oxford (2017)
41. Maruyama, Y.: The dynamics of duality: a fresh look at the philosophy of duality. In: RIMS Kokyuroku (Proceedings of RIMS, Kyoto Univesity), vol. 2050, pp. 77–99 (2017)
42. Maruyama, Y.: Compositionality and contextuality: the symbolic and statistical theories of meaning. In: Bella, G., Bouquet, P. (eds.) CONTEXT 2019. LNCS (LNAI), vol. 11939, pp. 161–174. Springer, Cham (2019). https://doi.org/10.1007/978-3-030-34974-5_14
43. Maruyama, Y.: Foundations of mathematics: from Hilbert and Wittgenstein to the categorical unity of science. In: Wuppuluri, S., da Costa, N. (eds.) WITTGENSTEINIAN (adj.). TFC, pp. 245–274. Springer, Cham (2020). https://doi.org/10.1007/978-3-030-27569-3_15
44. Maruyama, Y.: The conditions of artificial general intelligence: logic, autonomy, resilience, integrity, morality, emotion, embodiment, and embeddedness. In: Goertzel, B., Panov, A.I., Potapov, A., Yampolskiy, R. (eds.) AGI 2020. LNCS (LNAI), vol. 12177, pp. 242–251. Springer, Cham (2020). https://doi.org/10.1007/978-3-030-52152-3_25
45. Maruyama, Y.: Topological duality via maximal spectrum functor. Comm. Algebra **48**, 2616–2623 (2020)
46. Maruyama, Y.: Universal stone duality via the concept of topological dualizability and its applications to many-valued logic. In: Proceedings of FUZZ-IEEE. IEEE Computer Society (2020)
47. Maruyama, Y.: Symbolic and statistical theories of cognition: towards integrated artificial intelligence. In: Cleophas, L., Massink, M. (eds.) SEFM 2020. LNCS, vol. 12524, pp. 129–146. Springer, Cham (2021). https://doi.org/10.1007/978-3-030-67220-1_11
48. Maruyama, Y.: Duality, Intensionality, and Contextuality, accepted for publication in a volume of Outstanding Contributions to Logic. Springer (2021)
49. Mochizuki, S.: Inter-Universal Teichmuller Theory I-IV (2012). http://www.kurims.kyoto-u.ac.jp/motizuki/. Accessed 12 Feb 2021
50. Reichenbach, H.: Selected Writings: 1909–1953, Reidel (1978)
51. Tait, W.: Finitism. J. Philos. **78**, 524–546 (1981)
52. Terui, K.: A flaw in R.B. White's article "The consistency of the axiom of comprehension in the infinite-valued predicate logic of Łukasiewicz" (2014). http://www.kurims.kyoto-u.ac.jp/terui/whitenew.pdf. Accessed 12 Feb 2020
53. Thurston, W.P.: On proof and progress in mathematics. Bull. AMS **30**, 161–177 (1994)
54. Univalent Foundations Program, Homotopy Type Theory: Univalent Foundations of Mathematics, Princeton IAS (2013)
55. Voevodsky, V.: The Origins and Motivations of Univalent Foundations, Princeton IAS (2014). https://www.ias.edu/ideas/2014/voevodsky-origins. Accessed 10 Feb 2021
56. Weingart, P.: A short history of knowledge formations. In: The Oxford Handbook of Interdisciplinarity, pp. 3–14. Oxford University Press (2010)
57. White, R.B.: The consistency of the axiom of comprehension in the infinite-valued predicate logic of Łukasiewicz. J. Philos. Log. **8**, 509–534 (1979)

Generalization Training Support System Promoting Focusing Target Changes

Kosuke Minai[1]($\boxtimes$) and Tomoko Kojiri[2]

[1] Graduate School of Science and Engineering, Kansai University, 3-3-35 Yamate-cho, Suita, Osaka 564-8680, Japan
k418139@kansai-u.ac.jp
[2] Faculty of Engineering Science, Kansai University, 3-3-35 Yamate-cho, Suita, Osaka 564-8680, Japan
kojiri@kansai-u.ac.jp

Abstract. Generalization extracts common features from target concepts and rephrases them into an abstract concept. This operation is often used to acquire knowledge from examples that use it. For instance, when we grasp the usage situation of an English word, we generalize the words that are often used with a target English word (target concepts) to derive the word that represents the usage situation (abstract concept). However, sometimes we are not able to determine the common features and cannot derive the abstract concept, especially when the number of target concepts is large. For such cases, focusing on a subset of target concepts provides an opportunity to notice common features, since it is easier to find common features with a small number of target concepts. To establish this technique of minimizing the focus targets, this research aims to develop a generalization training support system that provides target concepts and promotes focusing on their subsets when we fail to derive an abstract concept from the given target concepts.

Keywords: Generalization support · Training system · Focusing target change · English word learning

1 Introduction

Generalization extracts common features from target concepts and rephrases them into an abstract concept [1]. This operation is often used when we acquire new knowledge from examples or organize knowledge that we understand as target concepts [2, 3]. By grasping the common features of examples as new knowledge, we are able to apply that new knowledge to other situations that have the same features.

One learning situation that utilizes this generalization is words learning during language learning, e.g., the learning of English words. Words have a situation to which they can apply, so it is important to understand the scenes or situations in which the words can be used. When we learn English, we often use dictionaries [4]. Dictionaries provide definitions and translations of words, and example sentences, but often do not clearly

© Springer Nature Switzerland AG 2021
S. Yamamoto and H. Mori (Eds.): HCII 2021, LNCS 12766, pp. 92–103, 2021.
https://doi.org/10.1007/978-3-030-78361-7_8

describe the usage situation of the words. As a result, we cannot properly use English words that are translated into Japanese. Bijami et al. introduced peer feedback activities between learners to point out the inappropriate use of English words [5]. In this method, whether the learners are able to acquire the correct use of the English words depends on their partners, so correct usage situations are not always learned. We need a learning method for acquiring the usage situation.

Example sentences represent examples of usage situation. If we can generalize the situation of the example sentences, we are able to discriminate the usage situation of the English words even if they have the same definition.

Our previous study proposed an English-words learning method to extract words (keywords) that represent usage situations from example sentences and generalize them. In addition, we developed a learning support system to learn English words by following our proposed method [6]. This system was effective in discriminating the usage situation of English words of the same definition compared with other English words in memorization support systems [7]. However, if we are not able to generalize keywords, we cannot grasp the usage situation. To address this, our system provides sentences that explain the concepts of keywords as hints. Despite the hints, however, it is sometimes still difficult for us to generalize keywords even if we know their meaning. Additional support for monitoring the generalization process and deriving one abstract concept is necessary. This research clarifies an effective method for deriving the abstract concept and describes the design of the generalization training system based on this method.

Several researchers have endeavored to support a generalization process [8, 9]. These studies developed systems that give learners concrete and abstract concepts, and let the learners connect them by generalization relations: for example, concepts of the names of plants and their types. When learners connect incorrect concepts, the systems create images that represent the incorrect phenomena based on the incorrect relationship and show them to the learners. Based on the images, learners are able to understand the generalization relations of given concepts, but are not able to generate abstract concepts by themselves.

The generalization process extracts the common features (from here, we call these features *attributes*) of target concepts and replaces them with abstract concepts that contain these attributes. From this viewpoint, one reason for not deriving the abstract concept is that we cannot recognize attributes that are common to all given target concepts. On the other hand, we might be able to derive common attributes if the number of target concepts is small. If we could derive the common attributes from a subset of the given target concepts, and these common attributes happen to be the common attributes of the rest of the target concepts as well, they become the attributes of the abstract concept. Based on this idea, we propose a mechanism that monitors the generalization process, promotes focusing on a subset of target concepts from which we have not derived the abstract concept, and finds the common attributes when we meet an impasse situation.

This research focuses on generalization for understanding the usage situation of English words [6] and develops a generalization training system based on the given English words. When we select English words, this system gives us the words in example sentences that represent the usage situation as target concepts to assist us in learning the usage situation. It also holds the hierarchy of concepts from the abstract concept to the target concepts as the correct answer. In the correct answer, the intermediate nodes correspond to the abstract concepts that can be derived from the subset of the given concepts. The attributes of such intermediate nodes can be found easily. Therefore, the proposed system points out the child nodes of the intermediate node as focusing target concepts.

2 Approach for Supporting Generalization

2.1 Generalization Difficulties and Method to Overcome These Difficulties

In generalization, common attributes of target concepts are extracted to form an abstract concept. The abstract concept is a concept that has attribute values common to all target concepts. Figure 1 shows an example of generalization when *brick*, *cookie*, *bread*, and *cake* are given as target concepts. It is assumed that there are three attributes, specifically, *the way to generate*, *hardness*, and *the way to use*. Since all target concepts have the same attribute value "baking" for the attribute *the way to generate*, *something baked* is generated as their abstract concept.

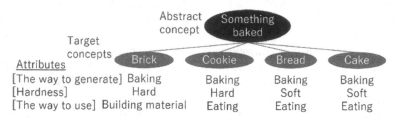

Fig. 1. Example of generalization

When the attributes that are common to all target concepts are not obvious, we cannot generate the abstract concept properly. In such case, if we focus on a subset of the target concepts and derive their abstract concept, we may notice the common attribute that can be applied to the rest of the target concepts. For instance, let us suppose that we fail to notice the attribute *the way to generate* of *brick*. When we focus on *bread* and *cake*, find that they are both baked goods, and derive *something baked* as their abstract concept, we can see *brick* from the viewpoint of *the way to generate* and may find that *brick* is also baked. Then, *something baked* becomes the abstract concept of *brick* as well. In this way, in order to recognize attributes that are not noticed, it is effective to focus on a subset of target concepts and apply discovered attributes to other concepts.

2.2 Overview of Generalization Training Support System

In this research, we develop a generalization training system that provides awareness of new attributes by letting us focus on a subset of target concepts. We then verify the effectiveness of this proposed awareness method. The target domain is to understand the usage situation of English words.

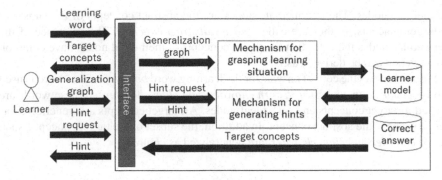

Fig. 2. System configuration

Figure 2 shows the system configuration. The user of the system is called a learner, since he/she trains to acquire the generalization method using the system.

In order to support generalization, the system must know which abstract concepts are derived from given target concepts and indicate the subset of the target concepts whose abstract concept may be easier to derive. To do so, the system has a correct usage situation (*correct answer*) that indicates the relations between given target concepts and their abstract concept for the learning word. It also has abstract concepts of the subsets of the target concepts. The correct answer is prepared for each learning word using a concept dictionary that describes the superordinate and subordinate concepts of the concepts.

The system starts when a learner selects a learning word to obtain the usage situation as training contents. Currently, the learner must select a word from the list of available words whose correct answers are already in the system. When the learning word is chosen, the system gets the words that represent the usage situation as target concepts from the correct answer and presents them to the learner.

The interface provides an environment where a learner can externalize the process of generalization using a graph structure called a *generalization graph*, which was proposed in our previous research [6]. When a learner is not able to derive the abstract concept by himself/herself and requests a hint, the mechanism for grasping the learning situation compares the learner's generalization graph with the correct answer and creates a learner model. According to the learner model, the mechanism for generating hints determines a subset of target concepts and provides it as hints.

3 Generalization Training Support System

3.1 Correct Answer

The correct answer represents the relations between the learning word's usage situation (*abstract concept*) and the keywords that represent the example situation (*target concepts*). It forms a tree structure, where the root node corresponds to the abstract concept and leaf nodes show the target concepts. The link represents the generalization relation, which means that the parent node is derived by generalizing its child nodes. It also has intermediate nodes. The intermediate nodes are the abstract concepts of the subset of the target concepts, so they are called *partial-abstract concepts*. The existence of the intermediate nodes indicates that the target concepts of their child nodes have common attributes that can be derived easily.

Figure 3 shows the correct answer for the learning word *boil down*. This word is used with *vegetable soup*, *vichyssoise*, *corn chowder*, and *clam chowder*, so these words are selected as target concepts and set as leaf nodes. All target concepts are generalized as *soup*, so *soup* is the abstract concept. In addition, the subset of the target concepts, such as *corn chowder* and *clam chowder*, are generalized as *chowder*.

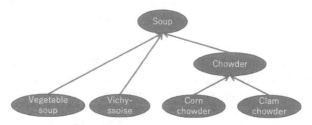

Fig. 3. Example of correct answer

3.2 Generalization Graph

The generalization graph represents the generalized relations between concepts and is created when learners generalize target concepts. The generalization graph consists of nodes that represent concepts and directed links that show the generalization relation. Nodes at the bottom of the directed link correspond with the target concepts to be generalized and the top of the directed link is the abstract concept. Figure 4 shows an example of a generalization graph. It shows that *corn chowder* and *clam chowder* are generalized, and the partial-abstract concept *chowder* is generated.

Fig. 4. Example of generalization graph

At the beginning of the learning, only the target concept nodes are prepared on the generalization graph. The learner can add nodes by generalizing existing nodes and the generalized nodes become the bottom of the directed link. The generalization graph is completed when the node that is connected to all nodes of the target concepts given at the beginning is generated.

3.3 Learner Model

The learner model represents whether a learner can derive the abstract concept and partial-abstract concepts in the correct answer. Each node other than the leaf nodes in the correct answer takes three values: *derived*, *not-derived*, and *misunderstanding*.

The learner model compares the correct answer with the learner's generalized graph. When nodes are created by the learner, the target concepts linked to the nodes in the generalization graph and the target concepts that are descendant nodes of each intermediate node in the correct answer are compared. If their target concepts are the same, the corresponding intermediate nodes in the correct answer are considered to be derived and are set as *derived*. If the target concepts in the correct answer are the subset of those in the learner's generalization graph, the value of the node is set as *misunderstanding*. For all other cases, the values of the nodes are set as *not-derived*.

3.4 Mechanism for Generating Hints

Narrowing down the target concepts to focus on is effective for detecting the common attributes. Based on this assumption, the mechanism for generating hints selects the subset of target nodes to consider generalization according to the learner model.

The leaf nodes of the descendant of the *not-derived* and *misunderstanding* intermediate nodes are candidates of the hint. If there are multiple intermediate nodes whose values are *not-derived* or *misunderstanding*, the *misunderstanding* nodes are selected prior to the *not-derived* nodes, because it may be easier for learners to find additional attributes. If there is more than one *not-derived* node or *misunderstanding* node, the one whose number of leaf nodes in their descendant nodes is the smallest is chosen because it is easier to find common attributes when the number of target concepts is small. If the number of leaf nodes is the same, one is randomly selected.

Figure 5a shows the correct answer and Fig. 5b is the generalization graph created by the learner. In this example, node A in the correct answer is derived because the same target concepts are connected to A and A'. Nodes B, C, D, and E in the correct answer are judged as *not-derived*, so their leaf nodes are hint candidates. There are two leaf nodes for nodes B and C, four for D, and six for E, so the leaf nodes of either B or C are given as hints.

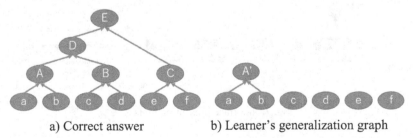

a) Correct answer   b) Learner's generalization graph

Fig. 5. Examples of correct answer and learner's generalization graph

4   Prototype System

We implemented the proposed system with C#. When the system starts, the start screen is displayed and an English word of which the learners can learn the usage situation can be selected from a word list. After the word is selected, the interface for creating the generalization graph appears (Fig. 6). At this time, the leaf nodes of the correct answer are displayed as target concepts in the generalization graph display area. Example sentences using each target concept are shown in the example display area.

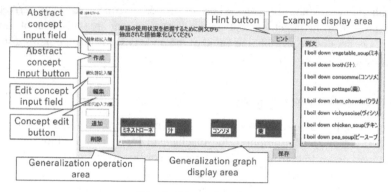

Fig. 6. System interface

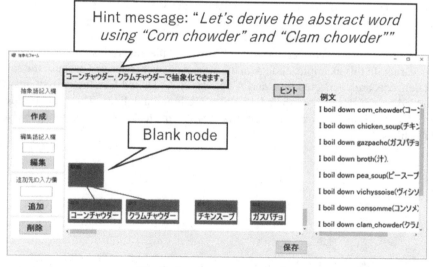

Fig. 7. Interface presenting hints

By selecting the nodes in the generalization graph, inputting the abstract concept in the abstract concept input field, and pushing the abstract concept input button in the generalization operation area, a node of the abstract concept is created in the generalization graph display area and links are attached from the selected nodes to the created node. When one node is selected, a new concept is entered in the concept edit input field, and the concept edit button is pressed, the concept of the selected node is edited.

When the hint button is pushed, the system judges the learner's generalization graph and presents a hint. Figure 7 shows an interface in which a hint is presented. It indicates the subset of the leaf nodes to focus on by the message. In addition, a blank node corresponding to the intermediate node that the learner should derive based on the message is displayed in the generalization graph display area.

5 Evaluation Experiment

5.1 Overview

We conducted an experiment to evaluate the effectiveness of the proposed hint. To verify the hint's effectiveness, we prepared another system without the mechanism for generating hints. We call our proposed system System A and the system without the mechanism for generating hints System B. We asked nine university students to learn the usage situation of English words twice using Systems A and B.

Table 1 shows the English words that were prepared as learning words. In the experiment, the students were first asked to derive the abstract concept of given words using

Table 1. Table captions should be placed above the tables.

ID	Learning word	Target concepts	Abstract concept
1	Write	Missive, Simple sentence, Complex sentence, Compound sentence, Plain sentence, Question, Encyclopedia, Fan letter, Form letter, Public, Open letter, Chain letter, Aviation letter, Solicitation, Commercial letter of credit, Traveler letter of credit, Balance sheet, Checkbook, General ledger, Subledger, Diary inventory, Wage payment roster	Document
2	Draw	Pen painting, Cityscape, Smear, Landscape, Mural, Oil painting, Sand painting, Seascape, Still life, Trompe l'oeil, Watercolor, Argyle, Linoleum print, Polka dot, Pyrograph, Triskelion, Floor plan, Venn diagram, Design, Diagram, Draft, Spots, Pirate skull, Dots, Pictograms, Stars and Stripes, Nobori, Pirate flag, National flag, Confederate flag, White flag	Drawing
3	Win	Popularity voting, Chess match, Dive, Final, Quarterfinals, Semifinals, Test match, Wrestling, Games, Races, Wins, Field tests, Spelling contests, Selection Games, Road games, Home games, Practice games, Double headers, Bicycle races, Dog races, Suburbs, Horse races, Scratch races, Continuation, Loser revival, Grand prix, Rally	Match
4	Defeat	Athlete, Gymnast, Professional, Runner, Sniper, Skater, Skier, Soccer player, Striker, Swimmer, Golfer, Seed, Stringer, Victor, Champion, King, Winner, Enemy, Batter, Major leaguer, Kicker, Linebacker, Lineman, Infielder, Outfielder, Southpaw, Right arm pitcher	Contestant

System B (Step 1). If the students were able to derive the abstract concept, which means they had already acquired the usage situation of the word, their learning word was changed. If the students were not able to derive the abstract concept, they were asked to derive the abstract words of the same word using System A (Step 2). After completing Step 2, they were asked to answer a questionnaire (Step 3).

The questionnaire asked about the effectiveness of the presented hints for generalization and the operability of the system. Table 2 shows the items in the questionnaire. Question 1 asks whether the presented hints are effective and Question 2 asks whether the system was easy to use. For both questions, students were asked to select "Yes" or "No" and to describe their reasoning.

Table 2. Questionnaire items

Question	Content
1	Did you find any helpful hints about generalization?
2	Was it easy to manipulate the interface?

5.2 Results

One student was able to derive an abstract concept for all learning words prepared in Table 1. We therefore discuss our results for the other eight students. Tables 3 and 4 show the results of Step 2. Table 5 shows the number of times the hint button was pushed. Table 6 indicates the average time taken for all operations and that for operations just after using the hint function. Table 7 describes the questionnaire results.

Table 3. Learning result of Step 2 (Students 1 to 4)

Student	1	2	3	4
Learning word ID	4	2	4	1
Generated abstract concept	Characteristic	Pattern	Human	Write

As shown in Tables 3 and 4, seven students succeeded in deriving one abstract concept in Step 2. Although Student 7 generated the same abstract concept with the correct answer, almost all abstract concepts generated by the students seemed related to the correct answer.

Table 5 shows the number of times that students used the hint function and Table 6 shows the average time (seconds) for taking every operation and that for taking operations just after the hints were provided. As shown in Table 5, all students used the hint functions

Table 4. Learning result of Step 2 (Students 5 to 8)

Student	5	6	7	8
Learning word	2	1	3	2
Generated abstract concept	Picture	Sentences	Match	–

Table 5. Number of times the hint button was used

Student	1	2	3	4	5	6	7	8
Number of times the hint button was used	3	3	5	5	8	4	3	5

Table 6. Average time (seconds) for each operation and for operations just after pushing the hint button

Student	1	2	3	4	5	6	7	8
All operations	42.05	58.8	58.43	47.04	97.65	114.9	87	57.72
Operations after hint button	23.5	93	70.4	80.6	87.25	152	79.66	21.5

Table 7. Questionnaire results

Student	1	2	3	4	5	6	7	8
Question 1	Y	Y	Y	Y	Y	Y	N	N
Question 2	Y	N	N	N	Y	Y	N	N

more than three times. However, as shown in Table 6, the time for taking operations decreased for only four students. On the other hand, according to Question 1 in Table 7, six out of the eight students who derived an abstract concept answered that the hints given by the system were helpful. For example, Student 1 commented that "By deriving the abstract concept based on the given hints, I could derive abstract concepts of the other target concepts as well." This demonstrates that the student felt that the given hints were effective. These results show that hints that encourage us to change focusing target concepts might be effective for deriving an abstract concept that is similar to the correct answer, but that it was not easy to derive the abstract concept immediately.

Turning to the results of Student 8, who could not derive an abstract concept in Step 2, this student was unable to generalize target concepts even after hints were presented. Figure 8 shows a part of the learner's generalization graph, which was finally created by Student 8, and Fig. 9 shows a part of the correct answer of *Draw*. Student 8 generated *Pattern* and *Symbol*, which matched the correct answer. However, these were derived from different target concepts than those in the correct answer. Therefore, the system judged that *Pattern* and *Symbol* were not derived yet and presented hints to encourage the derivation of these words. This indicates the method's limitation of judging the derived abstract concepts only by the number of correct leaf nodes.

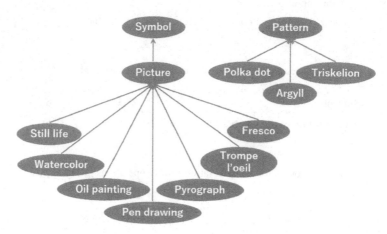

Fig. 8. Part of student 8's generalization graph

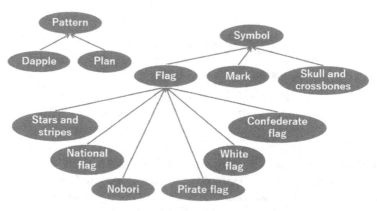

Fig. 9. Part of correct answer of Draw

Let's evaluate the operability of the system. According to the result of question 2 in Table 7, six out of eight students thought our system was difficult to use. Many comments were given to the generalization graph display area. Since the generalization graph display area of this system cannot be enlarged or reduced, the whole generalization graph cannot be seen at a glance when its size got large. In addition, since all links are drawn with the same color, it was difficult to recognize which nodes were connected to which links. In the future, it is necessary to improve the visibility of the generalization graph.

6 Conclusion

In this research, in order to support the acquisition of generalization methods, this research proposed the hints for changing the focusing targets by indicating the subset of target concepts. In addition, this research developed the generalization training support system that gives the target concepts to generalize and promotes focusing target changes to subsets of them in the context of learning the usage situation of English words. As a result of the evaluation experiment, the proposed hints were effective in overcoming the deadlock of the generalization. However, since the number of the participants of the experiment was small, we need further experiments to evaluate the effectiveness of the hints and the system.

In the evaluation experiment, many students could not fully understand the words given as target concepts and searched meaning of them through the Internet. We cannot generalize the words that we do not understand the exact meaning of. In order to cope with the situation, the mechanism for proposing the meaning of the concepts as hints should be developed and be embedded in the system.

References

1. Angryk, R.A., Petry, F.E.: Consistent fuzzy concept hierarchies for attribute generalization. In: Proceedings of the IASTED International Conference on Information and Knowledge Sharing, pp. 158–163 (2003)
2. Crandall, K.L., Wickenheiser, A.M.: Controlling parent systems through swarms using abstraction. IEEE Trans. Control Netw. Syst. 7(1), 210–220 (2020)
3. Thain, D., Moretti, C., Bui, H., Yu, L., Chawla, N.P.: Flynn: Using small abstractions to program large distributed systems. In: IEEE Fourth International Conference on eScience, pp. 723–724 (2008)
4. Chen, N.-S., Quadir, B., Teng, D.C.: A novel approach of learning english with robot for elementary school students. In: Chang, M., Hwang, W.Y., Chen, M.-P., Müller, W. (eds.) Edutainment 2011. LNCS, vol. 6872, pp. 309–316. Springer, Heidelberg (2011). https://doi.org/10.1007/978-3-642-23456-9_58
5. Bijami, M., Kashef, S.H., Sharafinejad, M.: Peer feedback in learning english writing: advantages and disadvantages. J. Stud. Educ. 3(4), 91–97 (2013)
6. Kojiri, T., Yamada, T.: Generalization support environment for understanding ways to use english words. Res. Pract. Technol. Enhanced Learn. 15(22) (2020)
7. Wicha, S., Tangmongkhonnam, K., Saelim, K., Jongkorklang, T., Khant, K.: The developing of active english learning system for local entrepreneurs. In: International Conference on Digital Arts, Media and Technology, pp. 183–188 (2017)
8. Tomoto, T., Imai, I., Horiguchi, T., Hirashima, T.: Error-based simulation in concept mapping for learning about meaning of class structure. In: Proceedings of 20th International Conference on Computers in Education, pp. 9–11 (2012)
9. Horiguchi, T., Imai, I., Tomoto, T., Hirashima, T.: Error-based simulation for error-awareness in learning mechanics: an evaluation. J. Educ. Technol. Soc. 17(3), 1–13 (2014)

Proposal of Learning Support System for Improving Skills in Inferring Background Knowledge in Conversation

Tomohiro Mogi[1], Kento Koike[1], Takahito Tomoto[2]([✉]), Tomoya Horiguchi[3], and Tsukasa Hirashima[4]

[1] Graduate School of Engineering, Tokyo Polytechnic University, Atsugi, Kanagawa, Japan
[2] Faculty of Engineering, Tokyo Polytechnic University, Atsugi, Kanagawa, Japan
[3] Graduate School of Maritime Sciences, Kobe University, Kobe, Hyogo, Japan
[4] Graduate School of Advanced Science and Engineering, Hiroshima University, Higashi-Hiroshima, Japan

Abstract. In communication, a claim should be conveyed to others correctly. However, establishing such communication is not easy. In this study, we define miscommunication as a situation where a claim is conveyed incorrectly. We discuss how to resolve miscommunication and propose a learning support system designed to help resolve miscommunication.

In considering how to resolve miscommunication, we constructed a dialogue model consisting of three elements: claim, background knowledge, and utterance. The claim is an individual's internal demands, the background knowledge is information for constructing claims, and the utterance is the text for conveying claims to others. In dialogue, speakers convey claims to listeners. In conveying a claim, the speaker constructs an utterance(s) based on their background knowledge. The listener receives the utterance(s) and infers the intended meaning of the speaker's claim based on their own background knowledge. Therefore, the difference in the claim conveyed and the claim received is a difference in background knowledge or a difference in interpretation of the utterance or error of inferring.

In this paper, we focus on the difference in background knowledge and propose a learning support system for improving skills in inferring others' background knowledge. This system involves an example of miscommunication between a speaker and a listener, where learners constructs the listener's background knowledge.

Keywords: Resolving miscommunication · Inferring background knowledge

1 Introduction

In communication, a claim should be conveyed to others correctly. However, establishing such communication can be difficult. In this paper, we define miscommunication as a situation where a claim is not correctly conveyed. We discuss

S. Yamamoto and H. Mori (Eds.): HCII 2021, LNCS 12766, pp. 104–114, 2021.
https://doi.org/10.1007/978-3-030-78361-7_9

how to resolve miscommunication and how to learn skills for resolving miscommunication.

Mere recognition of a difference between our claim and another person's understanding of the claim cannot resolve miscommunication. In conversation, the listener infers the speaker's claim from their interpretation of the speaker's utterance and their own background knowledge. Therefore, the claim conveyed by the speaker and the claim received by the listener differ in background knowledge or interpretation of the utterance, which can lead to miscommunication. In this paper, we attempt to resolve such miscommunication by focusing on the difference in background knowledge. Further, we propose a learning support system for improving skills in inferring others' background knowledge.

We describe this system by using examples of miscommunication between a speaker and a listener. Learners construct the listener's background knowledge using the Kit-Build concept map proposed by Hirashima et al. [3].

2 Cause of Miscommunication and How to Resolve It

In this section, we present the model of a conversation and describe how to resolve miscommunication.

2.1 Triangular Model of Conversation

There is a model that gives outputs by processing inputs using an inference engine and using a knowledge base as a common information process model. In this paper, we use this model as a base in constructing a triangular model of conversation (Fig. 1).

The triangular model consists of three elements: claim, background knowledge, and utterance. The claim is an individual's internal demands, the background knowledge is information for constructing claims, and the utterance is the text for conveying claims to others. In dialogue, a speaker conveys their claim by constructing an utterance based on their background knowledge. On the other hand, a listener receives the utterance and infers the intended meaning

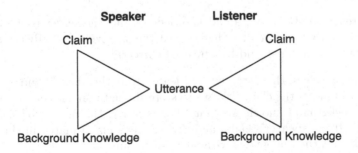

Fig. 1. Triangular model in dialogue

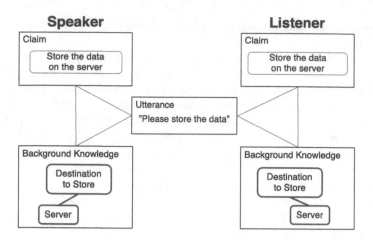

Fig. 2. Dialogue example using the triangular model

of the speaker's claim based on the utterance and their own background knowledge. In other words, the speaker constructs the utterance using the claim and their background knowledge, and the listener infers the intended meaning of the claim from the utterance and their own background knowledge.

In addition, when the speaker constructs the utterance, they consider "What kind of utterance is needed to convey the claim correctly?" The utterance itself assumes the background knowledge of the listener. The speaker confirms that the listener infers the same claim based on this background knowledge and utterance. This consideration is coherent with the listener's consideration of "inferring the intended meaning of the claim from the utterance and their own background knowledge". In this way, the speaker and the listener carry out different activities in the dialogue, but they have the same consideration in the consideration process.

We explain this model in the following example (Fig. 2). A speaker's claim is, "Want to store the data on the server." In order to convey this claim to the listener, the speaker says, "Please store the data." The speaker considers their utterance as follows.

> The listener has the background knowledge that "the server is the place where the data are stored." Therefore, if the speaker says, "Please store the data," the claim should be conveyed correctly.

The listener receives the utterance, "Please store the data," and infers the intended meaning of the claim, "Want to store the data on the server" based on their own background knowledge that "The server is the place where the data are stored." If the speaker's claim and the listener's claim match in this way, it can be said that the dialogue is without miscommunication.

2.2   Miscommunication and Background Knowledge

In this study, we define miscommunication as a speaker's claim that is not well communicated to the listener. Hirashima's framework of empathic understanding [1] is useful in explaining such miscommunication. Empathic understanding is the understanding of other's understanding states by tracing the understanding process. Hirashima explains empathic understanding as follows: (Fig. 3)

(i) Observe the difference between our claims and others' claims.
(ii) Suppose that others rationally infer others' claims, just as we rationally infer our claims.
(iii) Recognize others' knowledge states in comparison with our knowledge state.

Hirashima explains that differences in knowledge state cause differences in the interpretation of the claim.

We can explain miscommunication using the dialogue model and the framework of empathic understanding.

(i) Consider the case where the speaker and the listener have different claims.
(ii) Suppose that the speaker's claim based on their utterance and background knowledge is the same as that inferred by the listener.
(iii) The listener recognizes the speaker's knowledge status (utterance and background knowledge) and compares it with their own knowledge status.

In dialogue, utterances are common between the speaker and the listener. Therefore, differences in background knowledge are the likely cause of differences in understanding claims.

We explain the causation of miscommunication in the following example (Fig. 4). Suppose a situation where a speaker says to a listener, "Please store the data." The speaker wants to "store some data on a server," but the listener stores the data on a USB storage device. The speaker's knowledge state is "a server is where the data are stored", whereas the listener's knowledge state is "a USB storage device where the data are stored." This example shows that if the speaker's background knowledge differs from the listener's background knowledge, even though they infer from the same utterance, they interpret different claims, which results in miscommunication.

We consider that there are two types of "differences in background knowledge."

(1) The other person does not have the required knowledge.
(2) Both have the required knowledge, but both activate different background knowledge.

To resolve case (1), it is necessary to teach the missing knowledge itself. In this study, we focus on case (2), where the only difference is in the background knowledge that is activated.

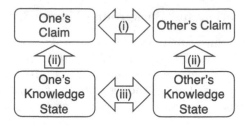

Fig. 3. Hirashima's framework of empathic understanding [1]

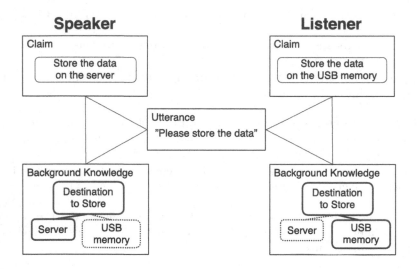

Fig. 4. Example of miscommunication by difference in background knowledge

2.3   How to Solve Miscommunication

Miscommunication is a situation where the speaker and the listener have different claims. To resolve the miscommunication, the speaker needs to modify the utterance so that it is received without miscommunication. We consider the process of resolving the miscommunication as follows:

(1) Infer the listener's background knowledge.
(2) Modify the utterance so that the intended meaning of the claim can be inferred correctly.

In other words, to modify the utterance, the speaker needs the skill of inferring the listener's background knowledge. Therefore, our aim in this paper is to improve the skill of inferring others' background knowledge as a component of a larger set of skills required in resolving miscommunication.

3   Learning Activity for Resolving Miscommunication

We propose a learning method where learners infer the listener's background knowledge in the situation of miscommunication. We also develop a system based on this learning method. This system shows utterances and claims in miscommunication. The learners construct the listener's background knowledge so that the listener can infer the intended meaning of the claim. This system helps learners understand the mechanism that "different claims generate different background knowledge" and improves their skill in inferring others' background knowledge.

3.1   Proposed Method

To improve skills in inferring others' background knowledge, we propose the following learning method. First, we prepare two agents: a speaker and a listener. The speaker has a claim and directs an utterance at the listener. However, the listener concludes a different claim. So, the learners are required to observe two different claims based on one utterance. In addition, the learners are required to infer others' background knowledge, which means they must infer different claims. In our proposed method, the learners infer the difference in background knowledge in miscommunication. We explain the learning flow of this method in the following example.

A speaker's claim is "Want to store the data on the server." The speaker says, "Please store the data." However, a listener guesses that the speaker's claim is, "Want to store the data on a USB storage device." The system shows the utterance and the two different claims. Then, the speaker's background knowledge is shown, such as, "the server is the place where the data are stored." Finally, the system requires the learners to infer the listener's background knowledge. If the listener has the same background knowledge, that is, "the server is the place where the data are stored", they can guess the speaker's claim correctly as "Want to store the data on the server." However, if the listener interprets the claim as"Want to store the data on a USB storage device," the learners infer that the listener has a different background knowledge, such as, "the USB storage device is the place where the data are stored." In this method, the system shows the situation of miscommunication and requires the learners to construct background knowledge. Through this activity, the learners consider "Why the claims are different even though they are listening to the same utterance." Therefore, the learners comprehend that, "If the background knowledge different, the claims differ."

3.2   Proposed System

We explain the interface of the proposed system (Fig. 5).

In this system, the learners construct the background knowledge using a Kit-Build concept map [3]. The system shows the utterance in Fig. 5-① and the claim of the speaker and that of the listener below. In the example in the figure, the speaker utters the claim, "I want the listener to answer with 'four'," and the

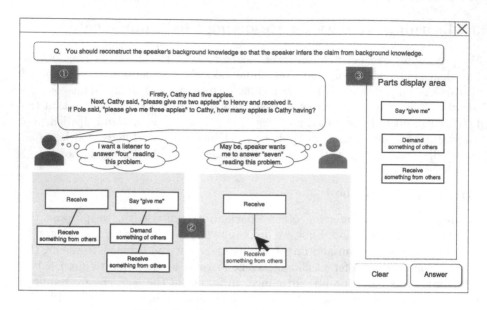

Fig. 5. Interface of the proposed system

listener receives the speaker's claim as "I want you to answer with 'seven'." This miscommunication is due to a difference in background knowledge between the speaker and the listener. In other words, the speaker has the background knowledge that the listener will give something to the speaker simply by the words "Please give me," whereas the listener has the background knowledge that the speaker will not give something to the speaker. Accordingly, the system shows the background knowledge of each person in the Fig. 5-②. In the initial state, the correct background knowledge of the speaker is displayed, and the background knowledge of the listener is also displayed on the listener's side. Next, the learner uses the parts in the parts display area of the Fig. 5-③ and reconstructs the listener's background knowledge. The learner selects the answer button to confirm whether their understanding of the claim is correct or incorrect.

4   Discussion and Future Prospects

4.1   Empathic Understanding and Triangular Model

In learning, it is important that the learner has empathic understanding of the teacher. Through this activity, the learner can understand more learning content. However, this activity is difficult for the learner. Therefore, Kit-Build concept maps can be implemented to encourage empathic understanding, as explained in Hirashima's study (Fig. 6).

(I) A teacher externalizes their own knowledge state about learning material as a concept map.

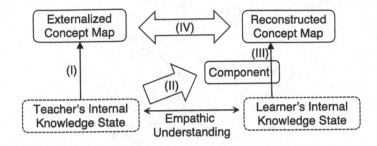

Fig. 6. Empathic understanding using Kit-Build method [1]

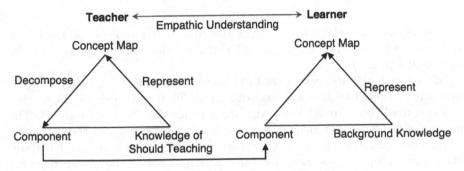

Fig. 7. Empathic understanding using the triangular model

(II) A system deconstructs the concept map into smaller components and relations to generate component.

(III) A learner uses the components to construct a concept map.

(IV) The learner compares their own concept map with the teacher's concept map.

The learner can acquire empathic understanding of the teacher through a simple process of reconstructing components using the Kit-Build concept map [3].

Figure 7 shows the empathic understanding derived by the Kit-Build method in the triangular model. In the Kit-Build method, the teacher represents the knowledge that they want to teach as a concept map. Next, the system deconstructs the concept map into smaller components that are shown to the learner as a problem. The learner constructs a concept map using the received components and their own background knowledge. In this activity, the concept map expresses what the teacher wants to teach. In other words, a special case is presented where the background knowledge and the claim are equal. Therefore, in the case where the learner constructs the same concept map as that of the teacher, the background knowledge of the teacher and that of the learner can be regarded as equal. Hirashima calls such a state empathic understanding.

In the system proposed in this paper, the learner uses background knowledge to reconstruct the concept map. However, in Hirashima's Kit-Build concept map,

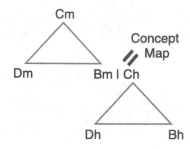

Fig. 8. Differences between the Kit-Build method and the proposed system

the learner uses the claim to construct the concept map. These activities are considered different. However, these different activities can be expressed by the same model (Fig. 8).

In dialogue, the speaker wants to convey a claim (Cm) and they want to convey it by using background knowledge (Bm). On the other hand, the teacher wants to teach background knowledge itself using the Kit-Build method. The purpose of the Kit-Build method is to teach this knowledge, and the claim and background are almost the same (Ch $\fallingdotseq$ Bh). Therefore, we consider the Kit-Build method and proposal system as the same activity because they both construct background knowledge.

4.2   Consideration of the Triangular Model

In the definition of miscommunication described in Subsect. 2.2, it was assumed that "Utterances are common between the speaker and the listener." We explained that "the listener infers the claim from the utterance and background knowledge," but the utterance cannot change and cannot be used for inferences. We explain the process of inferring the intended meaning of claims from utterances and background knowledge using the figure of the problem-solving process in Hirashima et al. [2].

Hirashima et al. explain the process of solving arithmetic and mathematical word problems and physics problems as follows:

(1) Read objects, attributes, and relationships between objects from the problem statement and generate a surface structure.
(2) Generate a formulated structure by transforming the surface structure so that it can be used in problem-solving.
(3) Generate a goal structure by transforming a constraint structure, with all of the quantitative relationships that exist in the situation targeted by the problem by using the necessary quantity relations.

This process can be regarded as the process of inferring the intended meaning of the claim from utterances and background knowledge. In other words, the problem statement serves as the utterance, the constraint structure as the background knowledge, and the goal structure as the claim.

The premise of this paper, "Utterances are common between the speaker and the listener," means that the information used for inference is the same for the speaker and the listener. In other words, the premise was that the formulated structure was common between the speaker and the listener. Therefore, the reason for different claims is not only the difference in background knowledge, but also:

(1) Error in the process of generating surface structures from utterances.
(2) Error in the process of generating the formulated structure from the surface structure.

In the future, we intend to consider the necessity of providing support for solving these problems.

4.3 Consideration of the Proposed System

The system proposed in this paper takes only a correct vs incorrect judgment function as a feedback function. However, the learner could be unsure of how to recognize and subsequently modify their own mistakes. Therefore, we consider a feedback function such as "changing the claim in response to the reconstructed background knowledge." Such a function in the system would help the learner to recognize their own mistakes.

Also, in Subsect. 2.3, we stated that "To resolve the miscommunication, the speaker needs to modify the utterance so that it is received without miscommunication." Therefore, we plan to consider how to improve skills to modify the utterance in the future.

4.4 Relation to Our Ongoing Study

We have been working on a study that involves a structure called the is-achieved-by hierarchy [6]. The structure is a hierarchical relationship of a combination of tasks that are to be achieved [4]. The is-achieved-by hierarchy is a link between requirements and executable primitive knowledge. Conveying the claim as executable is important for mutual understanding. Therefore, we plan to visualize the inference process using the is-achieved-by hierarchy in the future.

We attempt to explain this study based on psychological findings on the reading process. Kintsch describes two levels of reading comprehension: textbase and situational model [5]. According to Kintsch's study, the textbase is understanding of the surface structure in text, and the situational model is comprehension that corresponds to a deeper level of understanding. The situational model is constructed by integrating the text information and background knowledge.

Construction of the situational model is equivalent to construction of the background knowledge in our system. Therefore, we consider that our system can provide a deeper level of understanding for learners.

5   Conclusion

In this paper, we have shown that it is important to recognize the differences in background knowledge in order to resolve miscommunication. In addition, we proposed a system for understanding different background knowledge results in different claims. However, the inference process is not discussed in this paper. To address this limitation, we plan to combine our ongoing work on the is-achieved-by hierarchy with the present study.

References

1. Hiarshima, T.: Learning through empathic understanding: Tasking empathic understanding for learners. In: The 45th Annual Conference of Japanese Society for Information and Systems in Education, pp. 169–170 (2020), (in Japanese)
2. Hirashima, T., Kashihara, A., Toyoda, J.: A formulation of auxiliary problems and its evaluations. Proc. of AIED95, pp. 186–193 (1995)
3. Hirashima, T., Yamasaki, K., Fukuda, H., Funaoi, H.: Framework of kit-build concept map for automatic diagnosis and its preliminary use. Res. Pract. Technol. Enhanced Learn. **10**(1), 1–21 (2015). https://doi.org/10.1186/s41039-015-0018-9
4. Ishikawa, S., Kubo, S., Kozaki, K., Kitamura, Y., Mizoguchi, R.: Design and development of a guide system for building an ontology based on task/domain role concepts. Trans. Japan. Soc. Artif. Intell. **17**(5), 585–597 (2002), (in Japanese)
5. Kintsch, W.: Text comprehension, memory, and learning. Am. Psychol. **49**(4), 294–303 (1994)
6. Mogi, T., Koike, K., Tomoto, T.: Evaluation of feedback in a learning environment to improve requirement analysis skills. In: The 34th Annual Conference of the Japanese Society for Artificial Intelligence, pp. 1G4-ES-5-05 (2020)

Development of a Learning Support System for Electromagnetics Using Haptic Devices

Konoki Tei[1]([✉]), Toru Kano[2], and Takako Akakura[2]

[1] Department of Information and Computer Technology, Graduate School of Engineering, Tokyo University of Science, 6-3-1 Niijuku, Katsushika-ku, Tokyo 125-8585, Japan
4620519@ed.tus.ac.jp
[2] Department of Information and Computer Technology, Faculty of Engineering, Tokyo University of Science, 6-3-1 Niijuku, Katsushika-ku, Tokyo 125-8585, Japan
{kano,akakura}@rs.tus.ac.jp

Abstract. Many high school students are not good at studying the field of electromagnetics. Three major reasons have been given for this: "hard to see the overall structure of electromagnetics," "hard to understand the concept of fields," and "hard to perform intuitive experiments that can be visualized." To solve these problems, some studies have been conducted on experiential learning for physics using haptic devices that allow users to experience force feedback. However, fewer studies have used haptic devices for electromagnetics compared with mechanics, and only basic content has been implemented. Therefore, we developed advanced electromagnetic learning support systems using haptic devices. These systems simulate electromagnetic phenomena according to the parameters set by a learner and can help students "feel" forces of electric and magnetic field vectors that are difficult to experience in reality. We developed two systems. The first system allows learners to experience Ampere's force and magnetic flux density, and the second system allows learners to experience the magnetic field and vector potential generated around currents. Four university students in the Faculty of Engineering at Tokyo University of Science participated in an evaluation experiment and used the second system. The experience was highly rated by the participants, suggesting that our system using haptic devices is effective for intuitive learning of electromagnetics.

Keywords: Haptic devices · Learning support system · Electromagnetism

1 Introduction

1.1 Current State of Electromagnetics Education

According to a national survey in Japan, since the second half of the 1980s, Japanese students have become less interested in science and the low scientific literacy of citizens is becoming more serious; for example, the academic ability of applicants for the faculties of science and engineering at Japanese universities has been declining [1]. Also, many high school students are not good at studying the field of electromagnetics [2].

© Springer Nature Switzerland AG 2021
S. Yamamoto and H. Mori (Eds.): HCII 2021, LNCS 12766, pp. 115–127, 2021.
https://doi.org/10.1007/978-3-030-78361-7_10

Three major reasons have been given for this: "hard to see the overall structure of electromagnetics," "hard to understand the concept of fields," and "hard to perform intuitive experiments that can be visualized." To solve these problems, education using visual information, such as diagrams and simulation videos, has been provided. Furthermore, some studies have been conducted on experiential learning of physics using not only visual simulations but also haptics for tactile feedback.

1.2 Related Research

Many studies that incorporate force feedback into learning have used haptic devices that allow users to experience force feedback. Studies by Okimi et al. [3] and Matsubara et al. [4] have focused on learning of pulley movement by experiencing pulley behavior in a virtual environment by operating them with haptic devices (Fig. 1). In the experiment by Okimi et al., learners commented that "the content was interesting" and "the content we experienced was useful for learning." In the experiment by Matsubara et al., learners' test scores improved after the learning exercise. Thus, it was shown that effective experiential learning of physics is possible by using a system incorporating haptic devices.

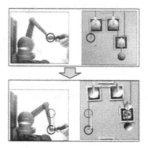

Fig. 1. Learning system for pulley movement [3].

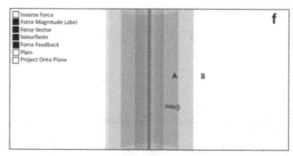

Fig. 2. Learning system using haptic devices to impart understanding of electric fields [5].

In electromagnetism, where it is difficult to understand the concept of fields, Magana et al. [5] developed a learning system using haptic devices to impart understanding of electric fields (Fig. 2). Their system simulates the force acting on a charge in the electric field generated by, for example, point charges and line charges. However, fewer studies have used haptic devices for electromagnetics compared with mechanics, and only basic content has been implemented.

1.3 Purpose of This Research

Based on the current state of electromagnetic education and related research, this study aimed to develop advanced electromagnetic learning support systems using haptic devices. Specifically, in this study, we developed systems that employ a stylus as the haptic device. These systems are designed to simulate electromagnetic phenomena according to parameters set by a learner and can simulate forces of electric and magnetic field vectors that are difficult to experience in reality.

1.4 Structure of This Paper

We describe the developed learning support systems for electromagnetics using haptic devices. The remainder of this paper is organized as follows. Section 2 gives information about the haptic devices used in this study and describes our two systems. Section 3 gives an overview of experiments that evaluated the second system as well as results and discussion. Section 4 summarizes this study and discusses future work.

2 Development of Systems

2.1 Haptic Devices

For the haptic device in our system, we used Touch (Fig. 3), developed by 3D Systems. This device controls the three-dimensional movement of a stylus, which provides force feedback. The system further gives the values of coordinates on the x, y, and z axes, and rotation information (roll, pitch, and yaw) on each axis. Figure 4 shows the axis coordinates and their rotation, and Table 1 lists the main specifications of Touch.

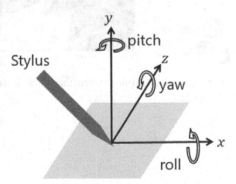

Fig. 3. Touch device [6].   **Fig. 4.** Axes and rotation directions of Touch.

Table 1. Main specifications of Touch [6].

Workspace	160 W × 120 H × 70 D mm
Nominal position resolution	0.055 mm
Maximum exertable force	3.3 N
Stiffness	x-axis > 1.26 N/mm
	y-axis > 2.31 N/mm
	z-axis > 5.9 N/mm

2.2 First System: Ampere's Force and Magnetic Flux Density

System Overview. The first system we developed allows learners to experience Ampere's force and magnetic flux density (Fig. 5). Learners first set the magnitude and direction of a linear current. Then, by setting the parameters of the magnetic flux density, learners can feel Ampere's force through the haptic device. They can also experience the corresponding magnetic flux density by setting Ampere's force. Simultaneously, Ampere's force and magnetic flux density are visualized in proportion to their magnitudes. Figure 6 shows an image of the situation in which learners choose items to experience and set parameters, and Fig. 7 shows an image of the situation in which a learner feels force feedback.

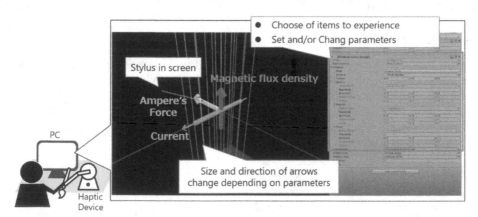

Fig. 5. Outline of learning system that allows learners to experience Ampere's force and magnetic flux density.

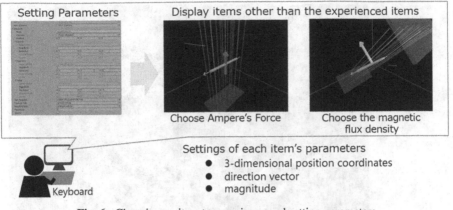

Fig. 6. Choosing an item to experience and setting parameters.

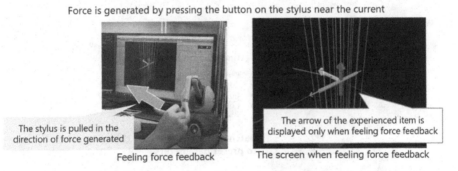

Fig. 7. Feeling force feedback of experienced item.

2.3 Second System: Magnetic Field and Vector Potential

System Overview. The second system we developed allows learners to experience the magnetic field and vector potential generated around currents. Because the magnetic flux density implemented in the first system is expressed as a vector sum, learners cannot see the influence of the surrounding magnetic field, current, and vector potential. Therefore, the second system simulates the magnetic field and vector potential, which change according to arbitrary current parameters. This system visualizes the magnetic field and vector potential in detail and provides force feedback for them by using linear currents and permeability $\mu = 1.3 \times 10^{-6}$ N/A^2. Figure 8 shows the second system's user interface.

Functions. Figure 9 shows the learner operation screen and content. Up to five currents can be set, and each current has the following parameters: three-dimensional position coordinates, direction vector, magnitude [A], and length [mm]. If the learner selects the batch setting button (single, parallel, parallel [reverse], cross, or random) for current parameters, specified parameters are entered into the system and reflected on the screen.

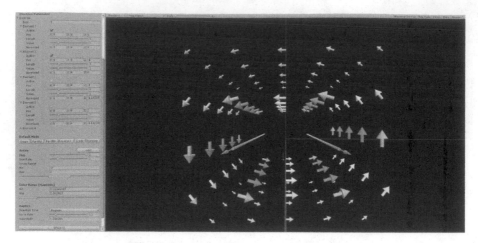

Fig. 8. Magnetic field system user interface.

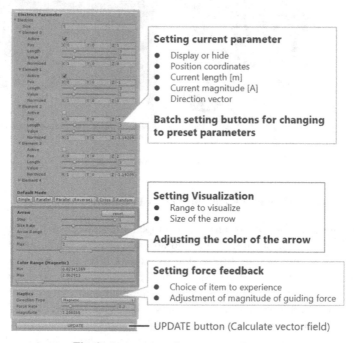

Fig. 9. Learner interface screen and content.

Table 2 shows the features controlled by this button. After setting the current parameters, learners choose whether to visualize the magnetic field or vector potential. In both of these visualizations, arrows are drawn around currents according to each vector field. The arrow sizes and directions follow the vector field, and the arrow colors change according to the magnitude of the vector. By adjusting the visualization range, size, and color, it is possible to easily confirm small changes in the vectors.

After pressing the button on the tip of the haptic device's stylus, the stylus moves along the trajectory of the target vector and provides force feedback. When learners receive feedback for magnetic field force, the stylus moves as if writing magnetic field lines. The force F_p to guide the stylus when the learner feels the vector V_p in position coordinates p of the stylus can be expressed by Eq. (1) using the rate of increase or decrease R_F that adjusts the magnitude of the guiding force. As shown in Eq. (1), the directions of F_p and V_p are the same, and their magnitude changes depending on the value selected by the system or the learner. Here, the upper limit of the magnitude of the guiding force is 0.5 N.

$$F_p = \begin{cases} V_p \cdot R_F \times 10^6 & (|V_p| \cdot R_F \leq 0.5) \\ \frac{V_p}{|V_p|} \cdot 0.5 \times 10^6 & (|V_p| \cdot R_F > 0.5) \end{cases} . \tag{1}$$

Also, when learners change the item to experience while using this system, the system can change the display of the vector field and the force used to guide the stylus. Furthermore, this system can move and change the viewpoint via mouse wheel and keyboard operation. Table 3 shows the input operations for moving the viewpoint. The directions of stylus instructions are with respect to the initial position. Figure 10 shows the operation flow during one simulation in this system using these functions.

Table 2. Effect of batch setting button on current parameters.

Name	Effect
Single	One current is placed at the origin
Parallel	Two currents are arranged in parallel in the same direction
Parallel (Reverse)	Two currents are arranged in parallel and opposite directions
Cross	Two currents are arranged to intersect vertically
Random	The number, position, and direction of currents are determined by random numbers

Table 3. Operations for moving the viewpoint.

Input	Moving content
Mouse wheel	Move the viewpoint back and forth
Arrow key	Move the viewpoint up, down, left, or right
Key 1, Space bar key	Return to the initial position
Key 2	Move to the opposite side of the initial position
Key 3	Move to the left of the initial position
Key 4	Move to the right of the initial position
Key 5	Move up from the initial position
Key 6	Move down from the initial position

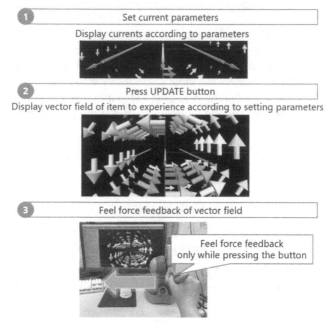

Fig. 10. Operation flow during one simulation in this system.

3 Evaluation Experiments

3.1 Experimental Setup

Four university students in the Faculty of Engineering of Tokyo University of Science participated in the evaluation experiment and used the second system (Sect. 2.3). Figure 11 shows the actual experimental environment.

This experiment was conducted according to the following procedure:

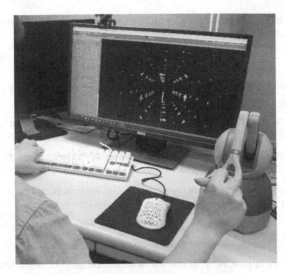

Fig. 11. Experimental environment.

(1) Pre-experiment questionnaire (3 min)
(2) Description of system (5 min)
(3) System use (10–15 min)
(4) Post-experiment questionnaire (5–10 min)

As shown in Table 4, the pre-experiment questionnaire asked how much the participants understood about electromagnetics, including magnetic fields and vector potentials. We then described our system to the participants and they used the system. Table 5 shows the post-experiment questionnaire, which focused on the learning perspective. All questions shown in Tables 3 and 4 used a 5-point scale, with 1 to 5 corresponding to negative to positive, respectively.

Table 4. Pre-experiment questionnaire (5-point scale, where 5 = positive).

No.	Question
A-1	Do you understand electromagnetism?
A-2	Are you interested in electromagnetism?
A-3	Do you understand the relationship between current and magnetic field?
A-4	Do you understand the relationship between current and vector potential?
A-5	Do you understand the relationship between magnetic field and vector potential?
A-6	Are you interested in the relationship between current, magnetic field, and vector potential?

Table 5. Post-experiment questionnaire (focusing on the learning perspective) (5-point scale, where 5 = positive).

No.	Question
B-1	Did you deepen your understanding of the relationship between current and magnetic field?
B-2	Did you deepen your understanding of the relationship between current and vector potential?
B-3	Did you deepen your understanding of the relationship between magnetic fields and vector potentials?
B-4	Do you think the simulation of this system is useful for understanding the vector field of magnetic field and vector potential?
B-5	Do you expect enhanced learning in the field of electromagnetics using this system?
B-6	Do you think the guidance of this system is useful for understanding vector fields?
B-7	Did this experiment increase your interest in the relationship between current, magnetic field, and vector potential?
B-8	Do you want to use this system for learning electromagnetics in the future?

3.2 Experimental Results

Table 6 shows the results of pre- and post-experiment questionnaires. The pre-experiment questionnaires showed that all participants were not interested in electromagnetism, and even less interested in the relationship between current, magnetic field, and vector potential contained in electromagnetism. However, the post-experiment questionnaires showed that they became interested in the relationship between current, magnetic field, and vector potential in electromagnetism and acquired a deeper understanding.

Table 6. Results of pre/post-experiment questionnaires.

(i) Pre-experiment

No.	Avg. (SD)
A-1	1.75 (0.433)
A-2	2.50 (0.866)
A-3	2.00 (0.707)
A-4	1.00 (0.000)
A-5	1.25 (0.433)
A-6	2.25 (1.299)

(ii) Post-experiment

No.	Avg. (SD)
B-1	4.25 (0.433)
B-2	4.00 (0.000)
B-3	4.25 (0.829)
B-4	4.25 (0.829)
B-5	3.75 (0.433)
B-6	4.00 (0.707)
B-7	3.75 (0.829)
B-8	4.25 (0.829)

Understanding the Relationships. Here, we focus on participant understanding of three relationships: current–magnetic field, current–vector potential, and magnetic field–vector potential. Figure 12 compares pre- and post-experiment results for participants' understanding of the three relationships. From Fig. 12, their understanding of all relationships was low before the experiment, but increased after the experiment. Also, the result of question B-4, "Do you think the simulation of this system is useful for understanding the vector field of magnetic field and vector potential?" was highly rated at 4.25. Therefore, these results suggest that this system is useful for understanding the relationship between current, magnetic field, and vector potential, and it is possible to obtain a deeper understanding by using it.

Interest in the Relationships. Here, we focus on interest in the relationship between current, magnetic field, and vector potential. Figure 13 compares pre- and post-experiment results for interest in this relationship. From Fig. 13, participants' interest in the relationship was low before the experiment, but improved after the experiment. Also, the results of question B-5, "Do you expect enhanced learning in the field of electromagnetics by using this system?" and B-8, "Do you want to use this system for learning electromagnetics in the future?" were highly rated at 3.75 and 4.25, respectively. These results suggest that this system allows learners to increase their interest in the relationship between current, magnetic field, and vector potential and to expect enhanced learning for them in the future.

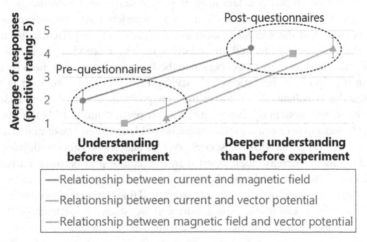

Fig. 12. Comparison of pre- and post-experiment questionnaire results on understanding of three electromagnetism relationships.

Opinion of the System. We received several negative comments, such as "Parameter setting is troublesome," "The position of the stylus on the screen is difficult to see," and "It is difficult to see the position of the current viewpoint." Accordingly, these comments indicate areas where we should improve the system. On the other hand, we received

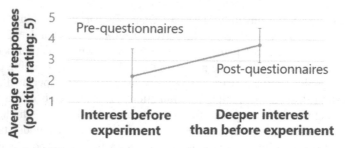

Fig. 13. Comparison of pre- and post-experiment questionnaire results on interest in relationship between current, magnetic field, and vector potential.

several positive comments, including "It is easy to understand visually," "I think it helps to understand complex magnetic fields," and "We could learn all levels from the basics level to the advanced level by using this system." These comments indicate that this system is effective for learning about the relationship between current, magnetic field, and vector potential.

4   Conclusion

4.1 Summary

In this study, we developed two learning support systems for electromagnetics using haptic devices. The first system allows learners to experience Ampere's force and magnetic flux density, and the second system allows learners to experience the magnetic field and vector potential generated around currents. These are visualized according to input parameters, and learners can experience the force feedback of an item by pressing a button on the tip of the haptic device's stylus. In the second system, it is possible to customize the visualization and move the viewpoint, unlike the former system. We evaluated the second system by measuring whether participants could effectively learn about the relationship between current, magnetic field, and vector potential. The results of questionnaires suggested that the second system enables learners to develop deeper understanding and to increase their interest in the relationship between current, magnetic field, and vector potential, and the system is expected to facilitate learning about them. In addition, several positive opinions suggested that the second system is effective for intuitive learning in electromagnetics. Furthermore, studying electromagnetics using haptic devices was considered to be effective from this viewpoint.

4.2 Future Work

We plan to improve aspects pointed out in the evaluation experiment using the second system, such as operability and visualization, and to integrate our systems toward the realization of a more complete learning support system. Also, for use in actual learning, we will introduce a tutorial for our system and implement nonlinear current, such as circular or coil flow. After system improvement, we will evaluate whether the system is effective for learning electromagnetics using similar pre- and post-test questionnaires.

References

1. Naganuma, S.: A Study of Research Trends in "Decline in students' positive attitude toward science": focusing on its current conditions and causes. J. Sci. Educ. Jpn. **39**(2), 114–123 (2015). (in Japanese)
2. Shinmura, K., Ishihara, S., Niwase, K.: Denjiki-gaku ni okeru Ba no Gainennkeisei wo mezasita Jiryokusen-kaiseki ni tsuite (About magnetic field line analysis aiming at the concept formation of the field in electromagnetism). In: 58th Annual Meeting of Society of Japan Science Teaching, 260 (2008). (in Japanese)
3. Okimi, Y., Matsubara, Y.: Learning support system for pulley arrangement experiments using augmented reality type markers. Jpn. J. Educ. Technol. **37**(2), 107–116 (2013). (in Japanese)
4. Matsubara, Y., Kono, T., Okamoto, M.: Pulley learning support system with feedback based on pseudo-haptics. Jpn. J. Educ. Technol. **43**(Suppl.), 89–92 (2020). (in Japanese)
5. Magana, A.J., Balachandran, S.: Students' development of representational competence through the sense of touch. J. Sci. Educ. Technol. **26**(3), 332–346 (2017)
6. 3D SYSTEMS: Touch Haptic Device User Guide. https://ja.3dsystems.com/sites/default/files/2017-12/3DSystems-Touch-UserGuide.pdf. Accessed 28 Jan 2021

Features Analysis of a Patent Act Based on Legal Condition–Effect Structure: Conversion of Law Texts into Logical Formulas for a Learning Support System

Akihisa Tomita[1]([✉]), Masashi Komatsh[1], Toru Kano[2], and Takako Akakura[2]

[1] Graduate School of Engineering, Tokyo University of Science, 6-3-1 Nijuku, Katsushika-ku, Tokyo 125-8585, Japan
{4620522,4419511}@ed.tus.ac.jp
[2] Faculty of Engineering,
Tokyo University of Science, 6-3-1 Nijuku, Katsushika-ku, Tokyo 125-8585, Japan
{kano,akakura}@rs.tus.ac.jp

Abstract. With the development of information and communications technology, intellectual property education is expected to become increasingly important. However, it has been shown that intellectual property education is insufficiently conducted in university education faculties of engineering. Therefore, we previously focused on engineering students learning logic circuits to create an e-learning system that displays articles as logic circuits. Evaluation experiments demonstrated the learning effect of this system, but it could not handle all intellectual property laws because it required manually converting law texts into logic circuits in the problem creation process. To address this problem, in this paper we examine a method for converting intellectual property laws into logical formulas. Previous studies have converted law texts into logical formulas to perform consistent tests of law texts, whereas this study aims at more human-comprehensible visualizations. We divide law texts into constituents based on a legal condition–effect structure and convert them into propositional calculus. This paper presents the results of an attempt to convert 101 law texts of typical patent acts in intellectual property law into logical formulas. From the results of integrating the logical formulas into our law text learning system, we describe future policies.

Keywords: Patent act · Learning support system · Propositional logic

1 Background

1.1 Importance of Intellectual Property Law Education

With the development of information and communications technologies, sometimes called the Fifth Industrial Revolution, many technologies using AI and IoT are being put into practical use. In the future, new technical ideas will be created in a 5G environment. Therefore, to strengthen the international competitiveness of domestic industries, it is

© Springer Nature Switzerland AG 2021
S. Yamamoto and H. Mori (Eds.): HCII 2021, LNCS 12766, pp. 128–140, 2021.
https://doi.org/10.1007/978-3-030-78361-7_11

necessary to develop human resources who can generate and protect intellectual property. As a country that lacks natural resources, this is considered particularly important in Japan, and industry expects students to acquire knowledge about intellectual property. The Japanese government has thus established the Intellectual Property Strategy Headquarters, a Cabinet department that establishes strategies for promoting utilization of intellectual property and enhancing intellectual property education [1].

1.2 Intellectual Property Education in Faculties of Engineering

In addition to government and industry, universities too recognize the importance of intellectual property education. However, the results of a survey of faculty of engineering syllabi at Japanese national universities revealed that current intellectual property education is insufficient [2]. This is likely because the curriculum is generally limited to exercises such as experiments, and intellectual property is only partially treated in ethics classes.

Therefore, the authors have been developing a learning support system for intellectual property law for engineering students. To facilitate use by anyone without restrictions on time and place, we developed our e-learning system as a web application and introduced it in actual classes.

2 Previous Research

We considered a mechanism for promoting understanding of law texts as needed for faculty of engineering students not specializing in law. Considering that such students learn logic circuits, we developed a system that can display law texts as logic circuits [3]. However, in an e-learning system without an instructor, it is difficult for learners to notice mistakes on their own. To address this problem, we focused on error-based simulation and improved the system so that when learners make mistakes, an animation that can intuitively indicate the error is displayed [4]. Figure 1 shows the system interface, which displays a logic circuit that utilizes the fact that Article 2 Paragraph 1 of the Patent Act ("'Invention' in this Act means the highly advanced creation of technical ideas utilizing the laws of nature") can be represented as a propositional formula: "(1) Utilizing the laws of nature ∧ (2) Technical ideas ∧ (3) Creation ∧ (4) Advanced → (5) Invention." The learner can thus see the requirements for "invention" by connecting (1) through (4) to the logical conjunction element and connecting that element to (5).

We introduced this system into an actual course on intellectual property law and conducted an evaluation experiment regarding its learning effects. Felder's learning-style-based analysis [5], which defines the learning styles of science students, suggests that this system would be particularly effective for visual learners, rather than for verbal learners.

However, this system required manually converting law texts into logic circuits in the problem creation process, making it difficult to comprehensively handle all of intellectual property law. Therefore, in this study, we examined a method for converting intellectual property law into logical formulas and showing the results of integrating the converted formulas into the system.

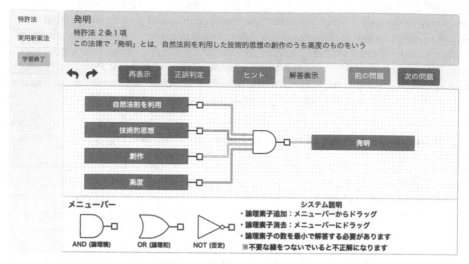

Fig. 1. Interface of the law text learning system using logic circuits [3].

3 Purpose

Some studies on converting law texts into logical formulas have been conducted in the field of expert systems, where law texts are converted into logical formulas based on predicate logic to mechanically perform consistency tests for the texts. In other words, the conventional conversion method does not assume learning and is not a visualization method for ease of comprehension. Moreover, no method for converting predicate logic into logic circuits has been established. Therefore, this study focuses on the legal condition–effect structure of law texts to convert text into a propositional calculus, then logic circuits. As a first step, in this paper we show the results of converting the Patent Act to logical formulas and their integration into the system.

4 Analysis Method

This study was carried out according to the following procedure.

1. Get law text data.
2. Preprocess the data.
3. Select target texts to be analyzed.
4. Conduct morphological analysis and dependency analysis.
5. Examine constituent identification patterns based on the legal condition–effect structure [6].
6. Identify and tag the constituents by pattern matching.
7. Create formulas by regarding clauses or phrases enclosed in tags as propositional variables.
8. Judge the correctness of the result.
9. Integrate formulas into the system.

The legal condition–effect structure is a logical structure in which the law text consists of five constituents: a subject part, a condition part, a target part, a content part, and a regulation part. Figure 2 shows an overview.

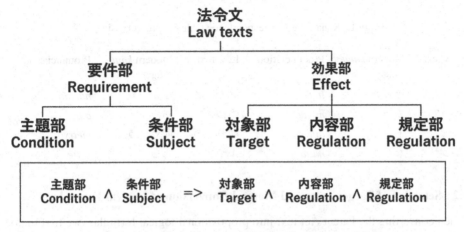

Fig. 2. Outline of the legal condition–effect structure [6].

Law texts consist of an effect part that expresses rights and obligations, and a requirement part that expresses the conditions under which the effect part is applied. The requirement part further comprises a subject part, which is the subject of the law text, and a condition part, which is the condition of the law text. In addition, the effect part comprises a regulation part, which is a predicate, a target part, which is an object, and a content part. The law text thus becomes a logical formula, "Subject $\land$ Condition $\rightarrow$ Target $\land$ Content $\land$ Regulation." Law texts can consist of any combination of these five constituents, and there are cases where multiple constituents are contained or some are omitted.

4.1 Acquisition and Preprocessing of Text Data

Law text data is obtained from the administrative information portal site "e-Gov," operated by the Japanese government. The raw data is an extensible markup language (XML)-format file, so we extract only the textual part for conversion into a comma-separated values (CSV)-format file. When there is parenthesized text for supplementary explanations, it is necessary to separately analyze the range of the parentheses and the dependency relationship between the main text and the parenthetical text. Since the establishment of such an analysis method is beyond the scope of this study, we removed parenthetical text in this study.

Another issue is that law texts, including the Patent Act, often make special use of the Japanese *kana* syllabary. For example, modern Japanese uses a small *tsu* character (っ) to express a double consonant and other small kana characters to express specific sounds. Law texts, however, always use full-size kana, such as the text "*mono no hatsumei ni atte wa*" (物の発明にあつては, which should be written as 物の発明にあっては in modern Japanese) in Article 2, Paragraph 3, Item 1 of the Patent Act. Because this hinders accurate morphological analysis, in preprocessing we convert such special kana usage to modern usage. In this study, pretreatment is performed according to the contents of Table 1.

Table 1. Kana usage correspondence table for preprocessing.

Law text	Modern *kana* usage	Pronunciation	Law text	Modern *kana* usage	Pronunciation
至つた	至った	*itatta*	なかつた	なかった	*nakatta*
もつて	もって	*motte*	あつた	あった	*atta*
あつて	あって	*atte*	明りよう	明りょう	*meiryo*
なつた	なった	*natta*	よつて	よって	*yotte*

4.2 Selection of Target Texts and Manual Conversion of Logical Formulas

When converting the Patent Act text into propositional logical formulas, we first manually created the logical formulas and asked an expert to confirm their correctness. The Patent Act has 290 articles, excluding those deleted through amendments and supplementary provisions. We manually selected 34 articles (comprising 101 texts) that are considered particularly important and frequently used in intellectual property management skill tests, and converted them into logical formulas. Table 2 shows the selected texts and their captions.

Table 2. .

No.	Article number	Caption
1	Article 2	Definition
2	Article 17-2	Amendment of specification, claims or drawings attached to the application
3	Article 29, Article 29-2	Patent requirements
4	Article 30	Exceptions to loss of novelty of invention
5	Article 35	Employee inventions
6	Article 39	First applications
7	Article 41	Priority claim based on patent applications, etc.
8	Article 48	Patent applications by a method claiming that the previous patent application should be referred to
9	Article 49	Assessment of refusal
10	Article 50	Notification of reasons for refusal

(*continued*)

Table 2. (*continued*)

No.	Article number	Caption
11	Article 51	Patent decision
12	Article 64	Publication of application
13	Article 64-2	Request for publication of application
14	Article 66	Registration of patent right setting
15	Article 67	Duration
16	Article 68	Effectiveness of patent rights
17	Article 73	Patent rights related to sharing
18	Article 77	Exclusive license
19	Article 78	Non-exclusive license
20	Article 79	Non-exclusive license for prior use
21	Article 83	Decision to set non-executive license in case of non-implementation
22	Article 98	Effect of registration
23	Article 100	Right to request an injunction
24	Article 104	Estimation of production method
25	Article 105	Credit recovery measures
26	Article 112-3	Limitation of the effect of the restored patent right
27	Article 113	Patent opposition
28	Article 121	Trial against decision of refusal
29	Article 123	Patent invalidation trial
30	Article 168	Relationship with proceedings
31	Article 169	Burden of costs in refereeing
32	Article 170	Enforcement power to determine the amount of expenses
33	Article 178	Appeals against trial decisions, etc.
34	Article 196	Offense of infringement

Next, based on the result of manual conversion from law texts to logical formulas, we examined the identification pattern of the constituents. Figures 3 and 4 show examples of the law texts that were manually converted into logical formulas.

Patent Act, Article 78, Paragraph 2

[Original sentence]
　通常実施権者は、この法律の規定により又は設定行為で定めた範囲内において、業としてその特許発明の実施をする権利を有する。

[Meaning]
　A non-exclusive licensee shall have a right to work the patented invention as a business to the extent prescribed by this Act or permitted by the contract granting the license.

[Converted into logical formula]
　通常実施権者 ∧ {この法律の規定により定めた範囲内 ∨ 設定行為で定めた範囲内}
　=> 業として特許発明の実施をする権利を有する

Fig. 3. Well-formed logical formula of Article 78, Paragraph 2 of the Patent Act.

Patent Act, Article 168, Paragraph 6

[Original sentence]
　特許庁長官は、前項に規定する通知を受けたときは、裁判所に対し、当該訴訟の訴訟記録のうちその審判において審判官が必要と認める書面の写しの送付を求めることができる。

[Meaning]
　Where the Commissioner of the Patent Office receives the notice as provided in the preceding paragraph, the Commissioner of the Patent Office may request the court to deliver copies of any record of the said action which the trial examiner considers necessary for the trial.

[Conversion into logical formula]
　特許庁長官 ∧ 前項に規定する通知を受けた
　=> 裁判所に対し、当該訴訟の訴訟記録のうちその審判において審判官が必要と認める書面の写しの送付を求めることができる

Fig. 4. Patent Act Article 168, Paragraph 6.

4.3 Analysis of Articles and Examination of Constituent Identification Patterns

The morphological analyzer uses JUMAN [7], which is suitable for analyzing proper nouns and technical terms, and KNP [8] for dependency analysis. We examined identification patterns of the constituents by comparing the manually converted logical formulas with the results of text analysis. Constituents are tagged using the identified identification patterns by comparing the manually converted logical formula with the results of text analysis. The subject part in the law text is enclosed by the tags <Subject> </Subject>, and the condition part is enclosed by the tags <Condition> </Condition>. The target part, content part, and regulation part are collectively enclosed by the tags <Effect> </Effect> as the effect part to prevent the logic circuit from becoming too complicated.

5   Results and Discussion

5.1   Result of Constituent Identification

Using the results of morphological analysis and dependency analysis for 34 articles, we extracted morphemes with high frequency of appearance and their combinations as constituent identification patterns. Table 3 shows the identification patterns and the number of appearances.

Table 3. Identification patterns and number of appearances.

Constituent	Identification pattern	Number of appearances
Subject	Common noun + (と)は, / Common noun + が,	42
Condition	～ *baai (wa)* 場合(は), / ～ *toki (wa)* とき(は), / ～ *ni oite (wa)* において(は), / ～ *ni tsuite (wa)* について(は),	73
Content	～*o* を	117
Target	Common noun + *ni (taishi)* に(対し),	5
Regulation	～ *to suru* とする。/ ～ *suru* する。/ ～ *dekiru* できる。/ (Other verbs)。	125

Table 4 shows the results of identifying the text constituents by pattern matching based on Table 3.

Table 4. Results of identifying the constituents.

Correct	47
Wrong	10
Lack of definition	48
Need preprocessing	5

Successful Examples of Constituent Identification. As a result of the constituent identification of 101 documents in 34 Articles, about half of the constituents could be identified as intended (see Table 4). Figures 5 and 6 show examples in which constituent identification was performed as intended.

<u>**Patent Act, Article 168, Paragraph 6**</u>

[Original sentence]
　特許庁長官は、前項に規定する通知を受けたときは、裁判所に対し、当該訴訟の訴訟記録のうちその審判において審判官が必要と認める書面の写しの送付を求めることができる。

[Conversion]
　　<Subject>特許庁長官は、</Subject>
　　<Condition>前項に規定する通知を受けたときは、</Condition>
　　<Effect>　<Target>裁判所に対し、</Target>当該訴訟の訴訟記録のうちその審判において審判官が必要と認める書面の写しの送付を求めることができる。</Effect>

Fig. 5. Constituent identification results for Article 168, Paragraph 6 of the Patent Act.

<u>**Patent Act, Article 39, Paragraph 7**</u>

[Original sentence]
　特許庁長官は、前項の規定により指定した期間内に同行の規定による届出がないときは、第二項又は第四項の協議が成立しなかったものと見なすことができる。

[Conversion]
　　<Subject>特許庁長官は、</Subject>
　　<Condition>前項の規定により指定した期間内に同項の規定による届出がないときは、</Condition>
　　<Effect>第二項又は第四項の協議が成立しなかったものと見なすことができる。</Effect>

Fig. 6. Constituent identification results for Article 39, Paragraph 7 of the Patent Act.

Failure Examples of Constituent Identification. Figures 7 and 8 show examples in which the constituents could not be identified as intended.

The law text in Fig. 7 is based on a context meaning "exclusive licenses can be transferred only if the conditions are met." Therefore, an "exclusive license" is considered to be a constituent that originally corresponds to Content, not Subject. In this way, when the noun corresponding to the content part was used as the subject for a passive verb, we found that an erroneous judgment was made in our identification pattern. In addition, we considered that the combination of morphemes "*ni kagiri*" (に限り, "only when") can be used for identification of the condition part, but this was undefined as an identification pattern because the number of appearances was relatively small.

Patent Act, Article 77, Paragraph 3

[Original sentence]
　専用実施権は、実施の事業とともにする場合、特許権者の承諾を
得た場合及び相続その他の一般継承の場合に限り、移転することが
できる。

[Conversion]
　<Subject>専用実施権は、</Subject>
　<Condition>実施の事業とともにする場合、</Condition>
　<Effect>特許権者の承諾を得た場合及び相続その他の一般継承の
場合に限り、移転することができる。</Effect>

Fig. 7. Constituent identification results for Article 77, Paragraph 3 of the Patent Act.

Patent Act Article 2, Paragraph 3

[Original sentence]
　この法律で発明について実施とは、次に掲げる行為をいう。

[Conversion]
　<Effect>この法律で発明について実施とは、次に掲げる行為をい
う。</Effect>

Fig. 8. Constituent identification results for Patent Act Article 2, Paragraph 3.

In the case of the law text in Fig. 8, the context is that "the following acts are the implementation of the invention," so the subject part should be "*tsugi ni kakageru koi*" (次に掲げる行為, "the following acts"), and the effect part should be "*hatsumei ni tsuite jisshi*" (発明について実施, "implementation of the invention"). However, this interpretation was difficult to identify with our simple rules. Therefore, it is considered that a separate feature for specifying the text of a description format similar to Article 2, Paragraph 3 of the Patent Act is required.

5.2   Integration with Learning Support System

Figures 9 and 10 show the results of integrating the logical formulas into the system. Figure 9 shows the example of integrating Article 168, Paragraph 6 of the Patent Act, in which the constituents were identified as intended, into the system. Figure 10 shows the example of integrating Article 77, Paragraph 3 of the Patent Act, which failed to identify constituents, into the system.

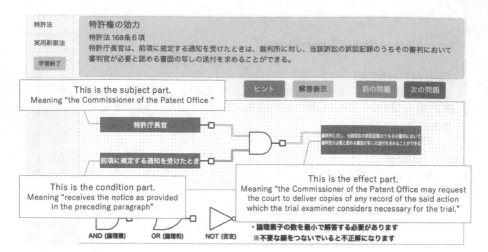

Fig. 9. Example correct logic circuit (Patent Act Article 168, Paragraph 6).

Figure 9 shows that the proposed method can integrate a law text with a simple logical structure into the system. When the effect part is very long, however, it is difficult to understand the content. Therefore, it is considered necessary to devise measures such as dividing the target and content parts according to the numbers of characters and phrases in the effect part.

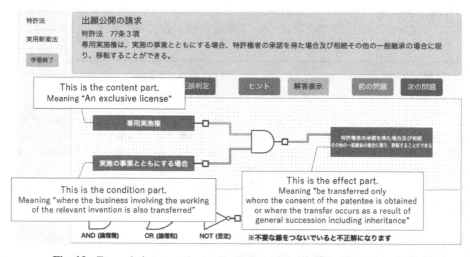

Fig. 10. Example incorrect logic circuit (Patent Act Article 77, Paragraph 3).

Figure 10 shows that "*sen'yo jisshi ken*" (専用実施権, "exclusive license") is part of the requirement part, because it was mistakenly identified as the subject part. In addition, "*tokkyo ken ja no syodaku o eta baai oyobi sozoku sonota no ippan keisyo no baai*" (特許権者の承諾を得た場合及び相続その他の一般承継の場合, "where the consent of the patentee is obtained or where the transfer occurs as a result of general succession including inheritance") is included in the effect part. From the above, this logic circuit is incorrect. Figure 11 shows a logic circuit when conversion to a correct logical formula can be performed.

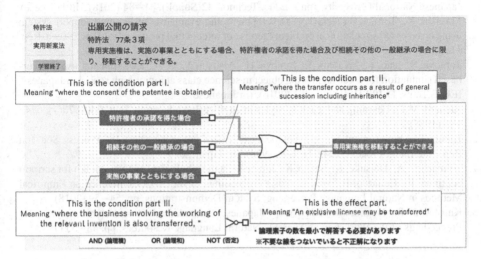

Fig. 11. Correct logic circuit (Patent Act Article 77, Paragraph 3).

It is necessary to modify the algorithm in the future so that the logic circuit shown in Fig. 11 can be created. Other future tasks include increasing the number of rules for identifying constituents and improving accuracy, such as adding part-of-speech and dependency information to existing rules. In addition, when conjunctions such as "*mata wa*" (又は, "or"), "*katsu*" (かつ, "and"), and "*oyobi*" (及び, "and/or") are included, as in Fig. 7, it is necessary to divide the parallel relationship so that it is easy to understand.

6   Conclusion

We investigated a method for automatically converting law texts into propositional calculus to support a law text learning system using logic circuits. As a result of analysis based on legal condition–effect structures, it was possible to tag law texts having relatively simple structures, as intended.

In the future, to improve the identification accuracy of constituents, we will consider identification patterns that utilize morpheme category information, etc., and perform machine learning using manually converted texts as learning data to automatically formulate logical formulas. We will also divide the condition part in consideration of parallel relationships such as "*oyobi*" (及び, "and/or") and "*katsu*" (かつ, "and").

Acknowledgments. This work was supported by JSPS KAKENHI Grant Number 20H01730.

References

1. Intellectual Property Promotion Plan 2020 Homepage. https://www.kantei.go.jp/jp/singi/tit eki2/kettei/chizaikeikaku20200527.pdf. Accessed 7 Feb 2021. (in Japanese)
2. Takako, A., Shuya, N., Koichiro, K.: Topic analysis of syllabus for faculty of engineering in the Japanese National University. Jpn J. Educ. Technol. **42**(Suppl.), 81−84 (2018). (in Japanese)
3. Masashi, K., Toru, K., Takako, A.: Development and evaluation of learning support system using error-based simulation in problem exercise of intellectual property law. IEICE Tech. Rep. **119**(331), 33–36 (2019). (in Japanese)
4. Tomoya, S., Isao, I., Takahito, T., Tomoya, H., Atsushi, Y., et al.: Experimental use of error-based simulation for force on moving object in science class at junior high school in Japanese. IEICE Trans. D **J99-D**(4), 439–451 (2016). (in Japanese)
5. Richard, M.F.: Learning and teaching styles in engineering education. Eng. Educ. **78**(7), 674–681 (1988)
6. Kikuo, T.: About semantic function of the legal - effect's restrictive part. Inf. Process. Soc. Jpn Rep. Nat. Lang. Process. **124**(21), 1–8 (1998). (in Japanese)
7. Tolmachev, A., Daisuke, K., Sadao, K.: Juman++: a morphological analysis toolkit for scriptio continua. In: Eduardo, B., Wei, L. (eds.) Proceedings of the 2018 Conference on Empirical Methods in Natural Language Processing: System Demonstrations, pp. 54−59 (2018)
8. Kurohashi, S., Nagao, M.: KN parser: Japanese dependency/case structure analyzer. In: Proceedings of the Workshop on Sharable Natural Language Resources, pp. 48−55 (1994)

Using User-Guided Development to Teach Complex Scientific Tasks Through a Graphical User Interface

Alexis R. Tudor$^{(\boxtimes)}$, Richard M. Plotkin, Aarran W. Shaw, Ava E. Covington, and Sergiu Dascalu

University of Nevada, Reno, Reno, NV 89557, USA

Abstract. As more and more data are collected from the night sky, it becomes increasingly important to be able to analyze the data precisely and quickly by using computer programs. Given the importance of data analysis pipelines for telescopes we have developed a photometric pipeline, Photometry+, for the Great Basin Observatory (GBO), a 0.7-m robotic telescope located in the Great Basin National Park in Nevada. This photometric pipeline takes raw images of the night sky and measures the brightness of a star in the image. Studying the changes in the brightness of a star over time is crucial for learning more about variable objects such as supernovae and binary star systems. Photometry+ focuses on human-computer interaction (HCI) in addition to scientific results. The HCI goals of the proposed pipeline are to create a graphical user interface (GUI) that is easy to use, gives astronomers control of and confidence in the results of the program, and teaches students the process of differential photometry through use. User studies show that Photometry+ achieves these goals, cementing it as a new tool for professional astronomers looking to reduce the time they spend on data analysis while still obtaining publication-quality results and for students looking to learn the process alike. The program is publicly available and while its open source code has been designed for the GBO telescope it is flexible enough for use with data from any observatory.

Keywords: Astrophysics · Photometry · Education · UX design · User study

1 Introduction

The importance of data analysis in astrophysics has become indisputable as data gathering techniques have gotten larger and faster. The spotlight has thus begun to shine on data science and software development as key supporting fields of astrophysics. Given the importance of data analysis pipelines for telescopes of all kinds, we have developed a photometric pipeline, Photometry+, for the Great Basin Observatory (GBO), a 0.7-m robotic telescope located in the Great Basin National Park in Nevada [1]. The GBO is the first research grade observatory

© Springer Nature Switzerland AG 2021
S. Yamamoto and H. Mori (Eds.): HCII 2021, LNCS 12766, pp. 141–155, 2021.
https://doi.org/10.1007/978-3-030-78361-7_12

located in a U.S. National Park, shown in Fig. 1, enjoying dark skies free of light pollution. It partners with universities in order to inspire researchers and students alike to enjoy astrophysics.

The goal of a photometric pipeline is to analyze raw images of the night sky that are taken by counting photons hitting a charge coupled device (CCD) to calculate the magnitude, a measure of the flux or brightness of a target star or celestial object (this paper will refer solely to stars going forward). The measurement of fluxes represents one of the most basic deliverables from astronomical images, which in most cases is one of the key pieces of information to determine the physics driving astronomical phenomena. For example, supernovae represent exploding stars, which are discovered via the sudden appearance of a bright source in the sky. Or, monitoring changes in the flux of a star over time can (sometimes) indicate changes in its surface temperature and/or radius, or provide information on the orbital parameters of certain binary systems. However, in between those images and the result are several steps that can be tedious to do by hand. For each sky image there are an additional two to three calibration files that are used to remove noise and pixel-to-pixel variations from the raw CCD images. After the noise is removed, noise from cosmic and terrestrial background radiation needs to be subtracted as well by taking a median of photons counted from "blank" sky. Once the error is reduced by removing noise, the magnitude of a target star can be calculated by comparing it to other stars of known magnitude and taking an average of the results calculated for each comparison. The process of comparing a target object to multiple reference stars can take up to a half hour per image to do by hand. However, by automating the process Photometry+ can perform these same tasks in less than 20 s per image.

To prevent Photometry+ from being a black box tool, we focus on the human-computer interaction (HCI) components of the program. The HCI goals of the proposed pipeline are to create a graphical user interface (GUI) that is easy to use, gives astronomers control over the program, increases confidence in the results of the program, and can be used to teach students the process of differential photometry. To validate the accomplishment of these goals three user studies were conducted, two of which have been used to guide the development of Photometry+, and a final user study to validate that Photometry+ can be used as a teaching tool for the complex task of differential photometry. The first two user studies tested how long it takes inexperienced and experienced astronomers, respectively, to use the GUI to complete the task, the parts of the process they found confusing, their confidence in the tool, and how much they feel they learned about differential photometry through using the tool.

Using the feedback received from the first two user studies, a public-release version of Photometry+ was developed and the final user study was completed with this version. The final user study tests the hypothesis that user-guided development of a GUI can be used to create scientific tools that are useful for (i) experienced astronomers completing routine results generation, and (ii) beginners looking to learn more about the process. User confidence in the results was measured both in terms of the control users feel they have over the program,

Fig. 1. The Great Basin Observatory, Nevada (courtesy of the Great Basin Observatory).

and in their confidence in the accuracy of the results obtained. We also present examples of the application of Photometry+ for monitoring variable objects. Photometry+ provides a new look at photometric pipelines with the user and HCI principles in mind. This user-oriented design allows Photometry+ not just to be a tool for experienced astronomers, but also a teaching tool for students and others looking to learn differential photometry. While Photometry+ was designed with a specific scientific process target, this approach is generalizable enough to be used on any tool seeking to teach a difficult scientific concept through performing a task.

2 Background and Related Works

The age of big data has changed the way many fields are able to operate, including astronomy and astrophysics. Telescopes around the world produce a colossal amount of data, with some telescopes producing data in the exabyte range [26]. It is only natural that the large amount of data needing to be processed has put an emphasis on data analysis pipelines of all sorts. One kind of data analysis pipeline, the photometric pipeline, focuses on performing different kinds of photometry on telescope images to calculate the flux of stars. Most of these photometric pipelines are not generalized, but rather built with a single telescope or telescope system in mind (with only a few exceptions [17]). Some of these pipelines are open source and, although they are designed for a specific telescope they allow for other researchers to use modified versions of their pipeline. An example of this is the Legacy Survey of Space and Time (LSST) Science Pipeline [11], which is designed for the Vera C. Rubin Observatory but whose code is available and modifiable for anyone interested in it. One of the broadest photometric pipelines available is designed for the All Sky Automated Survey for SuperNovae (ASAS-SN), which is not a single telescope but a network of telescopes designed to work together to image the entire night sky [12]. The ASAS-SN photometric pipeline works through a web portal that allows users to generate a light curve of anywhere in the night sky, assuming that there is data for that space at the time when the user wants to observe. However, large telescopes and surveys are not the only systems with automatic pipelines. Smaller telescopes for different purposes, like the Watcher robotic telescope in Boyden Observatory, have photometric pipelines designed for them [7]. Some photometric pipelines are even designed with a backlog already in mind, such as the pipeline created for the Robotic Optical Transient Search Experiment (ROTSE)-IIId archival data [8]. That photometric pipeline is used almost exclusively for archival data, though that is not always the case for pipelines designed to handle archival data. The pipeline for the Wide Field Astronomy Unit (WFAU) is built to parse data fast enough to continually process new data in addition to processing archival data that has backed up [6]. Clearly the creation of photometric pipelines for telescopes around the world is widespread, and with Photometry+ there is now a new pipeline for the GBO telescope as well [24].

While the general goal of all photometric pipelines is to perform photometry on images from telescopes, many pipelines are made with additional goals in mind. For instance, some pipelines are designed to cater to specific types of stellar objects rather than a telescope. One such example, the Pippin pipeline, is an open source pipeline designed for supernova-based analysis [9]. However, not all of the pipelines with additional goals are focused on certain stellar objects. Some of these pipelines instead direct their attention toward data quality or other mechanical parts of the astrophotography process. One such example is a pipeline that uses a convolutional kernel to reduce the effect blurry images have on the final photometric calculation [10]. Like these other pipelines, Photometry+ includes more than the standard goal of performing photometry. Unlike these other pipelines however, the additional goal of Photometry+ does not focus on space or data correction, but rather on the human element of interacting with the pipeline.

Scientific software and usability have always had a complicated history. Software developers can often be entirely absent when it comes to making the computational tools that scientists use on a daily basis. Thus, good design practice can often be neglected. This problem goes back to the early days of software being used as a scientific tool with observers noting that the creation of user interfaces (UIs) for scientific tools are ill-funded, poorly understood, and less emphasized [5]. And although it is not a focus in scientific software, usability-centered design can have many benefits including reducing user errors, reducing the time it takes to learn to use a tool, and making software more generalizable. Adding user-centered design principles to scientific software doesn't have to be difficult either, as studies have shown beginning the process doesn't take very long and brings many benefits [16]. In recent years usability has become a focus of some astronomy developers, such as in visualization software for radio astronomy [21]. Rampersad et al. used user-guided development to create their visualization tool, holding user studies in between prototypes and molding it to be more user-friendly and easy to use. We also argue that this can be taken a step further by combining these development user studies with research studies that validate what a pipeline can do for the user. Pipelines can be more than just user-friendly; they can be a valuable teaching tool for students looking to learn complicated scientific processes. Photometry+ is a new step in the combination of HCI and astronomy, as a tool that obtains high quality results and is easy to use. It is also a teaching tool for those looking to learn about differential photometry.

3   Photometry+ Design

Photometry+ is a photometric pipeline that performs differential photometry using Python. It can be used in one of two ways, with both methods working independently of each other. The code that runs the system can be run in the Python terminal, and the backend of the program is fully functional on its own. The second method, that this paper covers in more detail, is the GUI for Photometry+. The GUI makes the program accessible even to inexperienced users and is focused on making differential photometry usable and easy to learn.

3.1   System Design

Photometry+ performs all the stages of differential photometry with minimal user input. Figure 2 shows a flowchart representing the steps of differential photometry performed by the program. To begin, users simply need to upload a telescope image and the stellar coordinates for the target star whose magnitude will be calculated. At this stage users can also optionally add calibration files for automatic calibration of their images and change the default settings of the program. Examples of the settings that can be changed include setting an Astrometry.net API key, choosing how to calculate the radius of the target star, and choosing which VizieR [18] catalog (or SIMBAD [25]) to search for reference stars. Once the user has chosen their settings the program can be run.

Autonomous differential photometry follows the same steps as manual differential photometry. These steps are calibration of the telescope image, finding background radiation noise to subtract out, locating reference stars of known magnitude in the image, and comparing the reference stars to the target star to calculate a comparative magnitude of the target star. These individually calculated target star magnitudes are averaged together to create the final target star magnitude for that image. An error is also calculated for this magnitude through

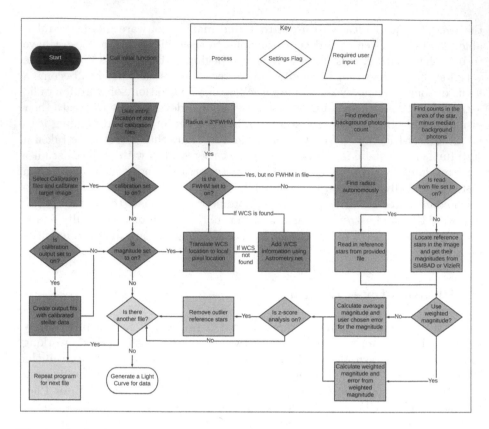

Fig. 2. Abridged version of the steps Photometry+ takes to perform differential photometry.

a user's choice of standard deviation, weighted magnitude, or a jackknife method for photometric uncertainties [2]. This process is repeated for many images taken at different points in time. After calculating the magnitudes for every image in a set, Photometry+ generates a publication-quality light curve (like the light curve in Fig. 3, a graph of the magnitude of a star over time.

To create Photometry+ and allow it to be robust required several external resources. Like many other astronomy tools, Photometry+ used the Astropy library [3,23], photutils [4], and DAOPHOT [22]. Additionally, Photometry+ pulls information from the APIs for Astrometry.net [15], VizieR, and SIMBAD. These external dependencies are shown in the context diagram presented in Fig. 4.

3.2   User Interface Design

The user interface for Photometry+ was designed with open source PyQt5 [20]. The main components of the user interface include a page to create a new project,

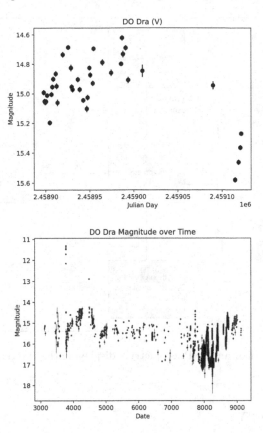

Fig. 3. Light curve made with Photometry+ utilizing GBO data (top) matched with data from AAVSO, where the Photometry+ results are green and AAVSO results are blue (bottom). The match in the bottom figure demonstrates that Photometry+ works with a comparable accuracy to other top photometric pipelines.

shown in Fig. 5, a "My Projects" page where users can view their already created projects, an "About" page where users can learn more about the program and its creators, a page where users can change their default settings, and a page with frequently asked questions and a contact form. This user interface was designed with user-guided development, following the style of user testing outlined by Steve Krug [13,14]. Two development user studies were conducted with 3 and 4 participants respectively, and feedback from those user studies were used to improve the GUI to better accomplish the HCI goals of the program.

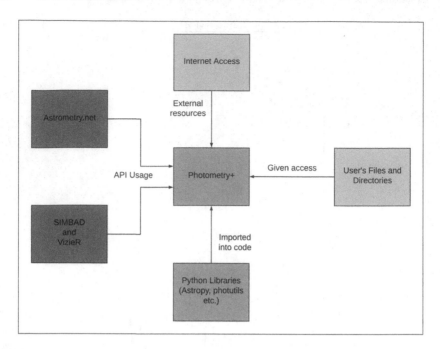

Fig. 4. The context diagram for Photometry+ displaying the external dependencies of the system.

4   Methodology

The main experiment described in this paper involves a user study wherein participants were asked to perform tasks related to differential photometry with the fully developed Photometry+. These tasks were done with data from the GBO telescope and a SIMBAD page, shown in Fig. 6, containing location information for the star DO Dra.

4.1   Participants

The recruitment for this user study targeted physics and astrophysics students, faculty, and researchers. Recruitment messages were sent out at the 237th meeting of the American Astronomical Society, to the Great Basin Observatory users committee, to the University of Nevada, Reno (UNR), Department of Physics, the UNR astronomy club, and other local astronomy groups. This targeted recruitment ensured that the participants using Photometry+ were a part of its final target audience in order to accurately test whether astrophysics students and researchers who may not use differential photometry often can perform the process with this tool. Participants filled out a pre-study survey that collected demographic information, including gender, education level, astronomy experience, and photometry experience.

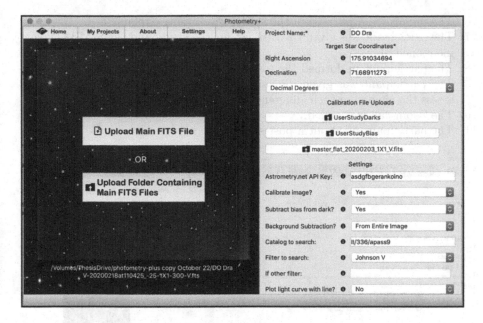

Fig. 5. The "New Project" page of Photometry+ filled out.

4.2 Apparatus

Due to the unfortunate COVID-19 pandemic, all user studies for this research were conducted remotely via the video and messaging application Zoom [27]. Participants were asked to take remote control over the study administrators computer to take a brief quiz, perform some tasks on the program and then take another brief quiz. The tasks performed with Photometry+ were based entirely on the user interface of the program and no interaction with code or Python was required. Each user study took less than forty-five minutes in total.

4.3 Procedure

To maintain consistency between every study, a script was followed when performing the user studies and all emails sent to participants were the same. This ensured that each participant had the same experience to minimize confounding variables. Every study followed the following procedure:

1. The participant was asked to sign a consent form and recording release.
2. The participant filled out a pre-study survey with a unique participant ID.
3. The participant joined a Zoom call with the study administrator.
4. The participant was given remote access to the testing machine with the quizzes and Photometry+ available.
5. The participant was given a differential photometry quiz that briefly assessed their prior differential photometry knowledge.

6. The premise and purpose of the study were briefly explained.
7. The participant was given the task list for the study and the SIMBAD page mentioned above.
8. The participant performed the tasks on the list using Photometry+.
9. The participant was given the same quiz as they took at the beginning to assess the change in their differential photometry knowledge.
10. The Zoom call was ended.
11. The participant filled out a post-study survey.

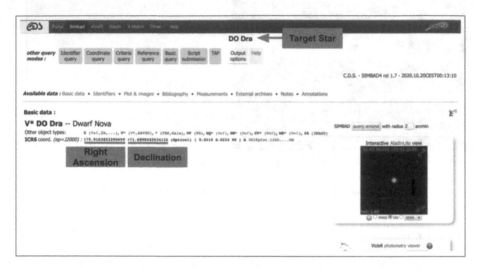

Fig. 6. The example SIMBAD page that was provided to participants of the user study.

The pre-study survey participants filled out concerned demographic information such as age, gender, education, and level of astronomy and photometry knowledge. The differential photometry quiz scored users out of 12 based on questions about photometric calibration, differential photometry steps, and other related knowledge. This quiz was given twice. The tasks the participants were asked to perform included creating a new Photometry+ project targeting DO Dra, changing default settings, and observing the results of their project. After the users finished performing tasks and retook the quiz, they were given a post-study survey that asked questions concerning the look and feel of Photometry+, their confidence in its results, and whether they learned more about differential photometry by using it.

4.4   Experimental Design

Independent variable: Prior use of Photometry+
Name: Photometry+ Exposure
Levels: Before use, after use
Dependent variable: Differential photometry knowledge

The independent variable being manipulated was whether participants had been exposed to Photometry+ before or not. Thus, participants were measured on differential photometry knowledge before and after using the program for the first time. Changing the Photometry+ Exposure variable should produce a change in the dependent variable, differential photometry knowledge, as our hypothesis was that Photometry+ can teach differential photometry.

The amount of entry in this experiment is 12 participants ×2 administered quizzes for 24 phases. Thus this is a 12×2 within-subjects design.

5   Experimental Results

For each of the twelve research user study participants, demographic information was collected through the use of a pre-study survey, with the results shown in Fig. 7. 75% of the participants were in the 18–24 age range, with a few participants in the 25–34 and 45–54 age ranges. Additionally, 75% of the participants were male, similar to the demographics in the physics field [19]. Users came from a variety of education levels ranging from undergraduate students to graduate degree holders. The predominant operating system was Windows. As expected from our targeted recruitment, all participants had at least a little experience with astronomy, though a large percentage were less experienced with photometry.

Using the post-study survey, we collected data from the participants concerning how easy it was to use Photometry+. For statements like "Photometry+ is easy to use", "The user interface of Photometry+ is well designed", "Photometry+ is intuitive", and "Photometry+ is easy to navigate", users consistently rated their agreement with the statement between "Strongly Agree" or "Agree", which were 5 and 4 respectively, on our Likert scale. The average participant scores for those statements were 4.58 for "Photometry+ is easy to use" and 4.33 for "The user interface of Photometry+ is well designed", "Photometry+ is intuitive", and "Photometry+ is easy to navigate". When asked questions concerning the aesthetics of Photometry+, users rated them 4.33 on average overall. Additionally, timing the user study showed that participants took an average of 10.66 min to complete their first photometry project, despite never having used the software prior.

The primary HCI goal of Photometry+ is to teach students differential photometry in addition to being an analysis tool. To assess this we administered a short quiz on differential photometry before and after the participants used Photometry+. As shown in Fig. 8, the mean score on the quiz that participants took after using Photometry+ measured at 81%, which is 15% more than the 66% mean score from before participants used Photometry+. This difference, when analyzed with ANOVA, is statistically significant ($F = 7.54$, $p < .05$). Additionally, on the post-study survey, participants were asked to agree or disagree with the statement "Photometry+ taught me more about performing differential photometry" on a Likert scale. The average value of the responses was 4.08 on a scale where five points was the maximum.

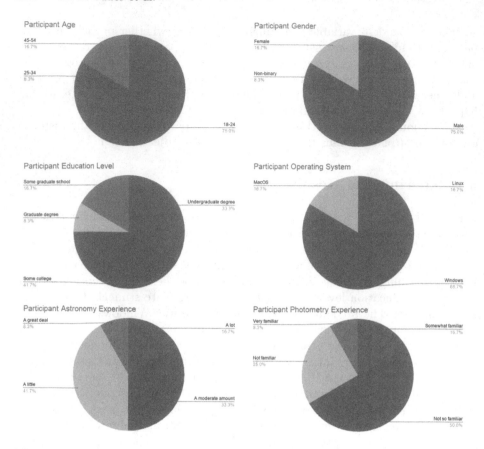

Fig. 7. Pie charts representing the demographics of the study participants based on the pre-study survey each participant filled out.

6 Discussion

The data gained from the experiments shows that Photometry+ achieves its HCI goals of being easy to use and of teaching differential photometry. Through directly measuring use time, we can ascertain that, even with little experience with photometry and no experience with Photometry+, participants could still perform differential photometry in a reasonable time span, with many of the participants expressing the sentiment that they could repeat the process more quickly if they needed to use the software again. By directly measuring improvement in differential photometry knowledge with the quizzes, we conclude that there is a statistically meaningful knowledge boost associated with using Photometry+. It is apparent that both HCI goals were achieved when looking at the directly measured data.

Photometry+ not only accomplished these goals, but also convinced users that these objectives were met. In addition to being able to use the program

Participant	Photometry+ Exposure Level	
	Before	After
1	92%	83%
2	67%	75%
3	58%	75%
4	50%	100%
5	75%	75%
6	75%	100%
7	50%	83%
8	58%	67%
9	83%	67%
10	75%	92%
11	50%	83%
12	58%	67%
Mean	66%	81%
SD	14%	12%

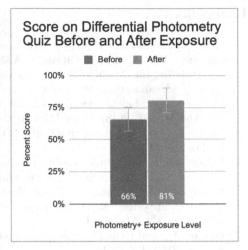

Fig. 8. Detailed information on the performance of participants on a differential photometry quiz before and after exposure to Photometry+.

in about ten minutes, participants directly ranked Photometry+ as being easy to use and intuitive in the post-study survey. Likewise, participants on average agreed with the statement that they learned more about differential photometry from using Photometry+, which means that users are aware of the learning potential of Photometry+. Participants both measurably increasing their learning and feeling that they learned more effectively is a great endorsement of the power of software to support teaching and performing complex scientific tasks.

7   Conclusion

In conclusion, Photometry+ is the result of the combination of successful user-guided development techniques and HCI research into making an easy-to-use software tool that can double as a teaching tool for complex scientific tasks. This addresses a clear need for scientific software designed with end-users in mind, and can decrease the difficulty involved with learning new scientific methods. The methodology detailed in this paper could be used to create software for any variety of scientific tasks in a broad variety of fields, and our results show that it works for scientists of all levels of experience. Photometry+ is an open source program that will continue to be worked on, expanded and adjusted. Its ability to create accurate, high-quality light curves and teach students differential photometry makes it an excellent candidate for adoption by other telescopes or projects.

Acknowledgements. Great thanks to the Great Basin Observatory, Nevada, for their support of this project and the use of their telescope.

References

1. Great basin observatory. https://greatbasinobservatory.org/
2. Anderson, W.L., Smith, S., Gillen, D.: A simple and direct measure of photometric uncertainties. Int. Amateur-Prof. Photoelectr. Photom. Commu. **81**, 16–21 (2000)
3. Astropy Collaboration, Price-Whelan, A.M., et al.: Astropy contributors: the astropy project: building an open-science project and status of the v2.0 Core Package. **156**(3), 123 (2018). https://doi.org/10.3847/1538-3881/aabc4f
4. Bradley, L., et al.: Astropy/photutils: 1.0.0, September 2020. https://doi.org/10.5281/zenodo.4044744
5. Chiozzi, G., et al.: Trends in software for large astronomy projects (2007)
6. Cross, N., et al.: A matched aperture photometry pipeline incorporated into the WFAU archives. In: Manset, N., Forshay, P. (eds.) Astronomical Data Analysis Software and Systems XXIII. Astronomical Society of the Pacific Conference Series, vol. 485, p. 371, May 2014
7. Ferrero, A., et al.: The photometry pipeline of the watcher robotic telescope. Adv. Astron. **2010**, 1–5 (2010)
8. Güçsav, B.B., et al.: A pipeline for the rotse–iiid archival data. Exper. Astro. **33**(1), 197–209 (2012)
9. Hinton, S., Brout, D.: Pippin: a pipeline for supernova cosmology. J. Open Source Software **5**(47), 2122 (2020). https://doi.org/10.21105/joss.02122
10. Huang, W., et al.: Robust automated photometry pipeline for blurred images **132**(1013) (2020). https://doi.org/10.1088/1538-3873/ab8e9b
11. Ivezić, Z., et al.: LSST: from science drivers to reference design and anticipated data products. Astrophys. J. **873**(2), 111 (2019). https://doi.org/10.3847/1538-4357/ab042c
12. Kochanek, C.S., et al.: The all-sky automated survey for supernovae (ASAS-SN) light curve server v1.0. Publications of the Astronomical Society of the Pacific **129**(980), 104502 (2017). https://doi.org/10.1088/1538-3873/aa80d9
13. Krug, S.: Don't Make Me Think: A Common Sense Approach to Web Usability. Voices That Matter, Pearson Education (2009)
14. Krug, S.: Rocket Surgery Made Easy: The Do-It-Yourself Guide to Finding and Fixing Usability Problems. Voices That Matter, Pearson Education (2009)
15. Lang, D., Hogg, D.W., Mierle, K., Blanton, M., Roweis, S.: Astrometrynet: Blind astrometric calibration of arbitrary astronomical images. Astronom. J. **139**(5), 1782–1800 (2010)
16. Macaulay, C., et al.: Usability and user-centered design in scientific software development. IEEE Software **26**, 96–102 (2009). https://doi.org/10.1109/MS.2009.27
17. Mommert, M.: Photometrypipeline: an automated pipeline for calibrated photometry. Astron. Comput. **18**, 47–53 (2017). https://doi.org/10.1016/j.ascom.2016.11.002, http://www.sciencedirect.com/science/article/pii/S2213133716300816
18. Ochsenbein, F., Bauer, P., Marcout, J.: The VizieR database of astronomical catalogues. **143**, 23–32 (2000). https://doi.org/10.1051/aas:2000169
19. Porter, A.M., Ivie, R., American Institute of Physics, S.R.C.: Women in physics and astronomy, 2019. Technical report, AIP Statistical Research Center (2019)
20. PyQT: Pyqt reference guide (2012). http://www.riverbankcomputing.com/static/Docs/PyQt4/html/index.html

21. Rampersad, L., Blyth, S., Elson, E., Kuttel, M.M.: Improving the usability of scientific software with participatory design: a new interface design for radio astronomy visualisation software. In: Proceedings of the South African Institute of Computer Scientists and Information Technologists. SAICSIT 2017, New York, NY, USA. Association for Computing Machinery (2017). https://doi.org/10.1145/3129416.3129899
22. Stetson, P.B.: DAOPHOT: a computer program for crowded-field stellar photometry **99**, 191 (1987). https://doi.org/10.1086/131977
23. The Astropy Collaboration, Robitaille, T.P., et al.: Astropy: a community python package for astronomy. A&A 558, A33 (2013). https://doi.org/10.1051/0004-6361/201322068
24. Tudor, A., Plotkin, R., Shaw, A., Covington, A., Dascalu, S.: User-guided development of a photometric pipeline for the great basin observatory robotic telescope. In: Poster Presentation at the 237th Meeting of the AAS (2021)
25. Wenger, M., et al.: The SIMBAD astronomical database. CDS Reference Database Astronom. Object. **143**, 9–22 (2000). https://doi.org/10.1051/aas:2000332
26. Zhang, Y., Zhao, Y.: Astron. Big Data Era. Data Sci. J. **14**, 11 (2015). https://doi.org/10.5334/dsj-2015-011
27. Zoom Video Communications Inc.: Video conferencing, web conferencing, webinars, screen sharing - zoom. https://zoom.us/. Accessed 20 Jan 2021

Preparing Undergraduate Students for Summer Research Experiences and Graduate School Applications in a Pandemic Environment: Development and Implementation of Online Modules

Kim-Phuong L. Vu(✉), Chi-Ah Chun, Keisha Chin Goosby, Young-Hee Cho, Jesse Dillon, and Panadda Marayong

California State University Long Beach, Long Beach, CA 90804, USA
{Kim.Vu,Chi-Ah.Chun,Keisha.ChinGoosby,Young-Hee.Cho,
Jesse.Dillon,Panadda.Marayong}@csulb.edu

Abstract. Engaging students in research is a high impact practice that improves student retention and persistence in behavioral and biomedical sciences and engineering. The California State University Long Beach (CSULB) Building Infrastructure Leading to Diversity (BUILD) Program offers an intensive research training experience to undergraduate students from a wide range of health-related disciplines. The goal of this program is to provide students with research skills, psychosocial resources, and graduate school application guidance that will make them competitive for Ph.D. programs. With the COVID-19 pandemic forcing the campus closure of many universities, including CSULB, our student training had to transition from in-person training to online training. This paper discusses the development and implementation of a series of eight online modules for guiding students through the application process for summer research experiences and graduate schools. Overall, the BUILD trainees were positive about the online modules. Specifically, they indicated that the modules were useful, informative, easy to access/use, good use of their time, and a good supplemental activity to their learning community activities. Most trainees indicated that they preferred the modules to be implemented in a hybrid format, where the students can view the modules on their own first and then have an opportunity to engage in in-person/synchronous online discussions.

Keywords: Undergraduate training · Online modules · Professional development

1 Professional Development for Undergraduate Students

1.1 The CSULB BUILD Program and Background

Engaging students in research is a high impact practice that has been shown to improve student retention and persistence in STEM fields [1]. Funded by the National Institutes

© Springer Nature Switzerland AG 2021
S. Yamamoto and H. Mori (Eds.): HCII 2021, LNCS 12766, pp. 156–176, 2021.
https://doi.org/10.1007/978-3-030-78361-7_13

of Health (NIH), the California State University Long Beach BUilding Infrastructure Leading to Diversity (CSULB BUILD) Program offers an intensive research training experience to undergraduate students from a wide range of disciplines from behavioral, health and natural sciences to engineering (for more information about the program, see [2]). CSULB BUILD offers two training programs: Scholars and Fellows. The Scholars Program provides 2 years of training for undergraduates who are starting their junior year, and Fellows is a 1-year program for graduating seniors. The training curriculum was designed to prepare students to apply to graduate schools and pursue a research career in health-related disciplines. In addition to the hands-on research experience that trainees gain from working with their faculty mentors, it covers professional development activities to enrich the students' training experience. This paper describes the creation, implementation, and evaluation of online modules that prepare students for their search and application to summer research experiences (SREs) and graduate schools.

The professional development modules on application for SREs and graduate schools were initially developed for in-person delivery as part of a learning community for CSULB BUILD trainees. The learning community format was intended to provide students, especially those from underrepresented backgrounds, with the knowledge and resources needed to apply to SREs and graduate schools in a culturally relevant and supportive context. Scholars and Fellows participate in the learning community with members of their own cohort.

Starting in March 2020, the COVID-19 pandemic forced the campus closure of many universities, including CSULB. The switch to remote or alternative modes of instruction meant that our student training activities had to transition from an in-person format to an online format. Fortunately, the CSULB BUILD Program leadership was already in the process of converting the modules relating to application for SREs and graduate schools to an online format as part of the broader plan for institutionalization of our grant-funded training curriculum. The content of the online modules, which consist of lecture and activities, was intended to be used as a starting point for in-person discussion during the BUILD learning community or with one-on-one meetings with the BUILD training directors and graduate assistants (called graduate mentors hereafter). An important advantage of the online format is that it allowed students the opportunity to re-visit the information at their own time and pace. This provided BUILD students with flexibility in viewing the modules since many students have very busy schedules. Moreover, research has shown that underrepresented students and students with family commitments have a greater preference for online course materials [3] because they are able to access the course materials outside of classes, especially during the night [4].

In the 2018–2019 academic year, the CSULB BUILD team worked with Academic Technology Services (ATS) on campus to create the first set of five online modules relating to graduate school preparation. These modules were designed to provide BUILD students with an overview of the graduate school application process and help them develop a SMART (Specific, Measurable, Achievable, Relatable, Time-based) [5] action plan that they can implement. In the 2019–2020 academic year, three additional online modules, *Individual Development Plan (IDP), Summer Research Experience (SRE),* and *How to Interview Successfully for Graduate School,* were developed.

Beginning spring 2021 all of these professional development modules were also made available to other undergraduate students at CSULB who are interested in learning about research opportunities and pursuing training at the graduate levels. Our goal is to expand their use on our campus and disseminate them to other institutions that serve diverse undergraduate students. Although the transition of these professional development modules to an online format was originally intended for sustainability and dissemination, the use of these modules proved to be highly instrumental during the shift to online learning due to COVID-19. This paper discusses the development and implementation of the eight online modules for guiding students through the application process for SREs and graduate schools before and during the pandemic. At the end of the paper, we provide lessons learned and recommendations for implementation at our campus and other universities.

1.2 Topics for the Online Modules in Support of Applications for SREs and Graduate Schools

A series of eight online modules (Table 1) were developed to support students with their applications for SREs and graduate schools. The modules vary in length and number of videos and quizzes.

Table 1. Module names, durations and contents.

Module name	Duration	# of Videos	# of Quizzes
Individual Development Plan (IDP)	19 m 19 s	14	1
Graduate School Application Process	36 m 53 s	9	6
Curriculum Vitae and Statement of Purpose (CV & SOP)	41 m 35 s	20	1
Letter of Recommendation (LOR)	24 m 4 s	7	1
Summer Research Experience (SRE)	21 m 32 s	10	1
GRE Preparation and Expectations	59 m 5 s	18	2
How to Interview Successfully for Graduate School	24 m 28 s	13	1
Seeking Financial Support for Graduate Schools	20 m 49 s	6	1

The online module series begins with a module on the *IDP* that was designed to help students set goals to guide them through the undergraduate research training process. Originally created to support the professional development of postdoctoral fellows, IDP is now regarded as an effective tool for undergraduate students' preparation for graduate education and research careers [6]. Our IDP module explains what an IDP is; the difference between short-term, intermediate, and long-term goals; the importance of setting goals and re-visiting/up-dating them; how to identify and assess skills; tips for bridging gaps in desired skills; and how to get input from mentors, peers, and family members. The module encourages students to pause at various timepoints to access the templates related to goal setting and skill assessment. At the end of the module, students are expected to produce their own IDPs.

Because our training program is geared towards preparing students for a doctoral program that leads to a research career, the module on the *Graduate School Application Process* provides students with a step-by-step overview of the graduate school application process, describes the different types of masters and doctoral degrees available in health-related disciplines, and discusses important factors to consider when researching and selecting potential graduate programs. The module also includes the importance of having a "Plan B," in case students do not get into a Ph.D. program the first time that they apply.

The next module was designed to provide students with information on preparing a *Curriculum Vitae (CV) and Statement of Purpose (SOP)*, essential elements of both SRE and graduate school applications. The *CV & SOP* module was divided into two sub-modules. The CV sub-module explains how to present biographical information, education, research activities, teaching activities, additional professional experiences, grants, honors and awards, service and publications and provides specific examples. The SOP sub-module explains the purpose and structure of the SOP and provides strategies to compose and revise one with specific examples and hands-on writing activities for each step of the writing process.

The *Letters of Recommendation (LOR)* module was designed to help students learn about the materials and processes they should use for obtaining LOR from their research mentors and course instructors to accompany their applications. This module also includes: what programs look for in LOR, who is qualified to write letters, the request timeline, as well as examples for an application portfolio that they can provide their letter writers. Trainees create an application portfolio with an IDP, CV, and SOP for use when requesting LOR.

The portfolio also provides the foundation to help students find external research opportunities such as SRE. The *SRE* module provides students with guidance and tips on how to find and apply to rigorous and competitive SRE programs at research-intensive universities, government laboratories or industry settings. The *SRE* module explains what an SRE is, the benefits of undergraduate research, where to look for SRE programs, how to apply, the SRE application timeline, and how to discuss SRE programs with family members who may be hesitant with their college student traveling and staying away from home for an extended period of time. The module also includes additional tips and video testimonials from past student trainees who participated in an SRE.

The remaining three modules are specifically targeted toward graduate school applications: preparing students for the GRE, interviewing, and financing graduate school. The *GRE* module provides an overview of the exam and its process and explains how the GRE scores are typically used in graduate program admissions. Specific topics in this module include: how to create an ETS account, what to expect on the day of testing, the structure of the computer delivered/online test, a discussion of when to take the GRE, and a description of each section of the test. In addition, students are introduced to fee reduction programs as well as given guidance for test preparation and how to select and send their scores to a graduate program. The module also addresses some of the factors that may influence underrepresented minority students' preparation for the exam (e.g.

cost of preparation courses or materials) and performance on the exam (e.g. test anxiety) and what students can do to mitigate their impact.

The *How to Interview Successfully for Graduate School* module discusses what students should expect and plan for when interviewing for graduate school. Specific topics include: the purpose of the interview (i.e., why the interview is important), typical components of an interview, how to prepare for an interview, and what to expect in terms of logistics and financial support for the interview day and/or travel to the programs. This module also includes video testimonials from past student trainees who shared tips and recommendations based on their personal experiences.

Finally, the *Seeking Financial Support* module provides an overview of the timeline for financial aid and other types of funding mechanisms. It also describes the differences in funding options available to students for graduate school such as fellowships, grants, and teaching and research appointments and explains the advantages and disadvantages of each type of funding option. Finally, it explains how students should evaluate different kinds of funding packages that graduate programs typically offer.

As indicated in Table 1, the modules contain quizzes that assess students' understanding of the content and serve as an indication of completion to progress to the next module in the series. Although the modules have been described above in a specific order, each was designed to be a stand-alone module and can be assigned to students in any order. In the CSULB BUILD Fellows Program and Scholars Program, modules are selected to cover appropriate topics based on the curriculum of the specific training program in which a trainee participates. For example, the activities for Fellows who are graduating seniors primarily focus on preparing them for graduate school application, whereas the activities for Scholars focus on application to SREs in their first year of the program and graduate school application during their second year.

2 Method

2.1 Subject Matter Experts

The subject matter experts (SMEs) that created the content of the online modules were recruited from the training directors of the CSULB BUILD Student Training Program and other staff members at the university's Graduate Studies Resource Center. Training directors include the Principal Investigators and Associate Director of the BUILD Program as well as faculty members from four colleges (Engineering, Health and Human Services, Liberal Arts, and Natural Sciences and Mathematics) participating in the BUILD Program. SMEs also recruited students who completed SREs and graduate interviews to share their experience and advice. Training directors developed and refined the content of each of the learning community modules that were delivered in-person. All SMEs have extensive experience in the topic areas that they covered, are active mentors to undergraduate students, and have the knowledge, skills, and abilities to generate content appropriate for the online modules.

2.2 Module Creation and Editing

A BUILD module coordinator worked with the SMEs and instructional designers from ATS to create the modules. The SMEs and instructional designers were paired to work on specific modules together. The role of the coordinator was to provide continuity of the module development across the different SMEs and instructional designers. The following activities outline the general process used for creating and editing the modules. The specific activities that the coordinator, SMEs, and instructional designers engaged in varied slightly from one module to another module.

1. Development of each module began with a "kick-off" meeting with the coordinator, the SME(s), and instructional designers assigned to the module. The kick-off meeting was intended to allow the various individuals working on the project to meet each other and to set up expectations about what would be involved in the module creation.
2. The SMEs worked with their assigned instructional designers to create an initial conceptual map that typically went through several iterations.
3. The SMEs provided content for the module to the instructional designers. The content included PowerPoint™ lecture slides, web resources, documents, worksheets and a script (i.e., narration for the videos). When the SMEs and recruited students (for testimonials) completed the script writing and/or presentation slides, the designated instructional designers used them to create storyboards to capture the instructional designers' vision for the module design. Next, they met with the SMEs and students to map out the parts that would be video recorded or audio recorded with graphic slides and videos created by the instructional designers. All slides were converted to either Prezi or other graphic presentation format.
4. The instructional designers selected the initial graphic content, scheduled and edited the audio and video recordings, and formatted other materials (e.g., quizzes, handouts, web pages). For graphic presentations, photo images or video files were selected to enhance the delivery of content along with text summaries. All images, videos, and text displays were reviewed and approved by the SMEs.
5. All modules included a combination of video-recorded introductions and voice-over Prezi or graphic presentations. For each module, the introduction video featured one of the SMEs who prepared the module so that the students would know what the "presenters" look like and make the module relatable. At least one more segment was video recorded with the SMEs to break the monotony of the voice-recorded graphic presentations.
6. The instructional designers delivered drafts of the modules and their supplemental material for the SMEs and the coordinator to review and provide feedback. This step was an iterative process. Some modules (e.g., *How to Interview Successfully for Graduate School*) contained videos with student testimonials, and the student presenters approved the use of their videos.

7. The instructional designers uploaded the "full" versions of the modules into the learning management system for pilot testing.
8. Each module was reviewed for clarity and appropriateness by the 2019–2020 cohorts of BUILD trainees who used the beta versions as part of their learning community activities.
9. The instructional designers uploaded the "final" versions of the modules, with closed captioning added, into the learning management system.

2.3 Implementation in Course Management System

Once all the modules were developed, the instructional designers uploaded them into BeachBoard, the Desire-2-Learn (D2L)-based learning management system used at CSULB. The module coordinator and SMEs checked the components in the modules and made revision requests to ATS, if necessary. Figure 1 illustrates the homepage for the course, and Fig. 2 is a screen shot of the content for one of the modules.

Fig. 1. Screenshot of the BUILD online module homepage implemented in CSULB's learning management system.

BUILD training directors are able to export the entire content of the module from the host course or any of its components into their own course for use in a particular learning community.

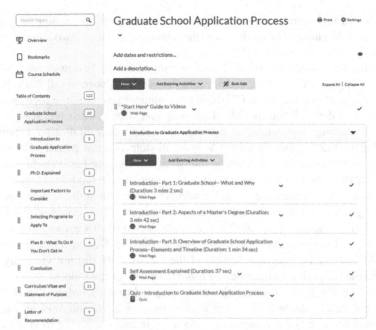

Fig. 2. Screen shot of the *Graduate School Application Process* module implemented in CSULB's learning management system.

3   Implementation

Both the Fellows Program and Scholars Program begin with an eight-week intensive summer training session called Summer Undergraduate Research Gateway to Excellence (SURGE). SURGE consists of a weekly commitment of 40 h, including a 3-h-long twice-a-week summer learning community run by their respective training directors. During the academic year, the commitment is reduced to 15–20 h weekly, with a 1-h-long weekly learning community. The online professional development modules were incorporated into the learning community curriculum.

3.1   2019 Pilot Testing of Beta Versions

The pilot testing was conducted in summer and fall of 2019 with the beta version of four of the first module set: *Graduate School Application Process, LOR, CV & SOP,* and *Seeking Financial Support.* Fellows (n = 15) who were in their final year at CSULB viewed all four modules. They began with two modules that were completed in summer 2019: *Graduate School Application Process* and *LOR.* Trainees were instructed to first watch the video recordings on their own time. The viewing of the modules was supplemented by in-person lectures and a homework assignment. For homework, the trainees were instructed to conduct research on potential graduate programs that they might be interested in applying to and develop their "Preliminary List of Graduate Programs" using the criteria explained in the *Graduate School Application Process* module. All

Fellows viewed the entire *Graduate School Application Process* module. All but one Fellow viewed the entire *LOR* module, and the remaining trainee viewed more than 70% of the videos.

Following the completion of the initial two modules, the Fellows cohort watched the next two modules, *CV & SOP* and *Seeking Financial Support,* in fall 2019. Because students had already created their CV during the summer program, the focus in the fall semester was on the SOP sub-module. The group had three in-class breakout activities during their learning community to develop and refine their SOP after viewing the module. Lastly, the *Seeking Financial Support* module was not paired with a formal discussion about the topic immediately following the viewing because their contents were self-explanatory. Students were required to complete the module quizzes for both modules. The quizzes were used to track students' completion of the modules and were part of the graded activities for the learning community. Two-thirds of the Fellows watched all of the videos for the *SOP* sub-module, 20% did not view any of the videos, and 13% viewed between 30–60% of the videos. For the *Seeking Financial Support* module, 80% of the Fellows watched all of the videos, 13% did not view any of the videos, and the remaining trainee viewed more than 80% of the videos.

The first year Scholars trainees (hereafter referred to as Scholars 1; n = 16) did not pilot test the *Graduate School Application Process*, *LOR* and *Seeking Financial Support* modules as those contents were meant for trainees applying to graduate programs. Instead, the Scholars 1 cohort focused on the *CV & SOP* module, which was delivered in fall 2019 in a fully hybrid format consisting of asynchronous online and in-person instructions. Specifically, in preparation for their SRE applications, the Scholars 1 trainees were assigned to view the entire *CV & SOP* module on their own, created their first draft CV and SOP, and refined each two more times with the advice of their training director. The Scholars 1 cohort had one in-class and one outside-of-class feedback session on CV and two in-class breakout activities and two outside-of-class feedback sessions to refine their SOP. Even though the *CV & SOP* module was assigned, students were not required to complete the quizzes and their viewing was not part of their grade. The Scholars 1 trainees were also encouraged to view the remaining modules on their own as they became available, but these modules were not graded for their learning community. Implications of this "volunteer" form of delivery will be discussed later along with the evaluation survey results for this cohort.

In terms of usage, 43% of the Scholars 1 cohort viewed all CV videos and 56% of them viewed at least half of the CV videos. Only 19% of the Scholars 1 cohort viewed all SOP videos and 43% viewed at least half of the SOP videos. The lower viewership of the CV & SOP videos for this cohort may be the result of these modules not being part of the graded learning community activities. Also, only one Scholars 1 trainee viewed all of the graduate application process videos and 2 additional students viewed one of those videos (i.e., only 19% of the students viewed any videos for this module).

Despite the lower usage rate for the Scholars 1 cohort, feedback from a BUILD program evaluation focus group and informal conversations with the Scholars and Fellows, their near-peer graduate mentors, and the training directors who used the modules in their learning community revealed that the modules were promising. The trainees generally found the module content helpful and preferred to keep each sub-module video in a shorter length. Some problems with viewing the modules and the quizzes on Beach-Board were reported and resolved for the subsequent versions. The training director of the Scholars 1 Program shared that the modules ran smoothly and the trainees produced an excellent second draft CV. For many Scholars 1, the second draft was good enough to be their final CV for their SRE application.

3.2 2020 Implementation of the Full Set of Online Modules During Remote Learning Instruction Period

Due to the pandemic, CSULB pivoted to fully remote instruction beginning mid-March of 2020. Accordingly, the CSULB BUILD Program had to finish its in-person training activities for the academic year of 2019–2020 in a virtual format and modify the training curriculum to make it fully virtual for 2020–2021 academic year. The online professional development modules provided much-needed flexibility in delivery, while allowing students to have remote access to critical information. By June 2020, the remaining modules, *IDP, SRE,* and *How to Interview Successfully for Graduate School,* were completed. Therefore, we were able to implement the full set of online modules for the virtual Fellows Program and Scholars Program beginning summer 2020.

A new cohort of Fellows trainees (n = 15) began the virtual SURGE training in June 2020. Six of the online modules were assigned as required asynchronous assignments outside of the twice-a-week synchronous learning community meetings. Those modules were: *Graduate School Application Process, GRE, CV & SOP, LOR, IDP,* and *Seeking Financial Support.* Fellows watched the modules in the order listed above over the period of eight weeks of SURGE. Following students' asynchronous viewing of each module, the next synchronous session provided "in class" time for discussion, sharing of examples and templates, drafting of documents and statements, and feedback from the training team on student drafts. The SME who created the *Seeking Financial Support* provided a Q&A session with the trainees following the module. The only module that did not include a focused discussion during SURGE was the *LOR* module. This topic was part of a synchronous discussion later in the fall term, when students began requesting letters from faculty.

In fall 2020, Fellows viewed the *How to Interview Successfully for Graduate School* module during the final weeks of the semester. During the last synchronous learning community of the fall semester in December 2020, training directors provided more details and tips for interviewing. By the time students viewed this module, they had finalized a list of prospective graduate schools and had already begun submitting applications. Since invitations to interview would soon follow, the timing of this module and the subsequent discussion were appropriate.

The new cohort of Scholars 1 (n = 16) also began with a virtual SURGE training in June 2020. They first viewed the *IDP* module asynchronously, followed by synchronous discussion of their IDP with other Scholars during a breakout session. In the fall, three additional online modules were assigned: *CV & SOP, SRE,* and *LOR.* The *CV & SOP* and *SRE* modules were covered in a hybrid format that consists of asynchronous viewing of the video modules followed by synchronous virtual class activities. For example, after viewing the module videos on their own, Scholars 1 trainees created the first draft CV and SOP, and refined each two more times in preparation for their application for the SRE next summer. As in the Fellows cohort, the group had one in-class and one outside of class feedback session on CV and four in-class breakout activities and two outside of class feedback to refine their SOP. Each draft of CV and SOP was graded by the graduate mentors. Training directors and students' faculty research mentors also provided feedback on the last two drafts of CV and SOP. Unlike the pilot testing of the beta versions in 2019–2020, the 2020–2021 Scholars 1 cohort was required to take a quiz for each module as graded activities for the BUILD learning community.

As in the pilot testing of the beta version, we continued to gather feedback in class from the BUILD trainees. Many trainees commented that the people in the photos and videos were often mostly or all White and/or represented non-academic, business, corporate or commercial settings as they were from standard stockpile images accessible by ATS. In order to address this group feedback, a group of BUILD trainees volunteered in fall 2020 to give more detailed review and feedback, with a particular focus on the photo and video images to make sure that the images of people are representative of our diverse student body and relatable for our students. In response, the ATS purchased or created original images of individuals that are more diverse and reflective of academic settings and contexts. Any images replaced by the instructional designer were then reviewed and approved by the SMEs of the corresponding module or by the module coordinator.

4   Evaluation of 2020 Virtual Module Implementations

4.1   Data Source

Evaluation of the virtual implementation of the online modules was based on (a) instructor feedback, (b) student usage data from the course management system and (c) student self-report data from an online evaluation survey. The online evaluation survey was administered in January 2021 to trainees currently in the program to assess trainees' general experiences with the online modules on their informativeness, usefulness, accessibility, length, etc. Trainees consist of the 2019–2020 Scholars 1 cohort (referred to as 2019 Scholars 1, Pilot), 2020–2021 Fellows cohort (2020 Fellows), and 2020–2021 Scholars 1 cohort (2020 Scholars 1). Note that the 2019 Scholars 1, currently in the second year of the program, are referred to as the Pilot group that serves as a comparison group for the fully virtual implementation of the modules. Unlike the 2020 cohorts who have been remotely trained due to the pandemic, the pilot group viewed the beta version of the online modules asynchronously and discussed the materials synchronously in person. The 2019–2020 Fellows cohort who also viewed the beta version did not participate in the online survey as they already completed the BUILD training in May 2020 and graduated from CSULB.

4.2   Instructor Feedback

Training directors reported that the use of the online modules during SURGE 2020 was beneficial to students in three ways. First, it helped to reduce the number of hours that students had to participate in synchronous virtual lectures, and it allowed training directors to allocate more time for interactive activities. Second, it provided students with ongoing access to important foundational information outside of formal meeting times. Third, students gained more time to spend on guided practice and to receive feedback during synchronous meetings with their training directors and graduate mentors.

In addition, the modules provided sufficient foundational knowledge so that trainees could draft meaningful versions of their IDP, CV, and SOP before the SRE and graduate school application season began. After receiving feedback from training directors and graduate mentors, trainees had drafts to review with their research faculty mentors when they met to discuss their applications.

4.3 Student Usage and Feedback

Only a subset of the three cohorts of trainees enrolled in the BUILD learning community during spring 2021 completed the survey: 2019 Scholars 1, Pilot (n = 11), 2020 Scholars 1 (n = 13), and 2020 Fellows (n = 15).

Usage Data. Usage data obtained from the course management system were analyzed by examining the percentage of trainees that accessed the modules (i.e., viewed at least one video), the percentage of trainees that viewed the entire module (i.e., viewed all videos), and average percentage of videos viewed by trainees.

During SURGE, the 2020 Fellows cohort was assigned 6 modules consisting of 97 videos/documents. The Fellows viewed on average 96% of all module materials, with 73% of Fellows trainees viewing all of the content in the modules. The 2020 Scholars 1 cohort was assigned the *IDP* module consisting of 20 video/documents. The trainees viewed on average 92% of all *IDP* module materials, with 69% of Scholars trainees viewing all of the content in the modules.

In fall 2020, additional modules were assigned as part of the learning communities for all three BUILD cohorts. The 2020 Fellows were assigned one module consisting of 14 video/documents. They viewed on average 80% of all module materials, with 60% of trainees viewing all of the content in that module. The 2020 Scholars 1 were assigned three modules consisting of 75 video/documents. Trainees viewed on average 67% of all module materials. No trainee viewed all of the content in the modules, but 2 trainees (12.5%) viewed more than 90% of the materials and 5 trainees (31%) viewed more than 70% of the materials. The 2019 Scholars 1 (Pilot), now in their senior year, were not assigned specific modules. Instead they were recommended to review the modules in preparation of their graduate school applications and the quizzes were not enforced. Only 50% of these trainees accessed any of the modules during their 2nd year.

Trainees were also asked to report on the online survey which of the eight modules that they viewed during SURGE and during the academic year learning communities. The percentage of trainees in each cohort that viewed a particular module is illustrated in Fig. 3a–c. These self-report data matched the usage data obtained from the course management system described above.

Subjective Feedback. On the online survey, trainees were asked a series of questions with the stem, "Based on your experience with the online module(s) you have viewed, please indicate your level of agreement for each of the following statements about the module(s)" on a 5-point Likert-like scale (1 = strongly disagree, 2 = somewhat disagree, 3 = neither agree nor disagree, 4 = somewhat agree; 5 = strongly agree). One sample

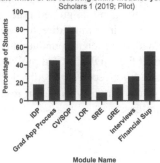

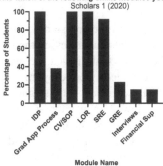

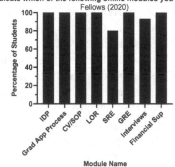

Fig. 3. Percentage of BUILD trainees who viewed each of the specific online module topics: a) 2019 Scholars 1 (Pilot); b) 2020 Scholars 1; c) 2020 Fellows

t-tests were performed on the ratings for each question, collapsed across cohorts, against a test value of 4 (somewhat agree) to gauge the strength of trainees' overall endorsement for each item. Table 2 shows the mean ratings and the results of t-tests. One-way analyses of variances (ANOVAs) were also run for each question with the BUILD cohort (2019 Scholars 1, Pilot; 2020 Scholars 1; or 2020 Fellows) as a factor to determine whether there is a significant difference between the pilot implementation of the beta versions of the online modules and the fully virtual implementation of the revised modules. The *F*-ratio and *p*-value for each analysis are also provided in Table 2. The alpha-level was set as 0.05 for statistical significance. Figure 4 (a–h) illustrates the mean ratings by cohort for questions showing a significant effect of cohort.

Table 2. Ratings on a 5-point Likert-like scale (1 = strongly disagree to 5 = strongly agree) to each survey question. Statistics for the one sample t-tests and ANOVAs are listed in the last two columns. Significant effects are highlighted in bold.

Question	Mean	St. Dev	Test value = 4.0	Effect of Cohort
The module(s) was/were **informative** (i.e., the module(s) covered all the information that I would need to know about this topic and/or I learned a lot about the topic)	4.65	0.58	**t(39) = 7.09, p < 0.001**	**F(2,36) = 6.13, p = 0.005**
The module(s) was/were **useful** (i.e., the information is relevant and I have/will be able to use the information. For example, I learned to prepare applications for summer research experiences/graduate schools)	4.53	0.68	**t(39) = 4.89, p < 0.001**	**F(2,36) = 5.31, p = 0.010**
The module(s) was/were **easy to use** (e.g., easy to navigate through)	4.58	0.71	**t(39) = 5.11, p < 0.001**	F(2,36) = 2.57, p = 0.091
The module(s) was/were **easy to access** (e.g., accessible from computer or mobile device)	4.60	0.81	**t(39) = 4.68, p < 0.001**	F(2,36) = 0.94, p = 0.401
The module(s) was/were **appropriate in length** (i.e., not too long or too short)	4.38	1.03	**t(39) = 2.30, p = 0.027**	F(2,36) = 1.36, p = 0.270
The module(s) was/were a **good supplement to the learning community activities**	4.55	0.85	**t(39) = 4.11, p < 0.001**	F(2,36) = 2.30, p = 0.114

(continued)

Table 2. (*continued*)

Question	Mean	St. Dev	Test value = 4.0	Effect of Cohort
The module(s) was/were **appropriate as a stand-alone learning activity** (i.e., I can fully use the information presented in the module(s) without additional guidance or activities)	4.23	0.87	$t(38) = 1.65, p = 0.107$	$F(2,35) = 1.66, p = 0.205$
The module(s) was/were a **good use of my time** (i.e., it saved my time by providing information that would have taken more time for me to find on my own)	4.60	0.59	$t(39) = 6.43, p < 0.001$	$F(2,36) = 12.08, p < 0.001$
The **graphics/videos in the module(s) were appropriate** for the topics being covered	4.67	0.58	$t(38) = 7.21, p < 0.001$	$F(2,35) = 6.81, p = 0.003$
The **graphics/videos in the module(s) were "professional"** looking	4.62	0.63	$t(38) = 6.07, p < 0.001$	$F(2,35) = 4.07, p = 0.026$
The **graphics/videos in the module(s) were relatable** to me	4.33	0.81	$t(38) = 2.58, p = 0.014$	$F(2,35) = 3.52, p = 0.040$
The **graphics/videos in the module(s) were representative of students at CSULB**	4.33	0.87	$t(38) = 2.40, p < 0.022$	$F(2,35) = 2.83, p = 0.073$
The **quiz or quizzes in the module(s) fairly assessed my familiarity, knowledge and understanding** of the content of the module(s)	4.30	0.82	$t(39) = 2.31, p = 0.027$	$F(2,36) = 6.78, p = 0.003$
I would recommend the module(s) to a friend who wants to learn more about the topic(s) covered by the module(s)	4.55	0.71	$t(39) = 4.87, p < 0.001$	$F(2,36) = 12.36, p < 0.001$

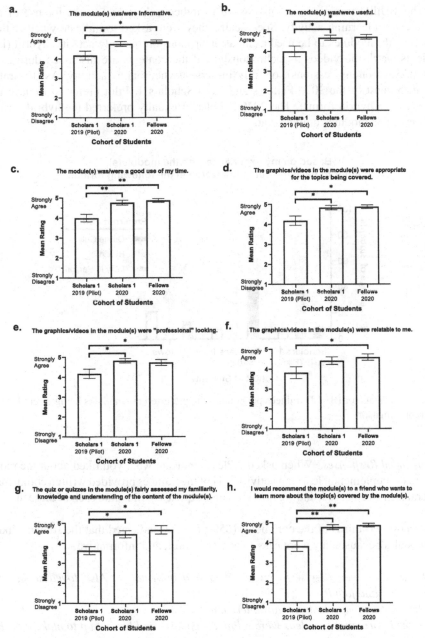

Fig. 4. Mean rating of the module(s) by cohort for a) informativeness, b) usefulness, c) good use of time, d) appropriate graphics/videos, e) professional looking, f) being relatable, g) fairness of quizzes, and h) recommend to a friend. Post-hoc Bonferroni pairwise analyses were conducted and illustrated as * for $p < 0.05$ and ** for $p \leq 0.001$.

The BUILD trainees were also asked to indicate their preference for use of the modules as a learning activity. Specifically, they were asked to indicate whether they preferred the modules to be used as an asynchronous online only activity, hybrid (i.e., students watch the videos asynchronously and the contents are discussed during in-person/synchronous sessions), or fully in-person/synchronous activity. As illustrated in Fig. 5, most of the 2020 Fellows and 2019 Scholars 1, Pilot preferred to have the modules in a hybrid format. The 2020 Scholars 1 equally preferred the hybrid format and the online modules only format.

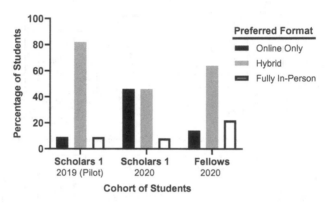

Fig. 5. Percentage of BUILD trainees per cohort who preferred the modules being offered in the different formats.

Open-Ended Responses. When asked, "Please indicate what you liked about the module(s) as a supplemental learning activity", 34 of the trainees provided written comments. Several themes emerged, and we provide sample quotes to illustrate each of these themes below.

Almost two-thirds of the comments (65%; n = 22) indicated that the students liked the modules because they were easy to access, useful, and informative:

1. *I liked how well they were put together and informative. Also loved seeing my directors and faculty.*
2. *Provided a comprehensive introduction to the topics.*
3. *… the informational videos were relatively concise and broken up to make it easier to digest information.*
4. *They provide essential information step-by-step. I have utilized many of the advice when applying for summer research programs or drafting my SOP and CV.*

Over one-third of the comments (35%; n = 12) indicated that the students liked the ability to view the modules at their own pace and/or revisit the modules:

1. *I highly appreciate that we can go back to modules for future reference.*
2. *I liked being able to complete them at my own pace. It allowed for me to be familiar with the material and prepare questions for the follow-up meetings rather than using the time to introduce the topic.*
3. *It is helpful that you can pause, slow down and go back in the video modules to re-grasp the information provided. Also, I always use the CC because I tend to miss things when I hear them but when I can read it as well, it is beneficial for my understanding.*

When asked, "Please indicate what you did not like about the module(s) as a supplemental learning activity. Can you think about a way (or ways) to improve BUILD's use of the module(s)?", 29 out of 37 trainees provided written comments. The following quotes are organized by themes.

Almost one-quarter of the comments (24%; n = 7) indicated that the students did not dislike anything or did not have suggestions for improvement:

1. *The videos/modules were good as is!*
2. *... these modules provided very important information and were great in every way. Although I would have liked everything in person, the internet is a great tool because I was able to access the information on my own time and multiple times if I needed to.*

Almost one-quarter of the comments (24%; n = 7) indicated that the students did not like the number of short videos or wanted to know how long it would take to view the entire module:

1. *I did not like having to change the page in between videos, and not knowing how long the whole module was going to take before I started working on it.*
2. *I did not like how the videos were split up into multiple short sections.*
3. *The way the videos were broken up. I think some could have been combined.*

Some students (17%; n = 5) indicated that the modules were too basic or too general, and did not have enough specific examples:

1. *I believe this is a general view of the processes that take place. If there was a bit more of more unique situations being shown, that would be great.*
2. *Some modules should include more extensive information.*
3. *The information that was covered was mostly introductory/basic*

Some students (17%; n = 5) indicated that the modules needed to be part of discussions of the learning communities so that students can ask questions:

1. *I liked the modules as a supplemental learning activity, however, I think there may be room for discussion in an LC (learning community) session.*
2. *Incorporating the modules as assignments or as part of the LC presentations could motivate more participation in using the modules.*

3. *The only issue with the modules is that if I have questions, I am unable to have those questions answered right away...*

A few students (10%; n = 3) indicated that they would have liked a summary added to the modules:

1. *I would suggest providing a summary sheet of the info covered, like in bullet point format. That way students can reread the summary in the future without clicking through all the videos.*
2. *... the graphics could/should be combined to create flyers to summarize key points.*
3. *... The quizzes for some modules could do with more questions; the quiz was helpful in summarizing/reminding me of what I learned, so only having 5 questions is not enough to remind me of most of the covered information.*

Two students (7%; n = 2) provided other comments:

1. *I do think some of it was repetitive. I think we go over a lot of it in LC so it makes the modules a little redundant[1]*
2. *Just to make sure to have CC on all the videos uploaded for accessibility*

5 Discussion

The online modules on the topics relating to applying for graduate schools and SREs were viewed by students who participated in the BUILD Program between summer 2019 and fall 2020. More trainees viewed the modules when they were not only assigned to them, but when there was also a grade assigned to the activity. Overall, the BUILD trainees were positive about the modules that they viewed. Specifically, they agreed that the modules were useful, informative, easy to access/use, a good use of their time and a good supplemental activity to their learning community activities. The trainees also found the video/graphics to be appropriate, professional looking, and relatable. The only question with which trainees did not agree was, "The module(s) was/were appropriate as a stand-alone learning activity...". This finding is consistent with the preference for a hybrid approach to using the modules from two of the cohorts.

Our results are also consistent with a meta-analysis of studies comparing online, hybrid, and traditional in-person courses performed by the US ED [7], that found hybrid courses (instruction that combines online and in-person components) to be more effective than purely in-person and purely online instruction. Moreover, the use of online modules in a hybrid format provides students with more flexibility in their schedules. Thus, even when in-person classes resume, we will explore continuing to use the online modules in a hybrid format. They can continue to be assigned prior to an in-class discussion about the topic and/or used at appropriate times in the semester as a way to review the information prior to taking a specific step in the SRE or graduate school application.

---

[1] This comment was from a trainee in the 2019 Scholars 1, Pilot cohort. This cohort received in-person instruction on the topics that were covered in some of the modules.

Finally, the online modules themselves can be further improved by expanding the quizzes and providing a summary sheet for each module's highlights that students can view in one place and could also be downloaded and/or printed.

5.1 Lessons Learned

When using the modules in the future, trainee feedback shows that instructors should explain that some modules are intended to provide an introduction to the topic. In addition, students should take notes and record their questions to be addressed during the next in-person or synchronous session to maximize the learning. Students who are unfamiliar with hybrid learning may simply forget to use some of the strategies that they normally use during in-person classes. Instructors should therefore provide tips for using educational videos.

The timing of most module assignments aligned well with the discussions that were planned for the synchronous sessions. However, it may be more beneficial for graduating trainees to view the LOR module at the beginning of the fall semester, rather than during the summer term. There is more discussion about requesting LOR in fall when faculty return to campus and are available to receive student requests.

Another finding from our use of online modules as a part of student training is that enforcing the quizzes helps to ensure that trainees complete the modules in their entirety. The results indicate that students who were required to view the modules and complete the quizzes did so at a much higher rate than trainees who were encouraged but not required to do so. More importantly, these trainees perceived the modules more favorably in all regards compared to the 2019 Scholars 1, Pilot cohort who did not view the videos as part of grading requirement (refer to Fig. 4 a through h). Feedback to expand quizzes provided by a trainee also revealed that the assessments help trainees reinforce the content they just learned from viewing the videos.

Lastly, simply having access to online modules did not lead to sufficient utilization. The 2019 Scholars 1, Pilot group's lower usage as well as lower perceptions of helpfulness of the modules suggest that if implemented, modules need to be a required activity with grading consequences. This can ensure that students view sufficient content to benefit from the modules.

5.2 Recommendations for Dissemination and Adoption

The successful development and implementation of online modules depend on a coordinated team effort. Involving faculty, staff, and resources that are available through the campus contributes to successful collaboration. The results also show that students appreciate seeing and hearing familiar faces and voices (i.e., diverse representation) when viewing the modules.

Because development began ahead of the pandemic, the online modules were completed and ready for student use when there was a sudden need to move to remote learning. Creating tools such as the online modules can provide greater flexibility both in times of crisis and when serving students with diverse needs. There is now an opportunity for universities to develop and introduce online modules so that instructors and students can use them in ways that enhance in-person meetings.

One strategy that may improve the experience of using the online modules as a fully virtual learning tool is the use of an online discussion board. This strategy was not employed in this study. However, our trainees expressed their need to pose questions or ask for clarification while viewing. Instructors can determine whether the discussion boards can be used for students to post questions, relevant examples, and/or additional information and resources related to the topic.

While many campuses now use a learning management system, it is still important to stress that the interface should be user-friendly for both the instructor who manages the content and the students who will access the content. Accessibility concerns also include student access to technology, high-speed internet, and a physical space that is conducive to remote learning. Just as important is ensuring that students who are hearing and/or visually impaired can receive full benefit from module contents. Finally, when the course ends, instructors will need to ensure that students continue to have access to the modules so that they can refer to them in the future as needed.

Acknowledgments. We thank the SMEs and CSULB's ATS department and their instructional designers for their work creating the online modules. We also thank the BUILD training directors, staff, graduate mentors, and student trainees who help implement or use the online modules as part of the BUILD training curriculum. Last but not least, we thank the Center for Evaluation and Educational Effectiveness (CEEE) and Dr. Nada Rayyes, the BUILD Program Evaluator for their evaluation work.

This work was supported by the National Institute of General Medical Sciences of the National Institutes of Health under Award Numbers UL1GM118979, TL4GM118980, and RL5GM118978. The content is solely the responsibility of the authors and does not necessarily represent the official views of the National Institutes of Health.

References

1. Hippel, W., Lerner, J., Gregerman, S., Nagda, B., Jonides, J.: Undergraduate student-faculty research partnerships affect student retention. Rev. Higher Educ. **22**, 55–72 (1998)
2. Urizar, G.G., et al.: Advancing research opportunities and promoting pathways in graduate education: a systemic approach to BUILD training at California State University, Long Beach (CSULB). BioMed Central (BMC) Proceedings **11**(12), 26–40 (2017)
3. Pontes, M.C.F., Hasit, C., Pontes, N.M.H., Lewis, P.A., Siefring, K.T.: Variables related to undergraduate students' preference for distance education classes. Online J. Distan. Learn. Adm. **13**, 1556–3847 (2010)
4. Bosch, N., et al.: Modeling key differences in underrepresented students' interactions with an online STEM course. In: Proceedings of the Technology, Mind, and Society. ACM (2018)
5. Doran, G.T.: There's a SMART way to write management's goals and objectives. Manage. Rev **70**(11), 35–36 (1981)
6. Bosch, C.G.: Building your Individual Development Plan (IDP): A guide for undergraduate students. STEM and Culture Chronicle. SACNAS (2013)
7. Means, B., Toyama, Y., Murphy, R., Bakia, M., Jones, K.: Evaluation of evidence-based practices in online learning: a meta-analysis and review of online learning studies. Washington, D.C.: U.S. Dept. of Education (2009)

Advancing Inclusive Mentoring Through an Online Mentor Training Program and Coordinated Discussion Group

Kelly A. Young[1](✉), Malcolm A. Finney[2], Panadda Marayong[3], and Kim-Phuong L. Vu[4]

[1] Department of Biological Sciences, California State University Long Beach, Long Beach, CA 90840, USA
Kelly.Young@csulb.edu
[2] Department of Linguistics, California State University Long Beach, Long Beach, CA 90840, USA
Malcolm.Finney@csulb.edu
[3] Department of Mechanical and Aerospace Engineering, California State University Long Beach, Long Beach, CA 90840, USA
Panadda.Marayong@csulb.edu
[4] Department of Psychology, California State University Long Beach, Long Beach, CA 90840, USA
Kim.Vu@csulb.edu

Abstract. Mentoring is key to ensure success of the high impact practice of undergraduate-led research and scholarly activities; however, most faculty and staff members are not trained in the best practices of mentoring undergraduate students. The National Institutes of Health-funded Building Infrastructure Leading to Diversity (NIH BUILD) Initiative at California State University Long Beach is developing an online mentor training program with a coordinated discussion group to refine mentoring skills across faculty and staff from all disciplines. Faculty and staff members participated in two pilots of the Advancing Inclusive Mentoring (AIM) Program, where participants watched training videos and came together to discuss mentoring: either face-to-face (spring 2020) or virtually (fall 2020). Participants indicated that the videos and discussion were engaging and reported that AIM provided useful information on communicating with their own mentees as well as with any student on campus. Participants also reported that AIM provided strategies to work with students from diverse backgrounds and strengthened their commitment to inclusive mentoring. Finally, participants indicated that they would recommend AIM to colleagues and that the program was not only beneficial to their mentoring, but also that they would put into practice techniques that they had learned. There were some differences in usage, but no significant differences in participants' ratings of the program across the two delivery formats. Thus, the AIM Program with facilitated discussion appears to provide a useful mentor training experience in both in-person and virtual formats. Because this unique program is intentionally inclusive to faculty and staff mentors across all disciplines, the goal is that this training will ultimately benefit student success across campus.

Keywords: Mentor training · Faculty development · Online learning

© Springer Nature Switzerland AG 2021
S. Yamamoto and H. Mori (Eds.): HCII 2021, LNCS 12766, pp. 177–194, 2021.
https://doi.org/10.1007/978-3-030-78361-7_14

1 Introduction

1.1 Impact of Mentoring

Mentoring is key to ensuring the success of the high impact practice of hands-on undergraduate research and scholarly activities. Trainees report that strong mentorship is critical to their success and contributes to their productivity, in addition to providing long term career benefits post-graduation [1–4]. Faculty mentors can influence student persistence in their undergraduate degree as well as a mentee's decision to continue in the field [5, 6]. Positive and inclusive mentoring experiences are of particular importance to mentees of historically marginalized groups [7–9]. Students who work closely with a faculty member on research or other scholarly or creative projects are more engaged and more likely to consider faculty mentors as resources [10, 11].

While mentoring is expected of most faculty members and many staff members on university campuses, few professionals have been formally trained in best practices in mentoring. Indeed, the definition of what constitutes mentoring can vary broadly both in practice and by researchers [12]. Recent definitions of mentorship include reference to a longer-term supportive relationship inclusive of both psychosocial and professional development for the purpose of enhancing mentee self-efficacy and success [13]. These modern definitions build upon earlier ones that include training of specific skills, presenting final products to professionals in the field, and other aspects of both career building, advice and support [14]. However, in actual practice mentoring received by students can differ substantially across mentors. Some mentors view the mentoring role as one dedicated solely to the training or development of discipline-specific skills, whereas others also include mentee growth and development as key aspects of a mentoring practice [6]. Indeed, the mere presence of a mentor itself may not be enough to generate the positive effects on mentees, particularly in terms of persistence to graduation and staying in the field from students belonging to historically marginalized groups [15, 16]. More important for these outcomes is the type of mentoring a student receives, speaking to the need of mentor training programs; however, most faculty and staff members are not trained in the best practices of mentoring undergraduate students [17, 18].

1.2 Mentor Training Programs

Targeted and formalized training for mentors of research students benefits both mentees and mentors. Mentors who completed training enhanced key mentoring skills, including communicating with mentees, promoting mentee professional development and independence, and ethical mentorship [18]. Students of mentors who have completed a formal mentor training program reported that their mentors provided a better mentoring experience, acknowledged their contributions more, and increased their motivation as compared to students of non-trained mentors [19]. Recent mentor training programs have been specifically developed for medical schools or large research institutions, PhD students, and post-doctoral fellows, providing critical mentor training to these specific groups [20, 21]. However, the needs of mentors at largely undergraduate institutions differ, as mentors of undergraduate researchers introduce inexperienced students with a high turn-over rate and limited time to conduct research to their disciplines [19].

To address both the need of a formal mentor training program and the requirement that it serves experienced mentors of primarily undergraduate research students, California State University Long Beach (CSULB) developed a mentor training program as part of the National Institutes of Health-funded Building Infrastructure Leading to Diversity (NIH BUILD) initiative. The CSULB BUILD program is designed to increase diversity in health-related research careers by supporting sites such as CSULB, a Hispanic Serving Institution (HSI) and Asian American Native American Pacific Islander Serving Institution (AANAPISI). The CSULB BUILD Mentoring Program was established in 2015 and successfully trained 93 faculty members across four Colleges (College of Engineering, College of Health and Human Services, College of Liberal Arts, and College of Natural Sciences and Mathematics) and 24 different Departments [19]. As part of the CSULB BUILD initiative, this training focused primarily on faculty mentors of undergraduate students in the health-related disciplines from the four participating colleges. However, interest from faculty and staff members outside of these disciplines, in addition to the desire to develop discussion of equity and inclusion in more detail, prompted an expansion of the program to our campus community as part of institutionalization efforts, and the Advancing Inclusive Mentoring (AIM) Program was created. Because time and accessibility are always factors to consider in the development of any training program, it was decided to create an online training course, with complementary discussion sessions to allow cohorts of faculty and staff working through the online course a venue to discuss the training material and share their experiences. In 2020, the CSULB BUILD program partnered with the Faculty Center on campus to pilot the implementation of the first two modules of this program. Originally, the intent was to have the complementary discussion sessions for the program held in-person to promote engagement and community within the university, which occurred in the first pilot of the program in spring 2020. However, due to the COVID-19 campus closure, the discussion sessions were held remotely during the fall 2020 semester. In this paper, we will compare the participants' viewing behaviors and ratings of the pilot program across semesters to determine whether the format of the discussion delivery impacts the overall effectiveness of the training experience.

1.3 Development of the Advancing Inclusive Mentoring (AIM) Program

The AIM Program includes six different modules with 35 episodes on communicating with students, inclusive mentoring, mentee growth and development, mentee health and wellbeing, mentee-centered mentoring, and a mentoring toolbox of tips (see Table 1). In addition to enlisting faculty and students in film production, different faculty members and administrators 'host' each episode to bring a feeling of shared ownership to AIM. These hosts introduce topics and tips, with additional suggestions provided by a narrator. Actors reenacted actual mentoring-related stories from CSULB students and faculty members, with names and affiliations changed, in order to engage viewers and provide context for the mentoring tips. As of fall 2019, the first two modules of the online AIM mentor training program had been developed. We piloted these two modules in the spring 2020 semester to obtain feedback about the content and appropriateness of the episodes. Moreover, to ensure that training had impact, we supplemented the two hours of video episodes from the modules with 3 hours of discussion (1.5-hours sessions followed the viewing of each of the two modules) led by the Director of the CSULB Faculty Center. The combined time for watching the videos and attending the discussion sessions exceeded the recommended minimum mentor training duration threshold of four hours, which was previously empirically determined to have impact on mentoring outcomes [22]. For the CSULB implementation of the AIM Program, the goal is to reward faculty members who complete the training with certificates of completion that provide a priority status when competing for select internal awards, such as the CSULB Summer Undergraduate Research Fellowship. For internal branding purposes and to engage the campus community, the AIM Program is called the 'Beach Mentor Program' at CSULB. The content of the Beach Mentor Program is identical in content to the AIM Program, which is designed for broader dissemination.

The implementation of the spring 2020 pilot was completed before the CSULB COVID-19 campus closure in March of 2020, but the closure delayed the filming and production of the subsequent modules that were intended to be piloted in fall 2020. In fall 2020, CSULB was open to remote instruction so the same two modules were piloted again, this time using a virtual discussion format with a new cohort of participants. The goal of this paper is to describe the implementation of AIM in both formats and compare participants' viewing behaviors and subjective evaluation of the modules across the different formats (i.e., in-person discussion vs. online discussions in a virtual environment).

Table 1. Modules in the Advancing Inclusive Mentoring Program

Module name	Number of Episodes
I. Communicating with your mentees	9
II. Inclusive mentoring	6
III. Cultivating mentee growth and development	5
IV. Supporting mentee health and wellbeing	5
V. Mentee-centered mentoring	5
VI. Mentoring toolbox	5

2 Implementation of the AIM Program Pilots

2.1 Participants

While the goal of the AIM Program is to be open to all faculty and staff who work with students in a mentoring role, participants for the pilots were more targeted. That is, participants were recruited from the CSULB BUILD faculty mentors (their mentees participate in a formal undergraduate research training program), staff with student advising roles who were recommended by their supervisors, and tenured/tenure-track faculty who were recruited directly by the Faculty Center. The groups included 15 participants (11 faculty and 4 staff members) in spring 2020 and 16 participants (11 faculty and 5 staff members) in fall 2020. The 31 total participants were from 27 different departments or programs across seven different colleges at CSULB.

2.2 Training Activities

For the pilot of the AIM Program, each cohort participated in two sessions, where participants watched the different episodes of the two modules on their own and came together every other week in a group led by the Director of the CSULB Faculty Center to discuss mentoring either: face-to-face (spring 2020) or virtually via online video conferencing (fall 2020). The first two modules of the AIM Program include the following episodes:

Module I, 'Communicating with your Mentees':

1. Active Listening
2. Constructive Feedback
3. Favoritism
4. Virtual Mentoring
5. Personalities and Communication
6. Nonverbal Communication
7. Power Differentials
8. Professional Limits in Mentoring
9. Communication Across Differences

Module II, 'Inclusive Mentoring':

1. Why Equity and Inclusion Matter
2. Identifying and Minimizing Unconscious Bias
3. Combating Discrimination
4. Strategies for Culturally Aware Mentoring
5. Understanding Privilege
6. Microaggressions in Mentoring

To facilitate participant access to the training materials, the AIM videos and supplementary resources were posted on a BeachBoard site, the Desire-2-Learn (D2L) learning management system used by CSULB. The participants' commitment involved watching the two modules (40–50 min each) and taking a short quiz to demonstrate understanding at the end of each module (2 quizzes total, with 9 and 7 questions, respectively, for Module I and II). To move onto the next module, participants were required to complete the quiz with a 50% success rate within 2 attempts.

Following module viewing and completing the quiz, participants engaged in a ninety-minute group discussion of each module. Participants in the spring 2020 group met in the CSULB Faculty Center for these discussions and in fall 2020 the discussions were held on the Zoom platform. During the sessions, faculty and staff members shared ways in which they could incorporate information shared in the episodes in their mentoring of students. The initial session with each cohort started with introductions during which participants were asked to share challenges (if any) they have had in mentoring diverse students. This provided participants the opportunity to identify biases they might harbor (with the explicit acknowledgment that everyone harbors biases). Group norms were also established, including making space for others to contribute, and maintaining confidentiality about personal information shared, while still using knowledge gained to inform future practice and actions.

At the start of each session, participants were asked to share major take-aways (the great, good, bad, and ugly) from the videos in terms of content and production, including whether they "saw themselves" depicted in the videos showing examples of both positive and unconstructive mentoring styles. Faculty Center handouts with additional information and case studies were made available to the participants prior to the discussion session. Each module contained several learning objectives, which were discussed independently or in conjunction with other objectives that addressed similar themes. The group discussed recommendations made for each objective and explored ways in which faculty/staff could become more effective mentors to mentees of diverse backgrounds, personality traits, abilities, and levels of academic and professional preparedness. Ideas were exchanged on lessons learned and how to address or avoid pitfalls identified in the videos. Participants were further encouraged to share examples of challenges relevant to each objective they had experienced in interacting with students, strategies they adopted in attempts to overcome such challenges, and whether there were indications that such strategies were effective.

Participants were reminded of the potential effects (positive and negative) mentors' practices could have on mentees, especially given the power dynamics that exist in the mentor/mentee relationship. Participants were reminded of verbal and non-verbal cues to be cognizant of as indicators of the efficacy of mentoring interaction. Each session additionally engaged participants in group discussion of activities (scenarios or real-life occurrences) relevant to learning objectives and the module in general. Major take-aways were reported to the entire group. Participants were also directed to the supplemental resources for each module made available through the learning management system. Each session ended with "final thoughts" during which participants were encouraged to identify one major takeaway from the module and to share something specific (if any) they planned to do differently when interacting with mentees in the future.

Following the completion of the program, participants were asked to complete a brief Qualtrics survey to assess the impact of the training program. For both the spring 2020 and fall 2020 cohorts, a third session was scheduled to obtain participant feedback about the program.

2.3 Data Sources and Statistical Analysis

Data for the two pilot modules of the AIM Program included usage data (number of videos in the module viewed, number of supplemental materials in the modules viewed, viewing dates, etc.) obtained from the learning management system. Quiz scores for each module were also obtained to measure participants' retention and comprehension of the topics covered. Participants' subjective ratings about the quality of the content and videos in the modules, as well as other open-ended comments were obtained through an online Qualtrics survey administered to the participants after completion of the two module discussion sections. Finally, a third discussion session was held on the Zoom platform as a focus group to collect comments from participants. Because the feedback from comments in the focus group was consistent with the survey feedback, results from the evaluation session will not be presented in the present paper due to space constraints. Descriptive and inferential statics were performed on the different dependent measures, and the specific analyses used will be described in the appropriate results section below. The alpha level for statistical significance for all analyses was set to $p \leq 0.05$.

3 Results

3.1 Participants' Viewing Behaviors and Module Quiz Scores

Participants' viewing data from the learning management system was analyzed to determine if there was an association between viewing behaviors and the format of the pilot program based on the semester of participation. Participants in spring 2020 experienced the discussion in an in-person format and participants in fall 2020 in a virtual format. Chi-Square analyses were performed to determine whether a relationship existed between the semester and when participants watched the videos in the modules and whether they watched the videos in one or multiple sessions, see Figs. 1 and 2.

For Module I, there was an association between the semester and when participants viewed the videos, $X^2 (4) = 9.498, p = 0.05$. More participants watched the videos before the discussion day in spring 2020 when it was held in-person than in fall 2020 when the discussions were held virtually. For Module II, no association was found between the semester and when participants viewed the videos, $X^2 (5) = 6.474, p = 0.263$.

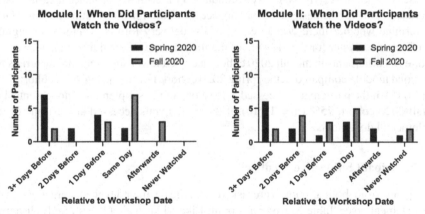

Fig. 1. Timing of video viewing by spring 2020 (n = 15) and fall 2020 (n = 16) participants relative to date of discussion for Module I, Communicating with your Mentees, and Module II, Inclusive Mentoring.

No association was found between semester and whether the participants viewed the videos in one session, multiple sessions, or never viewed the videos for Module I, $X^2 (1) = 0.354, p = 0.552$, or Module II, $X^2 (2) = 1.00, p = 0.606$. Participants tended to view the videos in one session instead of multiple sessions. Most participants viewed all of the episode videos in the modules. Three participants (one from spring 2020 and 2 from fall 2020) did not view any of the videos in Module II. Because all the episodes must be viewed in their entirety before the participants could access the quiz for the respective module, not all participants completed the quiz (i.e., 2 participants in each cohort failed to complete the quiz).

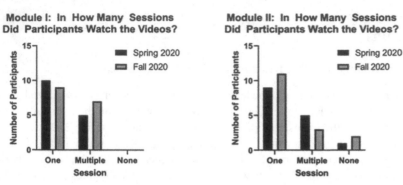

Fig. 2. Number of participants who viewed the videos in the modules in one session, multiple sessions, or none by semester (spring 2020 or fall 2020) for Module I, Communicating with your Mentees, and Module II, Inclusive Mentoring.

The participants' performance and usage data are summarized in Table 2 by semester (spring 2020, in-person discussions vs. fall 2020, online discussions). One-way Analyses of Variances (ANOVAs) were conducted for each performance measure listed in Table 2, with the semester as a factor (see last column for F-ratios and p-values) to determine whether there was an effect of the delivery format. There was a significant effect of semester for the measure of number of supplemental materials viewed for Module II. Participants in the fall 2020 cohort accessed fewer supplemental materials for the second module compared to the spring 2020 cohort. For the spring 2020 cohort, 73% (n = 11/15) of the participants accessed at least one of the supplemental documents. For the fall 2020 cohort, 75% (n = 12/16) of the participants accessed at least one of the supplemental documents.

3.2 Participant Subjective Feedback

Participants from both groups were asked to indicate their level of agreement with nine statements (see Table 3) using a 4-point Likert-like scale (1 = strongly disagree, 2 = disagree, 3 = agree, and 4 = strongly agree), and provide answers to open-ended questions about the modules. Only a subset of the program participants responded to the survey (n = 10 from spring 2020 and n = 14 from fall 2020), and not all survey respondents answered every question.

A series of ANOVAs were also conducted to determine whether there were significant group differences in ratings across the two semesters, see last column of Table 3. No effects of semester were obtained, indicating that the ratings were similar across groups, despite differences in discussion format (online vs in person), therefore data from the two cohorts were combined for subsequent analyses. For each statement listed in Table 3, the participants' ratings were submitted to one sample t-tests, using a test-value of 3.0 (agree). For all but one question, the ratings were significantly above the test value of 3.0 (see column 4 of Table 3), indicating agreement with the statement.

Table 2. Participant performance and usage data (means and standard deviations) for the two groups of participants. The F-statistics for the ANOVAs showing the effect of Group is in the last column (significant effects in bold and indicated by *statements).

Performance Measure	Spring 2020 (hybrid)		Fall 2020 (online)		Effect of Semester
	Mean	Std Dev	Mean	Std Dev	
Module I: Quiz Score (percent correct)	83.52 (n = 13)	5.36	82.65 (n = 14)	6.08	$F(1,25) =$ 0.152, $p = 0.70$
Module I: Number of videos viewed (out of 9)	9.00 (n = 15)	0.00	8.50 (n = 16)	1.55	$F(1,29) =$ 1.559, $p = 0.222$
Module I: Number of supplemental materials viewed (out of 9)	4.47 (n = 15)	3.78	3.56 (n = 16)	3.42	$F(1,29) =$ 0.489, $p = 0.490$
Module II: Quiz Score (percent correct)	84.00 (n = 13)	7.37	85.00 (n = 14)	6.50	$F(1,27) =$ 0.149, $p = 0.702$
Module II: Number of videos viewed (out of 6)	5.67 (n = 15)	1.29	5.25 (n = 16)	2.05	$F(1,29) =$ 0.451, $p = 0.507$
*Module II: Number of supplemental materials viewed (out of 17)	6.60 (n = 15)	5.90	0.88 (n = 16)	2.28	**$F(1,29) =$ 13.016, $p < 0.001$**

3.3 Additional Questions from the Fall 2020 Cohort Survey

The fall 2020 survey included several additional questions (see Table 4). For each of these additional statements, the participants' ratings were submitted to one sample t-tests, using as test-value of 3.0 (agree or good). Participant ratings were significantly higher than 3.0 for three of the questions. Specifically, the participants agreed with the statement relating to being able to use the information gleaned from the modules in their online mentoring and indicated that the level of engagement of the videos for both Modules I and II were better than 'good'.

Table 3. Mean ratings (1 = strongly disagree; 4 = strongly agree) to statements about the modules that were given to both spring 2020 and fall 2020 participants. t and F statistics are provided in the last two columns (significant effects in bold and indicated by *statements)

Statement	n	Mean	Std Dev	Test Value = 3.0	Effect of Semester
*After viewing Module I, I feel more confident about ways to effectively communicate with my mentee(s)	23	3.22	0.42	**t(22) = 2.472, p = 0.022, Cohen's d = 0.42**	F(1,21) = 0.002, p = 0.97
*Module I provided information that I can use about effectively communicating with my mentee(s)	23	3.35	0.49	**t(22) = 3.425, p = 0.002, Cohen's d = 0.49**	F(1,21) = 0.196, p = 0.663
*Module I provided information that I can use about effectively communicating with any student on campus	23	3.39	0.50	**t(22) = 3.761, p = 0.001, Cohen's d = 0.50**	F(1,21) = 0.161, p = 0.692
*Viewing Module II has strengthened my commitment to mentoring with inclusive practices	23	3.48	0.51	**t(22) = 4.491, p < 0.001, Cohen's d = 0.51**	F(1,21) = 0.062, p = 0.806
*Module II provided me with strategies for working with my mentees from diverse backgrounds	23	3.35	0.49	**t(22) = 3.425, p = 0.002, Cohen's d = 0.49**	F(1,21) = 0.571, p = 0.458
*I would recommend Module I to a colleague	24	3.38	0.49	**t(23) = 3.715, p = 0 .001, Cohen's d = 0.49**	F(1,21) = 0.384, p = 0.542
*I would recommend Module II to a colleague	22	3.41	0.50	**t(21) = 3.813, p = 0 .001, Cohen's d = 0.45**	F(1,21) = 0 .334, p = 0.570
I plan to make concrete changes to my mentoring approaches as a result of these modules	22	3.14	0.77	t(21) = 0.826, p = 0.418, Cohen's d = 0.77	F(1,21) = 0.180, p = 0.676
*Participating in this beta test was beneficial to my mentoring practice	22	3.41	0.50	**t(21) = 3.813, p = .001, Cohen's d = 0.52**	F(1,21) = 1.309, p = 0.266

Table 4. Mean ratings to statements about the modules that were given only to the fall 2020 participants. The t-statistics are provided in the last column (significant effects above 3.0 for 'good' are in bold and indicated by * statements).

Statement	n	Mean	Std Dev	Test Value = 3.0
Please indicate the extent to which you agree or disagree with the following statements (1 = strongly disagree; 4 = strongly agree):				
The facilitated discussions added to my understanding of the topics addressed in the videos	13	3.23	0.725	$t(12) = 1.148$, $p = 0.273$, Cohen's d = 0.73
The facilitated discussions were useful to my mentoring practice	13	3.15	0.689	$t(12) = 0.805$, $p = 0.436$, Cohen's d = 0.43
*I will be able to put the information gleaned from the modules into my ONLINE mentoring practice	13	3.38	0.506	**$t(12) = 2.74$, $p = 0.018$, Cohen's d = 0.51**
Please rate the quality of the following (5 = Excellent; 3 = Good; 1 = Poor)				
*Engagement of videos in Module I	14	4.29	0.726	**$t(13) = 6.624$, $p < 0.001$, Cohen's d = 0.73**
Usefulness of Module I handouts	14	3.43	1.158	$t(13) = 1.385$, $p = 0.189$, Cohen's d = 1.16
*Engagement of videos in Module II	14	4.14	1.099	**$t(13) = 3.889$, $p = 0.002$, Cohen's d = 1.10**
Usefulness of Module II handouts	14	3.43	1.089	$t(13) = 1.472$, $p = 0.165$, Cohen's d = 1.158

3.4 Comments from Spring 2020 Cohort Survey

Six out of the 10 survey respondents from the spring 2020 cohort provided comments in an open field for 'Other Comments'.

- Three participants expressed appreciation of the material/topics being presented.
- Two participants asked for additional supplemental material.
- One indicated that there was redundant information that could be reduced and that the discussion handouts could be of higher resolution (i.e., better quality).
- One participant indicated that the volume of the videos was not consistent across episodes and the closed-captioning was not accurate.
- One participant noted that the section on power relationship was critical to address because, "*while we all may realize this differential exist, we may not often think about concrete effects it has on students.*"
- One participant indicated that the "*modules on implicit bias and confronting bias were particularly meaningful to me*".
- One participant said that s/he would e-mail the workshop facilitator specific comments and did not include them in the survey.

3.5 Comments from Fall 2020 Cohort Survey

While the spring 2020 cohort was only asked to provide any other comments in one question of the survey, the fall 2020 cohort was asked four specific open-ended questions in addition to being provided with a field for entering any other comments.When asked, 'What suggestions or recommendations do you have for improving Module I (Communication)?', 10 of the 14 participants provided comments.

- Three participants indicated that the videos should consists of more scenarios for discussion practice, with some suggesting the use of more subtle situations.
- Three participants also had comments relating to the discussion component of the workshop: One participant suggesting having a clear list of topics to discuss, another suggested that the meeting should include *"re-watching and discussing videos"*, and the last one wanted to invite experts from outside the university to lead the discussion of specific topics and have more time discussion among group members.
- One participant suggested spending more time on non-verbal communication, especially when communicating virtually.
- One participant indicated that the number of handouts and supplemental materials included was too much and that only a few materials should be included that do not compete with the video content.
- One participant suggested that the actors be less scripted.
- One participant indicated that s/he liked this module [I] better of the two that were assigned.

When asked, 'What suggestions or recommendations do you have for improving Module II (Inclusive Mentoring)?', six of the 14 participants provided comments.

- One participant indicated that, "This one was great! I really liked learning about microaggressions, I felt there was a lot of new info for me."
- One participant wanted to have "additional resources or tools that faculty can use or read to fill in the problem areas they find."
- Four participants made similar comments to those that they provided for Module I: more scenarios for discussion practice, use videos in the discussions, reduce amount of handouts/supplemental material, and have the role-playing appear to be less scripted.

Participants were also asked, 'We are currently in the process of broadening and deepening our Module II discussion on how systemic racism and structural inequities may affect mentees. Additional videos are being created. Do you have any examples of topics you think would be critical to address these or other key topics to promote social justice?' Five of the 14 participants provided suggestions for including examples of:

- Housing inequities, indicating that *"Some of our students' families are renting properties and not homeowners. This completely changes the family's wealth. Systemic racism plays a big role in this, when white families could buy homes and black families were excluded. The trickle down of this unfairness is huge."*
- Research to demonstrate systemic racism exists since *"I think it's a great way to open conversation."*

- Fallacies associated with grit, stating: *Some of the mentors in smaller discussions expressed a lot of ideas along the lines of "if they can't handle the work then they just need to work harder"; "I'm not hand holding since real life is out there". I think we often times fall into that trap of believing that it's not our problem (e.g., it's a lack of preparation elsewhere in the pipeline).*
- Information from presentations done on campus. *"This should absolutely include statements of how/what they are doing to minimize the impacts of structural racism on faculty, staff, and students."*
- Teaching moments: *"Before starting the last meeting one of the participants made a statement saying a group of people being stupid to the facilitator/group over zoom... Leading me to see that the practicing part is even harder to do even when you are trended and teaching what we learned to be mindful educators."*

When asked, '*How can we improve the discussion sessions associated with the mentoring modules?*,' nine of the participants provided comments. In addition to the comments covered in previous questions relating to having more scenarios for discussion practice, re-watching videos as part of the discussion, allowing more group discussion, participants suggested:

- Having more breakout groups. (n = 2)
- Having more structured discussions. (n = 2)
- Having a video illustrating a moment when you mess up or how to handle a situation when someone else says something inappropriate. (n = 1)

The only substantive "other" comment provided by one participant was that the supplemental documents were dated and the content (i.e., videos with no social distancing, no masks) does not represent the current COVID 19 situation.

4 Discussion

4.1 Effectiveness of the Pilot Modules

Overall, the online AIM Program with a facilitated discussion appears to provide a useful mentor training experience. Because this unique program is intentionally inclusive to faculty and staff mentors across all disciplines, we believe that this training will ultimately benefit student success across campus. The first two modules of the AIM Program focus on communication with student mentees as well as actively promoting culturally aware and inclusive mentoring. These two modules were the first to be pilot tested based on results from the prior CSULB BUILD mentor training program. When surveyed, our BUILD trainees often rated mentors who had received mentor training more highly on mentoring skills compared to non-trained mentors; however, no differences were noted between mentor groups in key aspects of communication or respecting cultural differences [19]. In addition, when mentors in a large academic mentoring study were asked to self-assess on skills, 'pursing strategies to improve communication' and 'accounting for biases and prejudices' received the lowest ratings [23]. Incorporating culturally aware mentoring skills to mentor training programs does positively impact awareness, beliefs, and mentoring methods to trained mentors [24], and mentor training on key communication skills can also change mentoring practices employed [17]. As a result, the learning goals for this pilot included the two modules focusing on these essential topics of communication and equity and inclusion.

Ratings provided by the participants in the current study (see Tables 3 and 4) suggest that the modules met our learning goals for the pilot project. Faculty and staff members found that the modules provided useful information on both communicating with their own mentees as well as with any student on campus. The insignificant group effect shown in Table 3 indicated that the format of the discussion (in-person vs. online) does not significantly affect participants' perception on the quality of the program. Participants also reported that the modules provided strategies to work with students from a diversity of backgrounds and that the modules strengthened the commitment of individual faculty members to mentor with inclusive practices. Assessments of mentor training programs on our campus and others suggest that training mentors does change the skill set and self-evaluated competency of mentors, and that mentors report that they will or have made changes to their mentoring practice as a result of training [19, 25].

While participants in the current study indicated that they would recommend the modules to colleagues and found that the program was beneficial to their mentoring, collectively, they did not significantly agree with the statement that they would make concrete changes in their mentoring as a result of the course. It is unclear why the response to the program would be positive and the fall 2020 participants would indicated significant agreement to the question asking them if they will put the information learned in the course to use in their online mentoring practice; yet the commitment to concrete changes for the cohorts did not reach significant agreement. It may be that the use of the phrase 'make concrete changes' suggested more of a commitment than the more typical and generic 'make changes'. It may also be that participants had learned the material but were not ready to make a specific change because the spring 2020 group had just transitioned online at the time of taking the survey, and the fall 2020 group were in the middle of the first full semester of remote instruction and mentoring.

In addition to assessing the learning goals and impact of the program, the training materials were also rated by faculty and staff in the fall 2020 cohort. Participants indicated that the videos for both modules were engaging. Comments from spring 2020 participants indicated that there were issues with consistent sound levels or closed captioning errors were addressed in episode revisions that took place between cohorts, and these comments were not observed in fall 2020.

The participants of the fall 2020 cohort did not significantly agree with statements regarding the usefulness of both the facilitated discussion and the handouts provided by the Faculty Center for the discussion sessions for either Module I or Module II. In the evaluation session, participants in the fall 2020 semester commented that aligning the discussion to the videos would be preferred to using handouts with additional case studies or information not linked directly with the videos. Relating the discussion directly to the videos may prove to be beneficial in the learning process, as when the viewing data were assessed, participants tended to watch the videos back-to-back, often in one viewing session, in close proximity to the discussion day (see Figs. 1 and 2). In addition, while the number of participants who watched the videos 'on time' declined among those in the fall 2020 cohort, a few of the faculty and staff in the spring 2020 cohort also did not complete the viewing as requested, which was prior to the shutdown induced by the COVID-19 pandemic. Because the total duration of the videos in the modules is under one hour (50 min total for Module I; 40 min total for Module II), watching an entire module right before the discussion does not meet the 3-h criteria for 'binge-watching'. However, because binge watching does reduce both retention and enjoyment of the media content [26], the tendency for faculty to watch all episodes of one module over a short period of time may impact what they learn and retain, and may have contributed to the quiz scores being around 83% rather than closer to 100%. While this average quiz score is similar to scores obtained in other studies [27], the quizzes were short and were focused on lower-level retention questions; so, it may be that watching the episodes in succession reduced overall comprehension or retention.

4.2 Lessons Learned and Recommendations for Future Implementations

Allowing faculty to fully engage in the module on their schedule is one benefit of self-paced faculty development courses [27]; however multiple benefits can be derived from taking part in a live discussion group or having other face-to-face interaction that complements online learning material and reduces the steep attrition observed in voluntary online training modules [28–30]. Once the entire AIM/Beach Mentor Program is rolled out, comparing future quiz scores from faculty members who opt for the self-paced option as compared to those who select the facilitated discussion may elucidate if the pressure to watch the videos 'on time' to meet the discussion deadline reduces retention about the material presented.

The participants in the fall 2020 semester also commented on the number and variety of supplementary resources, including weblinks and journal articles related to the episode topics, which were provided on the learning management system. The amount of available supplemental material provided may have deterred the fall 2020 participants from actually looking at the material. Access of the supplementary resources differed by semester, with a wider range of supplemental materials accessed and a lower average of number of materials accessed for Module II in the fall 2020 as compared to spring 2020 cohort. In general, comments from some of the fall 2020 participants indicated a larger workload than did most participants in the spring 2020 semester, which may speak to the perception of online work as compared to in-person format, in addition to the additional responsibilities incurred by participants during the 2020 pandemic. To address the comments of participants, we are implementing another pilot in spring 2021 that includes streamlined handouts and a discussion leader's manual that are interconnected with the videos. Other lessons learned centered around the look of individuals in stock photos; spring 2020 participants found the individuals in business suits distracting. Based on this feedback, these images were replaced to better reflect a university atmosphere and these types of comments did not resurface in the fall 2020 pilot.

While both cohorts included real-time discussion sessions (face-to-face in spring 2020 or via Zoom in fall 2020), the introduction of topics and ideas occurred primarily through viewing the videos embedded within CSULB's learning management system. Unlike similar participant ratings of the effectiveness of the two modules, there were differences in the number of episodes viewed, with all nine of Module I episodes on communication with mentees viewed; however only an average of 5.7 out of the 6 episodes viewed for inclusive mentoring in Module II (see Table 4). Sessions for both cohorts were intentionally held in the middle of the semester so the program did not overlap with either the first weeks of instruction or final exams. Attrition in voluntary online training programs has been attributed to lack of professional and personal time, as opposed to a lack of interest in the material [30], and it may be that as AIM/Beach Mentor course continued, participants were more pressed for time. Completion of online training is also contingent upon the need or perceived value of the course by faculty members [31], making advertising of the program important to achieve buy-in by key stakeholders on campus. The perceived benefits of the materials are also critical factors to consider for the roll out of this mentor training program. Although the drop-off in viewing activity for the episodes was limited in the two pilots, it will be an important element for future assessment when all six AIM/Beach Mentor modules are included as part of the program.

5 Conclusion

Mentoring during a pandemic is obviously just as critical, if not more important than mentoring during a typical academic year. The practices needed for inclusive mentoring remained the same prior to and during the COVID-19 pandemic; however, mentors and mentees were more likely to feel overwhelmed and overworked during this global medical and economic disaster [32]. The present study compares two cohorts, where all learning materials were presented in online modules, but one cohort had the discussions take place an in-person format prior to the campus shutdown in March 2020 and the other in a Zoom format during the fall 2020 semester. For the latter platform, faculty and staff members participating had to navigate a rapidly changing and demanding environment brought about by remote or alternative modes of teaching, advising and/or mentoring. Interestingly, there were no significant differences between the spring 2020 and fall 2020 cohort in terms of ratings given to the program or its effectiveness; however, differences in viewing behavior for both video episodes as well as the supplemental materials declined in fall 2020. Because mentor training can refine mentoring practices and induce change in how students are mentored [25], it was important to continue the program despite the campus closure. Despite the serious situation, results from the present study suggest that this choice to continue mentor training was useful to participants and provided key skills to help the participants work with students in the future. These pilots also allowed for the refinement of the program, notably connecting the discussion and handouts to the videos, prior to the full series of modules being debuted to the campus. As the full six-module, 35-episode AIM/Beach Mentor Program is introduced to CSULB, future studies are planned to continue to gauge its usefulness to a broader spectrum of both faculty and staff members and improve its effectiveness in helping mentors interact with students in a more equitable and inclusive manner.

Acknowledgments. We thank Nada Rayyes, the CSULB BUILD program evaluator, for conducting the evaluation sessions and administering the evaluation survey. We also thank the participants of the Beach Mentor Program pilots along with the actors, editors, and producers of the AIM series, including producer and director, Nick Oceano.

This work was supported by the National Institute of General Medical Sciences of the National Institutes of Health under Award Numbers UL1GM118979, and RL5GM118978. The content is solely the responsibility of the authors and does not necessarily represent the official views of the National Institutes of Health.

References

1. Jacob, R.R., Gacad, A., Pfund, C., et al.: The "secret sauce" for a mentored training program: qualitative perspectives of trainees in implementation research for cancer control. BMC Med. Educ. **20**, 237 (2020). https://doi.org/10.1186/s12909-020-02153-x
2. Cohen, J.G., et al.: Characteristics of success in mentoring and research productivity - a case-control study of academic centers. Gynecol. Oncol. **125**(2), 8–13 (2012)
3. Pascarella, E.T., Wolniak, G.C., Seifert, T.A.D., Cruce, T.M., Blaich, C.F.: Liberal arts colleges and liberal arts education: new evidence on impacts. ASHE High. Educ. Rep. **31**(3), 1–148 (2005)
4. Ray, J., Kafka, S.: Life in college matters for life after college. 11 Jan 2021 (2014). http://www.gallup.com/poll/168848/life-college-matters-life-college.aspx
5. Gloria, A.M., Robinson Kurpius, S.E.: Influences of self-beliefs, social support, and comfort in the university environment on the academic nonpersistence decisions of American Indian undergraduates. Cultur. Divers. Ethnic Minor. Psychol. **7**(1), 88–102 (2001)
6. Hathaway, R.S., Nagda, B.A., Gregerman, S.R.: The relationship of undergraduate research participation to graduate and professional education pursuit: an empirical study. J. Coll. Stud. Dev. **43**, 614–631 (2002)
7. Stolle-McAllister, K., Sto Domingo, M.R., Carrillo, A.: The Meyerhoff way: how the Meyerhoff scholarship program helps black students succeed in the sciences. J. Sci. Educ. Technol. **20**(1), 5–16 (2011)
8. Cora-Bramble, D., Zhang, K., Castillo-Page, L.: Minority faculty members' resilience and academic productivity: are they related? Acad. Med. **85**(9), 1492–1498 (2010)
9. Estrada, M., Woodcock, A., Hernandez, P.R., Schultz, P.W.: Toward a model of social influence that explains minority student integration into the scientific community. J. Educ. Psychol. **103**(1), 206–222 (2011)
10. Kuh, G.D.: High-Impact Educational Practices: What They Are, Who Has Access to Them, and Why They Matter. AAC&U, Washington, D.C. (2008). 34 p.
11. Russell, S.H., Hancock, M.P., McCullough, J.: Benefits of undergraduate research experiences. Science **316**, 548–549 (2007)
12. Crisp, G., Cruz, I.: Mentoring college students: a critical review of the literature between 1990 and 2007. Res. High. Educ. **50**(6), 525–545 (2009). https://doi.org/10.1007/s11162-009-9130-2
13. National Academies of Sciences, Engineering, and Medicine; Policy and Global Affairs; Board on Higher Education and Workforce; Committee on Effective Mentoring in STEMM. Dahlberg, M.L., Byars-Winston, A. (eds.): The Science of Effective Mentorship in STEMM. National Academies Press, Washington (DC) (2019)
14. Kram, K.E.: Phases of the mentor relationship. Acad. Manag. J. **26**(4), 608–625 (1983)
15. Haring, M.J.: The case for a conceptual base for minority mentoring programs. Peabody J. Educ. **74**(2), 5–14 (1999)
16. Schultz, P.W., et al.: Patching the pipeline: reducing educational disparities in the sciences through minority training programs. Educ. Eval. Policy Anal. **33**(1), 95–114 (2011)
17. Pfund, C., Pribbenow, C.M., Branchaw, J., Lauffer, S.M., Handelsman, J.: The merits of training mentors. Science **311**, 473–474 (2006)

18. Pfund, C., et al.: Training mentors of clinical and translational research scholars: a randomized controlled trial. Acad. Med.: J. Assoc. Am. Med. Coll. **89**(5), 774–782 (2014)
19. Young, K.A., Stormes, K.N.: The BUILD mentor community at CSULB: a mentor training program designed to enhance mentoring skills in experienced mentors. Underst. Interv. **11**(1) (2020)
20. Pfund, C., et al.: A research mentor training curriculum for clinical and translational researchers. Clin. Transl. Sci. **6**, 26–33 (2013)
21. Johnson, M.O., Subak, L., Brown, J., Lee, K., Feldman, M.: An innovative program to train health sciences researchers to be effective clinical and translational-research mentors. Acad. Med. **85**(3), 484–489 (2010)
22. Rogers, J., Branchaw, J., Weber-Main, A.M., Spencer, K., Pfund, C.: How much is enough? The impact of training dosage and previous mentoring experience on the effectiveness of a research mentor training intervention. Underst. Interv. **11**(1) (2020)
23. Fleming, M., et al.: The mentoring competency assessment: validation of a new instrument to evaluate skills of research mentors. Acad. Med. **88**(7), 1002–1008 (2013)
24. Womack, V.Y., et al.: The ASPET mentoring network: enhancing diversity and inclusion through career coaching groups within a scientific society. CBE—Life Sci. Educ. **19**(3) (2020)
25. House, S.C., Spencer, K.C., Pfund, C.: Understanding how diversity training impacts faculty mentors' awareness and behavior. Int. J. Mentor. Coach. Educ. **7**(1), 72–86 (2018)
26. Horvath, J.C., Horton, A.J., Lodge, J.M., Hattie, J.A.C.: The impact of binge watching on memory and perceived comprehension. First Monday **22**(9) (2017). https://firstmonday.org/ojs/index.php/fm/article/download/7729/6532
27. Rizzuto, M.: Design recommendations for self-paced online faculty development courses. TechTrends **61**(1), 77–86 (2016). https://doi.org/10.1007/s11528-016-0130-8
28. Galbraith, K., Choi, S., Parry, M., Hill, F.: MEDUSA: a blended approach to staff development at Southampton. Learn. Teach. Med. Dent. Vet. Med. **1**, 18–19 (2012)
29. Sherer, P.D., Shea, T.P., Kristensen, E.: Online communities of practice: a catalyst for faculty development. Innov. High. Educ. **27**, 183–194 (2003)
30. Long, L., Dubois, C., Faley, R.: A case study analysis of factors that influence attrition rates in voluntary online training programs. Int. J. E-Learn. **8**(3), 347–359 (2009)
31. Steinert, Y., McLeod, P., Conochie, L., Nasmith, L.: An online discussion for medical faculty: an experiment that failed. Acad. Med. **77**, 939–940 (2002)
32. Cameron, K.A., Daniels, L.A., Traw, E., McGee, R.: Mentoring in crisis does not need to put mentorship in crisis: realigning expectations. J. Clin. Transl. Sci. **5**(1), E16 (2021). https://doi.org/10.1017/cts.2020.508

Supporting Work, Collaboration and Design

Information Technology Creative Discussion Method for Collective Wellbeing

Hideyuki Ando[1]([⊠]), Dominique Chen[2]([⊠]), Junji Watanabe[3]([⊠]),
and Kyosuke Sakakura[4]([⊠])

[1] Osaka University of Arts, 469 Higasiyama, Kanan-chou,
Minamikawachi-gun, Osaka 585-8555, Japan
`hidryuki.a@osaka-geidai.ac.jp`
[2] Waseda University, Tokyo, Japan
[3] NTT Communication Science Labs, Kanagawa, Japan
`watanabe.junji@lab.ntt.co.jp`
[4] Tokyo City University, Tokyo, Japan
`kyosuke@sakakura.jp`

Abstract. The types of wellbeing can be broadly divided into medical health, entertainment pleasures, and a sustainable good state of mind. In particular, the third sustainable good state of mind can easily worsen the condition depending on the IT equipment (smartphone application, etc.) used daily. However, it is difficult for designers to predict many of these problems in advance. To address these issues, we have considered workshop methods and created manuals that work in situations where creative ideas are presented in the form of a hackathon. In this method, not only the IT designer, user, accounting, professional, creator, to form a group of the various positions, such as artists. Initially, from the beginning as a usual hackathon, not to consider the ideas towards the goal. We are in for a test bench of this approach, gathered members of such companies and students and local governments, we conducted seven workshops. And, for the ideas that were conceived using these techniques, we will introduce.

Keywords: Wellbeing · Workshop · New IT design

1 Introduction

There is a global trend in rethinking the role and assessing the potential risk of technology in the society in general. Dedicated institutions such the Future of Humanity Institute [1], Future of Life Institute [2] are good examples of efforts to deploy not only academic but also public discussions on the impact of digital technology on human society. This trend coincides with an arising public interest in pursuing mental wellness, as in active coverage of terms like Mindfulness by the press (see for an example [3]). In recent years, as a paradigm shift in the measurement of human psychological wellness occurred, the notion of Happiness has been rendered with higher resolution (Fig. 1), based on multi-dimensional evaluation including a quantifiable axis such as in the form of the PERMA

S. Yamamoto and H. Mori (Eds.): HCII 2021, LNCS 12766, pp. 197–207, 2021.
https://doi.org/10.1007/978-3-030-78361-7_15

model in Positive Psychology [4]. The problem of the human-machine relation has been specifically explored by research areas such as Calm Technology [5], Affective Computing [6]. Positive Computing [7], which have provided important grounds for designing human computer interface. However, it is debatable whether the design principles established in the Western cultures can be applied to the collectivist cultures directly, and whether such difference can lead us to a different technology design principles. For example, it is known that positive-psychology interventions (PPIs) are more effective in individualist cultures, in mainly Western regions. Therefore, we have been running a project to develop technology guidelines for promoting wellbeing, with focus on value systems observed in collectivist cultures, and especially Japan, where we are based [8].

As a result, we thought about what a "good intervention" in order to produce the wellbeing. It concluded that it should be noted therein for six points "individual", "autonomy", "latent", "cooperativity", "affinity", "sustained".

"Consideration of the individuality" is that it should not be too generalized elements of wellbeing. This is because varies with the individual life stages. Also, instead of everyone even in the decision-making in the case of large number of people gather to agree by the same values, it is important to aim for agreement on the premise of the difference of individual wellbeing. The "consideration of autonomy", wellbeing is intended to act noticed on its own rather than what is given to someone. As in the technique called technique is referred to as a "nudge" and "gaming", you need to consider the intervention of the user's autonomous sexual decision. The "consideration of the latency", but to the human decision-making is both conscious thing and the unconscious ones, it should scoop up information from the unconscious system. Someone to perform the same task together, encourage the sharing of empathy and values by the sharing of experiences, "consideration of the joint property" is also necessary. Positive emotions also exist modest feeling of when to relax not only the emotion of strong excitement by entertainment. "Consideration for affinity" is to intervene in good balance the two. If results in short term goals of wellbeing, in the long term may inhibit the wellbeing. For example, given the external reward for the promotion of voluntary activities, would for the purpose of activities reward. For this reason, "consideration of sustainability" is necessary.

We examined in light of these 6 points, the physical sympathy processes and co-creation arena the emphasis was wellbeing concept methods. As this initiative method, we have proposed a workshop such as hackathons. In addition, we created a work manual for carrying out the wellbeing workshop smoothly.

In this method, not only the IT designer, user, accounting, professional, creator, to form a group of the various positions, such as artists. Initially, from the beginning as a usual hackathon, not to consider the ideas towards the goal. First of all, so that we can understand the individuality of each other. To that end, export the map of favorite things and dislike things, and replace it with each other. At this time, the ideas and preferences of others are not different from their own, we will try to accept the positive . After that, each member will write three elements of the Wellbeing of for yourself. These contents also share with each other, we will endeavor to accept that there is a diversity. After this process, to solve the original problem or dislike things. And to proceed with the discussion on how to realize that satisfy the elements of the Wellbeing. This method of discussion, offers something unique. For example, as a prediction of when using the new technology, in portions of the story to the time as 'RENGA (poetic dialogue in japan)', each of the members using, for example, how to write in order. Using these methods, do the ideas design of new technologies and applications. We are in for a test bench of this approach, gathered members of such companies and students and local governments, we conducted seven workshops. And, for the ideas that were conceived using these techniques, we will introduce.

2   Workshop: Creative Discussion Method for Collective Wellbeing

In this section, we will be described with reference to the order in which the elements of a specific workshop. The methodology of the workshop has been proposed in our project, it has been opened to the public in the WEB.

Here we will explain the flow and mindset of an actual workshop. The first half is a phase about delving deeply into the well-being of participants and sharing this information. The second half involves expanding upon ideas based on those elements of well-being discovered in the previous phase. The composition of this workshop was made in reference to the ideas behind Theory U, a framework proposed by MIT professor Otto Scharmer for producing changes that are truly necessary. Rather than look to patterns that have succeeded in the past or the common sense of the day as a quick source of ideas, Theory U involves focusing on things taking place now and heightening dialogue to sense signs of change, and then from there producing a future everyone finds desirable. At the outset of a workshop, everyone must let go of the practical sense or fear of change they have now and deepen their value of well-being in accordance with the ideas of each phase. As long as you are with comrades who share a profound vision towards well-being, this should lead to fresh lines of thinking.

Once all the participants are assembled, it's time to get the workshop rolling. While the themes and composition of members of the workshop will likely be different in nearly every case, please have the organizer convey the topics discussed by thinking about well-being together. The next step is to endeavor to create an atmosphere that is as warm, relaxing, and conducive to speaking as possible. Before getting into to the actual work, it can also prove effective to conduct a sort of "check-in" with self-introductions, an icebreaker activity, and a short talk about what is hoped to come from the workshop.

2.1   Task1: Heartbeat Picnic

When we conduct a well-being workshop, what we employ as our first task is a "heartbeat picnic". Using a tool that makes it possible to feel a heart beating with the palm of the hand, participants gain a deep awareness of their own existence, along with that of their fellow participants as living beings in that space. The intent of this task to get everyone to let go of their usual thought patterns and adopt a stance of directing their eyes and ears

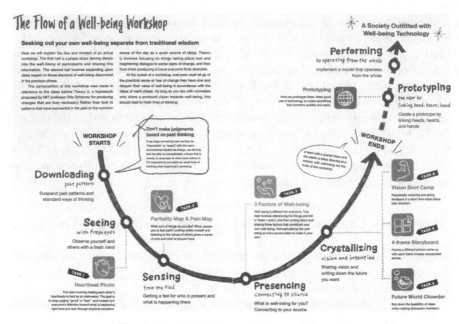

Fig. 1. The FLOW of a wellbeing workshop [9]

towards what is happening before them right here and now instead of judging things as good or bad according to conventional wisdom. So, another activity that similarly gets participants in tune with each other's current feelings and physical state can also be substituted in the heartbeat picnic. Our bodies react subconsciously to the things in front of us. Our hearts beat harder and more rapidly when we're excited or nervous, and beat more slowly and irregularly when we are relaxed. What situations have felt comfortable or uncomfortable for you before now (Fig. 2)?

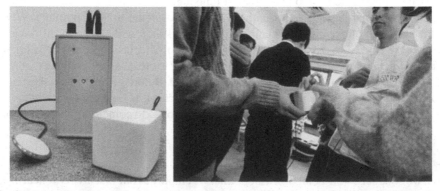

Fig. 2. A heartbeat picnic is a workshop activity meant to give us renewed awareness of our hearts, which work incessantly to keep us alive from the moment we are born, by bringing them outside of our bodies, in a sense. Participants gain a sound feel for their own heartbeats, then speak with other members of the workshop while exchanging hearts to feel what makes them different [9].

2.2   Task2: Partiality Map and Pain Map

Now that things have loosened up a bit, it's time to deepen the discussion. Having everyone reflect on things their likes or dislikes and then sharing them with each other can lead to the discovery of unexpected differences or things in common. The "partiality map" is activity in which everyone puts down things they like or prefer on a single piece of paper in words and pictures before presenting them to the rest of the group. Next, we make a "pain map" in the same manner, except that it depicts things a person doesn't like or finds unpleasant. Making these maps provides an opportunity to learn about oneself and disclose this information to others. Not only does this make everyone aware that we're all different, but hearing the other members of the workshop speak about their preferences helps it really sink in that people with disparate values exist (Fig. 3).

Fig. 3. A The partiality map is a communication method proposed by educationist Takashi Saito in his book "The Partiality Map-A Communication Method for Helping You like Everyone" (2004, NTT Publications) [9]

2.3   Task3: 3 Factors of Well-Being

By this point the mood of the workshop should be quite congenial and relaxed. In the third activity, "3 factors of well-being", everyone names three factors in their well-being. It can also prove effective to have a lecture on what sort of mindset well-being is before beginning this activity. One good method of doing this is to read through and discuss pages 2 to 5 of this pamphlet together. The important thing is that the activity be conducted in a setting where everyone recognizes not only that well-being is not the same as a state of physical health and that everyone isn't going to necessarily have the same standards, but also of acceptance towards each participant's unique factors and the reasons for them. Once everyone is on the same page in these regards, it's time to write down three factors that equate to well-being for you. When doing so, make sure to also include specific details for each factor, along with your reasons for choosing them. Once everyone is finished, it's time to share. Read your three factors and the reasons behind them to the rest of the group. Everyone who was listening then provides what they feel hearing these factors as feedback. Another effective technique building relativity towards one's own well-being is to have participants listen to another person's factors and then introduce said person to the group in their place.

Putting everyone's idea of well-being into words helps clarify what exactly needs to change or be made. Furthermore, the time the group members spend discussing well-being produces a setting filled with it (Fig. 4).

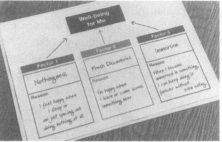

Fig. 4. By this point the mood of the workshop should be quite congenial and relaxed. In the third activity, "3 factors of well-being", everyone names three factors in their well- being [9].

2.4   Task4: Vision Boot Camp

The next three activities are meant to write a story based upon each person's well-being factors that they told to the group and in doing so produce a shared vision and the means of implementing it. It's fine to not do every activity and instead just choose the ones that fit the theme of the workshop best. The fundamental idea behind all of them is to have people with different values work together on solving a common issue. The "vision boot camp" is an activity where each participant creates a problem and then brainstorms about ways to solve it. They come up with an idea within the time limit, and then the other members of the group provide comments. After refining their idea and explaining it, they then receive more feedback. This process is repeated several times. It's fine if things are vague as long as everyone is sharing and providing comments so ideas take shape. Moving forward in this process at full speed without thinking too deeply may provide glimpses of directions you never would have thought in yourself (Fig. 5).

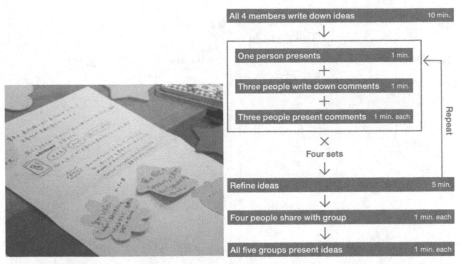

Fig. 5. A sample schedule if there are five groups of four people each. Write your idea on the top half of the paper, and then the three listeners write their comments on notes and attach them to the lower half. Once everyone has presented, ideas are repeatedly brushed-up, with the best one being shared with everyone at the end of the activity [9].

2.5   Task5: 4-Frame Storyboard

The "4-frame storyboard" is an activity about taking ideas in unanticipated directions.

Participants are split into groups of four, with each group having a worksheet split into four sections. Start by having one member draw a comic depicting themselves in a troubled state with a problem they need solved in the first frame. Then, hand the sheet to the next person and have them draw the next development in the story in the second frame. The goal here is to create as unexpected of a story as possible. There's no need to take responsibility here, since someone else is going to be coming up with the ending. Have the next person over then fill in the third frame. This frame is where we suggest methods or technology that might solve the previous issue and realize a state of well-being. This is the most thrilling scene in this activity. Pass the sheet on again to the fourth group member so they can draw the conclusion of the story in the final frame, and then we're done. After that, you present the story with your ending to the group. Since this activity involves putting together a story with an idea from a different member of the group in each frame, it can lead to approaches or tales for solutions that one could never come up with alone (Fig. 6).

Fig. 6. The "4-frame storyboard" is an activity about taking ideas in unanticipated directions [9].

2.6 Task6: Future World Chowder

"Future world chowder" is a world-cafe style ideation technique in which a rotating group of people discuss solutions to a single problem. Everyone is split into groups of four to six people, and then each table decides upon a theme they wish to ponder. Write down the ideas you talk about onto imitation paper at the table. Once a good amount of ideas have been assembled, one person stays behind while everyone else moves to a different table. The person who remained at the table then explains the table's theme and the ideas that have been come up with to the newcomers before expanding upon them with the new group. Decide upon a time limit and repeat this change two or three times to keep growing the ideas. Then everyone returns to their original table, bringing back the ideas and thinking they experienced at other tables with them then put together a story of how to solve the problem. The idea is that each table is like a pot with all kinds of people coming along and adding ingredients to the mix. This eventually creates a chowder unique to each of them. The activity comes to close with each group presenting their results (Fig. 7).

Fig. 7. "Future world chowder" is a world-cafe style ideation technique in which a rotating group of people discuss solutions to a single problem [9].

2.7 Prototyping

Once all activities have been completed, the workshop comes to a close with everyone doing a "checkout" where they speak of their thoughts at the end of the day.

Aside from full-on programs spanning several days, most workshops will also include portions for coming up with ideas for sharing vision and solving problems. In order to give shape to the ideas that emerge from the workshop, there needs to be a phase where each organization prototypes these ideas with an eye towards implementing them in society.

While we can't go into specifics on methods here What we have presented here is just one example of the content and flow of a well-being workshop, and it is of course possible to customize such workshops in a variety of manners to fit specific themes or participant compositions. However, we hope that you will adhere to the original principle of learning about the well-being of you and the other members, view as something given how much they can vary depending on the type of service or technology, we can introduce "a letter from the universe" as one means of intuitive guidance for evaluating prototyping. This is an activity that involves writing words of gratitude as a thank-you letter from the Earth (or the entire universe) that arrives once the service everyone made together comes into being. Doing so helps to reaffirm the value of those providing said service. Reflecting on whether the prototyping is of sufficient merit to warrant the arrival of such a letter can provide a compass while designing.

3 Workshop "well-being dojo"

We went enterprises, educational institutions, on an ongoing basis once a month during the half-year Wellbeing workshop the "well-being dojo" that target the NPO at Fab Cafe. The purpose of this workshop, the design of products and services based on the Japanese Wellbeing, about how to create the value of in society, specifically considered the scenario together with the people of the company, to have a place to share there were. For example, a person responsible for the business, such as new business support and web design and space design, participated in the discussion about the "ways of working". Alternatively, for how to practice the "Wellbeing as a company" by the electrical equipment manufacturer, it was also the month in which the participation of employees became the center to carry out the business plan. In addition, by the food and beverage industry and science communicators were also examined, such as the way of the company. Progress and final conclusion of the discussion are summarized as a graphic recording.

As an example of the quest theme it has been made raised a problem that the "Subordinate do not have the motivation of the work". A problem that is not able to foster a sense of accomplishment in the discussions were emerge. So, it was issued the idea of following. It is required multifaceted of the evaluation method. The boss to improve the motivation of subordinates by having the mind to expand the approved range. Furthermore, with card created to visualize thanks, be solved by creating a culture that mutually feed. Other quest theme "My time by SNS is taken away, I feel gloomy." "Time by thus opening the SNS in unawareness is wasted. Also thereby, a vicious cycle would increase the stress occurs. Physically it may be necessary to set a time that does not touch such as smart phones. From animals (such as cats), such as learning how to live in my own pace without any relation with such SNS it has been discussed."

Thus, it could be shown that it is possible to create a smooth discussion and specific method proposed for enhancing Wellbeing (Fig. 8).

Fig. 8. Shows the state of "well-being dojo" Workshop. I was traveling along the workshop manual.

4   Conclusion

General guidelines are based on the assumption methodology such as "it is desirable… to" ban law and such as "the must not be…". However, those feeling of Wellbeing is different for each individual. Therefore, we are what it was noticed that it is important to be determined whether the Wellbeing on their own.

Also, in terms of information presentation, the user can easily obtain symbolic answers such as searching for an answer on the net. While the user need not be considered a hard time when to act on the answer, the user is likely to become blindly follow the machine. Therefore, the user there is a risk of becoming a stop thinking and machine dependent in exchange for convenience. So, we came to the conclusion that their own autonomous understanding and judgment of the human subject that produce the meaning and the question is what is important, what can repeat the process that causes moderate "consciousness" to question the meaning is the essence. "That is, in the creation of general guidelines that could become a form of pressing it became obvious that cannot cope. Therefore, we consider a methodology for thinking autonomously about the workings of their own well-being. That concluded the establishment of practices, such as the workshop kit that can DIY the well-being theory to function as guidelines. Finally, we have implemented the workshop manual for the practice of this idea.

And, it was conducted a workshop based on this workshop manual for the various stakeholders.Results are still not so many that led to the practice of the specific prototype. However, experience who are able to realize the importance of this process itself, is considered to progress in the essential understanding of Wellbeing.

Acknowledgments. Our project is working under the support of Human Information Technology Ecosystem (HITE). HITE is a research and development (R&D) focus area delivered by the Research Institute of Science and Technology for Society (RISTEX), Japan Science and Technology Agency (JST).

References

1. Dedicated institutions such the Future of Humanity Institute. https://www.fhi.ox.ac.uk/. Accessed 11 Feb 2021
2. Future of Life Institute. https://futureoflife.org/. Accessed 11 Feb 2021
3. The Mindfulness Project. https://www.londonmindful.com/press. Accessed 11 Feb 2021
4. Seligman, M.: Flourish. Atria (2012)
5. Wiser, M., Brown, J.S.: Designing Calm Technology. Xerox PARC (1995)
6. Picard, R.: Affective Computing. MIT Press, Cambridge (1998)
7. Calvo, R., Peters, D.: Positive Computing. MIT Press, Cambridge (2014)
8. Ando, H., Watanube, J., Chen, H.D., Sakakura, K.: Development of information technology guidelines for promoting wellbeing in Japanese culture. In: Computing and Mental Health workshop at CHI 2017 (2017)
9. Wellbeing-Technology Homepage. http://wellbeing-technology.jp/. Accessed 11 Feb 2021
10. Scharmer, O.: Theory U: Leading from the Future as It Emerges. Berrett-Koehler Publishers, San Francisco (2009)

Development of a Survey Instrument to Explore Telehealth Adoption in the Healthcare Domain

Avijit Chowdhury[✉] ⓘ, Abdul Hafeez-Baig, and Raj Gururajan

University of Southern Queensland, Toowoomba, QLD 4350, Australia

Abstract. The purpose of this paper is to present a validated and reliable survey instrument to explore the determinants of telehealth adoption by healthcare professionals in developing countries. The survey instrument has been procreated for measuring the determinants of telehealth adoption in the Indian healthcare domain. A research design was conceived whereby three stages of methodologies were applied to establish and confirm the determinants. The stages are literature review, qualitative data collection and analysis, and finally, a survey for quantitative analysis generalising the findings over a large population to validate the findings of the first two stages. While the literature review and qualitative findings validated the perceived determinants or the items of the survey, the internal consistency or reliability of the items has been established by the survey conducted in India in the month of January to February 2020. A total of 11 responses were received by the online survey out of which 7 were full responses. Further, in the paper mode survey, 1,000 surveys were distributed among the Indian healthcare professionals out of which 343 completed responses were collected afterwards. The outcome of the pilot stage survey that stemmed out from the survey development process was a comprehensive 97-item survey instrument, based on 5 point Likert-scale, along with acceptable levels of internal consistency and validity. The contribution of the paper lies with providing a validated, and reliable survey instrument which could be utilised for telehealth adoption or ICT adoption research in healthcare domains in developing countries.

Keywords: Telehealth adoption · Indian healthcare · Survey instrument

1 Introduction

Healthcare challenges are a known phenomenon in developing countries. The challenges in healthcare can be in the form of inequalities and accessibility to the normal healthcare system. The lack of infrastructure, physical and ICT, coupled with the shortage of healthcare professionals in the rural and remote areas are additional challenges of the healthcare system in the developing countries. The introduction and success of communication technologies in the modern era has the potential to ease such effects. Regarding healthcare, the applications of ICT stemming into Telehealth/telemedicine/M-health etc. have a potential to serve as a useful alternative or as an associated healthcare service to eliminate such challenges, inequalities, and accessibility (Chandwani and Dwivedi

© Springer Nature Switzerland AG 2021
S. Yamamoto and H. Mori (Eds.): HCII 2021, LNCS 12766, pp. 208–225, 2021.
https://doi.org/10.1007/978-3-030-78361-7_16

2015). The developed countries such as USA, Canada, UK, Australia, New Zealand, Scandinavian countries had already built up and utilised their ICT infrastructure capacity to cater to the healthcare sector at its farthest (Anwar and Prasad 2018; Raza et al. 2017). In India, there have been telehealth and telemedicine service providers, but little information is known about the determinants or the factors influencing the telehealth adoption process by the healthcare professionals and healthcare organisations (Chowdhury et al. 2019). The most important thing is to determine the adoption process by Indian healthcare professionals and healthcare organisations, by identifying the significant factors influencing telehealth adoption.

The purpose of this research paper is to describe the process of developing a validated and reliable survey instrument to explore the determinants of telehealth adoption in the healthcare domain. Technical and contextual differences are significant shortcomings in the previously developed tools for exploring telehealth adoption (Rani et al. 2019). Further, previous studies focus on the patients' telehealth adoption (Paslakis et al. 2019) or the studies focussed on the adoption of specialised telehealth services (Janda et al. 2019; Zhou et al. 2019). While surveys are the usual method for exploring healthcare professionals' telehealth adoption, shortfalls in conducting and reporting survey studies are expected (Langbecker et al. 2017; Whitten et al. 2007). Furthermore, tools for measuring telehealth adoption in the context of developing countries are few (Chowdhury et al. 2019; Ghia et al. 2013). The development of a survey instrument is imperative to measure the determinants of telehealth adoption by healthcare professionals in developing countries. To establish such perceived drivers and barriers a research design was conceived whereby three stages of methodologies were applied to establish and confirm the determinants. The stages are literature review, qualitative data collection and analysis, and finally a survey for quantitative analysis generalising the findings over a large population to validate the findings of the first two stages.

The first stage was an extant literature review whereby the general perceived drivers and barriers and the adoption models of telehealth around the world have been reviewed.

The qualitative part of the research conducted semi-structured interviews of the healthcare professionals in India. The interviews were transcribed, and the data were analysed, and the perceived determinants were interpreted from the data. The process of the qualitative analysis was done with rigour so as to establish content validity and construct validity. The qualitative analysis involved two stages of manual coding, and NVivo coding. Hence, the resultant themes of manual coding process were matched with CAQDAS (Computer Assisted Qualitative Data Analysis Software) and thus, the content and construct validity of the qualitative analysis has been established.

The perceived determinants comprise of several items, which would be the basis of the next stage of the research. The next stage of the research would evolve into a survey of healthcare professionals in India, to measure and validate the perceived determinants interpreted from the literature review and the qualitative data. Further, the relationship between the perceived determinants can be conceived.

For quantitative data collection, a survey instrument has been prepared with the literature review and the qualitative analysis as the base. The themes, along with the items will be measured with the help of the survey instrument. The measurement will be done on a Likert scale with scales ranging from 0 to 5 denoting "strongly disagree" to "strongly agree". The following diagram shows the development process of the survey (Fig. 1).

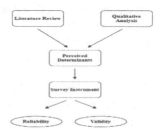

Fig. 1. Development process of the survey instrument

2   First Stage: Literature Review[1]

The literature review proposed a conceptual framework after exploring a range of published articles and theories on telehealth and ICT adoption in healthcare domains worldwide. Technology-Organisation-Environment Model (TOE) (Depietro et al. 1990) has been tested in organisational settings in various domains of ICT adoptions including healthcare. TOE is a comprehensive framework (Hu et al. 2002) and yields a consistent conclusion or results, regarding ICT adoption in the healthcare and other domains. This is supported by the researches of (Ahmadi et al. 2015; Alaboudi et al. 2016; Brancheau and Wetherbe 1990; Bretschneider 1990; Cooper and Zmud 1990; Fichman 1992; Ghani and Jaber 2015; Kimberly and Evanisko 1981; Lian et al. 2014; Zmud 1982). The different knowledge and technological barriers found through literature review (Adamson 2016; Faber et al. 2017; Paul et al. 1999; Tanriverdi and Iacono 1998; Zailani et al. 2014) are well represented through the TOE framework. Since the study aims to identify the different drivers and barriers of telehealth technology adoption in an organisational setting, the TOE framework adapted from Depietro et al. (1990); Hu et al. (2002) can lend a hand to modify and create a new theoretical framework for telehealth technology adoption in the Indian healthcare domain. The different constructs of the TOE framework are ease of use, technology safety, service benefits, service risks, collective attitude of healthcare staff, organisational policies and management, and service needs (Hu et al. 2002).

---

[1] The literature review section has been published previously in APDSI Conference, Brisbane, 2019.

The themes formulated for the conceptual framework to study Indian telehealth adoption are Technology, Organisation, Environment, Knowledge, Innovation and, Healthcare Specific.

Technology
The ease of use construct has been criticised by Chismar and Wiley-Patton (2003); Hu et al. (2002); Keil et al. (1995). The researchers were of the view that the physicians rely on the usefulness of ICT instead of relying on the ease of using it. The physicians' emphasis is more on the utility, functionality and effective patient outcomes. The results obtained by (Lin et al. 2012) show that usefulness has a greater impact than ease of use.

Technology safety can be a hindrance in influencing an organisation's ICT adoption. Physicians are concerned with the safety of the equipment and technology used in their patient's care (Hu et al. 2002). A technology which can affect patient's care outcome can be considered as risky.

In India, although the urban ICT infrastructure has improved significantly, there is still scope of improvement in broadband speed and increasing rural connectivity which is still low (Confederation of Indian Industry & KPMG 2017).

Organisation
Collective attitude of healthcare staff was found to be the most significant factor influencing ICT adoption in telehealth environment (Hu et al. 2002). The same research concludes that organisation policies and management was non-significant. The collective attitude of the healthcare staff towards telehealth can regulate an organisation's readiness for adopting ICT. The collective attitude may include willingness to share knowledge as well as willingness to learn from training.

A healthcare organisation's main purpose is to provide service to the people who need medical services because of service access or quality. In India there prevails a tremendous health inequality as observed by Balarajan et al. (2011). Exploring alternative arrangements for service delivery is one of the priority for a healthcare organisation.

Environment
The vast rural and remote areas of India are plagued by accessibility to healthcare and shortage of healthcare professionals (Rathi 2017). A standardised government policy and framework regarding telehealth can foster telehealth adoption in India catering to a larger section of the society (Singh 2005). Further, the demographics and disease profile in urban and rural areas can be a significant driver for adoption of telehealth (West and Milio 2004).

Knowledge

Easy access to information for healthcare professionals, patients and healthcare workers is the need of the day for adoption of telehealth in India (Dwivedi et al. 2001). Further, the training needs of the healthcare workers and for non tech savvy healthcare professionals are also significant barriers to adoption of telehealth in India (Chandwani and Dwivedi 2015; Dwivedi et al. 2001). Interestingly, majority of the healthcare professionals are willing to share their knowledge and participate in the telehealth adoption process (Ghia et al. 2013).

Innovation

The majority of the efforts in the telehealth environment in India are late adopters (Kumar and Ahmad 2015). The competitive advantage of telehealth, as to, face-to-face consultations, need to be studied in details (Cho et al. 2009). The scope of innovation in providing telehealth services in various forms such as telemedicine for primary care, online consultations by physicians, dietitians etc. and the adoption rates varies according to the domain (Cho et al. 2007).

Healthcare Specific

In India there have been efforts to provide telemedicine services in the rural areas focussing on primary healthcare (Kumar and Ahmad 2015). Various healthcare professionals including physicians, surgeons, dietitians, dentists, physiotherapists have started to provide online consultations in the urban areas, at least in the initial level of consultation. The online consultations has a broad outreach at a pan-India level (Brindha 2013; Sivagurunathan et al. 2015). As such, future study of telehealth adoption in specific healthcare domains may extend the viability of such efforts.

The conceptual framework which emerged by thematically arranging the drivers and barriers are presented below (Fig. 2).

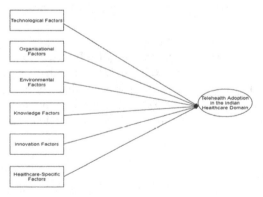

Fig. 2. Conceptual framework for telehealth adoption

3   Second Stage: Qualitative Data Collection and Analysis

The second stage of the research developed a qualitative framework to assist in recognising the measurable constructs. An open-ended, semi-structured, and in-depth interview questionnaire was developed with the help of the themes generated from the literature review. The interviews of healthcare professionals in India were conducted from the month of February 2019 to May 2019. A total of 12 interviews were conducted. The framework was developed after analysing the qualitative interviews in 2 stages: Manual Analysis and NVivo coding. The manual analysis yielded some a-priori codes which was helpful in analysing the data through NVivo. The themes were divided into drivers and barriers and consists of several concepts or items which would become the basis of measurement of the perceived constructs. The final coding revealed a framework consisting of meso, macro and micro level themes which is presented below (Table 1).

Table 1. Emerging themes from qualitative analysis

Perceived driver themes	Perceived barrier themes
1. Healthcare Practices (Mcso level)	1. Technology Inhibitors (Meso level)
2. Patient Awareness (Meso level)	2. Organisational Issues (Meso level)
3. Usefulness (Micro level)	3. State Leadership (Macro level)
4. Healthcare Facilities (Meso level)	4. Communication Issues (Micro level)
5. Healthcare Professional (HCP) Awareness (Meso level)	
6. Technology Motivators (Meso level)	
7. Competitiveness (Meso level)	

4   Third Stage: Survey Instrument Development

Altogether, 1000 healthcare professionals were approached either by sending online survey links or sending the paper survey to them, along with the participant information sheet. In both cases, the head of the hospital or private medical centre was consulted beforehand. The primary investigator also took a leadership approach to initiate the data collection by personally visiting the hospitals and private medical centres. The paper surveys were later collected in person, scanned copy email, or by post. An initial examination of the paper and online surveys revealed that 343 completed responses were received which was 34.3% of the total population targeted by the survey, which is in conformity to standard response rates according to published healthcare research literature (Cunningham et al. 2015). Further, the low response rates in online mode (only 11 completed responses) indicate that, though the online operation of the survey is significantly low in cost, it is still way behind the success rates of a paper-based survey in the Indian healthcare domain (Hohwü et al. 2013).

5 Findings and Discussion

The final outcome of the pilot stage survey that stemmed out from the survey development process was a comprehensive 97-item survey instrument, based on 5 point Likert-scale, along with acceptable levels of both content and construct validity as well as internal consistency.

Pre-testing

An initial content validity test was conducted before administering the survey instrument (Haynes et al. 1995; Wynd et al. 2003). Experts in healthcare research as well as health-care professionals were consulted by presenting a comprehensive survey instrument with 134 items. The participants for the pre-testing were asked to indicate their comfortability to answer the questionnaire survey. Their opinions were considered and 97 items (independent and dependent variables) and 6 demographic questions were finally included in the administered instrument.

Pilot-Testing

A pilot testing was conducted by taking the initial results of the survey into account. The first 30 responses were captured to find out the Cronbach's Alpha it generated. The Cronbach Alpha value was **.902** for all the 97 items of the survey for the first 30 cases. The Cronbach's Alpha values for overall items and the perceived factors which were measured by the survey instrument are presented below (Table 2).

Table 2. Cronbach's Alpha for pilot test

Perceived factors	No. of items	Cronbach's alpha	No. of cases
Overall	97	.902	30
Healthcare practices	15	.956	30
Patient awareness	5	.953	30
Healthcare facilities	8	.710	30
HCP awareness	6	.689	30
Technology motivators	7	.727	30
Competitive advantage	8	.871	30
Technology issues	14	.940	30
Organisational issues	6	.960	30
State leadership	6	.831	30
Communication issues	5	.699	30
Telehealth adoption (DV)	17	.752	30

Source: Developed for the study using IBM SPSS Statistics

As, **.902** was a highly satisfactory overall value the survey was decided to continue without altering any of the items or demographic questions. The perceived factors yielded values ranging from **.689** to **.956** which were also satisfactory figures for continuation of the survey without altering any items.

Principal Component Analysis

After the final data collection was over and the data was cleaned and prepared for analysis, a principal component analysis with varimax rotation technique was employed. Finally, 9 factors (including the DV) were retained and inspecting the measuring variables several new constructs had emerged either by rejecting the original factors or by breaking the factors into two. The rotation of the items emerged into 9 composite variables which were renamed accordingly as to their significance of what they are actually measuring.

The KMO measure of sampling adequacy and Barlett's test of sphericity proved to be of significant values. The KMO of .760 is an acceptable measure of sample adequacy and **p = .000** denotes the validity of the rotated component matrix (Hair et al. 1998) (Table 3).

Table 3. KMO and Bartlett's test

Kaiser-Meyer-Olkin Measure of Sampling Adequacy		.760
Bartlett's Test of Sphericity	Approx. Chi-Square	8226.730
	df	780
	Sig.	.000

Source: IBM SPSS Statistics 26 output

The extracted factors were renamed as Healthcare Practices [HP], Patient Awareness [PA], Technology Issues – ICT [TI-ICT], Organisational Readiness [OR], Competitive Advantage [CA], Technology Motivators [TM], Technology Issues – Security [TI-SEC], Organisational Support [OS], and the DV Telehealth Adoption [TA].

Reliability Analysis of Composites

The internal reliability of the composites were tested by Cronbach's Alpha values which resulted in significant values ranging from **.761** to **.791**. The overall Cronbach's Alpha of the composites stood at **.856** which is a good overall score and establishes the reliability of the constructs (Hair et al. 1998) (Table 4).

Table 4. Cronbach's Alpha of Composites

Composites	No. of items	Cronbach's alpha	No. of cases
Overall	40	.856	295
Healthcare practices [HP]	9	.901	295
Patient awareness [PA]	6	.845	295
Technology issues – ICT [TI-ICT]	4	.838	295
Organisational readiness [OR]	5	.802	295
Competitive advantage [CA]	3	.788	295
Technology motivators [TM]	3	.793	295
Technology issues – security [TI-SEC]	4	.791	295
Organisational support [OS]	3	.761	295
Telehealth adoption (DV) [TA]	3	.790	295

Source: Developed for this study using IBM SPSS Statistics 26

6 Discussion

For establishing and demonstrating rigour in preparation of survey instruments, validity and reliability should be established before and after the data collection process (Dwivedi et al. 2006; Straub et al. 2004). The recommended validity and reliability that were followed in to create a new survey instrument were construct validity, content validity, and reliability. After the pilot test the survey was continued without deleting any items, and afterwards, the principal component analysis confirmed 40 items out of the original 97 items.

The final 40 items of the survey culminated into several constructs. One difference is that the survey focussed on the determinants instead of measuring behavioural intention and attitude. This is because of the fact that telehealth is already in use at a certain level in Indian healthcare. Instead, HCP Awareness was found to be an accurate determinant to measure and predict the adoption levels. Globally, TAM and UTAUT were used extensively for ICT adoption studies and generated almost the same results, except differing from cultural variations. This study, focussed on finding the drivers and barriers to telehealth adoption.

The resultant 40 items can predict various determinants of telehealth adoption such as patient awareness, hcp awareness, technology motivators and inhibitors etc. The determinants can thus be explained from the lens of the T-O-E framework. Further, healthcare-specific determinants are identified, along with medical education, and state leadership, which can be measured. Though innovation was found to be significant in the literature review, it was found to be somewhat dependent on the determinants of telehealth adoption in Indian circumstances. Though knowledge was measured in the original instrument as HCP Awareness it was found insignificant in PCA. As such, the resulting 40 items had the potential to predict variance in telehealth adoption in developing countries.

7   Limitations

The survey was procreated as there are limited research regarding the determinants of Indian telehealth adoption. The exploratory survey was prepared dealing in stages with content and construct validity, pre and pilot testing and principal component analysis. The suggested validities for a newly constructed survey are content and construct validity, internal consistency and reliability, manipulation validity and common method bias (Straub et al. 2004). This research paper dealt with the above mentioned requirements except for manipulation validity and common method bias. A further confirmatory factor analysis and structural equation modelling can only confirm the constructs of the survey thus created. The relationship between the variables also need to be understood. The resultant framework needs further testing and generalisations over large populations, and in diverse contexts.

8   Conclusion

The contribution of the paper lies with providing a validated, and reliable survey instrument which could be utilised for telehealth adoption or ICT adoption research in health-care domains in developing countries. Further, the comprehensive nature of the instrument can provide researchers on telehealth or ICT adoption in healthcare domain, a validated and reliable instrument measuring diverse constructs of ICT adoption in a single survey instrument.

Acknowledgement. The authors acknowledge the support received by Avijit Chowdhury from the University of Southern Queensland in the form of fees research scholarship for PhD studies.

Appendix A

SURVEY FORM
Exploring the determinants of telehealth adoption by Healthcare Professionals (HCPs) in India

PLEASE CIRCLE THE ONE APPLICABLE TO YOU

1. Age Bracket (in years):   (a) 20-29   (b) 30-39   (c) 40-49
(d) ≥50
2. Gender: (a) Male   (b) Female
3. Educational Qualifications: (a) Under Graduate   (b) Post Graduate
4. Occupation: (a) Doctor   (b) Paramedics   (c) Healthcare Admin   (d)
Healthcare Technical Support   (e) Other ....
5. Experience (in years):   (a) 0-9   (b) 10-19   (c) 20-29
(d) ≥30
6. Employment: (a) Public   (b) Private

No.	PLEASE CIRCLE THE RESPONSE APPLICABLE TO YOUR ENVIRONMENT SD=Strongly Disagree 1, D=Disagree 2, N=Neither Agree nor Disagree 3, A=Agree 4, and SA=Strongly Agree 5	SD	D	N	A	SA
1.	**Telehealth/online services** can be beneficial to get to know the patient profile	1	2	3	4	5
2.	can be beneficial to provide preliminary information to the patients	1	2	3	4	5
3.	can be beneficial to view reports online	1	2	3	4	5
4.	can be beneficial for early detection of patient conditions	1	2	3	4	5
5.	can expedite referrals in rural/remote areas for long-term care patients	1	2	3	4	5
6.	facilitate the referral services, for the emergency conditions of patients	1	2	3	4	5
7.	facilitate to provide information regarding the prevention of diseases	1	2	3	4	5
8.	can facilitate early treatment of the patient by using examining cameras	1	2	3	4	5
9.	can facilitate to verify patient conditions by using examining cameras	1	2	3	4	5
10.	can facilitate to prescribe diagnostic reports for the patients	1	2	3	4	5
11.	can facilitate prescribing medicines to the patients	1	2	3	4	5
12.	can facilitate the scheduling of appointments, for follow-up patients	1	2	3	4	5
13.	can be convenient, for monitoring patients	1	2	3	4	5

14.		can be beneficial for post-treatment counselling	1 2 3 4 5
15.	rehabilitation services	can be beneficial for providing post-treatment	1 2 3 4 5
16.	cation	can be beneficial to promote patient health edu-	1 2 3 4 5
17.	diseases	can be beneficial to promote the prevention of	1 2 3 4 5
18.		can be beneficial to promote healthy diets	1 2 3 4 5
19.		promote self-management of diseases	1 2 3 4 5
20.	outcomes	can be beneficial to promote improved health	1 2 3 4 5
21.		help to improve the care I give to my patients	1 2 3 4 5
22.		increase the effectiveness of healthcare delivery	1 2 3 4 5
23.	**Using telehealth/online services** would make it easier to do my job		1 2 3 4 5
24.		would increase my job efficiency	1 2 3 4 5
25.	**Telehealth/online services** increase productivity in healthcare delivery		1 2 3 4 5
26.		may facilitate improvement in the area of my job	1 2 3 4 5
27.	patients	facilitate improved health outcomes for the	1 2 3 4 5
28.	Viewing medical report is easy using telehealth/online services		1 2 3 4 5
29.	Analysing medical report is easy using telehealth/online services		1 2 3 4 5
30.	I understand the nuances of technologies involved in providing telehealth/online services		1 2 3 4 5
31.	My interaction with telehealth/online services applications is clear and understandable		1 2 3 4 5
32.	Learning to provide telehealth/online services would be easy for me		1 2 3 4 5
33.	The disease profile in rural and remote areas encourages to provide telehealth/online services		1 2 3 4 5
34.	**Telehealth/online services** can facilitate promoting nutrition and hygiene in the rural/remote areas		1 2 3 4 5
35.	the rural/remote areas	can facilitate in providing emergency services in	1 2 3 4 5
36.	The lack of facilities in rural/remote areas encourage the provision of telehealth/online services		1 2 3 4 5
37.	The distance to the nearest hospital in rural/remote areas can encourage telehealth/online services		1 2 3 4 5
38.	**Telehealth/online services** can lessen the cost of healthcare services		1 2 3 4 5
39.	the rural/remote areas	can facilitate providing affordable healthcare to	1 2 3 4 5
40.	to the rural/remote areas	can be beneficial to provide accessible healthcare	1 2 3 4 5
41.		help easy access to information	1 2 3 4 5
42.	**There is enough support** for the health workers training in telehealth/online services		1 2 3 4 5

43.	for the health professionals training in tele-health/online services	1	2	3	4	5
44.	Medical education can be improved through telehealth/online services	1	2	3	4	5
45.	Doctor-doctor collaboration is more critical in telehealth/online services than patient involvement	1	2	3	4	5
46.	Expert opinion/second opinion can be solicited easily through the use of telehealth/online services	1	2	3	4	5
47.	The broadband services used for telehealth/online services in the urban areas are satisfactory	1	2	3	4	5
48.	The ICT infrastructure is robust in urban areas which can motivate to use telehealth/online services	1	2	3	4	5
49.	There are several telehealth/online services applications to choose from	1	2	3	4	5
50.	**Telehealth/online services** have the potential to be the alternative support solution to health services	1	2	3	4	5
51.	can facilitate services to immova-ble/disabled/specially abled patients	1	2	3	4	5
52.	can be the alternative support solution for ru-ral/remote areas	1	2	3	4	5
53.	can be the alternative support solution during natural disasters	1	2	3	4	5
54.	**Providing telehealth/online services** is time-saving for healthcare profes-sionals	1	2	3	4	5
55.	is time-saving for the patients	1	2	3	4	5
56.	The shortage of doctors in rural/remote areas can encourage providing tele-health/online services	1	2	3	4	5
57.	**Telehealth/online services** can cater to overseas Indians	1	2	3	4	5
58.	can provide information about treatment in India to overseas persons	1	2	3	4	5
59.	prove to be economical both for the HCPs and the patients	1	2	3	4	5
60.	save travelling distances both for the HCPs and the patients	1	2	3	4	5
61.	can be a useful tool to provide allied healthcare services	1	2	3	4	5
62.	I am using telehealth/online services for a considerable period of time	1	2	3	4	5
63.	I consider myself as a forerunner in Indian telehealth/online services	1	2	3	4	5
64.	**Telehealth/online services** are going to be an essential part of healthcare services in the near future	1	2	3	4	5
65.	applications provide me a better understanding of the patient profile	1	2	3	4	5
66.	I do not consider telehealth/online services as a requirement in healthcare practice	1	2	3	4	5
67.	A reliable ICT infrastructure is important for telehealth/online services usage	1	2	3	4	5
68.	Robust ICT infra (e.g. Broadband speed, towers) can be encouraging for telehealth/online services	1	2	3	4	5

69.	Uninterrupted video link makes it comfortable to use telehealth/online services	1	2	3	4	5
70.	Rural areas/remote areas need improved broadband services to provide telehealth/online services	1	2	3	4	5
71.	Enough technical support is required to provide telehealth/online services	1	2	3	4	5
72.	The inconvenience of using technology hinders telehealth/online services usage	1	2	3	4	5
73.	**Telehealth/online services** platforms should be technologically upgraded for better online services	1	2	3	4	5
74.	usage can increase if the online platforms are easy to use	1	2	3	4	5
75.	Information security plays a major role in telehealth/online services usage	1	2	3	4	5
76.	Confidentiality of information is necessary to start using telehealth/online services	1	2	3	4	5
77.	Hacking of health data hinders telehealth/online services usage	1	2	3	4	5
78.	Lack of ethical standards hinder telehealth/online services usage	1	2	3	4	5
79.	Validation of doctors' credential is essential to provide telehealth/online services	1	2	3	4	5
80.	There is a risk for the patient to get ill advice from quacks posing as HCPs online	1	2	3	4	5
81.	The organisational ICT infrastructure is sufficient to provide telehealth/online services delivery	1	2	3	4	5
82.	Additional remuneration is required to provide telehealth/online services	1	2	3	4	5
83.	Adequate staff training facilities are provided for training in telehealth/online services	1	2	3	4	5
84.	Organisation top management is encouraging enough to use telehealth/online services	1	2	3	4	5
85.	The organisation provides support to acquire new skills in telehealth/online services/technology	1	2	3	4	5
86.	There is a requirement for organisational policy for telehealth/online services	1	2	3	4	5
87.	Standardised guidelines are required for providing telehealth/online services	1	2	3	4	5
88.	There is a requirement for practical government policy on telehealth/online services	1	2	3	4	5
89.	**The government** can influence the demand for telehealth/online services	1	2	3	4	5
90.	can influence the supply of telehealth/online services	1	2	3	4	5
91.	can promote the benefits of telehealth/online services	1	2	3	4	5
92.	The current Government policy of promoting telehealth/online services is impractical	1	2	3	4	5
93.	I prefer face-to-face communications though I am not against using telehealth/online services	1	2	3	4	5
94.	I am reluctant to provide telehealth/online services	1	2	3	4	5
95.	**Telehealth/online services** may facilitate providing misleading information to the patients	1	2	3	4	5
96.	can be beneficial only for viewing diagnostic reports	1	2	3	4	5
97.	can be beneficial only for scheduling appointments	1	2	3	4	5

Healthcare Practices (HP 1-HP15) Items 1-15
Patient Awareness (PA1-PA5) Items 16-20
Healthcare Facilities (HF1-HF8) Items 21-28
HCP Awareness (HA1-HA6) Items 29-34
Technology Motivators (TM1-TM7) Items 35-41
Competitive Advantage (CA1-CA8) Items 42-49
Technology Issues (TI1-TI14) Items 50-63
Organisational Issues (OI1-OI6) Items 64-69
State Leadership (SL1-S6) Items70-75
Communication Issues (CI1-C5) Items 76-80
Telehealth Adoption (Dependent Variable) (TA1-TA17) Items 81-97

Appendix B

Principal Component Analysis.

Rotated Component Matrix[a]

Indicators	HP[1]	PA[2]	TI-ICT[3]OR[4]	CA[5]	TM[6]	TI-SEC[7]	OS[8]	TA (DV)[9]
HP13 Monitoring patients	.795							
HP2 Preliminary information to the patients	.787							
HP10 Beneficial to view reports online	.772							
HP12 Scheduling of appointments	.764							
HP4 Early detection of patient conditions	.764							
HP11 Prescribing medicines	.755							
HP6 Referral services for emergency patients	.743							
HP7 Information regarding prevention of diseases	.706							
HP5 Referral services for long term care patients	.627							
PA3 Promoting healthy diets		.815						
HP14 Post-treatment counselling		.813						
PA1 Promote patient health education		.758						
HP15 Post-treatment rehabilitation services		.676						
SL5 The government can promote the benefits of tele-health		.620						
SL3 The government can influence the demand for tele-health		.569						
TI3 Uninterrupted video link makes it comfortable to use telehealth			.816					
TI6 Inconvenience of technology hinders telehealth usage			.748					
TI5 Enough technical support is required			.732					
TI2 Robust ICT Infra can be encouraging			.653					

TA16 Provide a better understanding of the patient profile	.760							
OI2 Additional remuneration is required	.724							
TA15 Going to be an essential part of healthcare services in future	.714							
HF2 Can facilitate promoting health and hygiene	.696							
TI1 A reliable ICT infrastructure is important	.649							
CA4 Can cater to overseas Indians		.824						
CA8 Useful tool to provide allied healthcare services		.821						
TM7 Can be an alternative support solution during natural disasters		.747						
HA1 help easy access to inforamtion			.837					
TI8 Telehealth usage can increase if online platforms are easy to use			.732					
TM3 There are several telehealth applications to choose from			.697					
TI14 Risk of getting ill advice from quacks				.853				
TI13 Validation of doctors credential is essential				.784				
TI12 Lack of ethical standards hinders telehealth usage				.717				
TI10 Confidentiality of information is necessary				.591				
OI5 The organisation provides support to acquire new skills					.767			
TA9 Analysing medical report is easy					.590			
CA2 time saving for the patients					.551			
TA3 Telehealth would make it easier to do the job						.852		
TA4 Telehealth would increase job efficiency						.805		
TA7 Telehealth facilitates improved health outcomes for the patient						.755		

Extraction Method: Principal Component Analysis.
Rotation Method: Varimax with Kaiser Normalization. [a]
a. Rotation converged in 8 iterations.

1. **HP** Healthcare Practices	4. **OR** Organisational Readiness	7. **TI_SEC** Technology Issues-Security (TI-SEC)
2. **PA** Patient Awareness	5. **CA** Competitive Advantage	8. **OS** Organisational Support (OS)
3. **TI_ICT** Technology Issues – ICT	6. **TM** Technology Motivators	9. **TA** (**DV**) Telehealth Adoption (Dependent Variable)

References

Adamson, G.: The persistent challenge of health informatics. Inf. Commun. Soc. **19**(4), 551–558 (2016). https://doi.org/10.1080/1369118X.2015.1118523

Ahmadi, H., Nilashi, M., Ibrahim, O.: Prioritizing critical factors to successful adoption of total hospital information system. J. Soft Comput. Decis. Support Syst. **2**(4), 6–16 (2015)

Alaboudi, A., Atkins, A., Sharp, B., Balkhair, A., Alzahrani, M., Sunbul, T.: Barriers and challenges in adopting Saudi telemedicine network: the perceptions of decision makers of healthcare facilities in Saudi Arabia. J. Inf. Public Health **9**(6), 725–733 (2016)

Anwar, S., Prasad, R.: Framework for future telemedicine planning and infrastructure using 5G technology. Wireless Pers. Commun. **100**(1), 193–208 (2018)

Balarajan, Y., Selvaraj, S., Subramanian, S.V.: Health care and equity in India. Lancet **377**(9764), 505–515 (2011). https://doi.org/10.1016/S0140-6736(10)61894-6

Brancheau, J.C., Wetherbe, J.C.: The adoption of spreadsheet software: testing innovation diffusion theory in the context of end-user computing. Inf. Syst. Res. **1**(2), 115–143 (1990)

Bretschneider, S.: Management information systems in public and private organizations: an empirical test. Public Admin. Rev. 536–545 (1990)

Brindha, G.: Emerging trends of telemedicine in India. Indian J. Sci. Technol. **6**(sup 5) (2013)

Chandwani, R.K., Dwivedi, Y.K.: Telemedicine in India: current state, challenges and opportunities. Transform. Govern. People Process Policy **9**(4), 393–400 (2015)

Chismar, W.G., Wiley-Patton, S.: Does the extended technology acceptance model apply to physicians. Paper presented at the Proceedings of the 36th Annual Hawaii International Conference on System Sciences 2003 (2003)

Cho, S., Mathiassen, L., Gallivan, M.: Crossing the diffusion chasm: from invention to penetration of a telehealth innovation. Inf. Technol. People **22**(4), 351–366 (2009). https://doi.org/10.1108/09593840911002450

Cho, S., Mathiassen, L., Robey, D.: Dialectics of resilience: a multi-level analysis of a telehealth innovation. J. Inf. Technol. **22**(1), 24–35 (2007). https://doi.org/10.1057/palgrave.jit.2000088

Chowdhury, A., Hafeez-Baig, A., Gururajan, R., Chakraborty, S.: Conceptual framework for telehealth adoption in Indian healthcare. Paper presented at the 24th Annual Conference of the Asia Pacific Decision Sciences Institute: Full papers (2019)

Confederation of Indian Industry, & KPMG. Building ICT Infrastructure - Connecting the unconnected (2017)

Cooper, R.B., Zmud, R.W.: Information technology implementation research: a technological diffusion approach. Manage. Sci. **36**(2), 123–139 (1990)

Cunningham, C.T., et al.: Exploring physician specialist response rates to web-based surveys. BMC Med. Res. Methodol. **15**(1), 32 (2015)

Depietro, R., Wiarda, E., Fleischer, M.: The context for change: organization, technology and environment. In: Tornatzky, L.G., Fleischer, M. (eds.) The processes of technological innovation, pp. 151–175. Lexington Books, Lexington, MA (1990)

Dwivedi, A., Bali, R.K., James, A.E., Naguib, R.N.G.: Telehealth systems: considering knowledge management and ICT issues. Paper presented at the 2001 Conference Proceedings of the 23rd Annual International Conference of the IEEE Engineering in Medicine and Biology Society (2001)

Dwivedi, Y.K., Choudrie, J., Brinkman, W.P.: Development of a survey instrument to examine consumer adoption of broadband. Ind. Manag. Data Syst. (2006)

Faber, S., Van Geenhulzen, M., de Reuver, M.: eHealth adoption factors in medical hospitals: a focus on the Netherlands. Int. J. Med. Informatics **100**, 77–89 (2017). https://doi.org/10.1016/j.ijmedinf.2017.01.009

Fichman, R.G.: Information technology diffusion: a review of empirical research. Paper presented at the ICIS (1992)

Ghani, M.K.A., Jaber, M.M.: Willingness to adopt telemedicine in major Iraqi hospitals: a pilot study. Int. J. Telemed. Appl. **2015**, 6 (2015)

Ghia, C.J., Ved, J.K., Jha, R.K.: Benefits of Telemedicine and Barriers to its Effective Implementation in Rural India: A Multicentric E-Survey (2013)

Hair, J.F., Black, W.C., Babin, B.J., Anderson, R.E., Tatham, R.L.: Multivariate Data Analysis, 5 edn. Prentice Hall, Upper Saddle River (1998)

Haynes, S.N., Richard, D., Kubany, E.S.: Content validity in psychological assessment: a functional approach to concepts and methods. Psychol. Assess. **7**(3), 238 (1995)

Hohwü, L., Lyshol, H., Gissler, M., Jonsson, S.H., Petzold, M., Obel, C.: Web-based versus traditional paper questionnaires: a mixed-mode survey with a nordic perspective. J. Med. Internet Res. **15**(8), e173 (2013). https://doi.org/10.2196/jmir.2595

Hu, P.J.-H., Chau, P.Y.K., Liu Sheng, O.R.: Adoption of telemedicine technology by health care organizations: an exploratory study. J. Organ. Comput. Electron. Commer. **12**(3), 197–221 (2002)

Janda, M., et al.: Evaluating healthcare practitioners' views on store-and-forward teledermoscopy services for the diagnosis of skin cancer. Digit. Health **5**, 2055207619828225 (2019)

Keil, M., Beranek, P.M., Konsynski, B.R.: Usefulness and ease of use: field study evidence regarding task considerations. Decis. Support Syst. **13**(1), 75–91 (1995)

Kimberly, J.R., Evanisko, M.J.: Organizational innovation: the influence of individual, organizational, and contextual factors on hospital adoption of technological and administrative innovations. Acad. Manag. J. **24**(4), 689–713 (1981)

Kumar, A., Ahmad, S.: A review study on utilization of telemedicine and e-health services in public health. Asian Pac. J. Health Sci. **2**(1), 60–68 (2015)

Langbecker, D., Caffery, L.J., Gillespie, N., Smith, A.C.: Using survey methods in telehealth research: A practical guide. J. Telemed. Telecare **23**(9), 770–779 (2017)

Lian, J.-W., Yen, D.C., Wang, Y.-T.: An exploratory study to understand the critical factors affecting the decision to adopt cloud computing in Taiwan hospital. Int. J. Inf. Manage. **34**(1), 28–36 (2014)

Lin, C., Lin, I.C., Roan, J.: Barriers to physicians' adoption of healthcare information technology: an empirical study on multiple hospitals. J. Med. Syst. **36**(3), 1965–1977 (2012). https://doi.org/10.1007/s10916-011-9656-7

Paslakis, G., et al.: Assessment of use and preferences regarding internet-based health care delivery: cross-sectional questionnaire study. J. Med. Internet Res. **21**(5), e12416 (2019). https://doi.org/10.2196/12416

Paul, D.L., Pearlson, K.E., McDaniel, R.R.: Assessing technological barriers to telemedicine: technology-management implications. IEEE Trans. Eng. Manage. **46**(3), 279–288 (1999)

Rani, V., Hafeez-Baig, A., Gururajan, R.: Understanding factors influencing adoption of mobile devices in telehealth: a quantitative study. Paper presented at the 24th Annual Conference of the Asia Pacific Decision Sciences Institute: Full papers (2019)

Rathi, A.: Inequalities in financing of healthcare in India. Trends Immunotherapy **1**(1), 50–51 (2017). https://doi.org/10.24294/ti.v1i1.44

Raza, M., Le, M.H., Aslam, N., Le, C.H., Le, N.T., Le, T.L.: Telehealth technology: Potentials, challenges and research directions for developing countries. Paper presented at the International Conference on the Development of Biomedical Engineering in Vietnam (2017)

Singh, K.: Biotelemetry: could technological developments assist healthcare in rural India. Rural Remote Health **5**(2), 234 (2005). www.rrh.org.au/journal/article/234

Sivagurunathan, C., Umadevi, R., Rama, R., Gopalakrishnan, S.: Adolescent health: present status and its related programmes in India. Are we in the right direction? J. Clinic. Diag. Res. JCDR **9**(3), LE01 (2015)

Straub, D., Boudreau, M.-C., Gefen, D.: Validation guidelines for IS positivist research. Commun. Assoc. Inf. Syst. **13**(1), 24 (2004)

Tanriverdi, H., Iacono, C.S.: Knowledge Barriers to Diffusion of Telemedicine. Paper presented at the Proceedings of the International Conference on Information systems (1998)

West, V., Milio, N.: Organizational and environmental factors affecting the utilization of telemedicine in rural home healthcare. Home Health Care Serv. Quar. **23**(4), 49–67 (2004). https://doi.org/10.1300/J027v23n04_04

Whitten, P., Johannessen, L.K., Soerensen, T., Gammon, D., Mackert, M.: A systematic review of research methodology in telemedicine studies. J. Telemed. Telecare **13**(5), 230–235 (2007)

Wynd, C.A., Schmidt, B., Schaefer, M.A.: Two quantitative approaches for estimating content validity. West. J. Nurs. Res. **25**(5), 508–518 (2003)

Zailani, S., Gilani, M.S., Nikbin, D., Iranmanesh, M.: Determinants of telemedicine acceptance in selected public hospitals in Malaysia: clinical perspective. J. Med. Syst. **38**(9), 1–12 (2014). https://doi.org/10.1007/s10916-014-0111-4

Zhou, L., Thieret, R., Watzlaf, V., DeAlmeida, D., Parmanto, B.: A telehealth privacy and security self-assessment questionnaire for telehealth providers: development and validation. Int. J. Telerehabil. **11**(1), 3–14 (2019)

Zmud, R.W.: Diffusion of modern software practices: influence of centralization and formalization. Manage. Sci. **28**(12), 1421–1431 (1982)

Structural Changes in Discussions Using Design Thinking and Their Effect on Creativity

Mayumi Kawase[1](✉), Kazumi Matsumoto[2], Hiroshi Kamabe[3], Hidekazu Fukai[3], and Kazunori Terada[3]

[1] Department of Engineering Science, Gifu University, 1-1 Yanagido, Gifu 501-1193, Japan
`mkawase@gifu-u.ac.jp`
[2] Hitachi Ltd., Tokyo 140-8572, Japan
[3] Gifu University, 1-1 Yanagido, Gifu 501-1193, Japan

Abstract. This study examines the effect of the discussion process on the creativity of output when students discuss and solve problems in groups using design thinking proposed by d.school Stanford University. According to the design thinking, students were instructed to develop novel and useful communication digital tools according to the design thinking five steps. Microsoft Teams chatbox was used to have voice-based discussions and to keep text data of their discussions. Nine components were extracted from the discussion process, i.e., 'information gathering', 'problem analysis', 'needs', 'functions for realization', 'prototype', 'expectation', 'information sharing', 'confirmation', and 'agreement'. For each group's output, the level of creativity was evaluated using subscales of 'novelty' and 'usefulness'. Regression analysis was used to examine the effects of each component on 'novelty' and 'usefulness'. The results showed that 'problem analysis', 'prototype', and 'confirmation' components influenced 'novelty' on creativity.

Keywords: Creativity · Design thinking · Collaboration · High human resources development in engineering

1 Introduction

In 2018, the Japanese Cabinet Office announced its policy to promote Society 5.0 as the successor of Society 4.0, the information society, to bring about a significant paradigm shift by advancing innovative digital technologies such as AI, IoT, and big data [1].

In this phase of significant change, the next generation of advanced engineers will be required to master existing technologies and be highly creative in developing new values. The Graduate School of Natural Science and Technology, Gifu University, to which the authors belong, considers fostering the next generation of advanced engineers to be its mission and is already working on an educational program to foster creativity within the framework of design thinking [2]. The program is focused on human-centered design. In this educational program, the theory of design thinking is explained, and difficult problems with high uncertainty are given as exercises. Through group discussions, students will acquire the ability to redefine issues through subjective evaluation and analysis of various problems that arise when people use artifacts such as products and systems.

© Springer Nature Switzerland AG 2021
S. Yamamoto and H. Mori (Eds.): HCII 2021, LNCS 12766, pp. 226–241, 2021.
https://doi.org/10.1007/978-3-030-78361-7_17

According to Stanford University d.school [3], the design thinking five steps has Empathize, Define, Ideate, Prototype, and Test, which comprise the essential frame for problem-solving. In Society 5.0, integrating cyberspace and physical space will be a challenge. Therefore, as a practical task to cultivate creativity, we address creatively solving problems by using design thinking to integrate cyberspace and physical space.

In creative problem-solving, groups use design thinking to discuss and formulate creative output under almost identical conditions. However, when groups are asked to solve problems using design thinking creatively, the group's creative output's creativity differs. In order to develop a program to foster creativity, it is essential to elucidate the relationship between the type of discussion that takes place and the type of creativity that is evoked when participants engage in creative problem-solving using design thinking.

In this paper, we report how each group discussion element in our design thinking education program contributed to the creativity manifested.

2 Method

2.1 Research Target

The class analyzed in this study was a class of the second term of the 2020 academic year in the required course, Design Thinking Introduction, at the Graduate School of Natural Science and Technology, Gifu University. A total of 99 students were divided into 25 groups of 4 students each. The groups were organized such that the students' courses and majors would not overlap.

2.2 Design Thinking Introduction: Class Design and Contents

The first half of the class consisted of classroom lectures, and the second half consisted of group work. In the first half of the class, students studied the basic theory of design thinking and learned about specific problem-solving examples for design thinking introduced by corporate designers at Yahoo! JAPAN and Hitachi Ltd. (Fig. 1).

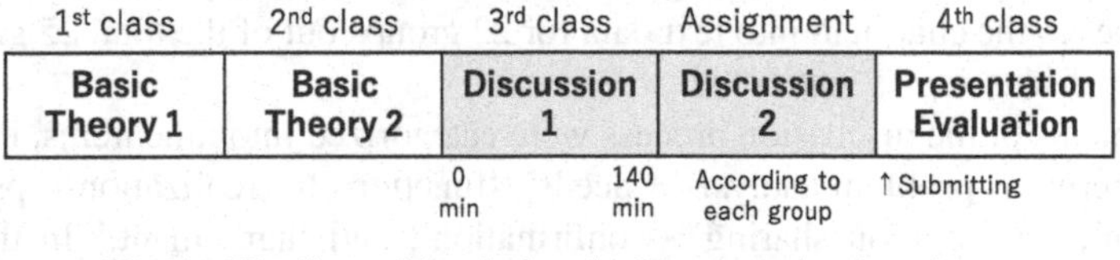

1st class	2nd class	3rd class	Assignment	4th class
Basic Theory 1	Basic Theory 2	Discussion 1	Discussion 2	Presentation Evaluation
		0 min	140 min	According to each group	↑ Submitting

Fig. 1. The flow of the design thinking introduction classes

All group work was conducted online using Microsoft Teams for a total of 166–1095 min, including lecture time and homework.

The group work assignments for the 2020 academic year were as follows:

"This year's group assignment is to discuss and work on a product development task online. However, as we communicated online, the discussion did not proceed as expected, and we felt more and more uncomfortable. Identify the feeling of discomfort you felt and develop and propose an artifact that solves it by making it easier to achieve the goal."

Along with the presentation of the task, the groups were showed how to proceed with the discussion as follows:

- Use the design thinking five steps
- Be aware of divergence and convergence when proceeding with the five steps
- When analyzing the problem, generating ideas, and summarizing the ideas, the group should simultaneously edit the relevant PowerPoint presentation
- [Divergent] Analyze the situations used by the user
- [Convergent] Describe the current problems and issues in one sentence
- [Convergent] Decide on users who would use an artifact and create personas
- [Divergent] Identify needs of the persona
- [Convergent] Describe the needs of the persona in one sentence
- [Divergent] Combine functions that meet the needs
- [Divergent] Create a usability-conscious prototype that is easy to use
- [Convergent] Evaluate the quality of use of the prototype by assuming a situation where it will be practically used
- [Convergent] Propose a new artifact by creating a two-minute presentation video

When discussing using Teams, we prepared a private channel for the group to develop the discussion. As for the students who did not participate in the discussion, they were asked to share their ideas and keep a record of their opinions in the group channel's posting section so that they could look back on the discussion later.

In the last session of the 4th class, the students were asked to watch the other groups' videos, consider the contents' accuracy following the design thinking five steps, and evaluate the other groups.

2.3 Text Data of Discussion Content, Structuring of Content Analysis

To examine what kind of ideas were generated in the discussion process, we converted the utterances in the chat field into text data for 22 groups out of the total 25 groups that recorded the discussion as instructed.

The contents of the discussion process were categorized into nine items, i.e., 'information gathering', 'problem analysis', 'needs', 'functions for realization', 'prototype', 'expectation', 'information sharing', 'confirmation', and 'agreement.' In this Table, 'information gathering' is about obtaining information sources for generating ideas from outside oneself, 'problem analysis' to 'expectation' are about analyzing problems from a human-centered (user-centered) perspective and creating new values to meet the 'needs', and 'information sharing', 'confirmation' and 'agreement' are about managing discussions for group design activities (Table 1).

Table 1. Classification lists and contents of discussion extracted from utterances analysis.

	Lists	Contents
1.	Information Gathering	Gathering information from outside and interacting with it.
2.	Problem Analysis	Analyzing the user's problem.
3.	Needs	Having a dialogue about the user's needs.
4.	Functions for Realization	Having a dialogue about the combination of functions in realizing the needs and providing a new service.
5.	Prototype	Having a dialogue by visualizing and checking the idea.
6.	Expectation	Expecating situations in which users are using the new service.
7.	Information Sharing	Sharing information to help others understand.
8.	Confirmation	Confirming what should be done next to solve the problem.
9.	Agreement	Understanding the other person's proposal and accepting the idea.

2.4 Measurement of Creativity

Although many studies have examined the abilities and activity processes of individuals who have generated innovative products [4], there is often no single definition of creativity [5]. Mumford defined creativity as the generation of products with novelty and usefulness by an individual [6]. Therefore, in this study, 'novelty' and usefulness were set as the survey scale when measuring the creativity of creative outputs (creations), and they were used as subscales of creativity [7]. To examine the subscales of creativity, two instructors in charge of the class independently rated the 'novelty' and 'usefulness' on a 10-point scale. 'novelty' implies a new value that did not exist before the discussion. 'usefulness' implies whether it is useful to the user as well as other people.

2.5 Measuring the Effect of Discussion on Creativity

A regression analysis was conducted to examine the effect of the nine items of discussion content on creativity subscales. SPSS, IBM's analysis software, was used for the analysis.

First, in order to compare the effects of the nine items of discussion on the 'novelty' of creativity, the nine items of discussion were set as the independent variables and 'novelty' as the dependent variable, and regression analysis was conducted. Similarly, to examine the nine items' effect on 'usefulness', a regression analysis was conducted for each item.

3 Results

3.1 Structuring the Discussion by Content Analysis: Aggregation of Nine Items and Number of Utterances

Table 2 categorizes the nine items of discussion content and compares the number of utterances in each group. Figure 2 shows the total number of utterances for each of the nine items. In the early stages of the group discussions, most of the groups discussed problem analysis, which accounted for 32.3% of the total discussion times.

Table 2. Discussion categories and number of utterances per group

	1 Information Gathering	2 Problem Analysis	3 Needs	4 Function for Re-alization	5 Proto-type	6 Expecta-tion	7 Infor-mation Sharing	8 Confir-mation	9 Agree-ment
Group 1	1	34	19	8	5	0	0	8	10
Group 2	1	5	6	6	5	0	1	2	0
Group 3	0	12	18	5	6	0	8	2	4
Group 4	2	26	20	7	14	0	18	8	7
Group 5	1	26	18	5	4	12	4	1	2
Group 6	0	19	12	5	4	3	2	8	0
Group 7	0	26	7	3	1	0	15	4	0
Group 8	0	7	10	4	4	0	13	3	8
Group 9	0	19	33	17	0	0	4	1	0
Group 10	0	35	32	12	0	0	2	4	3
Group 11	2	94	7	27	12	37	48	56	183
Group 12	2	33	20	9	3	4	3	3	4
Group 13	0	67	12	34	8	3	4	1	3
Group 14	0	44	25	19	0	0	7	1	2
Group 15	2	0	5	2	3	0	0	3	1
Group 16	3	25	10	22	3	0	0	2	4
Group 17	3	27	7	2	0	0	5	1	0
Group 18	0	53	10	13	4	0	1	2	0
Group 19	5	66	12	19	14	30	14	29	82
Group 20	0	23	39	24	0	5	0	5	3
Group 21	0	28	15	7	4	0	4	13	17
Group 22	0	59	33	19	17	10	2	5	0
Total	22	728	370	269	111	104	155	162	333
%	1.0	32.3	16.4	11.9	4.9	4.6	6.9	7.2	14.8

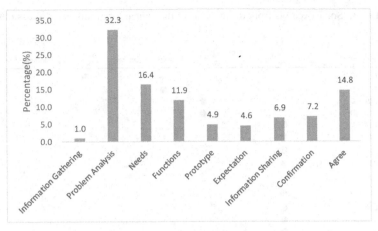

Fig. 2. Comparison of results of the content analysis of discussions

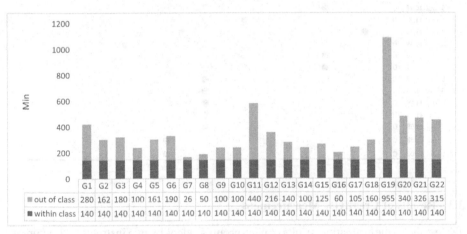

Fig. 3. Comparison of total discussion time for each group

3.2   A Concrete Example of Structural Analysis of Utterances Content: Group 19

Table 3 shows the content analysis of the discussions that took place in Group 19 in chronological order. The reason for choosing Group 19 was that it had much content related to problem analysis and prototyping in its discussions, a large number of hours of discussion, and was an overall well-balanced group.

The following are the items and the number of times they appeared in the actual discussions: items for obtaining information from outside ('information gathering') were mentioned once, 'problem analysis' 12 times, 'needs' zero, 'functions for realization' 5 times, 'prototype' 6 times, 'expectation' twice and 'information sharing' twice.

Table 3. Some excerpts from the analysis of the content of group 19's discussions

Date	Time	Speaker	1 Information Gathering	2 Problem Analysis	3 Needs	4 Function for Realization	5 Prototype	6 Expectation	7 Information Sharing	8 Confirmation	9 Agreement
8-Jul	10:19	D							●		
8-Jul	10:20	D					●				
8-Jul	10:21	D				●					
8-Jul	10:23	D				●					
8-Jul	10:26	C		●							
8-Jul	10:27	A		●							
8-Jul	10:27	D		●							
8-Jul	10:27	D		●							
8-Jul	10:30	A		●							
8-Jul	10:32	D		●							
8-Jul	10:34	D		●							
8-Jul	10:36	A		●							
8-Jul	10:38	C		●							
8-Jul	10:40	A				●					
8-Jul	10:41	C				●					
8-Jul	10:42	D		●							
8-Jul	11:20	D				●					
8-Jul	11:49	C	●								
8-Jul	11:49	D							●		
8-Jul	11:57	D		●							
8-Jul	11:57	D		●							
8-Jul	11:58	C					●				
8-Jul	11:58	C					●				
8-Jul	11:58	C					●				
8-Jul	11:58	D					●				
8-Jul	11:58	D					●				
8-Jul	11:59	C						●			
8-Jul	12:00	C						●			

3.3 Results of Creativity Measurement

Table 4 shows the evaluation results of each group's videos by two instructors (Lecture A, Lecture B) in charge. In order to determine the reliability of the evaluations, Cronbach's alpha coefficient was used; the result for 'novelty' was 0.86 and for 'usefulness' was 0.65 (Table 5).

3.4 Results of the Analysis of the Effect of Discussion on Creativity

We examined the relationship between the nine items of discussion and the two subscales of creativity. The results of the regression analysis for 'novelty' as the dependent variable and nine items as explanatory variables are shown in Table 6; values above 0.3 were found for 'problem analysis', 'prototype', 'expectation', and 'confirmation'. On the other hand, no values above 0.3 were found for 'usefulness' (Fig. 4).

Table 4. Evaluation of the creativity ('novelty' and 'usefulness') of the creation by two lecturers

Novelty		G1	G2	G3	G4	G5	G6	G7	G8	G9	G 10	G 11
	Lecturer A	7	6	8	7	6	7	5	4	5	6	8
	Lecturer B	6	7	8	7	6	8	6	3	5	7	7
Total		13	13	16	14	12	15	11	7	10	13	15
		G 12	G 13	G 14	G 15	G 16	G 17	G 18	G 19	G 20	G 21	G 22
	Lecturer A	6	6	6	6	7	6	8	8	7	7	7
	Lecturer B	7	7	5	6	6	7	8	8	8	8	7
Total		13	13	11	12	13	13	16	16	15	15	14

Usefulness		G1	G2	G3	G4	G5	G6	G7	G8	G9	G 10	G 11
	Lecturer A	8	8	10	8	8	8	7	7	8	7	6
	Lecturer B	5	6	9	6	7	8	7	7	6	7	7
Total		13	14	19	14	15	16	14	14	14	14	13
		G 12	G 13	G 14	G 15	G 16	G 17	G 18	G 19	G 20	G 21	G 22
	Lecturer A	8	9	8	8	8	6	8	8	7	8	8
	Lecturer B	8	8	6	8	8	4	8	7	7	8	9
Total		16	17	14	16	16	10	16	15	14	16	17

Table 5. Reliability evaluation of 'novelty' and 'usefulness' on creativity

	List number	Cronbach's α coefficient
Novelty	2	0.86
Usefulness	2	0.65

Table 6. Comparison of results of the regression analysis of the sub-items of discussion and creativity

	Information Gathering	Problem Analysis	Needs	Functions for Realization	Prototype	Expectation	Information Sharing	Confirmation	Agreement
Novelty									
R Squared	0.22	0.39	0.01	0.21	0.39	0.35	0.06	0.37	0.29
Reliability Coefficient	0.32	0.07	0.96	0.34	0.07	0.11	0.78	0.09	0.18
Usefulness									
R Squared	0.26	0.02	0.07	0.14	0.27	0.08	0.26	0.18	0.20
Reliability Coefficient	0.24	0.93	0.77	0.54	0.22	0.71	0.24	0.42	0.38

3.5 Analytical Result of the Total Time for Discussion Per Group and Creativity ('novelty')

A regression analysis was conducted to compare the effect of total discussion time on the 'novelty' per group without group 19. Group 19 was excluded from the regression analysis because the total number of hours was clearly higher than the other groups. The result showed $R2 = 0.586$, $p \leq 0.05$. Figure 5 shows the distribution of total discussion time and 'novelty' per group.

3.6 Relationship Between Each Group's Discussion ('problem Analysis', 'prototype') and Creativity ('novelty')

Figure 6 is a radar chart visualizing the breakdown of creativity ('novelty') and discussion structure for all 22 groups. The relationship between 'novelty' and discussion components ('problem analysis' and 'prototype') is visualized on a radar chart. The number of 'problem analysis' items has been multiplied by a factor of ten for easier comparison. The units are aligned with those of the other scales. The number in the lower right corner of the radar chart for each group indicates the total time for discussion.

Of the 22 groups, those in orange indicate a 'novelty' score of 70% or higher. These groups accounted for 68% of the total. All 15 groups with a 'novelty' score of 70% or higher made statements about 'problem analysis'.

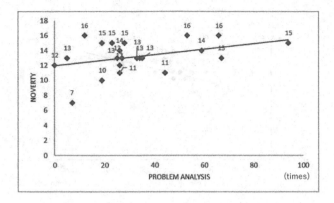

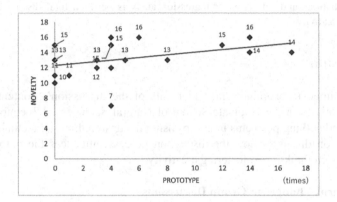

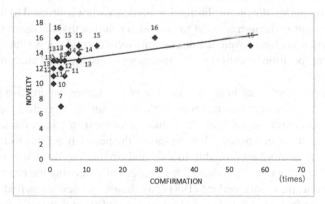

Fig. 4. Distributions and line plots of regression analysis for 'problem analysis', 'prototype' and 'confirmation', and 'novelty' on Creativity for the 22 groups

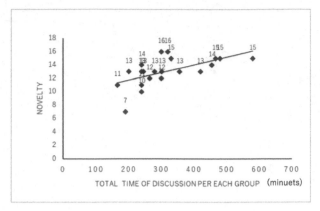

Fig. 5. Distributions and line plots of regression analysis between total discussion time and 'novelty' on creativity

4   Discussion

This study aimed to examine which elements of the discussion's content influence students' creativity in the Graduate School of Natural Science and Technology when discussing and solving problems in groups using the design thinking method.

This section discusses how the discussion process influences the output and the impact of design thinking on fostering creativity.

4.1   Structural Changes in Group Discussions

Students were instructed to use the design thinking five steps as a workflow for creative problem-solving during the online discussion. Students were instructed to find different problems that occur to the user in order to propose a solution that the user expects. After the above instructions were given, the discussions were carried out within class and out of class. The composition of the group utterances was classified and analyzed about the creative process.

Table 2 summarizes what happened in each group during the creative process and the components of the discussion. From Table 2, it can be seen that the discussion process involved analyzing the user's task and the context in which the user uses the artifact to extract the user's needs. Then, to satisfy the needs, functions were combined, the form was made more comfortable to use, and finally, the form was reconsidered from the user's perspective. This showed the process of proposing the desirable artifact (digital communication tool). Perkins (1981) has shown that new ideas find information in memory used as material for ideas and integrating it [8]. In this study, the utterances in which information is collected from Table 2 are 1% of the total utterances, so the utterances and ideas in this study's discussions are consistent with Perkins' theory.

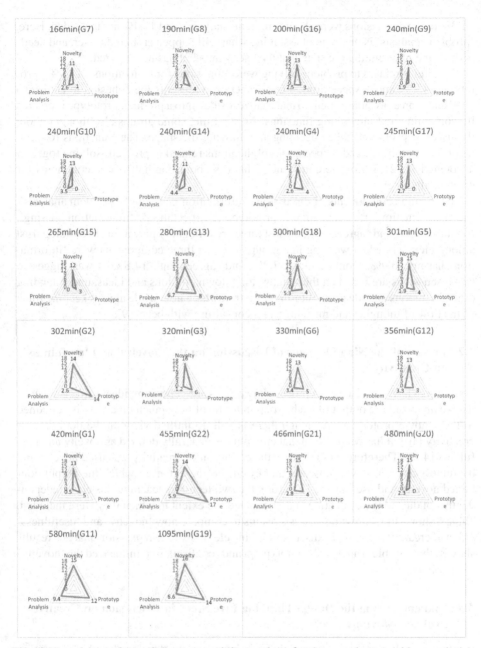

Fig. 6. Comparison of 'novelty' scores and the number of utterances about 'problem analysis' and 'prototype' in the order of total number of discussions

Design thinking is an approach to problem discovery and solution regarding human-centered issues. Looking at the nine components from this perspective, analyzing problems that occur to people and needs to have the problems solved is part of the five steps.

32.3% of the discussions were about 'problem analysis', and 16.4% about needed. Here, 'problem analysis' is the stage of assuming what will happen around the user, and needs is the stage of assuming the state that the user wants but has not realized.

The items related to problem-solving were 'functions for realizations', 11.9%, 'prototype', 4.9%, and 'expectation', 4.6%. Function represents the cohesion to achieve a need and is an unavoidable item to materialize an idea into a product. Prototype is created by combining and integrating functions. At this time, some groups also thought about the user's expectations when deciding and drawing the shape. The 'functions for realization', 'prototype', and 'expectation' of the items related to problem-solving together accounted for 21.4% of the comments, which is about one-half of the comments for problem discovery.

Of the nine components of discussion, 'information gathering', 'problem analysis', 'needs', 'functions for realization', 'prototype', 'expectation', 'information sharing', 'confirmation', and 'agreement', the last three are thought to play a role in building trust among members when working in a group. The last three components were 'information sharing', 6.9%, 'confirmation', 7.2%, and 'agreement', 14.8%. It was suggested that discussions are based on thinking, writing down opinions and ideas, understanding others' opinions and ideas, monitoring what to work on next while always keeping track of the flow of thoughts and meanings, and consulting with peers [9].

4.2 Impact of the Nine Elements of Discussion on the 'novelty' and 'usefulness' on Creativity

To examine how the discussion process (the process of generating ideas) affects creativity, we analyzed the output of each group in terms of how much creativity is contained in their movie prototypes. Although there is still no unified view on the definition of creativity [10], it has been shown that creativity is generally defined as novelty and usefulness [4, 5]. Therefore, in this study, the definition of creativity was used novelty and usefulness as creativity's subscales and evaluated the extent to which the output contained novelty and usefulness. Therefore, the two lecturers teaching this class independently conducted the evaluation and eliminated the extent to which they were included. Table 6 shows the regression analysis results to compare how 'novelty' and 'usefulness' affected creativity among the discussion's nine elements. The regression analysis results showed that 'problem analysis', prototyping, and 'confirmation' influenced the 'novelty' of creativity.

4.3 Influence Using the Design Thinking Five Steps in Discussion on Creative Problem-Solving

In order to solve problems creatively, it is necessary to develop the idea generation process in a group by setting up a situation similar to real-world activities [11]. In this study, in order to analyze the extent to which the creative problem space related to the users in the group was expanded, the total discussion time in the group for the users' problem-solving statements was investigated and tabulated concerning the times recorded at the start and end of the Teams chat (Fig. 3). The common class time was set at 140 min, and the time spent on independent design activities can be said to be the time excluding this 140 min. Figure 5 shows the results of the regression analysis, which showed that R2 = 0.586, p ≤ 0.05. This indicates that the more time a group spends on 'problem analysis' and prototyping, the more it affects the quality of 'novelty'.

Laakso (2014) shows the importance of engaging students in the community and continuous learning beyond the class time when promoting Design-Based Learning [11]. In this study, group discussions were conducted online, which allowed members to develop discussions independently whenever they were available. The group could think of solutions that were desirable to the user, extend the problem space individually according to the user's situation, and set up specific discussion situations in the chatbox for continuous learning. This indicates that the Active Learning environment described by Laakso could have been provided.

The design thinking five steps are Empathize, Define, Ideate, and Prototype, which correspond to Problem Finding, and Problem Solving. Since this research uses these five steps as a framework for thinking, it is not challenging to deviate from the path from problem discovery to problem-solving. However, searching for users' problems is a wicked way to tackle the problem of finding only one problem at a time [12]. Searching for a user's problem is tackling a wicked problem in which only one problem can be identified at a time. Therefore, when discussing problems, we use thinking frameworks such as the 5 Steps of Design Thinking, a thinking operation that involves divergent thinking about one problem, exploring the entire problem space, and convergent thinking that examines selects and integrates the essential items in the problem space. Simultaneously, it is possible to juxtapose the user-centered analysis of the problem with the thought process of integrating the problem to achieve the goal, leading to the creation of new ideas.

5   Conclusion

In this study, we examined the impact of the discussion process on the creativity of output when students discussed and solved problems in groups using the five steps of Stanford University's d.school. Students were instructed to follow the design thinking five steps in class to develop a novel and useful communication digital tool.

Analysis of the discussion process of developing a usable digital communication tool using design thinking revealed nine components: 'information gathering', 'problem analysis', 'needs', functions to be realized, 'prototype', 'expectation', 'information sharing', 'confirmation', and 'agreement'.

The nine components revealed that group members might have identified user needs based on their personal experiences and evaluated them subjectively when analyzing usage in discussions.

The creativity of the development task artifacts was evaluated in terms of 'novelty' and 'usefulness'. A regression analysis was conducted to compare how the discussion's nine elements affected creativity's 'novelty' and 'usefulness'. The results indicated that 'problem analysis', prototyping, and 'confirmation' had an impact on 'novelty'. Besides, the group with higher points for 'novelty' may have spent more time on 'problem analysis' and 'prototype'.

The design thinking five steps of the Creative Thinking Development Program may play a role in thinking. The use of the design thinking five steps may have encouraged individuals to monitor their thinking and communicate with each other while confirming the purpose of the discussion when solving problems by one by one about step, thus promoting understanding and utilization. Postings to the chatbox included sharing information, agreeing with what the other person said, and confirming the next task, in addition to the content to be problem-solved. When using an online program to foster creative thinking, it is possible that participants were confirming consensus and co-constructing meaning by increasing the number of posts and writings on the collaborative editing PowerPoint to bridge the gap between face-to-face and online communication students. The nine items in the discussion indicated that meaning construction and meaning confirmation were conducted for each statement to generate new ideas. The participants were trying to jointly construct value creation for the product value that the users were unconsciously seeking.

This experiment was the first step in a planned series of studies on design thinking education in this study. This experiment's subject was data from discussions held in 22 groups, with only two evaluators, but we plan to increase the number of samples and evaluators in the future. In the future, we would like to conduct more research on identifying issues in design thinking education and on designing learning environments that enhance creativity.

Acknowledgment. I would like to express my sincere gratitude to Ms. Narae Lee and Ms. Rie Shingai, who are designers belonging to Yahoo Japan Corporation, together with Mr. Kazumi Matsumoto, who is a designer belonging to Hitachi, Ltd., for their valuable advice and significant contribution to the creation of the content for the Design Thinking Introduction's lecture for first-year master's students of the Graduate School of Natural Science and Technology, Gifu University.

I would also like to express my sincere gratitude to my colleague, Prof. Junji Moribe, who consulted with me from the beginning to the end on running the class and working with me to make it happen. I would like to express my sincere appreciation for your sincere efforts.

References

1. Society 5.0. https://www8.cao.go.jp/cstp/english/society5_0/index.html. Accessed 09 Feb 2021
2. Brown, T.: Design thinking. Harv. Bus. Rev. **86**(6), 84 (2008)
3. d.school Stanford University. https://dschool.stanford.edu/resources/getting-started-with-design-thinking. Accessed 06 Feb 2021
4. Shimizu, D.: Introduction of review papers on creativity frameworks and measurement methods. Cogn. Stud. **26**(2), 293–290 (2019). (in Japanese)
5. Kondo, K., Nagai, Y.: A study of creativity in groupwork. In: The 32nd General Meeting of the Japan Society of Cognitive Science OS08-2, pp. 877–884 (2015). (in Japanese)
6. Mumford, M.D., Mobley, M.I., Reiter-Palmon, R., Uhlman, C.E., Doares, L.M.: Process analytic models of creative capacities. Creat. Res. J. **4**(2), 91–122 (1991)
7. Yoshida, Y.: Defining and grading creativity based on creative outputs. Ritsumeikan Human Science Research, no. 8 (2005). (in Japanese)
8. Perkins, D.N.: The Mind's Best Work. Harvard University Press, Cambridge (1981)

9. Kawase, M., Ozeki T.: Evaluation and understanding degree analysis by visualization of design thinking process using divergence-convergence curve. Jpn. Soc. Eng. Educ. **67-1**, 48–53 (2019). (in Japanese)
10. Hennessey, B.A., Amabile, T.M.: Creativity. Ann. Rev. Psychol. **61**, 569–598 (2010)
11. Laakso, M., Clavert, M.: Promoting creativity and design thinking skills among university students. Aalto Univ. Des. Factory **104**, 215–228 (2014)
12. Buchanan, R.: Design research and the new learning. Des. Issues **17**(4), 13–23 (2001)

Evaluation of the Current State of Nippon Professional Baseball in Digitalization

Masaru Kondo[1]([⊠]) and Yumi Asahi[2]

[1] School of Information and Telecommunication Engineering, Course of Information Telecommunication Engineering, Tokai University, Tokyo, Japan
Ocjnm008@mail.u-tokai.jp
[2] School of Business Administration Department of Business Administration, Tokyo University of Science, Tokyo, Japan
asahi@rs.tus.ac.jp

Abstract. This survey is a survey on the evaluation of Japanese professional baseball players. Due to the corona epidemic, many sports around the world are affecting the management of organizations. In Japan, we were able to accommodate spectators for a while, but the number of people is limited. As a result, many professional baseball teams that were already in the red during the off-season were announced. Severe business conditions are affecting not only Nippon Professional Baseball but also sports such as soccer and basketball. Also, this applies not only to Japan but to the rest of the world. There are various sales composition ratios to make money in sports competitions. In Nippon Professional Baseball, ticket income, broadcasting rights income, sponsor income, goods sales, fan clubs, etc. You can see how much the coronavirus has an impact, as most of the sales come from ticket revenue. Looking at other sports, in the J-League of soccer, there are teams centered on sponsor income, which may reduce the impact of ticket income, but it is difficult to decide the direction immediately. When it becomes difficult to manage teams, the salary of player is also affected. In fact, at Japan Professional Baseball Players Association, we ask the team to give relative evaluations, such as giving serious management explanations and wanting them to stop intentionally lowering their annual salary. But the real problem is the evaluation is clearly different when looking at the annual salary by role. Especially young pitchers, even if they pitch in many games, may be lower than veteran players. Therefore, I conducted a survey on the current evaluation of pitchers in Nippon Professional Baseball. Multiple regression analysis was performed using the player's annual salary as the axis of the dependent variable, and the total results up to 2019 as the independent variable, and the results of 2019 including the number of pitches and the number of wins. By performing multiple regression analysis, we were able to find out what was evaluated by many teams and what was the cause of the increase in annual salary. In addition to the results of this analysis, we will propose businesses and initiatives that Nippon Professional Baseball should work on in the future based on online events held all over the world.

Keywords: Sports marketing · Multiple regression analysis · Pitching · Evaluation method · Business strategy

© Springer Nature Switzerland AG 2021
S. Yamamoto and H. Mori (Eds.): HCII 2021, LNCS 12766, pp. 242–252, 2021.
https://doi.org/10.1007/978-3-030-78361-7_18

1 Introduction

Today, the world is facing a difficult situation in conducting professional sports competitions.

With the new coronavirus, the spread of the infection makes it impossible to enter the audience at the request of the government and local governments.

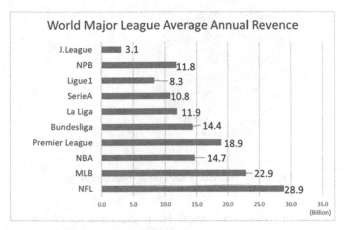

Fig. 1. World major league average annual revenue [1]

The table above shows the average annual income of the major leagues in the world. Among them, Japanese sports organizations are NPB and J-League. (Fig. 1) This is the data before being affected by the coronavirus, so the figures may change in the future.

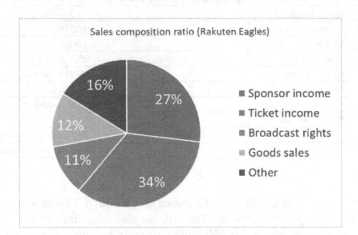

Fig. 2. Rakuten Eagles sales composition ratio [2]

Figure 2 shows the sales composition ratio data of one Nippon Professional Baseball team called Rakuten Eagles. Comparing this with the world-famous soccer team

Barcelona in Fig. 3, we can see that the percentage of match-related matters is high. From this, it is very difficult to obtain a revenue of past of professional sports performance.

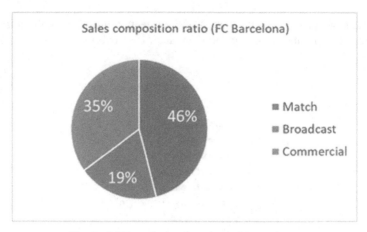

Fig. 3. FC Barcelona sales composition ratio [3]

It is important to improve management, but in that case, the player's annual salary must be considered. As you can see, the top athletes in the world introduced by Forbes [4].

Table 1. Top athletes in the world

Rank	Player	annual salary(million dolloars)	Competition
1	Roger Federer	106.3	Tennis
2	Cristiano Ronaldo	105	Soccer
3	Lionel Messi	104	Soccer
4	Neymar	95.5	Soccer
5	Lebron James	88.2	Basketball
6	Stephen Curry	74.4	Basketball
7	Kevin Durant	63.9	Basketball
8	Tiger Woods	62.3	Golf
9	Kirk Cousins	60.5	American Football
10	Carson Wentz	59.1	American Football

From this, we can see that the player's annual salary is high. This survey is about the annual salary of Nippon Professional Baseball, but since the maximum annual salary of Nippon Professional Baseball is 650 million yen (six million dollars), there is a big difference, but I would like to mention it. In any case, order to improve management, we must consider the annual salary of the players.

However, in Nippon Professional Baseball, there are concerns from the players' association that the decrease in the number of games will have a significant impact on the player's annual salary. In fact, in this year's contract renewal, opinions are expressed in the form of "explanation of business conditions." Furthermore, there is a big problem not only in management by coronavirus but also in the part where the evaluation criteria of players are ambiguous.

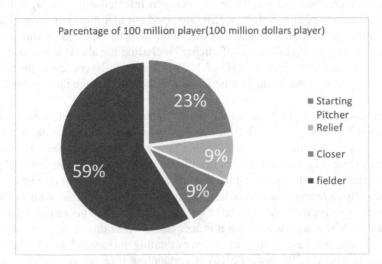

Fig. 4. Percentage of 100 million yens players in Nippon Professional Baseball ($ 1 million player)

From Fig. 4, we can see that the percentage of fielders is high. The remaining 40% are pitchers but starting pitchers account for the next ratio.

You can see that starting pitchers and fielders are mainly evaluated first.

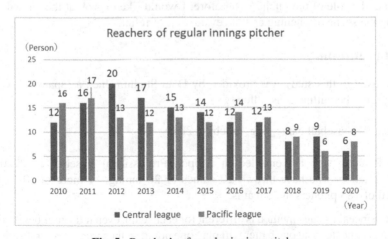

Fig. 5. Reacher's of regular innings pitcher

However, from Fig. 5, the number of "regulated innings reached pitchers", which is one of the starting pitchers' indicators, is decreasing. On the other hand, the burden on relief pitchers is increasing, and in 2019 there were 48 players in 2 leagues and more than 50 pitchers in 143 games. It is difficult to evaluate when creating your own rules with coronavirus.

For example, manager must think about various things such as increasing the number of bench members and replacing players if a player is infected with corona. In the major leagues, the starting pitcher called "opener" dropped out in a short inning and has been pitching since the start of the game, but the batter may be replaced by three innings. Therefore, the evaluation of the "relief pitcher" including the above-mentioned opener is complicated. In this study, we surveyed 100 million-yen players across the team and evaluated the pitchers and found that there was a clear difference in the relief before the pitchers.

In particular, the highest annual salary for Japanese middle-relief pitchers is in Nippon-Ham Naoki Miyanishi's 200 million yen (estimated), and he has already pitched 50 games for 13 consecutive years in 2020, but he is off every year. They take risks such as refraining from surgery in off season. In addition, the pitcher who pitched in 81 games last year is the best, and considering the risk in case of breakdown, it also bears a large risk. Especially in recent years, there have been cases where a pitcher who has pitched 50 games in a row for multiple years has a major breakdown and his annual salary drops at once. From this, it is presumed that it is necessary to take this opportunity to review.

Various methods have been studied for evaluating the annual salary of baseball. Among them, Shizuka Watanabe (2016) is conducting research on the evaluation of fielders called "analysis of factors that affect the annual salary of Japanese professional baseball players" [5]. In particular, Watanabe was conducting research on pitchers, but since her indicators are mainly starting pitchers and titles, and there is no part of the total results, she wants to focus on this time.

In this study, the role of the pitcher changes as the times changes. In 2019, there is a case where Nippon Ham implemented the "opener" in earnest, and it is difficult to evaluate the role of the pitcher. Therefore, I would like to look at the annual salary including the scene of pitching and the evaluation of relief.

2   Data Summary

The data used in this study was provided by Data Stadium Inc., a Japanese corporate company, and the outline is as follows.

Data used: 01_baseball game_ log_ pitching 2019

Target: Pitchers who are enrolled in Nippon Professional Baseball in 2020, and Japanese pitchers who have thrown 20 games or 20 innings or more in 2019. There are a total of 183 pitchers in 12 teams.

Reason: Since the usage method is different for each team, even if the number of pitches is large, it is expected that one batter will play one point, so the target was set. In addition, to investigate the total performance and annual salary of pitchers enrolled in 2020, we also used the contract renewal data posted on the official website of Nippon Professional Baseball [6] and the official website of Nikkan Sports [7].

Table 2. Sample data

Number	Pitchers name	Teams	2019 Number of pitches	Year sala	Professional years	· · ·	Wins game	Lose game
11	Tatsuya Imai	Seibu	23	3500	4	· · ·	11	12
13	Mitsunari Takahashi	Seibu	21	4000	6	· · ·	13	8
21	Ken Togame	Seibu	19	7000	9	· · ·	7	11
45	Keisuke Honda	Seibu	16	1600	5	· · ·	9	7
17	Wataru Matsumoto	Seibu	16	2100	2	· · ·	8	8

3   Analysis Result

3.1   Analysis Result: Basic Aggregation

In this study, as shown in Table 3, when we investigated changes in pitcher's annual salary, we found that the total pitcher's annual salary tended to increase for all teams. Yakult, which was the worst team in 2019, increased by about 45 million yen, and Orix increased by about 190 million yen. For ORIX, expectations for the next term and the dynamics of young people can be considered. You can see that from the average professional years in the following Table 3.

Table 3. Total annual salary for each pitcher

Teams	Number of players	Increase / decrease in the previous year(yen)	last year(yen)	this year(yen)
DeNA	16	293.35 million	701.4 million	994.75 million
Orix	16	189.9 million	623.4 million	813.3 million
Softbank	16	467 million	954 million	1421 million
Yakult	13	45 million	512 million	557 million
Lotte	16	243.7 million	646.3 million	890 million
Rakuten	17	150 million	1238.5 million	1388.5 million
Giant	12	166.25 million	1032.15 million	1198.4 million
Hiroshima	14	78.7 million	725.3 million	804 million
Hanshin	13	136.5 million	62.5 million	809 million
Seibu	13	194.5 million	433.5 million	628 million
Chunichi	18	62 million	549 million	611 million
Nippon ham	18	201.2 million	899.8 million	1101 million

Examining the average professional years of the target pitchers, it can be seen from Table 4 that ORIX and Seibu were appointed as relatively young pitchers. From the two tables, we were able to see the number of years of professional and the increase/decrease in annual salary.

Table 4. Average professional years and last year's ranking

Teams	Number of players	Average professional year	Last year's ranking
DeNA	16	6.13	Central League 2nd
Orix	16	5.81	Pacific League 6th
Softbank	16	7.31	Pacific League 2nd
Yakult	13	8.92	Central League 6th
Lotte	16	6.88	Pacific League 4th
Rakuten	17	8.71	Pacific League 3rd
Giant	12	8.17	Central League 1st
Hiroshima	14	7.00	Central League 4th
Hanshin	13	9.23	Central League 3rd
Seibu	13	5.77	Pacific League 1st
Chunichi	18	6.67	Central League 5th
Nippon ham	18	7.06	Pacific League 5th

3.2 Analysis Result: Nippon Professional Baseball Player Evaluation

In this study, the 2020 salary of the target pitcher was used as the dependent variable, and the following independent variables were used to perform multiple regression analysis by the stepwise method.

Dependent variable: Annual salary for 2020.
Independent variables: Annual salary in 2019, total results up to 2019 (total number of pitches, total number of wins and losses, total HP, total save, total earned run, total goals) 2019 results (number of pitches, wins and losses, pitching role, Number, number of saves, QS, HQS, complete game, shutout, number of pitches, number of pitches, hitter, hits, home base hits, four dead balls, violent throws, runs, earned runs, no runs, wins, loses.

The result is as follows.

Table 5. Multiple regression analysis results (overall)

Independent variable	b	β	SE	t
(constant)	16967437		5522342	3.073
Total number of wins	4209198	1.488	418104	10.067
2019 saves	6404891	0.48	557533.9	11.488
Total earned run	-513739	-1.076	69960.39	-7.343
Complete game	44822004	0.3	6548988	6.844
2019 HP numbers	1248605	0.137	390166.8	3.2
R^2	0.7			
F (5,181)	85.394			

p<.05,*p<0.05

Table 5 shows that the numbers that can contribute to victory, such as the number of saves in 2019, are high as an overall evaluation. However, when the predicted value is given, there are problems such as a negative value can be obtained even for pitchers who pitched in 2019. While the numbers are relatively stable in the Pacific League, there are large errors in the Central League.

Table 6. Total team error of regression model

Central League		Pacific League	
Giants	-235.4 million yen	Seibu	72.18 million yen
DeNA	-77.91 million yen	Softbank	-59.72 million yen
Hanshin	217.74 million yen	Rakuten	-128.86 million yen
Hiroshima	-100.82 million yen	Lotte	1.8 million yen
Chunichi	193.88 million yen	Nippon ham	-4.82 million yen
Yakult	169.57 million yen	Orix	-47.62 million yen
+ Is less than the number			
-Is more annual salary than the number			

As shown in Table 6, since there is a problem of large error in the entire team, the annual salary in 2020 and the annual salary in 2019 were compared, and the increase/decrease value of the annual salary was used as the dependent variable for regression analysis. The independent variable is the 2019 results.

Table 7. Multiple regression analysis results (2019 results)

Independent variable	b	β	SE	t
(constant)	-4892112		2478037	-1.974
2019 saves	2416709	0.543	224350.4	10.772
Strikeout	440664.7	0.587	68460.14	6.437
Conceded	-475851	-0.319	143061.9	-3.326
2019 wins	2525981	0.281	757553.6	3.334
2019 defeats	-1857581	-0.169	912527.2	-2.036
R^2	0.627			
F(5,181)	61.885			
p<.05,*p<0.05				

From Table 7, it was found that the data on winning and losing and strikeouts in 2019 and the number of runs are related.

However, since the intermediate evaluation such as the number of HP does not apply, it is necessary to improve this part.

Compared with the actual increase/decrease value, the correct answer rate is 66%, but it can be said that there are other than intermediate evaluation and results (mood maker).

3.3   Analysis Result: Current Management Perspective

After looking at the annual salary, the next thing to think about is improving management. Unfortunately, it is difficult to evaluate the current situation because Nippon Professional Baseball has not been officially announced about its management. Furthermore, please be aware that many teams in the world can only grasp sales and annual salary of players, which is extremely difficult to see from this point of view.

Table 8. Sales and broadcast rights revenues for major sports in Japan and the world

Teams	Sales (dollar)	Match related (dollar)
NPB/Eagles(2017)	125,908,962	55,977,465
Jleague/Urawa Reds(2019)	78209317	21,890,135
Premium.league/FC Balecona(2019.9)	805920732	185,424,879
B.league/Chiba Jets(2019)	16771821	3,963,250
MLB/Yankees (2018)	668000000	295000000(2013)

The above shows Table 8 regarding the main sales and broadcasting rights revenue [8–11]. Specifically, broadcasting rights revenue, game-related revenue including ticket revenue, sponsors, products, etc. occupy, but the amount is rarely officially disclosed, so the forecast is just a guide. Next, looking at the broadcasting rights, the amount of money for the Yankees and the B League, which is a professional basketball league in Japan, has not been disclosed. However, estimates suggest that the Yankees were estimated at $ 85 million in 2013 [12], but in recent years the Yankees have purchased shares in the "Yes network" company as a broadcaster, so the numbers are not accurate. In addition, since the J. League has signed a broadcasting rights from 2017 with a flat-rate video distribution service specializing in sports operated by the DAZN group called DAZN, the broadcasting rights revenue is distributed throughout the J. League. Since broadcasting rights revenue is complicated in this way, it is not possible to obtain accurate figures.

Table 9. Percentage of ticket revenue and sales and annual salary of athletes

Teams	Sales (dollar)	Match related (dollar)
NPB/Eagles(2017)	125,908,962	55,977,465
Jleague/Urawa Reds(2019)	78209317	21,890,135
Premium.league/FC Balecona(2019.9)	805920732	185,424,879
B.league/Chiba Jets(2019)	16771821	3,963,250
MLB/Yankees (2018)	668000000	295000000(2013)
Teams	**Player annual salary(dollar)**	**Ticket revenue ratio of sales**
NPB/Eagles(2017)	21,651,407	44%
Jleague/Urawa Reds(2019)	15,010,710	28%
Premium.league/FC Balecona(2019.9)	606,666,148	23%
B.league/Chiba Jets(2019)	Unpublished	24%
MLB/Yankees (2018)	241,850,000	44%

However, the following Table 9 shows that an athlete's annual salary is affected if many sports are unable to mobilize spectators. In fact, in many sports, team managers need to approve player salary reductions, so to maintain a player's salary, new business strategies need to be found.

4 Interpretation and Ideas Based on Analysis Result

4.1 Consideration of Nippon Professional Baseball Evaluation

In this study, we conducted a survey on the annual salary of 12 teams, and found that the starting pitchers and relief pitchers, which are the main force, are properly evaluated. However, as a problem, how to evaluate pitchers with many pitches will be a future issue. In the case of Nippon-Ham in Table 10, the fact that even if the annual salary is the same, the contribution of winning, the number of pitches, and the number of professional years is different is also taken into consideration. Seibu's example also pitches in the same winning match, but the number of pitches is clearly different. (Table 11) I think this also considers the number of years of profession. Given the maximum annual salary, I think active pitchers should be paid a reasonable salary.

Table 10. Comparison of annual salary (Example of Nippon Ham)

Team name	Pitcher	Winning game	Number of pitches	Estimated annual salary
Nippon ham	Mizuki Hori	21	53	21000000
	Takahiro Nishimura	6	35	21000000

Table 11. Comparison of annual salary (Example of Seibu)

Team name	Pitcher	Winning game	Number of pitches	Estimated annual salary
Seibu	Katsunori Hirai	57	81	100000000
	Tatsushi Masuda	58	65	190000000

4.2 Team May Help Fans by Publishing Data

This time, it was difficult to know how much team management is currently being done, other than assessing the player's annual salary. However, many fans believe that they need to watch the game locally. Especially for players in team who push fans, you can invest more than you need. Therefore, fans may be able to supplement the player's annual salary by proactively disclosing it without hiding the team management aspect. Until the coronavirus is over, I think it's okay to have a business that fans can help. Therefore, fans should be provided with the right to know the team business situation.

5 Conclusion

In this study, we conducted a study on the pitcher's annual salary, but tried various variables. However, it only understands how it is currently being evaluated.

Some teams have serious errors due to lack of coefficients for each team, so I would like to consider this part as a problem. Still, I was able to interpret the current evaluation points. Except that the title holders and award winners have higher annual salaries, I think they have seen the evaluation that they should have, and I think it is a necessary prediction model for future evaluation. However, from a global perspective, many sports teams do not disclose management or sales structure. Regarding baseball, as future issues, it is easy to continue research from the next time, such as course analysis and proposals for evaluation methods for each part. Baseball player data has various indicators, so it is easy to interpret, but I think it is difficult to evaluate in other sports. Based on these, the next task is to complete a sample model of baseball or other sports.

References

1. Sports Agency Ministry of Economy, Trade and Industry (2016): Sports Future Development Conference Interim Report
2. Background of Rakuten Eagles "Sales profitability by increasing audience" Toyo Keizai Online. https://toyokeizai.net/articles/-/21397. Accessed 11 Feb 2021
3. Eye on the prize Football Money League-Deloitte Sports Business Group, January 2020
4. Highest-paid athletes in the world-Forbes. https://www.forbes.com/athletes/?utm_source=TWITTER&utm_medium=social&utm_content=3380563832&utm_campaign=sprinklrForbesMainTwitter#269eb07855ae. Accessed 11 Feb 2021
5. Watanabe, S., Asahi, Y.: Analysis of factors affecting annual salary of Nippon professional baseball players. In: Proceedings of the 30th Symposium of the Japan Society for Computer Statistics, pp. 35–36 (2016)
6. NPB.jp-Nippon Professional Baseball Organization. https://npb.jp/games/2020/. Accessed 10 Nov 2020
7. Contract Renewal: Professional Baseball-Nikkan Sports. https://www.nikkansports.com/baseball/professional/koukai/. Accessed 10 Nov 2020
8. US Professional Sports Market-Chiba Bank (2019)
9. ANNUAL REPORT 2018/19-FC Barcelona
10. J-Club Individual Management Information Disclosure Material (2019)-J. League
11. Chiba Jets Funabashi Co., Ltd. (10th term) Financial results information-Chiba Jets. https://chibajets.jp/ir/. Accessed 11 Feb 2021
12. Why the Yankees can pay 18.2 billion yen-The PAGE. https://news.yahoo.co.jp/articles/82e25229b651a19d8406b34bf476691563eec701?page=3. Accessed 11 Feb 2021

Digitizing the FlexIA Toolkit
- Transforming a Paper-Based Method
into a Flexible Web App

Christian Kruse[✉], Daniela Becks, and Sebastian Venhuis

Westfälische Hochschule Gelsenkirchen, Bocholt, Recklinghausen, Münsterstraße 265, 46397 Bocholt, Germany
{christian.kruse,daniela.becks,sebastian.venhuis}@w-hs.de
https://www.w-hs.de

Abstract. Digitization of everything is the main driver in today's economy. The constantly growing proliferation of digital tools makes it increasingly important to properly analyze and document which information is needed in which processes throughout a company. Information management competencies are a key enabler on the path to data generated value creation.

The FlexIA toolkit described in this paper assists in such an analysis. One of its highlights is that it comprises both a method and a tool to investigate information flows within small and medium-sized companies. It focuses on pragmatic objectives and aims to empower workers in the domain of mechanical engineering to create an analysis independently. Starting out as paper-based prototype it soon became necessary to transform the tool into a digital web app.

The first section of this paper illustrates the context in which the FlexIA toolkit was created and describes its core concepts. Afterwards, related work is reviewed and the FlexIA is delineated from other tools and methods. The third section discusses the motivation behind the FlexIA toolkit, elaborates on further use cases and reasons why a digital tool was needed. The major part of this paper covers the step wise process of digitizing the FlexIA toolkit. Mock ups and wire framing were used to capture the user requirements. Subsequently, implementation aspects are illustrated. A short discussion as well as an overview of future steps concludes this article.

Keywords: Evaluating information · Information flow analysis · Digitization · GUI design · User-centered design · Service applications

---

This research and development project is funded by the European Social Fund (ESF) and the German Federal Ministry of Education and Research (BMBF) within the program "Future of work" (02L18B000) and implemented by the Project Management Agency Karlsruhe (PTKA). The authors are responsible for the content of this publication.

S. Yamamoto and H. Mori (Eds.): HCII 2021, LNCS 12766, pp. 253–268, 2021.
https://doi.org/10.1007/978-3-030-78361-7_19

1   Introduction

The trend towards digital workplaces has been around for several years - recently being boosted by the COVID-19 pandemic. The relevance of an all encompassing digitization has shifted from nice-to-have to a must-have status. The daily work routines for both white and blue collar workers are dominated by accessing internal and external digital resources, conducting virtual meetings and interacting digitally with suppliers and clients. Hence, more than ever the accessibility of a company's information assets as well as the information literacy of its workers have become essential factors for success. As a result, many small and medium-sized companies (SMCs) are forced to invest into the digitization of their processes and working environments. Utilizing digital assistants and intelligent tools that support them during the shift from analog to digital work have become more and more important.

One particular tool that helps SMCs in their digitization processes, is the FlexIA (Flexible Information Analysis) toolkit. It comprises both a methodological approach to information modeling as well as a web based tool. The FlexIA toolkit is being developed as part of the FlexDeMo suite[1] [1]. The goal of this research project is to support SMCs in optimizing their manufacturing performance with the help of participatory assembly planning and simulation.

An essential prerequisite for conducting simulation experiments is a robust information model that adequately represents all relevant data. Hence, a thorough initial analysis of the current assembly processes, the information landscape as well as existing data and parameters for the assembly simulation is of paramount importance. Soon after the project start it became apparent, that the workers' knowledge on the shop floor and the assembly lines needed to be extracted properly. After initially conducting the FlexIA analysis with paper-based forms the demand for digitizing the information analysis activities surfaced. Having applied the paper-based approach multiple times for different processes throughout the factory, a mature, well-suited methodology for conducting the information analysis established. Subsequently, the plan was to transfer it into a web-based tool that can easily be used by workers.

Initially, this paper reviews related work in the field of information modeling and analysis and briefly explains the need for yet another approach. Subsequently, the motivation for developing the FlexIA tool and its transformation into a web app are discussed. Section four outlines in detail different aspects and challenges in doing so. Finally, a brief discussion and outlook conclude the paper.

2   Related Work

There are literally countless research activities with respect to modeling and analyzing process-related information flows. A comprehensive overview can be found in [2]. This section focuses on projects and prior work with relevance to the development of the FlexIA toolkit and its distinct features.

---

[1] https://www.flexdemo.eu.

2.1   General Methods to Visualize the Information Flow

To facilitate information flow analysis, general modeling methodologies and notations like ARIS [10], UML [7] or BPMN [9] are being used widely. These are well suited to visualize information flows or processes in general but do not adequately address day-to-day requirements of the information users in manufacturing environments. The notations were not designed with factory workers in mind. As such, they are often too complex comprising many different symbols, status and options to visualize the information flow. Additionally, to be applied effectively, they need to be used in combination with a graphical editor - adding to the already complex methods an additional reason for their modest adaption.

Generalized graphical editors like diagrams.net[2] or Microsoft Visio[3] work well with most of the above mentioned modeling notations but they do not offer sufficient guidance and help functionalities. Thus, they can not be easily used to create information flows especially by novice users. Specialized tools for information and process modeling, such as Signavio[4], are designed for experts. As a consequence, they are too complex to be used for short, infrequent analysis typically found in incremental information system adaptions.

FlexIA has been designed with a set of specifically tailored functions to create an information analysis that can easily be used by untrained personnel with a minimal training effort. It combines aspects of modeling languages, general graphical editors and specialized tools.

2.2   Similar Work

Information flow analysis is a well known technique that is performed within different domains. For example [13] used information demand analysis to investigate processes within producing companies with the goal to provide context-relevant information to employees. Thereby, the focus is particularly set on analyzing the importance of information for specific users/roles and their relevant working processes. Additional factors such as general events are also included into the analysis. Similar to the FlexIA approach, the authors also implement a user-centered design and strongly involve users. But information analysis is restricted to gain further insights into information handling. They do develop a tool to assist employees in decision making and not to assist information analysis itself.

Another interesting approach that is closely related to the development process of FlexIA is presented in [11]. Although the authors did not conduct an information analysis in the classical sense, they used a fairly similar way to develop software. They also concentrated on the domain of mechanical engineering and implemented a user-centered as well as participatory approach to design a prototype for the technical documentation within the construction department.

---

[2] https://www.diagrams.net/.

[3] https://www.microsoft.com/en-us/microsoft-365/visio/flowchart-software.

[4] https://www.signavio.com/.

A very similar method to that underlying the FlexIA toolkit is FLOW described in [12]. In comparison to the FlexIA method the main overlapping aspects are:

- Processes and specific activities are analyzed.
- Explicit and implicit information is considered.
- Participatory workshops and interviews are executed.
- Paper-based forms and utilities to facilitate the information analysis are provided.

The main difference between the FlexIA toolkit and FLOW is the provision of tools. While FLOW is only performed with paper-based forms, FlexIA is used in combination with a digital tool.

There are much more related approaches in the literature, but digital tools can be scarily found. So the combination of method and digital tool for information flow analysis is one special feature of FlexIA.

2.3 Further USPs

Addressing the domain requirements of shop floor environments is of paramount importance for the tool's aptitude. Hence, methodological and tool complexity were reduced as much as possible. Rather than being an academic exercise the main purpose is to digitally support the workers' information management competencies and their information literacy. Both the FlexIA method and web-based tool emphasize the concept of domain events - a modeling perspective specifically addressed in the method of Domain Driven Design [14]. Domain events occur during daily operations on the shop floor and are particularly important to be incorporated in the modeling approach. Typically, this can be disrupting events which require the worker to reschedule her activities (i.e. unavailability of material, machine tool break down) or events that require further action (i.e. requesting the valid version of CAD drawing). Hence the tool explicitly caters for the capture of domain events in its components.

An additional unique feature of the FlexIA web-tool is the integration into the FlexDeMo suite. Through this, the tool can not only be used to carry out information analysis, but also support in the creation of an assembly form simulation with the FlexDeMo suite. There it can be used in the initial analysis phase to gather available information pools. It will also be able to share information with other tools of the suite to increase the efficiency of the tools.

3   FlexIA - A Tool for Analyzing the Information Flow

In this section, the motivation for developing the FlexIA tool and the transformation to a web app are discussed.

3.1   Motivation

Running a successful simulation requires well prepared input. Input data and decision parameters have to be as realistic and complete as possible. This typically includes aspects like factory layout, work load, routing, resource information, capacities, work stations, shift information and timings. Unfortunately, they are often not readily available in a coherent and consistent form. As a consequence, the FlexIA tool was developed to help SMCs to prepare data for the simulation.

This is achieved by providing the SMCs with a tool combining different functional components as well as methods to investigate the information flows, sources and possible disrupting events. Many existing approaches either focus on a specific document and its life cycle or one selected process. While FlexIA mainly focuses on process-based information analysis, aspects of the document life cycle (e.g. the creation and modification of document types) are also included. In this context the focus is particularly set on the workers demands as it is recommended by [8].

While developing and testing the initial prototype, it became quickly evident that the FlexIA toolkit is not only suitable to gather data for the simulation, but also fits many other applications. Some of them are presented in the next paragraph.

3.2   Added Value by FlexIA Tool

The tool has been thoroughly utilized and evaluated in one company in the domain of mechanical engineering. Due to the tool's comprehensible approach it was well received by the workers. During the workshops the following additional uses cases emerged.

Bridging information islands. FlexIA is considered useful to identify numerous encapsulated information sources. To bridge these information islands it is essential to analyze the existing information landscape in detail - e.g. in some cases certain instances of attribute values of information objects result in a complete re-scheduling of the work sequences.

Optimize information supply. As with any tool to analyze the information flow in and between processes (or departments), the FlexIA tool may be used to optimize the information supply within processes and for workers. This can be achieved by an additional analysis step in the existing interview component. It was noticed that with the help of the tool the workers became increasingly "information aware" and started to pull hitherto unused information bits.

Introduce software systems. Additionally, FlexIA may be used in preparation of software projects like e.g. the introduction of a new ERP system. The tool helps to gather all necessary information objects, groups them according to process step and user groups so that necessary permissions and additional views may be derived. The increased level of information literacy enabled the workers to actively participate in mock-up sessions to modify and optimize existing software systems.

3.3   From Paper-Based to Digital - Reasons to Transform FlexIA

The paper-based version of the FlexIA tool has been tested within the context of mechanical engineering. As outlined above, it soon became apparent, that a web app could significantly improve the FlexIA tool with regard to the following aspects.

Lack of space. Early on in the interview phase of the FlexIA method, it was noticed, that the available space on the paper forms was too restricted. Trying to squeeze in all the information would result in barely legible notes. It would also mean, that people with vision impairments could have problems reading the contents of the form. A web app could easily adapt to the amount of information by providing more space through scrolling.

Difficult to archive and retrieve. The paper based approach produced many pages of paper. Which means not only waste, but also additional work to digitize these documents and storage space to store them.

Cumbersome manual analysis. As the FlexIA method does not define a prescribed analysis process, the analysis will always be done manually. This could be partly improved by providing some automated stochastic analysis tools as well as guidance and recommendations.

Poor user experience. While functional, the use of multiple paper forms during and after the workshops did not provide for a good user experience. It could drastically be improved to transforming the process to a web-based app. Additional benefits like the ability to share and cooperate on analysis results accrue.

Limited consistency. Any software tool may provide additional help functions, assistants and automatism which not only could reduce user errors but also improve usability and efficiency of the FlexIA tool.

4   The Digitization of FlexIA

As outlined above the paper-based version of FlexIA posed a couple of challenges with regard to the efficiency of the information analysis. As described in [4] each analog form was evaluated and updated multiple times to improve its structure and to ease the transformation of FlexIA into a web based app, which is described subsequently.

4.1   Creating Initial HTML Mock Ups

Based on the optimized forms a non-functional mock up was created to sketch a possible design of the user interface and to define the technical requirements including necessary input elements and the structure of navigation. This simple mock up was developed with HTML and CSS. These technologies allow a quick transformation into a web tool and can be easily extended later on.

4.2   Defining a Digitization Strategy

Based upon the first mock ups a plan for transforming the constituting components of FlexIA was devised. Again, an iterative development process was chosen to allow repeated testing of the application within real settings. This approach also aligned with one of the main goals of the FlexDeMo project to develop tools and methods through participation of the accompanying companies.

Beside the participatory design it has been important to strictly focus on the users demands. One of the major findings of the initial analysis was that the demands of multiple heterogeneous user groups, very specific work settings and the characteristics of the underlying domain needed to be addressed [4].

In mind of these aspects, the development focused on the core components of FlexIA. The objective was to quickly create a testable prototype of the software. Subsequently, a general overview was needed to integrate these forms into a coherent tool and to allow navigation between the different components.

4.3   Determining Functional and Non Functional Requirements

During the design process various functional and non-functional requirements were specified. The most important ones are listed below.

Architecture. The architecture of the FlexIA tool needed to be compatible to the test architecture developed in the overarching FlexDeMo suite. It is based on micro services which are connected to a REST API server and linked to each other via AMQP[5]. The REST API acts as a gateway and forwards requests to the RabbitMQ[6] AMQP server which in turn acts as a load balancer for the micro services. Each individual FlexDeMo tool will be implemented in this test architecture as a micro service. The front end of the toolkit is designed as a single React[7] application, which the FlexIA user interface will be included in.

Save anytime. With respect to the anticipated user groups and domain context it is essential that results may be saved anytime [4]. Thus, the FlexIA tool is supposed to allow saving the progress continuously and to avoid loss of data in case an analysis workshop needs to be paused or postponed.

Available on desktop and tablet. Currently, the FlexIA tool is mainly used on desktops, laptops and bigger tablets. As a consequence, the web app is supposed to support these different devices. A typical mobile application running e.g. on smart phones will not be realized right now.

Usability. Usability plays a vital role during the digitization of the digital prototype. As the tool is to be used by different users having heterogeneous levels of technical knowledge and information literacy the web app needs to be designed for intuitive usage. Thus, a user-centered approach involving actual users in wire framing or evaluation was crucial.

---

[5] Advanced Message Queuing Protocol https://www.amqp.org/.

[6] https://www.rabbitmq.com/.

[7] https://reactjs.org/.

4.4   Creating Detailed Mock Ups

While the initial mock ups were used to provide a generic look and feel, more detailed and thorough versions were needed. They took into account the experiences made with the paper-based prototype, the initial HTML mock ups and the digitization strategy. These new mock ups were created using Balsamiq wireframes[8].

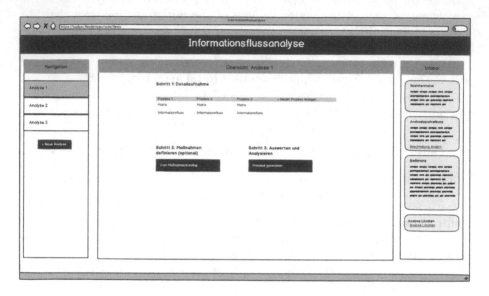

Fig. 1. Mock up of the dashboard

Figure 1 visualizes the mock up for the envisioned dashboard. As can be seen each view is divided into three sections: a navigation panel on the left, the main section in the middle and an info bar on the right. The navigation bar allows the user to switch between different analysis or create a new one. Further information, meta data and hints can be found on the right side of each view. The main content of the selected component or view will be displayed in the middle section. For example, the dashboard contains a general overview over all processes.

4.5   Developing the FlexIA Core Components

In the next step the FlexIA components were developed in a first iteration. The main focus was set on the functionality of the information matrix and information flow views, which were then combined with the help of a dashboard.

---

[8] https://balsamiq.com/wireframes/.

To implement these components, React[9] was used, which not only works well with the architecture described in Sect. 4.3, but also allows for the components to be highly dynamic and responsive to user actions.

To allow an easy and intuitive use of the digital tool especially for users not familiar with the FlexIA method additional tool tips and hints were added in each view.

Information Matrix. The goal of the information matrix is to document information objects, resources and possible interrupting events. It focuses on the structural aspects of information analysis.

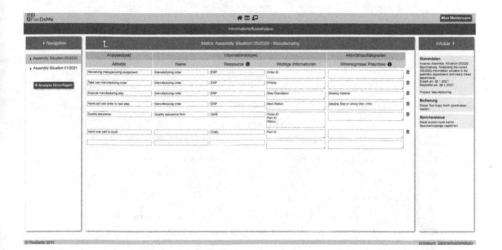

Fig. 2. Information matrix form

In case of the digital version of the information matrix the design of the mock up as well as the original paper-based form was nearly fully adopted. As can be seen in Fig. 2 it follows the tabular structure of the prototype. The major improvement with respect to the paper-based version is, that it allows for dynamically adapting to the needed space for numerous process steps. Additionally, some fields were implemented as HTML `textarea` inputs to provide more space for fields with multiple lines of input. The user can increase the size of these fields vertically as necessary. Functionally, the data will be saved automatically on the server whenever the user leaves an input field.

Information Flow Diagram. This component is used to collect data about the information flow of the process focusing on its dynamic aspects. To ease the implementation, but also to increase the usability and clarity of the information

---

[9] https://reactjs.org/.

flow the visualization of the paper-based prototype has been split into a table on the left, and a diagram on the right. This can be seen in Fig. 3a.

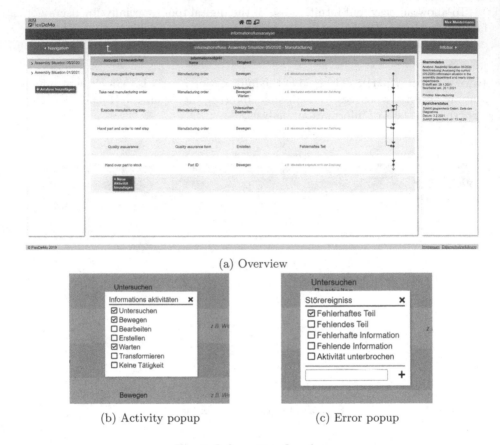

(a) Overview

(b) Activity popup   (c) Error popup

Fig. 3. Information flow form

The table was implemented similarly to that of the matrix component. In addition to normal text input fields two multi selects were introduced. As can be seen in Fig. 3b the field *Tätigkeit*[10] opens a small dialog in which the user can select applicable activities. Similarly, the field *Störereignisse*[11] will open a list of predefined disruptive events which the user can select from or add custom events if needed. This is presented in Fig. 3c.

The diagram was moved into a separate region to the right of the table. It was implemented in d3[12], which allows straightforward rendering of SVG diagrams. Each process step is visualized by a large dot in the center of the

---

[10] The activity on the information object.

[11] Disruptive events.

[12] https://d3js.org/.

row it represents and may be moved horizontally to illustrate parallel processes. If moved vertically the user can link different process steps. These links can be moved or removed by clicking and dragging on the end of an arrow. Additionally, further options for a process step can be accessed by hovering the cursor over a step and clicking on the fields that will appear to the right of the step.

Analysis Result Form. While developing the first iteration of the digital FlexIA components it became evident that the paper-based analysis result form is not as useful as assumed. It became obvious that - from a user's perspective - quantitative results (e.g. the number of total transformations) where not as significant and meaningful as the derived qualitative results. As such, the result form has been replaced by an automatically generated protocol.

Dashboard. The dashboard component acts as the main navigation element. As can be seen in Fig. 4 it offers three functionalities. First, a user may add processes to the selected analysis or navigate to the relevant information flow or matrix.

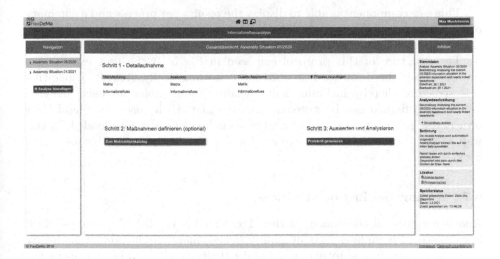

Fig. 4. Dashboard

Furthermore, the users may navigate to the additional components: the list of defined measures[13] and the protocol[14].

FlexIA Back End. As mentioned in Sect. 4.3 the server components needed to be compatible with the test architecture of the FlexDeMo suite. Accordingly,

---

[13] See Sect. 4.7.
[14] See Sect. 4.6.

the back end was implemented as a NodeJS[15] server communicating with the FlexDeMo RabbitMQ server via AMQP. To connect the back end to the front end, the REST API gateway of the existing test architecture was extended to encompass the new functionality. The main function of the gateway is to transform REST requests into AMQP messages. It can also authenticate and prevalidate requests.

The data of each performed analysis of the FlexIA service is stored into a PostgreSQL[16] database. This service is deployed via Docker[17] and can be configured to connect to different databases or RabbitMQ servers with the help of a configuration file.

4.6 Protocol

Each of the methodological components described so far was part of the analog version of FlexIA and was transferred into digital forms. The original analysis result sheet was replaced by a protocol because, as stated in Sect. 4.5, it did not prove to be a suitable mean to present the quantitative as well as qualitative results.

This new component is able to display the results per process and a summary of all results as well. The protocol might be exported into a file, that can be saved independently of the FlexDeMo suit.

The structure of this protocol can seen in Fig. 5. If the user exports the protocol from the dashboard, a word file is automatically generated following this structure thereby including some headlines and tables for each analysis. While some figures can be automatically calculated, the users may add their own notes, interview reports and analysis conclusions once downloaded. In this way, the protocol can be easily extended which better fits the flexible aspects of FlexIA.

4.7 Adding the List of Measures

Another additional component of the FlexIA tool is the list of measures which is supposed to include aspects of quality management. Right now, it is already possible to identify disrupting events and potentials within a process using the FlexIA tool. These will be collected in a list and the user will be given the option to add a suitable measure and priorities to each. Furthermore, the defined measures may be integrated into the protocol to complete the analysis.

4.8 Evaluation of the Prototype

As stated before, the driving aspect of the FlexIA toolkit is to provide the user with a tool that can be used easily and intuitively. To reach this objective

---

[15] https://nodejs.org/.

[16] https://www.postgresql.org.

[17] https://www.docker.com/.

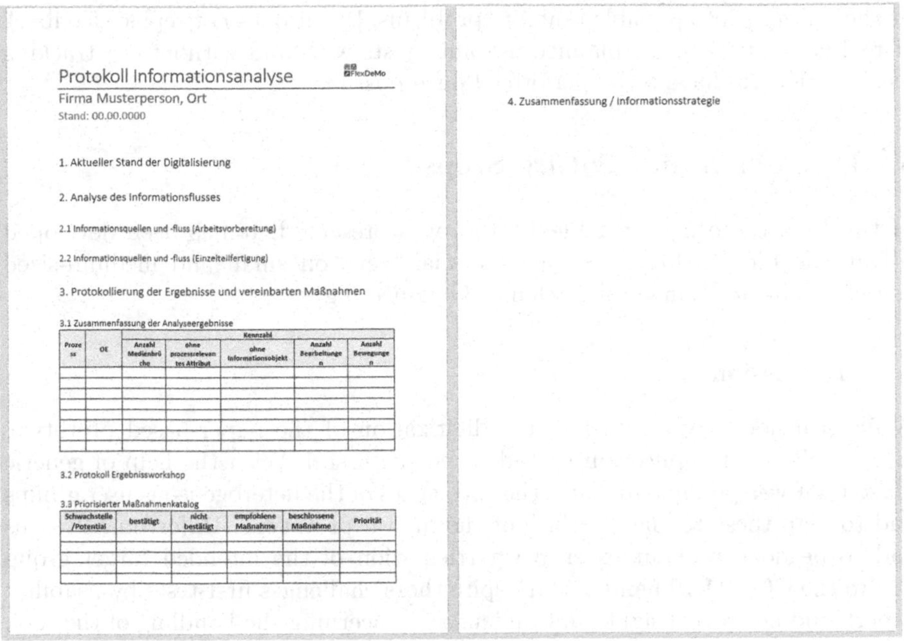

Protokoll Informationsanalyse

FlexDeMo

Firma Musterperson, Ort

Stand: 00.00.0000

1. Aktueller Stand der Digitalisierung

2. Analyse des Informationsflusses

2.1 Informationsquellen und -fluss (Arbeitsvorbereitung)

2.2 Informationsquellen und -fluss (Einzelteilfertigung)

3. Protokollierung der Ergebnisse und vereinbarten Maßnahmen

3.1 Zusammenfassung der Analyseergebnisse

Prozess	OE	Kennzahl				
		Anzahl Medienbrüche	ohne prozessrelevantes Attribut	ohne Informationsobjekt	Anzahl Bearbeitungen	Anzahl Bewegungen

3.2 Protokoll Ergebnissworkshop

3.3 Priorisierter Maßnahmenkatalog

Schwachstelle /Potential	bestätigt	nicht bestätigt	empfohlene Maßnahme	beschlossene Maßnahme	Priorität

4. Zusammenfassung / Informationsstrategie

Fig. 5. Blank protocol

evaluation is of great importance. As a consequence, a mixed iterative evaluation set up was designed comprising the following activities:

1. Evaluate the basic design of the initial FlexIA forms (paper-based prototype)
2. Assess the functionality and scope of the underlying FlexIA method (see [1])
3. Evaluate the digital prototype in real user settings and by real users
4. Evaluate the navigation and design of the web app using eye tracking

A first evaluation to rate the basic design and to check the suitability of the underlying FlexIA method was performed incorporating a medium-sized company in the domain of mechanical engineering. Multiple processes where analyzed ranging from the construction of a machine to its final assembly. Numerous employees were involved in the tests and gave important insights into the work context and the specialties of the domain.

Although the results of this test were promising small changes were made concerning the design of the information matrix and the information flow diagram [4]. These changes were already incorporated into the development of the digital prototype. Unfortunately, the first modified and digitized FlexIA tool could not yet be tested with real users and under real settings because the COVID-19 pandemic severely restricted physical cooperation with the partnering companies. As a consequence, these evaluation steps are still pending.

An alternative that does not require cooperation with users is the heuristic evaluation following Nielsen [6]. This is planned in a future iteration to gain further insights into possible usability problems. But it does not replace feedback of real users, so that the planned usability tests with and without eye tracking technologies will have to be performed once possible.

5   Discussion and Future Steps

In this article the digitized FlexIA tool was presented. It has been developed within the FlexDeMo project with special focus on small and medium-sized companies in the domain of mechanical engineering.

5.1   Discussion

While still not fully completed, the digitization of the paper-based prototype into a web-based application proved to be successful. With the help of generic personas it was possible to define the specialties of the heterogeneous user groups and to map these to the interface of the digital prototype. Unfortunately, this had to be done without extensive participation of the intended target group due to the COVID-19 pandemic. Despite these challenges first tests by usability experts did not reveal significant difficulties concerning the handling of the tool. Still, there are steps to be performed in the near future. These will be discussed in the next section.

5.2   Future Steps

Some tasks concerning the final evaluation and the completion of the tool are pending and need to be completed. This include the following:

Tool Polish. Although the core components of FlexIA have successfully been transformed, some functionalities need to be added. This particularly refers to the protocol and the list of measures. To better address the different target groups specific views need to be implemented, so that a user is only provided with relevant information and thus may efficiently perform an analysis. Furthermore, it is planned to integrate additional functionalities and recommendations to assist the user in handling the web app and ensure an intuitive usage.

Evaluation. Until now, little progress could be made to evaluate the digital prototype with real users and simulate real work conditions. Only the paper-based version has already been tested extensively, so that in the future broader evaluation studies will be necessary to gain further insights into the functionality and suitability of the FlexIA tool. This includes performing information analysis within different domains because first results simply focused on the domain of mechanical engineering.

Currently, multiple evaluation alternatives are assessed. These are:

1. **Simply wait.** The evaluation with users could be postponed until it is safe enough to visit partners. The major advantage of this option would be, that the initially planned eye tracking scenario could also be set up.
2. **Remote evaluation.** A remote evaluation could be performed. Depending on the exact procedure a lot more preparation is needed. Not only does the participating company need to setup the application, but also install a screen capturing software and if possible capture a webcam stream. If the tests are moderated, it would be preferable to setup an additional Video conference system.

Integration into FlexDeMo. One major step left is to integrate the developed web app into the FlexDeMo suite which will comprise:

- Reconfiguring the UI to match the FlexDeMo suite design.
- Connecting the authentication method of the suite to the web app.
- Separating and modularizing the FlexIA web app from the test architecture.
- Sharing analysis results with other tools of the suite.

The integration into the encompassing FlexDeMo suite is one of the major unique selling points of FlexIA, as the results will not only be usable within the tool itself. They may also be used in or by other FlexDeMo tools. As such the AHP[18] tool included may use the measures defined in the FlexIA tool as possible business objectives [5]. Alternatively, the analysis results of the value stream mapping [3] tool, may be used in FlexIA to predetermine possible processes to analyze.

References

1. Becks, D., Kruse, C., Venhuis, S.: Flexia - a toolkit for the participatory information analysis in small and medium-sized companies. https://doi.org/10.18420/ECSCW2020_P07
2. Durugbo, C., Tiwari, A., Alcock, J.R.: Modelling information flow for organisations: a review of approaches and future challenges. Int. J. Inf. Manag. **33**(3), 597–610 (2013). https://doi.org/10.1016/j.ijinfomgt.2013.01.009
3. Erlach, K.: Wertstromdesign: Der Weg zur schlanken Fabrik. VDI-Buch, 2nd edn, bearb. und erweiterte aufl. edn. Springer, New York (2010)
4. Kruse, C., Becks, D., Venhuis, S.: Information analysis with FlexIA - reconciling design challenges through user participation. In: Stephanidis, C., Antona, M., Ntoa, S. (eds.) HCII 2020. CCIS, vol. 1293, pp. 62–69. Springer, Cham (2020). https://doi.org/10.1007/978-3-030-60700-5_8
5. Latos, B.A., Holtkötter, C., Brinkjans, J., Przybysz, P.M., Mütze-Niewöhner, S., Schlick, C.: Partizipatives und simulationsgestütztes Vorgehen zur Konzeption einer flexiblen und demografierobusten Montagelinie bei einem Hersteller von weißer Ware. Universitätsbibliothek der RWTH Aachen, Aachen (2017)

---

[18] Analytic Hierarchy Process.

6. Nielsen, J., Molich, R.: Heuristic evaluation of user interfaces. In: Proceedings of the SIGCHI Conference on Human Factors in Computing Systems, pp. 249–256 (1990)
7. Oestereich, B.: Die UML-Kurzreferenz 2.5 für die Praxis: Kurz, bündig, ballastfrei. 6. auflage edn. De Gruyter Oldenbourg, München (2014)
8. O'Shea, M., Pawellek, G., Schramm, A.: Durch maßgeschneiderte Informationsversorgung zu mehr Usability. Wirtschaftsinformatik Manag. 5(6), 104–114 (2013). https://doi.org/10.1365/s35764-013-0370-8
9. Rücker, B., Freund, J.: Praxishandbuch BPMN 2.0: Mit Einführung in DMN. 6, aktualisierte auflage edn. Carl Hanser Verlag GmbH & Co. KG, München (2019)
10. Scheer, A.W.: Wirtschaftsinformatik: Referenzmodelle für industrielle Geschäftsprozesse. 7, durchges. aufl. edn. Springer, Berlin (1997)
11. Schwab, M., Wack, K.J.: Digitalisierung der kontsruktion im sondermaschinenbau - ein erfahrungsbericht zur nutzerzentrierten gestaltung & usability-evaluation einer individuallösung. https://doi.org/10.18420/muc2019-up-0359
12. Stapel, K., Schneider, K.: Flow-methode - methodenbeschreibung zur anwendung von flow. CoRR abs/1202.5919 (2012)
13. Unger, H., Börner, F., Müller, E.: Context related information provision in industry 4.0 environments. Procedia Manuf. 11, 796–805 (2017). https://doi.org/10.1016/j.promfg.2017.07.181
14. Vernon, V., Evans, E.: Implementing domain-driven design, 4th Printing edn. Addison-Wesley, Upper Saddle River (2015)

Analyzing Early Stage of Forming a Consensus from Viewpoint of Majority/Minority Decision in Online-Barnga

Yoshimiki Maekawa[1]([✉]), Tomohiro Yamaguchi[2], and Keiki Takadama[1]

[1] The University of Electro-Communications, Chofugaoka 1-5-1, Chofu, Tokyo, Japan
yoshimiki.maekawa@uec.ac.jp, keiki@inf.uec.ac.jp
[2] National Institute of Technology, Nara College, 22 Yata-cho,
Yamatokoriyama, Nara, Japan
yamaguch@info.nara-k.ac.jp

Abstract. This paper focuses on the "early stage" of the online communication to investigate what kind of factors that contribute to forming a consensus among people who have their own way of thinking. For this purpose, this paper employs Barnga as the cross-cultural game where the players should select the winner according to their own rules, and analyzes one key person that can adapt to her/his group from the viewpoint of majority and minority decisions (*i.e.*, her/his selected winner tends to become the majority rather than the minority). Through the human subject experiment on the online version of Barnga, the following implications have been revealed: (1) the key player can change her/his initial rule to the shared rule among the players by recognizing the difference of the rules of other players; (2) the change of the rule of the key player derives the situation where the winner selected according to the shared rule becomes majority; and (3) such a situation promotes the other players to declare their intents, which is needed to from a consensus.

Keywords: Online communication · Barnga · Consensus · Majority/Minority

1 Introduction

Recently, many online communication tools have been developed and become a part of our lives. For example, the chat services enable us to keep in touch with our friends who are far from us, and the Social Network Services (SNSs) enable us to communicate with many people via the Internet. In addition to such one-to-one or one-to-many communication, many-to-many communication such as Zoom and Google meets, becomes indispensable for the group communication since the COVID-19 pandemic of 2020. However, these online communications are based on the *non*-face-to-face communication which is hard to deeply

© Springer Nature Switzerland AG 2021
S. Yamamoto and H. Mori (Eds.): HCII 2021, LNCS 12766, pp. 269–285, 2021.
https://doi.org/10.1007/978-3-030-78361-7_20

understand what the partners think in comparison with the face-to-face communication. Although both communications are based on not only the verbal information (*i.e.*, words) but also the non-verbal information (*e.g.*, facial expressions and gestures), the quality and quantity of the non-verbal information in the non-face-to-face communication are lower and fewer than those in the face-to-face communication. Due to this fact, the online communication easily causes problems of misunderstanding, which may change a consequence of communication and may become a trigger to break the relationships among partners. Nevertheless, it is difficult to recognize such situations. In chat communication, for example, it is easy for a sender to imagine that partners understand sent messages correctly, and the above problems happen easily among partners [4]. In addition, since online communications like SNSs are based on one-to-many communication, it is difficult for users to control the amount or kinds of information. If the coming information includes negative contents, the pots of the users tend to be negative, and a consequence or a message of communication can be changed [3].

However, it is difficult for people to recognize and solve misunderstandings in online communication where relationships among partners tend to be weak. In contrast, the more intimate the interpersonal relationships are, the more likely it is that misunderstandings can be solved. In addition, in the field of social psychology, this intimate interpersonal relationship has been discussed. Thibaut et al. proposed that in order to build intimate interpersonal relationships, it is necessary for communicators to give rewards to each other [8]. However, in online communications, which is usually a one-to-many communication format, many users who simply take advantage of the rewards given by the other users and do not give rewards themselves exist, and it is not an environment that can efficiently realize intimate interpersonal relationships. Furthermore, Levenger et al. proposed that interaction in the early stages of communication plays a major role in the realization of intimate interpersonal relationships [5]. Concretely, Levenger divided the process from the beginning of communications to the realization of intimate interpersonal relationships into four stages. In particular, 2nd stage is a situation that "noticing the other person, but do not communicate", and the impressions and evaluations in this stage play an important role in the realization of intimate interpersonal relationships.

To tackle this problem, this paper analyzes a process of "forming a consensus" among people who have their own way of thinking in the online communication. This is because we can roughly regard that people have the good relationships without misunderstanding if they can form a consensus. For this purpose, this paper focuses on the "early stage" of the online communication to investigate what kind of factors contribute to forming a consensus. Note that the "early stage" of the online communication is very important because it gives a big influence to determine whether people can form a consensus. To analyze such a process, this paper employs the cross-cultural game called Barnga, which is the card game that the players should determine the winner according to their own rules. Since the players are not allowed to speak in Barnga, it is difficult to fully communicate among players. Such a situation is often caused in the online communication. As the concrete analysis of Barnga, this paper analyzes one key person that can adapt to her/his group from the viewpoint of *majority* and *minority* decisions (*i.e.*, her/his determined winner tends to become the majority rather than the minority).

This paper is organized as follows: Sect. 2 explains Barnga employed in the human subject experiments, and Sect. 3 describes the results of previous experiments. Section 4 analyzes a process of forming a consensus from the viewpoint of the majority and the minority, and Sect. 5 discusses the key player clarified in Sect. 4. Finally, our conclusion is given in Sect. 6.

2 Barnga: Cross Clutural Game

2.1 Overview

Barnga is the card game proposed by Thiagarajan [7]. The main purpose of Barnga is to provide not only an experience of the difficulty of communicating with people who have the different cultural backgrounds (*e.g.*, culture shock) but also an experience of the trial and error to resolve such differences. The number and suit of playing cards used in Barnga are 28, which covers from Ace to seven with all suits. Basically, the suit of the firstly discarded card is stronger than the other suits, but the trump suit (determined beforehand) is the strongest among the four suits, (*i.e.*, the other suits < the suit of the firstly discarded card < the trump suit). For example, if the firstly discarded card is a certain number (*e.g.*, Ace) of Spade and the trump suit is Spade, the Spade cards are strong in the game. If the firstly discarded card is a certain number (*c.g.*, Ace) of Spade but the trump suit is Heart, the Heart cards are strong in the game. Among the same suit, the strength of number is the ordinal ascending order (*i.e.*, Ace < 2 < 3 < 4 < 5 < 6 < 7) or the Ace prioritized ascending order (*i.e.*, 2 < 3 < 4 < 5 < 6 < 7 < Ace). What should be noted here is that the players have their "own rules" which are not recognized by the other players. For example, the rule of the player A is the ordinal ascending order with the Spade trump suit, while the rule of the player B is the Ace prioritized ascending order with the Heart trump suit. Since the players are not allowed to communicate verbally while playing Barnga, *i.e.*, the players cannot speak or write words on paper, the players may select the different winner due to the different rules. What the players can do in such a situation is to express their minds or decisions by gesture, which corresponds to the cross-cultural experience.

2.2   Procedure

The basic procedure of the Barnga is summarized as follows: (1) 28/(the number of players) cards are distributed to each player; (2) the players discard their cards in turn one by one (*i.e.*, each player discards one card from her/his hand and discards it on the field); (3) After the four cards are discarded on the field, the players select their own winners who play the strongest card among the four discarded cards according to their own rules; (4) one game completes if the players select the same winner (*i.e.*, one winner is determined by the same winner selection among the players), otherwise the players should select the winner again until one winner is determined by forming a consensus; and (5) return to (2) with starting to discard a card by the winner player when the cards are remain in hand while return to (1) when all cards are discarded. In Barnga, "one game" is counted every cycle from the procedures (2) to (5), while "one turn" is counted by repeating the winner selection within the procedure (4). Note that the players do not have to select their winners, meaning that the winner may be determined by the only players who select their winners (see Fig. 1 (c)).

Since the procedures (3) and (4) are important in Barnga, let us explain them in detail. Figure 1 shows the different situations of the winner selection. In detail, Fig. 1 (a), (b) and (c) respectively show the situation when all players select the same winner, when the players select the different winner, and when the players select the winner again after the different winner selection. Considering that the Players 1, 2, 3, and 4 respectively discard the three of Spade, the two of Heart, the five of Club, and the seven of Spade in turn, Player 4 is selected as the winner if all players have the same rule which is the ascending order with the Spade trump suit (Fig. 1 (a)), while Players 2 and 4 are selected as the winner if Player 1 has the rule which is the ascending order with the Spade trump suit and the other players have the different rule which is the ascending order with the Heart trump suit (Fig. 1 (b)). In the latter case shown in Fig. 1 (b), the players should select the winner again because of selecting the different winners, and Player 2 is selected as the winner in the next turn if Player 1 does not select the winner as shown in Fig. 1 (c) or Player 1 selects Player 2 as the winner.

2.3   Online-Barnga

To investigate the difficulty of the online communication, our previous research developed online-Barnga [6], which enables the players to play Barnga via Internet.

Figure 2 (a) shows the displayed image of Online-Barnga after the players discard their cards. In this figure, the face images in the four corners represent the players, *i.e.*, Players 1, 2, 3, and 4 are shown in the upper left, the upper right, the lower right, and the lower left, respectively. The red box in the lower area represents the cards of the player in her/his hand, and the player can discard by clicking the card. After selecting the winner selection, the displayed image of Online-Barnga changes as shown in Fig. 2 (b), which shows that the players point their fingers at the winner. In this figure, Players 1, 2, and 4 select Player

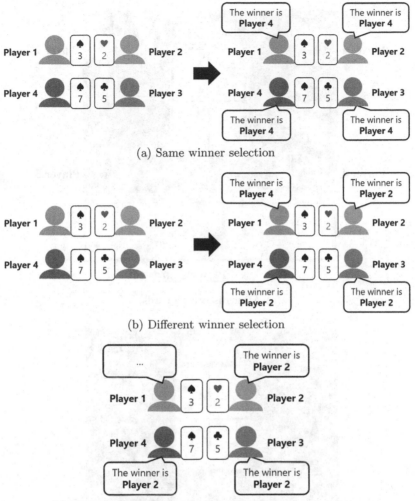

(a) Same winner selection

(b) Different winner selection

(c) Winner selection again after different winner selection

Fig. 1. Winner selection

3 as the winner, while Player 3 selects Player 2 as the winner, which causes the situation where the winner is not determined. In such a situation, the players can select the emotional panels shown in the yellow box in the middle area to express their emotions (*e.g.*, the happy panel in the case of the same winner selection while the anger panel in the case of the different winner selection). The players should select the winner again until the same winner is selected.

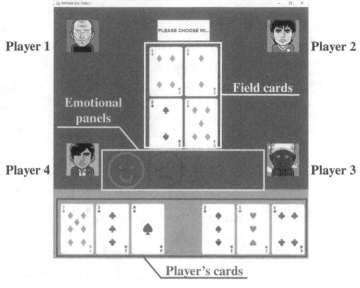

(a) After discarding cards

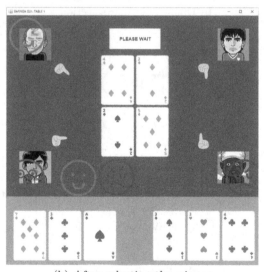

(b) After selecting the winner

Fig. 2. Displayed images of Online-Barnga (Color figure online)

3   Previous Experiment

This section describes our previous experimental result that we analyze in this paper. Since the previous result clarified the situation where the players could form a consensus in the online-Barnga, this paper investigates what kind of factors contribute to forming a consensus by analyzing the previous result.

3.1   Experimental Design

The previous experiment was conducted with the following conditions: (1) Barnga with the four human players who have the different rules (Case 1); (2) Barnga with the three human players who have the different rules and the agent that does not select the winner (*i.e.*, the quiet agent) (Case 2). The rules of the human players are summarized in Table 1.

Table 1. The rules of the players

	The strength of number	The strongest suit
Player 1	7 < 6 < 5 < 4 < 3 < 2 < Ace	Heart
Player 2	Ace < 2 < 3 < 4 < 5 < 6 < 7	Club
Player 3	7 < 6 < 5 < 4 < 3 < 2 < Ace	Diamond
Player 4	Ace < 2 < 3 < 4 < 5 < 6 < 7	Spade

The previous experiment evaluated whether the players form a consensus according to (1) the efficiency of the game progress and (2) the rate of the declaration of one's intent, and defined that the players could form a consensus in the case of the high value of both the criteria (1) and (2). In detail, we regard that the players form a consensus when they select the same winner quickly with many winner selections. For this issue, the criterion (1) is based on the number of turns in one game (N_{TURN}) that needs to determine the winner and is calculated by the Eq. (1). In this equation, the larger the N_{TURN} value is, the worse the efficiency is, because the players are hard to form a consensus in the case of the large N_{TURN}. Since the minimum N_{TURN} is 1, the maximum efficiency of the game progress is 1.

$$\text{Efficiency} = \frac{1}{N_{TURN}} \tag{1}$$

The criterion (2), on the other hand, is based on the number of the declaration of one's intent (*i.e.*, the number of the winner selections ($N_{declaration}$) in one game and is calculated by the Eq. (2). This criterion investigates whether the players declare their intents regardless of whether they win or lose.

$$\text{Rate of declaration} = \frac{N_{declaration}}{N_{TURN}} \tag{2}$$

3.2 Results

Figure 3 shows the efficiency of the game progress, where the vertical axis indicates the number of games while the horizontal axis indicates the number of turns. In this figure, the blue, orange, and green lines indicate the results of Case 1, 2 and the reference line with the slope 1, respectively. Comparing the results of Cases 1 and 2, (1) the number of turns in Case 2 (*i.e.*, the orange line) is larger than that in Case 1 (*i.e.*, the blue line) because its number is different in the same hour. This difference indicates that the players in Case 2 played the more games than Case 1; and (2) the slope of Case 2 after the 20 games is mostly 1 (which is parallel to the green line) while the slope of Case 1 is less than 1. This difference indicates that the players in Case 2 select the winner with one turn in one game while those in Case 1 select the winner with many turns in one game.

Figure 4, on the other hand, shows the rate of declaration of one's intent, where the vertical axis indicates a change in the rate of declaration of intent while the horizontal axis indicates a change in the rate of winning. In this figure, the blue and orange plots indicate the results of Cases 1 and 2, respectively. Note that the plots in the first and second quadrants mean that the rate of declaration of intent is positive (*i.e.*, the players declare more their intents than in the previous game), and the plots in the first and fourth quadrants mean that the rate of winning is positive (*i.e.*, the players win more than in the previous game). From Fig. 4, the number of plots in the third and fourth quadrants in Case 2 are fewer than in Case 1 (*i.e.*, 10 plots in Case 1 and 3 plots in Case 2), which suggests that most of the players in Case 2 keep to declare their intents regardless of whether they win or lose.

From the above results in Figs. 3 and 4, our previous research confirmed that the players in Case 2 form a consensus because they select the winner with one turn in one game (from Fig. 3) with declaring their intents (*i.e.*, the determined winner). In other words, the players in Case 2 do not determine one winner by the small number of (powerful or overbearing) players but by all players without a lot of conflicts of the winner selection.

4 Analysis

To investigate what kind of factors contribute to forming a consensus in the online-Barnga, this section analyzes the result of Case 2 in the previous experiment described in Sect. 3. To address this issue, this paper conducts the following steps: (step 1) the "early stage" of the game is focused on because it gives a big influence to determine whether the players can form a consensus as described in Sect. 1. This hypothesizes that something occurs before sharing the rules among the players to form a consensus. From this hypothesis, this paper starts to find the timing when the rule is shared; (step 2) the players are analyzed from the viewpoint of majority and minority decisions (*i.e.*, the selected winner is the majority or the minority) to find the key player who can select the winner based on the shared rule; and (step 3) the key player in the group is analyzed from the viewpoint of how s/he contributes to forming a consensus.

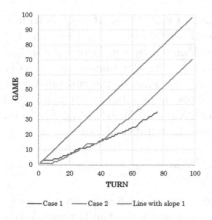

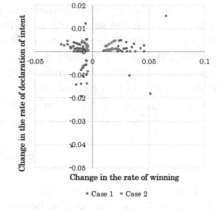

Fig. 3. Efficiency of GAME progression (Color figure online)

Fig. 4. Relationship between change in the rate of declaration and the rate of winning (Color figure online)

4.1   Step 1: Timing When Rule is Shared

To estimate the timing when the rule is shared, we investigate whether the suit of cards used for the winner selection becomes to be the same among the players. Considering the situation of Fig. 5 where the Ace of Spade is firstly discarded by Player 1, followed by the two of Heart (by Player 2), the five of Club (by Player 3), and the three of Heart (by Player 4) and the winner of this game is Player 1, for example, the following trump suit can be considered in the shared rule: (1) Firstly, Spade is considered as one of the trump suits in the shared rules because Player 1 wins the game; and (2) The other players may not have the Spade cards because they discards the cards that are not Spade. However, Heart and Club are not the trump suits in the shared rules because Player 2, 3, or 4 who discards the Heart or Club cards is not the winner. From these two points, the rule is shard to have the trump suite of Spade or Diamond which is not discarded by the players. Considering the other example when Player 3 who discards the five of Club is the winner, the rule is shard to have the trump suite of Club because Player 3 is not the first player who discards a card.

Fig. 5. Situation in playing sequence

After estimating the trump suit in the shared rule, the next issue is to find the timing when the same rule is shared. For this issue, we calculate the rate of suit used for the winner selection, which is calculated by the following Eq. (3), analyze which suit is shared as a trump suit among the players, and finally extract the timing of the shared rule from the viewpoint of the convergence of the rate of suit. In this equation, N_{suit} indicates the number of each suit used for the winner selection (*i.e.*, N_{suit} for Spade, N_{suit} for Heart, N_{suit} for Club, and N_{suit} for Diamond) and N_{GAME} indicates the number of game.

$$\text{Rate of suit} = \frac{N_{suit}}{N_{GAME}} \tag{3}$$

Figure 6 shows the transition in the rate of suit used for the winner selection, where the vertical axis indicates the rate of suit while the horizontal axis indicates the number of turns. In this figure, the blue, orange, green, and yellow lines indicate the rate of Spade, Heart, Club, and Diamond used for the winner selection, respectively. From this figure, the rate of Heart increases after the 40 turns while the rates of the other suits decrease, which suggests that the 40 turns is the timing when the rule is shared.

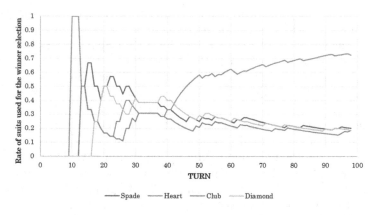

Fig. 6. Transition of winning rate of suits (Color figure online)

4.2 Step 2: Key Player Who Can Select the Winner Based on the Shared Rule

Since Sect. 4.1 found the timing when the rule is shared, this subsection finds the key player who can select the winner based on the shared rule. For this issue, we hypothesize that the key player can quickly notice how her/his rule is different from others in comparison with the others and can recognize how the different rules are merged into one rule shared among the players. From this hypothesis, the players are analyzed from the viewpoint of whether their selected winners are the majority or minority, supposing that the number of the selected majority winner of key player is larger than others. To confirm it, we analyze the players as follows.

Player 1 and Player 2: Figures 7 (a) and (b) respectively show the transition in the rate of declaration of intent rate of Players 1 and 2 and the turn when her/his decision (*i.e.*, the selected winner) is the majority/minority, where the upper figure shows the majority case while the lower figure shows the minority case. In these figures, the vertical axis indicates the rate of declaration of intent and the horizontal axis indicates the number of turns. The orange line indicates the rate of declaration of intent, and the blue line indicates the turn when the decision of the player is the majority/minority. Focusing on the turns until 40 (which is the timing when the rule is shared among the players (see Sect. 4.1)), the rate of declaration of intent of both players increases/keeps when their decision is the majority and decreases when decision is the minority.

Player 3: Figure 7 (c) shows the case of Players 3, where the upper/lower figure, the vertical and horizontal axes, and the orange and blue lines have the same meaning of Figs. 7 (a) and (b). Focusing on the turns until 40 as the same as Players 1 and 2, the rate of declaration of intent of both players increases when their decision is the majority but does *not decrease* when decision is the minority. More importantly, the number of turns when the decision of Player 3 is the majority/minority is larger/fewer than those of the other players. These results suggest that Player 3 can belong to the majority by selecting the winner based on the shared rule, meaning that Players 3 can adapt to her/his group from the viewpoint of majority and minority decisions.

However, the above result cannot ensure that Player 3 selects the majority winner *consciously* but not *consequently*. To verify it, Player 3 is analyzed from the viewpoint of whether s/he selects the winner according to her/his initial rule (which trump suit is Spade) or one of the other players' rules. In detail, we regard that (a) Player 3 selects the majority winner *consequently* if selecting it according to her/his initial rule, while Player 3 selects the majority winner *consciously* if selecting it according to one of the other players' rules. We also regard that (b) Player 3 recognizes the rule shared among the players if the suit used for the winner selection in Player 3 changes quickly to the suit in the shard rule.

Regarding the viewpoint (a), Fig. 8 shows the transition in the rate of declaration of intent and the turn when selecting the winner according to the initial/different rule of Player 3, where the vertical and horizontal axes, and the orange line have the same meaning of Figs. 7 (c). As the difference between Fig. 7 (c) and Fig. 8, the upper/lower figures in Fig. 8 show the winner selection according to the initial/different rule and the blue line in Fig. 8 indicates the turn when selecting the winner according to the initial/different rule. From the upper figure in Fig. 8, Player 3 applied her/his initial rule in the first several turns because all players including Player 3 do not notice that the other players

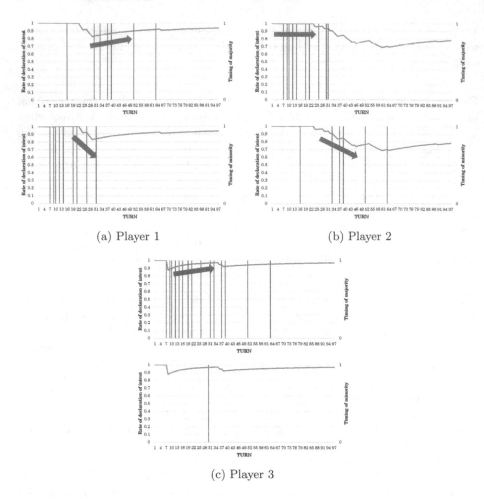

(a) Player 1   (b) Player 2

(c) Player 3

Fig. 7. Rate of declaration of intent and turn in the case of majority (upper figure)/minority (lower figure) (Color figure online)

have the different rules and thus they select the winner according to their initial rules. From the lower figure in Fig. 8, however, Player 3 changed to not to select the winner according the *initial* rule but select it according to the *different* rule after the 7th turn by recognizing the different rules of the other players (note that this change can be seen in Fig. 9 discussed later). Furthermore, the number of applying the different rule is three times larger than that of applying the initial rule, meaning that Player 3 selected the majority winner *consciously*. Needless to say, this implies that Player 3 selected the winner according to the shared rule among the players.

Regarding the viewpoint (b), Fig. 9 shows the rate of suits used for the winner selection, where the vertical axis indicates the rate of used suit while the horizontal axis indicates the number of turns. In this figure, the blue, orange, green, and yellow lines indicate the rate of using Spade, Heart, Club, and Diamond as the trump suits, respectively. From Fig. 9, the rate of using Spade become high because the trump suit of the initial rule of Player 3 is Spade and decreases after the 7th turn by recognizing the different rules of the other players. Although the rate of all used suits become similar until the 40th turns, the rate of using Heart become high from the 40th turn when the rule with the HERAT trump suit is shared among the players. This result means that Player 3 finally determined to select the winner according to the different rules.

From the above analyses of (a) and (b), Player 3 is the key player who can adapt to her/his group by selecting the majority winner consciously through a change from the initial rule to the different rule of the other players. Such a capability of Player 3 contributes to forming a consensus in comparison with Players 1 and 2.

4.3   Step 3: Analyzing Key Player to Find Factors for Forming a Consensus

Since Sect. 4.1 found the timing when the rule is shared and Sect. 4.2 extracted the key player who can select the majority winner after the rule is shared, this subsection analyzes the key players to find factors that contribute to forming a consensus, considering that the rate of declaration of intent of players generally increase/decreases when the selected winner is the majority/minority (which are found in Players 1 and 2 described in Sect. 4.2).

As described in Sect. 4.2, Player 3 changed to apply the different rule with the Heart trump suit after the 40th turn as shown in Fig. 9, which derives the situation where Player 1 whose trump suit in the initial rule is Heart belongs to the majority (because two players (Players 1 and 3) shared the rule with the Heart trump suit). As a result, the rate of declaration of intent of Player 1 (*i.e.*, the orange line in Fig. 8 (a)) starts to increase slightly before the 40th turn because the her/his selected winner becomes the majority. This situation contributes to forming a consensus by increasing the number of players who declare their intents.

What should be noted here is that the change of the rule in Player 3 affect not only Player 1 but also Player 2. As described above, the selected winner of both Players 1 and 3 becomes majority slightly before the 40th turn, which derives the situation where the selected winner of Player 2 becomes minority. As a result, the rate of declaration of intent of Player 2 (*i.e.*, the orange line in Fig. 9 (b)) decreases around the same turn. However, the rate of declaration of intent of Player 2 increases after the 63th turn. To investigate this issue, Fig. 10 shows the transition in the rate of suits user for the winner selection in Player 2, where the vertical and horizontal axes, and four colored lines have the same meaning of Fig. 9. This figure suggests that the timing (around the 63th turn) when the rate of declaration of intents increases in Fig. 9 (b) is the same as the timing when

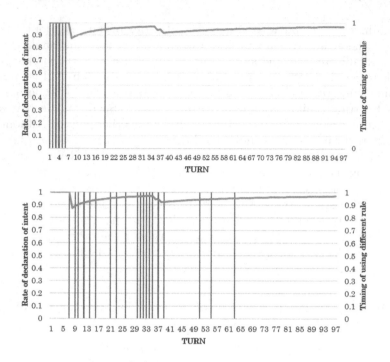

Fig. 8. Timing when Player 3 applied initial/different rule (Color figure online)

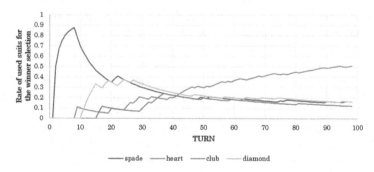

Fig. 9. The rate of the used suits for the winner selection of Player 3 (Color figure online)

Player 2 applies the rule with the Heart trump suit in Fig. 10. This phenomenon of Player 2 is considered as a result of the conformity of a group. Note that the conformity of a group is divided into the *external* and *internal* conformity, where the former conformity forces people to conform a group without their consents, while the latter conformity incorporates the intention of others [1, 2]. Since Barnga does not have the mechanism of the external conformity, the phenomenon of Player 2 causes because of the internal conformity. Considering that Player 3 and 2 started to apply the rule with the Heart trump suit after the

40th and 63th turns respectively, Player 2 started to conform internally from the 40th to 63th turn and completed to conform internally at the 63th turn. Such an internal conformity of a group is occurred indirectly by Player 3, which also contributes to forming a consensus by increasing the number of players who declare their intents.

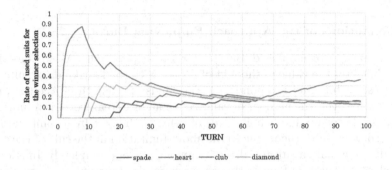

Fig. 10. The rate of the used suits for the winner selection of Player 2

5 Discussion

5.1 Design of Agent Toward Forming a Consensus

Since the agent player is needed in the case of no key human player, this section explores to design the agent player who contributes to form a consensus in the group composed of the agent and human players.

Agent Player Like Player 3: From the analysis in Sect. 4, the agent players can be designed to imitate the behavior of the key player (Player 3) to provide the same effect of the key player. Concretely, this agent is expected to select the winner according to the shared rule in the case of no key human players in the group. For this purpose, the agent is required to record the histories of the winner selections to estimate the rules of the other players and select the majority winner. Such an agent contributes to increasing the rate of declaration of intent of the human players, which is indispensable for forming a consensus.

Agent Player Who Supports Human Players: From the different viewpoint of the agent design, the agent players should be designed to take care of the human players whose rate of declaration of intent is low (such as the players who select the minority winner or the players who often lose the game). Since the declaration of intent by many players are needed to form a consensus (because a consensus is hard to be formed by the small number of players), the aim of the agent is to increase the rate of declaration of intent of the above types of human players (Note that the agent players are not required to support the human players like Player 3 because s/he can declare her/his intent by oneself). For this purpose, the agent is also required to recode the histories of the winner selections to select the same winner of such human players in order not for their decisions to become the minority in the their group. This kind of the winner selection is important because the rate of declaration of intent highly depends on whether the player's decision is majority or minority.

5.2   Limitations of the Approach Employing Barnga

In this research, we employed Barnga for the experiment. As we described, Barnga simulates the value of thought of people with the four kinds of suits (*i.e.*, Spade, Heart, Club, and Diamond) and two kinds of strength of Ace (*i.e.*, weak or strong). However, the number of values of thought in real-world is infinity, and it is impossible to simulate whole kinds of value of thought by a combination of two kinds of rules in Barnga. Due to the above limitation in the rule of Barnga, it is difficult to simulate a cultural diversity among players completely. In addition, the number of players is four in this research, while the number of members in real communications is fluid because members drop out from or come into groups during communications. Therefore, the implications of this research may not be reproduced depending on the number of rules and the number of players. Furthermore, since participants of the human subject experiment are all Japanese, this research could not consider the cultural diversity in the real-world. However, it is Barnga's characteristic to simulate the different cultural background even if the players have the same cultural background. On the other hand, a situation, where the players have different cultural backgrounds in the real-world and the players have different rules in Barnga, is an interest of future researches.

6   Conclusion

This paper focused on the "early stage" of the online communication to investigate what kind of factors contribute to forming a consensus among people who have their own way of thinking (*i.e.*, the rule in Barnga). For this purpose, this paper employed Barnga as the cross-cultural game where the players should select the winner according to their own rules, and analyzed the one key person who can select the winner which tends to become the majority rather than the minority. Through the human subject experiment on the online version of Barnga, the following implications have been revealed: (1) the key player can change her/his initial rule to the shared rule among the players by quickly recognizing the difference of the rules of other players in comparison with other players; (2) the change of the rule of the key player derives the situation where the winner selected according to the shared rule becomes majority; and (3) such a situation promotes the other players to declare their intents, which is needed to from a consensus. In detail, the players who select the majority winner increases the rate of the declaration of intent, while the players who select the minority winner also increases by the internal conformity of a group. Furthermore, this paper discussed how the agent should be designed to support the players to form a consensus among them, and provided the following directions: (1) the agent that imitates behaviors of the key player who can adapt to her/his group in order to provide the same effect of the key player, (2) the agent that supports the players who do not tend to declare intents in order not for their decisions to become the minority in the their group.

What should be noticed here is that the results have only been obtained from the small number of the human subject experiment of Barnga, and therefore the further careful qualifications and justifications, such as an analysis of the results based on other subjects, are needed to generalize our implications. Such important directions must be pursued in the near future in addition to the following research: (1) an investigation of the size effect (*i.e.*, an increase/decrease of the number of players in Barnga) to verify how the key player affects to form a consensus; and (2) an investigation of online-Barnga which is composed of the agent and human players.

References

1. Deutsch, M., Gerard, H.: A study of normative and informational social influences upon individual judgement. J. Abnorm. Psychol. **51**(3), 629–36 (1955)
2. Kelman, H.: Processes of opinion change. Public Opin. Q. **25**, 57–78 (1961)
3. Kramer, A.D.I., Guillory, J.E., Hancock, J.T.: Experimental evidence of massive-scale emotional contagion through social networks. Proc. Natl. Acad. Sci. **111**(24), 8788–8790 (2014). https://doi.org/10.1073/pnas.1320040111. https://www.pnas.org/content/111/24/8788
4. Kruger, J., Epley, N., Parker, J., Ng, Z.W.: Egocentrism over e-mail: can we communicate as well as we think? J. Pers. Soc. Psychol. **89**(6), 925–936 (2005). https://doi.org/10.1037/0022-3514.89.6.925
5. Levinger, G., Snoek, J.D.: Attraction in relationship: a new look at interpersonal attraction (1972)
6. Maekawa, Y., Uwano, F., Kitajima, E., Takadama, K.: How to emote for consensus building in virtual communication. In: Yamamoto, S., Mori, H. (eds.) HCII 2020. LNCS, vol. 12185, pp. 194–205. Springer, Cham (2020). https://doi.org/10.1007/978-3-030-50017-7_13
7. Thiagarajan, S., Steinwachs, B.: Barnga: A Simulation Game on Cultural Clashes. Intercultural Press (1990)
8. Thibaut, J., Editors, R., Kelley, H.: The Social Psychology of Groups. Wiley (1959). https://books.google.co.jp/books?id=B6dEAAAAIAAJ

Classification of Automotive Industry Salesmen

Yoshio Matsuyama(✉) and Yumi Asahi

Graduate School of Management, Department of Management, Tokyo University of Science,
1-11-2, Fujimi, Chiyoda-ku 102-0071, Tokyo, Japan
8620507@ed.tus.ac.jp, asahi@tsc.u-tokai.ac.jp

Abstract. Looking at the total ratio of Japan's top 10 exports, the total export value in 2018 was 81,478.8 billion yen, of which automobiles accounted for the top of the total export value. In addition, automobiles and automobiles Assuming that parts and prime movers are related to automobiles, automobile-related accounts for 23.6% of Japan's total exports. It turns out that the automobile industry has been in a very large position in Japan's domestic economy in recent years, and the automobile industry is It can be said that it is the cornerstone of Japanese industry. However, when checking the number of automobiles in Japan, it is on a downward trend, and in terms of ownership rate, it can be confirmed that the passenger automobile ownership rate has been on a downward trend after peaking in 2013. From the above, in order not to shrink or decline the automobile industry in the future, it is necessary to respond more reliably to the decreasing demand than ever before. For that purpose, the automobile dealers first classified sales positions, but since there was a problem with the classification, we will create a classification standard in this research. Sales position classification is performed by three methods: hierarchical cluster analysis, non-hierarchical cluster analysis, and EM algorithm. The data classified by this classification is divided by salespeople classified by three methods. Multiple regression analysis is performed on each result, comparison is made between excellent sales staff and non-excellent sales staff, and proposals are made as specific sales methods.

Keywords: Automobiles · Classification · Salesman

1 Introduction

1.1 Japan's Domestic Economic Situation

In October 2019, the consumption tax rate was raised to 10% in Japan. It has been five and a half years since it was raised to 8% in April 2014. However, considering the 17-year period from 5% in April 1997 to 8% in April 2014, the pace of consumption tax hike is fast. And, at the same time that the consumption tax rate has been raised to 10%, a reduced tax rate has been introduced to reduce the burden on daily life [1].

The consumption tax rate for food and drink and newspapers, excluding alcohol and eating out, remains unchanged at 8%, but it still increases as the tax rate changes from 8% to 10%, and the burden on the average household is annual. At 45,000 yen [2], the burden on households is not small. Furthermore, on November 25, 2019, the

© Springer Nature Switzerland AG 2021
S. Yamamoto and H. Mori (Eds.): HCII 2021, LNCS 12766, pp. 286–299, 2021.
https://doi.org/10.1007/978-3-030-78361-7_21

International Monetary Fund (IMF) published a 2019 report analyzing the Japanese economy [3]. This report was written which the consumption tax needs to be raised to 15% by 2030 and raised to 20% by 2050 to cover the increasing social security costs of medical care and long-term care. It is predicted that Japan will enter an aging society with a very low birthrate, the proportion of elderly people will increase, and the proportion of working-age population will decrease. In this respect, the recommendations of the International Monetary Fund are not wrong, but they are one of the external factors that cannot be ignored in the automobile industry.

1.2 Japan Domestic Automobile Situation

In this section, we will confirm the actual position of the domestic automobile industry. First, check the economic situation of the automobile industry.

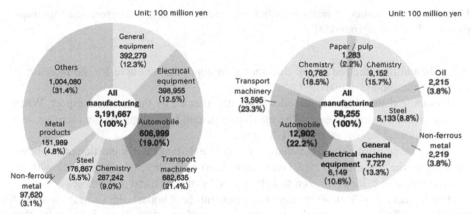

Fig. 1. Shipments of manufactured goods (left) and capital investment in major manufacturing industries (right) [4]

Figure 1 shows the shipment value of manufactured goods (2017) and the capital investment value (FY2017) of major manufacturing industries in Japan. The automobile sector accounts for 88.9% of the shipment value of manufactured goods, and 19.0% for all manufacturing industries. Of the capital investment, the automobile sector accounts for 94.9% of transportation machinery, and the total manufacturing industry accounts for 22.2%.

Figure 2 shows the R & D expenses of major manufacturing industries in Japan (FY2017) and the export value of each major product based on FOB (2018). From Fig. 2 here, the automobile sector accounts for 95.6% of transportation machinery and 24.5% of the total manufacturing industry in R & D expenses. Furthermore, of the FOB-based export value by major commodities, the automobile sector accounts for 88.5% of transportation equipment, and the total manufacturing industry accounts for 20.5%.

Then, what about the demand for automobiles? Fig. 2 shows changes in domestic demand for automobiles by vehicle type. However, in 2002, only light vehicle data existed for both passenger cars and trucks, so it is omitted, and 2018 is the estimated

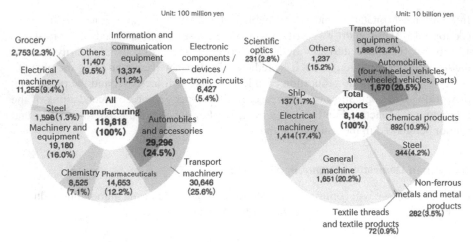

Fig. 2. R & D expenses of major manufacturing industries (left) and export value by major products (F.O.B basis) (right) [4]

value. In addition, the red dotted line shows an approximate curve for the increase in domestic automobile demand.

Domestic demand for automobiles is greatly affected by the financial aspect. When the tax increase is implemented, the maximum demand is before the tax increase, and then the demand has decreased for two years.

Here, we confirm the approximate curve of the demand for domestic automobiles. Looking at the transition for 18 years from 2000 to 2019 (excluding 2002) with an approximate curve, it can be seen that there is a downward trend as a whole.

Furthermore, Fig. 3 shows changes in the percentage of households owning passenger cars in Japan by region. Since the transition is viewed as a percentage, it is a value that does not depend on the declining birthrate and aging population, which is being called out today. Looking at the whole and local areas, it can be confirmed that the passenger car ownership rate has been declining since peaking in 2013. Especially in the metropolitan area, it has been decreasing since 2011. In the Tokyo metropolitan area of Japan, the development of public transportation is remarkable, and it can be inferred that the biggest factor in the decline in the ownership rate is the environment in which people can live without owning a car.

Furthermore, Fig. 4 shows changes in the percentage of households owning passenger cars in Japan by region. Since the transition is viewed as a percentage, it is a value that does not depend on the declining birthrate and aging population, which is being called out today. Looking at the whole and local areas, it can be confirmed that the passenger car ownership rate has been declining since peaking in 2013. Especially in the metropolitan area, it has been decreasing since 2011. In the Tokyo metropolitan area of Japan, the development of public transportation is remarkable, and it can be inferred that the biggest factor in the decline in the ownership rate is the environment in which people can live without owning a car.

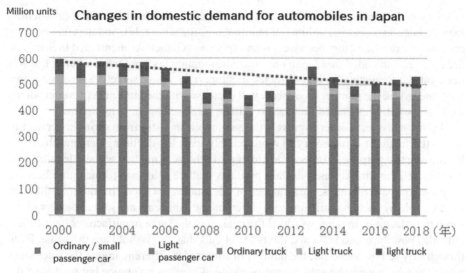

Fig. 3. Domestic demand for automobiles by vehicle type

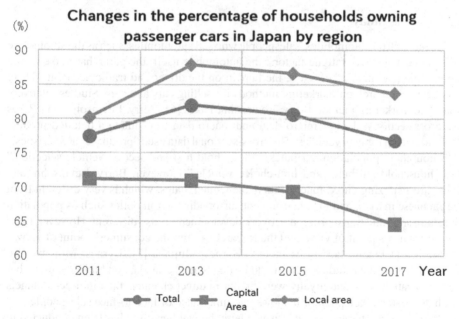

Fig. 4. Changes in the percentage of households owning passenger cars in Japan by region [5]

From the viewpoint of domestic automobile demand and ownership rate in Figs. 3 and 4, it is estimated that the automobile industry will shrink or decline. Furthermore, the younger generation's departure from automobiles, which will be the main target of automobile sales in the future [5], is also a factor in the speculation that the automobile industry will shrink or decline. In addition, as can be confirmed from the production, export, sales, and demand volume of automobiles, the automobile industry is very susceptible to external factors because it is an expensive product. As mentioned in Sect. 1.1, the IMF recommended that Japan raise the consumption tax even more when it had just been raised. Realistically, it is difficult to support an aging society with a very low birthrate, where the number of workers will decrease with the current tax revenue alone, so it can be easily estimated that the tax will be increased again in the future.

From the above, in order to prevent the automobile industry from shrinking or declining in the future, it is necessary to more reliably meet the declining demand than ever before. For that purpose, it is necessary to improve the sales method of the sales staff who actually sell the car. Automobiles are products that are sold face-to-face, and because they are expensive products, the influence of sales staff is not small. In addition, although the cars sold by each manufacturer are different, the same cars are sold at dealers of the same manufacturer. In other words, if the dealers of the same manufacturer have different sales positions who sell cars, the types of cars that can be sold are the same. Even though they sell the same car, the number of cars sold is different among the sales staff. Since the cars that can be sold cannot be changed, there is no choice but to change the sales method of the sales staff.

1.3 Previous Study

As for research on automobiles, salespeople who sell automobiles, such as the automobile failure rate and driver fatigue factors, the automobile itself, the parts that make up the automobile (engine, brakes, etc.), the burden on the driver and traffic accidents There is not much research on marketing methods for selling cars and cars. Studies relatively related to marketing include Berry, Levinsohn, Pakes [6]. Berry, Levinsohn, and Pakes use cross-sectional data of micro data and macro data to estimate a detailed product demand system for new vehicles. The cross-sectional data used "product characteristics," "US household population attributes," "household first and second vehicle selection," and "household attributes and first-choice vehicle." However, Berry, Levinsohn, and Pakes are analyzing micro-macro data in the United States, which is very different from the Japanese market, and the environment surrounding automobiles such as population size, land area, and transportation network development is also different. However, there is no salesman's point of view, and the research is from the consumer's point of view.

Studies in face-to-face sales include Byrnes, Mujtaba [7]. Byrnes, Mujtaba also reported that the data studied were in the United States, Canada, and Latin America, but customer satisfaction and loyalty were higher in direct channels than indirect channels (such as email and telephone). It shows the importance of face-to-face salespeople.

Two previous studies were confirmed here, but neither study has been conducted in Japan.

Studies in face-to-face sales include Byrnes, Mujtaba [7]. Byrnes, Mujtaba also reported that the data studied were in the United States, Canada, and Latin America, but customer satisfaction and loyalty were higher in direct channels than indirect channels (such as email and telephone). It shows the importance of face-to-face salespeople.

Two previous studies were confirmed here, but neither study has been conducted in Japan.

1.4 Purpose of Study

This research is a joint research with automobile dealers A and B Co., Ltd. Data provider A classifies sales positions into excellent and non-excellent. This index was created based on the number of new cars sold each month as one index, but it is known that it is only inferred from the experience of selling so far. Therefore, it is hard to say that it is a very exact value. In this research, we present one method to classify sales positions that sell new cars to general customers into mathematically excellent sales positions and non-excellent sales positions based on the number of new cars sold in recent years. From there, analyze the customers owned by excellent sales positions and non-excellent sales positions. Then, the purpose is to confirm what kind of customers can be increased to increase the number of new cars sold. If you are at the same car dealership, you can sell the same car, and there are no restrictions depending on the products you own.

2 Analytical Data

The data used in this study are owned customer data, new car sales record data, and insurance transaction history data provided by automobile dealer A. In addition, there were various masters about products, services, and sales staff in the form of accompanying these data. The number of sales positions analyzed is 134, the customer data is 12,407, the new car sales record data is 7,361, and the insurance transaction history data is 36,164. The target period of the owned customer data is 2011/10/29 to 2019/06/14, the target period of the new car sales record data is 2017/04/01 to 2019/03/31, the target period of the insurance transaction history data is 2009/04/02–2019/06/14. See later sections for more details on the data.

3 Salesman Evaluation

3.1 Background

The car dealer A, who received the data, also provided the rank of the sales position. Car dealer A ranks sales positions based on its own criteria, and makes a judgment based on the number of new cars sold as an index. However, when checking the details of the data, it was found that the longer the sales position has passed since the company joined the company, the higher the rank.

In order to see the purpose of this study, "improving the number of new cars sold from the factors of excellent sales staff," on a sales staff basis, analysis using ranks that do not decline may lead to incorrect conclusions is there. Therefore, instead of using this rank, we will create a new index to classify excellent and non-excellent based on the number of new cars sold. In addition, data providers had a customary index to classify excellent sales positions and non-excellent sales positions. However, it is known that this index is an index decided by human beings and is not strictly determined. In this study, we mathematically create an index to classify the excel-lent sales position and the non-excellent sales position, and present one method for considering this classification.

3.2 Salesman Classification Method

In Sect. 3.1, we confirmed the necessity of classifying sales positions into excellent and non-excellent. By analyzing the sales method performed by the excellent sales position and the sales method performed by the non-excellent sales position, the sales method of the excellent sales position that the non-excellent sales position should perform and the excellent sales position You will be able to think about improving sales methods, such as avoiding sales methods that you have not done.

Similarly, as confirmed in Sect. 3.1, it is difficult to use the existing sales position classification index for analysis. Since the purpose of this study is to improve the number of new cars sold, we consider a method of classifying sales positions based on the number of new cars sold. However, by not using the existing salesman classification index, the classification is unsupervised. Salesperson classification is performed by three methods: (1) hierarchical cluster analysis, (2) non-hierarchical cluster analysis, and (3) EM algorithm. The number of classifications is "2" because it is a binary value of excellent and non-excellent.

3.3 Salesman Classification Results

The classification results of sales positions are shown in Table 1.

Table 1. The classification results of sales positions

Classification method	Hierarchical cluster analysis	Non-hierarchical cluster analysis	EM algorithm
Classification discrimination number	1.625	2.000	0.875

In particular, the parameters estimated by the EM algorithm are shown in Table 2.

Table 2. The parameters estimated by the EM algorithm

Parameters	Class 2 (non-excellence)	Class 1 (excellence)
$\gamma(z_{nk})$	0.287722	0.712278
μ	0.295122	3.372788
Σ	0.155633	1.123059

Figure 5 shows the results of allocating the monthly new car sales of each sales position to the one with the highest maximum a posteriori probability belonging to each class.

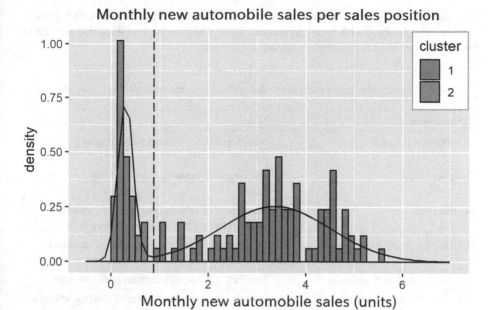

Fig. 5. Monthly new car sales volume EM algorithm analysis result histogram for each sales position after discrimination

4 Consumer Analysis

4.1 Multiple Regression Analysis Data Used

The data is divided by the salespeople classified by the three methods presented in Sect. 3. (1) Excellent cluster in hierarchical cluster analysis, (2) Non-excellent cluster in hierarchical cluster analysis, (3) Excellent cluster in non-hierarchical cluster analysis, (4) Non-excellent cluster in non-hierarchical cluster analysis, (5) Excellent cluster in EM algorithm analysis, (6) EM algorithm We created the above 6 datasets of non-excellent clusters in the analysis. Table 3 shows the number of sales staff, along with the classification criteria for each classification method.

Table 3. The number of sales staff, along with the classification criteria for each classification method

Classification method	Classification criteria	Non-excellent	Excellent
Hierarchical cluster analysis	1.625	48	86
Non-hierarchical cluster analysis	2.000	40	94
EM algorithm	0.875	51	83

The objective variable in multiple regression analysis is the number of new cars sold each month, and in order to avoid multicollinearity, the explanatory variables are removed one by one in order from the one with the highest correlation coefficient until there are no variables with high correlation. Table 4 shows the variables that remain in the end and are used for multiple regression analysis.

Table 4. The variables that remain in the end and are used for multiple regression analysis

Variable name	Detail
Monthly new car sales	Number of new cars sold by each sales position in a month
Male percentage	Percentage of customers who sold new cars were male
Normal ratio	Percentage of vehicles purchased by customers who sold new vehicles were ordinary vehicles
Vehicle type classification 3 ratio	Percentage of vehicles purchased by customers who sold new vehicles were classified as 3
Product A Number of contracts	Number of product A contracts per customer
Vehicle class alias – S ratio	Percentage of vehicle layer alias S when selling a new car
Vehicle layer alias – D ratio	Percentage of vehicle layer alias D when selling a new car
Total number of payments	Total number of installment payments per customer with installments. Cash payment was set to 0
Insurance – Renewal rate	Percentage The percentage of insurance reception category values that were renewed halfway when contracting for insurance
Insurance – New Percentage	Percentage of new insurance acceptance category values when contracting insurance
Insurance-New Percentage of Other Companies	Percentage of new insurance reception category values when contracting insurance
Insurance-Mid-term renewal rate	Percentage of insurance reception category values that were renewed halfway when contracting insurance

4.2   Multiple Regression Analysis Results

Tables 5, 6 and 7 show the results of multiple regression analysis of the six clusters classified by each classification method. The numbers in parentheses in Tables 5, 6 and 7 represent the standard error. The objective variable used in each multiple regression analysis is the monthly new car sales. As for the explanatory variables, the combination of explanatory variables that minimizes AIC is adopted in each model using the stepwise method based on AIC, with the state in which all the variables shown in Table 4 are input as the initial state.

Table 5.   Results of classification multiple regression analysis in hierarchical cluster analysis

	Objective variable	
	Monthly new car sales	
	Non-excellent	Excellence
Vehicle class alias – S ratio	0.105** (0.050)	
Vehicle layer alias – D ratio		0.266^{***} (0.110)
Total number of payments		0.774^{***} (0.211)
Insurance – Renewal rate	0.070^{*} (0.041)	0.403^{**} (0.190)
Insurance-New Percentage of Other Companies	0.055 (0.040)	
Intercept	0.606^{***} (0.076)	3.392^{***} (0.105)
Observations	48	86
R^2	0.156	0.186
Adjusted R^2	0.099	0.157
Residual Std. Error	0.372 (df = 44)	0.816 (df = 82)
F Statistic	2.715^{*} (df = 3; 44)	6.262^{***} (df = 3; 82)

Note: *p < 0.1; **p < 0.05; ***p < 0.01

Table 7. Results of classification multiple regression analysis by EM algorithm

	Objective variable	
	Monthly new car sales	
	Non-excellent	Excellence
Vehicle class alias – S ratio		1.207***
		(0.050)
Vehicle layer alias – D ratio	0.093***	0.514***
	(0.032)	(0.108)
Insurance-Mid-term renewal rate	0.034**	
	(0.014)	
Total number of payments		0.561***
		(0.198)
Intercept	0.357***	2.675***
	(0.030)	(0.153)
Observations	40	94
R^2	0.270	0.334
Adjusted R^2	0.230	0.311
Residual Std. Error	0.147 (df = 37)	0.898 (df = 90)
F Statistic	6.827*** (df = 2; 37)	15.016*** (df = 3; 90)

Note: *p < 0.1; **p < 0.05; ***p < 0.01

Table 6. Results of classification multiple regression analysis in non-hierarchical cluster analysis

	Objective variable	
	Monthly new car sales	
	Non-excellent	Excellence
Vehicle class alias – S ratio	0.178***	
	(0.058)	
Vehicle layer alias – D ratio		0.208*
		(0.107)
Total number of payments		0.658***
		(0.207)
Insurance – Renewal rate	0.092*	0.382**
	(0.049)	(0.183)
Insurance-New Percentage of Other Companies	0.076	
	(0.047)	
Intercept	0.752***	3.475***
	(0.084)	(0.104)
Observations	51	83
R^2	0.241	0.153
Adjusted R^2	0.192	0.120
Residual Std. Error	0.448 (df = 47)	0.782 (df = 79)
F Statistic	4.969*** (df = 3; 47)	4.742*** (df = 3; 79)

Note: *p < 0.1; **p < 0.05; ***p < 0.01

5 Conclusion

5.1 Discussion

From the results of multiple regression analysis in Sect. 4, it is shown that the EM algorithm is the best classification method among the three methods for classifying excellent sales positions and non-excellent sales positions based on the number of new cars sold each month. It was done. Looking at the results of multiple regression analysis with the EM algorithm, in order to increase the number of new cars sold, excellent salespeople first increase the number of customers whose vehicle layer alias is S, and the second and third are almost It was shown that, with the same degree of priority, the number of customers with a large number of "total payment frequency installments" and the number of customers with a "vehicle layer alias" of D should be increased. On the other hand, the non-excellent salesman showed that in order to increase the number of new cars sold, the number of customers whose "vehicle class alias" is D and the number of customers who are "mid-term renewal" of insurance are to be increased. However, looking at the influence of the explanatory variables of the non-excellent sales position, it is very small compared to the influence of the excellent sales position. From here, it is difficult to discuss the customers that should be increased based on the influence of the explanatory variables of the non-excellent sales staff. Therefore, we make recommendations based on the influence of the explanatory variables of excellent sales staff.

For excellent sales staff, the fact that there are many customers whose vehicle layer alias is S has a great influence on the number of new vehicles sold. There are five vehicle layer aliases from S to D, and the closer to S, the more customers receive goods. The warehousing is to go to the car dealer for inspection or maintenance, and the ratio of customers who have a large number of warehousing is high for excellent sales staff. Since this value is divided by the number of owned customers for each sales position, there is no effect on the number of owned customers. Therefore, in order to increase the number of new cars sold, it was shown that it is most important to increase the number of times customers receive goods and increase the number of customers who receive many times. In addition, the large number of customers with a vehicle layer alias of D affects the number of new vehicles sold.

This is in contrast to the many customers whose vehicle class alias is S, which was mentioned earlier, and is a customer who does not receive much goods. Considering this in combination with increasing the number of customers who have received a large number of warehousing, it means that not only the number of warehousing of customers will be increased, but also the number of newly acquired customers will be large. Furthermore, excellent sales staff are customers who make installment payments, and the fact that there are many customers who make installment payments affects the number of new cars sold. Since automobiles are expensive products, their impact on households is not small. You can't afford to lose your life by buying a car. Therefore, even if the total payment amount increases a little, it is speculated that increasing the number of installments will reduce the monthly burden and make it easier to purchase expensive automobiles.

Based on the above, in order to increase the number of new cars sold, the number of warehousing times for a single customer is increased to increase the number of customers with a large number of warehousing times. Installment payments with a large number of installments should be recommended in order to reduce the burden on customers and make them easier to purchase.

5.2 Future Works

Here are three remaining issues that need to be addressed in the future.

First, the data mainly used in this research are new car sales performance data and owned customer data. Since these are not the data collected for analysis, only the information when the car was sold, such as the customer's information when the car was actually sold, what the car was sold, etc. It didn't exist. From this data alone, it is not possible to find out who has left the car, which is an expensive product. The reason for the customer who did not buy the car at the car dealership and went to another car dealership cannot be traced. We believe that the availability of such data will provide deeper insights into increasing new car sales.

Second, in this study, we analyzed from the perspective of a salesperson. When comparing the sales methods of excellent sales positions and non-excellent sales positions and trying to imitate the actual behavior of excellent sales positions with a large number of new car sales, by using the behavior variables of sales positions, excellent sales I think that we can find the difference between the sales method of the man and the non-excellent salesman, and discover the action to increase the number of new cars sold.

Finally, the improvement of the model. Excellent salespeople and non-excellent salespeople were classified by the three methods presented in this study, and multiple regression analysis was performed for each, but even with the EM algorithm that created the most explanatory model, the degree of freedom was adjusted. In terms of coefficient, excellent: 0.311, non-excellent: 0.230, which is hard to say as a highly explanatory model. Since automobiles, which are expensive products, are strongly influenced by external factors such as the economy, it seems to be a relatively high value when considered together with the number of explanatory variables, but the influence of external factors is further increased. There is still room for improvement as a model, such as introducing new variables to lower the value.

References

1. The official website of the Government of Japan: About reduced tax rate system.https://www. gov-online.go.jp/cam/shouhizei/keigenzeiritsu/. Accessed 09 Feb 2021
2. Nagahama, T.: Macro impact of the consumption tax rate hike again (revised edition). Daiichi Life Research Institute Inc., Japan (2019)
3. International Monetary Fund: Japan: Staff Concluding Statement of the 2019 Article IV Mission. https://www.imf.org/en/News/Articles/2019/11/24/mcs-japan-staff-concludingst atement-of-the-2019-article-iv-mission. Accessed 09 Feb 2021
4. Japan Automobile Manufacturers Association: Automobile manufacturing as an institutional industry. http://www.jama.or.jp/industry/industry/index.html. Accessed 09 Feb 2021

5. Japan Automobile Manufacturers Association: Changes in domestic demand for automobiles. http://www.jama.or.jp/stats/outlook/20190325/PDF/change2019fy.pdf. Accessed 09 Feb 2021
6. Berry, S., Levinsohn, J., Pakes, A.: Differentiated products demand systems from a combination of micro and macro data: the new car market. J. Polit. Econ. **112**(1), 68–105 (2004)
7. Byrnes, T.J., Mujtaba, B.G.: The value of B2B face-to-face sales interaction in the United States, Canada and Latin America. Int. Bus. Econ. Res. J. **7**(3), 79–90 (2008)

Impact of Task Cycle Pattern on Project Success in Software Crowdsourcing

Razieh Saremi[1]($\boxtimes$), Marzieh Lotfalian Saremi[2], Sanam Jena[1],
Robert Anzalone[1], and Ahmed Bahabry[1]

[1] Stevens Institute of Technology, Hoboken, NJ, USA
{rsaremi,sjena,ranzalon,abahabry}@stevens.edu
[2] Concordia University, Montreal, QC, Canada
m.lotfa@encs.concordia.ca

Abstract. Software projects have begun to accept crowdsourcing in several different phases of software design and production. Ideally, mass parallel production through Crowdsourcing could be an option to rapid acquisition in software engineering by leveraging on infinite worker resource on the internet. It is important to understand the patterns and strategies of decomposing and uploading parallel tasks in order to maintain stable worker supply as well as satisfactory task completion rate.

To address that end this research reports an empirical analysis on the available tasks' lifecycle patterns in crowdsourcing. Following waterfall model in Crowdsourced Software Development (CSD), this research identified four patterns for sequence of task arrival per project: 1) Prior Cycle, 2) Current Cycle, 3) Orbit Cycle and 4) Fresh Cycle.

Keywords: Crowdsourcing · Topcoder · Task lifecycle · Task failure ratio

1 Introduction

The interest on crowdsourcing software development(CSD) is rapidly increasing in both industry and academia. In crowdsourcing, jobs that were traditionally done in-house, would be distributed among a large, distributed group of crowd workers [7]. Software projects are using crowdsourcing methods in different phases of software design and production [28]. While understanding the patterns and strategies of decomposing and scheduling crowdsourced is important to maintain stable worker supply as well as satisfactory task completion rate, much of existing studies are only focusing on individual task level, such as task pricing, task similarity, and task diversity [1,5,16,22], and worker recommendation and behavior models [12,24,25]. Crowd workers usually choose to register, work, and submit for certain tasks with satisfactory award and comfortable level of dedicated effort, as award typically represents degree of task complexity as well as required competition levels [2,5]. Although sometimes Award

S. Yamamoto and H. Mori (Eds.): HCII 2021, LNCS 12766, pp. 300–311, 2021.
https://doi.org/10.1007/978-3-030-78361-7_22

is simply representing a specific required skill to perform the task, it is one of the main factors influence on crowd software workers in terms of number of registrants and consequently number of submissions [32]. Therefore, pricing tasks could be a huge challenge in decomposing the projects to mini-tasks and time of uploading them in the platform, yet by uploading more number of parallel tasks, crowd workers would have more choice of utilized tasks to register for and consequently the chance of receiving more number of completed tasks is higher [26]. Since existing studies on general crowdsourcing reported limited or unpredictable results [2,5,12], it is a good opportunity to focus on parallelism on uploading same project tasks.

For software managers, utilizing external unknown, uncontrollable, crowd workers would put their projects under greater uncertainty and risk compared with in-house development [12,32]. Understanding crowd worker's sensitivity to the project stability and failure rate, becomes extremely important for managers to make trade-offs among cost saving, degree of competition, and expected quality in the deliverable [32]. To address these challenges, existing methods have explored various methods and techniques to bridge the information gap between demand and supply in crowdsourcing-based software development. These includes: studies towards developing better understanding of worker motivation and preferences in CSD [4–6,32], studies focusing on predicting task failure [9,10]; studies employing modeling and simulation techniques to optimize CSD task execution processes [21,23,29]; and studies for recommending the most suitable workers for tasks [31] and developing methods to create crowdsourced teams [30,33]. However, there is a lack of study on the task execution flow in the field of software crowdsourcing.

To develop better understanding of crowdsourcing-based software projects, this research reports an empirical study on analyzing Topcoder[1], largest software development crowdsourcing platform with an online community of 750000 Crowd Software workers. Topcoder intensively leverage crowdsourcing throughout the product implementation, testing, and assembly phases. Topcoder started to explore crowdsourcing tasks in the form of competitions for software development, in which workers would independently create a solution and winner will be chosen [25].

The remainder of this paper is structured as follows. Section 2 presents background and review of available works. Section 3 outlines our research design. Section 4 presents the empirical result. Section 5 discuss the findings and limitations and Section 6 presents the conclusion and outlines a number of directions for future work.

2   Research Background

2.1   Crowdsourced Platform Workflow

A successful crowdsourcing platform contains three determinants: the characteristics of the project; the composition of the crowd; and the relationship among key

---

[1] https://www.topcoder.com/.

players [13]. A systematic development process in such platform a starts from a requirements phase, where the project goals, task plan, and budget estimation are recognized. This will be performed through communication between the project manager, who may come from the crowd or the platform, and the requester, who pays for the solutions offered by the crowd. The outcome will be a set of requirements and specifications. These requirements are used as the input for the future architecture phase, while the application is decomposed into multiple components [17]. In CSD workflow, the requester company divides the project into many small tasks, prepares task descriptions, and distributes tasks through the platform. Each task is tagged with a pre-specified prize as the award [14,32] to winners and a required schedule deadline to complete. On average, most of the tasks have a life span of 2–4 weeks from the first day of registration.

Crowd software workers browse and register to work on selected tasks, and then submit the work products once completed. After workers submit the final submissions, the files will be evaluated by experts and experienced workers, through a peer review process, to check the code quality and/or document quality [13]. The number of submissions and the associated evaluated scores replicate the level of success in task success. In TopCoder, usually the award goes to the top 1 or 2 winners with the highest scores. If there are zero submissions, or no qualified submissions, the task will be treated as starved or cancelled. Figure 1 illustrates the CSD flow.

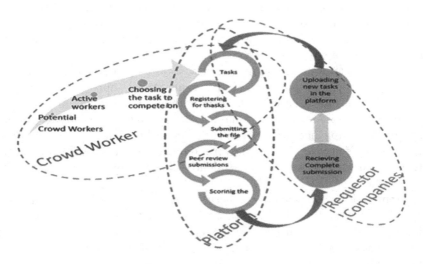

Fig. 1. Crowdsourcing software development flows [32]

2.2   Task Decomposition in Crowdsourcing

In general, projects in crowdsourcing can be decomposed and executed in both independent and dependent tasks. There are two methods of task decomposition: 1) horizontal task decomposition for independent subtasks and 2) vertical task decomposition for dependent sub-tasks [8]. In the horizontal decomposition method, workers dedicate efforts independently to their own subtasks for individual utility maximization, while in the vertical decomposition method, each subtask takes the output from the previous subtasks as input, and therefore the quality of each task is not only related to the worker's effort but also associated with the quality of the previous tasks [8].

Crowdsourcing complex tasks, i.e. software development tasks, generate heavy work-loads and require dedicated resources with high skill sets, which limit the pool of potential workers. In order to expand the qualified labor pool, it is essential to decompose software engineering tasks into smaller pieces. However, software engineering tasks are often concerned with their specific contexts, for which decomposition may be complicated. This fact opens a discussion on different ways of decomposition based on a hierarchy of workflow [27].

The key factors of decompositions considered in this research are: smaller size of micro-tasks, larger parallelism, reducing time to market, and a higher probability of communication overhead. The most common method in decomposing microtasks is asking individual workers to work on a task of specific artifact. This method will lead to some natural boundaries for software workers and there may be a need of defining new boundaries as well.

2.3 Task Flow in Crowdsourcing

Different characteristics of machine and human behavior create delays in product release [20]. This phenomenon leads to a lack of systematic processes to balance the delivery of features with the available resources [20]. Therefore, improper scheduling would result in task starvation [5]. Parallelism in scheduling is a great method to create the chance of utilizing a greater pool of workers [18,26]. Parallelism encourages workers to specialize and complete tasks in a shorter period. The method also promotes solutions that benefit the requester and can help researchers to clearly understand how workers decide to compete on a task and analyze the crowd workers performance [5]. Shorter schedule planning can be one of the most notable advantages of using CSD for managers [11].

Batching tasks in similar groups is another effective method to reduce the complexity of tasks and it can dramatically reduce costs [15]. Batching crowdsourcing tasks would lead to a faster result than approaches which keep workers separate [3]. There is a theoretical minimum batch size for every project according to the principles of product development flow [19]. To some extent, the success of software crowdsourcing is associated with reduced batch size in small tasks.

3   Empirical Study Design

3.1   Empirical Analysis

To develop better understanding on the dynamic patterns in task supply and execution, we formulated research question s below and investigated the different task cycle patterns in CSD and relationships among them in quantitative manners. The required steps to answer the proposed research questions is illustrated in Fig. 2.

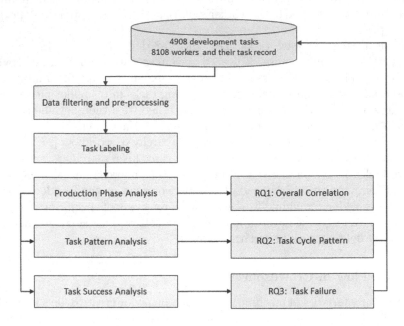

Fig. 2. Main flow of the proposed framework and relationship to research questions

To investigate the evaluation framework, the following research questions were formulated and studied in this paper:

1. *RQ1 (Overall Correlation)*: How does different task production phases correlate with task success?
   This research question aims at providing general overview of task success per software production phases in CSD platform;
2. *RQ2 (Task Cycle Pattern)*: Is there any task cycle pattern in CSD?
   Understanding task cycle patterns in CSD can be good measure to indicate project success;
3. *RQ3 (Task Failure)*: How does different task cycle patterns impact task Failure?
   The ratio of receiving not valid submission per task phase per task cycle pattern represents task success per identified task cycle.

3.2   Dataset

The dataset from TopCoder contains 403 individual projects including 4,907 component development tasks (ended up with 4,770 after removing tasks with incomplete information) and 8,108 workers from January 2014 to February 2015 (14 months). Tasks are uploaded as competitions in the platform, where Crowd software workers would register and complete the challenges. On average, most of the tasks have a life cycle of one and half months from first day of registration to the submission's deadline. When the workers submit the final files, it will be reviewed by experts to check the results and grant the scores.

The dataset contains tasks attributes such as technology, platform, task description, monetary prize, days to submit, registration date, submission date, and the time-period (month) on which the task was launched in the platform. Then, we used expert based method and labeled associated phase with each tasks. The tasks attributes used in the analysis are presented in top section of Table 1.

Moreover, Topcoder clustered different task type to 7 groups as bellow:

1. *First2Finish*: The first person to submit passing entry wins
2. *Assembly Competition*: Assemble previous tasks
3. *Bug Hunt*: Find and fix available Bugs
4. *Code*: Programming specific task
5. *UI Prototype*: User Interface prototyping is an analysis technique in which users are actively involved in the mocking-up of the UI for a system.
6. *Architecture*: This contest asks competitors to define the technical approach to implement the requirements. The output is a technical architecture document and finalized a plan for assembly contests.
7. *Test Suit*: Competitors produce automated test cases to validate the quality, accuracy, and performance of applications. The output is a suite of automated test cases.

4   Empirical Results

Overall Correlation (RQ1). It is reported that CSD platforms are following waterfall development model [27]. Therefore, all tasks in the platform will follow development phases of Requirements, Design, Implementation, Testing, and Maintenance one after the other. Figure 3 presents the distribution of failure ratio for different task types per task phase in the task life cycle.

As it is shown in Fig. 3, First2Finish cluster contains tasks from all different development phase. Highest task failure takes place in the implementation and testing phase with 64% and 23% respectively, while design and requirement are sharing less than 5% of task failure each. One reason can be a lower number of the available task in these phases. Interestingly maintenance is holding 7% of task failure in the platform. First2Finish tasks can be assigned to all different phases. As it is shown in Fig. 3, 90% of task failure in maintenance and 57% of task failure in testing phase belong to this task type. While in implementation, only 6% of task failure is under First2Finish task type, and interestingly 60% of task failure happens in assembly tasks.

Table 1. Summary of metrics definition

Metrics	Definition
Task registration start date (TR)	The first day of task arrival in the platform and when workers can start registering for it (mm/dd/yyyy)
Task submission end date (TS)	Deadline by which all workers who registered for task have to submit their final results (mm/dd/yyyy)
Task registration end date (TRE)	The last day that a task is available to be registered for (mm/dd/yyyy)
Monetary Prize (MP)	Monetary prize (USD) offered for completing the task and is found in task description. Range: $(0, \infty)$
Technology (Tech)	Required programming language to perform the task. Range: $(0, \# \text{ Tech})$
Platforms (PLT)	Number of platforms used in task. Range: $(0, \infty)$
Task Status	Completed or failed tasks
# Registration (R)	Number of registrants that sign up to compete in completing a task before registration deadline. Range: $(0, \infty)$
# Submissions (S)	Number of submissions that a task receives before submission deadline. Range: $(0, \# \text{ registrants}]$
# Valid Submissions (VS)	Number of submissions that a task receives by its submission deadline that have passed the peer review. Range: $(0, \# \text{ registrants}]$

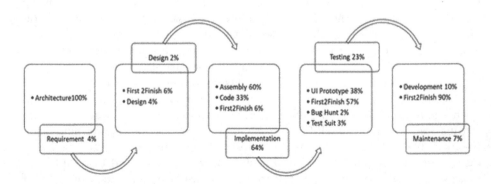

Fig. 3. Distribution of task failure ratio among different development phase in task lifecycle

Task Cycle Pattern (RQ2). Waterfall development model in CSD makes each batch of tasks be always from a prior batch and a fresh batch. Following this sequence of task arrival we identified four cluster of task cycle patterns per project in CSD. In this study, the patterns are named as four clusters of Prior Cycle, Current Cycle, Orbit Cycle and fresh Cycle, which are defined as below:

1. *Current Cycle* is the batch of tasks that are scheduled to complete following the initial task life cycle.
2. *Prior Cycle* is the batch of tasks that went into task life cycle before the batch of current cycle arrives at the platform.
3. *Fresh cycle* is the batch of tasks that will start their life cycle after the current cycle arrives at the platform.
4. *Orbit Cycle* is the batch of tasks that all following the same development phase in the task life cycle.

Figure 4 presents the summary of task cycles in a CSD platform.

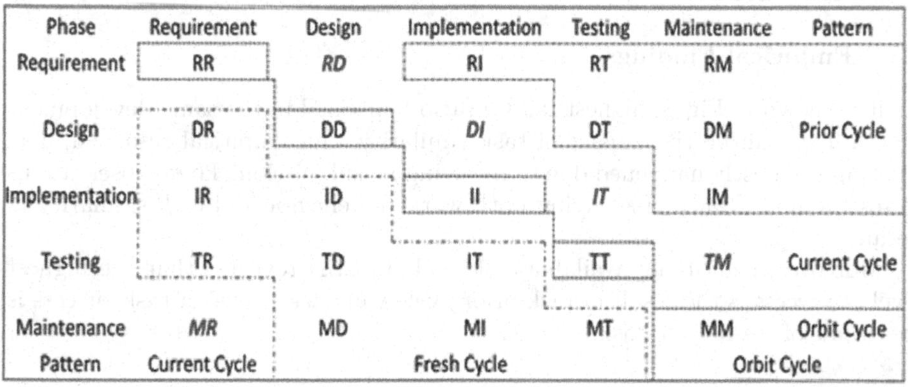

Phase	Requirement	Design	Implementation	Testing	Maintenance	Pattern
Requirement	RR	RD	RI	RT	RM	
Design	DR	DD	DI	DT	DM	Prior Cycle
Implementation	IR	ID	II	IT	IM	
Testing	TR	TD	IT	TT	TM	Current Cycle
Maintenance	MR	MD	MI	MT	MM	Orbit Cycle
Pattern	Current Cycle		Fresh Cycle		Orbit Cycle	

Fig. 4. Summary of task cycle in CSD projects

Task Failure (RQ3). Our analysis shows that on average 44% of tasks in Topcoder are in Fresh Cycle while only 4% of tasks are in the Prior cycle. Also, only 15% of tasks are in Current Cycle and 37% of tasks are in Orbit Cycle. 18% and 20% of task failure is respectively associated with Orbit Cycle and Fresh Cycle. Figure 5 illustrates the details of task failure pattern in different task cycles.

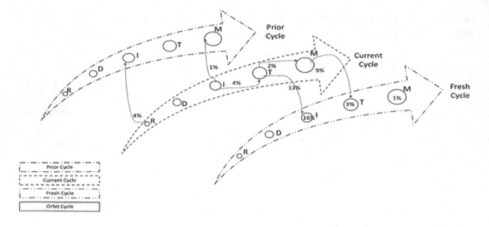

Fig. 5. Task Failure Pattern In Different Task Cycle

5 Discussion

5.1 Empirical Findings

As it is shown in Fig. 3, highest failure ratio happened in the same development phase. This can be the impact of task similarity. Our empirical result support that failure mostly happened due to receiving no submission. These observations raises the importance of studying both workers behavior and task similarity in details.

Moreover, identifying available task cycle in CSD revealed that the highest level of success is the result of task prior cycle while least level of task success is the result of fresh cycle task.

5.2 Threats to Validity

First, the study only focuses on competitive CSD tasks on the TopCoder platform. Many more platforms do exist, and even though the results achieved are based on a comprehensive set of about 5,000 development tasks, the results cannot be claimed to be externally valid. There is no guarantee the same results would remain exactly the same in other CSD platforms.

Second, there are many different factors that may influence task success, and task completion. Our task failure probability-focused approach is based on known task attributes in TopCoder. Different task failure probability-focused approaches may lead us to different, but similar results.

Third, the result is based on tasks description and completion only. Project level description and limitations are not considered in this research. In the future, we need to add this level of research to the existing one.

6   Conclusion and Future Work

To understand the probability of a tasks success in a crowdsource platform, one should understand the task cycle patterns in the platform. This research investigated available task cycle patterns in CSD. Then analyzed tasks failure ratio in both software production phase and identified task cycle.

This study identified four patterns for sequence of task arrival per project: 1) Prior Cycle, 2) Current Cycle, 3) Orbit Cycle and 4) Fresh Cycle. The empirical analysis support that the prior cycle led to the lowest task failure of 4% while fresh cycle resulted n the highest level of task failure (i.e. 44%).

In future, we would like to use the identified task cycle and test them via crowdsourced task scheduling methods.

References

1. Alelyani, T., Mao, K., Yang, Y.: Context-centric pricing: early pricing models for software crowdsourcing tasks. In: Proceedings of the 13th International Conference on Predictive Models and Data Analytics in Software Engineering, pp. 63–72 (2017)
2. Archak, N.: Money, glory and cheap talk: analyzing strategic behavior of contestants in simultaneous crowdsourcing contests on topcoder. com. In: Proceedings of the 19th International Conference on World Wide Web, pp. 21–30 (2010)
3. Bernstein, M.S., Brandt, J., Miller, R.C., Karger, D.R.: Crowds in two seconds: enabling realtime crowd-powered interfaces. In: Proceedings of the 24th Annual ACM Symposium on User Interface Software and Technology, pp. 33–42 (2011)
4. Difallah, D.E., Demartini, G., Cudré-Mauroux, P.: Scheduling human intelligence tasks in multi-tenant crowd-powered systems. In: Proceedings of the 25th International Conference on World Wide Web, pp. 855–865 (2016)
5. Faradani, S., Hartmann, B., Ipeirotis, P.G.: What's the right price? Pricing tasks for finishing on time. In: Workshops at the Twenty-Fifth AAAI Conference on Artificial Intelligence (2011)
6. Gordon, G.: A general purpose systems simulation program. In: Proceedings of the December 12–14, 1961, Eastern Joint Computer Conference: Computers-key to Total Systems Control, pp. 87–104 (1961)
7. Howe, J.: Crowdsourcing: How the power of the crowd is driving the future of business. Random House (2008)
8. Jiang, H., Matsubara, S.: Efficient task decomposition in crowdsourcing. In: Dam, H.K., Pitt, J., Xu, Y., Governatori, G., Ito, T. (eds.) PRIMA 2014. LNCS (LNAI), vol. 8861, pp. 65–73. Springer, Cham (2014). https://doi.org/10.1007/978-3-319-13191-7_6
9. Khanfor, A., Yang, Y., Vesonder, G., Ruhe, G., Messinger, D.: Failure prediction in crowdsourced software development. In: 2017 24th Asia-Pacific Software Engineering Conference (APSEC), pp. 495–504. IEEE (2017)
10. Khazankin, R., Psaier, H., Schall, D., Dustdar, S.: QoS-based task scheduling in crowdsourcing environments. In: Kappel, G., Maamar, Z., Motahari-Nezhad, H.R. (eds.) ICSOC 2011. LNCS, vol. 7084, pp. 297–311. Springer, Heidelberg (2011). https://doi.org/10.1007/978-3-642-25535-9_20
11. Lakhani, K.R., Garvin, D.A., Lonstein, E.: Topcoder (a): Developing software through crowdsourcing. Harvard Business School General Management Unit Case (610–032) (2010)

12. LaToza, T.D., Van Der Hoek, A.: Crowdsourcing in software engineering: models, motivations, and challenges. IEEE Softw. **33**(1), 74–80 (2015)
13. Mao, K., Capra, L., Harman, M., Jia, Y.: A survey of the use of crowdsourcing in software engineering. J. Syst. Softw. **126**, 57–84 (2017)
14. Mao, K., Yang, Y., Li, M., Harman, M.: Pricing crowdsourcing-based software development tasks. In: 2013 35th International Conference on Software Engineering (ICSE), pp. 1205–1208. IEEE (2013)
15. Marcus, A., Wu, E., Karger, D., Madden, S., Miller, R.: Human-powered sorts and joins. arXiv preprint arXiv:1109.6881 (2011)
16. Mejorado, D.M., Saremi, R., Yang, Y., Ramirez-Marquez, J.E.: Study on patterns and effect of task diversity in software crowdsourcing. In: Proceedings of the 14th ACM/IEEE International Symposium on Empirical Software Engineering and Measurement (ESEM), pp. 1–10 (2020)
17. Mingozzi, A., Maniezzo, V., Ricciardelli, S., Bianco, L.: An exact algorithm for the resource-constrained project scheduling problem based on a new mathematical formulation. Manag. Sci. **44**(5), 714–729 (1998)
18. Ngo-The, A., Ruhe, G.: Optimized resource allocation for software release planning. IEEE Trans. Softw. Eng. **35**(1), 109–123 (2008)
19. Reinertsen, D.G.: Celeritas publishing (2009)
20. Ruhe, G., Saliu, M.O.: The art and science of software release planning. IEEE Softw. **22**(6), 47–53 (2005)
21. Saremi, R.: A hybrid simulation model for crowdsourced software development. In: Proceedings of the 5th International Workshop on Crowd Sourcing in Software Engineering, pp. 28–29 (2018)
22. Saremi, R., Lotfalian Saremi, M., Desai, P., Anzalone, R.: Is this the right time to post my task? an empirical analysis on a task similarity arrival in topcoder. In: Yamamoto, S., Mori, H. (eds.) HCII 2020. LNCS, vol. 12185, pp. 96–110. Springer, Cham (2020). https://doi.org/10.1007/978-3-030-50017-7_7
23. Saremi, R., Yang, Y., Khanfor, A.: Ant colony optimization to reduce schedule acceleration in crowdsourcing software development. In: Yamamoto, S., Mori, H. (eds.) HCII 2019. LNCS, vol. 11570, pp. 286–300. Springer, Cham (2019). https://doi.org/10.1007/978-3-030-22649-7_23
24. Saremi, R.L., Yang, Y., Ruhe, G., Messinger, D.: Leveraging crowdsourcing for team elasticity: an empirical evaluation at topcoder. In: 2017 IEEE/ACM 39th International Conference on Software Engineering: Software Engineering in Practice Track (ICSE-SEIP), pp. 103–112. IEEE (2017)
25. Saremi, R.L., Yang, Y.: Dynamic simulation of software workers and task completion. In: 2015 IEEE/ACM 2nd International Workshop on CrowdSourcing in Software Engineering, pp. 17–23. IEEE (2015)
26. Saremi, R.L., Yang, Y.: Empirical analysis on parallel tasks in crowdsourcing software development. In: 2015 30th IEEE/ACM International Conference on Automated Software Engineering Workshop (ASEW), pp. 28–34. IEEE (2015)
27. Stol, K.J., Fitzgerald, B.: Two's company, three's a crowd: a case study of crowdsourcing software development. In: Proceedings of the 36th International Conference on Software Engineering, pp. 187–198 (2014)
28. Surowiecki, J.: The wisdom of crowds. Anchor (2005)
29. Urbaczek, J., Saremi, R., Saremi, M.L., Togelius, J.: Scheduling tasks for software crowdsourcing platforms to reduce task failure. arXiv preprint arXiv:2006.01048 (2020)

30. Wang, H., Ren, Z., Li, X., Jiang, H.: Solving team making problem for crowdsourcing with evolutionary strategy. In: 2018 5th International Conference on Dependable Systems and Their Applications (DSA), pp. 65–74. IEEE (2018)
31. Yang, Y., Karim, M.R., Saremi, R., Ruhe, G.: Who should take this task? dynamic decision support for crowd workers. In: Proceedings of the 10th ACM/IEEE International Symposium on Empirical Software Engineering and Measurement, pp. 1–10 (2016)
32. Yang, Y., Saremi, R.: Award vs. worker behaviors in competitive crowdsourcing tasks. In: 2015 ACM/IEEE International Symposium on Empirical Software Engineering and Measurement (ESEM), pp. 1–10. IEEE (2015)
33. Yue, T., Ali, S., Wang, S.: An evolutionary and automated virtual team making approach for crowdsourcing platforms. In: Li, W., Huhns, M.N., Tsai, W.-T., Wu, W. (eds.) Crowdsourcing. PI, pp. 113–130. Springer, Heidelberg (2015). https://doi.org/10.1007/978-3-662-47011-4_7

Can Community Point System Promote the Interaction Between Residents?

Yurika Shiozu[1]($\boxtimes$), Mizuki Tanaka[2], Ryo Shioya[2], and Katsunori Shimohara[2]

[1] Kyoto Sangyo University, Kyoto 603-8555, Japan
yshiozu@cc.kyoto-su.ac.jp
[2] Graduate School of Science and Engineering, Doshisha University,
Kyotanabe 610-0394, Japan

Abstract. Community currency was used throughout the world in the 1990s and 2000s, and is once again attracting attention. Today there is renewed interest in it as a digital community currency. Whether digital or not, most community currencies have two main purposes: to promote interaction between residents and to stimulate consumption within a region. To achieve both purposes is not easy. In this paper, we focus on the former, namely, to promote interaction between residents. To examine the effect of community currency, we built our original Gift and Circulation model as a community point system and performed a multi-agent simulation and social experiment. Based on the data of the social experiment, we considered the conditions for promoting donation by conditional logit analysis. The analysis confirmed that receiving from other participants strongly encourages donation behavior. Compare with the results of simulation, it suggests that the parameter of donation will be a key factor of the community point system.

Keywords: Gift and circulation model · Conditional logit · Community point system

1 Introduction

Community currency was used throughout the world in the 1990s and 2000s, and is once again attracting attention. Today there is renewed interest in it as a digital community currency. Whether digital or not, most community currencies have two main purposes: to promote interaction between residents and to stimulate consumption within a region. To achieve the two purposes, it is necessary to limit currency acquisition method and the range of use. The acquisition method is based on shopping at a private store or doing volunteer work within the same region; the range of usage is that one can only use the currency to pay for a service, such as housework or buy a commodity at private store. Since the purpose of community currency is to stimulate consumption within a region, the commodity that can be exchanged using a community currency is limited, making it unattractive to users from other regions. For a community currency that is expected to promote consumption within a region to be sustainable, someone must pay the discount amount.

S. Yamamoto and H. Mori (Eds.): HCII 2021, LNCS 12766, pp. 312–325, 2021.
https://doi.org/10.1007/978-3-030-78361-7_23

A previous study, other than the case study [2], described values such as altruism, reciprocity, and attachment to the community that would influence participation in volunteer activities using gaming and multi-agent simulation (MAS). The results clarified that with value change through the mediation of currency, the participation rate of volunteer activities is improved and it leads to an increase in purchasing behavior in the region. In addition, according to an analysis by agent-based model simulation [3], it is said that the increase in self-efficacy raises normative awareness and the surrounding people also participate in local community activities.

As previous studies have shown, it is useful to first change people's values, reshape the community, and then stimulate consumption through the introduction of a community currency. However, it is not easy to encourage interaction among local residents or to change behaviors and values. In recent years, research results in behavioral economics have shown that nudge can be used to encourage environmentally friendly behavior. However, it cannot be said that sufficient research has been accumulated on promoting interaction between local resident.

In our previous study, using MAS, we showed that a regional point system based on our own Gift and Circulation model (hereinafter referred to as GC model) promotes interaction between residents. The purpose of this paper is to verify whether the GC model, through a regional point system, would work well as a social experiment. As a result of the verification, it became clear that the probability of an occurrence of interaction between residents differed from the assumption of the GC model, and that the mechanism for promoting interaction did not function as intended. Based on the verification results, we will propose improvements to the GC model.

This paper consists of the following sections: Sect. 2 introduces the concept of the GC model and the results of the MAS; Sect. 3 presents an overview of the social experiment; in Sect. 4 we analyze the data of the social experiment using conditional logit; and in Sect. 5 we describe the conclusions and remarks.

2 Overview of Gift and Circulation (GC) Model

2.1 Structure of GC Model

The GC model is a simulation model which [4] developed. In the GC Model, participants gain relationality assets by interacting with people. Relationality assets have the function of visualizing the connections between people, but unlike currency, they do not have the function of exchanging goods and services. In economics, currency is defined as having three functions: a value exchange function, a storage function, and a calculation function. So a relationality asset is not a currency. Many commercial points, although more limited than currency, have a value exchange function and can be regarded as a pseudo-currency. In other words, a characteristic of relationality assets is that they do not have a value exchange function. In general, as game scores also do not have the value exchange function, relationality assets are like game scores.

The GC model consists of two departments: an individual (hereinafter referred to as an Agent) and a local government (hereinafter referred to as the Public Account).

Agents can acquire relationality assets by meeting and talking with other Agents, making phone calls and sending emails, and receive relationality assets from others.

Immutable attributes affect the number of relationality assets that can be acquired by acting on the length of stay and the number of steps in an area. It is assumed that all agents donate their points at the end of every period, however, the variable nature affects the number of relationality assets donated to others. In other words, the probability of donation is 100%.

The Public Account is responsible for visualizing the number of relationality assets of agents and other Public Accounts, and redistributing a certain percentage of the relationality assets accumulated in the Public Account to Agents. Figure 1 illustrates the relationship between *Agent A*, *Agent B*, and *Public Account*. Agent A and Agent B represent individuals with different attributes and personalities. Each Agent earns the relationality assets by interacting with other Agents. In Fig. 1, it is expressed as *Earnings*.

The GC model assumes the donation of relationality assets between agents. In Fig. 1, the arrow from Agent A to Agent B is displayed as a *Gift*. As for how much to donate, the model assumes that some of the relationality assets that agents own will be given in random proportions. The Gift rate is determined by a random value that follows a normal distribution based on 30%. The GC model assumes that agents always make a donation to another agent every day. This means that participants must communicate with each other once a day through the points system. And the same number of relationality assets donated between agents is stored virtually in the Public Account. In Fig. 1, it is indicated by an arrow labeled *Virtually Pooled* from below the Gift toward the Public Account. In this paper, for convenience, one step is referred to as one day. After seven steps, a proportion of the virtually stored points is redistributed to each agent. In Fig. 1 it is indicated by an arrow labeled Redistribution, and the redistribution rate is defined as Eq. (1), where x denotes the balance of the Public Account.

$$redistibution\ rate = 0.4(1 - e^{1.5*10^{-5}x}) \tag{1}$$

In this paper, for convenience, one step is referred to as one day and seven steps are referred to as one week.

At the end of t-week, the balance of the Public Account is represented by the following equation.

$$Public\ Account_t = \sum_{t=i}^{i+7} \sum_{n=1}^{200} donation_n^i - r \cdot \sum_{t=i}^{i+7} \sum_{n=1}^{200} donation_{n=1}^i \tag{2}$$

In Eq. (2), r means redistribution rate, n denotes an individual, and i shows a day.

In addition, a certain percentage of the balance of personal account relationality assets will leak after one step. In Fig. 1, it is displayed as a liquid dripping from a cylinder (A or B). The reason for assuming a leak is to encourage Gifts to other Agents.

We adopted a MAS. The total number of Agents is 200, and the property of an Agent is assumed by combining invariant ones during the simulation period, such as age, gender, walking speed, working status, and variable ones, such as aggressiveness, respect for others, and self-efficacy. The period is 90 days. At the beginning of period, every agent has 100 points as an endowment. Equation (2) defines that $i = 1, ..., 90$ and $t = 1, ..., 12$.

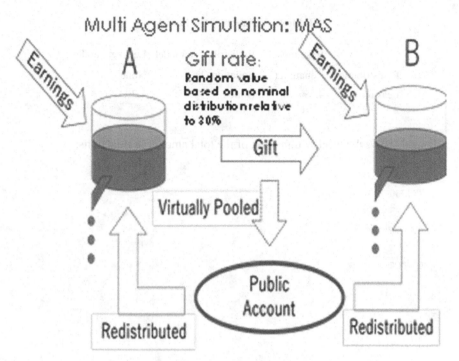

Fig. 1. Overview of the Gift and Circulation model

2.2 Result of MAS

In this paper, we assume that increasing the frequency of Gift in the GC model means revitalizing communication between the participants. Specifically, we focus on the fact that one participant's gift is another's relationality asset, and we represent the act as donation.

First, we assumed the base model. In the base model, agents always donate to one person once a day and the same number of relationality assets are stored in the Public Account. At the end of one day 4.3% of the balance of the Personal Account is leaked, and at the end of a week, a portion of the balance of the Public Account is redistributed equal in all the participants. Then we defined two variations of the base model. One is that the relationality assets of the Agent will not be leaked after the end of the day. We denoted this model as the redistribution model. The other one is that at the end of one period, 4.3% of the balance of the Personal Account leaks, and that the Public Account does not do redistribution. This model is defined as the leakage model. Table 1 shows a summary of each variation.

Table 1. Variation of GC Model

	Base model	Redistribution model	Leakage model
Redistribution	Equation (1)	Equation (1)	None
Leakage	4.3%	None	4.3%

Figure 2 shows the weekly transition of the total amount of donations.

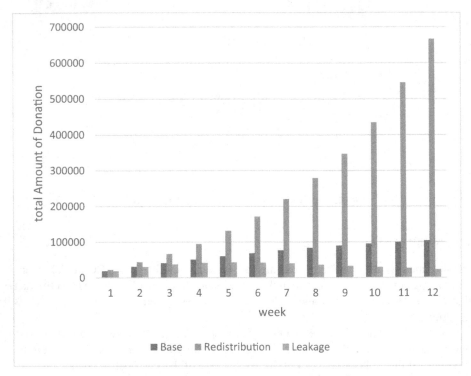

Fig. 2. Weekly transition of the total amount of donations

The total amount of donations in both the base model and the redistribution model increases over time (Fig. 2). Agents change the number of points they donate according to their personality, so the rate of change in total points for each week is not constant. Note that the simulation period is 90 days, so the 12th week is the cumulative total of donation points for 6 days. Table 2 shows the rate of change in donation points.

The rate of change in donations in the base model and the leakage model gradually decreases, however, the rate of the redistribution model has a saddle point at the 9th week.

Table 2. Percentage change in donations

Week	Base	Redistribution	Leakage
1			
2	66.7%	96.8%	63.6%
3	33.0%	51.7%	23.5%
4	23.0%	42.8%	10.8%
5	18.0%	38.1%	2.9%
6	14.3%	30.5%	−2.1%
7	11.8%	28.8%	−4.6%
8	8.8%	26.6%	−9.1%
9	7.2%	24.4%	−8.5%
10	6.4%	25.1%	−11.2%
11	4.9%	25.6%	−11.0%
12	3.8%	22.1%	−13.3%

Based on the settings, the number of points that flow into the Public Account are equal to the total number of points when the Agent makes a donation each week. As shown in Eq. (2), the week-end balance of the Public Account for week $t = (1 - r) \times$ the total number of Agent donation points in one week for week t, which is linear. Now, since r is a constant, the total of Public Accounts increases over time, but the rate of change can be said to be declining like the rate of change of donation points.

3 Social Experiment

To verify whether the point system devised by the simulation based on the GC model activates communication between local residents as intended, we conducted a social experiment.

3.1 Overview

We asked a member of Makishima Kizuna-no-kai, a non-profit organization in Kyoto prefecture in Japan, to conduct a regional point system experiment using an independently developed app[1] for 60 days from October 12, 2020 to December 12, 2020. The number of participants was 18.

The app is equipped with a point system created by simulation. At the start of the social experiment, all the participants have 100 points. As in the simulation, a percentage of individual points is lost (leaked) every day. The same number of points donated will be stored in the Public Account and after seven days, a certain percentage of the Public Account will be redistributed equally to all the participants.

---

[1] See [5] and [6] for more information on the app.

Based on the results of the preliminary experiment,[2] the following points were changed.

The leakage rate was changed from 4.3% to 5%. In addition, individuals could donate to other participants, but it was not always necessary to donate every day, and the number of points to donate could be freely decided. In other words, the probability of donation per a day was 100% or less. The redistribution rate was also changed as shown in Eq. (3), where x denotes the balance of Public Account.

$$redistribution\ rate = min(0.1 + 0.000008x, 0.4) \tag{3}$$

Table 3 summarizes the simulation and social experiment settings.

Table 3. Summary of settings

	Simulation	Social trial
Number of agents/participants	200	18
Period	90 days	60 days
Mean of earning points	Meeting another agent	Meeting another participant
	Visiting the community center	Visiting the community center
	Making a phone call	Joining the game
	Writing an email	Posting a photo
		Like on the app
		Walking
		Writing a message with donation
Leakage rate	4.3%	5%
Redistribution rate	Equation (2)	Equation (3)

3.2 Result

Figure 3 shows the daily changes in the total number of individual donation points for all participants.

---

[2] See [7] in details.

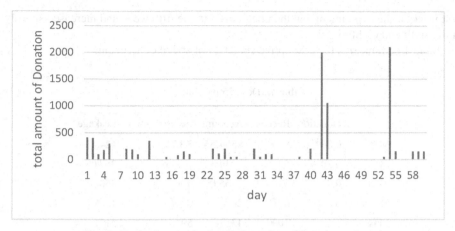

Fig. 3. Daily changes in the total number of donation points

Figure 3 shows that there were days when donations were not made. A sharp increase in the number of donation points was also observed on the 42nd, 43rd, and 54th days. From this result, it can be said that donations were concentrated on specific days rather than a certain amount of donations being generated every day.

Assuming participants were able to donate once a day, they could donate 60 times per person. Since there were 18 participants in the social experiment, the maximum number of donations that could be made was 1080. Since the number of actual donations was 66, the donation probability was about 6.1%.

Next, we confirmed the weekly transition of the total number of individual donation points in Fig. 4.

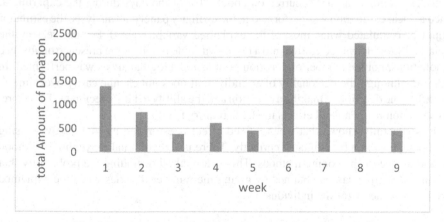

Fig. 4. Weekly changes in the total number of donation points

Note that the 9th week is the total number of donated points for 4 days because the experiment period is 60 days. Figure 4 shows that donations were actively made in the first week of the experiment, but then decreased in the fifth week and increased sharply in the sixth and eighth weeks.

Table 4 summarizes the descriptive statistics of social experiment.

Table 4. Descriptive statistics

	Donation	Receive	Account	Redistribution	Leakage
Mean	0.06	8.58	8564.55	3.15	424.44
SD	0.24	59.6	7234.13	10.06	367.08
Median	0.0	0.0	7065.0	0.0	350
Min	0	0	29	0	1
Max	1	1000	43578	59	2171
Range	1	1000	43549	59	2170
Skew	3.66	13.6	1.59	4.05	1.6
Kurtosis	11.48	214.54	3.4	17.31	3.37
SE	0.01	1.81	220.13	0.31	11.17

4 Analysis

In this section, we used panel data to confirm the factors behind the donations in the social experiment by conditional maximum likelihood logit analysis. As we saw in Sect. 3, donations had not occurred on about 94% of the days during the experiment. Since a linear estimation was performed in the ordinary panel data analysis, the estimator cannot be calculated when most of the explained variables are 0. For this reason, the explained variable was converted into a binary variable based on the presence or absence of donations, not the number of donation points, and a logit analysis was performed. In addition, although the personality of an individual does not change easily over time, it may affect the decision of making a donation and the ability to be the recipient. Therefore, an estimation using a fixed effects model is required.

It is generally known that when a fixed effect is estimated by logit analysis using panel data, it cannot be estimated correctly. There is a conditional maximum likelihood method as one of the coping methods. This is a method of finding the probability that the current sample can be obtained by giving the number of times when the explained variable becomes 1 for the individual i.

4.1 Effect of Receiving and Redistribution

When a person receives something from another person, he/she has the ability to return it to the other person. In psychology this is called the norm of reciprocity. In this social experiment, when a person receives points from another participant, it is assumed that points will be given to the donor. However, even if a participant wants to give the points, he/she cannot give them if he/she does not have a balance, so it is assumed that the balance affects the donation. First, we will verify whether donations are promoted depending on receiving. The formula is expressed by Eq. (4).

$$\log\frac{\hat{p}_t^i}{1-\hat{p}_t^i} = \alpha_i + \beta_i\,Personal\,Account + \beta_2\,receive + \beta_2\,redistribution + \varepsilon \quad (4)$$

The left side of Eq. (4) represents the odds ratio of the probability that a donation will occur, and the first term on the right side represents the intercept. *Personal Account* is the balance of the personal account, *receive* is a dummy variable for receiving the Gift, and *redistribution* is the number of redistribution points from the Public Account; ε is error term.

Suppose a participant makes a donation when his/her point balance increases, when the participant receives points from someone, or when redistributing occurs. In Eq. (4), it is assumed that the coefficients β_1 to β_3 all take positive values. The estimation results are shown in Table 5. Statistical analysis was performed with R Version 4.0.3.

Table 5. Estimation results of receiving dummy and redistribution

n=1080
number of events= 66

	coef	exp(coef)	se(coef)	z	Pr(>|z|)
Account	−2.625E-05	1.000	2.034E-05	−1.291	0.1967
Receive	2.845	17.19	0.3.416	8.328	<2e-16 ***
Redistribution	−2.030	0.1313	1.048	−1.938	0.0526+

Significance codes: 0 '***' 0.001 '**' 0.01 '*' 0.05 '+' 0.1

	exp(coef)	exp(-coef)	lower.95	upper.95
Leakage	1.0000	1.00003	0.99993	1.000
Receive	17.1943	0.05816	8.80323	33.584
Redistribution	0.1313	7.61436	0.01685	1.023

Concordance	0.7810	se=0.038	
Likelihood ratio test	89.77	on 3 df	p=<2e-16
Wald test	76.56	on 3 df	p=<2e-16
Score (logrank) test	112.20	on 3 df	p=<2e-16

Since β_2 is 2.845 and the z value is as close to 0 as possible, it is significant at the significance level of 1% or less. This means that donations are encouraged when Agents are receiving. From exp. (coef), it is also shown that the probability of donating is increased by about 17 times when there is a receiving activity. However, β_1 and β_3 are negative and the z value is not significant. That is, the balance of Personal Account and redistribution do not promote donations.

Next, the donation variable was changed to the number of points instead of the dummy to see if the number of points donated affects the donation. The estimation is the same as that of Eq. (4). The estimation results are shown in Table 6.

Table 6. Estimation results of receiving and redistribution

n=1080
number of events=66

	coef	exp(coef)	se(coef)	z	Pr(>|z|)
Account	−3.459E-05	1.000	1.802E-05	−1.919	0.05495+
Receive	0.005.009	1.005	0.001.727	2.900	0.00373 **
Redistribution	−0.2061	0.8137	0.09127	−2.258	0.02392 *

Significance codes: 0 '***' 0.001 '**' 0.01 '*' 0.05 '+' 0.1

	exp(coef)	exp(-coef)	Lower .95	Upper .95
Leakage	1.0000	1.000	0.9999	1.0000
Receive	1.0050	0.995	1.0016	1.0084
Redistribution	0.8137	1.229	0.6804	0.9731

Concordance	0.7460	se = 0.038	
Likelihood ratio test	26.64	on 3 df	p=7e-06
Wald test	12.24	on 3 df	p=0.007
Score (logrank) test	19.21	on 3 df	p=2e-04

Since β_2 is 0.005 and the z value is 0.00373, it is significant at the significance level of 1% or less. This means that donations are encouraged when there is a receiving activity. From exp. (coef.), it is also shown that receiving 1 point increases the probability of donating by about 1.005 times. Since β_1 is − 0.000003459 and the z value is 0.05495, it is significant at the significance level of 10%, and β_3 is − 0.2061 and the z value is 0.02392, which is significant at the 5% level. In other words, the individual point balance has almost no effect on donations, but redistribution has the effect of retarding donations. It shows that if 1 point is redistributed from the redistribution exp. (coef.), the probability of donating will decrease by about 20%.

4.2 Effect of Leakage and Redistribution

In the GC Model, leakage is set based on the assumption that individuals do not store points and actively donate points to others. We will verify whether leakage encourages donations with the data from social experiment in the same way as in the previous section. Since leakage is a fixed percentage of the balance of personal account, the balance of the personal account and the amount of leakage cannot be included in the estimation formula at the same time. Therefore, the personal point balance is excluded from Eq. (4) and the leakage points are substituted.

The estimation is expressed by formula (5).

$$\log \frac{\hat{p}_i^t}{1 - \hat{p}_i^t} = \alpha_i + \beta_1 \, Leakage + \beta_2 \, receive + \beta_3 \, redistribution + \varepsilon \qquad (5)$$

The left side of Eq. (5) represents the odds ratio of the probability that a donation will occur, and the first term on the right side represents the intercept, where *Leakage* is the amount of the leakage, *receive* is the amount of receiving the gift, and *redistribution* is the number of redistribution points from the Public Account, ε is error term. The estimation results are shown in Table 7.

Table 7. Estimation results of receiving and redistribution

n=1080
number of events=66

	coef	exp(coef)	se(coef)	z	Pr(>|z|)
Leakage	−0.0006843	0.9993160	0.0003500	−1.955	0.05058+
Receive	0.0050027	1.0050152	0.0017273	2.896	0.00378 **
Redistribution	−0.2069697	0.8130443	0.0915714	−2.26	0.02381 *

Significance codes: 0 '***' 0.001 '**' 0.01 '*' 0.05 '+' 0.1

	exp(coef)	exp(-coef)	lower.95	upper.95
Leakage	0.9993	1.001	0.9986	1.0000
Receive	1.0050	0.995	1.0016	1.0084
Redistribution	0.8130	1.230	0.6795	0.9729

Concordance	0.745	se=0.038	
Likelihood ratio test	26.78	on 3 df	p=7e-06
Wald test	12.36	on 3 df	p=0.006
Score (logrank) test	19.29	on 3 df	p=2e-04

Since β_2 is 0.0050027 and the z value is 0.00378, it is significant at the significance level of 1% or less. This means that donations are encouraged when there is a receiving activity. From exp (coef), it is also shown that receiving 1 point increases the probability of donating by about 1.005 times. Since β_1 is −0.0006843 and the z value is 0.05058, it is significant at the significance level of 10%, and β_3 is significant at the significance level of -0.20696971, and the z value is 0.02381 at the 5% significance level. In other words, leakage has little effect on donations, but redistribution has the effect of retarding donations. It shows that if 1 point is redistributed from the redistribution exp (coef), the probability of donating will decrease about 20%.

The results in Table 7 are consistent with the results in Table 6 because leakage is a portion of Personal Account.

5   Conclusion and Remarks

The result in Fig. 2 suggests that redistribution promotes donations. In the simulation model, it was assumed that everyone would make donations every day, and that the donation would be a certain percentage of the individual's point balance. In the redistribution-only simulation, the individual's balance can only increase, so the donation amount will increase accordingly. However, in the social experiment, each person was allowed to donate any number of points at any time, on other words, each person made a donation according to the norm of reciprocity, regardless of the balance of Personal account or point increase due to redistribution.

Considering the occurrence of donations as a Bernoulli trial, in the social experiment, 66 out of 1080 donations occurred in 60 days, so the probability of donations p is about 0.0611. At this time, assuming that the number of observation days n is sufficiently large and the donation probability is sufficiently small, the number of donations is considered to follow the Poisson distribution. If the parameter of the Poisson distribution is λ, in this case, λ is about 3.666 from $\lambda = np$. Similarly, in the simulation, λ is 90 because it is assumed that donations will occur with 100% probability in 90 days. It is known that the Poisson distribution follows the normal distribution as λ increases. In the simulation, it was assumed that donation follow the normal distribution, but in the social experiment, it should be pointed out that it may follow the Poisson distribution instead of the normal distribution.

In this paper, we defined frequent donations as active communication.

The results of social experiment clarified that the frequency of donation is not so much. Therefore, when revising the simulation model in the future, it is necessary to make improvements based on the actual donation probability.

This social experiment was done among acquaintances. Therefore, it is possible that the norm of reciprocity worked strongly. It is necessary to verify whether this GC model is a system that induces donations. In addition, the number of participants is as small as 18, and it cannot be said that it is a representative of the society. When the members are strangers or when the number of people increases, donations are not always made as in this social experiment.

Furthermore, the GC model assumes that points do not have a value exchange function. However, among community currencies, those that have almost no value exchange function have declined. The value exchange function is one of the factors that brings about utility, so this function is an important factor for a sustainable system. It is also an issue to consider assuming a point with an exchange function. In fact, points with a value exchange function are widely distributed. Even if the area that can be used is limited as seen in community currencies and the types of goods and services that can be exchanged for values are limited, when points have some economic value, it is routinely exchanged among local residents. It is not clear if the donation will be made with such community currency.

In future work, we will verify that donations will increase by refining the simulation model and explicitly incorporating a mechanism to encourage donations to the GC model, or donations between participants will be made on a daily basis even at points with a value exchange function.

Acknowledgements. The authors are grateful to the no-profit corporation Makishima Kizu-nanokai for their cooperation to the social experiment, and to Vitalify Asia Co., Ltd. for their collaboration to develop the applications.

References

1. Yosano, A., Kumano, T., Takase, T., Hayashi, N., Takano, I.: Summary Report on a Snowball Sampling Survey of Local Currency in Japan, On certain integrals of Lipschitz-Hankel type involving products of Bessel functions, Bulletein Bureau of Kansai University, Kansai Daigaku Shakaigakubu Kiyo, vol. 37, no. 3, pp. 293–317, (2006)
2. Kobayashi, S., Yoshida, M., Hashimoto, T.: Study on the mechanism of community currency circulation using gaming and multi-agent simulation. Stud. Simul. Gaming **23**(2), 1–11 (2015)
3. Yamada, H., Hashimoto, T.: Formation and expansion of community activity driven by subjective norm and self-efficacy. Trans. JSAI vol. 23, no. 2, SP-F, pp. 491–497 (2015)
4. Ogita, K., Kimura, K., Shiozu, Y., Yonezaki, K., Tanev, I., Shimohara, K.: Simulation for visualizing relationality assets in local community toward re-building of communities. In: 57th Annual Conference of the Society of Instrument and Control Engineers of Japan (SICE) 2018, pp. 670–673 (2018)
5. Shioya, R., Kimura, K., Shiozu, Y., Yonezaki, K., Tanev, I., Shimohara, K.: Regional revitalization through finding potential hazards by object detection. In: 2019 57th Annual Conference of the Society of Instrument and Control Engineers of Japan (SICE), pp. 498–502 (2019)
6. Shiozu, Y., Kimura, K., Shimohara, K., Yonezaki, K.: Relationship Between Difference of Motivation and Behavior, Human Interface and the Management of Information Part I, pp. 489–499 (2019)
7. Tanaka, M., Shioya, R., Yonezaki, K., Shiozu, Y., Tanev, I., Shimohara, K.: Visualizing relationality as assets toward communities vitalization. In: 7th IEEE CSDE 2020, the Asia-Pacific Conference on Computer Science and Data Engineering 2020, 6 pages (2020)

Research on the Smart Traditional Chinese Medicine Service System Based on Service Design

Junnan Ye[✉], Xu Liu, Jingyang Wang, Menglan Wang, and Siyao Zhu

East China University of Science and Technology, Shanghai 200237, China

Abstract. Traditional Chinese medicine (TCM) is a kind of medicine that has been passed down for thousands of years in China and is rich in cultural characteristics. Nowadays TCM is moving towards modernization and intelligence, and its status is constantly improving. Smart TCM is to realize the intellectualization of TCM diagnosis and treatment with the help of the concept and technology of smart medicine under the TCM system. However, in the process of TCM intellectualization, there are also some problems such as complicated hospital treatment process, imbalanced regional medical resources, and slow transmission of TCM knowledge.

In view of the above problems, this paper starts from the perspective of service design, and builds an ideal user behavior process in a smart TCM system with users based on the real scenario of users asking for doctors in TCM. Using the user journey graph to analyze the user's pain points and opportunities at each touch point, it is concluded that the optimization function of the smart Chinese medicine service system should have four functional modules: smart doctor, physiological test, disease feedback, and patient community. And this paper proposes the construction strategy of the service system, and finally presents the smart TCM service system design in the form of service blueprint. This research is an effective exploration of building smart TCM service system based on service design method, which has theoretical and practical significance for the future development of smart TCM.

Keywords: Smart TCM · Service design · Design methods

1   Introduction

COVID-19 is a test of a country's medical and health system. During China's fight against the epidemic, Chinese medicine has played an irreplaceable role. It is clinically verified that the combination of traditional Chinese medicine and modern medicine is effective in treating COVID-19, and the cure rate of patients may be positively correlated with the participation rate of TCM treatment [1]. In addition, studies have shown that the acceptance of TCM services among the population is relatively high, and TCM has room for development [2].

Smart TCM is an informatization upgrade of traditional Chinese medicine services. Although treatment methods are modernized, smart TCM does not abandon the characteristic thinking mode of traditional Chinese medicine holistic treatment and dialectical

S. Yamamoto and H. Mori (Eds.): HCII 2021, LNCS 12766, pp. 326–339, 2021.
https://doi.org/10.1007/978-3-030-78361-7_24

treatment. On the contrary, in the context of the current epidemic, it will promote the development of TCM and promote people's health care.

Because of its systematic characteristics, service design is very suitable for the construction of smart TCM system and create a good user experience. This study proposes a research strategy for smart TCM service system design from the perspective of service design, which has theoretical guiding significance for the future development direction of smart TCM, and also has practical guiding significance for today's epidemic prevention and control work.

2   A Summary of Smart TCM Literature

2.1   Status of Smart Chinese Medicine Platform

With the development of technology, there are more apps about smart TCM. From the data of Qimai, on the IOS platform, the number of TCM-related apps in the year from November 24, 2019 to November 24, 2020 fluctuates around 237. This paper considers downloads, application ratings and evaluations, and selects the top six smart Chinese medicine apps as the research objects: "Chinese medicine think tank", "Chinese medicine medical records", "Licorice Chinese medicine", "Xiaolu Chinese medicine", "Bailu Chinese medicine" and "Chinese medicine online". In order to make a comparison and find out the differences, this paper selects two comprehensive Internet Medical apps under the same standard, which are "Zhiyun health" and "Pingan good doctor".

Through comparative analysis, it is found that the functions of smart TCM platform are summarized as follows: information knowledge, online consultation, self-prescription, medicine mall, physique fitness test, electronic medical record and appointment registration (see Fig. 1).

APPs	Functional module							
	Information knowledge	Online consultation	Self-prescribing	Medical mall	Physical fitness test	Electronic medical record	Appointment registration	Total
Chinese medicine think tank	✓	✓	✓	✓	✗	✗	✗	4 items
Chinese medicine medical records	✓	✓	✗	✓	✗	✗	✗	3 items
Licorice Chinese medicine	✓	✓	✗	✓	✓	✗	✗	4 items
Xiaolu Chinese medicine	✗	✓	✗	✓	✗	✓	✓	4 items
Bailu Chinese medicine	✓	✓	✗	✗	✗	✓	✗	3 items
Chinese medicine online	✗	✓	✗	✗	✗	✓	✗	2 items
Zhiyun health	✓	✓	✗	✓	✓	✓	✗	5 items
Pingan good doctor	✓	✓	✗	✓	✓	✓	✓	6 items

Fig. 1.   Comparison of 8 APPs functional modules.

2.2 Existing Problems of Smart Chinese Medicine Platform

After deeply experiencing the smart TCM platform and visiting three hospitals in Shanghai, the author found that the overall service depth was not enough, and the smart TCM service system was not considered from a macro perspective, which could not meet the all-weather medical needs of users. The specific problems are shown in the following three aspects.

Hospital Treatment Process is Complex. The impact of COVID-19 has not dissipated, and the pressure on hospitals has not eased. With winter coming, the medical system will face a new round of tests. The author visited Longhua Hospital Shanghai University of Traditional Chinese Medicine, Shuguang Hospital Shanghai University of Traditional Chinese Medicine and Shanghai Hospital of traditional Chinese Medicine, and found that many management steps were added to the treatment process of each hospital under the influence of COVID-19, such as personal itinerary survey, filling in safety commitment, etc. These means of epidemic prevention and control are easy to queue up, which reduces the efficiency of patients' medical treatment and also reduces the user experience of medical consultation in low-risk areas.

Imbalance of Regional Medical Resources. As a kind of medical resources, TCM resources are also facing the problems of resource shortage and unbalanced distribution of regional resources. Hospitals have the majority of medical resources, and most hospitals with high-quality medical resources are concentrated in first-tier cities [3]. For example, comparing the resources of TCM hospitals in Shanghai and Xining City, Qinghai Province, there is a big gap in the number, level and reputation of TCM hospitals in the two places. Although the existing smart TCM platform is under the blessing of the Internet, it has expanded the scope of diagnosis and treatment of some TCM to a certain extent. However, the resources of TCM are limited, and it is still difficult to get out of the situation of "patients greater than doctors", and medical resources are still tight.

TCM Knowledge Spreads Slowly. Today's medical models mostly focus on the treatment of diseases, but the TCM's thinking on preventing diseases has not been paid attention to. The idea of "preventing disease" is one of the core theories of TCM, including three aspects: prevention before illness, prevention of transformation of existing illness, and rehabilitation after illness [4]. On the one hand, there is a lack of independent TCM health care institutions or departments, and the TCM preventive health services provided by other non-medical and health institutions also have problems such as irregularities, low quality, and single format [5]. On the other hand, the thought of preventing disease has not been popularized among the public. For a long time, people have been accustomed to the thinking of seeing a doctor only when they are ill. They have a low awareness of the thought of preventing disease and have not developed a sense of identity [6]. In the long run, it is easy to fall into a vicious circle, which is not conducive to the user experience of TCM.

2.3 Research on Related Technologies of Smart TCM

Most of the research on smart TCM focuses on the exploration of technology, including the intelligent four-diagnosis method of "seeing, hearing, asking and cutting", the establishment of TCM data sets and the application of artificial intelligence in smart TCM.In the context of technological development, the four-diagnosis technology of Chinese medicine has achieved informatization and objective application, and the hardware facilities are also developing in a more portable direction [7, 8]. Judging from the research status of intelligent four-diagnosis, it can basically meet the practical application needs of intelligent Chinese medicine.

Smart TCM also needs to use machine learning and other technologies to continuously adjust relevant plans based on changing patient conditions, which provides smart TCM with the ability to self-diagnose. Yuan Bing and others proposed to establish a data set that can be learned, through a standardized system of symptoms, signs, and detection indicators, and a unified information collection software platform for comprehensive information collection [9]. The resulting data set will become an important basis for smart Chinese medicine diagnosis. Chen Xintian and others proposed to use named entity recognition and relationship extraction technology to extract the key information of TCM text data, and use the knowledge graph to build a structured data model to reveal the dynamic laws of the medical field [10].

Artificial intelligence is the core technology of smart TCM. By using deep learning and other technologies, Qingchen Zhang and others have constructed a unified intelligent TCM framework based on edge cloud computing system to realize computer-aided syndrome differentiation and prescription recommendation, so as to provide patients with universal and personalized medical services [11].

This current situation of focusing only on technology and ignoring service design and user experience can easily cause its own market competitiveness to decline. Now, some people have explored relevant TCM services from the perspective of macro system in order to improve the user experience. Lei Hua and others have built an intelligent service platform of traditional Chinese medicine for intelligent health, which integrates the resources of hospitals, pharmacies, decocting centers, distribution centers, forms a service system of traditional Chinese medicine decocting, distribution and traceability system, and realizes the informatization, automation and standardization of TCM pharmaceutical service [12].

Although the exploration of Lei Hua and others has systematic and global thinking of service design, they did not use specific service design methods to study the relevant user needs and experience process, and did not form a specific service design research process, but this systematic thinking provides a basic idea for the construction of intelligent Chinese medicine service system.

2.4 Service Design

Service design emphasizes user-centered and user experience, and has a systematic and overall thinking. It pays more attention to the value brought by the entire service, not just the problems exposed by the technical side [13]. These concepts are in line with the development needs of the smart TCM service system that emphasizes human-computer interaction and user experience.

Service design has a certain significance for the development of smart medicine. Service design can optimize the patient treatment process and build a new interactive service platform. Liu Jun analyzed the pain points of the whole service process of Wuhan Central Hospital and proposed a self-service experience based on intelligent information terminals, which improved the efficiency of medical treatment. Service design helps smart medical to build a closed-loop service process and provide users with systematic and integrated services [14]. Lingjie Yu proposed the design of chronic disease management services in the context of smart medical care, using systematic services, visualized information, and emotional interaction to provide a new perspective for chronic disease management [15]. In the context of today's digital society, applying service design to online smart medical services can quickly and extensively improve the medical service experience that users enjoy.

There are various methods of service design, which can help researchers design and optimize a reasonable service process. Typical methods include user portraits, user journey maps, stakeholder maps, service system maps, and service blueprints. These methods can help researchers fully understand user needs, optimize user journeys, and build a holistic service experience, thereby helping smart TCM service systems reshape business processes and organizational forms.

3   Research Process

This paper puts forward the research route of smart TCM service system based on service design theory. The research route is divided into three stages: situational analysis, service innovation and design, organize implementation.

In the situational analysis stage, based on the real scenario, the stakeholders are determined, and the target user research is carried out to create an ideal behavior process with the user. In the service innovation and design stage, the user journey map method is used to analyze the pain points and opportunities to derive the function optimization plan. In the stage of organize implementation, systemic thinking is used to construct a service blueprint for a smart Chinese medicine service system (see Fig. 2).

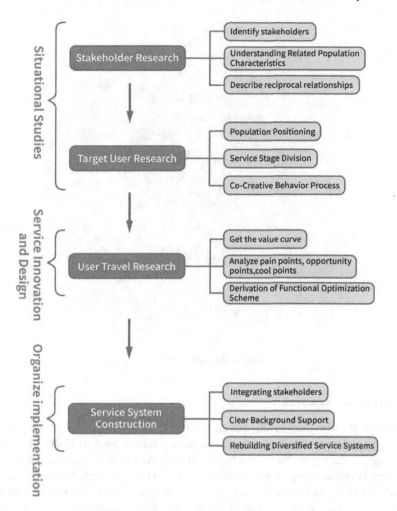

Fig. 2. Research roadmap.

4   Smart TCM Service System Based on Service Design

4.1   Stakeholder Analysis

Based on user research, combined with the functions of the existing smart TCM platform and service design concepts, this paper identifies the stakeholders of the smart TCM service system under the service design concept. The core users of the system include doctors, patients or family, and smart hardware. Other stakeholders in the system are offline medical staff, drug suppliers, courier personnel, insurance personnel, and platform operators. The core members provide users with professional services of TCM and rehabilitation guidance. Other related parties not only maintain the normal operation of the system, but also provide users with other services (see Fig. 3).

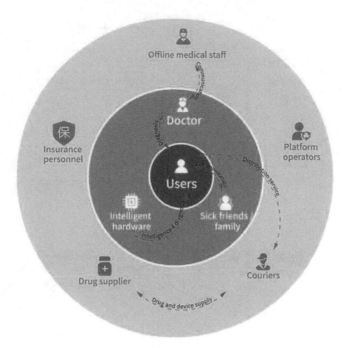

Fig. 3. Stakeholder map.

4.2 Target User Research

Target User Positioning. In this paper, the target users are young people who have a high degree of acceptance of Internet medicine. With regard to health, the trend of younger age is becoming more and more obvious. At the same time, more and more young people are showing greater interest in TCM [16]. Through the questionnaire, it is found that compared with the elderly, young people have lower satisfaction in the efficiency, convenience, and cost of TCM, and they have a higher degree of acceptance of Internet medicine. Young people have a strong interest in emerging technologies, and under the influence of COVID-19, the idea of TCM for preventing diseases has been deeply rooted in the hearts of the people. Therefore, young people are the core users of the smart TCM service system.

Co-create User Behavior Process. Designing with users is the source of service design innovation [17]. This paper selects 22 users who have a positive attitude towards Internet medical care and have offline TCM treatment experience, and their ages are distributed between 25 and 35 years old. Through user research, this paper constructs an idealized user behavior process of smart TCM service system from the perspective of sports medicine integration, which is divided into three stages: information acquisition, medical services, and self-management (see Fig. 4).

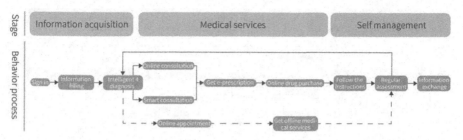

Fig. 4. Behavior flow chart.

On the one hand, the user behavior process of smart TCM service system based on service design attaches importance to the logic of online service, provides online TCM consultation service, electronic prescription and other services, and attaches importance to service feedback, thus bringing about a benign service cycle. On the other hand, it interacts with the offline hospitals to improve the offline medical experience, and integrates the intelligent hardware required by the intelligent four diagnosis into the system to build a new smart TCM service mode combining online and offline, which not only widens the service channels, but also improves its own differentiation and market competitiveness.

4.3   Target User Research

User Journey Map. Based on the co-creation of the ideal user behavior process, the user's emotional experience is depicted, and the user's pain points, opportunities points and cool points are analyzed according to each touch point (see Fig. 5).

Functional Module Optimization and Design Proposal. According to the analysis of the emotional experience curve in the user journey map, as well as the current situation of smart TCM and the content of user interviews, this paper analyzes the problems and needs of users, and puts forward the corresponding opportunity points and solutions, so as to put forward new optimization schemes on the basis of the basic function construction of the existing smart TCM service platform to increase new competitiveness.

The basic function modules include consultation knowledge, hospital service, medicine mall and health management. Consultation knowledge pushes the latest disease prevention and health knowledge for users. Hospital service is the intersection of online service and offline service. Users can book offline service at any time to get more comprehensive service and synchronize e-prescription. The medicine mall allows users to buy the medicines they need without leaving home. Health management is through the user's e-prescription to see the details and other physiological data records for later evaluation.

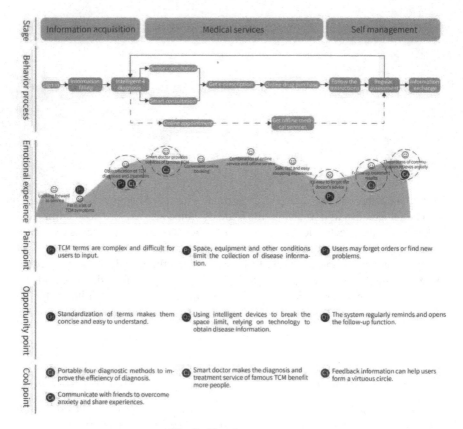

Fig. 5. User journey map.

The four new functions of smart TCM combined with service design concept are Smart Doctor, Physiological Test, Disease Feedback and Patient Community (see Fig. 6).

5   Build a Smart TCM Service System Based on Service Design

5.1   Service System Design Strategy

Guided TCM Consultation Service. The terminology of TCM embodies professionalism and history, but it also brings difficulties for users to understand, leading to poor user experience. TCM services cover a wide range and are complex. Non-professionals cannot accurately describe their needs in TCM terms, and most of them use colloquial expressions. For example, in response to common illnesses in the user's life, the app called "Zhiyun Health" uses colloquial words in the consultation service to ask users about their diseased parts, symptoms and other information, allowing users to do multiple-choice questions, reducing users' concerns, reducing the error rate of users when they input information.

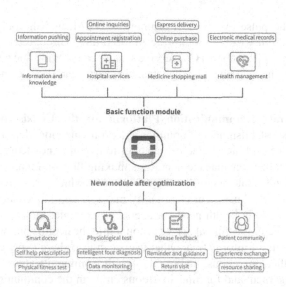

Fig. 6. Functional diagram of smart TCM service system based on service design.

Realize the Integration of Online and Offline Services. Medical services only rely on the Internet to do online services, which is easy to make the user's sense of participation is low, the channel for users to obtain services is single, and the service is difficult to innovate, and the simple online medical service is easy to make users have a sense of distrust. Therefore, we should pay attention to the offline multi scene medical and sports service experience, and realize the combination of online and offline information and contacts. For example, the app named "Xiaolu Chinese medicine" integrates the functions of online consultation and appointment registration into the doctor profile interface. Users can choose convenient online consultation services, and can also make appointment registration for offline diagnosis and treatment, so as to obtain more complete medical services under the guidance of the same doctor and ensure the fluency of the treatment process.

Technology Promotes the Development of Smart TCM. The data support of smart TCM service comes from the intelligent four diagnostic methods of "seeing, hearing, asking and cutting". With the development of technology, diagnostic instruments are developing towards the direction of portability and family. According to the research status of intelligent four diagnosis, it can basically meet the practical application needs of smart TCM. For example, the electronic nose system based on the theory of olfactory diagnosis, and the identification system of "five visceral sounds" related to acoustic diagnosis [18]. In addition, the photoelectric sensor used in the exercise bracelet has been applied in the pulse diagnosis instrument of TCM, and the pulse diagnosis is expected to achieve all-weather monitoring in the future. Through the combination of software and hardware, the smart TCM service system can provide fine medical services, and has a better monitoring effect on diabetes, coronary heart disease and other chronic diseases.

Build a Community Communication Platform for the Coexistence of Doctors and Patients. The establishment of community communication platform provides the users of smart TCM with an interactive channel to expand knowledge, exchange and share. Users can realize self-management, thus making the community social. Doctors share knowledge and refute rumors in the community, which adds professionalism to the community. This dual nature of community management mode can better meet the continuous and long-term health needs of users.For example, the app named "Pingan good doctor" introduces the official doctor account into the health community module to increase the authority of information. Other users can also share experience, emotional counseling and other operations, making the whole community more life-oriented in daily health management and forming a virtuous circle in the community.

5.2 Building Service Blueprint

Service blueprint is one of the important tools to present the results of service design. It helps service designers to sort out the basic resources and processes invisible to users through user journey map. Based on the research of idealized user behavior process and user journey map of smart TCM, this paper constructs the service blueprint of smart TCM service system from the perspective of service design (see Fig. 7).

The smart TCM service system based on service design divides the service into three stages: information acquisition, medical service, and self-management, which can provide systematic services to help users meet their daily health needs. Users can collect high-density physiological data through intelligent devices, such as temperature detection, pulse detection, and so on. Smart doctors will also feedback corresponding suggestions according to the detection results. Due to the characteristics of online and offline interconnection, the smart TCM service system will also cooperate with the hospital for rapid response, so as to deal with emergencies. The establishment of patient community is to make the smart TCM system more humanized, so that users can reflect their personal value in the process of experience sharing and medical resource sharing.

Systematic services not only expand the influence of traditional Chinese medicine, its good user experience and the backstage support from the service design make it useful for the daily management and prevention and control of diseases.

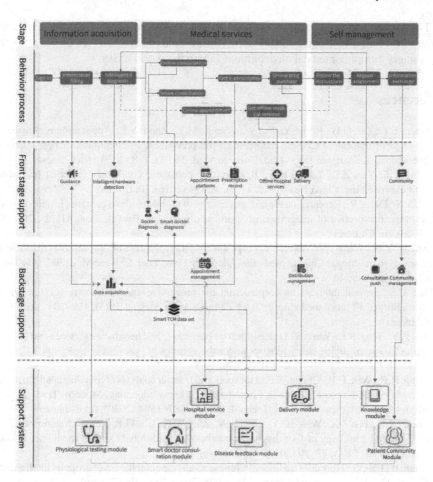

Fig. 7. Service blueprint.

6 Conclusion

With the rise of Internet medical care in recent years, people's attitudes towards Internet medical care have become more optimistic, and TCM has also ushered in a new opportunity for digital upgrade of its own services. From the perspective of service design, this paper finds that the existing smart TCM service platform has problems such as complicated hospital treatment process, imbalance of regional medical resources, and slow transmission of TCM knowledge. Based on these problems, this paper uses the method of service design to optimize the existing service system, and proposes four optimization modules: Smart Doctor, Physiological Test, Disease Feedback, and Patient community.

In the future, smart TCM should pay more attention to the combination of offline service and online service, and establish a buffer zone between users and hospitals, that is, the improvement of community TCM medical service, so as to gradually expand smart TCM users to the middle-aged and elderly groups in the future, and make them better adapt to the digital diagnosis and treatment experience provided by smart TCM.

The smart TCM service system based on service design is a new idea for the development of smart TCM and contributes a "Traditional + Modern" TCM force to the increasingly complex medical environment facing the world today.

References

1. Chen, L.L., Ge, G.B., Rong, Y., Fu, W., Zheng, M.Y., Zhao, Y.F.: Application and research progress of traditional Chinese medicine in the prevention and treatment of new coronary pneumonia. J. Shanghai Univ. Trad. Chinese Med. **34**(03), 1–8 (2020). (in Chinese)
2. Qiu, H.Z., Yan, Z.L., Liang, R.Q.: Research on consumer confidence index of traditional Chinese medicine. China Health Ind. **13**(5), 32–34 (2016). (in Chinese)
3. Li, S.X., Deng, R.: Research on the design strategy of mobile medical care for chronic diseases from the perspective of integration of sports and medicine. Packag. Eng. **41**(12), 202–206 (2020). (in Chinese)
4. Zhang, Z.B., Wang, Y.Y.: On the concept and scientific content of "preventive treatment of disease" in traditional Chinese medicine. J. Beijing Univ. Trad. Chinese Med. **30**(7), 440–444 (2007). (in Chinese)
5. Xu, L.S.: Several thoughts on constructing the preventive and health care service system of traditional Chinese medicine. J. Trad. Chinese Med. Manag. **19**(3), 199–201 (2011). (in Chinese)
6. Yu, X.Y., Tang, S.L., Wang, G.L.: Research on preventive and health care services and policies with Chinese medicine characteristics under the concept of "preventive treatment". Chinese J. Health Policy **8**(2), 71–75 (2015). (in Chinese)
7. Song, H.B., Wen, C.B., Cheng, X.E.: Hot spots and frontier analysis of four diagnostic methods of traditional Chinese medicine in China based on knowledge map. Modern. Trad. Chinese Med. Materia Medica-World Sci. Technol. **22**(5), 1587–1594 (2020). (in Chinese)
8. Wang, R.Q., Fan Z.X., Wang, C.Y., Zheng, W., Zhu, W.H., Liu, G.P.: Research status of digital acquisition technology of four diagnostic methods of traditional Chinese medicine. J. Trad. Chinese Med. **54**(1), 77–80 (2013). (in Chinese)
9. Yuan, B., Fan, G.: How does traditional Chinese medicine enter the era of artificial intelligence. China J. Trad. Chinese Med. Pharm. **33**(2), 698–703 (2018). (in Chinese)
10. Chen, X.F., Ruan, C.Y., Yu, G.Z., Zhang, Y.C.: Integrating ancient with present to build a new system of intelligent traditional Chinese medicine. Acad. J. Second Military Med. Univ. **39**(8), 826–829 (2018). (in Chinese)
11. Zhang, Q.C., Bai, C.C., Chen, Z.K., Li, P., Wang, S., Gao, H.: Smart Chinese medicine for hypertension treatment with a deep learning model. J. Netw. Comput. Appl. **129**, 1–8 (2019)
12. Hua, L., Ma, Y., Meng, X., Xu, B., Qi, J.: A Smart health-oriented traditional Chinese medicine pharmacy intelligent service platform. In: Wang, H., Siuly, S., Zhou, R., Martin-Sanchez, F., Zhang, Y., Huang, Z. (eds.) HIS 2019. LNCS, vol. 11837, pp. 23–34. Springer, Cham (2019). https://doi.org/10.1007/978-3-030-32962-4_3
13. Wang, G.S.: Service Design and Innovation, 2nd edn. China Architecture & Building Press, Beijing (2015). (in Chinese)
14. Liu, J., Liu, Q., Liu, Q.Q.: Research on the design of medical self-service based on smart medicine: a case study of Wuhan Central Hospital. J. Zhuangshi (12), 74–75 (2016). (in Chinese)
15. Yu, L.J., Zhang, X.: Research on the design of chronic disease health management service in the context of smart medicine. J. Des. (21), 56–58 (2018). (in Chinese)
16. Zhu, Z.X., Liu, Y.M., Liu, J.: Review of empirical research on mobile medical user adoption behavior. Sci. Technol. Manag. Res. **40**(22), 206–213 (2020). (in Chinese)

17. Huang, W.: Revolution Driven by Service Design: The Secret of User Following, 1st edn. China Machine Press, Beijing (2019). (in Chinese)
18. Wang, Y.Q., Li, F.F., Yan, H.X., Yao, D.: Review on the research status of digitalization of four diagnostic information of traditional Chinese medicine. Modern. Trad. Chinese Med. Materia Medica-World Sci. Technol. (3), 96–101 (2007). (in Chinese)

A Scenario-Based, Self-taught and Collaborative System for Human-Centered and Innovative Solutions

Der-Jang Yu[1,2(✉)], Wen-Chi Lin[1,2], Meng-Yu Wun[1,2], Tian Yeu Tiffany Lee[1,2], and Tao-Tao Yu[1,2]

[1] Providence University, 200, Sec. 7, Taiwan Boulevard, Shalu Dist., Taichung City 43301, Taiwan, R.O.C.
djyu@scenariolab.com.tw
[2] Scenariolab, Room 914, Innovation and Development Building, Tsinghua University, No. 101, Section 2, Guangfu Road, Hsinchu 30013, Taiwan, R.O.C.

Abstract. This article proposes a scenario-based, self-taught and collaborative system to assist an innovation team to perform design projects robustly. This system transforms the innovation process into a collection of screen-based storyboards consist of the facilitator, design method-induced tools, environment and activities. This system also includes: 1) a set of modular courses that follow the design process of start-adapt-evolve-conclude, based on narrative in Chinese literature, 2) a modular space that is constructed the same scene as in the storyboard, and 3) a quantitative and qualitative evaluation mechanism. Through this system, the innovation team can engage in the collaborative activities and innovate together seamlessly. This method has been used by nearly 100 persons, and the users' evaluation feedback of the innovation output is exceedingly positive, and the evaluation mechanism also provides new insights for continuous improvemens. This modular system has been proven effective in helping design teams more freely use proper methods to explore different innovative touch points, and to further inquire more human-centered design realms in the future.

Keywords: Scenario-based design · Human-centered design · Design thinking · Co-creation · Design method · Activity theory

1 Background

Human-centered design is nowadays a structured process widely used to guide teams at various scales to innovate. In human-centered design process, the two major activities are facilitating the process and designing innovative solutions, which are the responsibilities of the facilitator and the design participants. The facilitator guides the participants to enter the design context with pre-selected design methods, such as observation, affinity wall, customer journey, and paper prototypes, etc. Within this context, the participants as designers can share new ideas, generate insights, and build prototypes. A designer's goal is to come up with innovative solutions, whereas the facilitator's goal is to focus on

© Springer Nature Switzerland AG 2021
S. Yamamoto and H. Mori (Eds.): HCII 2021, LNCS 12766, pp. 340–349, 2021.
https://doi.org/10.1007/978-3-030-78361-7_25

ensuring the process proceed smoothly throughout the design workshop. In an optimal situation, empowering designers with effective guidance from the facilitator will produce promising solutions in this collaborative process [1].

In the real world, guest facilitators outside of a team do not possess the knowledge the designer team has acquired in their practice. This condition prevents facilitators from being fully engaged in the activities. On the other hand, if the designers serve as facilitators, they might not be as familiar with the methods as the facilitator. Additionally, the designers may have the difficulty in seeing the big picture as they may be constrained by their own perspectives.

The activity theory provides a framework to understand the dilemma in the scenario mentioned above [2]. In an activity in which a facilitator and designers cooperate, the designers' goal is to use appropriate methods in different stages in the human-centered design process to come up with creative solutions. Whereas, the facilitator's goal is to manage time and to ensure the fluency and productivity of the innovation process. The facilitator, who resembles the director of the team, proposes appropriate methods and controls the rhythm to guide the designers throughout the design process. The activity theory illustrates the competing goals between the designer and the facilitator (as shown in the Fig. 1 below).

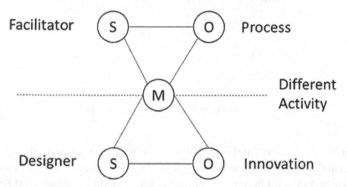

Fig. 1. The activity theory illustrates the difference in objects and goals between designer and facilitator using same mediator/method. S means Subject, O means object, M means Mediator.

2   A Scenario-Based, Self-taught and Collaborative System

In order to address the above-mentioned issues, in this ongoing research we propose a collaborative system based on self-learning and teamwork approaches to drive innovation. Through the assistance of the system, the team members can adopt different mindsets of the facilitator and designers and switch between the two roles.

The system includes two components: 1) a storyboard projected on a computer screen, which includes a fictional narrator acting as a facilitator, 2) a physical space that enables designers to collaborate and co-create, and 3) a quantitative and qualitative evaluation mechanism. A group of four to six designers would enter the modular space (as shown in the Fig. 2 and Fig. 3 below) and go through the design process using the storyboard.

Fig. 2. The story board of facilitating scenario for co-creation process.

Fig. 3. The modular space for co-creation process.

The storyboard can be categorized into three main scenes: activity scene, action scene [3, 4], and activating scene (as shown in the Fig. 4 below). In the activity scene, a team of designers would be introduced to the set of methods preselected for the team and familiarize themselves with the purpose of the methods. The action scene would lay out the step-by-step instructions on how the designers might carry out the activities. After understanding the methods, the designers would enter the activating scene where they will conduct hands-on activities and produce innovative solutions in the real-life physical environment that is set up to mirror the storyboards on the computer screen.

In this system, since the physical environment mirrors the storyboard displayed in the digital screen, the participants can switch over between the digital storyboard and the physical environment (see Fig. 5,) to gain clarifications on the design methods and to carry out the tasks they have been instructed to assume. Accordingly, the participants can smoothly transition between the roles of a facilitator and a designer.

Activity Scene   **Action Scene**   **Activating Scene**

Fig. 4. Activity scene for purpose and method, action scene for step-by step operations, and activating scene to start the real action.

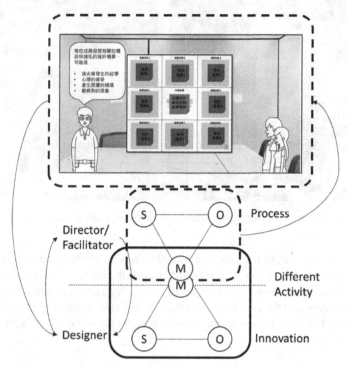

Fig. 5. The physical environment mirrors the storyboard environment provided on the digital screen enabling user to carry out the task.

3 Self-taught and Co-creation Activity

In actual operations, we found many new human-computer interaction behaviors, such as Fig. 6, from left top left of the activity photos, members of a team will watch the storyboards on the screen, and then start to work; after a period of time, some members will naturally volunteer to assume the roles of the characters in the storyboards. In the top right picture, for example, the member on the left in front of the screen will naturally read the instructions in the dialog boxes on the screen. He was actually imitating unconsciously and internalizing the behaviors of the virtual facilitator; on the lower left picture, the members will cooperate with the instructions on the screen, and then in real space, execute the behavior of the storyboards on the screen; and finally make unique innovations under the guidance of the storyboards, such as a digital media prototype made by the members, displayed on the lower right photo.

Fig. 6. Human-computer interaction of self-taught and collaborative behaviors

This self-taught system uses the storyboards, the virtual characters inside, and the same environment as the one on the screen for enacting the scenes, allowing the operating members to internalize the innovation process naturally and seamlessly through role-playing themselves into the characters and the team. Figure 7 shows the behavior of the team to record their final presentation, which is exactly the same as the behavior of the storyboard on the screen.

Fig. 7. The behavior of the team, which is exactly the same as the behavior of the storyboard on the screen.

One of the characteristics of this method is that members use their narrative ability to replicate the entire process [5, 6], while at the same time using another ability to innovate, as if we are running forward with our feet while throwing the ball into the basket with our hands. There is no conflict in the fluent attention switching of the mind.

Another feature is the set of virtual storyboards from the screen, which trigger a series of similar activities aimed at innovation in the physical space. Conversely, the innovative activities carried out by the members in this space can also help improve the efficacy of the virtual storyboards in the screen. How? Their ratings can be useful guide and reference for future participants to select the proper design methods available on the system. Just as the Chinese proverb goes, "Zhuang Zhou dreams of butterflies, butterfly dreams of Zhuang Zhou", this mutually reinforcing feature can be established by the measured data of selected methods and innovative output, so that the two worlds are more closely integrated.

4   Modular and Analyzable Courses

The system currently provides modular courses. Each course is based on a narrative structure, Start, Adapt, Evolve, Conclude, or Kishōtenketsu, the 4-element structure and development of classic Chinese narratives [7–9]. The preliminary plan we provide includes four courses and a total of 16 design methods.

This system is being implemented as curriculum and tested at Tsinghua University in Taiwan, and 99 users include undergraduate students, graduate students, and startup teams. Participants evaluate others' design outcomes in terms of usefulness, ease of use and novelty. The evaluation results are not unexpectedly positive scores around 3–4 out of 1 to 5 scale, shown on the Table 1. The results confirm that the teams have benefited from the outcomes to attain innovation they need. It is worth emphasizing that these outcomes are from each team's self-learning and co-creation activities, without any real facilitator's guidance.

Table 1. The evaluation result of the design outcomes.

Lesson ╲ feature	Useful	Easy to use	Novel
L1, Theme and scene	3.8	3.8	3.6
L2, Users and prototypes	3.5	3.5	3.6
L3, Value and presentation	3.4	3.0	3.6
L4, Experience and journey	3.3	3.4	3.4

The teams also evaluated the guidance methods in terms of usefulness, ease of use, and novelty, and most of the methods are above four out of 5, shown on the Table 2. This is not surprising, because these methods are effective and innovative methods that have been carefully selected for each individual team's needs. Among them, each star indicates the highest score for usefulness, ease of use, and novelty at each stage. For example, Brain Writing 653 is a very well-received method.

Table 2. The evaluation result of the methods used in the modules of the system.

	Start		Adapt		Evolve		Conclude	
L1 Theme and scene	Past scene Mandala Chart	Usefulness 4.3 Ease of Use 4.1 Novelty 3.9 ☆	Future scene Mandala Chart	Usefulness 4.4 Ease of Use 4.1 Novelty 4.0	5W1H Mandala Chart	Usefulness 4.2 Ease of Use 3.9 Novelty 4.0	Concept situation Form	Usefulness 4.1 Ease of Use 4.0 Novelty 4.0
L2 Users and prototypes	Observation	Usefulness 4.3 Ease of Use 4.1 Novelty 3.9 ☆	Persona	Usefulness 4.6 ☆ Ease of Use 4.4 ☆ Novelty 4.2	Brain writing 653	Usefulness 4.4 ☆ Ease of Use 4.3 ☆ Novelty 4.3 ☆	Paper mockup	Usefulness 4.1 Ease of Use 4.0 Novelty 4.2
L3 Value and presentation	Interview	Usefulness 4.1 Ease of Use 4.2 ☆ Novelty 3.9	Value Laddering	Usefulness 4.3 Ease of Use 4.3 Novelty 4.3 ☆	Innovation matrix	Usefulness 4.2 Ease of Use 4.2 Novelty 4.3 ☆	Digital mockup	Usefulness 4.0 Ease of Use 4.1 ☆ Novelty 4.0
L4 Experience and journey	Safari	Usefulness 4.4 ☆ Ease of Use 4.0 Novelty 3.8	AEIOU Pains and gains	Usefulness 4.4 Ease of Use 4.0 Novelty 4.0	Customer journey	Usefulness 4.0 Ease of Use 3.8 Novelty 4.0	Storyboard prototype	Usefulness 4.2 ☆ Ease of Use 3.9 Novelty 4.3 ☆
	Understanding		Insights		Ideation		Prototyping	

These evaluations also confirm the users' engagement in their own learning and reflect value after using these methods.

In addition, the scores are useful for future participants to choose the design methods provided in the system. Therefore, the system is attested as a promising tool for enabling both self-learning and co-creation which can drive innovative solutions.

What's more interesting is that we did a correlation analysis on methods utilized in the innovation process and innovation outcomes, and found that there are positive correlation, negative correlation, and low-degree correlation exist among the methods (Fig. 8, the thick box is positive correlation, the dashed thick box is negative correlation, others are non-related). Since designers all gave these methods very positive reviews, we believe they may not have found subtle insights in negative correlations. For example, shown as Table 3, in L2 courses, designers like Brain Writing 653 method of Evolve stage and paper mockup of Conclude stage, however the analysis shows that on each of these 2 methods there is a negative correlation between the methods evaluation and outcomes evaluation. To interpret this unexpected insight, we inspected the qualitative feedback of participants. The feedback reveal that Users might consider the ideas generated by Brain Writing 653 spans across a wide range of issues, which are rendered irrelevant when the ideas are passed into Paper Mockup. Why they are irrelevant? Because the subsequent Paper Mockup, thought a useful method, cannot successfully express these wide-ranging ideas properly.

Table 3. The correlation analysis of L2 course.

Methods / Outcomes	Observation			Persona			Brain writing 653			Paper mockup		
	usefulness	Ease of use	novelty	usefulness	Ease of use	novelty	usefulness	Ease of use	novelty	usefulness	Ease of use	novelty
usefulness	0.32	0.72	0.66	0.33	-0.04	0.11	-0.36	-0.13	0.06	-0.31	0.13	0.06
Ease of use	0.26	0.27	0.63	0.25	-0.09	0.05	-0.41	-0.14	0.00	-0.27	0.11	0.04
novelty	0.13	0.64	0.67	0.24	-0.10	0.02	-0.25	0.05	0.22	-0.25	0.03	0.12

In general, a facilitator arranges workshop processes for the teams based on his/her subjective experience of usefulness and ease of use as well as the feedback from previous

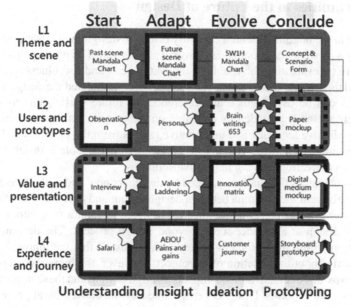

Fig. 8. The high-scoring stars are distributed in methods that are with positive, negative, and unrelated correlation.

users of the system. In Fig. 8, the high-scoring stars are distributed in methods that are with positive, negative, and unrelated correlation. This discovery reveals to us that users cannot distinguish subtle obstacles with positive use experience in the innovation process; however, through the measured quantitative data and qualitative responses, this system can determine the mutual suitability among the various methods in the process of combining them in special order for a more productive workshop, shown as Fig. 9.

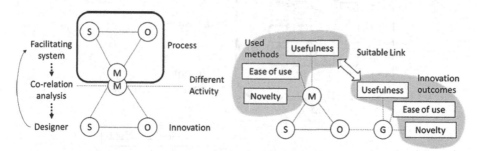

Fig. 9. This system, sifting through the measured quantitative data and qualitative responses, can determine the mutual suitability among the various methods in the process.

5   Opportunities in the Future of Design

This system in the ongoing research currently offers 16 design methods and is currently being tested with students at Tsinghua University in Taiwan. The participants contribute to the system by evaluating the usability, innovativeness, and usefulness of the design methods and the participants' design outcome after they completed the design workshop. Their ratings can be useful guide and reference for future participants to select the proper design methods provided by available on the system. To date, the evaluations, including qualitative feedback and quantitative ratings from the participants have been extremely positive. Hence, the system is a promising tool to enable both self-taught and collaborative co-creation, driving innovative solutions.

This system solves the challenges faced by designers now and in the future. As Dan Formosa put forward the dilemma between design output and design effect of designers [10], designers usually focus on the object of design and cannot take into account the influence of design at a broader scope beyond design process. The designer's linear process can only limit them to focus on key pain points, so that the innovations generated are mainly about the function of the object. However, the human-centered design vision is to provide better and holistic impacts through design, and these impacts will fall on ambiguous touch points. Designers constrained by the conventional process cannot explore and expand into potential realm of value proposition through design more freely. The system is envisioned to be a platform to facilitate design participants' onboarding in human-centered design process in a scenario-based, self-taught and collaborative virtual/physical hybrid environment. This deeply immersive experience during the innovation process would definitely ingrain in the participants the design thinking skills and mindset for their own innovation endeavors in the future.

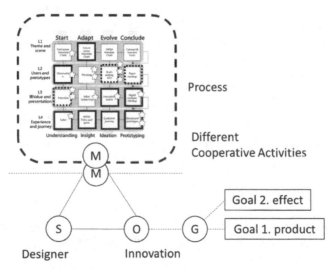

Fig. 10. Design teams can independently guide their own design exploration process to fit the product function an effect via different cooperative activities.

Using this set of self-taught collaborative system, design teams can independently guide their own design exploration process for an object or a service, combine several sets of different courses and procedures in special order, explore different impact goals, and then complete the design tasks in the end. They simultaneously can also address the design issues and impacts by the design, and abandon the product-first doctrine. In so doing the teams can ultimately achieve the goal of Human-centered design putting people first in their endeavors.

References

1. Yu, D.-J., Lin, W.-C.: Facilitating Idea Generation Using Personas. Human Centered Design (2009)
2. Nardi, B.A. (ed.): Context and Consciousness: Activity Theory and Human-Computer Interaction. MIT Press, Cambridge (1996)
3. Kurosu, M. (ed.): HCD 2009. LNCS, vol. 5619. Springer, Heidelberg (2009). https://doi.org/10.1007/978-3-642-02806-9
4. Yu, D.-J., Chuang, M.-C., Tseng, S.: Case Study for experience vision designing notebook PC. In: Human-Computer Interaction. Human-Centred Design (2013)
5. Schank, R.: Tell Me a Story: Narrative and Intelligence. Northwestern University Press, Evanston (1995, 2001)
6. Carroll, J.M.: Scenarios and design cognition. In: Proceedings of the IEEE Joint International Conference on Requirement Engineering (2002)
7. Yu, D.J., Lin, W.C., Wang, J.C.: Scenario-Oriented Design, Garden City, Taipei (2000)
8. Yu, D.-J., Yeh, H.-J.: Scenario-Based Product Design, a Real Case. In: Human-Computer Interaction. Interaction Design and Usability (2007)
9. Okamoto, M., Komatsu, H.: Participatory Design Using Scenarios in Different Cultures. In: Human-Computer Interaction (2007)
10. Formosa, D.: Thoughts on the future of design. Arch. Des. Res. 31(2) (2018)

Intelligent Information Environments

Proposal of Credit Risk Model Using Machine Learning in Motorcycle Sales

Ryota Fujinuma[✉] and Yumi Asahi

Graduate School of Business Administration, Tokyo University of Science, Tokyo, Japan
7bjm2219@star.tokai-u.jp, asahi@tsc.u-tokai.ac.jp

Abstract. While the new BIS regulations are reviewing the way of thinking about loans all over the world, many people in Central and South America still have a vague way of thinking about loans. It is due to the global recession. As a result, companies have not been able to recover their manufacturing costs. Therefore, in this study, we create a classification model of customers who default and customers who do not default. Also, explore the characteristics of the default customers. This is because it is thought that it will be easier for companies to improve the loan problem and secure profits.

In this study, we compare the accuracy of Random Forest and XG boost. Since the data handled in this study were unbalanced data, data expansion by Synthetic Minority Over-sampling Technique (SMOTE) was effective. Mainly the accuracy of Recall has increased by 30%. Feature selection is performed by correlation, which is one of the filter methods. This can be expected to have the effect of improving accuracy and the effect of improving the interpretability of the model. We were able to reduce it from 46 variables to 22 variables. Furthermore, the accuracy increased by 1% for Binary Accuracy and 1% for Recall. The accuracy decreased when the number of variables was reduced by 23 variables or more. This is probably because important features have been deleted. Shows the accuracy of the model. The accuracy of Random Forest is Binary Accuracy $= 61.3\%$, Recall $= 58.2\%$. The accuracy of XGboost is Binary Accuracy $= 60.3\%$, Recall $= 61.6\%$. Therefore, XG boost became the model that can identify the default of the customer than the random forest.

Finally, SHApley Additive exPlanations (SHAP) analyzes what variables contribute to the model. From this analysis result, we will explore the characteristics of what kind of person is the default customer. The variables with the highest contribution were the type of vehicle purchased, the area where the customer lives, and credit information. It turns out that customers who have gone loan bankruptcy in the past tend to be loan bankruptcy again.

Keywords: Loan · Loan bankruptcy · Credit risk model · Machine learning

1 Introduction

The US SPL problem, which became apparent in 2007, has resulted in turmoil in global financial markets. However, securitization and ratings are not the only problems that have

© Springer Nature Switzerland AG 2021
S. Yamamoto and H. Mori (Eds.): HCII 2021, LNCS 12766, pp. 353–363, 2021.
https://doi.org/10.1007/978-3-030-78361-7_26

become apparent in the SPL problem. What is important is that banks have embarked on extremely high-risk operations. Therefore, the idea of accurately predicting the default probability and securing profits commensurate with credit risk has become important. This is because the establishment and verification of an appropriate internal rating system has become a major issue for the introduction of the new BIS regulations. While the new BIS regulations are reviewing the way of thinking about loans all over the world, many people in Central and South America still have a vague way of thinking about loans. Behind this is the Lehman shock caused by the SPL problem. The Lehman shock brought a recession to the world. This event is no exception in Central and South America. From this event, the Central and South America government implemented an interest rate policy. This made it easier for the poor to get a loan. However, there are many customers who default due to lack of loan experience. And they often have a poor understanding of the contract. This is an international issue. If this situation deteriorates, manufacturers have difficulty in recovering manufacturing costs.

In this study, we use motorcycles sales data from Central and South America. This is because in Central and South America, where infrastructure development is not perfect, motorcycles have become indispensable for economic development such as commuting and agriculture as a practical means of transportation.

2 Data Summary

We use motorcycles sales data from in Central and South America in September 2010 to June 2012. There are 14,304 data and 359 variables. For example, borrowing amount, purchased motorcycles, resident state, revenue, career and whether the loan has been repaid or not.

And variables with a loss rate of more than 50% were deleted. A new dummy variable was created for the qualitative variable with the remaining missing values. It was complemented by substituting 0 here. This is because the data used in this study are rarely marked with 1. Therefore, it was judged that the data would not be biased even if 0 was substituted. Quantitative variables were complemented by stochastic regression imputation. With this, the number of data become 13,059.

In this study, a person who does not repay a loan is called a loan unpaid customer. A person who pays off a loan is called a loan paying customer. This is represented by the variable "Bad". "Bad" is a variable that indicates how long a customer has not paid a loan. The term is whether you have repaid the loan at 6,12,18 months. If you have not repaid, 1 will be entered in the data. Once you become a loan unpaid customer, it is difficult to return to a loan paying customer. Therefore, if you have not repaid the loan at 6 months, the data at 12 months and 18 months will also contain 1. As the number of data increases, it leads to more accurate analysis, thus we decided to focus on 18 months.

Central and South America has income inequality. Many poor people live in the north. Wealthy people live in the south. We have divided Central and South America into five regions. This is a category published by the government. Customers living in the north have an average income of 1446. Customers living in the northeast have an average income of 1245. Customers living in the Midwest have an average income of 1489. Customers living in the southeast have an average income of 1799. Customers living in the South had an average income of 1656. You can see that there is an economic disparity. But the economy of northeastern Brazil is currently growing. That is supporting the growth of the motorcycle market. Since there are many poor people in the north, it is not affected much by the Lehman shock. In fact, the number of purchases in the northeast was the highest.

Customers living in the South tend to buy relatively expensive motorcycles. Customers living in the southeast also tend to buy relatively expensive motorcycles. Conversely, customers living in the north and those living in the northeast tend to buy relatively cheap motorcycles.

The best-selling bike is product A. The price is 6747. The next selling bike is product B. The price is 5163. The two products account for about 80% of the total. Product C is a high-priced product. The price is 29504. Only about 100 units are sold.

Credit information ranges from 1 to 7. 1–3 are customers who have forgotten to repay their loan in the past. And it is a customer who is Loan bankruptcy. 4 to 7 are the bank usage history and the accuracy of the career.

Educational background is 1 to 3. 1 is the most highly educated, educational background decreases as becomes 3.

3 Purposes of This Study

Credit risk refers to "risk that the capital invested by loans, etc. does not return, such as when default occurs", and a model that quantifies credit risk is called a credit risk model. The risk factors of credit risk stipulated in the BIS regulation are PD (ease of default of the company. Default probability), LGD (expected loss when default occurs), EAD (credit exposure when default occurs) and Maturity (residual loan period). In this research, we focus on PD, which has been studied for some time. As a method for evaluating PD, an index that emphasizes the so-called hit rate, which is how much the default/non-default discrimination is correct, is often used (see Yamasita et al. 2003, Yamasita and Yoshiwa 2007). In this study, a customer who forgets to repay a loan once is defined as the default. For the default probability, create a model that determines whether you forgot to repay a loan once or paid it off.

Traditionally, credit risk models have used statistical methods such as Logistic Regression (LR). On the other hand, in recent years, various machine learning methods have been proposed, centering on deep learning. As a result, the accuracy is significantly improved. Along with this, there are increasing reports on building scoring models using machine learning methods (see Lessmanna et al. 2015).

Set the research purpose from these things. The first research purpose is to dis-cover the optimal machine learning method. Sawaki et al. (2017) constructed a cred-it risk model using various machine learning methods using Japanese SME data. As a result, we verified what kind of method can produce high accuracy. In machine learning, it is generally known that ensemble learning that combines multiple models often provides higher accuracy than learning only a single model. Therefore, in this study, we focused on ensemble learning. Neural Network, Gradient Boosting Decision Tree, Random Forest, and Support Vector Machine are typical machine learning methods that have been attracting attention in recent years. Each has its own characteristics, and which method is optimal depends on the field and the characteristics of the dataset. Therefore, it can be said that the discovery of a machine learning method suitable for the Brazilian loan problem has academic significance. In this study, we will focus random forests and Gradient Boosting Decision Tree (XGBoost). Compare the two precisions.

The second purpose of research is to understand the characteristics of customers. Find out which background information affects customers who are unpaid. Also, find out which background information affects the customers who pay off the loan. A second research objective can help find customers at high risk of loan bankruptcy in advance, as customers with late payments are very likely to lead to loan bankruptcy.

4   Main Experiment

The AR value (accuracy ratio) is a typical index that shows the discriminating power of the credit risk model that estimates the default probability. The AR value is an index that determines whether the default or non-default can be discriminated. Yamashita et al. (2011) show that many models created for large and medium-sized enterprises have a value of 60% to 80%. In this study, the AR value is used as a reference to evaluate the model performance using a confusion matrix. It can be considered that the correct determination of customers who will not pay the loan directly leads to the securing of profits for the company. However, identifying a customer who pays off a loan as an unpaid customer and not taking out a loan is the same as losing the opportunity to generate a profit. Therefore, in this study, with reference to Yamashita et al. (2011) the goal is to improve the precision of the recall rate (Recall) on the premise that the accuracy rate (Binary Accuracy, hereinafter Accuracy) is maintained at 60%.

4.1   Confusion Matrix Result

First, the results of the credit risk model by Random Forest and XG boost are shown. In this study, 0 represents a loan paying customer. And 1 represents a loan unpaid customer.

In this study, the accuracy is evaluated by the holdout method. It divides the learning data (learning) and the test data (test) in a ratio of 7:3 (see Uchida 2004). The analysis is performed by changing the data used in the training data and the test data each time. The results of machine learning change each time depending on the test data used. Therefore, the data is divided into learning data and test data, and the analysis is performed 5 times. The result of applying the model constructed from the training data to the test data appears as a confusion matrix. The Accuracy and Recall at that time is evaluated using the average of 5 analyzes (see Atsuki and Asahi 2018). Shows one of the analysis results of the confusion matrix (Figs. 1 and 2).

Looking at the results of Random Forest, Accuracy = 76.3% and Recall = 0%. All predicted values were determined to be 0, and none were predicted to be 1. This can be considered to be the result of overfitting to 0 data because the number of 0s in the training data is large. In fact, by discriminating all the data as 0, the accuracy of Accuracy was as high as 76.3%. However, it can be said that this analysis did not work well because it is a model in which no loan unpaid customer can be identified. Looking at the results of XGBoost, Accuracy = 75.7% and Recall = 11.6%. As with Random Forest, it can

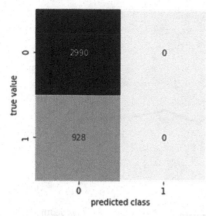

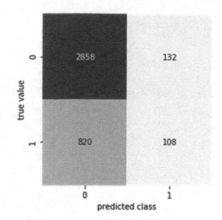

Fig. 1. Confusion matrix result of the Random Forest

Fig.2. Confusion matrix result of the XGBoost

be said that the analysis did not work well because it is a model that can hardly identify loan unpaid customer.

4.2 Model Tuning

In this study, SMOTE was used to process imbalanced data. The data has been extended by SMOTE. As a result, the data of loan paying customer was 7052, and the data of loan unpaid customer was 7052. The credit risk model is created as 50%: 50% data.

Next, tune the hyperparameters of Random Forest. In this study, we focus on the depth and number of trees in Random Forest for tuning. This is because these two are thought to have a significant effect on accuracy. It is known that the deeper the tree, the more overfitting occurs. Therefore, deepen them one by one and round up the learning before overfitting occurs. In other words, it takes early stopping to mitigate the effects of overfitting (see Prechelt 1998). Of the tree depths before overfitting, the one with the best recall accuracy is the optimum tree depth. The result is shown in Fig. 3.

The result was that a tree depth of 7 was optimal. The precision is Accuracy = 61.3% and Recall = 46.5%. When the depth of the tree exceeds 7, the Accuracy increases and the Recall decreases. You can see that overfitting occurs when the tree depth exceeds 7.

Next, set the depth of the tree to 7, and increase the number of trees. The results are shown in Fig. 4.

Accuracy increased as the number of trees increased. However, the Recall decreased. Therefore, the optimum hyperparameters are max depth = 7 and number of trees = 1. The precision of Random Forest after data expansion and hyperparameter tuning is Accuracy = 61.3% and Recall = 46.5%.

As with Random Forest, tune the hyperparameters for XGBoost. In this study, we focus on the number of rounds. This is because the number of rounds is considered to have a large effect on precision. It is known that overfitting occurs as the number of rounds increases. Therefore, the number of rounds is increased in order from 1. Apply Early stopping to XGBoost. Of the round numbers before overfitting, the one with the

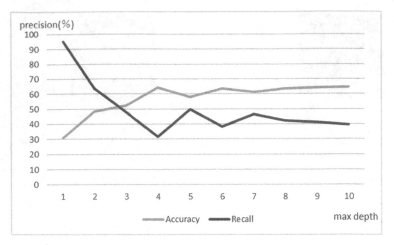

Fig. 3. Change the max depth

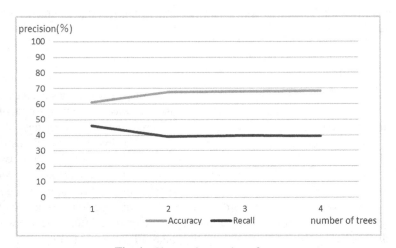

Fig. 4. Change the number of trees

best Recall is set as the optimum round number. In addition, Random Forest determines the threshold by majority voting of prediction results, but XGBoost sets the threshold by itself. Therefore, after grasping the optimum number of rounds, the threshold value is changed. The threshold is changed by 0.01. This is because the change in precision is easy to see and does not complicate the model. The result are shown in Fig. 5 and Fig. 6.

The result was that 2 was the optimum number of rounds. When the number of rounds exceeds 2, the Accuracy increases and the accuracy of Recall decreases. It can be expected that overfitting occurred from the number of rounds 2. Next, in order to improve the accuracy of the recall, the threshold was reduced from 0.5. As a result, when the threshold was 0.42, the Accuracy was less than 60%. Therefore, the optimal hyper parameter is round 2, the threshold is 0.43. The precision of XGBoost was Accuracy =

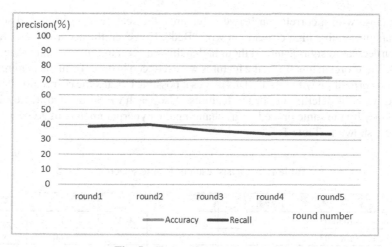

Fig. 5. Change the round number

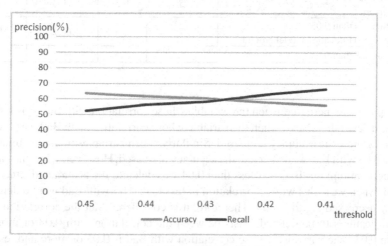

Fig. 6. Change the threshold

60.6% and Recall = 58.3%. From these facts, it was found that the credit risk model by XGBoost is a better model for the purpose of this study than Random Forest.

Feature selection is performed for the highly precision XGBoost. There are merits such as improvement of accuracy, improvement of interpretability, and reducing calculation cost by selecting features. In this study, features are selected by the filter method. Hall (1999) mentions the feature selection of machine learning by the correlation-based approach in the filter method. In many cases, the correlation-based filter method produces results comparable to the wrapper method. It is also suitable for large datasets such as this study because it runs many times faster than the wrapper method. Correlation-based filtering is based on the assumption that a good feature set contains features that are highly correlated with the objective variable but not correlated with each other.

For those with a correlation between features, the features were selected so as to leave variables with a high correlation with "Bad". However, the accuracy after feature selection decreased significantly. I thought that this was because important features were deleted. Therefore, in this study, the features were reduced in order from the features with the lowest correlation with "Bad". This makes it possible to relax the correlation between variables without deleting important features. Also, each time I deleted it, I evaluated the accuracy by the same procedure as changing the hyperparameters of XGBoost. The results are shown in Table 1.

Table 1. Analysis result of feature selection.

Deleted features	round number	threshold	Accuracy(%)	Recall(%)
Correlation less than 0.01	5	0.45	60.9	59.7
Correlation less than 0.02	6	0.5	60.6	60.0
Correlation less than 0.03	5	0.5	60.6	61.0
Correlation less than 0.03 +Civil servant	5	0.5	60.3	61.6
Correlation less than 0.03 +Civil servant +Educational Background 1	7	0.5	60.2	61.1
Correlation less than 0.04	6	0.5	60.2	60.8

The precision increased when the variable whose correlation with Bad was less than 0.01 was deleted first. Next, when the variable whose correlation with Bad was less than 0.02 was deleted, the accuracy increased. Similarly, when variables with a correlation of less than 0.03 with Bad were deleted, the accuracy increased. However, when the variable whose correlation with Bad was less than 0.04 was deleted, the accuracy decreased. In addition, when variables with a correlation of less than 0.05 with Bad were deleted, the accuracy decreased significantly. Therefore, it is considered that the correlation of the optimum features to be deleted exists between the correlation with 0.03 or more and less than 0.04. The variables whose correlation with Bad is 0.03 or more and less than 0.04 are the three variables of educational background 1, salaried workers, and civil servants. These three variables were deleted from the variables of civil servants with the lowest correlation with Bad, and the accuracy was evaluated one by one in order. The results were most accurate by re-moving variables with a correlation of less than 0.03 and variable of civil servant. Similar to XGBoost, Random Forest also deleted variables whose correlation with Bad was less than 0.03 and variables of civil servants and evaluated the accuracy. The highest accuracy was max depth 7 and number of trees 6, with Accuracy = 61.3% and Recall = 58.2%. After all, the credit risk model by XGBoost resulted in high precision.

4.3 SHAP Value

Finally, I will raise the interpretability of the model. It was adopted SHAP in this study. Targets highly precision XGBoost. SHAP is a framework that raises the interpretation of predictions for ensemble learning and deep learning, which are difficult to interpret models (see Lundberg and Lee 2017). In models using decision trees such as Random Forest and XGBoost, the feature importance can be defined using the trained model. But feature importance is heavily biased by the data (see Strobl et al. 2007). In experiments, Yoshikawa et al. (2020) showed that the feature importance of XGBoost in Gain may not be calculated correctly for the contribution rate of the model. Therefore, in this study, we adopted SHAP, which can calculate the contribution rate of the model more accurately than the importance. Improved interpretability makes it easier for companies to work with models. Because you can see the reason for the inference result of the model. Figure 7 shows the results of the contribution of the model.

The variable with the highest contribution to the model was product B. This is followed by product A, married, Credit information 7 and Iiving in the southeast. It was found that the variable product B has a higher contribution rate than other variables. Product B and product A are variables that represent of vehicle type, and the top two variables of the contribution rate are variables that represent vehicle type, so the variable of vehicle type is an important variable for the model. The variable of the area where they live also has a relatively high contribution rate.

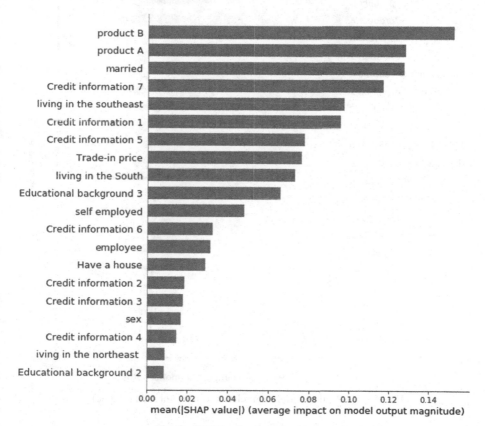

Fig. 7. SHAP value contribution rate

The result of the correlation relationship is shown in Fig. 8. For example, product B is data on whether product B has been purchased or not. The red plot indicates that product B has been purchased. The blue plot indicates that you have not purchased product B. The horizontal axis represents the correlation with Bad. If a positive value is taken for SHAP value, it means that there is a positive correlation with Bad. On the contrary, if the SHAP value is negative, it means that there is a negative correlation with Bad. In other words, with regard to product B, it can be seen that customers who have purchased product B tend to be loan-paid customers, and customers who have not purchased product B tend to be loan unpaid customers.

Of the variables that tend to be loan unpaid customers, the one with the highest contribution was product A. And credit information 1 to credit information 3 were both characteristics of loan unpaid customers. Other than that, self-employed customers also tend to be loan unpaid customers. You can see that the variables with low contributions have a mixture of plot colors. This has a low impact on the model and may affect both loan paying customers and loan unpaid customers.

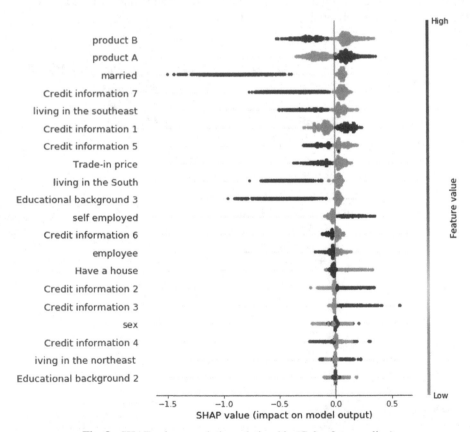

Fig. 8. SHAP value correlation relationship (Color figure online)

5 Discussion

In this study, we proposed a credit risk model by Random Forest and XGBoost. As a result, the accuracy of the model by XGBoost fits the purpose of this study and was adopted. The ability to change the threshold contributed to improving the accuracy of the recall. In addition, model tuning was able to greatly improve the precision. However, there are many other tuning methods. And there are other types of hyperparameters. Changing them may further improve the accuracy of the model.

Since SHAP can handle any method of machine learning, the interpretability of the model can be improved even if another method is considered. Looking at the contribution rate of the model, the top two variables were the variables of the vehicle type. Most of the Vehicle type purchased as a premise were product A and product B, and there was a bias. Therefore, many of the customers who purchase product A have unpaid loans, which may have contributed to the inference of the model. In fact, customers who buy product A have a higher percentage of unpaid customers than those who buy product B.

References

Yamashita, S., Kawaguchi, N., Tsuruga, T.: Consideration and comparison of credit risk model evaluation methods. Financial Research and Training Center discussion paper series (2003)

Yamashita, S., Yoshiba, T.: Credit risk considering additional financing: analytical solutions of EL and UL using structural models. Financ. Res. **26** (2007)

Lessmanna, S., Baesensb, B., Seowd, H., Thomas, L.C.: Benchmarking state-of-the-art classification algorithms for credit scoring: an update of research. Eur. J. Oper. Res. **247**(1), 124–136 (2015)

Sawaki, T., Tanaka, T., Kasahara, R.: Construction of credit scoring model for SMEs by machine learning. Mater. Japanese Soc. Artif. Intell. (2017)

Yamashita, S., Miura, K.: Prediction precision of credit risk model -AR value and evaluation index-, Asakura Shoten (2011)

Uchida, O.: Consideration and Proposal of Model Goodness of Fit Index in Logistic Regression Analysis. Tokyo University of Information Sciences, pp.9–14 (2004)

Mari, A., Yumi, A.: Analysis of the career of bankrupts of loans. Bull. Tokai Univ. Facul. Inf. Telecommun. Stud. **11**(2), 27–33 (2018)

Prechelt, L.: Early Stopping – but when? Fakultät für Informatik, Universität Karlsruhe, pp. 55–69 (1998)

Hall, M.A.: Correlation-based Feature Selection for Machine Learning. Department of Computer Science, Waikato University, New Zealand (1999)

Lundberg, S.M., Lee, S.-I.: A unified approach to interpreting model predictions. Adv. Neural Inf. Process. Syst. 4765–4774 (2017)

Strobl, C., Boulesteix, A.-L., Zeileis, A., Hothorn, T.: Bias in random forest variable importance measures: illustrations, sources and a solution. BMC Bioinform. **8**, 25 (2007)

Yoshikawa, H., Tajima, Y., Imai, Y.: Verification of the effectiveness of SHAP values in the interpretation of decision tree-based models. In: The 34th Annual Conference of the Japanese Society for Artificial Intelligence (2020)

Research on Supporting an Operator's Control for OriHime as a Telepresence Robot

Kosei Furukawa[1]([✉]), Madoka Takahara[2], and Hidetsugu Suto[2]

[1] Graduate School of Engineering, Muroran Institute of Technology, Hokkaido 050-8585, Japan
20043049@mmm.muroran-it.ac.jp
[2] College of Information and Systems, Muroran Institute of Technology,
Hokkaido 050-8585, Japan

Abstract. Recent years, classes, conferences and group works in companies and universities have been done as online, which means people don't have chances to hold them in person because of preventing infections of COVID-19. In regard to these ways of using an online meeting, there is a problem that people who attend online meetings have a strong tendency to have a cognitive load due to having burden behaviors such as discussing and operating PC, smartphone and tablet devices at the same time in comparison with in-person meeting. Particularly, when it comes to using telepresence robots, it is needed for operators to be required to pay much attention. In this study, for diminishing operators' cognitive load, a supporting system which operating telepresence robots OriHime by using the movement information of operators' head is proposed. Moreover, we identify that there is a chance to diminish operators' cognitive load through obtaining information of face position by using telepresence robot, although the effect of the proposed system is set to be revealed by conducting an experiment.

Keywords: COVID-19 · Remote meeting · Cognitive load · Bio-information

1 Introduction

Figure 1 shows that the number of people who conducts remote work and places transition. The subject of this survey, 1158 people via NTT.com Research Registration Monitor, and this survey was taken by NTT DATA INSTITUTE OF MANAGEMENT CONSULTING. N is the number of workers who are doing remote work besides this monitor is allowed multiple choices. Furthermore, dedicated satellite office represents the office space where can be used as only in-house or in-house group and shared satellite office represents the office space where can be used by sharing with multiple companies.

After February when COVID-19 infected people began to appear, the number of remote workers has been increasing 20% to 30% every month. Especially, telework (work from home) has been increasing significantly.

© Springer Nature Switzerland AG 2021
S. Yamamoto and H. Mori (Eds.): HCII 2021, LNCS 12766, pp. 364–372, 2021.
https://doi.org/10.1007/978-3-030-78361-7_27

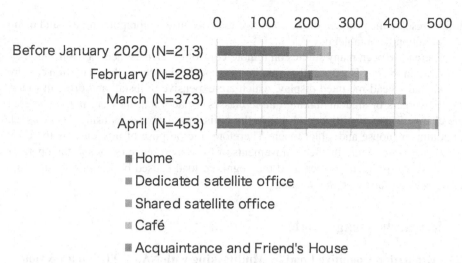

Fig. 1. The number of people who conducts remote work from January to April 2020. [1]

Table 1 shows the results of a survey on class methods in Japanese universities as of May 20th, 2020. This survey was conducted by the Ministry of Education, Culture, Sports, Science and Technology (MEXT), for 864 Japanese universities (86 national universities, 83 public universities, 638 private universities, and 57 technical schools) that were given classes at that time. The Japanese government announced a state of emergency for all prefectures from April 16th to May 14th, 2020. Although this announcement was already lifted on May 20, 837 schools, or 96.8% of the total, are forced to have online or combined online and face-to-face classes.

Table 1. The number of schools by class methods in Japanese universities on May 20, 2020 [2]

	Online class	Both remote class and face-to-face class	Face-to-face class
National university	0 schools	8 schools	78 schools
Public university	0 schools	7 schools	76 schools
Private university	26 schools	44 schools	568 schools
Technical school	1 school	0 schools	56 schools
Total	27 schools	59 schools	778 schools

In this kind of situation, the number of the people who feel stress cause of online works and seminars have been increasing [3]. The reason for this can be considered that increasing in a cognitive load due to performing multiple tasks of discussion and using devices simultaneously [4–6] and luck of non-verbal communications which are needed when communicate with people using body language [7]. There is a telepresence robot that is combined with video conferences, robots, and remote-control technology as an attempt to resolve the latter factor. However, operating typical telepresence robot is not able to resolve the problem of the cognitive load because of computer mouse and using touch motion from tablet devices.

There have been many studies on remote-control of telepresence robots using body information [8–11]. However, these studies use special devices such as a motion capture device and a head-mounted display, which are expensive to install and difficult to use by teleworkers or students taking online classes. In addition, they are not considered the change in the cognitive load due to the omission of processes using devices such as computer mouse and tablet touch. Therefore, the purpose of this study is to verify whether synchronizing the head movements of the telepresence robot and the operator can solve the problem of increased the cognitive load caused by both discussion and using devices during online meetings.

2   Research Background

2.1   Evaluation Cognitive Load by Multitasking with NASA-TLX in a Previous Study

NASA-TLX (Task Load Index) is a method to examine whether a particular task load imposes any demands or ecological burdens from a subjective perspective [12]. NASA-TLX consists of six rating scales: mental demand, physical demand, temporal demand, performance, effort, and frustration. There have been previous works [4–6] for evaluating the effect of a cognitive load by multitask using this method. For example, Okuwa et al. presented a method for estimating and quantifying the driver's cognitive load when driving a car and using in-vehicle information devices [4]. In this study, experiments were conducted on a simple driving simulator under a total of eight conditions, including driving only, driving and manual operation of in-vehicle information devices. In this study, experiments were conducted on a simple driving simulator under multiple conditions combining driving operation with manual operation of in-vehicle information devices and voice operation. As a result, it was confirmed that an increase in the load caused by driving and manual operation of in-vehicle information devices was observed. Therefore, an increase in a cognitive load is assumed due to both peripheral cognition and manual operation of the information device.

2.2   Remote-Control of Robots Using Physical Information in a Previous Study

Many studies [8–11] have been conducted on using body information to control telepresence robots. Among them, there is a study that aims to build a tele-education support system for children who have been hospitalized for a long time, in which the head movements of a robot can be controlled intuitively [11]. In this study, a system was proposed to operate the robot according to the number of times and duration of the inclination of the child's face in order to avoid the robot's head moving at unintended timing when the child moves their face to write notes during a remote class. For acquiring the head information, Euler angles of the child's head were focused on, and face direction was estimated by images acquired from the camera. The results of the user experiment showed that the accuracy that user operates the robot was 60% based on the number of tilts and 80% based on the time of the tilts. This study was only verified the accuracy of the proposed system, it was not considered how much cognitive load imposes on the operator by using the system. Therefore, we consider the degree of cognitive load by the system using operator's head movements.

2.3 Telepresence Robot

Telepresence robot is contrivance which make speaker who is in a remote place give presence as if it exists in the same place and speaker can control it as if their copy [13]. Various studies which are introduced telepresence robot for remote communication are conducted [8, 13]. Figure 2 shows that the situation of communicating speaker and robot operator via telepresence robot.

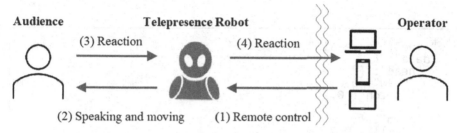

Fig. 2. Example of communication by using Telepresence Robot [14]

First, robot operator operates telepresence robot by using PC, smartphone and tablet devices (1). Speaker colloquize form of react to telepresence robot movements (2), (3). Speaker reaction is conveyed to devices which are operated by robot operator (4). In (4), it is possible to have a dialogue between robot operator and speaker who is in a remote place by viewing the dialogue contents which are obtained from devices. Nevertheless, operator's cognitive load tends to increase cause of leaping upward of the number of (1) process in comparison with face-to-face communication with speaker. Figure 3 is telepresence robot produced by Ory Laboratory. This is for helping ALS people who have difficulty in moving their body and helping an inpatient who occurred physical changes by effect of taking anticancer agent to take part in social involvement. Its features are considered that it can be communicated by operator's voice and movement of it.

The operation application API for PC version is disclosed and possible to obtain information of OriHime's motion control and whether OriHime in a call or not. According to the API specifications, all of the data for both sending and receiving are exchanged in JSON strings.

Figure 3 shows the parts of OriHime which is possible to control OriHime's motion by API [15]. In all parts, they can be conducted operation control from 0 to 1, head can move vertically and horizontally, left and right hands can adjust arm opening angle and move vertically. Additionally, id is used when specify which part is conducted operation control on. In Fig. 3 left, the posture of OriHime set as head-yaw 0.6, head-pitch 0.25, larm-roll 0, larm-pitch 1, rarm-roll 0.7, rarm-pitch 0. The JSON string to send the information to OriHime is shown below (Fig. 4).

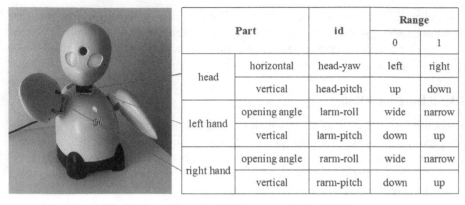

Part		id	Range	
			0	1
head	horizontal	head-yaw	left	right
	vertical	head-pitch	up	down
left hand	opening angle	larm-roll	wide	narrow
	vertical	larm-pitch	down	up
right hand	opening angle	rarm-roll	wide	narrow
	vertical	rarm-pitch	down	up

Fig. 3. Operable parts of Telepresence Robot OriHime

```
{
  "type": "move-all",
  "data": {
    "head": {
      "yaw": 0.6,
      "pitch": 0.25
    },
    "rarm": {
      "roll": 0.7,
      "pitch": 0
    },
    "larm": {
      "roll": 0,
      "pitch": 1
    }
  }
}
```

Fig. 4. The JSON string to send the information to OriHime

Thus, it is possible to control the operation of OriHime by assigning numerical values to the prescribed JSON strings and sending them via inter-process communication. In this study, OriHime is used for verification of methods.

3   Methods

Figure 5 shows the flow of the proposed system below.

1. Using Dlib [16], which is a python machine learning library, a face detection is performed on images acquired from a PC camera.
2. Landmark detection is performed on the faces detected in (1) using regression tree analysis. The learning model for the analysis is available from the official Dlib website (file name: shape_predictor_68_face_landmarks.dat.bz2) [17]. The Euler angles of the head are estimated from the facial six points: tip of the nose, chin, left

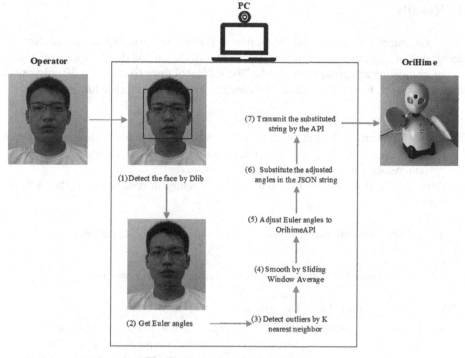

Fig. 5. Flow of the proposed system

corner of the left eye, right corner of the right eye, left corner of the mouth, and right corner of the mouth [18].

3. Since outliers may occur in the estimated values [11], outlier detection is performed using the K-nearest neighbor algorithm. In the case of the outlier, the previous frame's value is referenced.

4. In order to handle as the time series data, smoothing is performed using Simple Moving Average.

5. Decompose the Euler angles that are not outliers into the horizontal and vertical directions of OriHime's head shown in Fig. 3. Since the range of values for controlling OriHime defined in the API is 0 to 1, the normalization is carried out.

6. Substitute the numerical value which was calculated in (5) into the JSON string shown in 2.3 for controlling OriHime's operation. The horizontal id of the head is "yaw" in "head" and the vertical id is "pitch" in "head".

7. Send the prescribed JSON string to OriHime via inter-process communication, substituting the information about the Euler angle in (6).

Our research focuses on meetings such as remote conferences and group work. We propose a system that enables OriHime to move its head as much as the estimated face direction, because it is considered that there are few head movements that are not for the purpose of motion control of OriHime, such as head movements for writing notes, compared to the previous study [11].

4 Results

This experiment was conducted by proposed system for verifying the possibility of decreasing of cognitive load which is caused by discussion and device operation when an online meeting and groupwork is hold. The subject of this experiment is 30 university students who still have online classes and meeting. Experimental procedure is as follows.

1. Divide subjects into A group and B group.
2. People from group A operate an OriHime which is proposed system uninstalled, people from group B have an online meeting as operates OriHime which is proposed system installed in order, and then they take a survey.
3. After people from group B have an online meeting in reverse order, they take a survey.

Table 2 shows questionnaire contents which are used in this experience.

Table 2. Questionnaire contents of after each online meeting

Title	Endpoint	Descriptions
Mental demand	Low/High	How much perceptual activity did you need to turn to face your conversation partner? (example: Ask a question, Memorize conversations, or Think about what you will say)
Physical demand	Low/High	How much physical activity did you need to turn to face your conversation partner? (example: Move your head)
Temporal demand	Low/High	How much time pressure do you think you felt from the frequency or speed of this task to turn to face your conversation partner?
Performance	Good/Poor	How successful do you think you have been in meeting the task goal?
Effort	Low/High	How hard do you think you worked to maintain and accomplish the tasks you were given?
Frustration level	Low/High	How much frustration, anxiety, discouragement, stress, or worry did you feel during the work?

This questionnaire was designed based on the rating scale of NASA-TLX. It is necessary to simplify and concretize the evaluation scale enough for the public to understand, because NASA-TLX was developed for the purpose of measuring the mental load of astronauts. There are studies that have improved, simplified, and concretized the description of each rating scale [9, 19]. Based on these studies, we considered explanations that would be easy for the subjects to understand in this questionnaire as well. An example of the questionnaire items is shown in Fig. 6. The subject marks a circle on the line of the item with "Low/High" or "Good/Poor" polarity for the given task on the questionnaire using a rating scale. It allows his/her subjective evaluation to be quantified by converting it from 0 to 10 depending on where they wrote the circle on the line. In our research, the mean value of the six rating scales is used as the NASA-TLX total value, which is a measure of the load.

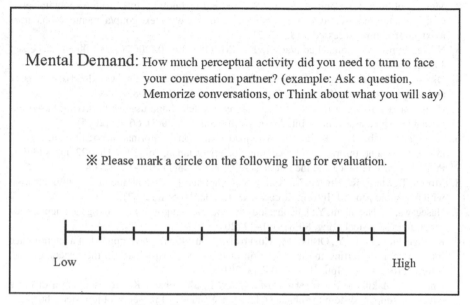

Fig. 6. Example of the questionnaire item

5 Conclusions

Nowadays, there have been many studies on using body information to control telepresence robots remotely [8–11]. However, they require special devices such as a motion capture device and a head-mounted display, which are expensive to implement and difficult to use by many people, such as teleworkers. In addition, it was not investigated that the change in the cognitive load caused by the decrease in the process of operating devices such as mouse and tablet touch. We focus on these two problems and propose a system which decrease a cognitive load cause of online meeting through controlling the motion of telepresence robot by face direction. The proposed system is assumed that the cognitive load is low because existing online meeting tools and telepresence robot abbreviate device operation compared with PC, smartphone and tablet devices. As for effectiveness, it is set to reveal through experiments.

The problem with the proposed system is that the arm movements of the telepresence robot are not synchronized with the operator's movements, so the issue of increased the cognitive load still remains when controlling the robot's arms. Thus, In the future work, we will solve the above problem by estimating postures such as shoulders and arms from the PC camera images in addition to face direction estimation and synchronizing them with the robot's arm movements.

References

1. NTT.Com Research. https://research.nttcoms.com/database/data/002151/. Accessed 17 Act 2020
2. Ministry of Education, Culture, Sports, Science and Technology, Information about universities, graduate schools, and technical colleges. https://www.mext.go.jp/a_menu/coronavirus/mext_00016.html. Accessed 29 Jan 2021
3. Nikkei. https://www.nikkei.com/article/DGXMZO59730520Z20C20A5CE0000/. Accessed 19 Act 2020
4. Okuwa, M., Ebe, K., Inagaki, H., Doi, S.: Evaluation of driver's mental workload due to visual and auditory cognition. Soc. Instr. Control Eng. **36**(12), 1079–1085 (2000)
5. Hagiwara, T., Tokugawa, A.R.: Effects of cellular telephone use while driving based om mental workload assessment. Int. Assoc. Traffic Saf. Sci. **30**(3), 66–73 (2005)
6. Iwata, T., Yamabe, T., Nakajima, T.: Workload evaluation of information cognition in a multi-task environment. Information Processing Society of Japan, vol. 2009-UBI-22, no. 8 (2009)
7. Pettit, P.: Trust, reliance and the internet. Anal. Kritik **26**(1), 108–121 (2004)
8. Morita, T., Mase, K., Hirano, Y., Kajita, S., Okadome, T.: Distant attention communication with humanoid robot. J. Inform. Process. **48**(12), 3849–3858 (2007)
9. Hasegawa, K., Nakauchi, Y.: Unconscious gestures that empower turn taking for telepresence robot. Jpn. Soc. Mech. Eng. **80**(819), 1–12 (2014)
10. Kawaguchi, I., Endo, Y., Otsuki, M., Kuzuoka, H., Suzuki, Y.: Development of a telepresence robot system supporting the participation of the remote participant in the teleconference. Inform. Process. Soc. Jpn. **2016**, 739–743 (2016)
11. Ohata, T., Makihara, E., Takahara, M., Tanev, I., Shimohara, K.: To establish a distance education support system to enhance telexistence and social presence of long-term hospitalized children - robot's head operation by proposed two recognition system of head motion. In: Products of the Society of Instrument and Control Engineers Annual Conference 2020, pp. 1961–1964. Online (2020)
12. Hart, S.G., Staveland, L.E.: Development of NASA-TLX (Task Load Index): results of empirical and theoretical research. In: Hancock, P.A., Meshkati, N. (eds.) Human Mental Workload, pp. 139–183. Elsevier Science Publishers B.V., Amsterdam (1988)
13. Yamamoto, R., Kubota, K., Kishi, M., Ueda, S.: A study of cooperation with outside personnel encouraging teacher's active behavior in special needs education school: from a case of tele-presence robot use. Media Stud. Educ. **24**(1), 89–104 (2017)
14. Yamamoto, R., Sekimoto, H., Kubota, K.: Studying a telepresence robot installed into a hospital classroom. Int. J. Educ. Media Technol. **10**(1), 53–62 (2016)
15. GitHub. https://github.com/OryLab/biz-ipcapi. Accessed 18 Act 2020
16. Dlib C++ Library. http://dlib.net. Accessed 29 Jan 2021
17. Dlib C++ Library Index of files. http://dlib.net/files/. Accessed 29 Jan 2021
18. Learn OpenCV Head Pose Estimation using OpenCV and Dlib. https://learnopencv.com/head-pose-estimation-using-opencv-and-dlib/. Accessed 29 Jan 2021
19. Miyake, S., Kumashiro, M.: Subjective mental workload assessment technique - an introduction to NASA-TLX and SWAT and a proposal of simple scoring methods. Jpn. J. Ergon. **29**(6), 399–408 (1993)

Factor Analysis of Continuous Use of Car Services in Japan by Machine Learning

Kenta Hara[✉] and Yumi Asahi

Graduate School of Management, Department of Management, Tokyo University of Science, Tokyo, Japan

8620504@ed.tus.ac.jp, asahi@rs.tus.ac.jp

Abstract. The automotive industry is an important industry for Japan and has a great impact on the Japanese economy. According to the Automotive Industry Strategy 2014 announced by the Ministry of Economy, five problems will occur in the next 10 to 20 years, and countermeasures are required. Five is-sues are increasing environmental and energy constraints, population growth and personal income growth, aging, urban overcrowding and depopulation, and changing values. Moreover, it is affected by external factors which is consumption tax increase, soaring gasoline and so on.

As a strategy to increase the number of cars sold, it is possible to develop products that meet the needs of customers. However, in the car industry, the same type of cars of the same manufacturing company are also sold by other sales corporations, and product development that makes a difference between products may involve enormous costs and risks. Therefore, in this re-search, we focus on customers who use car-related services rather than products to differentiate their services. The purpose of this study is to build a Bayesian network that can handle many missing values and difficult elements of observed data and can introduce expert knowledge into the network structure. In addition, we also show that Bayesian networks are useful by comparing them with multiple machine learning models. It used Logistic regression, Decision tree, XGBoost, and Random Forest. The conclusions of this study show that the Bayesian network is more accurate than other analyzes.

Keywords: Car · Machine learning · Bayesian network

1 Introduction

The automotive industry is an important industry for Japan and has a great impact on the Japanese economy. According to the Automotive Industry Strategy 2014 announced by the Ministry of Economy, five problems will occur in the next 10 to 20 years, and countermeasures are required [1]. Five issues are in-creasing environmental and energy constraints, population growth and personal income growth, aging, urban overcrowding and depopulation, and changing values. Moreover, it is affected by external factors which is consumption tax in-crease, soaring gasoline and so on. In fact, comparing the number of cars sold in 2014, when the consumption tax was increased in the JAMA (Japan

© Springer Nature Switzerland AG 2021
S. Yamamoto and H. Mori (Eds.): HCII 2021, LNCS 12766, pp. 373–384, 2021.
https://doi.org/10.1007/978-3-030-78361-7_28

Automobile Manufacturers Association) database [2], a temporary increase in demand can be seen from 2011 to 2013 before the tax increase and demand is declining from 2014 to 2015 after the tax increase. Hirose [3] suggests that the relationship between gasoline prices and unit sales is likely to significantly reduce consumer demand for passenger cars due to the decline in real income due to soaring gasoline prices. Today, Car sales are increasing, however the number of car inspection services is decreasing year by year [4], and in order to expand the scale of the Japanese automobile industry, it is necessary to increase the number of customers who use car-related services.

As a strategy to increase the number of cars sold, it is possible to develop products that meet the needs of customers. However, in the automotive industry, the same type of cars of the same manufacturing company are also sold by other sales corporations, and product development that makes a difference between products may involve enormous costs and risks. Therefore, in this research, we focus on customers who use car-related services rather than products, show the factors of customers who continue to use car-related services. Murakami et al. [5] are able to handle many missing value data and difficult to observe elements as a feature of the Bayesian network. They also point out that it is possible to introduce the knowledge of experts into the network structure. We have created Bayesian network that can flexibly respond to the influence of various external factors in the automotive industry. We also show that Bayesian networks are useful by comparing them with multiple machine learning models. It used Logistic regression, Decision tree, XGBoost, and Random Forest (Fig. 1).

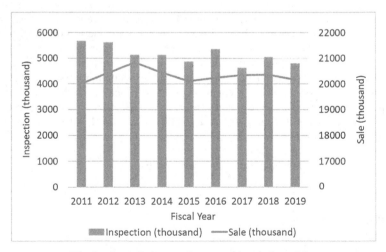

Fig. 1. Annual changes in car and inspections sales

2   Previous Study

There are many studies analyzing customers who buy cars in terms of consumer behavior. Shende [6] focuses on the Indian automobile industry, which is influenced by the presence of many national and multinational manufacturers, showing that car buyers have different priorities for action in each segment and car companies should adopt the "Think-Global, Act-Global". Alamgir et al. [7] investigates the relationship between brands and consumer decision-making processes, and reveals that brand names have a strong influence on car purchase decisions. [8] treats the user's emotional excitement as a data item for classification problems related to automobiles and consumers, and considers the types of question items related to it.

Some studies suggest optimal machine learning models by evaluating accuracy using multiple machine learnings. So et al. [9] are using rental property data, they use three techniques, Logistic Regression, Random Forest and XGBoost, to compare the accuracy of the types of property attributes queried by email. As a result, XGBoost has been shown to be more accurate than logistic regression, however if it has the same level of prediction accuracy, it is better to use logistic regression as a method to apply to business. Zuo et al. [10] evaluate the Bayesian network, linear discriminant analysis, and binomial logistic regression research proposal model through accuracy comparison using data on bread purchase, and show that the Bayesian network model is highly accurate.

3 Data Summary

3.1 Basic Aggregate

In this study, we used the data provided by the car sales corporation I, which sells the products of the car manufacturing corporation II. The number of data is 23,754 for all car information and 29,112 for all customer list, and the period is from January 1, 1991 to May 31, 2018.

The automobile industry is affected by external factors, so it is not good to use it as it is. Therefore, I processed the data and created a new dataset. In creating new a data set, we selected customers. First, the demand for cars is higher in the rural areas than in the metropolitan area, and it is estimated that the needs differ depending on the prefecture, so we limited the area of residence of customers and used prefecture A(76.8%), which is the home of car sales corporation I, and prefecture B(8.6%), which is an adjacent prefecture. Second, the data consists of the genders of male (52.4%), female (8.72%), Corporation (6.52%), and unknown (32.4%) customers. Corporations are believed to be using it as a business vehicle and may continue to use it or switch to another service provider by contract, which can lead to extreme usage trends. Therefore, we used only men and women to eliminate extreme usage trends. Figure 2 shows the types of automobiles of customers who use car sales corporation I are about 50% of popular cars such as minivans, compact cars, and sedans, it is possible that many customers own family cars. In addition, there is no difference in the types of cars owned by male and female (Fig. 2), so this study does not distinguish between genders. From the above, individual customers don't distinguish between male and female, and we set male and female who live in prefecture A and B. Third, since individual customers had direct transactions, sales, and unknowns, we limited them to direct transactions only. we limited it to individual customers who own one car. This was done to eliminate the impact of the possibility of varying frequency of scrutineering for each car owned by a person who owns multiple vehicles.

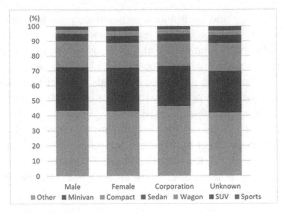

Fig. 2. Percentage of car types owned by gender

3.2 Data Cleaning and Processing

We found many missing and outliers in the data we used, so we cleaned and processed the data. First, we dealt with missing data. Since the data used is qualitative data, if there are missing data in the variables used for analysis, the method of deleting all data rows was used. Many studies have shown how to deal with missing data. However, there is no clear solution for polynomial qualitative variables, and compatibility problems have been pointed out [11]. Second, if there are few customers in charge of the data variable "Service Sales Representative ID", we decided that the employee with the same contact ID is not a sales representative, and selected and excluded the customer in charge.

Based on the customer selection, data cleaning and processing, we used 7024 individual customers who own one car that directly traded the target sample and purchased a new car.

4   Analysis

4.1   Dependent Variable

The purpose of this study is to identify the factors of customers who continue to use car inspections. Therefore, we need to create a variable for whether to visit for car inspection. Using the variable in the data, the car inspection expiration date, we created a dummy variable "observable" that will continue to use the car inspection. We have assigned it to 0 because it will not always be visited in future car inspections if the car inspection expiration date is within the data period. On the other hand, if it is outside the data period, 1 is substituted to continue using the inspection of the vehicle even after the data collection period ends.

When doing machine learning, creating a classifier with imbalanced data will prevent accurate evaluation. Observable is imbalanced data because 0 is 5025 and 1 is 1099. Therefore, it is necessary to make the data balanced. Chawla et al. [12] cite many studies and shows how to deal with imbalanced data. Random undersampling can potentially remove certain important examples, and random oversampling can lead to overfitting.

In addition, oversampling can introduce an additional computational task if the data set is already fairly large but imbalanced.

We have clustered samples with similar attribute characteristics to avoid losing their characteristics in order to avoid the possibility that certain important columns will be deleted. We determined the optimum number of clusters to be 3 from the transition of the residual sum of squares using the Gap statistic, performed non-hierarchical cluster analysis (Fig. 3), and undersampled.

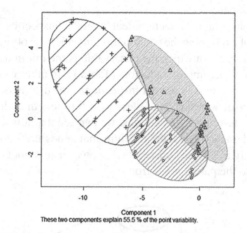

Fig. 3. Results of non-hierarchical cluster analysis

4.2 Independent Variable

Independent variables used in this study are dummy variables. We used "group", "kotei", "kei", "inspection", "DM", "Email", "TEL", and "Mail List" as independent variables. Group is a variable originally created by car sales corporation I, there are numbers from 1 to 7, and the closer it is to 1, the more likely it is to use the store. In that it, 1 accounted for 72%, and the other numbers were small, so I separated 1 and others and converted them to dummy variables. Kotei represents the attributes of customers and is classified into four types: fixed customers, semi-fixed customers, new car customers, and general customers. Kei represents 1 if customer own a light car and 0 if customer own a regular car. Inspection represents the actual number of warehouses. There are numbers from 1 to 5, with 1 accounting for 85% and the other numbers being small, so we separated the numbers 1 and the rest and converted them to dummy variables. DM, Email, and TEL indicate whether you can send or contact, and the Mail List indicates whether the customer is on the mailing list.

4.3 Bayesian Network

The Bayesian network is a probability model that uses Bayesian inference to express the dependency between random variables by the network structure and to express the relationship between each random variable by conditional probability. It provides flexible support regardless of the linearity or non-linearity of the data. If each variable to be processed is large enough data, it is easy to normalize the frequency of the state of each variable and get the probability value of each item. In the graph structure of the Bayesian network, the random variable of interest is a node, and their dependencies are represented by arrows that are directed links (directed acyclic graph). The link source is called the parent node and the link destination is called the child node. Nodes that do not have directed links between the nodes on the network graph indicate that they are conditionally independent.

Figure 4 shows "observable" directly affect "kotei", "inspection", and "group". Furthermore, as a result of examining the combination in which the observable is most likely to be 1 and the combination in which the observable is the minimum, it was found that "kotei" and "inspection" are important factors (Table 1). In other words, the characteristics of customers who continue to use car inspections are customers who frequently use stores and the number of warehousing is less than 5 times. In addition, since "group" is the parent node and has many connections, we can see that it is a variable created by connecting various elements. Also, the medium that sends the information to the customer does not directly affect the "observable", however it is not completely irrelevant because it is related to the parent node group.

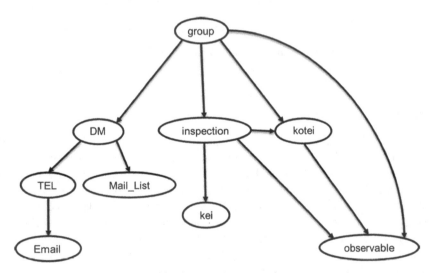

Fig. 4. Bayesian network

Table 1. Maximum and minimum combinations for the dependent variable

	Group	Kotei	Kei	Inspection	DM	Email	TEL	Mail list
Max	0	1	0	1	0	0	0	0
Min	0	0	0	0	0	0	0	0

4.4 Logistic Regression

Logistic regression is a type of regression analysis and is a parametric method that is premised on following a normal distribution. Logistic regression does not follow a normal distribution because it uses qualitative data for the dependent variable. However, it is possible to handle binomial and Poisson distributions other than the normal distribution by using a generalized linear model in which the linear model of regression analysis is linked to the exponential family via a link function. In addition, the odds which are the ratio of probabilities, are predictable and are expressed by the probability p that the independent variable of a certain dependent variable occurs and the probability 1-p that it does not occur. The logarithmic odds ratio probability, which measures the influence of the independent variable on the dependent variable, is expressed as an odds ratio. A value greater than 1 indicates a positive effect, and a value smaller than 1 indicates a negative effect.

We used the stepwise backward regression method of variable selection reduction method to reduce the variables until the optimal model based on AIC and continue until the optimal model with variable selection. Table 2 shows that "kotei", "Email", and "inspection" have a positive impact. In other words, the characteristics of customers who continue to use car inspections are customers who frequently use stores, allow them to send emails, and the number of warehousing is less than 5 times.

Table 2. Logistic regression analysis results

	β	SE	OR	95% Cl	P-value
Group	−0.257	0.176	0.774	0.548–1.093	0.145
Kotei	−0.987	0.179	2.682	1.887–3.812	0.000
Email	0.931	0.234	2.538	1.604–4.016	0.000
Inspection	1.008	0.154	2.739	2.024–3.705	0.000

4.5 Decision Tree

Decision tree is a data mining method used for regression and classification, and is a non-parametric method. It can handle both quantitative and qualitative data, and builds prediction and discrimination models by combining attributes with the influence of attributes as a turning point. By creating a model with a tree-like structure, it is possible to visually recognize the analysis results and display the effects in an easy-to-understand manner. However, overfitting that overfits the model is likely to occur, which makes pruning work to set the depth of the tree important.

We used CART in the split method and the Gini coefficient as the split criterion. In addition, the tree pruning method uses the Min + 1 × SE criterion, which is the minimum mean cross-validated misclassification rate + 1 × standard deviation. Figure 5 shows the dotted line indicates the Min + 1 × SE standard. We pruned at the 7th size, which is lower than the dotted line. Therefore, we set nsplit to 7 and CP as 0,03 (Table 3). Figure 6 shows that if the customer is a fixed customer, the number of car inspection warehouses is 5, and telephone contact is possible, the probability of becoming a continuously observable customer is about 63%.

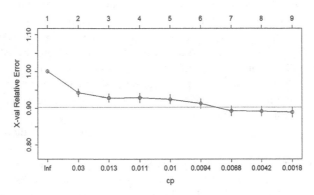

Fig. 5. Complexity per tree size

Table 3. List of pruning decision trees

nsplit	CP	rel error	xerror	xstd
0	0.059	1.000	1.00	0.003
1	0.015	0.941	0.944	0.011
2	0.011	0.926	0.935	0.012
3	0.010	0.915	0.933	0.013
4	0.010	0.904	0.926	0.014
5	0.009	0.894	0.915	0.014
6	0.005	0.886	0.897	0.014
7	0.003	0.880	0.895	0.014
8	0.001	0.877	0.893	0.014
9	0.001	0.876	0.895	0.014

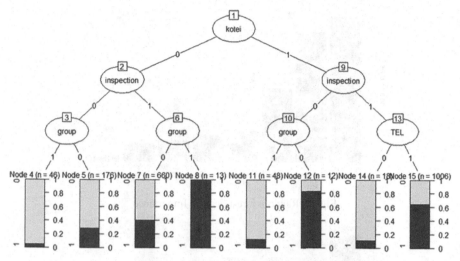

Fig. 6. Decision tree analysis results

4.6   Random Forest and XGBoost

Random forest is an ensemble learning process that uses multiple decision trees as weak discriminators and integrates the results. Decision trees used as weak discriminators in Random Forest tend to be less biased. Therefore, it can use randomness to reduce the correlation between decision trees, prevent overfitting, and obtain high generalization performance. On the other hand, XGBoost implements a decision tree gradient boosting algorithm. It creates a weak learner by sequentially using the results of the previously built model.

A grid search was used to adjust the parameters of the two models. It is a method to build a model of all patterns of given hyperparameter candidate values, and was used in this study because the number of high parameters is not so large.

Figure 7 and 8 show the feature importance of variables when performing a Random Forest and the feature importance of variables when performing XGBoost. "Kotei", "inspection", and "group" are higher in importance than both figures. Both results are similar to decision tree analysis. However, there are differences between Random Forest and XGBoost feature importance. For example, "Mail_list" is the fifth most feature important in Random Forest, while it is the least important in XGBoost. This is probably due to the difference in prediction accuracy before and after sorting by a reasonable measure of the importance of the variables [13].

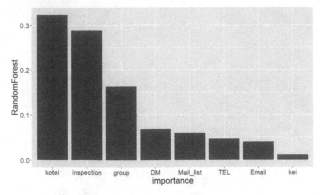

Fig. 7. Random forest Feature Importance

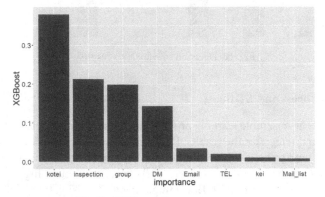

Fig. 8. XGBoost Feature Importance

4.7 Accuracy Evaluation

Table 4 shows that Bayesian networks are more accurate than other analyses. Logistic regression is the second most accurate after Bayesian networks. Decision tree, Random Forest, and XGBoost gave the lowest accuracy in this study. In addition, these three methods have the same accuracy for both Accuracy and F-measure. In general, it is considered unlikely that the accuracy of all three methods will be the same, but it is considered that this happened because the number of data used was small in this study.

Table 4. Accuracy and F-measure of each analysis

	Accuracy	F-measure
Bayesian network	0.631	0.640
Logistic regression	0.626	0.634
Decision tree	0.621	0.631
Random forest	0.621	0.631
XGBoost	0.621	0.631

5   Conclusion

The purpose of this study is to build a Bayesian network that can handle many missing values and difficult elements of observed data and can introduce expert knowledge into the network structure. In addition, we also show that Bayesian networks are useful by comparing them with multiple machine learning models. As a result, the accuracy of the Bayesian network proved to be higher than other analyzes. Each analysis shows that the factor of customers who continue to use car inspections has changed slightly, however Bayesian network and other analyzes have three things in common: "kotei", "inspection", and "group". In other words, the characteristics of customers who continue to use car inspections are customers who frequently use stores and the number of warehousing is less than 5 times. The medium that sends the information to the customer does not directly affect the "observable", however it is not completely irrelevant because it is related to the parent node group. This indicates that by using a medium that sends the information, it is possible that the vehicle will continue to be inspected.

6   Future Research

In this study, the accuracy of the Bayesian network was proved to be high, however the knowledge of actual experts was not introduced. Since this data is provided by car sales corporation I, it is possible that only the characteristics of car sales corporation I have been extracted. It is difficult for this result to be applied to other car sales corporation because the needs of automobiles differ from region to region. Therefore, it is necessary to incorporate the knowledge and experience of sales sellers as a future task. In addition, increasing the number of samples and variables is a future issue. In this study, due to imbalanced data, cluster analysis was performed and undersampling was performed so as not to lose features. As a result, less data was used and no difference was found in the Decision tree, Random Forest, and XGBoost. This can be interpreted as being well divided, however the three analyzes did not tell us which was the most accurate. From the above, it is necessary to improve the quality as a model that can flexibly support the Bayesian network by digitizing the knowledge and experience of other sales sellers and increasing the number of samples and variables.

References

1. Car industry strategy (2014). https://www.meti.go.jp/shingikai/sankoshin/seizo_sangyo/pdf/003_s02_02.pdf. Accessed 14 Jan 2021
2. Jama Active Matrix Database System. http://jamaserv.jama.or.jp/newdb/index.html. Accessed 14 Jan 2021
3. Hirose, A.: The analysis of the demand of automobiles with the price of gasoline. Bull. Saitama Gakuen Univ. **8**, 129–136 (2008)
4. Ministry of Land, Infrastructure, Transport and Tourism. https://www.mlit.go.jp/statistics/details/jidosha_list.html. Accessed 14 Jan 2021
5. Murakami, T., Suyama, A., Orihara, R.: TOSHIBA Corp. research & development center.: consumer behavior modeling using Bayesian networks. In: The 18th Annual Conference of the Japanese Society for Artificial Intelligence, p. 260 (2004)

6. Shende, V.: Analysis of research in consumer behavior of automobile passenger car customer. Int. J. Sci. Res. Publ. **4**(2), 1–8 (2014)
7. Alamgir, M., Nasir, T., Shamsuddoha, M., Nedelea, A.: Influence of brand name on consumer decision making process-an empirical study on car buyers. USV Ann. Econ. Publ. Admin. **10**(2), 142–153 (2011)
8. Sakurai, E., Motomura, Y., Yasumatsu, K., Michida, N., Sakamoto, K.: User modeling for car selection based on probabilistic methods. SIG-SAI **27**(2), 1–6 (2016)
9. Takeshi, S., Yuta, A.: Predicting inquiry from potential renters using property listing information - prediction accuracy and applicability to business. In: The 34th Annual Conference of the Japanese Society for Artificial Intelligence (2020)
10. Yi, Z., Yada, K.: Consumer behavior modeling using bayesian networks. Commun. Oper. Res. Soc. Jpn. **62**(12), 795–800 (2017)
11. Watanabe, M., Takahashi, M.: Missing data processing: single substitution method and multiple substitution method by R. Kyoritsu (2017)
12. Chawla, N.V., Japkowicz, N., Kotcz, A.: Special issue on learning from imbalanced data sets. ACM SIGKDD Explor. Newsl. **6**(1), 1–6 (2004)
13. Strobl, C., Boulesteix, A.L., Zeileis, A., Hothorn, T.: Bias in random forest variable importance measures: illustrations, sources and a solution. BMC Bioinform. **8**(1), 1–21 (2007)

Creative Design of Gaussian Sensor System with Encoding and Decoding

Yu-Hsiung Huang[1], Wei-Chun Chen[1], and Su-Chu Hsu[2(✉)]

[1] Department of New Media Art, Taipei National University of the Arts, Taipei 11201, Taiwan
eric@techart.tnua.edu.tw
[2] Research Center for Technology and Art, National Tsing Hua University,
Hsinchu 30013, Taiwan
suchu@mx.nthu.edu.tw

Abstract. Stuart Hall proposed the "encoding/decoding model of communication" for the theoretical method of media information production and dissemination in 1973. In 1980, he further proposed the research of classic contemporary culture titled "Encoding/Decoding", which explained how media producers can "encode" an object, feeling, and ideas. Message in the media to achieve the purpose of disseminating information. In addition, "decoding" is the process and method of how the media message can be perceived by the "receiver" after being transformed and translated. It has been explained that the concept of encoding and decoding has a great influence on the research of different cultural media communication from the analogy to the digital age through many kinds of research. However, with the rapid development of digital media technology, we are faced with the production methods of information in tangible and intangible media, and most of them are translated in virtual form in programming languages or digital symbols. Encoding and decoding of digital symbols and codes has gradually changed the way we understand perception.

In this paper, we propose the "Gaussian Sensor System", which consists of three parts: Gausstoys magnetic sensor module, video/audio encoding and decoding, and interactive installation art. We used damped oscillator magnetic balance and Gausstoys sensor as a tangible user interface (TUI), and integrated the Gaussian sensor into the interactive installation art. When the user intervenes with the floating magnet device and disturbs the magnetic field, the gaussian sensor will "encode" the human analogy behavior. Then the data of human behavior is transformed into visual video and sound feedback. The RGB color of visual video and frequency feedback of audio on the screen is the "decoding" of perception. Therefore, in our Gaussian Sensor System, "balance" is generated through the floating magnetic force in our artwork. After the user "intervenes", the entire behavior is transformed into a digital reproduction of video/audio and then transmitted to the user the perception feedback of color and sound. Our creative design has been shown to "Tsing Hua Effects 2020: STEM with A" Technology and Art Festival of Tsing Hua University in Taiwan and "Art Gallery, 2016 SIGGRAPH Asia" in Macau. In the past, many applications of Gaussian Sensor were used in interactive games or interactive learning, but our application was in "interactive installation art". We applied the damped oscillator magnetic balance as a tangible interface device, which is quite rare in HCI applications or interactive art. In the future,

© Springer Nature Switzerland AG 2021
S. Yamamoto and H. Mori (Eds.): HCII 2021, LNCS 12766, pp. 385–395, 2021.
https://doi.org/10.1007/978-3-030-78361-7_29

the media in the digital age that we are facing will gradually transform real-world cognitions through digital programming languages to produce new perceptions. At present, many kinds of research in HCI field have explained how to experience hearing, taste, and touch in digital media. The encoding and decoding of digital media will be one of the important topics in HCI in the future. Our creative design can be applied to more HCI or TUI research fields in the future and drive users to experience more diverse perceptions through digital media.

Keywords: Gaussian Sensor · Encoding and Decoding · Damped oscillation · Tangible User Interface · Interactive installation art

1 Introduction

In recent years, the influence of computer technology on economy, morality, politics and society has become more and more significant. How interactive technology affects human life has become an important issue [1]. At the same time, the way to understand media information in life has been fully digitized because of the rapid development of digital technology media. We face the production methods of all forms of media, which are mostly translated in a virtual way through programming languages or digital symbols. The encoding and decoding of digital symbols has gradually changed the way we understand perception. We have done many applications in the Tangible User Interface (TUI) and human-computer interaction interfaces in the past years [2]. We have created the works of "Forces in Equilibrium" [3], and was exhibited in the Art Gallery in SIGGRAPH Asia 2016 [3]. In 2020, it was also shown in the "Tsing Hua Effects 2020 - STEM with A" science and art festival at National Tsing Hua University in Taiwan [4]. In this study, we are discussing the system and TUI method behind the artwork. The system we developed is a TUI interactive interface formed by a combination of damped oscillator magnetic balance and Gausstoys sensor. It allows the audience to fiddle any magnet and generate magnetic field disturbances. We encode this interactive behavior, and then decode the change of gaussian value into digital representation and feedback as video and audio through the program. To discuss in the era of digital media, the digital programming language we are facing has transformed from human "analogous touching behavior" to "digital video and audio projection" in the real world through encoding and decoding, and people got the "analogous perception" feedback.

2 Related Work

This chapter will explain the transformation of the concept of encoding and decoding from the past analog media to the digital age. It brings different views on encoding and decoding in the future digital age. We will also discuss the related creation and research on the application of damped oscillator magnetic balance used in HCI.

2.1 Research on Encoding and Decoding

Stuart Hall proposed "encoding and decoding in the television discourse" in 1973 for the mode of media information [5]. Then in 1980, he proposed a classic contemporary cultural study entitled "Encoding/Decoding" (Encoding/Decoding). These studies influence the development of the media. From media, culture, politics, etc., a variety of media-oriented senders discussed how to "encode" an object, a perception, and an idea, and then integrate it into the message in the media to achieve the purpose of disseminating these messages [6]. And "decoding" is the process and method of translating the encoded media information to be understood and perceived by the "receiver". The research of Stuart Hall has been discussed in many traditional communication studies in the past. However, with the rapid development of digital media, we have also found that such encoding and decoding continue to be discussed from different perspectives in today's technology media.

Many studies so far have shown that encoding and decoding has many different opinions in today's digital age. Today's characters and symbols have been encoded by programming languages. For example, in the technical application of web pages, UTF-8 is used to encode the ASCII codes of different languages to solve the decoding and translation between different languages. As Ian Hutchby mentioned in 2001, the digital media will have different abilities through different processing of technologies. These abilities determine the difference in the way they may be "written" or "read" [7]. The same text language has many different encoding and decoding possibilities. Adrienne Shaw also pointed to encoding/decoding in the field of interactive media technology in 2017, proposing that digital media will change the way it is understood through programming technology. It contains a large number of digital images, games and multimedia, all of which produce many different sensory experiences due to digital programs [8]. In 2020, Marie Palmer also mentioned that modern media messages have largely changed our cognitive model through algorithmic calculations [9].

We must think about how our feelings and perceptions of digital media will change under the rapid development of digital technology. In our paper, we emphasized that digital signals are transmitted through the perception of TUI. It encodes and decodes human behavior and perception through programs to form a digital representation. In other words, our system transforms human's "analogous behavior" into "digital audio and video", and then transforms it into "analogous perception" feedback. It is an interactive art.

2.2 Gaussian Sensor

Gauss is a commonly used unit of magnetic field strength or magnetic flux. Quite a lot of sensors are designed as gaussian sensors and used in many different researches as magnetic sensors [10–13].

The gaussian sensor used in this paper is a magnetic sensing module, which is a series of studies developed in 2012 by the Communications and Multi-media Lab of the Institute of Information Networks and Multimedia, National Taiwan University. The main developer is Professor Rong-Hao Liang. Since 2012, the laboratory has proposed GaussSense [14], which installs a magnetic sensor with a thickness of about 2 cm on the back of a tablet or screen, and can sense the magnet installed in a stylus. Then in 2013 they proposed GaussBits [15] based on GaussSense sensing technology. GaussBits is a 3-dimensional interactive system that directly uses magnets and portable displays as near-surface. It uses thin and light Hall-sensors in the form of arrays and grids. It is neatly installed on the back of the sensor to track and process data such as magnetic position and three-dimensional direction [16]. Then the laboratory proposed GaussBricks [17] in 2014, which is a magnetic sensor module in the form of building blocks. It allows users to easily assemble and disassemble many shapes and through the physical interaction effects of the structure itself after the building blocks and magnets are assembled, such as squeezing and stretching with their hands. These actions can sense changes in the magnetic field through a magnetic sensor placed behind the tablet and generate feedback. The next year, after becoming more proficient in technology, they established a new Taiwan-based team "Gausstoys Le Magnetic Fun" in 2015 [18]. This series of sensors use magnets as a medium to interact with virtual computer programs in real time through magnetic users touching the physical magnet. It can be an interactive interface for location detection and has been used in many interactive apps for game-based learning. In the past, many applications of gaussian sensor were used in interactive games or interactive learning, but our application was in "interactive installation art".

2.3   Tangible User Interface, TUI

Since the Tangible Media Group of MIT Media Lab has devoted itself to the research and development of TUI, its vision is to add the rich physical properties of physical substances to the human-machine interface [19]. It attempts to link the perception of digital media from the appearance of the real world, and to find the perceptions that people have neglected due to the invention of computers and to rejoin the human-computer interaction [20]. Tangible Interactive Interface (TUI) has been a common human-computer interaction interface. Many TUI studies have been conducted on education and museums through HCI related fields [21, 22], but they are rarely applied in the field of artistic creation.

This paper uses Gaussian sensor combined with damped oscillator magnetic balance [23, 24] to construct TUI and drives the user to touch any magnet to produce different changes in the system. This paper will use the analog magnetic balance and imbalance designed in the interactive device of TUI to change the digital images and audio in the interactive situation. The real-time deformation of digital images and sound feeds back cognitive experience to participants.

3   Gaussian Sensor System

In order to realize our application of encoding and decoding human "analogous behavior" into "digital image" and "analogous perception" with digital programs. We propose Gaussian Sensor System. This chapter will introduce the Gausstoys magnetic sensing module, TUI module, video/audio encoding and decoding in this system. The Gausstoys sensing board has 192 magnetic sensing elements neatly arranged in an array. When a magnet is close, the position of the magnet and the strength of the magnetic sensing value can be determined and a virtual space sensed by magnetic force can be generated.

We also designed a TUI module by using damped oscillator magnetic balance installation and integrated Gausstoys magnetic sensor. Participants can touch any magnet that will disturb magnetic balance. We define this to be an analogous touch. The Gausstoys magnetic sensor module will detect the position of the touched magnet and the magnetic sensor value and then encode it into a projected digital audio and video screen. The real-time audio-visual changes of the picture can be decoded into the analog perception of RGB color and sound.

3.1 Structure of Gaussian Sensor System

Figure 1 describes our Gaussian Sensor system. We separately explain the Gausstoys magnetic sensing module, TUI device with damped oscillator magnetic balance installation, video/audio encoding and decoding in the system.

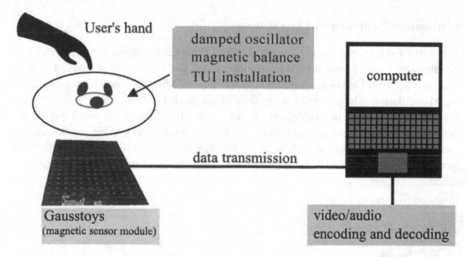

Fig. 1. Structure of Gaussian Sensor system

3.2 Gausstoys (Magnetic Sensor Module)

We used a 10-in. Gausstoy sensor board developed by CM Lab at NTU for our design. 192 magnetic sensor elements are arranged in a 16 × 12 matrix. The magnetic change values in the matrix range of the black development board can all be sensed. Gausstoys can determine the position of the magnet and calculate the relative distance between the magnet and the sensing board based on the magnitude of the magnetic force change. Based on these values, three-axis (x, y, z) axis virtual coordinates can be constructed. The matrix arrangement of Gausstoys sensors is shown in Fig. 2

Fig. 2. The matrix arrangement Gausstoys Sensor board

3.3   Magnetic Levitation TUI Installation

In the part of the interactive device, we applied damped oscillator magnetic balance installation as the user interface. We use three round flat magnets to be placed around the circular grooves. One of the magnets is fixed in the middle position to form a magnetic damped oscillation. The groove in the middle of the device is designed to make it easier for the magnet to stand in suspension. At the same time, there is an interlayer in the middle of the circular device, which hides the Gausstoys sensor board in the device. As shown in Fig. 3. The user can lightly touch the three semi-floating magnets with their fingers. The other two semi-floating magnets will also be disturbed when one magnet is touched.

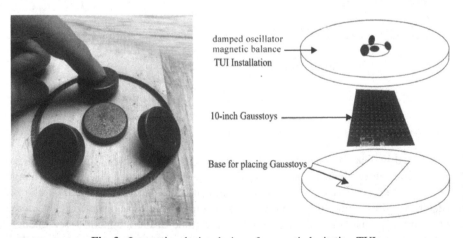

Fig. 3. Interactive device design of magnetic levitation TUI

3.4 Video/Audio Encoding and Decoding

When the user's hand touches any of the damped oscillator magnetic balance TUI installation, the Gaussian value sensed by Gausstoys will be collected by the microcontroller
(Teensy 2.0) and then "encoded". Teensy 2.0 is a controller similar and compatible with
Arduino. But the volume is relatively light and it supports transmission of multiple USB
connectors. With the feature that the magnet has positive and negative poles, the sensor
can interpret the tilt angle, rotation angle, and flipping motion of the magnet. Then transfer the data to the computer via USB. We receive Gaussian Data through the Processing
IDE on the computer and write the program, using the library provided by Gausstoys.
We divide three equal parts with the center point of the sensor board, corresponding
to the three colors of RGB. When the magnet in any range is lightly pressed and the
magnetic force increases beyond the threshold, the corresponding image shape, color
and sound will be changed at the same time. In this way, the Gaussian Data is "decoded"
into a "digital audio and video" that combines vision and hearing. The change of digital audio and video also stimulates the viewer's "analogous perception" of colors and
sounds (Fig. 4).

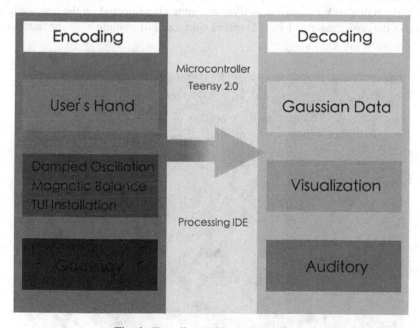

Fig. 4. Encoding and Decoding process

4 Implementations

This chapter describes how the Gaussian Sensor System proposed in this thesis generates "balance" through the damped oscillation of the magnet through our artwork,

and then "intervenes" by the user to transform the entire behavior into a video/audio representation. We introduce it with "Forces in Equilibrium".

4.1 Interactive Context of Forces in Equilibrium

The works of "Forces in Equilibrium" were exhibited in the Art Gallery of 2016 SIG-GRAPH Asia [3] and also in the "Tsing Hua Effects 2020: STEM with A" Technology and Art Festival at Tsinghua University, Taiwan in 2020. The work used "magnetic balance" as an interactive interface, where the participant touches a semi-floating magnet to create vibrations and trigger changes in sound and visual projection when the system is out of balance. It uses digital means to depict the struggle of analogy imbalance. We encode human intervention in the natural environment. It decodes through the Gaussian value of magnetic balance to reproduce a new digital perception. The art statement of the work emphasizes that under the destruction of human knowledge or ignorance, the environment is out of balance and the world is chaotic.

The interactive process of the works is as follows:

When the participant enters the exhibition space, they can see a stand with a circular platform above it. There are three semi-floating magnets on the platform and one magnet fixed in the center of the platform. A dynamic image is projected on the rear wall. The content of the projected image is a 3D sphere composed of a single light spot and moves faintly, as shown in Fig. 5.

Fig. 5. Public participation in interactive installation works

When the user touches the magnet lightly to cause a trigger, the magnetic force of the magnet will change with the force of pressing the magnet. At the same time, the system will generate sound feedback and the images will also change, as shown in Fig. 6.

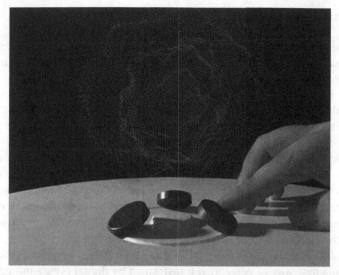

Fig. 6. The user touches the magnet which affects the projected image

We divide the center of the sensing area of the interactive device into three equal parts. The positions of the three magnets are allocated to the three areas. When the magnet in any range is touched or pressed down, the value of the magnetic force will increase if it exceeds the threshold. When the value is set, the logical expression is used to determine the sound and video to be shown. The colors of the three areas are red, green, and blue, as shown in Fig. 7 below. The three areas have different music file combinations. The screen corresponding to these areas may appear in three-color spheres and play three kinds of sounds.

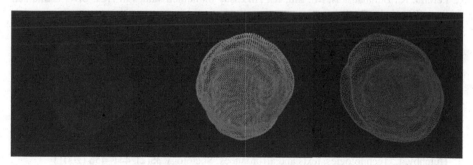

Fig. 7. The colors corresponding to the three magnetic sensing areas (Color figure online)

5 Conclusions

In the Gaussian Sensor System, we construct a "balanced" state through the encoding of damped oscillator magnetic balance and Gaussian value. After the user "intervenes", the entire behavior is transformed into a video/audio digital representation.

The user obtains perceptual feedback of color and sound through the program "decoding". In this way, the human "analogous behavior" in the real world is transformed into "digital audio and video" and then into "analogous perception". In the past, many applications of Gaussian Sensor were used in interactive games or interactive learning, but our application was in "interactive installation art". The work satirizes that people often destroy the balance of nature and the peace of the world intentionally or unintentionally. Our works have also received a lot of praise in the exhibition. In the past, most of the applications of magnetic force were mostly used to solve life problems, such as switches or general sensors. We designed magnetic levitation as a tangible user interface device, which is quite rare in HCI applications or interactive art.

The translation of media in the digital age has moved from cognition in the real world in the past to a new way of perception transformed by digital programming language. In the current HCI field, many studies have been discussing how to experience hearing, taste, and tactile sensations in digital media. Encoding/Decoding of this digital media is one of the important topics in HCI in the future. In the future our creative design can be applied in more HCI or TUI fields and can be used to connect the virtual and real world, for example, in natural science education, students can understand the invisible energy in the natural environment. This drives users to experience more diverse perceptions through digital audio and video.

References

1. Pereira, R., Baranauskas, M., Liu, K.: An essay on human values in HCI. SBC J. Interact. Syst. **9**(1), 4–16 (2018)
2. Hsu, S.C., Chang, C.Y., Shih, K.P.: TmP-The Study and Application of Tangible mobile-Phone Interface of Emerging Presentation in Culture Creative Industry. MOST 103-2627-E-119-001, Taiwan (2013)
3. Chen, W.C., Hsu, S.C., Huang, Y.H.: Forces in Equilibrium. Siggraph ASIA - Art Gallery, Macao (2016)
4. Tsing, H.: Effects 2020-Technology Art Festival "STEM with A", Hsichu City, Taiwan (2020)
5. Hall, S.: Encoding and Decoding in Television Discourse. CCCS Stencilled Paper no. 7; also in During, Simon (ed.) (1993). The Cultural Studies Reader (1973)
6. Hall, S.: Encoding/decoding. Media Cult. Stud. Keyworks **2**, 163–174 (2001)
7. Hutchby, I.: Technologies, texts and affordances. Sociology **35**(2), 441–456 (2001)
8. Shaw, A.: Encoding and decoding affordances: stuart hall and interactive media technologies. Media Cult. Soc. **39**(4), 592–602 (2017)
9. Palmer, M.: Facebook as a Meta-ideological Apparatus: Reassessing the Encoding/Decoding Model in the Context of Social Media. Diss (2020)
10. Berkelman, P., Tix, B., Abdul-Ghani, H.: Electromagnetic position sensing and force feedback for a magnetic stylus with an interactive display. IEEE Mag. Lett. **10**, 1–5 (2018)
11. Adel, A., Mansour, M., Micheal, M.M., Abdelmawla, A., Khalil, I.S., Misra, S.: Magnetic localization for an electromagnetic-based haptic interface. IEEE Mag. Lett. **10**, 1–5 (2019)

12. Langerak, T., Zárate, J.J., Lindlbauer, D., Holz, C., Hilliges, O.: Omni: volumetric sensing and actuation of passive magnetic tools for dynamic haptic feedback. In: Proceedings of the 33rd Annual ACM Symposium on User Interface Software and Technology, pp. 594–606 (2020)
13. Schütze, A., Helwig, N., Schneider, T.: Sensors 4.0–smart sensors and measurement technology enable Industry 4.0. J. Sens. Sens. Syst. **7**(1), 359–371 (2018)
14. Liang, R.H., Cheng, K.Y., Su, C.H., et al.: GaussSense: attachable stylus sensing using magnetic sensor grid. In: Proceedings of the 25th Annual ACM Symposium on User Interface Software and Technology, pp. 319–326 (2012)
15. Liang, R.H., Cheng, K.Y., Chan, L., et al.: GaussBits: magnetic tangible bits for portable and occlusion-free near-surface interactions. In: Proceedings of the SIGCHI Conference on Human Factors in Computing Systems, pp. 1391–1400 (2013)
16. Liang, R.H., Chan, L., Tseng, H.Y., et al.: GaussBricks: magnetic building blocks for constructive tangible interactions on portable displays. In: Proceedings of the SIGCHI Conference on Human Factors in Computing Systems, pp. 3153–3162 (2014)
17. Magnetic Field Record. http://www.kyouei-ltd.co.jp/magnetic_field_record.html. Accessed 14 Nov 2020
18. GaussToys Inc. http://gausstoys.com/. Accessed 20 July 2016
19. Ishii, H., Lakatos, D., Bonanni, L., Labrune, J.B.: Radical atoms: beyond tangible bits, toward transformable materials. Interactions **19**(1), 38–51 (2012)
20. Ishii, H., Ullmer, B.: Tangible bits: towards seamless interfaces between people, bits, and atoms. In: Proceedings of the ACM SIGCHI Conference on Human factors in computing systems, pp. 234–241 (1997)
21. Ávila-Soto, M., Valderrama-Bahamóndez, E., Schmidt, A.: TanMath: a tangible math application to support children with visual impairment to learn basic arithmetic. In: Proceedings of the 10th International Conference on PErvasive Technologies Related to Assistive Environments (2017)
22. Attard, G., Raffaele, C.D., Smith, S.: TangiBoard: a toolkit to reduce the implementation burden of tangible user interfaces in education. In: 2019 IEEE 13th International Conference on Application of Information and Communication Technologies (AICT). IEEE (2019)
23. Myers, E.D.: Magnetic damping of beam balances improves speed, increases accuracy, and affords permanency: the theory of maganetic damping. Nat. Sci. Teach. Assoc. **38**(7), 45–47 (1971)
24. The balance and oscillation of the magnet. https://www.youtube.com/watch?v=sU7Q26 N7MvY&ab_channel=%E5%9C%8B%E7%AB%8B%E7%A7%91%E5%AD%B8%E5% B7%A5%E8%97%9D%E5%8D%9A%E7%89%A9%E9%A4%A8%E7%A7%91%E5% AD%B8%E5%AD%B8%E7%BF%92%E4%B8%AD%E5%BF%83. Accessed 20 Dec 2019

Smart Speaker Interaction Through ARM-COMS for Health Monitoring Platform

Teruaki Ito[✉], Takashi Oyama, and Tomio Watanabe

Faculty of Computer Science and System Engineering, Okayama Prefectural University, 111 Kuboki Soja, Okayama 719-1197, Japan
tito@ss.oka-pu.ac.jp

Abstract. The authors have proposed an idea of augmented tele-presence system called ARM-COMS (ARm-supported eMbodied COmmunication Monitor System), which detects the orientation of a subject face by the face-detection tool based on an image processing technique, and mimics the head motion of a remote person to behave as if an avatar does during video communication. In addition to that, ARM-COMS makes appropriate reactions by audio signals during talk when a remote person speaks even without any significant motion in video communication. Based on the basic idea of ARM-COMS, this study focuses on AI speaker technology that answers questions in a natural language, and works on the development of an integrated system with health monitoring with ARM-COMS. This paper describes the prototype system developed in this study, shows some of the basic functions implemented in the prototype, and discusses how the combination of AI technology with ARM-COMS could work based on the experimental findings.

Keywords: Embodied communication · Augmented tele-presence robotic arm · AI speaker · Health monitoring

1 Introduction

The growing needs to personal health monitoring system [8], which provides health management information for daily life, shows the current trends in high health awareness. In fact, personal health management [2] is one of the critical topics in Japan and growing use of personal health monitoring system supports this observation. Today's modern technology is making it easier to take charge of your health and be alerted to any abnormal changes our bodies may be experiencing [9]. However, those systems are equipped with full of functions, which make it difficult to use for senior people or for those who are unfamiliar with ICT devices including smartphones.

This research focuses on AI speaker technology [13] that answers questions in natural language, and is working on the development of an integrated system with health monitoring. In addition to the user-friendly feature of natural language interface, it would be possible to build a system that would meet the individual needs by combining a variety of web service tools.

S. Yamamoto and H. Mori (Eds.): HCII 2021, LNCS 12766, pp. 396–405, 2021.
https://doi.org/10.1007/978-3-030-78361-7_30

On the other hand, there is a big demand to deal with the digital divide problem happening on the user side. Therefore, it would offer an effective approach to this issue if this research provides such a health monitoring system as anyone could easily use.

After briefly explaining the research background, this paper describes the system framework of the health management system which is the goal of this research. Then, this paper will introduce the prototype system which is currently under development, report the results of operation experiments conducted using this prototype system, and describe the effectiveness of the system framework.

2 Research Background

After Japan entered "an aging society" in 1970, the aging rate in Japan had risen very sharply, and entered "an aged society" in 1994, followed by "a super-aged society" in 2007 [10]. "A super-aged society" is defined as such a society where the proportion of the population aged over 65 accounts for 21% of the total population. Countries with a high aging rate include Sweden, Germany, France, the United Kingdom, and the United States, whereas Japan has a higher aging rate than any of these countries. Under these circumstances, it is an urgent issue for Japan to deal with the problems of the increasing elderly population, such as medical care and welfare amid the rapid increase of the elderly population.

Importance of appropriate health management is not only just for the elderly, but also is a great concern to anyone for enhancing the quality of life (QOL). There is a growing voice towards a wearable health monitoring system, which could analyze physical and mental health based on the biological information, such as heart rate, blood pressure, respiration, and body temperature [12]. In addition to that, manufacturers have released various digital health equipment as well as various home appliances that can be connected to home networks, which could be integrated with the health monitoring system. Under the integrated system environment, it would be expected to continuously review the measurement data regularly obtained from the activity meter, i.e., body temperature and blood pressure, while studying the long-term tendency of those data stored in database. However, it would difficult for general users to judge the health condition in such a way because it requires specialized knowledge. Therefore, there is a need towards a supporting service to understand health condition based on the measurement data even without advanced knowledge of data analysis nor IT tools.

In the meantime, the authors have proposed an idea of motion-enhanced display that utilizes the display itself as the communication media which mimics the motion of human head to enhance presence in remote communication. The idea has been implemented as an augmented tele-presence system called ARM-COMS (ARm-supported eMbodied COmmunication Monitor System) as shown in Fig. 1 [16]. In order to mimic the head motion using the display [3], ARM-COMS detects the orientation of a face by face-detection tool [11] based on an image processing technique [5]. However, ARM-COMS does not make appropriate reactions if a communication partner speaks without head motion in video communication. In order to solve these problems, the authors also proposed a voice signal usage [7] in local interaction so that ARM-COMS make an appropriate action even when the remote partner does not make any head motion [17].

Since this system is based on the remote communication support, remote healthcare for elder person is one of the biggest issues where ARM-COMS would be focused on. AI speaker function to ARM-COMS is a challenge to remote healthcare for ACM-COMS. Therefore, the introduction of AI speaker-based function is under study in this paper.

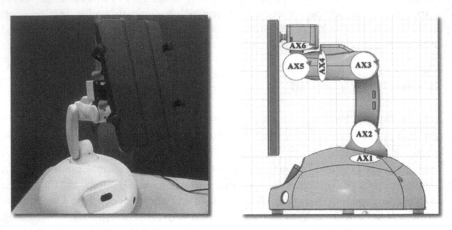

Fig. 1. Basic system configuration of ARM-COMS

3 System Reconfiguration

3.1 Basic Concept

Figure 2 shows the outline of the system framework of ARM-COMS health management system that is the goal of this research. ARM-COMS takes the role of remote communication core system, where communication participants enjoy the benefit of

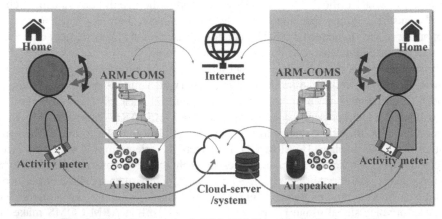

Fig. 2. Basic framework of ARM-COMS health monitoring system

telepresence communication. In addition to that, health monitoring system connected with AI speaker interface is integrated to ARM-COMS to share the health information between the communication participants.

Based on the collected data obtained from activity meter of a target person, AI speaker could answer such a question as would be related to the health monitoring of that parson. For example, a senior person who is hospital could monitor his/her health condition via natural language so that no technical skill is required to use AI speaker. For a remote diagnosis doctor, it would be possible to monitor the health condition of the remote patient either through AI speaker, or a remote monitoring system which could be offered to the doctor for more flexible monitoring functions. This paper focuses on the health monitoring module based on AI speaker.

3.2 System Configuration for a Prototype System

Basic configuration includes Data Collection Module (DCM) [1], Data Processing Module (DPM), Google-Spread Sheet Database (GSS DB), Data Analysis Module (DAM), AI Speaker Interface (AISIF), of which outline is shown in Fig. 3.

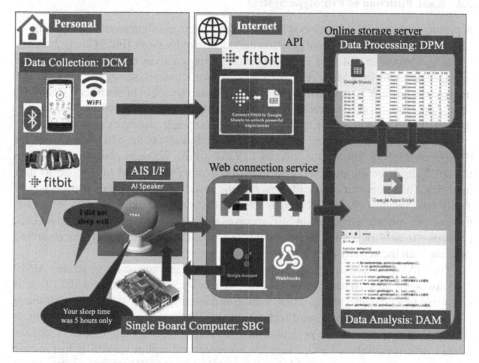

Fig. 3. Basic configuration of health monitoring function of ARM-COMS

DCM is composed of an activity meter worn on the user to collect basic activities. For example, an existing system such as Fitbit and Apple watch could be used as the activity meter. Biometric data required for health management, such as body temperature, blood pressure/heart rate, steps, calories, etc., are acquired from DCM, and are transmitted to GSS-DB for long-term storage.

DPM works for processing the collected data on GSS-DB, and feedbacks the required data according to the user's request. DPM can be performed with a device that provides an API for direct access to GSS-BD, but activities can be performed using web service linkage technology such as IFTTT [14]. GSS-DB is managed independently from the activity meter.

DAM is a collection of programs to make various analysis results. In order to respond to the user's request on health management, DAM performs the necessary analysis using the activity data, and prepares summary to provide it to the user.

As a solution to the digital divide problem, a smart speaker is integrated to the prototype system as a user interface as AISIF [15], which makes interactive conversation with the user in natural language. Although ordinary smart speakers cannot answer personal health data [1], the system proposed in this study makes it possible to have conversations with content tailored to the user because the biometric information regarding the user is available from GSS-DB.

3.3   Basic Function of Prototype System

A prototype system was developed based on the system configuration shown in Fig. 3. The basic component in the configuration includes, activity meter (FitbitCharge2: FBC), 3-axis accelerometer (Bitalino: BLN) for measuring user activity information, AI speaker interface (GoogleHomeMini: AIS) used by users for inquiries, sensor data storage and management which is composed of a cloud database (Google Spreadsheet: GSS-DB) [6] for operation, and a control program (Google AppScript: GAS) which operates the database based on inquiries from AIS and creates response sentences.

The above IoT devices and online services are linked via the SBC microcomputer (Raspberry PieB3). The web service (IFTTT) that links different platforms is used to automatically save the data obtained from the activity meter and to respond to user inquiries. The system automatically analyzes the saved data, creates a response, and lets AISIF talk. In addition, SBC is used as a server that receives and sends data from each component. A control program in SBC receives the generated response text from GAS, converts it to data for AISIF, and automatically sends it to the spreadsheet after receiving the data from the activity meter.

The GAS program analyzes the stored data, and automatically generates AISIF response sentences. When a user's inquiry is received from AISIF via IFTTT, it is converted to a character string. Then, a discriminant program is started to discriminate the presence or absence of a word with a responsive keyword in the character string. If an inquiry is responsible, the program reads the corresponding data from GSS, creates a reply sentence combined with a template sentence, and replies via AISIF. Just in case when the unrecognizable keyword is given, a reply sentence "There was no data about blah blah blah" will be created and be used in the reply.

– Scheduled Talking-to function (STF): This is a function of automatic talk-to to the user on a scheduled basis, where the system asks the user questions about their health condition at a scheduled time, and automatically records the reply contents from the user into a spreadsheet (Fig. 4).

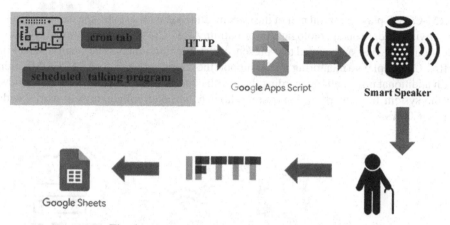

Fig. 4. Updated design of ARM-COMS system

– Alarmed Talking-to function (ATF): This is a function of emergency alarm talk, where AI speaker speaks through GAS if the system detects a sudden change of heart rate. With this function, a person with a heart disease can notify his/her family if a heart abnormality occurs (Fig. 5).

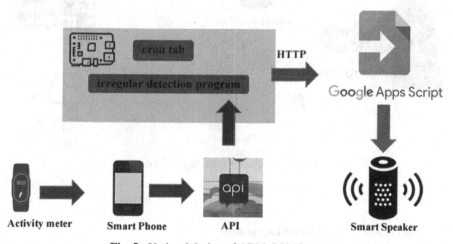

Fig. 5. Updated design of ARM-COMS system

4 Experiment

4.1 AI Speaker with ARM-COMS

ARM-COMS plays a central part of the system, attached with a smart-speaker connected to activity meter to obtain biological information. ARM-COMS supports virtual communication through an augmented tele-presence system environment. The smart-speaker in ARM-COMS plays a mentoring role to support the dialog between the ARM-COMS user with additional information regarding the health condition. Figure 6 shows the overview of the system framework to demonstrate how AI speaker collaboratively works with ARM-COMS.

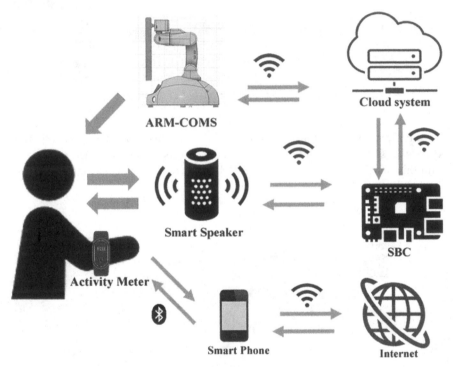

Fig. 6. AI speaker with ACM-COMS

4.2 Experimental Results and Discussion

This section shows how the prototype system works in AI speaker interaction. Figure 7 shows some examples of the contents of the inquiry and the contents of the response that actually made an inquiry to the AI speaker. Since the activity information is stored in GSS-DB, an inquiry regarding the basic information was correctly answered, for example, average calories burned last week, the maximum steps taken this month, etc. as shown in Fig. 7. These responses are not only the inquiry answer to the direct data query regarding the stored data in GSS-DB but also the calculation results based on the analysis of the stored information. However, if the question cannot be answered, the reply is given back with brief explanation. Therefore, it was confirmed that a function of a very basic conversation was implemented.

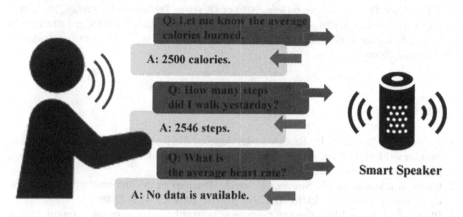

Fig. 7. Examples of AI speaker interaction

Implementation of STF function was confirmed in test conversation. When the user is asked questions about his/her health condition at a scheduled time, contents of the user-reply was automatically recorded to a spreadsheet. However, the user needs to say the wake-word all the time when he/she responses to the system. The interaction without the wake-word is one of the issues for the future work.

Implementation of ATF function was confirmed in test conversation. During the test run, the activity data was automatically transferred to GSS-DB successfully. When a heart-rate data exceeded the threshold was recorded by intentional hard exercise, ATF was initiated and emergency talk was given by the AI speaker. The response is performed at the time of crontab interval, not by a real-time reaction. It seems that the time delay in reaction is not a problem for this purpose. However, this topic will also be one of the issues to be studied in the future work.

5 Concluding Remarks

This paper briefly covers the idea of ARM-COMS, which detects the orientation of a subject face by the face-detection tool based on an image processing technique, and mimics the head motion of a remote partner in an effective manager. In addition to that, ARM-COMS makes appropriate reactions when a communication partner speaks even without any significant motion in video communication. ARM-COMS uses a voice signal usage in local interaction so that ARM-COMS makes an appropriate action even when the remote partner does not make any head motion.

This paper focuses on AI speaker technology that answers questions in natural language, and are working on the development of an integrated system with health monitoring. The idea is to integrate the AI speaker technology with ARM-COMS and to study how the idea should work. According to the experimental results with a prototype system, this paper clarified what could be done and what should be pursued in the future study.

Acknowledgement. This work was partly supported by JSPS KAKENHI Grant Numbers JP19K12082 and Original Research Grant 2020 of Okayama Prefectural University. The author would like to acknowledge Kengo Sadakane for implementing the basic modules, and all members of Kansei Information Engineering Labs at Okayama Prefectural University for their cooperation to conduct the experiments.

References

1. Bertrand, C., Bourdeau, L.: Research interviews by Skype: a new data collection method. In: Esteves, J. (Ed.) Proceedings from the 9th European Conference on Research Methods, pp. 70–79. IE Business School, Spain (2010)
2. Civan, A., Skeels, M.M., Stolyar, A., et al.: Personal health information management: consumers' perspectives. AMIA Ann. Symp. Proc. **2006**, 156–160 (2006)
3. Ekman, P., Friesen, W.V.: The repertoire or nonverbal behavior: categories, origins, usage, and coding. Semiotica **1**, 49–98 (1969)
4. Gerkey, B., Smart, W., Quigley, M.: Programming Robots with ROS. O'Reilly Media, Sebastopol (2015)
5. Ito, T., Watanabe, T.: Motion control algorithm of ARM-COMS for entrainment enhancement. In: Yamamoto, S. (ed.) HIMI 2016. LNCS, vol. 9734, pp. 339–346. Springer, Cham (2016). https://doi.org/10.1007/978-3-319-40349-6_32
6. Kumar, A., Haider, Y., Kumar, M., et al.: Using whatsapp as a quick-access personal logbook for maintaining clinical records and follow-up of orthopedic patients. Cureus **13**(1), e12900 (2021). https://doi.org/10.7759/cureus.12900
7. Lee, A., Kawahara, T.: Recent development of open-source speech recognition engine julius. In: Asia-Pacific Signal and Information Processing Association Annual Summit and Conference (APSIPA ASC) (2009)
8. Lokshina, I., Lanting, C.: A qualitative evaluation of iot-driven ehealth: knowledge management, business models and opportunities, deployment and evolution. In: Kryvinska, N., Greguš, M. (eds.) Data-Centric Business and Applications. LNDECT, vol. 20, pp. 23–52. Springer, Cham (2019). https://doi.org/10.1007/978-3-319-94117-2_2
9. Medical Alert Advice. www.medicalalertadvice.com. Accessed 23 Feb 2021
10. Muramatsu, N., Akiyama, H.: Japan: super-aging society preparing for the future. Gerontologist **51**(4), 425–432 (2011). https://doi.org/10.1093/geront/gnr067
11. Schoff, F., Kalenichenko, D., Philbin, J.: FaceNet: a unified embedding for face recognition and clustering. In: IEEE Conferences on CVPR 2015, pp. 815–823 (2015)
12. Society 5.0. https://www.japan.go.jp/abenomics/_userdata/abenomics/pdf/society_5.0.pdf. Accessed 23 Feb 2021
13. Stephen, J.: Understanding body language: birdwhistell's theory of kinesics. Corporate Communications an International Journal, September 2000. https://doi.org/10.1108/13563280010377518
14. Ovadia, S.: Automate the internet with "If This Then That" (IFTTT). Behav. Soc. Sci. Librarian **33**(4), 208–211 (2014). https://doi.org/10.1080/01639269.2014.964593

15. Sudharsan, B., Kumar, S.P., Dhakshinamurthy, R.: AI vision: smart speaker design and implementation with object detection custom skill and advanced voice interaction capability. In: 2019 11th International Conference on Advanced Computing (ICoAC), pp. 97–102. Chennai, India (2019). https://doi.org/10.1109/icoac48765.2019.247125
16. Watanabe, T.: Human-entrained embodied interaction and communication technology. In: Fukuda, S. (eds) Emotional Engineering, pp. 161–177. Springer, London (2011). https://doi.org/10.1007/978-1-84996-423-4_9
17. Web Speech API. https://developer.mozilla.org/en-US/docs/Web/API/Web_Speech_API. Accessed 23 Feb 2021

Proposal of Wisdom Science

Tetsuya Maeshiro[✉]

Faculty of Library, Information and Media Studies, University of Tsukuba,
Tsukuba 305-8550, Japan
maeshiro@slis.tsukuba.ac.jp

Abstract. This paper proposes a new field of knowledge that aims
to integrate explicit knowledge and tacit knowledge, with quantitative
treatment. The aim of wisdom science is to formulate a theory of knowledge based on brain activities, and on more detailed level, on neuron
functions. Tacit and explicit knowledge are treated as two facets that
represent knowledge of a person, differing from conventional interpretation of two independent entities. The hypernetwork model is used to
describe both tacit and explicit knowledge, which is capable of representing structures that cannot be described by conventional system models.
The concept of system science serves as the basic framework for the
modeling and analysis.

Keywords: Tacit knowledge · Explicit knowledge · Relationality ·
Quantitative · Facets · Brain

1 Introduction

This paper proposes a new field to study knowledge, which treats both explicit
knowledge and tacit knowledge as an integrated knowledge of a person. Explicit
knowledge and tacit knowledge have contrasting properties, where the former
can be explicitly described, is objective, can be communicated through text,
shared by a group of people, and represents a consensus of a group of people.
On the other hand, tacit knowledge cannot be described by text, is individual,
subjective and internal, thus not shared by people, and is strongly associated
with the body of each person and personal feelings.

The basic framework of wisdom science is that both explicit and tacit knowledge are facets of knowledge of a person, and the elements of knowledge of a
person is activated consciously for explicit knowledge or unconsciously for tacit
knowledge. The model of tacit and explicit knowledge that this paper is based
on is fundamentally different from the conventional frameworks where tacit and
explicit knowledge constitute knowledge of a person and the two types of knowledge are distinct elements of knowledge of a person (Fig. 1).

Wisdom science relies mainly on the concept by Polanyi [1] to define tacit
knowledge, as the scientific discovery is one of main topics in his discussions.
Other works on tacit knowledge exists, but they treat other targets rather than

S. Yamamoto and H. Mori (Eds.): HCII 2021, LNCS 12766, pp. 406–418, 2021.
https://doi.org/10.1007/978-3-030-78361-7_31

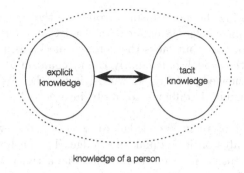

knowledge of a person

Fig. 1. Conventional interpretation of knowledge of a person

scientific discovery, vague and nonspecific intellectual activities or creative processes, which are on more abstract level than Polanyi's treatment Tacit knowledge is contrasted to explicit knowledge primarily on the describability by a text. Mathematical equations also belong to the category of texts, as a mathematical formula can be described verbally, although the precision is lost in some amount. Explicit knowledge and tacit knowledge are closely related with memory skill and imagination skill, respectively. While the memorization skill is related to rationality, imagination skill is related to emotions and feelings. However, memorization of images is also linked to emotions and feelings.

The conventional knowledge science mainly targeted explicit knowledge due to the easiness of its treatment, as knowledge described in text form provides a choice of methodologies from a wide range of analytical tools. Since almost all, if not all, today's science and humanities research fields rely on the class of explicit knowledge, it is natural that explicit knowledge received higher focus in the past. Simply put, however, explicit knowledge is easier to be studied than tacit knowledge. On the other hand, conventional studies on tacit knowledge was mainly qualitative analyses, trying to elucidate the general properties that is contrasting to explicit knowledge. Since it is individual knowledge, it is always under limitations of methodologies to prove the validity of results, particularly for qualitative analyses.

A focus of this paper is the integrated treatment of knowledge of a person. Activities using the knowledge, which is not limited to "intellectual" activities, is primarily an individual act. Obviously there are group activities, but it is an interaction of individual that employs each person's own knowledge. Any activity using the knowledge involves not only the explicit knowledge, but also the tacit knowledge. Conventional studies tend to treat explicit knowledge as an external layer of the tacit knowledge or explicit and tacit knowledge as two independent modules, but this paper treats the both explicit and tacit knowledge as two facets of the knowledge of a person.

From the facet related to the individuality of knowledge, Nonaka treated the tacit knowledge based on the innovation process of a group of individuals, and proposed the SECI model [2]. The SECI model connects the explicit and tacit knowledge by proposing the mechanisms involved in the endless cycle of explicit knowledge ⇒ tacit knowledge ⇒ explicit knowledge ⇒ tacit knowledge ⋯⋯. It offers a general framework, but lacks the detailed mechanism of individual processes described in the model, particularly the mechanism of transitions among tacit and explicit knowledge. In other words, it fits the observed process due to its abstract level, but is difficult to apply into actual situations to induce innovations.

The employment of tacit knowledge in scientific discovery described by Polanyi [1] concentrates on individual knowledge. The author agrees with this treatment, as the scientific discovery is an individual activity. Similar to Polanyi, Lorenz also arrived independently that the integration of elements is a possible basic mechanism of intellectual activity in scientific activity.

One of core concepts in Polanyi's tacit knowledge is the emergence. The emergence has long been a topic of system science, and innumerous examples have provided and discussed. The concept of emergence is accepted as a valid one, but attempts of quantitative theoretical formulation have failed, unfortunately, until today. Another central concept in Polanyi's formulation is the image or imagination, which is used in contrast to the explicit terms denoting concepts. Images cannot be described precisely, thus presenting opposite properties.

Polanyi proposed that the scientific discovery is a process of integration of particulars (elements), and is an emergence phenomenon (Fig. 2), driven by imagination. This integration process is self-driven and unconscious, as is uncontrollable by person. This paper employs the term "unconscious" to denote two meanings. First, it cannot be sensed or described by the person himself. The second meaning is the uncontrollability, and the person cannot control directly the referred entity. If the integrated image or concept or entity is a result of emergence, the integrated entity and the elements (particulars) constitute a hierarchical structure. This paper assumes that "emergence" becomes/constitutes a phenomenon when interpreted as a phenomenon by an observer (person). Thus the observer is an essential element when discussing emergence. Because a pattern recognized by the observer-A [person-A] might be interpreted as a random phenomena by a different observer-B. The recognition of an emergence phenomenon can also be defined as a viewpoint or a facet defined by an observer on how to describe the entities generating the phenomenon.

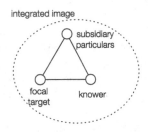

Fig. 2. Triad representation of Polanyi's tacit knowledge

Initially the target knowledge manipulation processes to investigate are question generation and scientific discovery. The target of the first process is clinical findings. On the other hand, the target of the latter process is broader with no specific research field, but limits to the field of science, excluding humanities. This exclusion is the relative vagueness of humanities field compared to the science field. The basic cycle of hypotheses generation and verification is accepted and executed daily by researchers.

2 Model of Knowledge of a Person

Compared to conventional interpretation of tacit and explicit knowledge as distinct entities (Fig. 1), the model illustrated in Fig. 3 explains better the transitions of knowledge pieces or elements between tacit and explicit knowledge. Wisdom science mainly focuses on phenomena in individuals, although social knowledge involving groups of people is also treated. If tacit and explicit knowledge are distinct entities as conventionally assumed, it is difficult to explain the transformation mechanism of tacit knowledge to explicit and vice-versa, as proposed by SECI model, without the existence of *something* that transitions between tacit and explicit knowledge.

Wisdom science also studies how knowledge elements are invoked as tacit or explicit knowledge, including temporal development of knowledge elements including their state and handling when deployed as tacit or explicit knowledge. The author proposes that both tacit and explicit knowledge are two facets of knowledge of a person, or *emerged* state of some of knowledge elements that belong to the core of knowledge of a person (Fig. 3). A defect of conventional interpretation (Fig. 1) is that knowledge elements, usually concepts at finest grain level, may not *emerge* from unconscious to conscious level, because some knowledge elements are employed simultaneously by both tacit and explicit knowledge.

Questioning and answering process is an example of knowledge elements being used in tacit or explicit knowledge depending on situation, represented as small circles in the bottom linked to explicit knowledge and tacit knowledge in Fig. 3. When a person is asked a question, for instance in a interview, the asked person sometimes say opinions, thoughts or ideas that the person has never said before or the person himself was not aware of. And the person himself feels surprised the recognize how the person was thinking about the asked issue. Formulating a sentence to talk involves gathering knowledge elements or concepts related to the content of the speech. In this (i) collecting process and (ii) the meaning generated by the formulated sentence invokes the knowledge elements that belonged to tacit knowledge. In conventional interpretation, this process is a tacit concept being transformed to an explicit concept. However, wisdom science models this process as a concept element that was already evoked as tacit knowledge became also evoked as explicit knowledge. As stated before, tacit knowledge and explicit knowledge are the representations of knowledge elements linked to the consciousness of the person possessing that knowledge.

Person-to-person discussions is analogous to interviews, particularly when participants discuss by speaking and in realtime without time lag, and possibly in face to face situations. In such situations, people often are able to generate and express new ideas, employing concepts and relationships among knowledge elements that were consciously unaware until that moment of sentence formulation. The act of discussing and of thinking alone, for instance when writing and sketching ideas, should share the same mechanism of invoking knowledge elements linked to tacit knowledge and linking to explicit knowledge by expressing them. At least this is in accordance with author's experiences. The process of integration of particulars proposed by Polanyi [1] can be explained with the same mechanism.

The author's viewpoint about the relationship between explicit and tacit knowledge is different from conventional standpoints. Conventionally the explicit and tacit knowledge are characterized as distinct entities. Figure 4 illustrates some possible interpretations of the structure of knowledge of a person.

Treating as two different facets of an entity implies that each of explicit knowledge and tacit knowledge can be treated as two independent systems. One viewpoint is to model the knowledge of a person as a system of systems. However, wisdom science treats the knowledge of a person as a different system that is the result of the fusion of explicit knowledge and tacit knowledge, and elements employed by tacit or explicit knowledge is stored in different entity.

Wisdom science also encompasses the knowledge shared among multiple individuals. Figure 6 is a rough sketch of the individual knowledge and social knowledge from the viewpoint of knowledge shared among individuals. In Fig. 6, knowledge of an individual is represented as a combination of explicit knowledge belonging to conscious level and tacit knowledge to unconscious level (Fig. 5). Knowledge at the unconscious level is personal and not shared, contrary to knowledge at the conscious level. In Fig. 6, social knowledge is represented as both *sharable* and *shared*. Only explicit knowledge is sharable due to its nature. Tacit knowledge cannot be described, thus it does not constitute social knowledge.

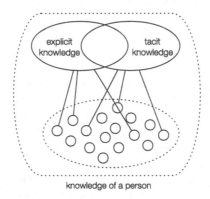

knowledge of a person

Fig. 3. Wisdom science interpretation of knowledge of a person. Bottom dotted circle represents the core of knowledge of a person, and small circles in the bottom dotted circle denote "knowledge elements".

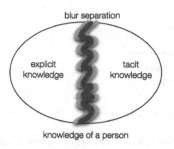
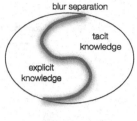

Fig. 4. Left: Explicit knowledge and tacit knowledge as two facets of knowledge of a person. Right: representation similar to tao icon

3   Decision Makings

Decision makings is a broad term, and involves all aspects and instances of human daily life. A main focus is decision makings of trained professionals, with enough time of training and experience that enable the person to have expertise on the [discussed] field and be called a *professional* in the field. As one of the main target of wisdom science treated in this paper is the scientific discovery, ˙the professional denotes a trained researcher in the field of science.

Two studies on decision makings that this paper relies on are those by Klein [3–5] and Kahneman [6], but mainly on the former. The RPD model [4] was proposed based on the decision making behavior of professionals under time constraints. It was suggested that the difference between professionals and novices is related to the generation process of decisions to be employed and executed. While the process of novices is algorithmic in a sense that steps that constitute the decision making process are clearly separated and can be described as a sequential flowchart, consisting of the step to generate decision candidates, followed by step to evaluate each decision and compare among other decisions, and finally the step to select a decision to execute. On the other hand, professionals think about a possible decision, check if this first decision candidate contains any flaw, and if not, execute this decision. If it contains, the person generates another decision candidate, and repeats the process. Although the activity of both professionals and novices are sequential, at least for the steps described explicitly by persons (interviewed participants), the granularity of the sequentialized tasks are different. The process of novices consists of three basic steps: (1) generate decision candidates; (2) evaluate the generated decisions; and (3) select the decision to execute. On the other hand, the process of professionals consists of two steps and constitute an execution loop, which is (1) generate one decision candidate; and (2) check the decision for any flow. Furthermore, the generation and check operations are more like parallel processes rather than sequential.

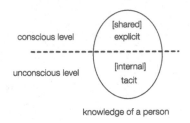

knowledge of a person

Fig. 5. Another representation of knowledge of a person, where explicit and tacit knowledge are associated with conscious level

Note that these are recognized processes by the decision maker or thinker himself. An important fact about the RPD model is that it is based on the conscious level of the decision maker. This limitation is primarily due to the employed methodology, the interviewing to the participants. A notable limitation of interviewing process related to the analysis of knowledge is that only the memory about feelings and employed knowledge at the conscious level, such as considered facts and used concepts, which the person was aware of, can be obtained in "experiments" from the participants. On the other hand, wisdom science targets the underlying process at the unconscious level. The author assumes . that the generation of decisions by professionals is an automated process involving unconscious level or sub-processes not explicitly detected by the decision maker himself.

This paper proposes that the basic process of decision generation ⇒ evaluation ⇒ selection is automated and executed at unconscious level. The execution is at least partially controlled by the cerebellum and basal ganglia, involving control mechanism similar to the motor control mechanism [7]. The basal ganglia is responsible for the reinforcement learning, and the cerebellum for supervised learning. Many studies can be found about the brain activity analyses of decision making [8], and they focus on the brain regions and functions involved in the context of each experimental settings such as perception and action. However, these studies do not analyze from the viewpoint of knowledge, how knowledge is employed in the analyzed decisions and the relation of knowledge with brain activity. The main target is the control mechanisms of decisions. As stated before, wisdom science aims to elucidate the relationship between knowledge and brain functions.

Wisdom science also employs physiological data from participants in order to detect the "thinking process" at the unconscious level. For instance we compared the decision making processes of experienced rugby players with novice players. Specific rugby game scenes with duration of two to five seconds were presented to the participants, and they were asked to decide the play they would execute. Participants wore a virtual reality (VR) headset, from which the game scenes were presented, and gaze data were collected. Along with the interview session after the experiment, the gaze patterns were analyzed to detect objects in the game scene that the participants have fixated, looked by the participant

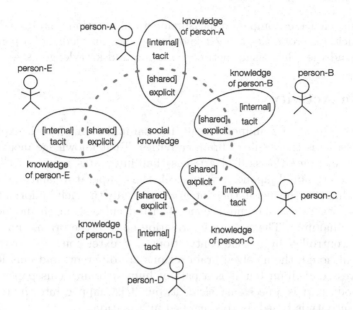

Fig. 6. Group knowledge shared among multiple persons

for a certain amount of time duration. We hypothesized that these objects were possibly recognized by the participants even unconsciously. Experienced players did not mention all the fixated objects in the interview, and these unreferred objects were unimportant and probably automatically discarded at the unconscious level. This suggests an automated process acquired through the experience.

Wisdom science incorporates emotion related factors to study knowledge, because emotion affects decision making process [9]. When expressing opinion in discussions, for instance, several decision makings are involved, both at conscious and unconscious levels. Selecting terms to formulate sentences, selecting concepts to construct opinions, agreeing or contradicting other persons' opinions, how to express own opinions, among many others. The author assumes that all these decisions are affected by emotion. Furthermore, emotion also affects generation of ideas. From the author's experience, it is difficult to generate ideas when the person is nervous or in extreme state.

These facts indicate that emotion cannot be ignored when investigating knowledge, particularly tacit knowledge that is personal and strongly related to personal experience and subjectiveness. Objectiveness is a mandatory condition of explicit knowledge, and the exclusion of subjectiveness empowers the sharing among different persons. The interpretations and subsequent understandings are person dependent, but the shared knowledge itself is identical. This is the reason emotion was not relevant in conventional knowledge studies. However, emotion becomes a requisite element, if not fundamental and essential, to understand tacit knowledge.

Wisdom science encompasses measurements of emotional state and uses its data to elucidate properties of tacit knowledge and knowledge of a person, and to understand the relationship between emotion and knowledge usage.

4 Brain Activity

The author is on the standpoint that the manipulation of both explicit and tacit knowledge is the result of brain activities. Tacit knowledge includes body motion, for instance the skill of artisans that integrates sensory feelings. For instance, the artisan of japanese swords feels the temperature and pressure, and see the condition of the metal, then integrate mentally the "felt" information, and executes body action to hammer the metal with decided strength and location to hit with the hammer. The sensory information goes to the brain, and the body movement controlled by muscle contractions and extensions are controlled by the brain, although the involved brain regions are different, and muscle control also involves cerebellum but it is a part of human brain. This paper assumes that the body part is a necessary element, but it is mapped into the brain, and the brain activity is based on this mapped information.

Therefore, wisdom science aims to investigate knowledge with theory and principles based on brain activity and on neuron function level. Currently, the mechanism of knowledge storage (or whatever more appropriate expression) in neurons is still unclear, but some evidences exist [10]. The author currently assumes that the physical entity, a single neuron or a collection of neurons, representing a concept and the neuron level constitute a hierarchical structure, when this viewpoint or facet of concept representation is extracted to study (Fig. 7).

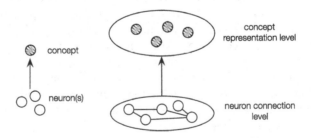

Fig. 7. Hierarchical structure of concept representation and neuron connection levels

fMRI and MEG are the current standard brain imaging instruments with human subjects. fMRI generates high space resolution images, with drawback of low temporal resolution. On the other hand, although its definitive analytical method has not been established yet, MEG generates high resolution data on time domain, but with low space resolution.

However, fMRI and MEG have limitations mainly on space resolution, unable to capture activity of small number neurons. The space resolution of fMRI is of millimeter order, which is approximately 200–1000 times larger than the neuron size (2–5 μm). The time resolution of MEG is millisecond, which seems to be sufficient to capture temporal variation of neuron activities.

Combined method using fMRI and MEG has been used in some studies to complement the low resolution data of each method, in order to obtain high resolution data on both space and times.

The combination of fMRI and MEG is currently the most promising brain activity imaging method to obtain neuron activity data related to the knowledge manipulation, particularly the tacit knowledge that cannot be described or expressed by the person manipulating the knowledge.

The brain imaging technique is a relatively simple problem. A harder problem is the experiment design to elucidate tacit knowledge.

Experiments that request participants to execute decision makings under strong time constraints is a possible experiment. Strong time constraints imply short time duration of one experiment, and since fMRI and MEG requires a repetition of experiments for statistical analysis, it is suited for brain activity imaging. A possible experiment is our study comparing experienced and novices. Similar experiment design enables to detect the different brain regions activated to operate or manipulate the tacit and explicit knowledge.

On the other hand, for longer time duration, the experiment is more difficult. At the moment, the author has no viable experiment design of brain activity measurement to investigate the use of tacit knowledge for longer time duration. One strong constraint is the maximum time duration and the number of repetitions imposed by fMRI and MEG experiments for one participant. A possible solution is to split long term, or long time duration, intellectual activities into a succession of shorter intellectual activities, exact characteristic conditions and design independent brain activity measurement experiments. It is unlikely that experiments with long time duration with the same participant will be allowed from ethical review committee, so the excision of different stages of tacit knowledge operation seems to be the most plausible solution.

Although the knowledge storage mechanism in brain, specifically at single neuron level, is still unknown, single neuron representation of concepts is a possibility [10]. When a non-invasive single neuron activity measurement instruments with enough time resolution become available, it is possible to elucidate the concept activation behavior related to the employment of tacit knowledge and explicit knowledge in decision makings. Once the activity of multiple neurons can be measured simultaneously, subject experiments of decision making tasks should provide the usage manner of the same set of concepts by experts and novices. Moreover, differences of the set of used concepts can also be detected.

5   Description Model

Tacit knowledge is so denoted because the person cannot describe his own tacit knowledge, particularly by natural language, and is even more difficult, if not impossible, to be described by the others. However, it is often possible to describe vaguely using images or feelings. The author agrees with Polanyi's statement that the inability of description does not negate its existence.

As stated in previous sections, the author assumes that tacit knowledge is based on neural activities. In the framework of system science, tacit knowledge can be interpreted as an emergence of neural activities. Polanyi also used the concept of emergence in the process of scientific discovery, the relationship between the elements (subsidiary particulars) and the image generated from the result of focusing the whole. The integrated image of the whole disappears if any of elements in Fig. 2 is focused. The tacit knowledge presents two properties. First, multiple facet, as an entity can be viewed or interpreted in multiple ways. Second, related to the first, the existence of multiple structures to represent.

A model framework with enough description capability is necessary to describe integrated personal knowledge of tacit and explicit knowledge. Namely, the model should be able to integrate multiple facets, no prerequisite of precise structure, and no fixed boundaries. The three features are interrelated. The last property, the boundary, is the elements belonging to one representation (facet) might differ from the elements employed in another representation (facet) (Fig. 8).

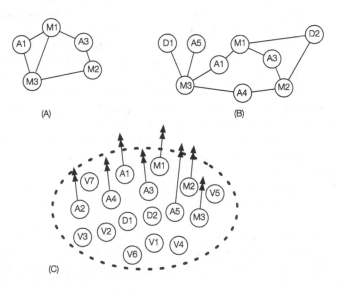

Fig. 8. Different elements in different facets

The hypernetwork model [11] is the model framework used to describe. No other conventional model framework presents the three properties related to multiple facets. No restrictions exist on what an element represents. It can be a concept described with terms, and image, or an abstract or a fuzzy entity.

The attempt of wisdom science to describe tacit knowledge does not conflict with the definition that tacit knowledge cannot be described even by the person owning that knowledge. The author assumes the inability of description is because tacit knowledge belong to the unconscious level and is more like an image. Tacit knowledge is, however, a phenomenon occurring as a result of neural activities in the brain. A phenomenon can be indirectly described based on elements that generate the phenomenon of interest, even if the phenomenon cannot be directly described. Moreover, one of goals of wisdom science is to elucidate the boundary between the describable and the non-describable features of tacit knowledge and of the integrated knowledge from tacit and explicit knowledge.

6 Conclusions

This paper proposes wisdom science, a new research field to investigate knowledge of a person using quantitative methods. Wisdom science integrates tacit and explicit knowledge to constitute a knowledge of a person. Tacit and explicit knowledge are treated as two facets that represent knowledge of a person, differing from conventional interpretation of two independent entities. The hypernetwork model is used to describe both tacit and explicit knowledge, which is capable of representing structures that cannot be described by conventional system models. The concept of system science serves as the basic framework for the modeling and analysis. Wisdom science aims to describe knowledge based on neuron level phenomena, differing from conventional knowledge studies that rely on vague and abstract level. Use of neuron activities permits quantitative investigation of knowledge of a person, which has not been done before. The aim of wisdom science is to formulate a theory based on brain activities, and on more detailed level, on neuron functions.

References

1. Polanyi, M.: Genius in science. Encounter **38**, 43–50 (1972)
2. Nonaka, I.: A dynamic theory of organizational knowledge creation. Organ. Sci. **5**, 14–37 (1994)
3. Klein, G.: Sources of Power: How People Make Decisions. MIT Press, Cambridge (2017)
4. Klein, G.: A recognition primed decision (RPD) model of rapid decision making. In: Klein, G.A., Orasanu, J., Calderwood, R., Zsambok, C.E. (eds.) Decision Making in Action, pp. 138–147. Ablex (1993)
5. Klein, G.A., Orasanu, J., Calderwood, R., Zsambok, C.E.: Decision Making in Action. Ablex (1993)
6. Kahneman, D.: Thinking, Fast and Slow. Farrar, Straus and Giroux (2011)

7. Doya, K.: Complementary roles of basal ganglia and cerebellum in learning and motor control. Curr. Opin. Neurobiol. **10**, 732–739 (2000)
8. Doya, K., Shadlen, M.N.: Decision making, editorial overview. Curr. Opin. Neurobiol. **22**, 911–913 (2002)
9. Damasio, A.: Descartes' Error: Emotion. Reason and the Human Brain. Grosset/Putnam (1994)
10. Quiroga, R.Q., Reddy, L., Kreiman, G., Koch, C., Fried, I.: Invariant visual representation by single neurons in the human brain. Nature **435**, 1102–1107 (2005)
11. Maeshiro, T.: Framework based on relationship to describe non-hierarchical, boundaryless and multi-perspective phenomena. SICE Journal of Control, Measurement, and System Integration **11**, 381–389 (2019)

Information Management System for Small Automatic Navigation Robot Ships

Kozono Rinto, Yutaro Tsurumi, Yasunori Nihei, and Ryosuke Saga(✉)

Osaka Prefecture University, 1-1 Gakuen-cho, Naka-ku, Sakai, Osaka, Japan
{saa01103,sub03075}@edu.osakafu-u.ac.jp,
nihei@marine.osakafu-u.ac.jp, saga@cs.osakafu-u.ac.jp

Abstract. Automatic navigation robot ships have large results in ocean data collection. Especially, small automatic navigation robot ships have low cost and can navigate precisely such that they have a merit in multiple operations. However, a problem in data collection by multiple small automatic navigation robot ships is that a great deal of labor is required in navigation planning, navigation management, and data analysis compared with the case of performing with a single vessel. In this paper, an information management system named robot ship information management system (RSIMS) for small automatic navigation robot ships is proposed to solve the above problem. RSIMS processes data sent by ships and users in real time. First, the processed data are divided into three types of information about ship, ocean, and cruise plan. Then, RSIMS shows users the latest information on the web GUI. The user can always browse the latest information because the information updated in real time is constantly updated by asynchronous communication even on the web GUI. RSIMS has high usefulness and usability in the operation of automatic navigation robot ships, which is expected to be made more effective by adding an application with high analytical ability to RSIMS.

Keywords: Information management system · Ocean data · Web GUI

1 Introduction

Much of the ocean data is out of the reach of humans. Therefore, helpful observational means must be used to obtain ocean information. Ocean data observation using a ship is one of the means. Freely navigating a huge range of sea areas and collecting data are possible. Smith et al. stated that any ship can be a useful tool in making ocean observations [1]. In addition, Aslam et al. stated that improvements in internet technology makes information about ships ubiquitous accessible [2]. Therefore, it can be said that data collection using ships has continued to increase in value in recent years. Automatic navigation ships have the advantage of reducing operating costs and improving safety [3]; thus, they will be an active field in the future. Among automatic navigation ships, small ones for ocean observation are excellent in cost and operability. They have the advantage of the ability to be operated effectively using multiple ships.

© Springer Nature Switzerland AG 2021
S. Yamamoto and H. Mori (Eds.): HCII 2021, LNCS 12766, pp. 419–428, 2021.
https://doi.org/10.1007/978-3-030-78361-7_32

However, as the number of automatic navigation ships in an operation increases, the following problem arises: The effort and considerations involved in navigation management, information analysis, and navigation planning increase. The authors believe that these problems could be solved by using a system to manage the information related to the operation of automatic navigation ships. Therefore, this paper aims to establish an information management system for automatic navigation robot ships to solve the above problems.

As research on a system for managing ship information, Li et al. Have proposed an intelligent ship management database [4]. This management database manages data about ships by dividing them into a ship information table, a user management table, a device information table, and an alarm point table. The user can then check the record of those data for each ship in the database from the browser. By using this system, users can check the details of the data related to the ship they want to check. However, this system a little influences the user's current decision making as not it focus on the latest information. On the other hand, Pieri et al. Have proposed A Marine Information System for Environmental Monitoring (ARGO-MIS) as a system for real-time monitoring of the ocean where multiple ships are congested [5]. ARGO-MIS is a system that aims to quickly detect oil spills that have occurred on vessels navigating the ocean. ARGO-MIS is a system that can proactively manage available resources and provide services that provide information obtained from the resources. What is required in this research is also a service that proactively manages the data generated from multiple sensors and provides the information obtained from them. However, the intended users of our system do not need to manage all automatic navigation robot ships in the ocean, but they manage the automatic navigation robot ships in the projects they are carrying out. This means that our system have to focus on specific automatic navigation robot ships and area. Based on the above research, the system proposed in this paper named robot ship information management system (RSIMS) manages information related to projects of automatic navigation robot ships based on data sent from users and ships, and provides information to users in real time. It was conceived for the purpose of a system to do. The contributions of this article are as follows:

- Proposal of a system for managing information related to the navigation of multiple automatic navigation ships
- Proposal of a system that integrates data sent from users and ships that have multiple measuring instruments
- Proposal of GUI that always provides users with the latest information on multiple automatic navigation robot ships by updating pages in real time by asynchronous communication

2 System Requirements

The purpose of RSIMS is to manage the information needed when collecting data by automatic navigation robot ships. The users assumed by RSIMS are engaged in a project for the purpose of collecting data by automatic navigation robot ships and want to manage information related to that project more easily. First, RSIMS integrates data sent from the ship in real time and data sent from the user, and displays the information of ships to the user on the GUI. Then, the information that RSIMS should manage is divided into three categories.

1. Information about operation of ships
2. Information about ocean data collected by ships
3. Information about cruise planning of ships

RSIMS is required to extract the three information from the input data and provide the information to users. In addition, the information related to the navigation of automatic navigation robot ships is related to the decision making regarding the management of automatic navigation robot ships in transit, and real-time information must always be provided. On the one hand, the information related to the ocean data collected by the automatic navigation robot ships is related to the analysis of the ocean data, and multiple information about the ocean can be viewed simultaneously. On the other hand, the information related to the navigation plan of the automatic navigation robot ships needs to influence the navigation plan requested by the user. Therefore, RSIMS must meet the following requirements:

- Users can understand the information about cruising automatic navigation robot ships in real time.
- Users can browse information related to data collected by automatic navigation robot ships in one display.
- Users can better plan the cruise of automatic navigation robot ships.

3 System Architecture

In this section, first, the RSIMS architecture is discussed. Next, the parts that compose RSIMS are explained. Finally, the web GUI that RSIMS shows users is presented.

3.1 System Architecture

Figure 1 shows the outline of RSIMS architecture. The web database accepts data from automatic navigation robot ships and users. On the one hand, data from ships are sent in real time. On the other hand, data from users are sent manually through the web GUI. The parts of grasping ship information, data integration, and route planning algorithm work according to the update of web database. The part of grasping ship information extracts information of the states and accidents of cruising automatic navigation robot ships based on the web database. The part of data integration extracts ocean information. The part of route planning algorithm extracts a route plan of automatic navigation robot ships. The ocean data page receives ocean data collected by ships and coordinate data the ships cruised from users, and shows users shows ocean information extracted by the part of data integration. The cruise planning page receives coordinate data ships will stop and shows a route plan extracted by the part of route planning algorithm. The ship information page shows the states and accidents of ships extracted by the part of grasping ship information.

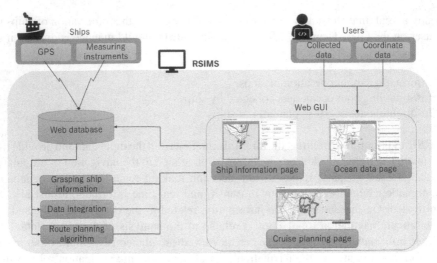

Fig. 1. Outline of the system architecture

3.2 Components of RSIMS

Grasping Ship Information. This part processes the latest data of cruising automatic navigation robot ships and outputs the states and accidents of ships. First, the ships' states (current coordinates of the ships, coordinates of the current destinations, distances to the current destinations, speeds of the ships, depths of the measuring equipment, sailing time, rotation speeds of the propellers, angles of the four ships that make up the ships, current direction of the ships, and whether the ship is collecting data) are extracted. Then, whether accidents occurred in the automatic navigation robot ships is determined based on the extracted data. Accidents found in this part are as follows.

- Unexpected speed down: The speed is below 0.3 m/s even though the ship is not collecting data.
- Sampling point holding abnormality: The distance from the current planned collection coordinates exceeds 0.26 m even though the ship is collecting data.
- Data not sent: All attributes of the latest data of the ships are "No Data" (when receiving and saving the data from the autonomous navigation ship, "No Data" is saved if no data are sent).

Extracted information about states and accidents of ships is output on the ship information page.

Data Integration. This part outputs ocean information by integrating ocean data collected by the automatic navigation robot ships entered by the user, coordinate data about sampled points, and state data of the ships stored in RSIMS. Data such as water temperature and salt obtained by each measuring instrument of the automatic navigation robot ships at a certain time are extracted from ocean data. Data about points the automatic navigation robot ships collect data are extracted from coordinate data. Data about points of the ships at a certain time are extracted from state data of coordinates. Information about when and which sampling points the automatic navigation robot ships are and data observed by the measuring instrument at that time are determined by combining these data. Finally, information about ocean that automatic navigation robot ships cruised is extracted by accumulating these information. Extracted information about ocean is output on the ocean data page.

Route Planning Algorithm [6]. This part extracts optimal routes based on coordinate data entered by users. To extract optimal routes, NSGA-II (nondominated sorting genetic algorithm-II) [7], one of the multi-objective optimization methods, is used. In this algorithm, evolutionary computation provides Pareto optimal solutions for two variables. Two variables that are Pareto optimized in this algorithm are about total distance and total power consumption. Extracted routes are output on the cruise planning page.

3.3   Web GUI

Ship Information Page. This page shows the states and accidents extracted in the part of grasping ship information as a dashboard (Fig. 2). The planned route points and current position of ships are displayed on the left side of the screen, and the current states of ships are displayed on the right side. In addition, when accidents occur, the accidents that occurred and the ships where the accidents occurred are displayed at the top of the screen. These information are constantly updated in real time. Therefore, users can always track the latest status of automatic navigation robot ships and what is currently happening in the ships by browsing this page.

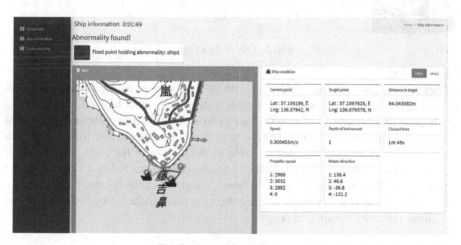

Fig. 2. Ship information page

Ocean Data Page. This page shows ocean information extracted in the part of data integration (Fig. 3). In addition, this page is responsible for receiving coordinate data

Fig. 3. Ocean data page

and ocean data. The map and coordinates with ships' corrected data are displayed on the left side of the screen, and ocean data (water temperature, salt, chl-a, σT, and DO) at a certain point are displayed as a graph. This graph displays the data corresponding to that point by clicking the icon displayed on the map. In addition, ocean data for all collection points are displayed as a bar graph or table at the bottom of the page. The colors of the bar graph and table change from blue to green, yellow, and red as it approaches the danger value. Therefore, users can effortlessly grasp the entire information of the sea area and the detailed information of the collection point gathered by the autonomous navigation vessel by viewing this page.

Cruise Planning Page. This page offer routes extracted in the part of route planning algorithm (Fig. 4). First, this page receives coordinate data and number of ships. Then, users can examine route planning algorithm. The result of the algorithm is shown with map in a display. If users prefer the offered routes, they can download the route file from this page.

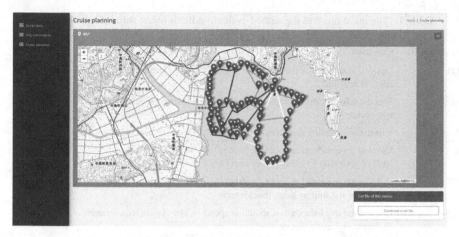

Fig. 4. Cruse planning page

4 Experiment

In this study, experiments were conducted to show that RSIMS meets the requirements and is usable. The contents of the experiment that asking the subject to use the system and answer the questionnaire after using it. This experiment was conducted to evaluate whether ship information page and the ocean data page meet the system requirements and are usable. For usability evaluation, Nielsen et al. proposed 10 heuristic evaluation items [8]. Therefore, in this experiment, questions corresponding to the heuristic evaluation items and the system requirements that each page should meet were created, and the subjects answered them to evaluate the satisfaction and usability of the system requirements for each page. Table 1 and Table 2 shows the questions and the related evaluation items based on 10 heuristic evaluation or the system requirements about ship information page and ocean data page. About ship information page, we created 5 questions that is corresponding to the heuristic evaluation items and 4 questions that is corresponding to the system requirements. In addition, we created 1 fake question to grasp whether the user is getting the information correctly. On the other hand, we created 6 questions that is corresponding to the heuristic evaluation items and 5 questions that is corresponding to the system requirements about ocean data page. All questions are rated on a 4-point scale from 1 to 4, with higher values being rated higher.

We conducted the questionnaire on a total of 7 people, 4 people who understand automatic navigation robot ships in detail and 3 people who are not understand automatic navigation robot ships. We expected people who understand automatic navigation robot ships in detail to help finding changes in data collection using RSIMS due to the use of the system. On the other hand, people who were not understand automatic navigation robot ships were expected to help grasping whether RSIMS is easy to use even for amateurs. In addition, all of the participants in the experiment were expected that to help grasping whether RSIMS is useful in operations of automatic navigation robot ships.

For the evaluation of the navigation planning page, users are referred to the paper by Saga et al. [6] who evaluated a similar system.

Table 1. The questions and the related evaluation items about ship information page

Question ID	Questions	Related evaluation items
Q1	Did you always check the condition of the ships in real time?	The system requirements
Q2	Was the information displayed sensuously appropriate?	User control and freedom
Q3	Was the information displayed is consistent?	Consistency and standards
Q4	Did you get information about the battery level of your ship by using this system?	The fake question
Q5	Did you get information about the current position of the ship by using this system?	The system requirements
Q6	Did you get any information about the speed of the ship by using this system?	The system requirements
Q7	Did you get any information about the anomalies that occurred on the ship by using this system?	The system requirements
Q8	Was the design good?	Aesthetic and minimalist design
Q9	Will this page make the operation of the ship more comfortable?	Flexibility and efficiency of use
Q10	Was the ship information available on this page appropriate?	Match between system and the real world

Table 2. The questions and the related evaluation items about ocean data page

Question ID	Questions	Related evaluation items
Q11	Was the information displayed properly?	Match between system and the real world
Q12	Did you operate smoothly?	User control and freedom
Q13	Was the information displayed is consistent?	Consistency and standards
Q14	Did you get the information efficiently?	Flexibility and efficiency of use
Q15	Was the design good?	Aesthetic and minimalist design
Q16	Is it comfortable to use this page to analyze the data collected by autonomous vessels?	The system requirements
Q17–21	Did you get information about the [temperature, salt, chl-a, σ-T, DO] in the ocean area from the collected data by using this system?	The system requirements

4.1 Result

Figure 5 shows the result of the experiment. Most of questions got high scored, therefore it can be said that RSIMS has been well received by users. Especially, questions that related the system requirements (Q1, Q5–7, Q16–17) tend to be evaluated well. Therefore, it can be said that RSIMS fully satisfies system requirements and RSIMS is useful method to solve problems in data correction with automatic navigation robot ships.

Both the expert and beginner responses received an average score of 3 or higher for most of the questions. Therefore, it can be said that RSIMS is a system for experts to expect good changes in the operation of autonomous ships, and for beginners to get information about the ocean and autonomous ships even if they have little understanding of autonomous ships.

On the other hand, in Q4, the fake question, expert users gave a low rating, while beginner users gave a high rating. This indicates that the information was not accurately received by the beginner users. Therefore, it will be necessary to provide the information of each autonomous ship in a more understandable form by using graphs.

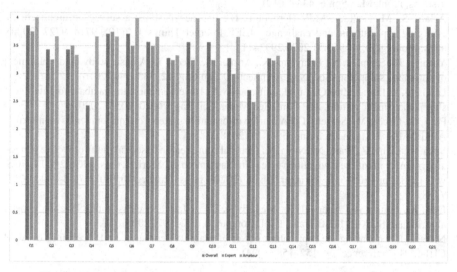

Fig. 5. The comparison results of questionnaires between expert and beginners

5   Conclusion

This paper has been proposed a robot ship information management system (RSIMS) to solve the labor problem of automatic navigation robot ships (AUVs). RSIMS processes data transmitted by autonomous ships and users in real time to provide information about navigation status, oceanographic data, and navigation plans to users participating in autonomous ship data collection projects. The page provided to the user is continuously updated through asynchronous communication, so that the user always has access to the latest information.

In this paper, we conducted an evaluation experiment to show that RSIMS meets the system requirements and is a usable system. The experiments show that RSIMS meets the system requirements well. In addition, the experiments showed that RSIMS is easy to use for experts and beginners of autonomous ships. However, we also found that the information displayed in RSIMS is not completely understood by the beginners of autonomous ships.

Future work will include resolving this shortcoming in the way information about the ship is provided in the experiment. In addition, research could include incorporating more specific ocean analysis (e.g., sparse estimation of ocean data and processing of images obtained by the autonomous ship) into RSIMS, as well as learning to make autonomous ship decisions based on real-time information from the autonomous ship.

References

1. Smith, S.R., et al.: Ship-based contributions to global ocean, weather, and climate observing systems. Front. Mar. Sci. **6**, 434 (2019)
2. Aslam, S., Michaelides, M.P., Herodotou, H.: Internet of ships: a survey on architectures, emerging applications, and challenges. IEEE Internet Things J. **7**(10), 9714–9727 (2020). https://doi.org/10.1109/JIOT.2020.2993411
3. Yoshida, K., Shimizu, N., Hirayama, K., Arima, M., Ikeda, Y.: A basic study on development of automatic ships. Jpn. Soc. Nav. Architects Ocean Eng. **22**, 335–340 (2016)
4. Li, G., Li, Y., Lan, J., Zhu, Q., Lu, H., Mitrouchev, P.: Development of the database for intelligent ship management system. IOP Conf. Ser. Mater. Sci. Eng. **768**, 042055 (2020)
5. Pieri, G., Cocco, M., Salvetti, O.: A marine information system for environmental monitoring: ARGO-MIS. J. Marine Sci. Eng. **6**(1), 15 (2018)
6. Saga, R., Liang, Z., Hara, N., Nihei, Y.: Optimal route search based on multi-objective genetic algorithm for maritime navigation vessels. In: Yamamoto, S., Mori, H. (eds.) HCII 2020. LNCS, vol. 12185, pp. 506–518. Springer, Cham (2020). https://doi.org/10.1007/978-3-030-50017-7_38
7. Deb, K., Pratap, A., Agarwal, S., Meyarivan, T.: A fast and elitist multiobjective genetic algorithm: NSGA-II. IEEE Trans. Evol. Comput. **6**, 182–197 (2002)
8. Nielsen, J.: Enhancing the explanatory power of usability heuristics. In: Proceedings of ACM CHI 1994 Conference, pp. 152–158 (1994)

Development of a Presentation Support System Using Group Pupil Response Interfaces

Yoshihiro Sejima[1]($\boxtimes$), Yoichiro Sato[2], and Tomio Watanabe[2]

[1] Faculty of Informatics, Kansai University, 2-1-1 Ryozenji-cho, Takatsuki-shi, Osaka 569-1095, Japan
sejima@kansai-u.ac.jp
[2] Faculty of Computer Science and Systems Engineering, Okayama Prefectural University, 111 Kuboki, Soja-shi, Okayama, Japan

Abstract. Since the presentation is a one-sided communication, it is difficult to realize an interactive communication while grasping the behavior of the audience. Therefore, a method that conveys audience's actions and affects such as interest and concern during the presentation is required. In this study, we focused on the dilated pupils which make favorable impression and developed a presentation support system using group pupil response interfaces. This system generates a dilated pupil response and a nodding motion based on voice input in each interface. Then, a communication experiment was conducted to evaluate the developed system under the condition that the system acts like audience. The effectiveness of the system was demonstrated by mean of sensory evaluations.

Keywords: Non-verbal communication · Affective expression · Dilated pupil · Interest

1 Introduction

In recent years, many presentations such as lectures and research presentation have been conducted. Since the presentation is a one-sided communication, it is difficult to realize an interactive communication while grasping the behavior of the audience. Originally, in human face-to-face communication, not only verbal messages but also non-verbal behaviors such as facial expressions, body movements, blinks, gazes, and pupil responses are rhythmically related and mutually synchronized between talkers [1]. This synchrony of embodied rhythms in communication, called entrainment [2], results in the interactive communication. Therefore, in the presentation as well, it is desired to realize an interactive communication by sharing embodied rhythms. However, in the actual presentation, it is not easy for the speaker to grasp the behavior and interests of the audience.

In order to support such presentation, many systems were developed so far. For instance, the previous research demonstrated that a sense of unity between the speaker and the audience was deepened by visualizing the listener's nodding response [3]. In addition, many studies have been conducted on methods such as an estimation in the

© Springer Nature Switzerland AG 2021
S. Yamamoto and H. Mori (Eds.): HCII 2021, LNCS 12766, pp. 429–438, 2021.
https://doi.org/10.1007/978-3-030-78361-7_33

degree of interest from the facial directions of the audience [4] and an expression in the audience's reaction based on the facial expression [5]. These systems and studies can support presentation by visualizing the virtual behavior of audience for the speaker. However, in order to improve on the performance or motivation of the speakers during the presentation, a method that conveys audience's interest and concern is required.

It is known that the dilated pupils make favorable impression [6]. Focusing on the dilated pupil, we have already developed a pupil response interface using hemispherical displays [7]. This interface seems like human eyeball and generates conspicuous pupil response based on voice input. In addition, the effectiveness of dilated pupil response during embodied interaction and communication was confirmed by using the interface.

In this study, focusing on the effects of dilated pupil response that easily conveys the degree of interest, we developed a system that supports the presentation using group pupil response interfaces. This system generates a dilated pupil response and a nodding motion based on voice input in each interface. The effectiveness of the system was demonstrated by mean of sensory evaluations.

2 Presentation Support System

2.1 Concept

It has been demonstrated that the human pupils dilate and contract depending on not only surrounding brightness [8] but also own emotions and interests [9]. In addition, dilated pupils give preferable and interesting impression to human [6]. We focused on the effects of dilated pupil response and have developed a pupil response interface that simulates the dilation and contraction of pupil response [7]. This interface projects CG models that mimic a pupil and an iris in a virtual space and can generate the conspicuous pupil response by voice input. Therefore, we applied this interface to the presentation system as a virtual audience.

Figure 1 shows the concept of the presentation support system. This system consists on group pupil response interfaces as a virtual audience. The CG models that play the role of pupil and iris generate a nodding motion based on the speaker's voice input, and the synchrony of embodied rhythm is promoted during a presentation. Furthermore, dilated pupil response in synchronization with the speaker's voice gives an impression as if the virtual audience is interested in the speaker. By dilating the pupil, the speaker can easily grasp the direction of the audience's gaze and interest and create an interactive and positive presentation. Thus, it is expected that a presentation environment will be improved by amplifying the dilated pupil response as audience's interest.

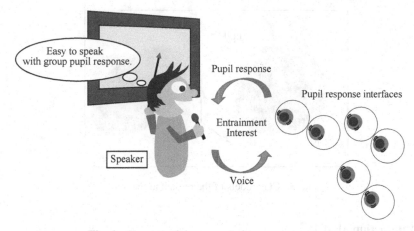

Fig. 1. Concept of the presentation support system.

2.2 Pupil Response Interface

We have already developed the pupil response interface using hemispherical displays [7]. Figure 2 shows the developed interface. The hemispherical display (Gakken WORLD-EYE) has a diameter of 250 mm, which is 10 times the size of an adult human eyeball (longitudinal diameter 24.2 mm, lateral diameter 23.7 mm) [10]. We regarded the hemispherical display as an eyeball and introduced CG models that play the role of the pupil and the iris (Fig. 3). The color of the iris is chosen to be blue because it is an easily distinguishable color to recognize the pupil response such as the dilation and contraction. The sclera of eyeball is simulated by painting the background of 3D space in white.

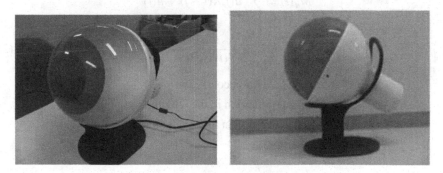

Fig. 2. Pupil response interface.

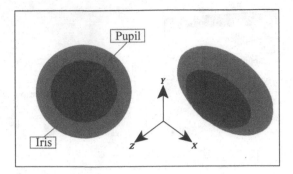

Fig. 3. CG models of the pupil and the iris.

2.3 Interaction Model

In order to support human interaction and communication, we have already developed an embodied communication technology called iRT that estimates listener's nodding response for promoting human communication [1]. The timing of nodding is predicted using a hierarchy model consisting of two stages - macro and micro (Fig. 4). The macro stage identifies a nodding response, if any, in a duration unit which consists of a talkspurt episode $T(i)$ and the following silence episode $S(i)$ with a hangover value of 4/30 s. The estimator $M_u(i)$ is a moving-average (MA) model, expressed as the weighted sum of unit speech activity $R(i)$ in Eqs. (1) and (2). When $M_u(i)$ exceeds a threshold value, nodding $M(i)$ is also an MA model, estimated as the weighted sum of the binary speech signal $V(i)$ in Eq. (3).

$$M_u(i) = \sum_{j=1}^{J} a(j)R(i-j) + u(i) \tag{1}$$

$$R(i) = \frac{T(i)}{T(i) + S(i)} \tag{2}$$

$a(j)$: linear prediction coefficient

$T(i)$: talkspurt duration in the i th duration unit

$S(i)$: silence duration in the i th duration unit

$u(i)$: noise

$$M(i) = \sum_{j=1}^{K} b(j)V(i-j) + w(i) \tag{3}$$

$b(j)$: linear prediction coefficient

$V(i)$: voice

$w(i)$: noise

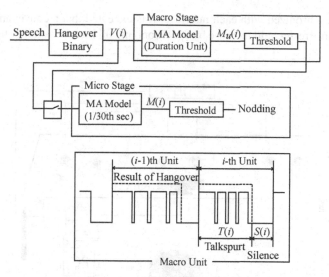

Fig. 4. Outline of the interaction model.

2.4 Presentation Support System

The outline of the developed presentation support system is shown in Fig. 5. This system has multiple pupil response interfaces connected to a workstation PC (CPU: Corei7 2.93 GHz, Memory: 8 GB, Graphics: NVIDIA Geforce GTS250) equipped with Windows. The frame rate at which the CG models are represented is 30 fps, using Microsoft DirectX 9.0 SDK (June 2010). The voice is sampled at 16bit 11 kHz by a handheld microphone (SONY F-V320).

The developed system generates a pupil response and a nodding motion based on the speaker's voice input. First, the pupil response in the system is generated as follows. When a speaker's voice is fed into the system, the absolute value of sound pressure in 30 Hz is calculated. If the value exceeds a threshold value, the voice signal is set as ON. When the voice signal is ON, the black pupil of CG model is moved in an anterior direction on the Z-axis. The velocity of movement is set at a speed of 5.2 mm/frame so that pupil response would not create a feeling of strangeness (Fig. 3). If the voice input is continuing, the dilated state of the pupil is maintained. When the voice input is finished, the pupil contracts to the normal size. Thus, the pupil response is generated in synchronization with voice.

Based on the interaction model, the nodding motion is realized by the CG models of both pupil and iris moving up and down at a speed of 0.25 rad/frame with respect to the Y-axis direction (Fig. 3). An example of pupil response and nodding motion is shown in Fig. 6. A distinct pupil response and nodding motion are observed.

In this system, a human detection sensor (Microsoft Kinect for Windows) is installed in front of the central pupil response interface to detect the position of the speaker. By moving the CG models based on the speaker's position, the system is realized eye contact with the speaker in real-time. In addition, both the pupil response and the nodding motion are synchronized with each interface. It is expected that a conveyance effect of emphasizing interest would increase by synchronizing all interfaces rather than reacting individually.

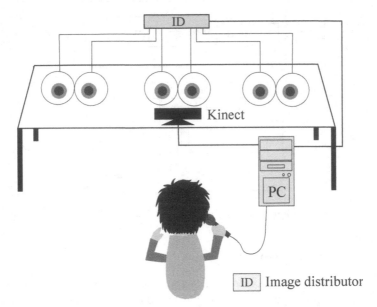

Fig. 5. Outline of the developed system.

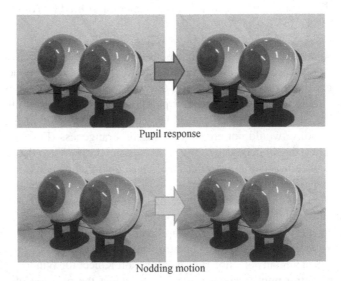

Fig. 6. Example of pupil response and nodding motion in the developed system.

3   Communication Experiment

In order to evaluate the effectiveness of the developed system, a communication experiment was conducted under the condition that the system acts like audience.

3.1   Experimental Method

In this experiment, participants spoke to a pupil response interface that acted as an audience, assuming a typical presentation (Fig. 7). Based on the results of previous studies [11], the distance between the participant and the three pupil response interfaces was arranged to consist of an equilateral triangle with a side of 2 m. The previous study confirmed that a visualizing listener's nodding response in a presentation supports embodied interactions [3]. Therefore, the following two modes were compared: (A) a mode that expresses only the nodding motion (nodding mode), and (B) a mode that expresses both the nodding motion and the pupil response (combined mode). The participants were 30 Japanese students (15 females and 15 males) who have never seen the system from 18 to 25 years old.

The experimental procedure was as follows. First, the participants used the system in each mode to understand the difference of modes. Next, the participants were told to talk on general conversational topics to three pupil response interfaces for 3 min (Fig. 8). The conversational topics were not specified, and they were instructed that the rate of their gaze was to be equally divided between the three pupil response interfaces. After the presentation, they evaluated each mode using a seven-point bipolar rating scale ranging from −3 (not at all) to 3 (extremely): 0 denotes the moderation. In this experiment, as important elements for presentation that form interactive interaction and communication,"(a) Enjoyment," "(b) Interaction," "(c) Unification," "(d) Familiarity," "(e) Relief," "(f)Empathy," "(g) Interest from audience" and "(h) Gaze from audience" were adopted. Finally, they were instructed to perform a paired comparison of modes. In the paired comparison experiment, based on their preferences, they selected the better mode. They were presented with the two modes that were counterbalanced in a random order.

3.2   Result of Experiment

The result of the paired comparison is shown in Fig. 9. The mode (B) was higher evaluated than the mode (A). Next, the questionnaire result is shown in Fig. 10. In the figure, the markers are the mean value, and the vertical bars show the standard deviation. Both (A) and (B) modes had a positive rating of 0 or higher, confirming a good impression of the developed system. Furthermore, in accordance with the result of the Wilcoxon signed rank test, all items had the significant difference of 1% between modes (A) and (B). Specially, in the items of "(g) Interest from the audience" and "(h) Gaze from audience", the average of the mode (B) exceeds 2.0, and it was confirmed that the interest from the audience is easily conveyed. For the mode (A), comments such as "I felt that the audience was calm and listening" and "I felt audience's eyes cold" were obtained. As for the mode (B), comments such as "I felt like steady listening," "I was delightful that the

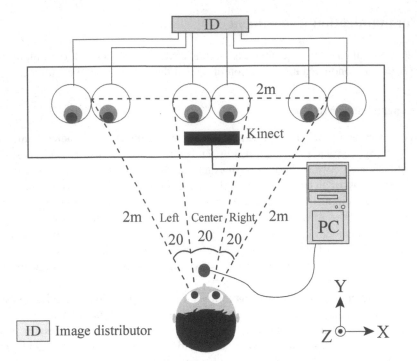

Fig. 7. Experimental setup of the communication experiment.

Fig. 8. Example of communication scene in the communication experiment.

eyes expanded due to my stories" and "I felt the audience was interested in my stories" were obtained.

These results demonstrate that the mode (B) that generates both pupil response and nodding motion are effective for supporting embodied interaction and communication in the presentation.

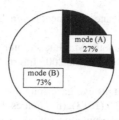

Fig. 9. Result of paired comparison.

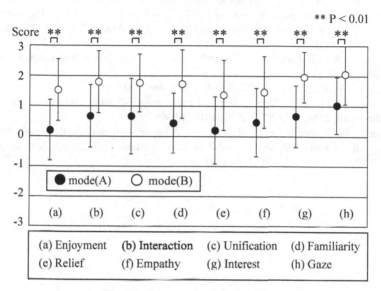

Fig. 10. Seven-points bipolar rating.

4 Conclusion

In this paper, we focused on the effect of dilated pupil that easily conveys the own interest and developed a presentation support system using group pupil response interfaces. This system generates a pupil response and a nodding motion based on voice input. By using the system, we conducted a communication experiment that emulates a presentation. The effectiveness of the developed system was demonstrated by sensory evaluations.

In the future, we plan to introduce the developed system into an actual presentation environment and verify effects of this system on the actual audience.

Acknowledgments. This work was supported by JSPS KAKENHI Grant Numbers 19K12890.

References

1. Watanabe, T., Okubo, M., Nakashige, M., Danbara, R.: Interactor: speech-driven embodied interactive actor. Int. J. Hum. Comput. Interact. **17**, 43–60 (2004)

2. Condon, W.S., Sander, L.W.: Neonate movement is synchronized with adult speech. Science **183**, 99–101 (1974)
3. Nagai, H., Watanabe, T., Yamamoto, M.: InterPointer: speech-driven embodied entrainment pointer system. In: Proceedings of the 2005 International Conference on Active Media Technology, pp. 213–218 (2005)
4. Takahashi, K., Takemura, K.: Multi eye-gaze tracking system using head pose direction. IEICE Tech. Rep. **113**(196), 63–69 (2013). (in Japanese)
5. Taniguchi, K., Hamakawa, R.: Presentation support system to visualize reactions of the audience. In: IPSJ Interaction 2018, 1B53, pp. 389–394 (2018)
6. Hess, E.H.: The role of pupil size in communication. Sci. Am. **233**, 116–119 (1975)
7. Sejima,Y., Egawa, S., Sato, Y., Watanabe, T.: A pupil response system using hemispherical displays for enhancing affective conveyance. J. Adv. Mech. Des. Syst. Manuf. **13**(2), JAMDSM0032 (2019)
8. Matthew, L.: Area and brightness of stimulus related to the pupillary light reflex. J. Opt. Soc. Am. **24**(5), 130 (1934)
9. Hess, E.H.: Attitude and pupil size. Sci. Am. **212**, 46–54 (1965)
10. Bekerman, I., Gottlieb, P., Vaiman, M.: Variations in eyeball diameters of the healthy adults. J. Ophthalmol. **2014**, 1–5 (2014). Article ID 503645
11. Sejima,Y., Watanabe, T. Jindai, M., Osa, A.: A speech-driven embodied group entrained system with an eyeball movement model for lecturer character. Trans. Jpn Soc. Mech. Eng. C **79**(799), 827–836 (2013). (in Japanese)

Extraction and Extended Analysis of Good Jobs from Safety Reports Using Text Mining - Focusing on the Voluntary Information Contributory to Enhancement of the Safety (VOICES) Data

Tsubasa Takagi[✉], Ayumu Osawa, and Miwa Nakanishi

Keio University, Yokohama, Kanagawa 223-8522, Japan
tkg283@keio.jp

Abstract. To incorporate Safety-II, which pertains to the continuation of stable operations, into safety management, we must understand why and how everyday operations are successfully carried out. However, there are no effective methods that enable such analysis since successful operations do not have to be reported in depth and are rarely analyzed. In this research, we extracted and undertook an additional analysis of the efforts or actions practiced at the sharp end to make things go right (Good Jobs) from safety reports describing events where an accident or a disaster had been successfully avoided or overcome. Specifically, we analyzed the Voluntary Information Contributory to Enhancement of the Safety (VOICES), which is one of the safety reports widely used in the field of Japanese aviation and is open to the public. In this paper, the discussions are focused on the practical analysis of the extracted Good Jobs so that they could be evaluated in depth.

Keywords: Safety reports · Safety-II · Good jobs · Text mining · Aviation

1 Introduction

Since the emergence of resilience engineering in the field of human factors, a new perspective on safety (Safety-II), which views the concept of safety differently from the traditional view (Safety-I), has been attracting a great deal of attention. As a result, various explanations have been provided to differentiate the two. In brief, while Safety-I focuses on minimizing undesirable consequences by removing the cause of errors and avoiding things that go wrong, Safety-II focuses on understanding why day-to-day operations are maintained stable and how things are ensured to go right [1].

Under Safety-I, conventional safety management focuses on analyzing the cause of unacceptable events such as accidents to prevent their recurrence. Meanwhile, human factor research has been focused on developing methods that enable such analysis. Because of these safety activities, as well as improvements in system performance, education, training, and regulations, accidents are less likely to occur.

© Springer Nature Switzerland AG 2021
S. Yamamoto and H. Mori (Eds.): HCII 2021, LNCS 12766, pp. 439–454, 2021.
https://doi.org/10.1007/978-3-030-78361-7_34

With regard to the reduced number of accident reports, safety reports related to minor hazardous events or close calls are used as a part of safety activities. Since obtaining a large amount of data from safety reports is easier, various methods have been proposed to support such activities. The examples here include research on methods for analyzing the factors that have resulted in undesirable outcomes in the medical field [2] and firefighting using the co-occurrence of words in the respective safety reports [3]. Meanwhile, in the aviation field, various methods have been proposed to analyze and predict operational risks using safety reports alongside the application of text mining [4].

However, applying Safety-II to safety management and understanding the key factors that enable stable daily operations is not as easy as extracting the causes of accidents. While there is some motivation for the application of Safety-II, there is no effective method that would allow us to analyze the positive activities that lead to successful everyday operations, making the application of the concepts of Safety-II in practice difficult. The main reason for this is that obtaining data related to the details and intentions of normal operations is extremely difficult, since successful operations do not need to be reported.

In our research, we shifted our perspective on safety reports from failures that almost led to accidents to successes that effectively avoided accidents. Using this perspective and the hypothesis that the actions are repeated throughout the operation, we attempted to extract activities that are practiced to ensure that things go right (referred to as "Good Jobs" in this research). Specifically, we used the data from the Voluntary Information Contributory to Enhancement of the Safety (VOICES), which has been operating since 2014.

The VOICES mainly aims to contribute to the improvement in aviation safety by collecting events that may have hindered aviation safety, sharing the information among operators, identifying factors that may be a threat to aviation safety, and proposing appropriate improvements [5]. The events need to be occurrences that were experienced or observed by an individual or an organization engaged in aviation activities [5]. As of August 26th, 2020, 2,000 reports from various aviation operations, including flight operations (commercial and general aviation), air traffic control (ATC), maintenance, and cabin operations, have been made available for public access [6].

In our previous related research, we introduced the process of extracting Good Jobs from VOICES data using text mining and discussed the meaning of the extracted Good Jobs to examine their applicability to safety management practices based on Safety-II [7]. In this paper, we will briefly explain the methods and the preliminary results from the previous report, before conducting further analysis by comparing the results among different aviation operations and analyzing the similarity and differences among the Good Job elements.

2 Construction of Good Job Extraction Model from VOICES Data

2.1 Method

Each safety report in the VOICES consists of free-narrative descriptions of events. Therefore, we attempted to analyze the data using text mining to extract the desired information from a large amount of text. All VOICES data are recorded in Japanese and for this paper, all the reports are translated into English, while the text mining procedures were conducted in Japanese and as certain text mining techniques were found to be limited to the Japanese language.

Data. We used 103 reports published by VOICES on November 27, 2018, as training data. The average number of sentences included in each report was 5.4 (standard deviation = 3.6 sentences). Table 1 shows examples of the reported data.

Table 1. Examples of VOICES reports [7].

Examples from training data
At the time of departure from AKJ (Asahikawa), push back was initiated after receiving a report of "Braking Action Medium to Good" following the completion of RWY snow removal. The weather at AKJ was −SHSN to SHSN. The aircraft began its takeoff from RWY34, and as soon as T/O thrust was applied, the aircraft started to slide and could not maintain directional control; thus, a ground turn-back was performed following an RTO. The snow continued to fall, and it was determined that if push back was commenced following the completion of the RWY snow sweep, the braking action would deteriorate during taxi. Following discussions with the flight operations department and the local staff, we decided to wait for the completion of the RWY snow sweep at the end of the RWY and to take off as soon as the plowing was completed while all safety checks were also completed. Although there was a significant delay, operations were completed safely due to the cooperation of all departments and staff.
When we approached the waypoint IKNAV on the Q935 over North America, the LNAV line was misaligned to the left and right, forming two straight lines that were connected in an N-shape. We checked the CDU, but it was not in discontinuity. To prevent any unintended behavior of the aircraft, I requested ATC to direct the aircraft to another waypoint ahead. The aircraft could tilt slightly at such a junction. While this is likely due to some deviation in the FMC, in this case, it was connected in an N-shape, and I thought I should pay attention to it.
While flying northbound at 1,000 ft east of the control area, I came into contact with a small aircraft attempting to land at the airport. When I tried to avoid the approach by turning right, the small aircraft also turned in the same direction, so I turned left and avoided further conflict.

Annotating Sentences with Good Jobs. In this study, we specifically defined Good Jobs as actions that demonstrate one or more resilience ability (i.e., anticipating, monitoring, responding, or learning) [8] and maintaining or improving a situation that is deteriorating or could have deteriorated. Specifically, a Good Job where the anticipating ability is exercised presents a case in which an individual predicts future threats and considers the necessary measures for dealing with them. Meanwhile, a Good Job where the monitoring ability is exercised presents a case in which an individual correctly recognizes the current situation and determines the potential threats, while in a case where the responding ability is exercised presents a case in which an individual has correctly responded to a threat in a timely manner. Last, a Good Job where the learning ability is exercised presents a case in which an individual reflects on and learns from what has happened to improve future operations.

Looking through the VOICES reports, we noted that they typically consist of an explanation of the background, what was seen and heard, the actions taken in response, the results, and the reflections. This structure can be observed in the examples shown in Table 1. From the safety reports, we also observed several actions that fit our definition of Good Jobs. Here, sentences such as "Following discussions with the flight operations department and the local staff, we decided to wait for the completion of the RWY snow sweep at the end of the RWY and to take off as soon as the plowing was completed, while all safety checks were also completed" and "When I tried to avoid the approach by turning right, the small aircraft also turned in the same direction; thus, I turned left and avoided further conflict" are examples of a Good Job.

With this in mind, we prepared the training data for text mining by looking at each sentence and annotating whether or not it presented a Good Job using the procedure described below (Fig. 1).

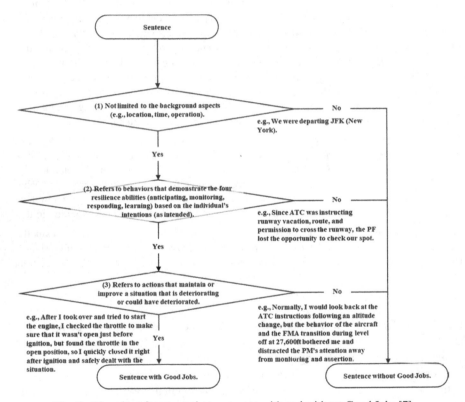

Fig. 1. Flowchart for annotating sentences with and without Good Jobs [7].

(1)   The details of the sentence are not limited to the background aspects (e.g., location, time, operation). If this is not the case, it is not a sentence with Good Jobs since it is a sentence explaining only the background.

(2) The sentence refers to behaviors that demonstrate the four resilience abilities (antic-ipating, monitoring, responding, learning) based on the individual's intentions (as intended). If the sentence met this criterion, we also annotated which of the four resilience abilities (anticipating, monitoring, responding, learning) were practiced (multiple abilities were annotated if multiple abilities were observed in a given sentence). If the sentence did not meet the criterion, it unavoidably occurred in the course of by mistake and was not a sentence with Good Jobs.

(3) The sentence refers to actions that maintain or improve a situation that is deteri-orating or could have deteriorated. If not, the sentence pertains to a behavior that worsens the situation and does not contain Good Jobs.

Using this procedure, 557 sentences from 103 reports were annotated. Of the 557 sentences, 208 were annotated as sentences with Good Jobs and 349 as sentences without Good Jobs. Following the annotation process, there were fewer sentences with Good Jobs pertaining to the anticipating and learning abilities. To balance the data, we used additional data from VOICES to supplement 54 sentences containing Good Jobs that fell under the anticipating and learning categories. Table 2 shows examples of sentences with Good Jobs, along with the final numbers for each category.

Table 2. Annotation results for the training data [7].

Annotations		Examples	Number of sentences
Sentences without Good Jobs		This event occurred during night after landing at RWY 34L at Haneda.	349
		I ended up accidently pressing the TOGA switch when diengaging the autothrottle.	
Sentences with Good Jobs	Anticipating	In order to try ENG run up while taxiing slowly to the ramp area, my copilot and I agreed that we would tell each other as soon as we started to slip and I advanced one of the ENG to 2 or 3 kts.	49
		Recently, I had been instructed to take off from D2, so I checked the OPT and set the assumed temperature with some margin so that I could take off from D2.	
	Monitoring	I made contact with the ground ATC after landing and headed for my assigned spot in the apron, but I saw another departing aircraft pushed back in the apron TWY.	96
		The arriving aircraft passed by and we tried to read back to the "OO1870, Resume Own Navigation Direct IKEMA" instruction, but another aircraft, OO 1770, read back instead and the controller did not make any corrections.	
	Responding	The B737-700 is generally lighter than the -800, and after redoing the OPT calculation with our tail number, the Vr and V2 of the OPT matched the FMC and we departed.	75
		We tried to check with the ground controller to see if we were the first aircraft to taxi, but due to frequent towing, we could not confirm and as a result, we had to stop before the W taxiway to let the other aircraft pass.	
	Learning	In any case, I realized once again that it is very important to check the results of the OPT calculations, including flaps, and to cross-check them with the FMS numbers.	70
		In addition, RWY 36, Spot 36, Spot 26, and other numbers that could be misheard were also a threat, and I think I needed to be more careful, especially when receiving long ATC instructions since it is easy to become uncertain.	

Construction of Filters to Identify Sentences with and without Good Jobs.
Using a total of 611 sentences from the training data, we constructed filters to identify sentences containing Good Jobs. We first applied morphological analysis to each of the sentences. Morphological analysis involves a series of processes in which a sentence is divided into words and where both the part of the speech and the original form of each word are identified [9]. We used the KH Coder [10] for the morphological analysis, while MeCab was adopted as the morphological analyzer.

We then used the three processes shown in Fig. 1 as a guide to create the filters. Regarding the sentences that were identified as sentences explaining only the background (criterion 1), 52.6% contained words related to airports (airport name or city name). Meanwhile, in terms of the sentences not limited to the background information, only 4.4% contained words related to airports. While other words related to time and operation were also analyzed, we could not identify any effective classifiers. Therefore, we decided to use airport-related words (e.g., Nagoya, Centrair, Chubu) recorded in Japanese as the first filter, and any sentences without those words were classified as sentences that may contain Good Jobs. Meanwhile, English words and airport codes were excluded from the airport-related words since they were used in sentences that were not limited to the background to refer to ATC instructions or charts.

To create a filter to identify sentences that refer to behaviors demonstrating the four resilience abilities based on the individual's intentions (criterion 2), we used 592 sentences that explained only the background or sentences that were classified to have details that were not limited to the background information. After listing all compound words, unnecessary words, and synonyms, we focused on the verbs, adverbs, and adjectives to focus on human behaviors and intentions. Furthermore, we observed that words that appeared three or more times throughout the sentences in the training data allowed us to effectively classify sentences that referred to the four resilience abilities and those that did not. Therefore, we set the percentage of sentences containing word i (verbs, adverbs, and adjectives that appeared three or more times throughout the sentences in the training data) that met criterion 2 as p_i and the percentage of sentences containing i that did not meet the criterion as q_i ($p_i + q_i = 1$). Applying these percentages, indices P_n and Q_n were calculated for each sentence n using Eq. (1) and Eq. (2), respectively [7].

$$P_n = \sum p_i \qquad (1)$$

$$Q_n = \sum q_i \qquad (2)$$

For each sentence n, if $P_n > Q_n$, the sentence was classified as a sentence that could contain Good Jobs.

Finally, we used 325 sentences that met criteria 1 and 2 to create a filter for criterion 3, that is, sentences that referred to actions that maintained or improved a situation that was deteriorating or could have deteriorated. In terms of the sentences that referred to behaviors that worsened the situation and did not contain Good Jobs, terms such as "ended up," "could not," and "without" were included in 50.8% of the sentences. Meanwhile, the percentage was 4.6% for sentences that met criterion 3. Therefore, we used the terms "ended up," "could not," and "without" for the third filter, and if the sentence did not contain any of these words, the sentence was classified as a one containing Good Jobs.

2.2 Results and Accuracy Verification

To verify the accuracy of the Good Job extraction model, recall, precision, and accuracy percentages were calculated in terms of the training data. Here, we used 24 reports (134 sentences) published on May 26, 2020, as the test data and calculated the recall, precision, and accuracy percentages after applying our model. The results are shown in Table 3, while the examples of extracted sentences with Good Jobs are provided in Table 4.

Table 3. Accuracy of Good Job extraction model in terms of training and test data [7].

	Training data	Test data
Recall	75.6%	75.0%
Precision	68.3%	65.2%
Accuracy	74.5%	70.9%

Table 4. Examples of Good Job sentences extracted from the test data [7].

Examples
The aircraft broke away from the towline and came to a stop.
It was almost midnight (around 13:00 Z), and my copilot and I were operating the aircraft with the utmost attention to ATC.
I often fly in this area, but I realized once again that any slight carelessness could lead to errors such as mishearing.
While paying attention to changes in the altimeter and speedometer, I climbed slowly, turned to the brighter side of my peripheral vision, and took off to the north of the wildfire smoke.
The pilot then maneuvered and landed the aircraft with the radio in his hand.
However, I prevented the wrong parts from being installed by comparing the AMM, the IPC, and the parts in the actual aircraft.

Although there were some cases where sentences without Good Jobs were extracted as sentences *with* Good Jobs, the accuracy of the model was over 70% for both the training and test data.

We also considered using machine learning techniques such as the random forest, naïve Bayes, and support vector machine; however, our proposed model demonstrated higher accuracy, especially when it was applied to the test data. Table 5 shows the accuracy values for the machine learning techniques. We concluded that the lower accuracy was likely due to the fact that our data corpus was not suitable for such methods. As a result, we decided to use our proposed Good Job extraction model for further analysis and discussion.

Table 5. Accuracy of Good Job extraction using the random forest, naïve Bayes and support vector machine [7].

Training data			
	Random forest	Naïve Bayes	Support vector machine
Recall	94.7%	56.9%	92.7%
Precision	97.6%	78.4%	97.2%
Accuracy	96.7%	74.8%	95.7%
Test data			
	Random forest	Naïve Bayes	Support vector machine
Recall	60.0%	33.3%	41.7%
Precision	65.5%	62.5%	62.5%
Accuracy	67.9%	61.2%	62.7%

2.3 Expansion of Model

During the annotation process, we also identified which of the four resilience abilities were practiced (multiple abilities were annotated if multiple abilities were observed in a given sentence). Using the 262 sentences from the training data that were classified as sentences with Good Jobs, we attempted to expand the model such that it could predict which of the four resilience abilities were present in each sentence.

Here, we used the same techniques as previously used to conduct the morphological analysis; that is, after identifying the compound words, unnecessary words, and synonyms, we focused on the verbs, adverbs, and adjectives of each sentence. Much like with the previous model, we observed that words that appeared three or more times throughout the sentences in the training data allowed us to effectively classify the sentences in terms of the four resilience abilities. Therefore, we set the percentage of sentences containing an ability-classifying word k that pertained to a specific ability j (j = anticipating, monitoring, responding, learning) as $r_{j,k}$ and after applying the percentages, index $Z_{m,j}$ was calculated for each sentence m using Eq. (3) [7].

$$Z_{m,j} = \Sigma r_{j,k} / (total\ number\ of\ verbs,\ adverbs,\ and\ adjectives\ in\ sentence\ m)$$

$$(3)$$

Last, we set the threshold value that would best maximize the recall, precision, and accuracy for all the abilities. Here, the threshold values were set at 0.27, 0.28, 0.19, and 0.25 for anticipating, monitoring, responding, and learning, respectively [7]. The sentence was deemed to relate to the corresponding ability if $Z_{m,j}$ was greater than the respective threshold value.

Using the same training and test data as previously used, the recall, precision, and accuracy percentages were calculated, and the results are shown in Table 6. Here, the recall was over 75% for the training data and over 60% for the test data. However, the values for precision and accuracy were lower, falling below 50% in certain cases. This means that, while the model was able to extract a good number of sentences that pertained to the correct categories, other sentences that pertained to a different category were also extracted. In reality, the definitions of the abilities tend to overlap each other, and the abilities are often practiced together rather than separately. While the model did not have demonstrate high accuracy, we believe the accuracy was high enough to roughly grasp the characteristics of sentences containing Good Jobs. We also considered the machine learning techniques for this model but chose to use the proposed model since our corpus was likely to be unsuitable for these techniques.

Table 6. Accuracy of ability estimation model for the training and test data [7].

Training data

	Anticipating	Monitoring	Responding	Learning
Recall	85.7%	76.0%	89.3%	88.6%
Precision	36.8%	59.8%	39.4%	47.3%
Accuracy	69.9%	72.5%	57.6%	70.6%

Test data

	Anticipating	Monitoring	Responding	Learning
Recall	62.5%	64.3%	68.2%	78.6%
Precision	20.8%	45.0%	57.7%	47.8%
Accuracy	55.1%	67.4%	63.3%	69.4%

Figure 2 presents an overview of the Good Job extraction process, while Fig. 3 shows the overall steps for the model expansion.

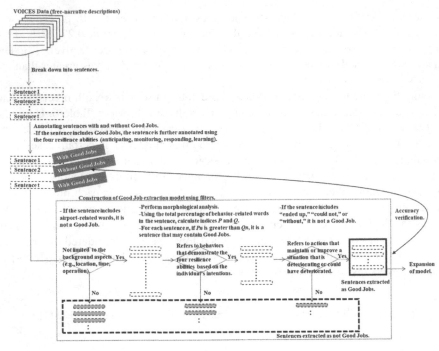

Fig. 2. Overview of the Good Job extraction model [7].

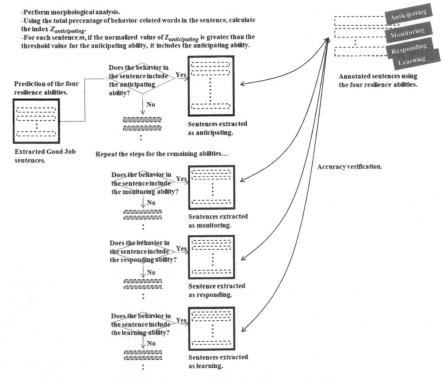

Fig. 3. Overview of the model expansion [7].

3   Application and Discussion of Good Job Extraction Model: Characteristics of Good Jobs in VOICES Safety Reports

3.1   Cluster Analysis

The models explained in Sect. 2 were applied to 1,594 reports (average = 7.1 sentences) published between December 25, 2014, and May 26, 2020, to analyze the characteristics of the extracted Good Jobs. Here, the data did not include reports used in the training or test data.

We extracted a total of 5,003 sentences with Good Jobs. Here, the number of sentences that demonstrated the anticipating, monitoring, responding, and learning abilities was 1,971, 1,731, 2,778, and 2,102, respectively. We then conducted cluster analysis to identify the characteristics of these sentences. Specifically, we calculated the *tf-idf* value for the verbs, adverbs, and adjectives. Next, the cosine similarity was calculated to ascertain the similarity among the sentences, while Ward's method was used for the hierarchical clustering analysis.

As a result, we identified five clusters for each of the four resilience abilities, with the specificity of the clusters interpreted from the sentences in each cluster. The results are shown in Table 7. Here, clusters related to the anticipating ability illustrated specific key points that are crucial to making effective preparations. Meanwhile, the clusters that are related to the monitoring ability involve breaking down the ways to improve the alertness and awareness of hazards, while Good Jobs related to the responding ability pertain to specific options for coping with irregular or deteriorating situations. Finally, the clusters for the learning ability highlight multiple approaches where the lessons learned are applied to future operations.

3.2   Extended Analysis of Good Jobs in Different Aviation Operations

As noted in Sect. 1, the VOICES data consists of reports from various aviation operations, including flight operations (commercial and general aviation), ATC, maintenance, and cabin operations. Specifically, the operations are divided into three categories: "commercial aviation (flight and ATC)," "general aviation (flight and ATC)," and "airport, cabin, and maintenance." To further analyze the similarities and differences among the Good Job clusters related to the various aviation operations, we calculated the ratio of each cluster by comparing the number of sentences in each cluster with the total number of Good Jobs for each aviation operation, with the results shown in Fig. 4. Since we allowed the annotation of multiple abilities, the sum of the ratios did not always add up to 100%. Meanwhile, we also focused on clusters that had operation categories of over 5%, which are indicated by the red boxes in Fig. 4. Moreover, if the ratio of a specific category was over 5% within these clusters, an example sentence was picked out. Table 8 presents the example sentences.

In terms of the third cluster in the anticipating ability, "recognizing and sharing information regarding delayed tasks as hazards," the ratios of all three categories were greater than 25%, while in terms of the commercial aviation category, the focus was on checking for delayed tasks related to flight plans and ATC instructions. Meanwhile, in terms of the general aviation category, the focus was on checking whether the individual's

Table 7. Cluster analysis results [7].

Abilities	Name of cluster	Examples
Anticipating	1-Confirming and sharing the recognition of self and others.	After telling the PM that "B is over there", we slowly continued down the E3 gateway.
	2-Checking for possible situations and responses to them.	The PF and PM had been discussing the possibility of both RWY A and RWY B since the briefing stage, and using the charts, they had confirmed that route 7 to 16R, route 9 to 16L, and possibly TWY T and U clockwise to 16L were also possible.
	3-Recognizing and sharing information regarding delayed tasks as hazards.	It was shared between the PF and PM that the clearance has not yet come.
	4-Recognizing and sharing situational and environmental changes as hazards.	The ETA on the CDU was 0540 Z, ILS 34L was set for ROUTE 2 in case of approach change, and the information was shared in the briefing.
	5-Checking for situations in which hazards increase.	During the takeoff briefing, we shared that it will be a short taxi and to be careful of task omissions.
Monitoring	1-Detecting damages and objects in abnormal conditions.	After stopping takeoff preparations, I went outside of the aircraft to check the exterior, and found that the pitot cover was still attached.
	2-Paying attention to information that cannot be obtained visually.	The trainee took over and pushed the throttle forward to take off immediately for a TGL training, but the engine sound was quieter than usual.
	3-Paying attention to the individual's internal conditions.	The separation, altitude, and speed were all fine, and when I was about to turn around Cape Kiyabu and align to final, I suddenly realized that my consciousness was heading slightly offshore from the land.
	4-Detecting the movements and changes of others.	While circling, I heard "Continue approach" and "No.1 now turning final," so I looked for the aircraft ahead of me and I found the aircraft on short final, so we proceeded to normal base.
	5-Detecting objects in unnatural conditions.	The chock operator set the chock on the nose tire when the aircraft arrived, but later, when the maintenance staff checked the status of the chock, the chock was not parallel with the tires.
Responding	1-Prioritizing the continuation of tasks.	A high-speed RTO crossed my mind for a moment, but judging from the ATC interaction, we were definitely cleared for takeoff and read back was performed properly, so I decided that it would be safer to continue the takeoff procedure than to execute a high-speed RTO.
	2-Cooperating with other departments and staff.	We notified the next shift about the defect, and the person in charge of the operation instructed the operator to check the status of the defect, plan for its maintenance, and look for spare parts.
	3-Stopping or delaying tasks.	As a precaution, I turned off at W9 using only the rudder, slowed down further, and confirmed that the steering was normal, so I blocked in at the spot as usual.
	4-Restarting tasks.	During the CAT II APCH, the autopilot disengaged near 1,000 ft AGL, so I performed a go-around.
	5-Changing plans or methods.	Thinking that aircraft A might not be able to clear the altitude limit at this rate, I instructed aircraft A to change the climb to FL280.
Learning	1-Coming up with specific procedures, plans, or tips that would enhance future operations.	In an approach such as SAN LOC 27, which is prone to high energy, it may be effective to share specific decisions with the PF and PM in advance, such as, "We will go-around if we are not at x with an altitude of xx ft and a speed of xxx kt."
	2-Reflecting on the individual's internal conditions (unfamiliarity, fatigue, etc.).	Since this was a new airport for me, I should have checked more carefully.
	3-Reflecting with others and sharing the lessons learned.	Also, while we were both verbally confirming the instructions, we both reflected that since taxi navigation had not been set, the PF should have stopped, and the PM should have urged him to stop.
	4-Gaining knowledge about hazardous situations such as high-workload situations.	Looking back, we had to handle the task with more margin and be careful during tasks related to visual approach such as tower handoff, mode change, and traffic.
	5-Adding options and responses.	Also, although we did not use the emergency checklist, we thought it was important to keep it readily available.

actions were appropriately carried out without delay, while for the airport, cabin, and maintenance category, the focus was on checking whether the tasks were completed on schedule. Given that efficiency is an important factor in aviation, it may have caused the percentage of this cluster to be higher than those among the other clusters in the anticipating ability.

In terms of the second cluster in the monitoring ability, only the ratio of the general aviation category was over 5%. This was likely because general aviation requires the attention of all five senses to detect any system or engine trouble, meaning this may be a characteristic that is unique to this category. In terms of the third cluster in the monitoring

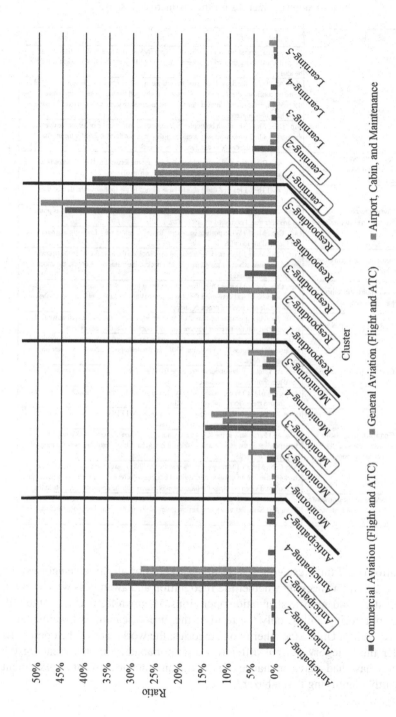

Fig. 4. Ratio of Good Job clusters for each aviation operation.

Table 8. Example sentences for the distinctive clusters.

Abilities	Name of cluster	Examples
Anticipating	3-Recognizing and sharing information regarding delayed tasks as hazards.	(Com. Av.) The wind was 8 kt at 190 deg., visibility was 10 km, and sky condition was FEW010, and during the landing briefing, the PM and I agreed that RWY insight was likely to be after 1,500 ft.
		(Gen. Av.) During the flight, I reported the change in en-route time and the amount of fuel on board by contacting the flight service center, and changed the flight plan, but the content was not reflected in the satellite airport operation management system, so a search and rescue could have been triggered.
		(Ap., Cab., Maint.) During a helicopter maintenance, a maintenance order for the overhaul of the main gear box was issued with a calendar deadline, but the time limit for the overhaul came earlier than the calendar deadline.
Monitoring	2-Paying attention to information that cannot be obtained visually.	(Gen. Av.) The trainee took over and pushed the throttle forward to take off immediately for a TGL training, but the engine sound was quieter than usual.
	3-Paying attention to the individual's internal conditions.	(Com. Av.) Then, I realized that I should have aligned to the spot along the dashed line instead of the solid line.
		(Gen. Av.) I thought I was going to T-4, so I did not realize my mistake until it was pointed out and after that, I corrected myself to T-4.
		(Ap., Cab., Maint.) While pushing back east, the pilots asked me if I was pushing back south and I realized my mistake.
	5-Detecting objects in unnatural conditions.	(Ap., Cab., Maint.) The chock operator set the chock on the nose tire when the aircraft arrived, but later, when the maintenance staff checked the status of the chock, the chock was not parallel with the tires.
Responding	2-Cooperating with other departments and staff.	(Ap., Cab., Maint.) During DEP, the container going to 09L was transferred to the cargo room, and when it was confirmed that it was loaded correctly, the container was on the auxiliary guide and was not properly strapped.
	3-Stopping or delaying tasks.	(Com. Av.) As a precaution, I turned off at W9 using only the rudder, slowed down further, and confirmed that the steering was normal, so I blocked in at the spot as usual.
	5-Changing plans or methods.	(Com. Av.) Due to the clouds in front of us and in the direction of the approach, we decided that it would be impossible to maintain VMC, so we deliberately changed our route and continued the flight.
		(Gen. Av.) Just as I was about to make the final turn, I spotted another aircraft (no.2) making a final turn from the opposite base.
		(Ap., Cab., Maint.) We explained the situation to the load controller through the load master and changed the position from 43R to 42L.
Learning	1-Coming up with specific procedures, plans, or tips that would enhance future operations.	(Com. Av.) From now on, I will try to press ACKNOWLEDGE and make sure that the screen changes before moving to the next screen.
		(Gen. Av.) Particularly in the KS4-5 area, not only is it impossible to receive radar service, but depending on the altitude and position, it is also hard to communicate with the terminal control area in charge.
		(Ap., Cab., Maint.) The reason for this may be that the baggage retrieval system was not checked when the information of unclaimed baggage was received, and the tag number was not confirmed when checking the baggage information with the baggage claim data at the gate.
	2-Reflecting on the individual's internal conditions (unfamiliarity, fatigue, etc.).	(Com. Av.) Since this was a new airport for me, I should have checked more carefully.

ability, the ratios of all three categories were above 10%. For all these categories, the actions were focused on checking whether the recognition and awareness were correct. Hence, this cluster could apply to all aviation operations. Meanwhile, in terms of the fifth cluster in the monitoring ability, only the ratio of the airport, cabin, and maintenance category exceeded 5%. Unlike the other two categories, the workplace of the operations that fell under this category did not differ (e.g., same hangar, airport), meaning the individuals may have had a greater chance of noticing an unnatural layout or placement and subsequently identifying it as a hazard.

In terms of the second cluster in the responding ability, only the ratio of the airport, cabin, and maintenance category was greater than 10%. Unlike with the other two categories, where the crew of the aircraft can and must deal with the majority of problems alone (e.g., during flight), here, the ground operations could significantly impact the departments and staff, which means that confirming that everyone is on the same page is a crucial factor in preventing any misunderstandings. In terms of the third cluster in the responding ability, only the ratio of the commercial aviation category was greater than 5%. Although the systems pertaining to this category are complex, the individuals that fall into this category tend to have a limited field of view, especially the pilots, which means halting or delaying the work is critical when something out of the ordinary is observed. In terms of the fifth cluster in the responding ability, the ratios of all three categories were over 40%. All these categories contained actions that involved changing the initial plan to cope with fluctuating or worsening conditions. This was especially the case with the commercial aviation and general aviation categories, which are related to flying, where the actions were focused on avoiding adverse weather conditions or other aircraft. Overall, the reason why the ratio of this cluster was the largest in each category was likely related to how it is difficult to stop and think during most aviation operations, which means making changes is the preferred means of responding.

In terms of the first cluster in the learning ability, the ratio was over 25% in all three categories. Here, the ratio was especially large in the commercial aviation category, which was likely because the tasks here tend to be well organized; thus, forming specific countermeasures is easier. However, the ratio was also higher than 25% in the other categories, meaning this behavior may be applicable to all aviation operations. In terms of the second cluster in the learning ability category, only the ratio of the commercial aviation category exceeded 5%. This was likely because the working hours tend to be longer in this area, which can lead to fatigue and means reflecting on the individual's internal conditions is crucial to maintaining safety.

4 Conclusion

In this research, we extracted and analyzed the Good Jobs that are practiced at the sharp end to make things go right from an aviation safety report database (VOICES) using text mining. In addition, we provided extended analysis related to the extracted Good Jobs by focusing on the similarities and differences among the various aviation operations. The analysis and discussions presented in this paper also shed some light on specific elements that could be used to evaluate actions and operations based on the Safety-II concept. While the accuracy of our extraction process was not particularly high and the research remains at the preliminary stage, we believe that this study could help guide practitioners and researchers toward the implementation of safety management using the concepts of Safety-II.

References

1. Hollnagel, E.: Safety-I and Safety-II: the Past and Future of Safety Management. CRC press, Boca Raton (2014)

2. Kimura, M., Ohkura, M., Tsuchiya, F.: Text mining analysis of medical near-miss reports. Jpn. J. Ergon. **42**(Supplement), 232–233 (2006)
3. Miyawaki, W., Kimura, M.: Analysis on a fire fighting incident database. In: Proceedings of the Institute of Electronics, Information and Communication Engineers General Conference, p. 298 (2012)
4. Zhang, X., Mahadevan, S.: Ensemble machine learning models for aviation incident risk prediction. Decis. Support Syst. **116**, 48–63 (2019)
5. Cabinet Office Homepage, https://www8.cao.go.jp/koutu/taisaku/h27kou_haku/english/pdf/t_8.pdf. Accessed 26 Aug 2020
6. VOICES FEEDBACK Homepage, http://www.jihatsu.jp/news/index.html. Accessed 26 Aug 2020
7. Osawa, A., Takagi, T., Nakanishi, M.: An attempt to extract good jobs from safety reports using text mining -analysis of voluntary information contributory to enhancement of the safety (VOICES) Data-. Hum. Factors Jpn. **25**(2) (in press) (2021)
8. Hollnagel, E.: Resilience Engineering in Practice: A guidebook. Ashgate, Farnham (2013)
9. Kudo, T.: Theory and implementation of morphological analysis. Kindai Kagakusha (2018)
10. Higuchi, K.: Quantitative text analysis for social research: toward the succession and development of content analysis. 2nd edn. Nakanishiya (2018)

Development and Evaluation
of a Gaze Information Collection System
in e-Testing for Examinee Authentication

Toru Tokunaga[1(✉)], Toru Kano[2], and Takako Akakura[2]

[1] Graduate School of Engineering, Tokyo University of Science, 6–3–1 Nijuku,
Katsushika-ku, Tokyo 125–8585, Japan
`4620520@ed.tus.ac.jp`
[2] Faculty of Engineering, Tokyo University of Science, 6–3–1 Nijuku, Katsushika-ku,
Tokyo 125-8585, Japan
`{kano,akakura}@rs.tus.ac.jp`

Abstract. With the development of communication technology, distance learning has improved to a point where it is comparable to in-person lectures and the demand for e-testing has increased. However, there are many challenges to e-testing, especially in preventing cheating. In this study, we develop and evaluate four systems that use different methods to collect gaze information during e-testing to authenticate examinees without interfering with natural responses. The results of the evaluation experiments show that the "gaze drawing system" is the most accurate and the load on the user is within an acceptable range, indicating that the system is the most appropriate method for collecting gaze information during e-testing.

Keywords: E-testing · E-learning · Personal authentication · Gaze information

1 Introduction

1.1 Research Background

Today, with depopulation in rural areas and populations concentrated in cities, change to a decentralized society is desirable, and distance education is attracting increased interest [1]. In addition, the need for remote work and education may increase due to sudden changes and events, such as the COVID-19 epidemic in 2020 [2]. In education, e-testing is a suitable solution to these social issues. In particular, these issues could be resolved if it were possible to remotely and asynchronously conduct tests that normally require large gatherings in one place. However, problems persist with the current e-testing system, including difficulty in detecting cheating and the ease of cheating, including spoofing attacks. These problems make accurate measurement of examinees' academic abilities impossible. In order to prevent such cheating, examinee authentication during e-testing

© Springer Nature Switzerland AG 2021
S. Yamamoto and H. Mori (Eds.): HCII 2021, LNCS 12766, pp. 455–467, 2021.
https://doi.org/10.1007/978-3-030-78361-7_35

is considered in the present study by evaluating gaze information and facial features. To our knowledge, no previous studies have investigated methods for collecting gaze information during e-testing. Thus, we considered it necessary to first establish a method for collecting gaze information that can efficiently show examinees' gaze movement characteristics without interfering with natural answering behavior. Therefore, the purpose of this study is to develop an e-testing system that implements gaze interaction to collect examinee gaze information. The study also aims to establish a method for collecting gaze information that satisfies the abovementioned conditions by calculating authentication accuracy based on gaze movement features obtained by the system.

1.2   Related Research

We refer to the related work of Mukai et al. [3]. Mukai et al. proposed an authentication method based on individual differences in the trajectories of letters and symbols drawn in the air by gazing. In their experiment, classification accuracy was verified for letters and symbols drawn with one's gaze. The results showed that the features of the drawn trajectories contributed to classification accuracy. The classification accuracy was over 90%, even when all the participants drew the same letters and symbols. These results suggest that this method could be used for personal authentication. On the other hand, there is room for further study on the combination of features to be used, and the effect of the difficulty of drawing letters and symbols with one's gaze on users should be considered. In the present study, we develop and evaluate four different systems that encourage examinees to make specific gaze movements during e-testing and extract features from their gaze trajectories. The systems create a discriminator based on these features and authenticates individuals so that examinees can confirm their identity simply by taking the test using the system. The systems aim to collect examinees' gaze information during the natural act of answering, without disturbance. We describe the results of evaluation experiments on these systems that implement different methods of collecting gaze information. In each system, gaze information is collected during e-testing by calculating authentication accuracy and examining the burden placed on examinees based on the results of user questionnaires.

2   Overview of Systems

In this study, we created four systems that use different methods of inducing specific gaze movements to collect gaze movement information during e-testing. These systems are designed to collect gaze information during gaze interaction at the time examinees answer a question. All of the systems use Unity [4] as the development platform, and Tobii Eye Tracker 4C [5] to collect gaze information. The details of each system are described in the following sections.

2.1   System 1: Select Choices in Four Corners by Gaze

System 1 was designed with a focus on the format of e-testing, where the user selects one answer from four choices.

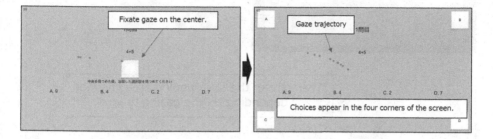

Fig. 1. System based on choices selected with one's gaze

Figure 1 shows how the system is used. The examinee reads the question, decides the answer from among four choices, and selects the "Start Answer" button. An area appears in the center of the screen, which the examinee gazes at to initiate choice selection. After gazing for about one second, the four answer choices appear in the four corners of the screen. The examinee gazes at their selection for about one second to confirm their answer. As the examinee holds their gaze, a gauge in the center of the screen indicates the duration of their gaze. Gazing at the center and then at each choice unifies the start and end points of the gaze movement. In addition, the gaze information is acquired frame by frame in synchronicity with the screen, so the frames per second (FPS) is fixed at 60. The collection of gaze information starts when the examinee finishes gazing at the center, and ends when they finish gazing at their answer for about one second.

The advantage of this system is that it collects the answer information and gaze information at the same time, which prevents prolonging the answer time and enables the collection of the answer information without interfering with the natural answering behavior of the examinee. The disadvantage of the system is that individual differences in the characteristics of the gaze information might be difficult to determine because the collection interval is relatively short.

2.2   System 2: Select a Screen Area that Is Divided into Four Sections

This system is a modification of System 1. In System 1, choices are located in the four corners of the screen, but in System 2, the entire screen is divided into four parts, and these parts are used as the answer choice areas. The interface of the system is shown in Fig. 2.

In this system, the examinee decides their answer choice and selects the "Start Answer" button. An area in the center of the screen appears to initiate

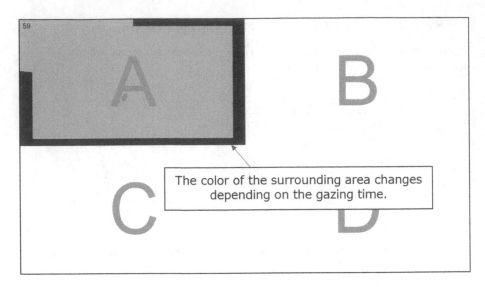

The color of the surrounding area changes depending on the gazing time.

Fig. 2. System with expanded choice areas

choice selection. Up to this point, System 2 is the same as System 1. However, beyond this point, the screen in System 2 is divided into four equal parts for choice selection. In this phase, because there is no screen area other than the choices, a short gaze time could trigger a selection error. Therefore, the gaze-holding time was set to be longer than that in System 1, and for easier visual comprehension for the examinee, the system draws a line around the selected choice as time passes. When the examinee's gaze fixates on a choice until the two ends of the line meet, the answer is confirmed and the examinee moves on to the next question. The system collects the gaze information from the time the examinee finishes gazing at the center to the time they finish gazing at their choice area.

The advantage of this system is that the area where the examinee fixates their gaze is larger than that in System 1, so the distribution of gaze movement is anticipated to be larger than that in System 1. This larger distribution makes gaze movement features appear more readily. In addition, System 2 does not require the examinee to move their gaze to the edge of the screen or to make complicated movements when answering the questions, thus reducing the burden on the examinee. The disadvantage is that the examinee's gaze could fixate on the choice numbers displayed in the choice areas instead of their answer choice. In addition, even though the choice areas are large, examinees could easily fixate on the center of the screen as a reference point when they are unsure of where to gaze. Thus, prolonged fixation on the center could prevent the features of gaze movement from appearing.

2.3   System 3: Follow Sorting with One's Gaze

This system differs from the previous two systems in that it targets sorting questions. Specifically, the system allows the examinee to select their intended answer by moving their gaze to the choice area in sorting order. The interface of the system is shown in Fig. 3.

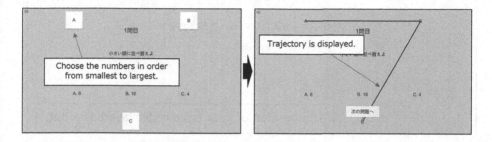

Fig. 3. System for selecting choices in a sorting order

In this system, the initial answering procedure by gazing is the same as that in the previous two systems, except that three choice areas appear, as shown in Fig. 3. Only three choices are provided because four permutations would mean 24 possible gaze movement patterns, which would be a heavy load on the examinee during training data collection. The examinee fixates on each choice area for about one second in their desired answer order. When the second or third choice is selected, a line is drawn between it and the previous choice, so that the examinee can visualize the order of their choices. The gaze information is collected from the time the examinee finishes gazing at the center to the time they finish gazing at their last choice.

The advantage of this system is that the distance of gaze movement is longer than that in the case of selecting a single choice, and the characteristics of the individual can be easily expressed. However, the disadvantage of this system is that a large number of gaze movements is required, which places a heavy burden on the examinee. In addition, the system is difficult to use because of the limited number of question types, so it may not be practical.

2.4   System 4: Draw a Symbol with One's Gaze When Moving onto a New Question

This system does not require gaze interaction when answering a question, but rather requires the examinee to draw a specific symbol with their gaze just before moving on to the next question. In order to make the design of this system easy to use for all examinees, we chose a four-choice question format and a simple circle as the symbol to be drawn. The interface of the system is shown in Fig. 4.

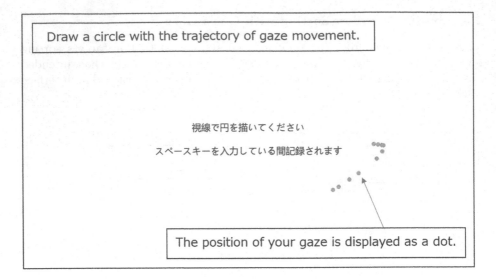

Fig. 4. System for drawing circles with gaze trajectory

In this system, the examinee answers questions as in a normal e-testing session; that is, after answering a question, they move on to the next question. The examinee draws a circle using the trajectory of the gaze movement before moving on to the next question. The gaze is visualized as a point, which serves as a reference as the examinee draws a circle. After completing the circle, the examinee presses the space bar. The gaze information is collected from the time the key is pressed until it is released.

One of the advantages of this system is that differences between individuals is expected to be large because even the shape and the way of drawing the symbols is expected to be distinctive. In addition, the system can be implemented in any format, making it highly versatile. However, a disadvantage of this system is that the act of drawing the symbols has nothing to do with the examination. Therefore, this system places a burden on the examinee and can result in decreased concentration.

3   Evaluation Experiments

We conducted evaluation experiments of the developed systems and calculated authentication accuracy based on the data obtained. A questionnaire survey on each system was also administered to determine their usability and load on examinees. Based on these results, we investigated the optimal method for collecting gaze information during e-testing.

3.1 Evaluation Summary

The evaluations involved seven undergraduate and graduate students. The evaluation procedure is shown in Fig. 5.

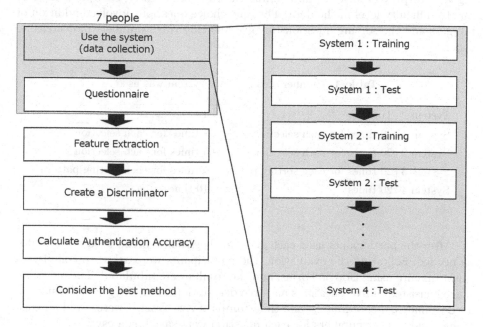

Fig. 5. Procedure of the evaluation experiment

The participants were taught how to use the system by the experimenter before using it themselves. First, they used the practice system to obtain training data and answered the questions with their gaze for a set number of times. Then they performed a simple test using the same system. This procedure was followed for all four systems and the participants completed a questionnaire about the experience. After collecting the data of all the participants, we extracted features from the data and created a discriminator to calculate authentication accuracy. Based on the authentication accuracy and the questionnaire, we compared the methods for collecting gaze information during e-testing.

3.2 Evaluation Experiment Set Up

The participants were seated with their faces positioned about 50 cm away from the display. The Tobii Eye Tracker 4C was calibrated to accurately track the participant's gaze. We used a 27-inch display and 60 FPS, and the screen resolution was set to 1920 × 1080 pixels. The order in which the systems were used was fixed: System 1 was used first, followed by System 2, System 3, and System 4. The number of questions (i.e., the number of times gaze information was obtained) in each system is shown in Table 1. To avoid confusing the participant while gaze information was collected, we designed the test so that the participant decided their answer before making a selection with their gaze. In addition, we used very simple questions in this test in order to prevent laborious answering and to prevent distress and confusion while answering. This prevents bias due to difficulty level in the data. The four-choice questions involved addition of integers and the sorting questions involved sorting three numbers in decreasing order.

Table 1. Number of times each system was used

System	Training	Test
System 1	20 times for each selection	5 times for each selection
System 2	20 times for each selection	5 times for each selection
System 3	20 times for each sorting pattern	5 times for each sorting pattern
System 4	20 times	10 times

After the participants used each system, they took a break for a few minutes as needed. Following the evaluation, the participants were asked to complete a questionnaire using Google Forms, and the results were tabulated. The questionnaire consisted of five questions and free descriptions. For the gaze information, x-coordinates, y-coordinates, and timestamps of Eye Tracker were saved for each frame, and answer numbers for each question were saved as a csv file.

3.3 Extraction of Gaze Features

We extracted the features of each participant's answers based on the collected gaze information. The classification accuracy was calculated multiple times while the combination of features in each system was changed. The features used in the combination were the same as those used in the study by Mukai et al. [3]: gaze coordinates, gaze trajectory size, drawing time, and gaze speed distribution. Each feature is described in the next section.

Gaze Coordinate. The trajectory of the participant's gaze during one answering action is considered one data set, and each data set is divided into the number of intervals for gaze information collection common to each system. The number of segments in System 1 is 22, whereas that in the other systems is 30. The number of segments is based on the related work of Mukai et al. [3]. The average of the x-coordinates and y-coordinates in each segment is used as the coordinates in that segment. Thus, there are as many dimensions as the number of divisions × coordinates; System 1 has 44 dimensions and Systems 2 to 4 have 60 dimensions. This feature shows the general shape of the gaze trajectory drawn by the participant.

Trajectory Size. The trajectory of the gaze drawn by the participant in a single act of answering is taken as one data set, and the trajectory size is the maximum x-coordinate minus the minimum x-coordinate and the maximum y-coordinate minus the minimum y-coordinate. This feature indicates the area where the examinee moved their gaze.

Drawing Time. We used the timestamp returned by Eye Tracker as the drawing time. The trajectory of the participant's gaze during a single answering action is defined as a single data set, and the drawing time for each data set is derived by subtracting the time of the end frame from the time of the start frame. This feature is one-dimensional data and represents the time required by the examinee to answer each question.

Distribution of Gazing Speed. The trajectory of the participant's gaze during a single answering action is considered a single data set, and the distance between frames in the time series data is used. We calculate the difference between the x-coordinate and the y-coordinate from a frame and the following frame, and calculate the Euclidean distance to obtain the distance traveled per frame. From the obtained data, the mean and standard deviation are calculated to obtain two-dimensional velocity distribution data. This feature shows the change in velocity when the participant draws the trajectory.

3.4   Calculation of Authentication Accuracy

We tested whether or not features that identify individuals were present in the gaze information acquired by each system using the accuracy of one-to-N class classification. We created a discriminator by extracting the aforementioned features in Sect. 3.3 from the participant's gaze data acquired by the training system and calculated the classification accuracy using the features extracted from the gaze data acquired by the test system. A Python library, scikit-learn [6], was used to create the discriminator and calculate the classification accuracy. The features were normalized so that the mean was 0 and the variance was 1 for each dimension of the training data set in each system, and the same parameters were used to normalize the data of each test. We performed N-class classification by a support vector machine (SVM) and N-class classification by logistic regression for the combination of the two features. The radial basis function (RBF) kernel was used as the kernel of the SVM, and the SVM parameters, (C, γ), were tuned by grid search. In the logistic regression classification, only parameters, C, were tuned by search.

3.5   Questionnaire

The purpose of this study is to authenticate examinees during e-testing, so it is necessary to consider not only the accuracy of authentication, but also the effect of gaze operation on examinees. Therefore, we conducted a user questionnaire for each system. The questionnaire contents are shown in Table 2. The contents of the questionnaire are the same for each system.

Table 2. Questionnaire for each system

For the five-point scale method, a positive rating was set to 5	
Question	Method
Q1. This system was easy to use.	Five-point scale
Q2. I was able to concentrate on the problem	Five-point scale
Q3. I didn't feel tired after using the system	Five-point scale
Q4. How many questions did you feel tired from?	Descriptive form
Q5. Other opinions and comments	Free description

4   Results and Discussion

Based on the classification accuracy of the data acquired by each system and the questionnaire, we investigated the best method for collecting gaze information during e-testing.

4.1   Results for Each System

Here, we show the features and discriminators used and their accuracy for each system. In each system, there are 7 classes to be classified; that is, the same as the number of participants. The confusion matrices of the two systems with the highest classification accuracy are also shown.

System 1. The features used were coordinate data (x, y) with 22 dimensions each for a total of 44 dimensions, trajectory size (x, y) with 2 dimensions, drawing time with 1 dimension, and gaze speed distribution, mean and standard deviation, with 2 dimensions. Thus, there was a total of 49 dimensions. As a result of classification using SVM, the classification accuracy was 38.6%.

System 2. The features used were coordinate data (x, y) with 30 dimensions each for a total of 60 dimensions, trajectory size (x, y) with 2 dimensions, drawing time with 1 dimension, and gaze speed distribution, mean and standard deviation, with 2 dimensions. Thus, there was a total of 65 dimensions. As a result of classification using SVM, the classification accuracy was 62.1%.

System 3. The features used consisted of 65 dimensions, as in System 2. As a result of classification using SVM, the classification accuracy was 64.3%. The confusion matrix of the classification results is shown in Table 3.

Table 3. Confusion matrix of classification results (System 3)

True[b]	Predicted[a]							ACC[c]
	1	2	3	4	5	6	7	
1	15	2	2	3	6	0	2	.50
2	1	18	11	0	0	0	0	.60
3	0	4	24	1	0	0	1	.80
4	0	4	1	23	0	2	0	.77
5	0	0	0	0	28	2	0	.93
6	0	1	0	2	6	16	5	.53
7	0	0	0	2	11	6	11	.37

[a] true value
[b] predicted value
[c] accuracy

System 4. The features used consisted of 65 dimensions, as in Systems 2 and 3. As a result of classification using SVM, the classification accuracy was 98.6%. The confusion matrix of the classification results is shown in Table 4.

Table 4. Confusion matrix of classification results (System 4)

True[b]	Predicted[a]							ACC[c]
	1	2	3	4	5	6	7	
1	9	0	0	1	0	0	0	.90
2	0	10	0	0	0	0	0	1
3	0	0	10	0	0	0	0	1
4	0	0	0	10	0	0	0	1
5	0	0	0	0	10	0	0	1
6	0	0	0	0	0	10	0	1
7	0	0	0	0	0	0	10	1

[a] true value
[b] predicted value
[c] accuracy

4.2 Discussion by Classification Accuracy

The classification accuracy of each system indicates that in the present experimental set-up, the classification based on the gaze movement of drawing symbols has the highest accuracy of 98.6%. In addition to the fact that the identification result of the system using only coordinates as the feature extracted from the gaze data was 86%, the accuracy was seen to improve dramatically depending on the trajectory size of the gaze, the drawing time, and the distribution of the gaze speed. Therefore, for complex human gaze movements, such as the symbol drawing in this study, not only the approximate shape of the trajectory, but also the size and speed of the drawing can be considered important features. After System 4, the next highest classification accuracy was shown by Systems 3 and 2, which were both greater than 60%. The high accuracy of these systems can be attributed to the fact that the gaze-based selection behavior was tolerant of differences among individuals. In System 2, the examinee could look anywhere within the area, and thus individual tendencies could have possibly appeared when gazing for a certain period of time. In addition, System 3 requires the examinee's gaze to move over a long distance, as in the case of drawing symbols with their gaze, so differences in speed and drawing time could have appeared. The classification accuracy of System 1 was 38.6%, which is not high. There are two factors that could be responsible for this result. One is that the drawing time was too short to begin with. Another is that the design was such that individual differences in starting and ending points were difficult to show, so the individual differences may not have appeared in the features used in this study. Considering the need for classification accuracy to enable the authentication of examinees during the e-testing process, an authentication accuracy of about 60% is considered impractical. Therefore, from the above results, we think that classification based on gaze movements of drawing symbols is the most suitable method for authentication of examinees during e-testing.

4.3   Discussion Including the Results of the Questionnaire

A summary of the results of the questionnaire is shown in Table 5. One-way analysis of variance was performed for each question, and a significant difference was found for question Q3, "Did you feel fatigue when using the system?" No significant differences were found for the other questions. The results of Q3 indicate that System 4 was less likely to cause fatigue than the other systems. This could be due to the difference in number of problems solved. However, a clear advantage of System 4 is that it requires only a single trajectory, and thus fewer questions require gaze information compared with four-choice questions or sorting questions. Therefore, the advantages of System 4 in the reduced number of questions and number of drawings outweigh the disadvantages of drawing symbols with one's gaze, which was a concern raised in Subsect. 2.4. In the other questions, System 4 was not shown to have a negative impact on examinees compared with the other systems. In addition, in the free description, one examinee commented that "System 4 was the easiest to work on because the answer method was the same as the normal e-testing". Considering that the act of drawing with one's gaze does not interfere with the act of answering the question itself, the "drawing of symbols with one's gaze" in System 4 is considered to be the most suitable method for collecting gaze information during e-testing.

Table 5. Questionnaire in each system

System	Average (standard deviation)		
	Q1	Q2	Q3*
1	3.57 (0.98)	3.57 (1.62)	3.00 (1,41)
2	3.71 (1.38)	3.57 (1.27)	3.14 (1.57)
3	3.14 (1.35)	2.71 (1.60)	1.71 (1.11)
4	3.71 (0.95)	4.43 (0.79)	4.14 (0.90)

* Significant difference at $P < 0.05$

5   Summary and Future Work

The purpose of this study was to develop a method for collecting gaze information from examinees during e-testing. From the results of evaluation experiments using four systems implementing different methods, and based on authentication accuracy and user questionnaires, we found that the most suitable system used gaze trajectory information derived from the drawing of symbols.

A future issue for investigation is the influence of the presence or absence of gaze trajectory on classification accuracy. In the questionnaire, there were some comments such as, "I became a little distracted by trying to draw a beautiful circle," and, "I could not concentrate on the circle because the trajectory was in the way". Therefore, we think that it is important to consider the necessity of gaze trajectory. Another comment was, "If I had limited time for the exam, I am not sure I would be able to draw the symbols carefully". Therefore, it is necessary to examine the influence of the time limit on the examinees. In addition, we plan to examine the possibility of improving the accuracy of authentication by improving the methods of Systems 1 to 3. As soon as we have established the gaze collection method, we intend to study it in combination with face images.

References

1. Prime Minister's Residence. https://www.kantei.go.jp/jp/98_abe/actions/202003/28corona.html. Accessed 2 Feb 2021 (in Japanese)
2. Japan Education News. https://www.kyoiku-press.com/post-210186/. Accessed 2 Feb 2021. (in Japanese)
3. Mukai, H., Ogawa, T.: Feature extraction of eye-gaze path for personal authentication. J. Inf. Proces. **4**(2), 27–35 (2016). (in Japanese)
4. Unity. https://unity.com/ja. Accessed 2 Feb 2021. (in Japanese)
5. Tobii Eye Tracker 4C. https://help.tobii.com/hc/en-us/articles/213414285-Specifications-for-the-Tobii-Eye-Tracker-4C. Accessed 2 Feb 2021
6. Pedregosa, F., et al.: Scikit-learn: machine learning in Python. J. Mach. Learn. Res. **12**, 2825–2830 (2011)

An Improved Optimized Route Selection Method for a Maritime Navigation Vessel

Yutaro Tsurumi$^{(\boxtimes)}$, Ryosuke Saga, Sharath Srinivasamurthy,
and Yasunori Nihei

Osaka Prefecture University, 1-1 Gakuen-cho, Naka-ku, Sakai, Osaka, Japan
sab03075@edu.osakafu-u.ac.jp, saga@cs.osakafu-u.ac.jp,
{sharath,nihei}@marine.osakafu-u.ac.jp

Abstract. In recent years, ocean measurements have been carried out by automated small vessels. Many of the places where measurement are taken are offshore farms such as oyster cultivation farm where water quality measurement is indispensable. However, there are many obstacles such as buoys and rafts in these sea areas, and vessels need to navigate the patrol route avoiding these obstacles. Furthermore, it is necessary to take disturbances such as waves and wind depending on the sea condition into consideration because the performance of the vessel changes due to the disturbances. In this research, the obstacle avoidance performance was improved by incorporating a program that automatically adds waypoints to the previously developed patrol route proposal system. In addition, waypoints with the shortest distance was selected from several possible obstacle avoiding routes between measurement points using Dijkstra fs algorithm. Furthermore, for the actual maritime test of this system, the values of the real sailing performance were introduced into the system. We simulated the improved system and confirmed whether an appropriate patrol route that avoids obstacles could be suggested.

Keywords: Ocean environmental survey · Optimal route · Obstacle avoidance

1 Introduction

Latest technology such as IoT and ICT have been introduced rapidly in Japan to various industries and advancements are targeted to help resource management, improve productivity and solve labor shortages. In the fisheries industry, an initiative called as g*smart suisangyo* h has commenced. For example, automatic feeder and smart buoy have been developed and are currently in use.

As an example of this g*smart suisangyo* h, Nihei et al. [1] aim to provide fisherman with results of water quality prediction by constructing big data in offshore farm and carry out simulation of seawater flow based on big data. In order to achieve this, high-density and high-frequency ocean measurements within the offshore farm are necessary. However, the conventional manual method of tying ropes

S. Yamamoto and H. Mori (Eds.): HCII 2021, LNCS 12766, pp. 468–481, 2021.
https://doi.org/10.1007/978-3-030-78361-7_36

to the measurement devices and pulling them at various locations in the seawater environment becomes tedious and costly. Therefore, an automatic navigation vessel gQuad-maran h was developed and studied that automatically patrols measurement points and measures water quality [2,3]. Figure 1 shows gQuad-maran h in sailing and Table 1 shows the principal particular of single hull. This vessel consists of four hulls, an upper deck that stores batteries and control boards, and four rotating devices that connects each hull to the upper deak. Furthermore, an elevated device can be attached to the upper deck, and a measurement device equipped with a wire-pulley arrangement can be connected to this elevated device. The wire-pulley arrangement helps in measuring water quality at various depths by dropping into the water and pulling up automatically. The greatest characteristic of this vessel is that the each hull can rotate independently. Because of this, as a shown in Fig. 2 it is possible to hold dynamic positioning during the measurement and helps to collect more accurate data. In addition, it can be used in narrow waterways in offshore farms because it can make small turns.

Fig. 1. *Quad-maran* sailing in Nanao Bay, Ishikawa, Japan

Table 1. Principal particular of single hull of *Quad-maran*

Length	1187	mm
Breath	300	mm
Height	280	mm
Mass	6.9	kg
Diameter of propeller	65	mm
Number of blades of propeller	5	–

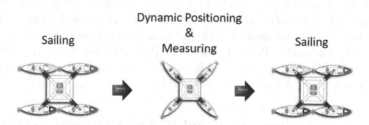

Fig. 2. Dynamic positioning during measuring

In August 2018 and September 2019, feasibility test were carried out and measurement work was demonstrated at Nanao Bay, Ishikawa, Japan using this vessel [4]. In particular, in the measurement in 2019, about 80 measurement points were set and measured on the sea route covering about 7 km. The total navigation and measurement took about 7 h. From this, the long-time and wide range operation of the vessel was demonstrated. However, of the obtained measurement data, the time taken between the first measurement and last measurement point is large, so it is not possible to compare hourly data. For ocean measurements, hourly data for the day is also important along with daily water quality data.

To address to this problem, in terms of the hardware, it is possible to improve navigation performance by changing the hull form to one with less resistance and operate multiple vessels at the same time. However, it is an expensive process and optimizing the measurement route in the software could also be a potential solution. Software optimization comes with its new challenges and Saga et al. [5] had previously proposed an optimal route search based on multi-objective genetic algorithm. This paper describes the following two points that have been improved for the implementation of the system developed by Saga et al.

1. Obstacle avoidance: By adding waypoints
2. Realistic sailing performance: By using velocity prediction program based on experimental database

For the first objective, in the conventional optimal route proposal system (see Sect. 2), the patrol route was suggested only by straight line motion between the measurement points. However, assuming the operation of this vessel in the offshore farm, there are many obstacles such as floating buoys and rafts. In the case when a measurement point is set at a point where these obstacles exist, it may not be possible to suggest a patrol route by this method and may lead to sea accidents. This can be solved by incorporating additional waypoint candidates, which are automatically created and selected, such that the route avoids obstacles and also minimizes the distance between the measurement points.

For the second objective, there are disturbances such as wind and waves in the real sea. In particular, because this vessel has an upper deck that exists above the water surface, the vessel speed changes as due to the wind hits the deck. Therefore, the vessel speed needs to be is extracted based on the predicted wind speed and wind direction obtained from experimental database for realistic route optimization. This experimental database is a compilation of values calculated using Velocity Prediction Program using the fluid coefficients obtained from the water tank test. The simulation is performed with the above improved optimized route selection method and the results are discussed.

2   The Conventional Optimal Route Proposal System

Before discussing the improved proposal system, we explain the conventional proposal system developed by Saga et al. This system aims to operate a vessel or multiple vessels at the same time and proposes a patrol route to each vessel. Furthermore, as a characteristic of traveling at sea, the speed and energy of the vessel are affected by disturbances such as wind and waves that change with time. Therefore, it can be said that the problem to be solved by this system is the time-dependent multiple traveling salesman problem (TDMTSP).

Normally, the multiple traveling salesman problem (MTSP) is a more complicated NP-hard problem than the traveling salesman problem (TSP), and it is generally solved by using the Genetic Algorithm (GA) or the Ant Colony Optimization Algorithm. This system simplifies TDMTSP into multiple simple TDTSP by classifying measurement points in advance using the K-means method. In addition, this makes it possible to avoid collisions between vessels due to the intersection of routes.

It is also necessary to consider various other conditions when suggesting a patrol route on the sea. For example, a route plan that minimizes energy consumption under a fixed time limit and a route plan that has the shortest navigation time under a fixed energy consumption limit. Therefore, the suggested optimized route is not unique and it is different under each situation. That is, the Pareto optimal solution set is suggested for users. Above all, this system adapted Genetic Algorithm NSGA-II [6] as a means to solve the TDMTSP, and propose the optimal route. Figure 3 shows examples of the suggested route using the conventional system for operating one vessel and two vessels. From Fig. 3 (b), it can be observed that there is no collision between the two vessels operating at the same time.

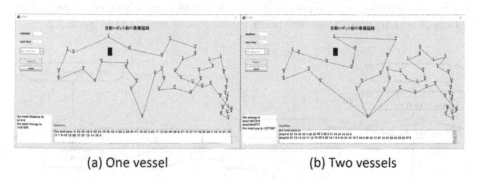

(a) One vessel   (b) Two vessels

Fig. 3. Examples of the suggested route by using the conventional system

3   Avoiding Obstacles

There are a lot of obstacles such as buoys and rafts in the sea area such as oyster farms. When the measurement points are set in an area as shown in Fig. 4 (a), it is not possible to move between measurement points in a straight line motion because every path has obstacles. Therefore, we improved the system so that path optimization can be implemented based on the route that avoids obstacles by adding waypoints like shown in Fig. 4 (b). In this section, methodology behind placing waypoints is explained and further, an example of a route between measurement points that avoids obstacles by adding waypoints is shown.

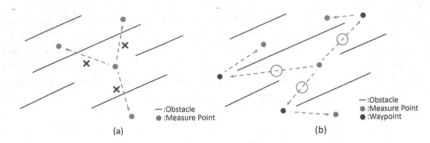

Fig. 4. Necessity of waypoints to avoid obstacles in aquaculture farms

3.1 Work Flow

Figure 5 shows the workflow for avoiding obstacles when moving between measurement points. First of all, it is judged whether or not straight line motion between measurement points is possible without contacting with obstacles. If it is possible, no waypoints are added and use this straight line as the route, and if it is not possible, set waypoint candidates between measurement points. The details of how to place these waypoint candidates is explained in Sect. 3.2.

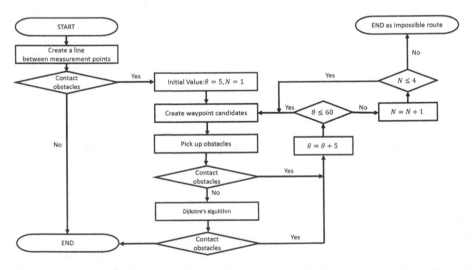

Fig. 5. Workflow of improved optimized route selection method

Secondly, identifying and picking up obstacles that exist between the measurement points is an important step. In this optimized method, the obstacles are picked up after adding waypoints as illustrated in Fig. 6. It can be observed that the path between measurement points A and B is divided into number of sections and obstacles in each section is identified. Furthermore, it is judged whether or not each route in the section contact with the picked up obstacles.

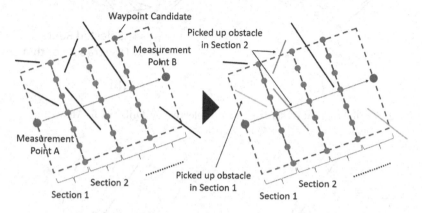

Fig. 6. Procedure to identify and pick up obstacles

If it is possible to move within all sections and find a path without obstacles (Fig. 7 (a)), then select waypoints that gives the shortest route by Dijkstra's algorithm (see Fig. 7 (b)). On the other hand, if it is not possible to find a path in any of the sections (for example, Sect. 2 in Fig. 8 (a)), increase the distance between waypoint candidates or the number of waypoint candidates and repeat the above method (Fig. 8 (b)). If it is not possible to avoid obstacles even after increasing the distance and the number of waypoint candidates to a certain level, the route between measurement points is considered as an impassable route. This method was executed between all measurement points, and based on this, a patrol route was created and genetic algorithm was executed.

3.2 Procedure to Place Waypoint Candidates

Figure 9 shows the procedure to place waypoint candidates. If straight line movement between measurement points is not possible, first place the midpoint on the line segment L1 with measurement point A and B as endpoints (a-1). Second, draw straight lines L2 and L3 which are at an angle θ with L1 and through the measurement point A (a-2). Then draw a straight line L4 that passes through midpoint and is perpendicular to L1. The intersections of L4 and L2, L4 and L1 (midpoint), and L4 and L3 are the waypoint candidates W1, W2 and W3 (a-3). The state in which these three waypoint candidates are placed is called $N = 1$ here.

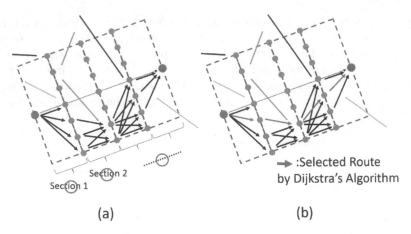

Fig. 7. Illustration of shortest route selected by Dijkstra fs Algorithm

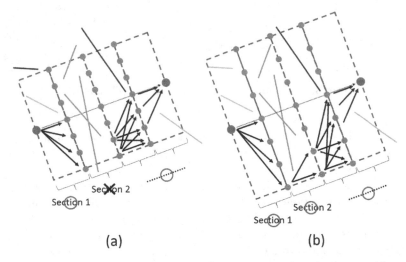

Fig. 8. Illustration of increasing distance between waypoints for impassable route

When it is not possible to avoid obstacles even if θ is increased to a certain value and the distance between waypoint candidates is increased, we focus on increasing the number of waypoint candidates. The number of waypoint candidates can be increased by placing the midpoints between the measurement point A and W2, and between W2 and measurement points B, and draw the line L5 and L6 that pass through these midpoints and are perpendicular to L1. The new waypoint candidates placed are as shown in Fig. 9 (b). This state is called $N = 2$. If the path cannot avoid obstacles even with $N = 2$, the above process is repeated to increase the number of waypoints candidates ($N = 3$, $N = 4$). Table 2 shows the summary of waypoint candidates indicating potential number of routes for each value of N. As mentioned above, this time we set the waypoint candidates based on midpoints. This is to simplify the model of avoiding obstacles and to be able to handle when obstacles exist at any position between measurement points.

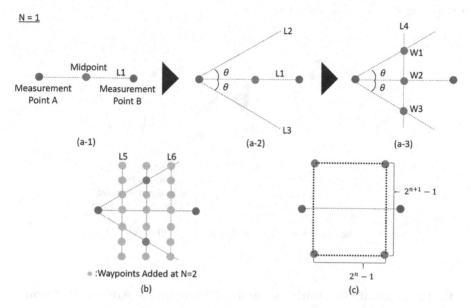

Fig. 9. Procedure to place waypoint candidates

3.3 Selecting Waypoints

Once the waypoint candidates are placed, the next step is to select the most optimized route (minimum distance between the measurement points after avoiding obstacles) by selecting the right waypoints. This is possible by using A$*$ algorithm or Dijkstra fs algorithm. However, since the distance between measurement points is long and the time-dependent vessel speed may have to be taken into consideration due to disturbances such as wind, in this study, we used Dijkstra fs algorithm to select the waypoints.

Table 2. Summary of waypoint candidates

N	Column	Row	Total candidates	Total routes
1	1	3	3	3
2	3	7	21	7^2
3	7	15	105	15^6
4	15	31	465	31^4
n	$2^n - 1$	$2^{n+1} - 1$	$(2^n - 1) \times (2^{n+1} - 1)$	$(2^{n+1} - 1)^{(2^n - 1) - 1}$

In addition, in the method described above, there is a possibility of selecting unnecessary waypoints on the straight line as shown in Fig. 10. Even though they have no direct effect on the distance and time, but after executing genetic algorithm and obtaining the optimum route, these waypoints are deleted by considering the slopes of the pathway.

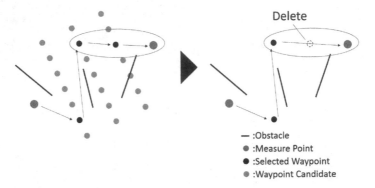

— :Obstacle
● :Measure Point
● :Selected Waypoint
● :Waypoint Candidate

Fig. 10. Deleted waypoint in a straight path

3.4 Example of the Route Avoiding Obstacles by Adding Waypoints

Figure 11 shows the example of the route between measurement points as explained above. In this case, $N = 2$ and $\theta = 35$. It can be seen that a route that avoids obstacles is generated.

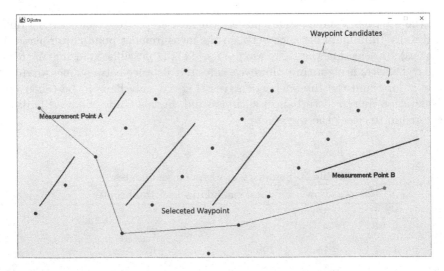

Fig. 11. Example of a route generated avoiding obstacles between measurement points

4 Realistic Sailing Performance

In the conventional suggested system, the vessel speed is treated as a constant, without considering the effect of disturbances such as wind and waves. However, in the case of sailing in the real sea, it changes due to these disturbances. In particular, because this gQuad-maran h has an upper deck that exists above the water surface, the vessel speed changes as wind hits the deck.

This vessel fs speed with respect to absolute wind direction and speed has been clarified by Nihei et al. [4], and the values are calculated using Velocity Prediction Program (VPP) using fluid coefficients obtained from the water tank test. The absolute wind direction is from 0° to 180° at an increment of 15°, and the absolute wind speed is from 0 to 10 m/s at steps of 0.5 m/s.

Figure 12 shows the coordinate system for VPP studies. $O - X_0Y_0$ is space-fixed coordinate system, and $o - x_0y_0$ is hull-fixed coordinate system. The result of VPP is shown in Fig. 13 as a polar curve. In this study, by inputting U_W (absolute wind speed) and θ_A (difference between the absolute wind direction and the azimuth of the vessel), the closest vessel speed was extracted from the database of VPP results and used to calculate the navigation time. Also, the absolute wind direction and speed refers to the hourly forecast values.

5 Simulation

5.1 Goal and Simulation Environment

The purpose of this simulation is to achieve the following:

1. The optimum patrol route in the area where many obstacles exist.
2. The navigation routes incorporating real marine environmental condition.

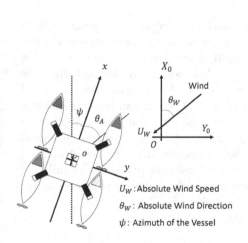

Fig. 12. Coordinate system

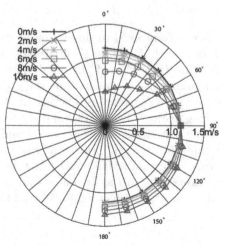

Fig. 13. Polar curve

In the simulation, a starting point, 20 measurement points and 10 obstacles were set, and surrounded by boundary line as an experiment area. The assumed obstacles are rows of oyster buoys arranged randomly in a total length of about 80 m. The measurement points and obstacles are input based on their latitude and longitude in the target sea area of Nanao Bay, Ishikawa, Japan. It is well noted here that the locations used in this simulation are for testing and those obstacles do not actually exist at these coordinates. Moreover, the simulation environment used a computer with a CPU Intel Core i7 3.4 GHz, 16 GB RAM, and Windows 10 OS. GA was executed with 100 generations and 1000 populations.

5.2   Results and Discussion

Figure 14 shows the simulation result in the case that the minimum distance was used as the objective function of GA. In this case the wind is calm (0 m/s). The result shows the best patrol route suggested by the improved optimized method avoiding all the 10 obstacles within the defined boundary line. The point circled in red is one of the added waypoints. Furthermore, the area surrounded by orange is the part that deleted unnecessary waypoints because they were on a straight-line path. Table 3 shows summary of the simulation and the total computational time is about 15 min. In addition, Fig. 15 shows the variation of minimum distance for each generation. It can be seen that when the number of generations is about 50, the value is converged.

Table 3. Summary of simulation for minimum distance

Cruising distance [m]	1693
Cruising time [s]	691
Computational time [s]	924

Now, we proceed to simulation of real marine environmental condition with a wind speed of 10 m/s. Figure 16 shows the results for (a) wind speed 10 m/s, wind direction 0°, and (b) wind speed 10 m/s, wind direction 90°, with the minimum cruising time used as the objective function. It can be seen that the patrol routes suggested is different from each other. When we compare the total cruising distance between wind directions of 0° and 90°, it can be seen that the cruising distance is longer for vessel under the wind direction of 90° (1922 m for 90° and 1748 m for 0°). However, when we compare the cruising times, the vessel in wind direction of 90° takes less time (807 s) compared to the vessel in wind direction of 0° (1016 s). It can be said that vessel speed increases due to tailwind in the case of wind blowing in 90° and therefore leads to shorter time even while

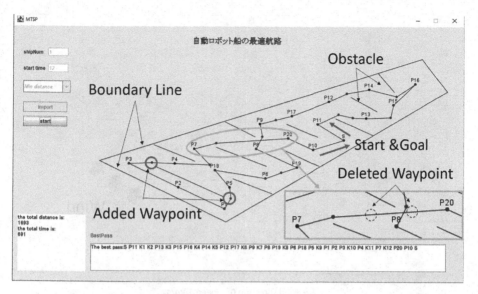

Fig. 14. Simulation result for the minimum distance (Color figure online)

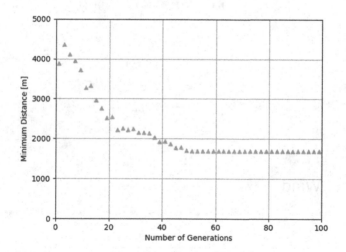

Fig. 15. Relationship between minimum distance and number of generations

cruising more distance. From this, it can be seen that the optimum patrol route can be selected using the proposed algorithm depending on the condition of the disturbance and setting the required objective.

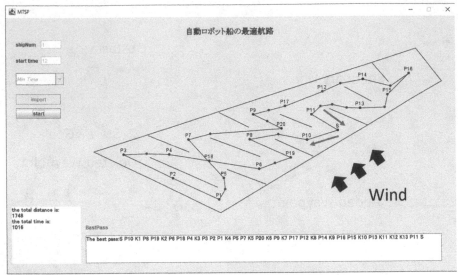

(a) Wind Direction 0°, Speed 10m/s

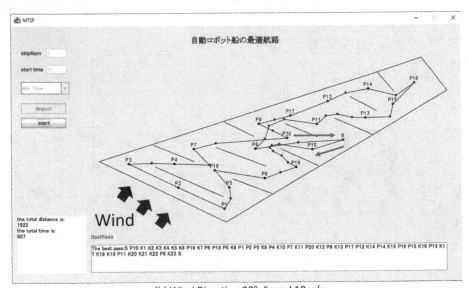

(b) Wind Direction 90°, Speed 10m/s

Fig. 16. Simulation for the minimum cruising time

6   Conclusion

In this research, we improved the performance of obstacles avoidance and introduced realistic sailing performance towards the implementation of the patrol route proposal system for a small vessel that collects water quality data at sea.

In the simulation, even if measurements points were set in the area where obstacles exist, the optimum patrol route that avoids obstacles was proposed by automatically adding waypoints. In addition, the proposed route changed due to the condition of disturbance. However, GA and Dijkstra fs algorithm have much calculating cost, and it is next task to reduce cost. In addition, it is necessary to verify the usefulness of the improved system by conducting the real sea tests.

References

1. Nihei, Y., Nakada, S., Hara, N., Harada K., Saga R.: Quad-maran automated vessel and its apprication to oyster farms. In: The 61th Japan Joint Automatic Control Conference, Aichi, pp. 83–89 (2018)
2. Zhang, C., Srinivasamurthy, S., Kitamura, S., Masuda, N., Park, C. S., Nihei, Y.: Energy Consumption of a Sailing Quad-maran Automated Vessel. In: Proceedings of ASME 2018 37th International Conference OMAE on Ocean, Offshore and Arctic Engineering, OMAE 2018-77946, Madrid, Spain (2018)
3. Srinivasamurthy, S., Sakamoto, H., Nishikawa, T., Nihei, Y.: Numerical hull resistance and hydrodynamic characteristics of an independently rotating multi-hull vessel. In: Proceedings of ASME 2018 37th International Conference OMAE on Ocean, Offshore and Arctic Engineering, OMAE 2019-95403, Glasgow, Scotland (2019)
4. Nihei, Y., et al.: Automatic and frequent measurement of water quality at multipoints using Quad maran. J. Japan Soc. Civ. Eng. Ser. B1 (Hydraul. Eng.) $76(2)$, I_1039–I_1044 (2020)
5. Saga, R., Liang, Z., Hara, N., Nihei, Y.: Optimal route search based on multiobjective genetic algorithm for maritime navigation vessels. In: Yamamoto, S., Mori, II. (eds.) HCII 2020, Part 2. LNCS, vol. 12185, pp. 506–518. Springer, Cham (2020). https://doi.org/10.1007/978-3-030-50017-7_38
6. Deb, K., Pratap, A., Agarwal, S., Meyarivan, T.: A fast and elitist multiobjective genetic algorithm: NSGA-II. IEEE Trans. Evol. Comput. $2(6)$, 182–197 (2002)

Novel Motion Display for Virtual Walking

Minori Unno[1], Ken Yamaoka[1], Vibol Yem[1], Tomohiro Amemiya[2],
Michiteru Kitazaki[3], and Yasushi Ikei[1,2(✉)]

[1] Tokyo Metropolitan University, Hino, Tokyo 1910065, Japan
{unno,yamaoka,yem}@vr.sd.tmu.ac.jp
[2] The University of Tokyo, Bunkyo, Tokyo 1138656, Japan
{amemiya,ikei}@vr.u-tokyo.ac.jp
[3] Toyohashi University of Technology, Toyohashi, Aichi 4418580, Japan
mich@tut.jp

Abstract. In this study, a novel motion display device, having 10 DOF (degrees of freedom) for virtual walking is developed. The device consists of a motion seat and a foot module. The device creates synchronous motions of the whole body and lower legs, imparting the straight and turn walking sensations. The motion seat has four-DOF motions of lifting, rolling, pitching, and yawing coordinated by three linear actuators and a DC motor. The three-DOF foot module consists of a pedal-like footrest, which rotates (pitch motion), slides (back and forth translation), and laterally shifts (yaw rotation). Besides, the motions are controlled by microcomputers and 3D space software (Unity).

Keywords: Body motion · Mechanical device · Sensation of motion · Walking motion · Virtual reality

1 Introduction

Virtual space transfer is a basic function for the user to exploit the space as a field of physical and social activities. The transfer in a real world is performed either by the physical motion of a body or a transport machine. The body motion of walking or machine operation provides a foundation for the perception of spatial transfer experience. The information introduced by spatial transfer due to body motion, which involves visual and vestibular sensations arising from self-motion and its relation to the world, is interpreted comprehensively. Usually, multisensory integrative perception must grasp the spatial transfer consistently.

Virtual space transfer requires the same multisensory information as in a real space. The lack of perceptual information leads to a severe problem in perceptual integration, motion sickness, which prohibits the practical use of the space. This problem frequently occurs when only visual information is provided for a virtual space experience.

In this study, we present a mechanical device for body motion presentation, which creates a self-motion sensation involved in virtual space transfer. This function is indispensable for virtual space transfer where the user does not physically move. The mechanisms of the motion device as a part of a multisensory display are also introduced.

© Springer Nature Switzerland AG 2021
S. Yamamoto and H. Mori (Eds.): HCII 2021, LNCS 12766, pp. 482–492, 2021.
https://doi.org/10.1007/978-3-030-78361-7_37

2 Multisensory Motion Display

A multisensory display (FiveStar) was developed for reliving past spatial experiences. The display imparts a walking sensation to the sitting user during virtual traveling in a reproduced realistic world [1]. Thus, the user can receive walking sensations without actually walking.

Figure 1 shows the display system presented in [2]. The display system includes a motion seat that principally produces the sensation of bipedal locomotion, and an audiovisual presentation of 360° visual scenes by an ordinary head mounted display and headphones. The somatosensory display consists of a seat for vestibular stimulus with an arm-swing device and a pedal-type lower limb stimulation device. These two somatosensory displays typically reproduce walking motion sensations of for the user seated on the device.

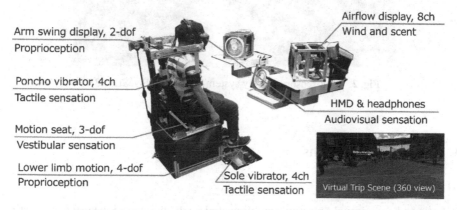

Arm swing display, 2-dof
Proprioception

Poncho vibrator, 4ch
Tactile sensation

Motion seat, 3-dof
Vestibular sensation

Lower limb motion, 4-dof
Proprioception

Airflow display, 8ch
Wind and scent

HMD & headphones
Audiovisual sensation

Sole vibrator, 4ch
Tactile sensation

Virtual Trip Scene (360 view)

Fig. 1. Multisensory display system, version 2 (FiveStar v2) [1].

The user can experience virtual walking without an active (voluntary) physical movement. The system creates a body motion of the user without its muscular activity. With the passive motion condition, only a considerable amount of the required body motion (~10% of the original walking motion) is added. The reduced motion ratio applies to the leg and resultant vertical body motions. However, for the arm-swing motion, the real amount (~100%) of the swing angle was appropriate. Swinging of the arms is not necessarily a voluntary motion but an almost passive motion, which is automatically generated to compensate for the angular inertia moment of the body. These ratios were adopted from our previous studies.

The tactile sensation at the foot sole for virtual contact with the ground at the beginning of the stance phase is impacted by the sole vibrators (at the heel, and the toe 10 ms after the heel). The tactile sensation at the face, arm skin, or other body surfaces is stimulated by the airflow, which occurs synchronously with arms swinging and virtual scene events. The wind also carries perfume, coffee, and fruit scents according to the travel scene. Also, large wind fluctuation of clothes is simulated by vibrators on the poncho.

Figure 2 shows the third version of the multisensory display, which novelly introduced a turning sensation allowing direction-free virtual walking. This version consists of a motion seat, which produces a four-degree of freedom (DOF) seat displacement, and a foot module, which creates a three-DOF motion for each foot. The design detail of this novel multisensory display is shown in the next section.

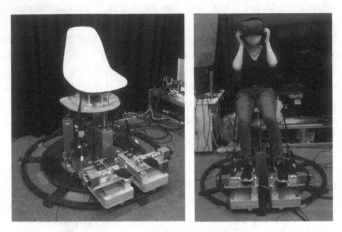

Fig. 2. Multisensory display system, version 3 (FiveStar v3).

3 Display Mechanisms

3.1 Body Motion System

Somatic and audiovisual sensations are impacted by the body motion system consisting of a motion seat and a foot motion module (Fig. 3). The motion seat has four motors, which produce lifting, rolling, pitching, and yawing motions, respectively, to impart the walking sensation. Three vertical linear actuators for three-DOF motion are placed under the seat that is rotated in the yaw direction by a single DC motor. Table 1 shows the motion and force range. The mechanical specification was determined by considering the sensation of running and walking. The foot module creates a three-dimensional (3D) trajectory of a foot like the real foot motion.

3.2 Motion Seat (Vestibular Display)

Three electric linear actuators (Fig. 4) were stationed from the front viewpoint at 320 mm width and depth, respectively. The front linear actuator rotates the body only in the pitch direction when the front and rear actuators are translated by a different length. The center guide axis unit moves only within the vertical direction, maintaining the center of the seat on the center axis line. The casing of the two rear actuators was allowed to rotate in the roll and pitch directions. The actuator axes were attached to the upper yaw actuator unit using universal joints.

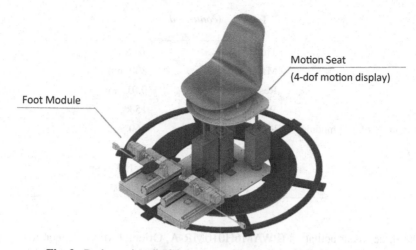

Fig. 3. Body motion display to move the whole body and lower legs.

Table 1. Specification of mechanisms

Linear actuator of motion seat	Range of linear motion	100 mm
	Resolution	0.01 mm
	Max. speed	200 mm/s
	Max. thrust (single unit)	1000 N
Yaw rotation actuator of motion seat	Range of rotation	∞
	Max. torque	3.8 N-m
	Free rotation speed	350 rpm
Seat motion	Range of roll angle	±17.4°
	Range of pitch angle	±17.4°
	Range of lift length	100 mm
	Max. lift speed	200 mm/s
	Max. roll speed	±0.625°/s
	Max. pitch speed	±0.625°/s
Pedal motion of foot module	Range of motion	−70.4 mm (−27°) to 141.3 mm (66°)
	Max. holding torque	8 N-m
	Max. lift force	133 N
	Allowable speed range	0 –60 r/min
	Resolution	0.0144°/pulse
Slider motion of foot module	Range of motion	0–200 mm

(continued)

Table 1. (*continued*)

	Thrust	70 N
	Max. speed	800 mm/s
	Resolution	0.012 mm/pulse
	Weight capacity	15 kg
Swing motion of foot module	Range of motion	360°
	Max. static torque	2 N-m
	Motor speed range	0–150 r/min
	Max. rotation speed	27.3°/s

The three linear actuators (PWAM6H010MR-A, Oriental Motor) generate vertical lift motion of the seat, ~100 mm, at a speed of 200 mm/s when they have the same translation. Whereas the pitch and roll rotations are controlled by different lengths of the rear actuators, ~± 17°. The yaw rotation is created by a single DC motor (RE40, Maxonmotor) connected to an orthogonal gearbox that drives a top disk under the seat.

The translation amplitude of lifting and the roll and pitch angles were 1.26 mm, 0.15°, and 0.13°, respectively, for the presentation of walking sensation to the sitting user. These values were optimally-obtained via experiments conducted for straight walking at 1.4 s walking cycle.

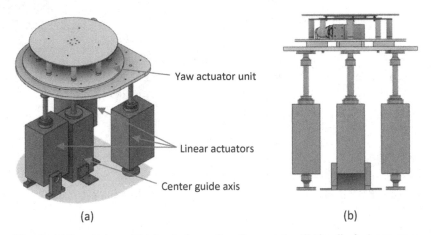

(a)   (b)

Fig. 4. (a) Isometric and (b) front views of motion seat (vestibular display) actuators.

3.3 Foot Module (Lower Limb Display)

The foot module (lower limbs display) consists of a pedal unit, a slider and a circular truck that carries the foot module (Fig. 5). The pedal mechanism on which the user places the foot rotates and raises the heel and lower leg periodically using a stepper motor (RKS564AA-PS50, Oriental Motor). The heel lift is ~24 mm for virtual walking. The slider mechanism moves the foot back and forth at about 60 mm synchronously with the pedal rotation, using a stepper motor (EAS4L(R)X-D020, Oriental Motor). The circular truck (Fig. 6) conveys the foot module on a circular rail of 495 mm radius around the motion seat to follow the body direction based on the virtual body walks. The chassis has a motor (ARM46AC-FC20L(R)A, Oriental Motor) and pinion gear under its bottom plate to mesh with a curved rack gear at the circular rail made of medium-density fiberboard.

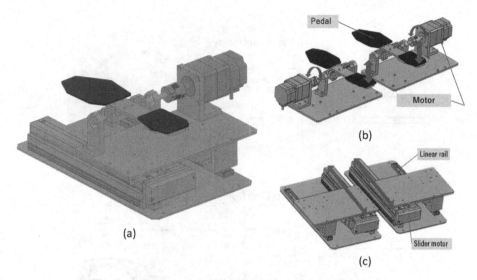

Fig. 5. (a) Foot module. Main parts: (b) pedal, (c) slider units.

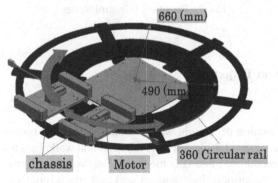

Fig. 6. Circular rail and chassis of the foot module.

3.4 Control System of the Multisensory Display (FiveStar V3)

The motion of 10 motors (four for the motion seat, and six for the foot module) is synchronously controlled by a trajectory generator in a 3D space engine (Unity) (Fig. 7). Every motor except for the yaw DC motor is pulsed by a microcomputer (ESP32, Espressif Systems) that receives a target angle and the time to get to the angle for one walking cycle via a user datagram protocol. The velocity of motion is set in a trapezoidal form. For the yaw rotation, a DC motor is controlled by a driver amp (Epos 70/10, Maxonmotor) in the profile position mode, receiving the target angle and the time to attain such an angle via a serial communication interface.

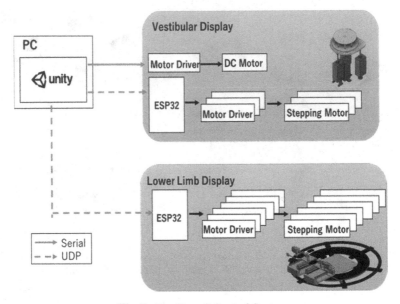

Fig. 7. FiveStar v3 Control System

3.5 Typical Motion Trajectory

Straight Walking

To produce the sensation of straight walking, the motion seat foot module move synchronously to trace sinusoidal-like curves. Although real walking is not a simple motion, the major sensations during walking come from head (vestibular sensation), leg (proprioception), and arm (proprioception) motions, and foot ground contact (tactile sensation), aside audiovisual sensation.

In actual walking, the head moves ~30 mm vertically while the footstep is around 600 mm. In a relaxed walk, when walking cycle time is 1400 ms, the heel elevation is ~230 mm. The optimal seat motion impacted by the multisensory display for the walking sensation is shown in Fig. 8, with a small motion compared to real walking.

The lifting is only 1.26 mm while the roll and pitch angles are 0.15 and 0.13° (forward-bent), respectively. This motion imparts the sensation of leg lifting and going forward eventually.

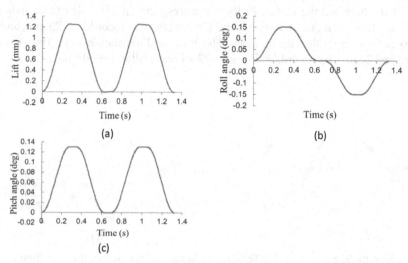

Fig. 8. Seat motion for straight walking at a 1400-ms cycle time. (a) Lift, (b) roll rotation, and (c) pitch rotation motions.

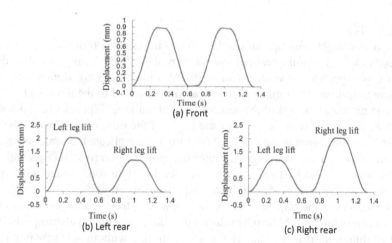

Fig. 9. Motion seat actuators' trajectory. Displacement (lift) of (a) front, (b) left rear, (c) right rear actuators.

Figure 9 shows the trajectory of each actuator for straight walking. The lift displacement of the front actuator is smaller than that of rear so that the seat bends forward in addition to the lifting motion. The rear actuator translates differently in magnitude to actualize left/right leg liftings. This difference causes a roll rotation of the seat. The trajectory is made of point-to-point motion segments, each comprising two quadratic curves and a mid-linear segment. The peak displacement lasts for a short time (0.1 s) of direction change.

Figure 10(a) shows the trajectory of the foot module when only the pedal and slider were provided for walking. The vertical (blue) and horizontal (orange) plots show the lifting of the heel and the motion of the slider, respectively. The plus value indicates upward and forward motions, respectively. The heel lift was recorded as 23 mm, and the down speed was faster than the up speed. The horizontal translation was 60 mm (38 mm forward and 22 mm backward, which are 10% of real walking conditions).

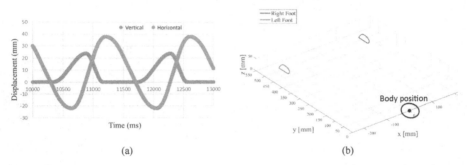

(a)   (b)

Fig. 10. Foot module trajectory. (a) Vertical and horizontal position of the heel from the rest position (origin). (b) Heel motion in the body coordinate (seat center). (Color figure online)

Turning Walking

In addition to straight walking, our display system impacts the turn walking sensation. The effective stimulus of the seat motion is a turn of the body (change the direction of the body), as expected. However, asymmetric roll rotation did not significantly affect the turning sensation. The turning motion was simply added to the three-DOF (lifting, rolling, and pitching) motion of the seat for straight walking. Figures 11a and b shows the optimal yaw rotation angle (~3°) of the seat and the difference between the inner and outer feet with regard to the center of the turning to replicate the same sensation as that of 2-m radius turning walking. The outer foot presentation rotated faster and larger than the inner foot. The seat yaw rotation for each left/right footstep did not return to the start angle but returns to 45% of the rotation to each start angle.

Figure 12 shows the trajectory of the heel resulting from combining the seat yaw motion to the foot module. Although the turning walking sensation is also impacted when the foot module returns to the start yaw angle each time without seat yaw motion, the turning sensation increases when the foot module follows the seat yaw swing (Fig. 11a).

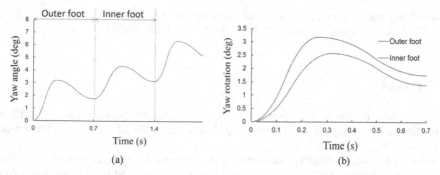

Fig. 11. Yaw rotation motion of the seat for turning walking. (a) Yaw angle of the seat and (b) yaw rotation angle for each step (outer and inner feet to the center of turning).

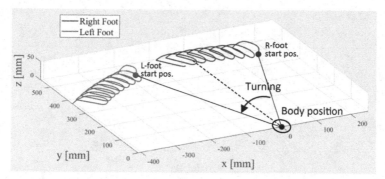

Fig. 12. Trajectory of the heel on the foot module in turning walking following the motion seat. Both heels started right in front of the body.

4   Conclusions

We described the mechanical structure and motion of a novel multisensory display designed to impart straight and turn walking sensation to a sitting user. Ten-DOF motions of the display were synchronously controlled to move the user's body, thus, rendering the walking sensation. Turn walking was achieved by introducing the body and foot turn mechanisms in the latest display system. Since the sitting posture is different from real standing walking, the amount of body motion was also different and small (~10% of the original motion). The motion stimuli were combined with audiovisual stimulation to form a subjective experience from a previously recorded motion and environment. The somatosensory information arising from active behavior forms the basis of acquiring audiovisual information. Thus, it must be involved in the experience before audiovisual information is obtained in a different space than the real environment in which the real body exists. Besides, the sensations are vital in establishing another space experience without the inconvenience of severe motion sickness.

As part of the future work, a mechanical structure that provides motion stimulus to the upper body and expands the range of experience of the user would be designed and built.

Acknowledgments. This research is partially supported by the MIC/SCOPE #191603003, JSPS KAKENHI Grant Number JP18H04118, JP18H03283, and JP26240029 projects.

References

1. Ikei, Y., Abe, K., Hirota, K., Amemiya, T.: A multisensory VR system exploring the Ultra-Reality. In: Proceedings of 18th International Conference on Virtual Systems and Multimedia (VSMM 2012), pp. 71–78 (2012)
2. Shimizu, K., et al.: FiveStar VR: shareable travel experience through multisensory stimulation to the whole body. In SIGGRAPH Asia 2018 Virtual & Augmented Reality (SA 2018), New York, NY, USA, pp. 1–2. ACM (2018). Article 2

Author Index

Agost, María-Jesús   I-3
Aikawa, Nonoka   II-3
Akakura, Takako   II-14, II-115, II-128, II-455
Alves, Erika   I-227
Amemiya, Tomohiro   I-247, I-322, I-357,
    II-482
Amos-Binks, Adam   I-218
Ando, Hideyuki   II-197
Anzalone, Robert   II-300
Aoyagi, Saizo   I-268
Aoyama, Kazuma   I-322, I-357
Ardissono, Liliana   I-206
Asahi, Yumi   II-242, II-286, II-353, II-373

Bahabry, Ahmed   II-300
Bayarri, Vicente   I-3
Becks, Daniela   II-253
Beringer, Joerg   I-163
Boaro, José   I-227
Bonacin, Rodrigo   I-143
Braasch, Jonas   I-257
Braz Junior, Geraldo   I-227
Briggs, Shannon   I-257

Chen, Dominique   II-197
Chen, Wei-Chun   II-385
Chen, Zi   I-369
Chin Goosby, Keisha   II-156
Cho, Young-Hee   II-156
Chowdhury, Avijit   II-208
Chun, Chi-Ah   II-156
Coursaris, Constantinos K.   I-163
Covington, Ava E.   II-141

Dascalu, Sergiu   I-28, II-141
de Almeida, Tatiana Aparecida   I-143
Dillon, Jesse   II-156
Divis, Kristin M.   I-192
Drozdal, Jaimie   I-257
Dwiputri Suciadi, Stephanie   I-16

Falconnet, Antoine   I-163
Fang, Rui   I-182
Finney, Malcolm A.   II-177

Flangas, Andrew   I-28
Flint, Isaac   I-218
Fujii, Ryoya   I-268
Fujinuma, Ryota   II-353
Fujishima, Yuki   II-63
Fujiwara, Hisashi   II-14
Fukai, Hidekazu   II-226
Furukawa, Kosei   II-364

Gastelum, Zoe N.   I-192
Goto, Takumi   I-306
Gračanin, Denis   I-337
Gururajan, Raj   II-208

Hafeez-Baig, Abdul   II-208
Hamaguchi, Jun   I-40
Hancock, Gabriella M.   II-27
Hara, Kenta   II-373
Harazono, Yuki   I-88
Harris Jr., Frederick C.   I-28
He, Entang   I-283
Hereasevich, Vitaly   I-218
Hirashima, Tsukasa   II-3, II-38, II-63, II-104
Hirose, Hayato   I-268
Hirose, Michitaka   I-322, I-357
Hirota, Koichi   I-306
Horiguchi, Tomoya   II-3, II-63, II-104
Howell, Breannan C.   I-192
Hsu, Su-Chu   II-385
Huang, Yu-Hsiung   II-385
Hung, Ya-Hsin   II-50

Ikei, Yasushi   II-482
Ishii, Hirotake   I-88
Ishii, Yutaka   I-297
Ito, Kenichiro   I-322
Ito, Teruaki   II-396
Izzi, Gianmarco   I-206

Jena, Sanam   II-300
Jones, Aaron P.   I-192

Kahu, Sampanna Yashwant   I-337
Kamabe, Hiroshi   II-226

Kano, Toru   II-14, II-115, II-128, II-455
Karavasili, Maria   I-49
Kataoka, Hitokatsu   I-101
Kawakita, Yuusuke   I-386
Kawase, Mayumi   II-226
Keeney, Natalie   I-218
Kimura, Nobuhito   I-306
Kitazaki, Michiteru   II-482
Koike, Kento   II-3, II-63, II-104
Kojiri, Tomoko   I-61, II-92
Komatsh, Masashi   II-128
Kondo, Masaru   II-242
Kruse, Christian   II-253
Kurokawa, Satoshi   I-297
Kuzuoka, Hideaki   I-357

Laufersweiler, Dawn   I-218
Lee, Tian Yeu Tiffany   II-340
Léger, Pierre-Majorique   I-163
Lin, Jing   I-283
Lin, Wen-Chi   II-340
Liu, Feng   I-182
Liu, Xu   II-326
Liu, Zhejun   I-283
Lotfalian Saremi, Marzieh   II-300
Lu, Qiang   I-182
Lucenteforte, Maurizio   I-206

Ma, Jiaxiu   I-76
Maekawa, Yoshimiki   II-269
Maeshiro, Tetsuya   II-406
Mallas, Andreas   I-49
Mano, Chonfua   I-61
Marayong, Panadda   II-156, II-177
Maruyama, Yoshihiro   II-75
Matković, Krešimir   I-337
Matsumoto, Kazumi   II-226
Matsuyama, Yoshio   II-286
Mattutino, Claudio   I-206
Matzen, Laura E.   I-192
Mauro, Noemi   I-206
Mendes, Marina   I-227
Minai, Kosuke   II-92
Mogi, Tomohiro   II-104
Moraes, Renato   I-227
Morishima, Shigeo   I-101

Nakanishi, Miwa   I-16, II-439
Narumi, Takuji   I-322, I-357
Nemeth, Christopher   I-218

Nihei, Yasunori   II-419, II-468
Nishihara, Yoko   I-76
Nishimura, Hiromitsu   I-386
Nojima, Takuya   I-306

Oka, Tokio   I-306
Oliveira, Milton   I-227
Osawa, Ayumu   II-439
Oyama, Takashi   II-396
Oyanagi, Akimi   I-322

Paiva, Anselmo   I-227
Peveler, Matthew   I-257
Pinevich, Yuliya   I-218
Plotkin, Richard M.   II-141
Portela, Carlos   I-227
Proctor, Robert W.   II-50

Rego, Venicius   I-227
Rinto, Kozono   II-419
Rivero, Luis   I-227
Rosa, Ferrucio de Franco   I-143
Rule, Gregory   I-218

Saga, Ryosuke   II-419, II-468
Sakakura, Kyosuke   II-197
Sakurai, Sho   I-306
Santos, Pedro   I-227
Sardana, Disha   I-337
Saremi, Razieh   II-300
Sato, Yoichiro   II-429
Segnan, Marino   I-206
Sejima, Yoshihiro   II-429
Shaw, Aarran W.   II-141
Shimoda, Hiroshi   I-88
Shimohara, Katsunori   I-113, II-312
Shinma, Daisuke   I-88
Shioya, Ryo   II-312
Shiozu, Yurika   II-312
Srinivasamurthy, Sharath   II-468
Stites, Mallory C.   I-192
Su, Hui   I-257
Suto, Hidetsugu   II-364
Suzuki, Ryota   I-101

Takada, Hideyuki   I-125
Takadama, Keiki   II-269
Takagi, Tsubasa   II-439
Takahara, Madoka   I-113, II-364
Takahashi, Nozomi   I-357

Tan, Hong Z.   I-369
Tanaka, Hiroshi   I-386
Tanaka, Mizuki   II-312
Tanev, Ivan   I-113
Tei, Konoki   II-115
Terada, Kazunori   II-226
Tokunaga, Toru   II-455
Tomita, Akihisa   II-128
Tomoto, Takahito   II-3, II-63, II-104
Torrielli, Federico   I-206
Trase, Ian   I-369
Trumbo, Michael C.   I-192
Tsurumi, Yutaro   II-419, II-468
Tudor, Alexis R.   I-28, II-141

Unno, Minori   II-482

Van Osch, Wietske   I-163
Venhuis, Sebastian   II-253
Vergara, Margarita   I-3
Vu, Kim-Phuong L.   II-156, II-177

Wakao, Tsukasa   I-386
Wang, Jingyang   II-326
Wang, Menglan   II-326
Warren, Christopher R.   II-27

Watanabe, Junji   II-197
Watanabe, Tomio   I-297, II-396, II-429
Wax, Amy   II-27
Wu, Hao   I-125
Wun, Meng-Yu   II-340

Xenos, Michalis   I-49
Xue, Dingming   I-88

Yamaguchi, Tomohiro   II-269
Yamamoto, Michiya   I-268
Yamamoto, Sakae   I-40
Yamamoto, Shintaro   I-101
Yamanishi, Ryosuke   I-76
Yamaoka, Ken   II-482
Ye, Junnan   II-326
Yem, Vibol   II-482
Yoshida, Satoko   I-113
Young, Kelly A.   II-177
Yu, Der-Jang   II-340
Yu, Tao-Tao   II-340

Zhang, John X. J.   I-369
Zhang, Yize   I-283
Zhou, Juan   I-125
Zhu, Siyao   II-326

Printed in the United States
by Baker & Taylor Publisher Services